The Handbook of Electronic Trading

Edited by Joseph Rosen

The Handbook of Electronic Trading

Edited by Joseph Rosen

Published in the United States by

Capital Markets Media Inc.
784 Morris Turnpike #394
Short Hills NJ 07078
www.capitalmarketsmedia.com

ISBN 978-0-9814646-0-2

Book jacket design by Lee Titone

**Dedicated to my wonderful family –
Rachel, Jonathan and Elisabeth**

Preface

'When I use a word', Humpty Dumpty said, in a rather scornful tone, 'it means just what I choose it to mean, neither more nor less'. 'The question is,' said Alice, 'whether you *can* make words mean so many different things.'

What is e-trading? Ask a sample of financial services industry professionals for a definition and like Humpty Dumpty you will probably receive a number of conflicting answers as they respond within their own context and experiences. Like the story of the blind men and the elephant, institutional or retail, buy side or sell side, front or back office, each has its own view. Completing the analogy, we are all looking at the same beast, created by forces going back over forty years. No, e-trading is not a recent revolution, but the result of regulation, industry initiatives and evolving, without intelligent design but reacting to market forces over four decades.

As recently as the 1960's the U. S. securities markets operated with slow, manual and paper based processes. Typically, an investor, retail or institutional, would make a trading decision then call their broker to place the order. Their broker would write up a paper order ticket, which would be delivered to the order room. Here a clerk would call the firm's clerk at an exchange or give the order to a dedicated trader to negotiate with a specialized dealer for that instrument, (e.g., bonds, OTC equities). Exchanges operated on floors where the clerk receiving the call hand wrote yet another order ticket. This would be given to a trader in the crowd where the instrument was traded and in a face-to-face auction like process the order could be executed. More paper tickets and phone calls would return the trade execution data back to all the parties and the brokerage firm's back office for clearance and settlement. In this last process, physical paper securities, stocks and bonds - and cash - would be exchanged each night between each pair of brokerage firms involved in the trade. The process was slow, manually intensive, risky and error prone.

In the late 1960's and early 70's trading days of 13 million shares caused the U.S. equity markets to close to handle the paper work. This resulted in the creation of clearing houses and depositories, (i.e., DTCC), the first steps in creating the environment for electronic trading. Eliminating paper and moving to book entry systems cut costs, time and risk and began the evolutionary process.

The SEC and Congress wanted the US markets to be fair and transparent. Their regulations were all aimed at improving the lot of the retail investor. In 1963 the SEC presented Congress with their *Special Study of Securities Markets*. It reviewed the over the counter (OTC – non exchange traded) equities market and identified wide spreads, high markups and profits by market makers, disadvantaging all clients. This was made possible by manual trading and phone-based quotes. The SEC's response -- The National Association of Securities Dealers Automated Quotations System – NASDAQ, began in 1971. It distributed quotes online from dealers for securities not traded on any exchange. It was an information only, quote-driven market with a multiple competing market makers model, but another step on the road.

New rules adopted in 1975 were directed at creating a National Markets System. Exchanges and dealers had to publish prices at which they would deal and had executed trades, and markets had to be linked electronically to access best prices. Broker/Dealers (B/D's) were obligated to obtain best execution for clients and the Inter-market Trading System created (ITS) was created to link all US equity exchanges enabling them to electronically route orders to the venue with the best price among the national markets. These regulatory requirements to increase fairness and transparency could only be met with transactions that were electronically routed and not by telephone calls and paper tickets.

In 1975 "May Day" eliminated fixed commissions; 1974 and 1981 brought us IRA and 401K legislation. These rules expanded the markets for trading as individuals had to invest for their own retirement. With it came the need to lower costs to remain profitable with lower commissions. Discount brokers such as Charles Schwab started in business, encouraging retail trading by independent, self directed traders. For both retail and institutional investors, lower costs enabled more frequent trading, as the friction of trading costs kept declining. Today institutions pay between 1¢ and 2¢ a share and retail investors about $8-12 a trade. Handling the growing volumes of trading and paper work could only be done economically by automating the processes. Markets were connected and could accept orders electronically, thus setting the stage for more electronic trading.

In 1996 the FIX protocol was established. This is a standard message format for a computer to send orders and execution data between institutional asset managers and their brokers. With a standard, institutional order management systems could more readily connect to multiple brokers and markets. Soon most order management systems implemented the standard and orders could be routed electronically, faster and more accurately than before. Exchanges and the new ECN's accepted their orders directly in the new standard, further increasing its value to the firms adopting it. By eliminating proprietary methods in connecting buyers, sellers and markets with a single common format, it reduced exclusivity of business relationships and encouraged the e-trading model on the institutional buy side. Versions of the FIX standard are now also used for fixed income, futures and options trading across the globe.

The late 1990's saw the SEC's order handling rules which fined market makers who traded ahead of their customer's order. In order to avoid these penalties, market makers began implementing "auto-ex" or automated execution strategies to ensure proper adherence to the rules. Another result was that traders who were responsible for making markets in 20 stocks were now able to trade over 100 issues. If a computer system could do as well as an experienced trader, why not expand the concept to markets.

To authorize completely automated matching systems and new market types, the SEC enacted Reg ATS in December 1998 which permitted and regulated Alternative Trading Systems (ATSs) and Electronic Communications Networks (ECNs). These markets accept orders, with limits, delivered electronically and the orders, *not* market makers (MMs) provide liquidity. Orders interact *directly* with each other. The system matches buy and sells automatically by price. It is implicitly fair, with no proprietary interests, and maintains the anonymity of traders. Success is dependent upon available liquidity. With the order book of unexecuted limit orders visible to all participants, it resulted in increased transparency as traders brought more trading to these markets. The result was additional new ECN's and fragmentation of markets amongst these trading venues; nine ECN's by 1999. NASDAQ lost 75% of its trading volume to these new markets. The NYSE eliminated Rule 390 which required all members to trade NYSE listed stock on the exchange or linked national markets. With its elimination, NYSE listed stock order flow also started moving to ECN's. We now have electronic trading of both market makers and these new market places.

The final major, regulatory change – prior to the recent onset of Reg NMS, whose impact is covered in later chapters – was in 2000, when the stock markets moved from fractional pricing to decimals. This caused a dramatic increase in quotes, with one cent, not six and a quarter cent price increments. This also decreased liquidity at each price point since there were 100 price points up from sixteen per dollar for similar trading interest. Traders now had to use many small order size trades to be consistent with the lowered available liquidity. The average trade size on the NYSE went from over 2000 shares to the current ~320 shares, producing a further increase of trading volume.

To address the issue of finding sufficient liquidity to meet institutional demand for trading large blocks, the algorithmic trading model came into wide usage. These are computer models based on historical data, set with parameters specific to the trader's strategy. To do this, large orders are sliced into small sizes (200-500 shares) and sent to market. The algorithms read real time data. If not immediately executable, they are canceled and replaced at different price levels. Their objectives are to find liquidity and leave no market impact or trail of their actions. The many small trades generate significantly more bid/asked quotes and market data. This type of trading, given penny price increments has impacted options and futures based on the underlying equities. This significantly increased the volumes of data all traders rely upon.

Using all that data is another type of algorithmic trading, sometimes referred to as block box trading. This strategy uses high frequency data analysis based on historical and real time data looking for trading opportunities. The techniques include statistical arbitrage and pairs trading. The models continuously look for violations of trends and try to buy an asset when it is cheap or sell it when it is perceived to be overpriced for periods of time measured in seconds or less.

For both of these types of algorithmic trading to exist required that all the previous market and technology enhancements be in place. Connectivity standards, fast electronic market places, cost effective computers and communications and paperless clearance and settlement. While not planned by a government or industry bureaucracy, we did achieve the environment we now have for e-trading.

What is e-trading? To the:

- retail investor it's using their PC and the internet to trade
- institutional investor it's direct access to many electronic markets and brokers with a single order management system
- entire investing public it's low cost, fair and transparent markets
- market maker it's automated quoting and execution of stocks and options
- institutional trader it's fast computers capable of algorithmic models to lower the impact of large trades or to find trading opportunities in vast amounts of real time data
- the back office it's almost real time clearance and settlement of trades with no paper, and a complete audit trail
- risk manager it's lower operational risk and better control of market and credit risk
- everyone it's the ability to increase returns in increasingly volatile markets

'That's a great deal to make one word mean,' Alice said in a thoughtful tone. 'When I make a word do a lot of work like that,' said Humpty Dumpty, 'I always pay it extra.'

Bernard S. Donefer 2008

Table of Contents

Section III - Technology & Electronic Trading

Editor's introduction

Wow! Now it's really here, the book I have always wanted to do. After all these years, and countless questions asked of many industry wise men/women at countless conferences and seminars– and not least, the year since we started this exciting project – at last *The Handbook of Electronic Trading* has been published.

Fifty notable industry friends and clients from 36 organizations were so giving of both their time and expertise to this project. The diversity of views and opinions that the reader will benefit from is clearly matched by the broad, cross-section of backgrounds, experience, responsibilities and subject matter expertise of the chapter contributors. In terms of organization type, geography, industry sector and asset class, as well as title, our participants cover the spectrum from equities and fixed income to derivatives, to buy-side as well as sell-side algo trading heads, to academic researchers, journalists and chief economists, to senior executives, such as CEO and CIO, at exchanges/ATSs/ECNs [defined below], consultants and vendors. Our approach, likewise, is a global one. A range of functional areas is also represented, including trading, operations, IT and compliance/regulation. It is fitting that we have such a stellar cast of contributors, as the subject of 'electronic trading' is such a broad one. We were as duly diligent in our selection of specific topics – and cognizant of the need to cover as broad a swathe as possible – as in inviting participants.

This is a most exciting time in the industry, with so much changing all at once. Some are calling this a perfect storm, buffeting the global securities industry with an unprecedented combination of forces. Hardly a week goes by without one or more articles about consolidation, convergence, dark pools and many other buzz words appearing in the *Financial Times, Wall Street Journal* or *Economist*. Much, if not most of this metamorphosis is related to the nearly exponential growth of 'electronic trading', which appears close to finally taking over the entire industry globally. One would be hard pressed to dispute that it's long touted benefits are more and more apparent, for example, reduction in errors, speedier order processing and customer service, more efficient and less pressured traders, and most importantly, cost savings that go straight to the bottom line.

When I started my Wall Street career some 25 years ago, and was fortunate enough to have actually written code for one of the first automatic execution systems for equities, the industry was a radically different place that would be unrecognizable today. In those days, it was all but a blank slate for trading automation, and 'electronic trading' meant many things, depending on who you asked. The first critical step was getting rid of the paper – the hand-written, order tickets, and the manual trade blotter. It is hard to imagine that at the time Wall Street – and the City -was still recovering from the 'back-office crunch' of the late '60s. As the trade magazine *Wall Street Computer Review* put it at the time, "Until nearly 1970, the securities business was wholly paper-based and manually processed. Ten or eleven million shares a day on the NYSE was a real back-breaker." ["Computer Speed May Eliminate Bargains in the Stock Market", *Wall Street Computer Review,* January 1984, p.38. This publication is now called *Wall Street & Technology.*]

Fast forward to the mid '00s. The first time I ever heard anyone talk about measuring price dissemination and order execution times in milliseconds was when I was serving as chairman of an industry conference on, what else, 'electronic trading'. And I naively thought that either they were joking, or I had misheard? Boy was I wrong; and they certainly weren't kidding! Now for better or worse, we already hear of some 'execution mechanisms', aka ECNs, ATSs, SIs, MLTFs, etc., claiming 'latencies', i.e. turn-around times, in microseconds, yes, *millionths* of a second. [For those who cannot wait for the above acronyms to be defined and described in chapters to follow, they stand for, respectively, 'Electronic Communications Network', 'Alternative Trading System', 'Systematic Internalizer', and 'Multi-Lateral Trading Facility'.]

At the same time that we have seen so much change, in some sense the more things change the more they stay the same, and nowhere more so than in the blurring of distinctions between players, and particularly, the growing competition for the trade execution business between exchanges and the multitudinous types of broker/dealer owned and operated trading systems, some of which are mentioned in the preceding paragraph. This phenomenon was quite elegantly and humorously captured some ten years ago by Ruben Lee, in the introduction to his book *What Is An Exchange? The Automation, Management, and Regulation of Financial Markets* (Oxford University Press, 1998), "... New technology, however, has led to the birth of a previously unknown type of institution, the 'MONSTER' (a Market-Oriented New System for Terrifying Exchanges and Regulators) ..... ." [page1]. Interestingly, if we go back another 15 years, it was already an issue on the regulators' radar screen. In a 1984 article dealing with 'automated systems' for trading, the *Wall Street Journal* writes "The commission [SEC] agreed with a staff recommendation not to force a decision on whether new systems allowing brokers to trade over-the-counter stocks electronically are really new stock exchanges. .... Technically, the staff said, the system operators could be deemed exchanges and be subject to the extensive regulation now applied to the New York and American stock exchanges." ["SEC to Encourage Automated Systems For OTC Trading", *Wall Street Journal*, October 5, 1984, p.53]. This is clearly one hot potato that has not gone away, and that the regulators must still figure out how to deal with.

Given the increasing pervasiveness of electronic trading, both globally and across asset classes, we expect that *The Handbook of Electronic Trading* will be useful to executives throughout the industry. The primary objective is to provide practical discussions – and actionable ideas - that will help seasoned executives as well as newcomers to the industry deal with both current and future challenges related to the growth of electronic trading.

For those readers who are not – yet – sufficiently mindful of how competitive forces can and do totally reshape industries and the 'pecking order' of players, let me share another cautionary tale back from the beginning of the PC revolution in the early 80's, and one that Joseph Schumpeter would have greatly appreciated. In those days, the market data business was basically controlled by the 'QRT' three [Quotron, Reuters and Telerate]. Two are gone, while the third has merged with another player that did not compete in the business segment then. Why one of the two disappeared becomes quite obvious when you read how one of their senior executives was quoted in a trade publication article at the time; you can't make this stuff up: "If I honestly believed that the solution was to place a personal computer on the desk of every account executive, I swear to God I would recommend it to this company. I do not believe it. I do not think it is practical. I do not think it is controllable. I do not think it's the way Wall Street should go!", ["Wall Street Back Offices Win Control of PCs", *Wall Street Computer Review*, September/October 1983, p.51]. The clear 'take-home' lesson here is do not be complacent, and certainly do not underestimate the potential impact that new technologies can have on the competitive landscape.

The 43 chapters that comprise *The Handbook of Electronic Trading* are organized into three sections, which will be familiar to readers of my two prior 'Handbooks' – *The Handbook of Investment Technology*[McGraw-Hill: 1997], and *The Handbook of Fixed Income Technology* [Summit Group Press: 1999]. The ten chapters in Section I, *Evolution of Electronic Trading*, together present a management level perspective on where the industry is, how we got here, and where we might be headed. Section II, *Electronic Trading Applications & Practices*, contains 23 chapters - a wide variety of case studies of business-segment-specific uses of electronic trading, everything from 'Algo Trading' and 'Dark Pools' to 'DMA' and 'EMSs', to 'MiFID', 'Reg NMS' and 'Smart Order Routing' among other topics. The ten chapters in Section III, *Technology & Electronic Trading*, discuss specific technologies – and related issues - that continue to facilitate the electronic trading revolution. Included are topics such as FIX, complex event processing [CEP], trading floor architecture, and 'Build Vs. Buy'. A couple of the chapters in this section are geared towards the more technically astute among us. You will know which chapters – and your level of technical astuteness - when you (try to) read them.

We originally expected some 15-20 chapters, and ended up with 43, which took much longer than we had anticipated. Let me therefore take the opportunity to thank all of the contributors and their organizations for their patience and for contributing to *The Handbook of Electronic Trading*:

4th Story, Steve Smith; Aleri, Don DeLoach, Jeff Wootton; Balatro Ltd., Chris Skinner; Baruch College, Robert Schwartz; BNY Mellon, Eric Karpman; BSG Alliance, Thomas Steinthal; Capital Markets Consulting, Don Mendelson, John Barun; Cisco Systems, Andy Kessler, Dave Malik, Mihaela Risca, Peter Robin; Cloverhill Enterprises, John Byrne; Credit Suisse, Dan Mathisson, James Doherty; Deutsche Bank, Udayan Goyal; Fidessa, Philip Beevers, Phil Slavin; FIX Protocol Ltd./Jordan & Jordan, Courtney Doyle, Daniella Baker; *Global Investment Technology*, Pavan Sahgal; Goldman Sachs, Dmitry Rakhlin, George Sofianos; Jay Gottlieb; Rick Holway; IBM, Piet Van de Velde; International Securities Exchange, Steven Wunsch; InvestTech Systems, Bennett Kaplan, Patrick Keough; Iowa (University of), Ashish Tiwari, Puneet Handa; Knight Group/EdgeTrade, Joseph Wald, Kyle Zasky; London Business School, Bruce Weber; John Lothian; Manhattan College, Janet Rovenpor; Nasdaq, Frank Hatheway; Nyfix, Howard Edelstein; NYU, Bernard Donefer; OM/NI Consulting, Wayne Wagner; Ordex, Bijan Monassebian; Charles Polk; Portware, Ary Khatchikian, Harrell Smith; Rockefeller & Co., David Bauman; Rosenblatt Securities, Joe Gawronski; Randy Schafer; Evan Schulman; Selero, Michael Wojcik; SIFMA; Sun Microsystems, Ambreesh Khanna; UBS, Robert Barnes; UNX, Michael Rosen; Westwater Corp., Jim Leman; Hua Zhu.

I'd like to thank Scott Porter, Publisher at Capital Markets Media, for commissioning this project, as well as Lee Titone, who designed the cover and layout of the book.

Let me close by acknowledging and thanking a number of Wall Street/City veterans that I've been fortunate to have worked with during my career: Bernie Weinstein; Bijan Monassebian; Henry Swieca and Peter Robin. They all taught me so much about the industry, and I owe them a lot. Thank you!

Joseph Rosen, September 2008

Section I –
Evolution of Electronic Trading

The Future Trader

By Chris Skinner, Chair, the Financial Services Club, Chief Executive, Balatro Ltd

Scenario: Lee Nixon, Future Trader, Water Commodities

Lee Nixon opened his eyes as the room's walls illuminated to intensity level 4[i]. The walls were set to brighten gradually from 1:45 a.m. and it was now 2:00. Another fifteen minutes and intensity level 10 would have been like a bright summer's day.

Lee liked the luminescent orange sunrise effect of the walls best as it made him feel warm and summery, even though the world outside was deep in the snows of winter and the dark of night. He usually woke at this time though, as he was known as a leader in futures trading in the world's rarest commodity: Water.

Water had been recognized as a potentially lucrative commodity market since the late 1990's, when the International Water Management Institute[ii] estimated that Earth would need 17% more water by 2025 than the water resources available at that time, in order to feed the world. The trouble was that no-one in the investment markets or elsewhere could really see how to capitalize on this opportunity until the 2011 Mercury Bomb when terrorists poured liquid mercury into Lake Meade, the largest reservoir in the USA. It was enough to wipe out all water supplies from the Lake for six months, and created a massive water shortage which cost the US Federal Reserve $35 billion to overcome.

This single incident led to water becoming the world's hottest commodity, thanks to the US Government's introduction of the Water Act in 2012. This Act allowed Water firms to not only trade as organizations, but also to trade their future water supplies based upon each of their water purification plants, reservoirs and facilities. The higher the government approved rating the water facility, the greater the liquidity of the stock in that facility, rather than in the water firm itself.

The implications of this Act were not realized in full until the investment markets picked up on the fact that they could now trade in parts of companies, not just the companies themselves. As a result, spread betting and exotic options markets appeared where traders would invest in the likelihood of a firm's tall buildings being impacted by flood or earthquake, and even on a company's key executives being kidnapped or departing due to ill health.

Such investment classes were not approved by government departments but, once firms realised how lucrative the potential returns could be, the impact was soon felt globally with most investment markets creating micro-stock alternative investment vehicles.

In addition, everything was so automated with news algorithmics that this had become the only way for many traders to leverage their returns. For example, Lee had heard the previous day of a news alert that a mini-Tsunami would hit San Diego at 10:12 PST that evening. Without even having to check his portfolio, his systems had automatically moved his investments with exposure to California water firms and micro-stocks to positions that reflected other water traders on the network. Such activity was simple and commonplace with the latest news algorithmics services on the network.

The final movement towards Water becoming the key trading commodity was the impact of the cost and management of water supplies worldwide. Water had become a scarce resource – even rarer than oil for many of the Earth's inhabitants – and now that the world's equities and future markets had worked out how to capitalize upon the opportunities of this commodity through highly automated trading facilities, where not only fractions of stocks could be traded but also fractions of firms, the introduction of the Water Act had led to an explosion of trading in Water.

Exotic water options trading on the Water Commodities Exchange (WCE) based in London became one of the most liquid markets, literally, and Lee was known as the world's leading Water options trader. It did not matter that Lee lived in Boston, although it is for that reason that he was getting up at 2:00 in the morning, not because he wanted to catch the opening of the markets as he would have done in the old days – there is no opening or closing of markets, markets trade 24 hours – but because he wanted to catch *WaterWorld*, the daily news update on the dedicated Water Channel, Water.net, which aired daily from London 8:00 to 8:30 GMT.

Of course, he could preset his view machine to catch *WaterWorld* and view it later on his watch or in his PTV[iii], but then he would miss the opportunity to catch the trading liquidity during the first half-hour after the programme's ending. The WCE literally spiked for an hour every day – from 8:00 until 9:00 GMT – during *WaterWorld*, after which everyone's positions were set for the next 24 hours as the algo services and news algorithmics took over. So, everyone watched *WaterWorld* if they were involved in the water commodities markets, whether it was 3:00 or 23:00 local time.

Lee began his day as usual with a fast all-round shower and air-dry whilst dealing with any urgent messages. The shower panels, doors, walls ... everything was built for connection in his purpose-built pod[iv]. Therefore, whilst showering, Lee was bringing up video screens in his Perspex-style shower screen simply by moving his hands around the screen to move different messages to where he wanted to see them or save them. As a result, he could check his messages easily whilst washing, with each message appearing in a specific space based upon where Lee pointed[v].

First there were a few video messages from other traders around the world, then a viewcard from his girlfriend who was travelling Asia and a commentary from his mother asking why he never viewed her[vi]. No change there.

After air-drying and pouring himself some Detox juice, the next part of the daily routine was to watch the market movements using "*Market Recorder*". *Market Recorder* is a service provided by his employer, Slate Street, and is designed to be used by all of their traders globally.

It does what it says on the tin: records the markets. All market data, brokers, prices, exchanges, execution venues, liquidity pools ... everything globally is recorded by *Market Recorder*.

The great thing is that each trader can then build dynamic trading strategies and test them through *Market Recorder* by fine tuning dealings they may have made over the last few hours, days, months and years.

Each trader would also use *Market Recorder* in a different way. For example, if you were dealing in energy futures then you would use *Market Recorder* to record the main execution venues for the energy desk, which typically came down to Enex: the merged Nymex and ICE exchange.

But water was far more important than oil or gas, and Lee used *Market Recorder* to record the WCE (the Water Commodities Exchange) as that was the only venue that counted for him, although he did use eBanyse, the eBay managed NYSE, as well because it was ideal for generic equity dealings in the world's water firms through a single low latency global connection.

The fact is that the unlimited storage and indexing facilities offered by *Market Recorder* meant that it could record all of these market movements across all of these trading venues. Not only that but it could retain market tick data and associated feeds for twelve months in real-time and for five years in near-time. That way any trader could review their dealings against the market movements for as far back as most of them ever wanted, on any market venue, for any stock, bond or commodity in the world.

In order to use *Market Recorder*, Lee began by asking the service to playback yesterday's markets, his dealings, trades executed and rejected, returns through the day and so forth. This sounds simple but is much more complex in practice.

For example, the first thing *Market Recorder* does is present Lee with screens on the video wall. The video wall he's using at this point is around six feet tall by nine feet wide, and there are six screens running.

The first screen linked to the WCE as well as his other primary water execution venues of interest such as eBanyse, the next showed his total Water portfolio, a third showed his position by each broker and venue, another showed his position against the other Slate Street water traders – he wasn't the only one, but was recognised as the leader of the Water Desk, a fifth showed his position of trading and return against each market over the past twelve months and a sixth showed projected water supplies, firms and purification plants news and forecasts released during the same period.

Lee assimilated all of this information in seconds – he was used to it – and then began to ask for simulations of actions he might have taken the previous day. *Market Recorder* not only played out his positions, but showed recommendations as to where he could have improved his position and portfolio, as well as marking his positive movements. The service allowed him to very quickly roll forward and roll back against positions to see how things would have worked out if he had made those decisions.

It even monitored his trades against his execution policy to alert him as to when he might want to consider updating a best execution policy for new execution venues, and would illustrate how his position would have changed for major trades by visually demonstrating the difference of returns each movement would have achieved against speed of execution, versus price, cost and likelihood of the trade being fulfilled.

Alongside these system and market changes another big change, from a technology viewpoint, is that all of his interactions with *Market Recorder* were being delivered through voice commands and hand movements – the keyboard had died out in the early 2010's as visual and touch communications became pervasive[vii] – and he was trying various ideas out before the *WaterWorld* broadcast to see how he could have improved his returns on the previous day.

The other big change in Lee's approach, compared to the way markets operated ten years before, is that he had no primary broker or sell-side firms to deal with[viii]. For a while, brokers had pushed technology heavily towards the buy-side with Execution Management Systems integrated with Order Management Systems, along with highly complex algo trading tools.

Lee's world was different, as all of these tools were built into *Market Recorder* which incorporated incredible smart routing intelligence. The result is that Lee did not even think about which firm or firms to trade through and did not check who executed which trades the day before. All trades were handled by *Market Recorder* itself, which basically would look at what Lee was trying to achieve and how, and then would route his requirements intelligently to any execution venue globally that could take the order based upon his requirements for speed, latency, price and cost[ix].

That is why, although WCE was his main choice of trading venue for Water commodities, it did not mean Lee traded there ... instead, he used the WCE to give him the best knowledge of what was happening in the Water markets. That is why Lee's orders in play at 2:00 in Boston were actually being routed direct to Hong Kong. But he had no interest in such mundane trivia, as the *Market Recorder* handled all of that for him.

Information was Lee's top priority.

Information to guide him in his investment process and strategy, and that is why Lee enjoyed the flexibility of the six-screen system which he could supplement with live news and other video services to enrich his knowledge base.

After half an hour of getting up to speed with the markets, *WaterWorld* came onto the Water Channel so he stopped playing with his portfolio and watched the feed coming in live. He also connected now with the other Slate Street water traders around the globe, with Yin in Kuala Lumpur, Dave in London, Theresa in Sydney and Sean in San Francisco.

The traders had no need to be based in the centres of water markets as information was their lifeblood. Nevertheless, as they were the key members of the Slate Street Water Trading Desk, they would meet at least once a day to trade knowledge on their investments, assets and portfolio, through a viewcall. Those meetings were always planned for three hours after *WaterWorld* but, during *WaterWorld*, they would talk using their video wall.

So, Lee now had a video wall next to his breakfast workout table that looked a little like a weird chess board, with six small screens from *Market Recorder* running in the lower portion of the wall, four 17" widescreen views of Yin, Dave, Theresa and Sean running across the top of the wall, and a large 60" screen of *WaterWorld* in the centre.

During the broadcast each of them made commentary. Their words were automatically being translated into subtitles by the intelligent voice recognition systems built into their systems. These subtitles appeared on-screen against each of their views.

Yin was commenting on China's Three Gorges Dam, run by Aqua America, and the fact the Government had ordered that the ageing processing plant needed to be upgraded by 2020, whilst Dave was sharing news that Russia's Gazprom had just made a bid to add the German utility RWE, which owned various water firms including the UK's Thames Water, to their portfolio. This would make Gazprom the world's largest integrated water and energy firm, and a further possible stranglehold on the markets.

Meantime, the Water Channel's *WaterWorld* broadcast was focusing on the breaking news of floods in California due to a mini-tsunami in San Diego. All eyes turned to Sean who was already on the case and reassured them that this had been forecast for 10:12 p.m. PST, but the fact it had hit at 10:14 would not cause an issue in their dealings.

As *WaterWorld* ended, they all returned to *Market Recorder* whilst leaving their video screens running. This was the way the 'team' worked – as a virtual team, all in touch via their video wall. Each could switch position to the other's *Market Recorder* view in real-time if required – in order to see the trading strategies of others in the network – or they could bring up a summary screen showing their position against the other Slate Street water traders as part of their main interface.

Lee programmed his trading, which included buying 1,000 shares short on Gazprom with an offset hedge of long on RWE in case the merger discussions failed, laying off Aqua America shares bundled with an increase in position in China's largest water processing utility, Sinowater. As part of his portfolio, *Market Recorder* recommended that he add a Yuan option as part of the Sinowater investment, as well as placing a bold hedge on water yields in the US markets post the tsunami and based upon the strength of the hit taken in San Diego.

This continued as a real-time dialogue with *Market Recorder* through the rest of day until 6:00 EST when, as per usual, the viewcalls for the day began[x].

Viewcalls delivered high quality communications that allowed the Water Desk team to come together as a virtual team each day. Effectively, if gave Lee a six foot tall by nine foot wide view of the other four guys in his group. Even though they were all spread around the world, they could just as easily have been there in the room with him, as the hi-definition three-dimensional connection felt real.

That is why no-one needed to meet or trade in an office block, but had the beauty of global, 24*7 trading facilitated from each of their personal pod spaces.

Summary

The Future Trader has:

- Unlimited bandwidth and storage allows complete market access, storage and knowledge
- Super-intelligent algo and multi-asset trading direct from the home, with smart order routing intelligence built into the network
- Trading in micro-stocks, parts of companies, rather than just equities is commonplace
- News algorithmics ensured that trading positions changed according to any breaking news on firms or markets
- Highly complex cross-asset class trading strategies delivered direct to the execution venues with no 'sell-side' broker-dealer involved – just trading and execution
- Broker-dealers now compete as execution venues with traditional exchanges whilst others have evolved to be specialist research analytics houses or boutique advisors
- Interactions with systems are intuitive and intelligent with voice and video interfaces, rather than mouse and keyboard
- Collaborative work with colleagues is through hi-definition video wall conferencing from home, rather than through 100-storey office blocks in downtown city venues

The Competitive Landscape for Global Exchanges: What Exchanges Must Do to Meet User Expectations

Peter Robin, Senior Director, Internet Business Solutions Group (IBSG), Cisco Systems

The Competitive Landscape for Global Exchanges
What exchanges must do to meet user expectations

Financial exchanges worldwide are being buffeted by an unprecedented combination of forces—to a large degree driven by changes in regulation, market turbulence, and technology—that are transforming the environment in which they compete to a remarkable degree. To gain insight into this evolving marketplace, the Cisco Internet Business Solutions Group (IBSG) conducted a research study, the Cisco Exchanges Survey, which included interviews with dozens of senior industry executives. These were performed in the first half of 2007 and since updated to highlight key capabilities required from a leading exchange. The survey examined performance, low-latency issues, and technology as it pertains to global exchanges.

Among the main conclusions and findings of the study:
- Exchanges have transformed from members' clubs to commercial, profit-making organizations listed on their own exchange.
- Liquidity is the most important capability that an exchange must have. It is, however, a consequence of performing well on other capabilities. An exchange needs to offer a reasonable tariff of charges to its users; a high-performance, low-latency platform for price dissemination; and an efficient order-execution system. There are dozens of capabilities that an exchange must have, many of which are not under its control.
- Banks and other institutions that used to own exchanges resent the fact that the exchanges now make profits from—and compete with—them. This conflict will intensify.

- Exchanges are competing with each other on a global basis to attract new listings and transaction flows.
- Mergers will continue, as exchanges have identified that "big is good" in an increasingly scalable business.
- Customers' expectations constantly are rising.
- Key exchange capabilities can be linked directly to increased revenue.
- New potential revenue sources exist for creative, forward-thinking exchanges.

> **What Must Exchanges Do to Meet User Expectations?**
>
> Reduce tariffs, improve latency performance, increase peak second transaction capacity, offer value-added services, increase transaction capacity through acquisitions and mergers, and stay two steps ahead of members.

Background to the Cisco Exchanges Survey

The 40 senior executives interviewed represent a cross-section of buy-side, sell-side, and exchanges/ATSs.[xi] Organizations invited to participate in the study included, among many others, major industry players such as AllianceBernstein; Cantor Fitzgerald/eSpeed; Credit Suisse; D.E. Shaw; Deutsche Börse; E*TRADE; Goldman Sachs; Highbridge Capital; HSBC Securities; ISE; ITG;[xii] Lehman Brothers; London Stock Exchange; Madoff Investment Securities; Morgan Stanley; and the New York Stock Exchange.

The individuals held a cross-section of senior roles. Titles included algorithmic trading head; CEO; CIO; electronic connectivity head; electronic execution/trading head; equity technology head; global operations head; head trader; institutional client group head; market data technology head; and prime brokerage head.

Cisco developed a series of questions that would enable participants to talk freely. Categories of questions included factors driving trading volumes; key capabilities of an exchange; impact of performance and latency; customer service; and the future of exchanges. Also, the survey asked, "What do you see as key differentiators of one exchange versus another in regards to trading technology, dealer support technology, regulatory structures, clearing, and settlement?"

The study's industry research included sources such as the World Federation of Exchanges, various analyst reports, and news services/press coverage.

We should note that a major part of the study took place before the following mergers: NYSE/Euronext; NASDAQ/OMX; Deutsche Börse/ISE; CME/CBOT; and LSE/Borsa Italiana. These firms, therefore, were evaluated as separate organizations.

Competitive Environment for Exchanges

It seems that a perfect storm of factors is now reshaping the global securities industry and the traditional exchange trading business more than any other segment. The trends and buzz words commonly cited, most of which are highly interrelated, include demutualization and IPOs; diversification; globalization; consolidation, mergers, and joint ventures; technology advances; explosive growth in algorithmic and electronic trading; de-/re-regulation; demanding customers and pricing pressures; aggressive new entrants; fragmentation of liquidity; and convergence.

Essentially, this translates into a confusing blurring of distinctions between and among segments and players, resulting in a near free-for-all, where almost everyone competes with everyone else. For example, most major investment banks have their own internalization and/or crossing engines, which siphon executions directly from exchanges; this is one manifestation of convergence.

But it gets more interesting as the competition between brokers and exchanges extends in more cases to the entire trading value chain, including the pre- and post-trade, in addition to the trade execution itself. By building and/or buying—and providing to customers—applications/functions such as order management systems (OMSs), transaction cost analysis (TCA), connectivity tools, and market data distribution platforms, these organizations give customers more reason to trade with them. This further manifestation of convergence, and its resultant, growing friction between the sell-side and exchanges, is an example of vertical diversification by both.

The entry of aggressive new competitors—in particular, various types of ATSs—has been facilitated, if not encouraged, by Reg NMS[xiii] in the United States and MiFID[xiv] in the European Union (EU), causing pricing pressure and, arguably, improvement in performance. And enter they have. According to a recent report by the research company Tabb Group, "...there are more than 55 different venues where buyers and sellers electronically trade U.S. equities."[xv]

Figure 1 lists a subset of 30 ATSs, a growing number of which now are active in both the United States and the European Union.

Figure 1. List of Players—Dark Pools[xvi]
U.S./European Dark Liquidity Pools—an Expanding List of Players

Sponsor	Dark Pool	Sponsor	Dark Pool
Pipeline Trading Systems	Pipeline Block Trading System	Morgan Stanley	ATS1
eSpeed	Aqua	BIDS Trading	BIDS ATS
Bloomberg	Block Hunter	Merrill Lynch/ITG	ML BLOCKalert
Automated Trading Desk	Institutional Match	Fidelity Brokerage	CrossStream
Investment Technology Group	POSIT Match	eBX	LeveL
Instinet	Instinet Global Crossing	State Street	Lattice
Liquidnet	Liquidnet	NASDAQ	Midpoint Reserve
Liquidnet	Liquidnet H₂O	NYSE	Matchpoint
BNY ConvergEx	VortEx	ISE	Midpoint Match
Investment Technology Group	POSIT Now	UBS	UBS PIN
Knight	Match	Goldman Sachs	SIGMA X
NYFIX	Millennium ATS	Merrill Lynch	MLXN
NYFIX	Euro Millennium	Morgan Stanley	MS Pool
River Cross	River Cross	Lehman Brothers	Liquidity Center Cross (LCX)
Credit Suisse	CrossFinder	Citi	LiquiFi

Source: Celent, 2007

New entrants also have been gaining traction. Nomura/Instinet-owned MTF
Chi-X in the European Union lately has been trading nearly 10 percent of the
London Stock Exchange (LSE) volume. Similarly, ECN BATS Trading in the
United States, which recently applied to the SEC for exchange status, has
been doing 11.3 percent of NASDAQ and 8 percent of NYSE volume. Many
new entrants, as well as some revamped older ones, have been created as
joint ventures of multi-firm consortia. The extent of this phenomenon, across
asset classes and geographies, and based on level of broker/dealer
participation, is illustrated on the next page.

Exchange Capabilities

Through interviews, discussions, and research, we determined more than 50
capabilities against which to measure an exchange's performance. Figure 3
contains 23 different capabilities; the capabilities toward the center are more
important than those at the outer edges of the diagram.

We focus on the 10 high-priority items that are in the middle circle, but also
will touch on some outside items. High performance, low latency is very
important, but isn't the most essential capability an exchange must have.
Our research showed that the most critical capability is liquidity, because
without it, you can't trade. In fact, liquidity is a consequence of getting
everything else correct. Some exchanges were surprised to find that they
weren't directly in control of liquidity. It was an eye-opener for some
exchanges to discover the capabilities they could control (investment
candidates) and those they could not.

Figure 2. The Altered Broker/Dealer Landscape

	Execution Platforms																										Post-trade Platforms								
	Equities	Rates	Credits	GF	Equities							FX and Commodities							Exchanges								Rates			Credit FX			Data		
Consortiums no longer dealer-controlled (a) Excludes shareholders of <1%	LiquidityHub	MTS-Bondvision(a)	Bonddesk	MarketAxess	Creditex(a)	QWIXX	RPWire	BIDS	LeVel	Turquoise	Archipelago	BATS	TradingScreen	EBS	FXall	Currenex	Volbroker	Climate Exchange	USFE	ISE	NSX	Chicago SE	Philidelphia SE	India National SE	Boston Options E	SwapsWire(a)	DTCC	Clearing Corporation	LCH Cleanet	Euroclear	T-Zero (Creditex)	CLS	BOAT	Markit	Thememarkets.com
ABN-AMRO	✓	✓	✓	✓									✓															✓			✓	✓		✓	✓	✓
Bank of America	✓		✓		✓				✓		✓	✓	✓		✓		✓		✓								✓	✓			✓	✓	✓	✓	✓	✓
Barclays Capital	✓	✓											✓															✓			✓	✓		✓		
Bear Stearns			✓	✓			✓											✓	✓	✓							✓	✓		✓	✓	✓		✓		
BNP PARIBAS	✓	✓								✓	✓																✓	✓			✓	✓			✓	
Citigroup	✓	✓			✓	✓	✓	✓			✓	✓		✓		✓		✓									✓	✓	✓	✓	✓	✓	✓	✓	✓	✓
Credit Suisse		✓				✓	✓	✓	✓	✓		✓	✓														✓	✓	✓	✓	✓	✓	✓	✓	✓	✓
Deutsche Bank	✓	✓		✓	✓	✓		✓	✓	✓		✓		✓			✓	✓									✓	✓	✓	✓	✓	✓	✓	✓	✓	✓
Goldman Sachs	✓	✓	✓		✓	✓	✓	✓		✓			✓	✓	✓	✓		✓		✓			✓		✓		✓	✓	✓	✓	✓	✓	✓	✓	✓
HSBC	✓	✓			✓								✓	✓													✓	✓			✓	✓		✓	✓	✓
JPMorgan	✓	✓			✓	✓		✓				✓	✓	✓													✓	✓	✓		✓	✓	✓	✓	✓	
Lehman Brothers	✓	✓		✓		✓	✓	✓	✓	✓		✓															✓	✓	✓	✓	✓	✓	✓		✓	✓
Merrill Lynch	✓						✓	✓	✓										✓				✓		✓		✓	✓	✓	✓	✓	✓	✓		✓	✓
Morgan Stanley	✓										✓							✓	✓			✓					✓	✓	✓	✓	✓	✓	✓	✓	✓	✓
RBS	✓	✓								✓	✓		✓														✓		✓	✓			✓			
Societe Generale	✓	✓																									✓		✓	✓	✓	✓				
UBS	✓		✓	✓			✓			✓			✓	✓			✓								✓		✓	✓	✓	✓	✓	✓	✓	✓	✓	✓

Source: Deutsche Bank, 2007

Since exchange customers and former members regret, to a large extent, that exchanges are making profits from them, they have been focusing on trying to convince exchanges to reduce costs. Our research, however, shows that the transaction cost element represented by an exchange in the total cost of buying, selling, and processing equities represents only about 4 percent of the total cost. So, members should focus on the other 96 percent of total costs.

We bundle several capabilities together in what we call "invariant execution" by the exchange. Users want the performance of an exchange—latency, distribution of prices, and processing of trades—to remain unchanged, no matter what the trade volume. It's easy to process just one transaction at a very high speed. But if you are processing 100,000 trades a day, and you have a surge that might put through another 20,000 trades, then it is not so easy to maintain a constant performance. Processing capacity and volume handling are very important to users. It also is critical that the exchange be available. If you look back over the past five or six years, there have been a number of failures of exchanges—some only for a few minutes, some for several hours. But whatever the situation, users want the exchange to remain available.

Figure 3. Key Capabilities Defining an Exchange

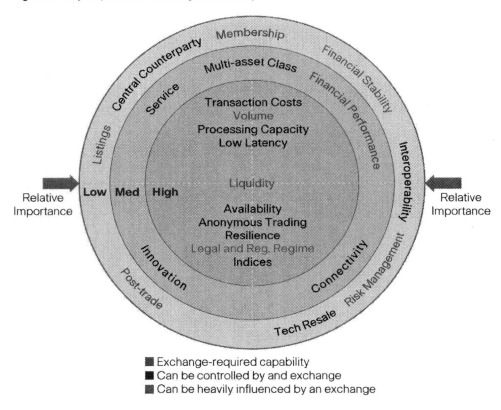

- ■ Exchange-required capability
- ■ Can be controlled by and exchange
- ■ Can be heavily influenced by an exchange

Source: Cisco IBSG, 2008

The exchanges to whom we spoke felt that they were in control of all the capabilities they needed, but manifestly they are not. Take, for example, the legal and regulatory regime. Many exchanges mentioned that they were in control of the rules, regulations, and laws that concern trading. We brought up the counter example of Sarbanes-Oxley, which prevented companies from listing on U.S. exchanges because it was too expensive to comply with the regulations. Similarly, in the United Kingdom, the government imposed an advanced corporation tax on share trading and stamp duty that has impacted the volume and cost of trading on the LSE. For each exchange, we can find an example where it is absolutely not in control of the regulatory regime. What exchange users want, however, is for the regime to be certain, even they do not find it perfectly favorable to their business situation. So, basically, the exchange is in control of letting its members know what the rules are.

Some exchanges were quite limited (trading, for example, only cash equities), whereas other exchanges trade the whole range of financial instruments. As part of their efforts to both diversify and grow the scale of their business, almost all the major players have been busy acquiring exchanges outside of their core. For example, Deutsche Börse bought ISE partly for its growing equities business, and NYSE acquired Euronext—a pan-European exchange based in Paris, with subsidiaries in Belgium, France, the Netherlands, Portugal, and the United Kingdom—largely to enable its diversification into the futures business via LIFFE Connect, a leading global derivatives trading system.

Most exchanges do not provide clearing and settlement functions, such as Central Counterparty, a financial institution that acts as an intermediary between security market participants. Those that do, however, gain a competitive advantage over other exchanges, including making more money. One of the reasons that the IntercontinentalExchange (ICE), which operates global commodity and financial products marketplaces, bought the New York Board Of Trade (NYBOT) was for its registered clearing license and business. In both the European Union and United States, sentiment among regulators seems to be away from the vertical silo model, whereby an exchange owns its clearing corporation. Regulators appear to be making threatening sounds to break up the vertical model. For example, the Chicago Mercantile Exchange (CME) is being examined to decide if it should divest its clearing business.

One more high-priority capability that must be considered is the exchange's peak second transaction volume capacity. Difficulties occur, and the throttles need to be applied, when all trades are trying to get through at one time. These peaks typically occur at the start and end of a trading session, or in response to news. They also emanate from the continued growth of algorithmic trading. An exchange's data distribution and trading systems must cope with ever-increasing frequency of peak seconds that put the greatest strains on capacity. In the words of a European exchange executive, "If an exchange is not prepared for the increased volume, it could take an exchange down."

Performance and Revenue Drivers

Key exchange capabilities can and must be linked to economic impact. In other words, what should be important is how to optimize revenues and profits. Exchanges, therefore, should focus investments on capabilities and factors over which they have control, and that will lead to higher volume of trades—the highest charging element for most exchanges. The proportion of an exchange's business that comes from algorithmic trading, largely from statistical arbitrage hedge funds and sell-side prop desks, already is high and rising. Estimates for the NYSE are that upwards of 60 percent of its trade volume is generated algorithmically, and it's even higher for NASDAQ. For the LSE at the end of 2007, it was greater than 50 percent. As the number of total orders increases, a result of algorithmic trading, so, too, does the need for improved latency in the exchange platform to process all the orders in the required time frame. On balance, the reduction in latency of an exchange's systems facilitates increased order and trade flow and, thus, more revenue. LSE, for example, noticed a 30 percent rise in trades when it introduced its new trading system, TradeElect. It's debatable whether this purely was because the exchange provided increased performance or if it was due, in part, to its improved volume-handling capacity as well.

What makes the investment decision for improving latency performance more interesting for an exchange is that, by and large, customer systems are nowhere as fast as those of the exchanges. So the question arises as to where to invest the money that would have been invested in further reducing latency? For some, the answer is easy. Exchanges need to ensure that the cancel processing is at least as good as the order-receive and execution processes. As it turns out, there are, by far, many more orders sent than trades executed. The ratios range from five orders to one execution for a typical equities-only exchange, to many hundreds or more at some derivatives exchanges. This also is a potential revenue opportunity for those exchanges not currently charging for cancels, since cancels are the main transaction type going through the exchange's system.

Our analysis suggests that it would be highly advisable for exchanges and customers to cooperate fully and disclose their technologies to each other. This will result in better performance and attract more flow to the exchange. This also could provide potential revenue for the exchange in the form of IT advisory services to its members, particularly as it relates to improving latency performance.

Exchanges should be aware of the operability of elasticity of demand in the trading business, i.e., that a reduction in price could lead to higher revenues if the volume increases at a higher ratio than the price cut. A case in point here is BATS Trading, which, via clever usage of price cuts, as well as extensive rebates for liquidity providers on its order book, cemented its position as the third-largest U.S. equity pool, after the NYSE and NASDAQ.

As part of our study, we asked interviewees to rank eight leading exchanges— CME, Deutsche Börse, Euronext, ISE, LSE, NASDAQ, the NYSE, and TSE—on a scale from 1 (poor) to 5 (excellent) based on the 10 high-priority capabilities of the inner circle in Figure 3. There was much clustering, but also interesting deficiencies and almost comical outliers on some attributes, especially regarding service, capacity, and performance/latency. We suspect that once the competitive impacts of MiFID are felt via, for example, Chi-X (the first order-driven pan-European equities multilateral trading facility) or Turquoise (an ATS in formation), there will be radical changes in the ratings.

Importance of Low Latency[xvii]

High-performance, low-latency trading is of great interest to all involved parties in a trading mechanism. Figure 4, on the following page, shows some of the key timings to be considered both by an exchange and its users.

The first thing we observed is that there are no uniform definitions for latency. One exchange can quote one millisecond for price formation, and another can quote two milliseconds, but they are not necessarily talking about the same thing. It would be useful for a central body to develop some uniform definitions for latency to facilitate comparisons.

From the exchange point of view, there were two important functions that we monitored: price dissemination/price distribution and order execution. On the member side, there's the opposite factor—how rapidly can prices received from the exchange be processed? We also have to consider the order-execution function.

Figure 4. Latency in an Exchange System

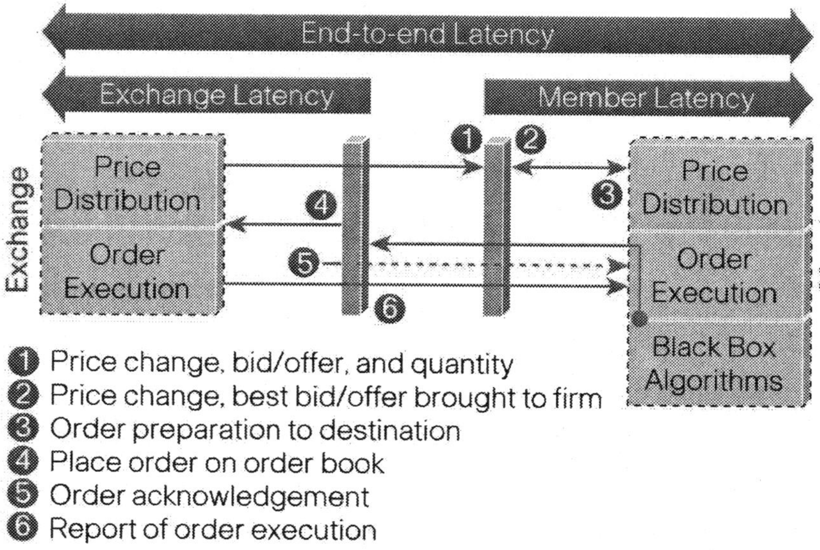

❶ Price change, bid/offer, and quantity
❷ Price change, best bid/offer brought to firm
❸ Order preparation to destination
❹ Place order on order book
❺ Order acknowledgement
❻ Report of order execution

Source: Cisco IBSG, 2008

In Figure 4, we've labeled the arrows. The first activity is that an exchange will publish the price at which trades are being done for a particular stock (arrow 1 in Figure 4). By now, most exchanges already perform pretty well, with a typical time range of between two to five milliseconds in terms of price dissemination. But times do vary, with very good times around one millisecond. NASDAQ, for example, claims that it disseminates prices within one millisecond of trades being done. To a very poor outlier exchange, which can take up to 18,000 milliseconds to disseminate the price of a trade, this is a very long time.

BATS Trading is faster still, disseminating prices in about 400 to 500 microseconds, and producing an order acknowledgement within 400 microseconds of order receipt. The LSE, for example, produces results in two milliseconds. The NYSE takes between three and five milliseconds, and it's working to reduce that to two milliseconds. Deutsche Börse distributes prices within two milliseconds.

The next element of time travel, along arrow 1 in Figure 4, is the transmission time from exchange to member. Typically, it's in the four- to five-millisecond range and, because of the laws of physics, cannot be improved much. Various techniques might help, such as employing dark fiber connections, or the famous collocation strategy. The idea is to put as much relevant processing as close as possible to the exchange, maybe even in the data center of the exchange itself, and as little as possible on your own premises if you are a member or an investment bank. Some exchanges have started to turn this into revenue, charging for the real estate in their data center.

We are reminded here of a Japanese proverb, which says that "nearer is farther." The principle is that the more functionality you put near the exchange, the farther you are from your user base for price. That is why you need a strategy. If you can receive price data within 500 microseconds, but you still can't distribute it to your user base in 20 milliseconds, you really haven't gained anything. Interestingly, not all hedge fund traders are requiring high speed if they are not involved in automated trading.

Members must be able to handle and process all prices that are received. In a reasonable high-performance trading venue, prices are generated in one or two milliseconds by the exchange and transmitted to members in four to six milliseconds.

A median response time for price-handling mechanisms is around 100 milliseconds. In this situation, there is little point in pushing the exchange for improved processing time until members upgrade their own systems. For some of the members to whom we spoke, this was quite a revelation. Exchanges shouldn't necessarily spend any more money improving latency performance. What they should be doing is improving capacity, because many members couldn't cope with an improvement in latency performance. We do see some members, however, claiming that they can handle prices within two or three milliseconds.

Typically, order-execution times are slower than price-dissemination times, although that's not invariably true. At the time of the survey, main board exchanges were achieving times between 25 milliseconds and 100 milliseconds for order execution. But, in fact, all exchanges have improved since the time of the survey. The LSE now executes at best within eight milliseconds, with a median of 14 milliseconds. The NYSE claims to execute at between 10 and 25 milliseconds. NASDAQ will claim to be within 15 milliseconds. BATS Trading is much faster than that, producing results within five milliseconds. By contrast, the outliers probably are around 250 to 500 milliseconds for execution. NASDAQ and NYSE latency performance improvements are largely due to their Inet[xviii] and Arca[xix] acquisitions, respectively.

In Figure 4, arrow 5 is important because of what the algorithms used by members require. It is an order acknowledgement, which they want as rapidly as possible. All exchanges send an acknowledgement to the originator to confirm that an order has been placed on the books, but some exchanges also provide an "order ack," which confirms only that the exchange has received the order. Black box strategies rely on the "order ack" to trigger the next response. BATS Trading, for example, claims 500 microseconds on this particular aspect, the LSE one millisecond, NASDAQ one millisecond, and the NYSE two milliseconds.

At the time of the survey, one of the participating exchanges surprisingly did not provide an order acknowledgement. As a result, it changed its policy to be more attractive to quantitative hedge funds.

All exchanges would like standardization and normalization of protocols used. The Financial Information eXchange (FIX) protocol seems to be the obvious candidate. FIX is a protocol of messaging specifications for the electronic communication of trade-related messages, but it is not a compressed protocol, whereas FAST is (FAST is FIX adapted for streaming). High-speed traders would like to receive pricing using the FAST protocol.

What people find useful is discussing where and how latency arises in the system. All things considered, the more you reduce the number of "hops" between systems, the lower latency you are likely to achieve. But it's important to measure what's happening here. Time-stamped transactions are highly important in understanding where delays are being incurred. Measuring time in itself is not going to improve performance, but it will tell you where to focus energy and effort.

Regarding accuracy, if we were in the old days, and times of a hundred milliseconds were being incurred, then perhaps measuring times to an accuracy of one millisecond would be perfectly adequate. In the current world, where some are talking of reducing latency to less than 100 microseconds, timings must be accurate to within microseconds.

One must distinguish between accuracy and precision. There are many devices along the chain, and all contain clocks that may generate time to within 10 decimal points. The time that's produced, however, may not be accurate unless it is in current time. In addition, the second you are measuring may not be the same duration as the second that you next measure.[xx] If you are looking for accuracy, you want each second to be identical in length and the same as real time. People have been searching for a universally recognized reference in terms of timing. Of course, the process of time stamping itself can add latency into the system, so you have to adjust for that. But at least you know whether you are going to focus on the firewall or your order management system in terms of reducing latency.

An important point to bear in mind is the existence of a positive feedback loop for well-performing exchanges, whereby low latency in data distribution triggers more electronic order flow as response time is narrowed.

Critical as low latency is to some, customer segments differ in views on just how important it is. For example, the global head of electronic trading at a sell-side firm said, "Latency affords bragging rights for exchanges; actual value isn't there. Once people can't perceive the difference, latency is immaterial." On the other hand, the competitive impact of poor latency performance on an exchange can be devastating. According to the global head of trading at a hedge fund, "Latency is very important to program trading . . . . It's easy to lose liquidity. AMEX lost exchange-traded funds (ETFs) because of latency. It took five seconds to get a fill."

Conclusion

Although exchanges have evolved from human-centered, paper-based institutions to high-speed, electronic platforms in a relatively short time period, they cannot afford to be complacent.

With their transformation into listed, quoted companies, exchanges need to seek value-adding revenues and profits from their members and users, and capture a greater share
of transaction flows on a global scale. This requirement has prompted the rash of merger and acquisition activity seen in recent years. In parallel, legislation and market forces have eased the development of alternative

trading systems (ATS). These newer trading vehicles are snapping at the heels of the established exchanges, making real inroads into the transaction flow.

Not only are exchanges competing with each other on a global basis to attract new listings and transaction flows, but banks and other institutions that used to own the exchanges now are in direct competition with them and are resentful of exchanges profiting from them. This conflict will intensify. Obviously, the environment for global exchanges shows no signs of becoming easier or less competitive.

With customer expectations constantly rising, improved capabilities must be provided to ease customers' processes. Exchanges must reduce tariffs, improve latency performance, increase peak second transaction capacity, offer value-added services, increase transaction capacity through acquisitions and mergers, and embrace newer technologies to maintain their position and stay two steps ahead of the competition.

In general, exchanges are doing an excellent job of meeting customer needs. To stay on top, however, exchanges must invest creatively in key capabilities that are under their control, and that can be linked directly to increased revenue opportunities.

Evolution of Electronic Trading:
Dealing with the Dimensions of Change

Wayne H Wagner, Principal, OM♦NI

Today's securities markets are changing at the fastest pace ever. The impetus driving toward the new market structures is primarily attributable to technological change, midwifed by regulator dictats in the U.S., the U.K., the E.U. and Canada. As has happened in so many other industries, major functions formerly operated by "carbon-based" (people-centric) systems are being taken over by "silicon-based" systems of heavy computing power and advanced communications.

In the process, familiar landmarks of market structure are virtually obliterated, or transmogrified into something barely recognizable. Nowhere is this more starkly apparent than on the floor of the New York Stock Exchange. What was once a teeming mass of humanity, humming busily at the symbolic heart of capitalism, is now depopulated to the point where rumors are that it was necessary to throw fake traders on to the floor to create a proper television backdrop for President Bush's early 2007 visit.

In the process, many old problems, even such simple procedural problems such as DK'd (Don't Know) trades failing to settle at significant rates, have virtually disappeared from the radar screen. In its place now is now a highly serious discussion of what, exactly, *is* a securities exchange? What is the goal we should be striving for in exchange "market micro-structure" design. In what dimensions do we define and measure the quality of the process that is supposed to produce the elusive "best execution" result? How are the various stake-holders – perhaps steak-holders might be a more revealing term – in the securities markets affected by the change? Who are the winners, and who are the losers?

Our understanding of these dimensions of market quality have been greatly advanced over recent years. Indeed, we now have a whole micro-community of academic specialists adding to our understanding of market microstructure. A fruitful interchange of ideas between practitioners and academicians has resulted, even though the surface has barely been scratched. Through this lens, we can approach such vital questions as:

- What is the goal we should be striving for in exchange "market micro-structure" design?
- How is "price discovery" to be enhanced and monitored?
- In what dimensions do we define and measure the quality of the process that produces the elusive "best execution" result?
- How are the various stake-holders affected by the change? Who will be the winners, and who are the losers?

Yet the answers to these questions are more than idle academic speculations; literally trillions of dollars of assets and transactions are affected.

This overview chapter identifies some key dimensions in which the new market structures are being defined. In alphabetical order, we will look into issues of (1) anonymity, (2) commoditization, (3) depth, (4) disintermediation, (5) fairness, (6) fragmentation, (7) franchise value, (8) internalization, (9) latency, (10) liquidity, (11) operating cost, (12) price discovery, (13) transparency, and (14) volatility.

For each issue, we define the domain, discuss how it's changing, what has improved, implications, real and potential serious consequences, and likely winners and losers among:

- exchanges, regulators, brokers (bulge bracket, electronic, 2nd tier, soft dollar);
- investment managers (buyside traders, hedge funds, portfolio managers, and individual traders); and
- wealth stewards (pension fund trustees, mutual fund and endowment boards.)

Finally, we will summarize the overall conclusions for dealing with the multiple dimensions of change.

Anonymity

Just what is at issue here?
Anonymity refers to the ability for an investor to submit orders and execute trades without its identity being revealed. If Joseph Rosen or Wayne Wagner's identity is revealed, who cares? However, if Fidelity Investments or George Soros's identity is revealed, it would make a great deal of difference to those who found out, and would assuredly be a major problem for Fidelity/Soros.

Why? Because the securities markets are filled with "prying eyes:" tape-watchers, free-riders, front-runners, signal stealers, day traders, etc. attempting to discover potentially valuable information about who is trading and why. What's the difference between Rosen/Wagner and Fidelity/Soros?[xxi] In a word, size; size of trading, especially indications of large unfilled trading interest. Such information can create a trading edge, an opportunity to benefit by trading on the information: buying in anticipation of the price jumps that inevitably arise in the face of sustained institutional buying.

From Fidelity/Soros's point of view, these prying eyes force prices to move against them without them the benefit of completing trades themselves. The liquidity they must capture to profit from their ideas is absconded by other traders whose ideas consist entirely of their ability to read endogenous market patterns and signals.

Markets ultimately need to attach to reality, the profit-making reality of the companies whose fortunes and futures their securities represent, in order to anchor market values to real values. The only thing that separates Wall Street from Las Vegas is the crucial function of linking security prices to economic reality in a sufficiently efficient market. Thus markets must encourage participants to do exogenous research by protecting their ability to profit from the fruits of their research. Anonymity of buyer and seller is essential to this wealth-enhancing quest.

What are the important changes?

Anonymity is not a new problem; it is inherent in any market: "Did you hear that Pythagoras is buying up millet?" The author agrees that this signal/rumor based trading is *essential* to market operations: without it liquidity could dry to the level of the real estate market, where anonymity is weak indeed.

That said, efforts to preserve anonymity are extremely important to large scale investors. Without anonymity, they become non-profit agents contributing to market efficiency without pecuniary gain. It is hard to envision a market where a message such as "a million shares just traded a nickel above the previous trade" doesn't represent a significant market signal. One would hope that whoever initiated that up-tick had filled their trading interest before transmitting such a blatant signal.

The traditional method for an institution to secure anonymity - once colorfully described as bearding the trade – was to use a broker to handle the trade while you remain hidden. This was less than 100% effective, since the broker was let in on the secret, and even though he was totally trustworthy, he had to make inquiries to try to find the seller on the other side of the trade. Hopefully those inquiries would be made only to potential sellers, but those potential "prying eyes" who received calls from the broker or others further down the daisy chain felt no obligation to protect the buyer.

Beginning with the crossing networks in the late 1980's, attempts were made to provide institutional investors with facilities to find the other side of the trade without revealing interest to the general public, the other side, nor their own brokers. Orders were placed into a "black box" computer which would search for matches against other anonymous submissions. Any matches that were found were crossed and printed, sometimes with a simple negotiation between the two anonymous parties. Any unmatched remainders were returned undisclosed.

In today's markets these are often referred to as "dark pools," and they are proliferating wildly, especially among bulge-bracket and retail brokers attempting to internalize the order to secure a commission on both sides of the trade. (More on internalization later.) These dark pools have two disadvantages, however. The success rate is low, with typical completion rates less than ten percent of the submitted orders. Secondly, they typically will set a price half way between the current bid and asked prices, and thus lack a pricing mechanism that would compensate for order imbalances. (More on price discovery later.)

In recent years, a new version of "bearding" has stormed onto the scene: chopping the big trades into small pieces of a few hundred shares that are individually indistinguishable from retail order flow, commonly referred to as 'algorithmic trading' (and covered in greater detail elsewhere in this book). By programming a computer to randomize the timing and size of trade, these "slice and dice" trading methods make it possible for a large institutional trade in a liquid stock to hide in plain sight.

Who is benefiting? Who is losing ground?
Today, perhaps as much as three-quarters of institutional trading in liquid names is traded through dark pools or hiding in plain sight. This type of trading can still leave tracks as supply/demand imbalances will still induce price movement. Yet it is more difficult to steal the signals and to profit by them. This would seem to be a significant benefit to wealth stewards and the managers they hire to run their funds.

Increased anonymity has destroyed much of the low hanging fruit for market insiders to profit by reading endogenous market signals, yet the practice still abounds and now succeeds by its ability to trade at lightening speed and low operating costs in order to profit from tiny pattern effects in the market.

Commoditization

Just what is at issue here?

Commoditization refers to the situation where an investor is unable to distinguish one broker from another by the quality of the executions. With algorithmic trading interacting with order flow through direct market access, trading reasonable size in liquid securities has become a commodity operation. When execution quality becomes a characteristic of the market rather than the individual broker, it is difficult for the vast number of brokerage firms to compete on execution quality. There are thousands of registered broker/dealers operating in the United States, and literally hundreds of them which specialize in providing services to institutional investors. Traditionally, these brokers cultivated "relationships" with investors through a variety of mechanisms, including research, contacts, IPO's, soft dollar mechanisms, superior execution and various not-always-above-the-board favors.

A confluence of negative factors is impinging on the business models of these brokers. Today's institutional investors increasingly [a] disdain street research as tainted, [b] consider broker-arranged contacts as less valuable, [c] find soft dollars diminishing and increasingly consolidated, and [d] see execution services reduced to a commodity. As with any commodity business, the advantage falls to the lowest cost producer. Thus the brokerage business finds itself in the uncomfortable position of being unable to create identifiable and differentiable value propositions to its most important clients. Plexus Group counts of brokers actively used by investment managers have declined 12% since the Order Handling Rules have been in effect.

What are the important changes?

The revealed truth appears to be that what had been peddled as a special relationship was for the vast bulk of the trading in liquid equities an unnecessary imposition of a middleman between buyer and seller. This interpositioning was manually intensive , slow, and expensive to provide, thus requiring a significant commission or a deep spread to compensate the market makers.

It gets worse. The commission is only the tip of the iceberg of transaction costs formerly borne by institutional investors. The added transaction steps and potential information leakage threw sand in the market mechanism. In addition to the inflated commission and spreads, separating buyer from seller through unneeded intermediation raised the more egregious costs of impact, delay and opportunity. When the Order Handling Rule changes and decimalization were implemented, these costs dropped precipitously. Plexus Group measured a reduction of total U.S. trading costs from 142 basis points in 2001 to 60 basis points in 2004. While some of that cost reduction was assuredly attributable to the demise of the internet/biotech boom, a significant portion can be attributed to streamlining of the former trading mechanism.

Who is benefiting? Who is losing ground?

A significant portion of the brokerage industry power has passed to the buyside, which is now able to directly control trading activity from initiation through settlement. The trading cost evidence suggests that electronic markets trump manual markets; which should not surprise us since almost all markets worldwide are electronic. Perhaps this will not hold true in times of extreme market turmoil, but so far, investors are the clear winner. Meanwhile, much of the brokerage industry has faced and will continue to face significant repositioning challenges to satisfy and retain clients.

Depth

Just what is at issue here?

Depth of market refers to the number of shares of a security that can be bought or sold at or near the bid and asked prices without causing a dramatic change in price. The deeper the market, the larger the trade that can be readily executed.

This common definition, however, scans only the surface waters of the market, and greater depth lies below. This depth of market can be thought of as lying in layers, with each layer of liquidity more difficult and more costly to access:

1. Revealed liquidity is the visible layer, the number of shares offered for sale or to buy through posted limit orders. Revealed liquidity can be accessed immediately.
2. Flow liquidity arising from a stream of traders posting limit or market orders. Flow liquidity can be accessed by waiting for its arrival. Flow liquidity is the same as revealed liquidity once it arrives, but a trader hoping to trade against it would have to wait for it to appear. "Slice and dice" trading algorithms rely on meeting flow liquidity.
3. Hidden liquidity is liquidity in committed decisions but not yet revealed. It is often institutional supply and demand, and is hidden to protect the information advantage. Dark pools have increased this type of liquidity considerably, mostly at the expense of Revealed and Flow liquidity. See Anonymity above and Transparency below.
4. Liquidity for hire is typified by a principal trade with a broker who buys the shares for his own account. Trading

with someone who would not otherwise trade can be thought of as buying liquidity.

5. Liquidity of last resort is deep pockets, deeply discounted liquidity offered solely in anticipation of significant profit. The author thinks of it as "down on your knees and begging for liquidity." Some examples of last resort providers would be deep contrarian managers, Warren Buffett's rescue efforts, and government bailouts.

6. Liquidity failure occurs when no buyers can be found at any price, as LTCM experienced with Russian Bonds and many banks experienced with Sub-Prime Mortgage CDOs.

An expansive view of market depth would encompass all of these layers, but discussions of depth usually revolve around how much *revealed* liquidity can be found in the market. A deep market is enhanced when traders are encouraged to expose trading interest, especially to expose it where it is visible and actionable, something which institutional traders are loathe to do. Dark pools attempt to overcome this barrier by making the orders actionable but not visible.

What are the important changes?

Traditionally, much of the exposed depth came from market makers and other market insiders who posted orders to profit from the bid-asked spread. For example, a broker, actually a dealer would simultaneously post an offer to buy at $10 and to sell at $10.125. Pairing up a buyer and a seller at these prices would lead to a gross 12½ ¢ profit on each completed buy/sell combination.

Anyone who posts a limit order subjects himself to some risk: price-affecting news might happen and the order hit before it can be modified. Note: this NEVER works in the favor of someone who posts a one-sided limit order.

Market spreads of an eight or a sixteenth used to be wide enough to protect against this contingency, but penny spreads create too little profit cushion and too much exposure for a dealer. What used to be an interesting business when spreads were an eighth or a sixteenth became unprofitable when spreads declined to a penny or two. Dealers began to reduce their depth to the mandated minimum 100 shares and managing the quotes electronically to decrease exposure. The net effect is that market depth as traditionally defined has decreased considerably. In fact, in a very real sense the *purpose* of the dealer quote part of market depth has changed: Ian Domowitz of ITG says "Quotes are not expressions of liquidity, they are tactical advertisements to draw liquidity out. " The liquidity is still there, however now lying in the deeper, trickier layers.

Who is benefiting? Who is losing ground?
Depth, as we have come to know it, seems dead, or at least moribund. The advantages that accrue to both those who place limit orders and lift them seem obsolete in today's fast paced trading. It is hard to see where any market participant would conclude that posting a large sized limit order would be a strategy that dominates an interactive playing out of a stream of small orders. They may retain some relevance as an advertising mechanism in less frequently traded stocks.

Of course, the dark pools are still capable of actuating depth.

Note that decreasing depth is not a signal of decreasing interest in trading. Rather, it indicates a decreasing willingness to expose that trading interest to the prying eyes in a public exchange.

The traditional definition of depth is static: as of one moment in time, suggestive of a more leisurely pace where it was possible to respond in a human-tempo. Perhaps a new definition of depth is in order; one more oriented toward the level of activity over short intervals, including draw-downs of hidden liquidity.

Bottom line, depth with immediacy has diminished, but the work-arounds appear to be capable of alleviating the problems.

Disintermediation

Just what is at issue here?
Disintermediation refers to the removal of intermediaries in a supply chain: "cutting out the middleman." The disappearance or diminishment of the middleman is occurring through out the economy, spurred by the fantastic increase in connectability achieved by the internet. Not only are existing distribution chains being twisted and broken, entirely new chains linking previously disparate parties are being forged: think eBay.

One tends to jump to the conclusion that contemporary discussions about disintermediation are all about the brokers, but the problem may be more pervasive. What we observe is the classic distinctions of an exchange, a broker, and a customer have been blurred in many dimensions. Through Direct Market Access, the exchanges are trying to disintermediate the broker. Through internalization, the brokers are trying to disintermediate the exchanges. Through ETFs and internally managed funds, the brokers are trying to disintermediate the investment management organization. Through institution-only dark pools, the institutions are trying to disintermediate both the exchanges and the brokers. Tim Mahoney, formerly of Merrill Lynch, and now CEO of BIDS Trading, is quoted as saying "It seems you can be a competitor, a client and a collaborator to everyone that you do business with." xxii

What are the important changes?

As Thomas Friedman pointed out in The World Is Flat,xxiii the distribution chains that served major connectivity functions, especially across time and geography, are becoming obsolete in many industries. As was pointed out earlier in this chapter, the
middlemen in the business of facilitating securities transactions is becoming unnecessary. The processes of connectivity are being simplified, and the costs are coming down.

Who is benefiting? Who is losing ground?

Eliminating unnecessary middlemen from a transaction benefits investors by significantly reducing trading costs. The party being disintermediated, however, is going to find Schumpeter's creative destruction unpleasant, at least in the short term. On the other hand, investors found themselves needing new methodologies and communications to efficiently access the markets. Brokers, service providers and exchanges who could meet these communication needs were in the position to dominate the provision of these services.

Fairness

Just what is at issue here?

Ah, the concept of *fairness* is a slippery one. The dictionary definition reads "neutral; free of favoritism or bias; impartial. Just and equitable to all parties." In the political realm, however, fairness often equates to an asserted right which may demand special treatment, often in new claims than implied in the dictionary definition.

The important dimensions of fairness in securities markets revolve around priority of trading and access to information. Most microstructure economists would agree that a market should provide "strict time and price priority." Time priority implies that if I get there first, I get treated first, Price priority means that I can jump the line by offering a better price, thus making the counterparty better off at my expense. Price priority trumps time priority.

What are the important changes?

The SEC's REG NMS market rules mandate strict time and price priority and state that a market center must meet the best price offered anywhere or route the order to the best price. The only caveat to this requirement is that only the best price offered anywhere is protected, which means that prices away from the best price do not receive the same mandated protection.

Priority in markets applies to both market orders and limit orders, but it is most important for encouraging limit orders. Market orders take offered liquidity by accepting the best price shown on the order book. The prices and size shown on the order book are *limit orders.* Thus markets are more robust and deeper if limit orders are encouraged. One way to encourage limit orders is to give them a better deal: allow orders that *supply liquidity* to transact for lower fees than orders that consume; i.e. purchase, liquidity.

Bigger problems arise when one considers other dimensions of best execution besides price. The issues for market order traders are [1] the fees associated with accessing that market; [2] the speed of response of that market (latency;) [3] the certainty of completing and clearing the trade in that market; and [4] most importantly for institutional traders, the size available in that market.

Who is benefiting? Who is losing ground?
At first thought, strict price time priority assures the individual investor of receiving the best price, a clear advantage. The advantages for other market players are not as clear.

Brokers seeking the most efficient means of execution would prefer to find the lowest fee trading venue. A hedge fund who needs to trade in a timeframe of microseconds could find their strategies compromised by latency. All traders would prefer to avoid markets with chronic clearing problems. Finally, institutional traders would prefer to deal in size without tipping their hands through repetitive small trades in public markets.

Many of these problems are not new. Large traders always had to "clear the book" before executing a large trade at a negotiated price away from the current market. But the problems have been accentuated by recent market and investor trends.

The SEC is charged first and foremost with protecting the interests of the individual investor. The individual investor is increasingly a marginal player in today's markets. The rules that protect the individual investor can hamper other traders, as suggested above.

Fragmentation

Just what is at issue here?
Market *fragmentation* arises when investors send their orders to one market where they cannot interact with orders sent to other markets.

Fragmentation is the all-time #1 favorite bogeyman of the organized exchanges: all investors are best served if every investor interacts with every other investor to establish price, so goes the litany. The underlying assumption here is that price is the only criteria and price discovery is the social good produced by an exchange. As discussed in the section on Fairness, price considerations are primary, but there may be other features that certain investors at certain times may be willing to pay up to acquire. You might buy this book for the cheapest price at WalMart, but you might be willing to pay the freight by having it shipped to you from Amazon. You may even enjoy a sojourn to your nearest Borders Books, where you can enjoy a good browse, a cup of latté and stimulating conversation with beautiful members of the opposite sex who are intrigued by your choice of intellectually stimulating material.

The truth is that fragmentation occurs when investors and their fiduciaries exercise freedom of choice and seek to maximize the utility of their trading. Trading only on a one-size-fits-all monopolistic market is like socialism: a solution that has to be imposed uniformly on a populace.

The proliferation of "dark pools" suggests that there are facilities (or profit opportunities) that lie beyond the structured facilities of the central exchanges.

What are the important changes?

Fragmented markets have been around forever; think of the street vendors on the fringes of farmers' markets, the black markets that spring up in any autocratic society, and the curb exchanges that spring up to trade stocks not approved for trading on the exchanges. These all enhance or create a liquid market where trading needs had not been met.

Market splinters began to appear before 1975 to get around the increasingly outrageous fixed commission schedule, but the process has greatly accelerated with the growing popularity of dark pools and "meet" markets.

As of this writing, the fractures in the US market place seem extreme: at last count there were over forty dark pools. Many of these seem duplicative, and at some point we foresee a consolidation into perhaps five to ten pools organized around robust trading communities with specific trading needs.

Is there any validity to the charge that this multiplicity of options means that a buyer might not be able to find a seller seeking liquidity in a different pool? There seems to be readily available technological solution to this problem.

An exchange is connected to its participants by fiber cables leading to the exchange in point-to-point connections. The eBay market, in contrast, is packet switched, with many possible sellers connected to many possible buyers. The connection points are determined by the complexity of the communication network, rather than by routing to a single collection point. Robust buyside software to query markets and route orders to exchanges is the analog to eBay: markets are centralizing at the point of order origination, rather than at the destination.

Who is benefiting? Who is losing ground?

Fractionalization occurs when structured markets fail to provide a class of investors with facilities that allow them to trade without exposing their information edge. Thus the clear losers are the organized exchanges trying to press a "one size fits all" regimen on diverse trading needs. The winners are those investors for whom the organized exchanges cannot – or will not – provide a structure that protects their information and trading interests.

Franchise value

Just what is at issue here?

Franchise Value can be thought of in several ways, a monopoly, a domain of expertise or marquee value. The New York Yankees playing in the Bronx is a monopoly. Bette Midler signing a two year Las Vegas contract is marquee value. Domain of expertise can be seen in the market share of trading desk displays held by Bloomberg.

What are the important changes?

A prime example of a marquee value in trading is the prestige that used to attach to the term "listed on the New York Stock Exchange." From this perspective, we can see that the NYSE monopoly has been eroding for many years, at least since 1975. Further erosion in franchise value is occurring with a reduction in the NYSE's market share of trading in their own listed stocks.

Franchise value attached to most exchanges has been greatly diminished. In today's market they must complete with alternative venues on price, time and value added. They must stake out the portion of the market where they perform best and vigorously defend it. The days of market dominance through rules, regulations and fiat are past.

Turning our attention to the broker/dealers, we find that franchise value can quickly disappear. Where is White Weld? Kuhn Loeb? Mitchell Hutchins? Barings? Salomon Brothers? They used to command wide market presence and great value. It appears to be easy to overstate the value of familiarity, as opposed to true franchise value.

Franchise value seems to exist only in the eye of the beholder. In an era of instant and intense celebrity, marquee value is more like ten minutes/years/decades of fame. Only a politically protected monopoly has any chance of holding against a firestorm of Schumpeterian creative destruction. And diminution of that power seems to come sudden and often complete. The fall of the USSR comes to mind. Or Kidder Peabody.

Who is benefiting? Who is losing ground?

To the extent that a franchise can demand monopoly profits or command a presence in spite of substandard performance and inefficiency, franchise value is largely a negative to the investing public, whose capital assets need to be deployed quickly, accurately, and inexpensively. As pointed out in the section on Commoditization, the externalities, the collateral spill-over damage done by monopolistic franchises far exceeds the monopoly profits.

Internalization

Just what is at issue here?

Internalization is the direction of order flow by a broker-dealer to an affiliated specialist or order flow executed by that broker-dealer as market maker. Internalization is one form of fragmentation. Brokers with large retail flow would prefer to match orders internally against their own flow because it reduces their operating cost and provides opportunities for increasing their commission volume.

Orders that are internalized cannot interact with orders placed through other brokers, so the concern is that price formation may be warped by internalization.

What are the important changes?

Through a variety of rules and regulations the exchanges have tried to preclude the internalization of orders. NYSE Rule 390 was the most effective rule, which said that all trades submitted to member broker/dealers had to be sent to a recognized exchange. B/D's who could not afford to lose trading rights at the NYSE were compelled to fall in line. Pressures to allow broker/dealers to trade in active off-exchange markets led to the rescission of Rule 390 in 2000, opening the door to internalization, a practice of far higher value to the broker/dealers.

Who is benefiting? Who is losing ground?

Clearly the broker dealers are gaining market share at the expense of the exchanges. If these savings are passed on to clients, clearly the clients are gaining. However, if this simply represents a transfer of pricing power from the exchange to powerful broker dealers, the interests of investors are not necessarily well served.

We expect to see the SEC keeping a sharp eye on developments in this area.

Latency

Just what is at issue here?

According to Wikipedia, *latency* is an engineering concept describing a time delay between the moment something is initiated and the moment one of its effects begins or becomes detectable. With respect to markets, the common usage refers to the ability to quickly liquidate or convert an asset through buying or selling without causing a significant movement in the price. Ten years ago the term was unknown. In the days of floor traders, latency was measured in minutes; in today's rapid fire markets latency is measured in thousandths of a second. In rough proportion, the difference between old and new is similar to the difference between messages sent by transatlantic cable compared to sending orders via a sailing vessel.

In today's markets latency needs reduce to raw speed. It blows the mind that for some market participants, locating a computer in facilities physically adjacent to the exchange reduces the trading disadvantage attributable to the speed of light

What are the important changes?
The speed of today's advanced jet fighter planes outstrips human reaction time; so it is with today's rapid-fire securities markets. The speed of today's markets bestows an advantage on those who are able to trade and respond extremely fast. This speed far eclipses the speed of the human mind (or eye) and can only be put to profitable use by tightly connected computers.

Who is benefiting? Who is losing ground?
This speed—the tem "supersonic" vastly understates it – clearly bestows advantage to "the fastest gun." (Which also vastly understates the speed.) Certainly, this microsecond reaction time clashes with the image of the studious CFA spending hours and days ferreting out the truth underlying the accounting statements.

The important distinction is in the decision horizon. The computer-driven trading algorithms focus on momentary advantage and the ability to react in super-human time frames. Market making today is a game of picking up pennies (in front of the steamroller, to complete the analogy), while the horizon of a security analyst extends to months, if not years or even decades. Yet they need to find a common facility to trade with one another. Compare this speed differential to a freeway, with fast cars moving quickly in the left lanes while trucks and old ladies lumber along in the right lanes. All receive value from the "freeway exchange"[xxiv] but the objective functions are entirely different.

Liquidity

Just what is at issue here?
Liquidity refers to the ability to quickly liquidate or convert an asset through buying or selling without causing a significant adverse movement in the price. Liquidity is good, it makes trading easy and inexpensive. It is especially good for institutional investors who wish to trade large amounts.

Liquidity in a stock results in large part from having many shareholders, especially shareholders who like to trade. This can be thought of as "natural liquidity" as an episodic flow of information creates a drift of opinion and triggers trading needs. It also comes from a matching off of buying and selling interests. A market of all sellers with no buyers is a market of zero liquidity.

The other source of liquidity is liquidity for sale, specifically from market insiders who hope to make a profit from selling liquidity to an anxious buyer or seller, then reversing the trade at a profit. This type of liquidity is essential to the functioning of a market; indeed for most stocks in most time frames it is the major source of liquidity.

These are the "prying eyes" we spoke of in the section on anonymity, but here seen from a different aspect. These tape-watchers, signal stealers, day traders, etc. watch the markets for signals of unfilled trading pressure on one side or the other. As we said earlier, such information can create an opportunity to benefit by buying in anticipation of the price rises that inevitably arise in the face of sustained institutional buying. These signals are not terribly difficult to discern, since they tend to create price movement and accelerated volume. The hazard for the liquidity seller is ending up with excess stock when the music stops.

What are the important changes?
Prior to Reg NMS, this kind of liquidity was provided by market makers and specialists, who made a nice living on one eighth and one sixteenth spreads. In order to make a profit in a penny spread market, the slow human beings have been replaced by fast-acting, profit seeking algorithms.

Who is benefiting? Who is losing ground?
Liquidity is clearly of value to investors and traders alike. However, the concept is most applicable to securities with natural liquidity, an inventory of shares that can be traded accompanied by a reasonable balance between buyers and sellers. Much ado was made of the "affirmative obligation" of the NYSE specialists to supply liquidity into unbalanced markets, but the mechanism was far too weak to stand ground in the face of large imbalances. A lack of liquidity would seem to lead to excessive volatility, discussed below. Today's markets seem to be highly liquid where interests are balanced, while more volatile in conditions of imbalance. Whether conditions today are better or worse than before is difficult to discern.

Operating cost

Just what is at issue here?
Operating cost refers to the costs to run an exchange or a brokerage operation, and can be defined as the amortized investment plus the on-going cost of providing and supporting a trading venue.

Two factors have historically prevented effective cost control in securities clearance:

1. High error rates arising from error-prone manual systems.
2. A lack of incentive for cost control under the umbrella of a plush commission.

Whatever can be said for or against manual systems, no one outside of a Florida election would suggest they are less error prone. In more benighted times, the selling broker would jot his understanding on a ticket and the buyer's broker would do the same. If they failed to match the trade would be "DK'd," as in "don't know." Error rates averaged around five percent of all trades, and each of these would require a clerk to get the two brokers together to resolve the problem. It probably cost an order or two of magnitude to clear these mismatched trades.

We have entered a single-entry era where all trading and clearing activity beyond the order origination is automated. Error rates have dropped to infinitesimal, although the errors that occur tend toward the spectacular. The lower cost of clearing is carried through to lower commissions.

What are the important changes?
Regarding cost control, the section on commoditization discussed how difficult it has become for brokers to distinguish themselves by the quality of their executions. When execution of routine orders becomes a commodity, price of execution supersedes quality of execution. In other words the lowest cost producer who will be able to be profitable at a lower commission rate can dominate the market for routine trading. Efficiency of process takes on a whole new importance.

Who is benefiting? Who is losing ground?
Operating cost must ultimately be passed on to the users of the facilities. Thus anything that lowers the cost of trading is of net benefit to those who trade; i.e. the investors.

Anything that lowers operating costs bestows a competitive advantage to a broker or an exchange.

Simply said, a well functioning, low cost low error trading environment makes everybody a winner. Resources consumed correcting avoidable errors is a dead loss activity.

Price Discovery

Just what is at issue here?

Price Discovery is often thought of as the primary *rasion d'etre* of an exchange: determining the price for a security by moving the price so that supply and demand are equalized. Generally the specialists or market makers will tweak the price up and down to find where the maximum trading volume can occur. This creates a wonderful synergy: the maximum trading volume of investors and traders are satisfied while the dealers simultaneously experience the maximum order flow *and* commission revenue.

But not all markets support price discovery. Most dark pools simply accept the prevailing market price and make no attempt to use price as an equilibrator of supply and demand.

The key issue is the increasing amount of trading that partially piggybacks upon the primary market for price discovery and crosses trades at this price, yet does not enable the trading to participate in the formation of prices. The problem is a tragedy of the commons.[xxv] The accurate pricing of securities becomes a free good, and the exchanges that bear the cost of producing economically meaningful prices do not share in the benefits of producing those prices.[xxvi]

What are the important changes?

Traditionally, price discovery was considered to be performed on "the primary market," which usually referred to the exchange on which the security was listed. In an era when the percentage of NYSE's trading in its own stocks has dropped below 50%, the concept of primacy seems to need redefinition. Price discovery is critical to the function of the market and the economy.

Unfortunately, it is difficult for an exchange to profit from the price discovery mechanism. Everybody wants efficient pricing, but no one seems willing to pay for it. The tragedy of the commons revisited.

Dark pools, including crossing networks and internalization of orders are almost wholly dependent on the open markets for the setting of prices of trades. This sounds like a potentially serious and nefarious problem but the deleterious effects might be considerably fewer than seems apparent.

Consider a trade where a 100 share buy order is paired off by the broker with a 100 share sell order and crossed internally. Neither trade participates in price formation, right? True, but not necessarily a problem! Suppose both trades were sent to the market: how would they have affected the setting of prices? Likely not at all. Prices are not changed when buy and sell volumes match, they are simply ticked off one against the other. Only trades that upset the buy/sell balance will have any effect on prices.

The same is true of crossing networks. Suppose a million shares of buying interest crosses against 100,000 shares of selling interest: what will happen. The match, 100,000 shares, will cross while the remaining 900,000 shares of buying interest will need to interact in the market, thus participating in price discovery.

Who is benefiting? Who is losing ground?
Inaccurate price discovery harms all market participants and compromises the pricing of assets and risks in the economy. Regulators seeking to protect the retail trader need to pay particular attention.

Transparency

Just what is at issue here?
Transparency describes a market in which (a) completed trades are promptly reported and (b) unfilled trading interest (limit orders) are publicly displayed. Transparency ties together with price discovery, which is pointless unless the results of recent transactions are widely known. Anyone who watches CNN, analyzes the records of current prices, or glances at the DJIA to see the current market trend relies on transparency information. Similarly, a trader would check the spread and depth of book to assess the likely price of a contemplated trade. Transparency is thus part information and part advertising. Information leads to informed decision making, while advertising creates a means of attracting new buyers and sellers. Think in terms of the advertising supplements in the Sunday newspapers, heralding prices and especially sale prices.

Transparency operates in opposition to anonymity, which we identified as valuable to institutional sized buyers and sellers. In markets governed by the Securities and Exchange Commission, quotes must be updated as quickly as possible and completed trades reported within seconds. For an institutional investor, this publicity can result in a partial disclosure of valuable private information, at least until the full order has been completed. Indeed, some non-US exchanges do not require immediate printing of a trade at the discretion of the dealer.

What are the important changes?
All markets and all ECNs are required to report existing trades within seconds. The dark pools, however are not required to reveal the orders placed into the system. Some, especially at the SEC, find this a disturbing inconsistency, because individuals cannot trade against the liquidity in

members-only dark pools. The dilemma is not easily solved: to require markets to expose their orders would invalidate the *rasion d'etre* of the dark pools.

Who is benefiting? Who is losing ground?
As with many of the topics, the question is not one of principle but of attaining a balance that accommodates the differing market needs. The resolution lies not in the principles, but in well balanced rules and regulations that govern trading activities.

Volatility

Just what is at issue here?
Volatility is the magnitude and frequency at which the price of a security moves up and down. There are three important sources of volatility: [1] changes in expectations or likelihood of expectations about the companies, industries and countries underlying the securities, [2] imbalance of buyers and sellers, and [3] poor market structures, potentially including fractionalized markets.

What are the important changes?
Volatility is an effect, not a cause. It is transmitted into the market through an imbalance of buyers and sellers. Under the old NYSE rules, the specialist was supposed to dampen volatility through the market continuity rules, but this was a finger in the dike at best. In the early 2000s volatility was very low, and rose later in the decade as the world began to show warning signs of economic recession.

Who is benefiting? Who is losing ground?
Dealers love volatility because it creates profit opportunities. Investors hate it because it creates uncertainty and risk.

Conclusion and Implications

What is this thing called a market? The dictionary definitions of a market or market place aren't especially insightful: e.g. "a body of persons carrying on extensive transactions in a specified commodity." Technically correct but not very illuminating.

To correctly understand markets, we need to think of "exchange" as a verb, not a noun.

The standard economists' model of an effective market describe a forum in which indications of trading interest are publicly displayed, ranked by price and time of submission within price, with the execution of orders strictly determined by this priority. In this model, all trades are interactions between visible limit orders and demands for immediacy in the form of market orders. Again, the focus is on the mechanics.

This model works when all traders are roughly the same size and arrive frequently enough to offset buying and selling interest. That might be a nice description of a farmer's market, but is deficient in describing today's equity markets for several reasons:

1. Institutional players need to trade in amounts that dwarf the trading desires of individual investors. This imbalance creates most of the difficult problems confronting market designers.
2. These traders are often more interested in size than price; they may be willing to forego better market prices at tiny volumes to get their enormous block done expeditiously.
3. They realize that displaying their trading interests would only serve to motivate frontrunners and copycats to jump ahead while causing potential trading partners to withdraw or delay until a clearer picture (and likely an inferior price) develops.
4. In a market where the best price may evaporate in a flash, certainty of execution might be more important than strict price priority.

Martin Sexton[xxvii] defines the purpose of an exchange as follows: ". . . [to] enable buyers and sellers to come together in a regulatory environment that ensures honest dealing but doesn't get in the way of growth." Again, focus on the mechanics.

A better starting point is from Picot[xxviii], "a discovery and learning process which rewards the best informed participants with the greatest knowledge arbitrage profits."

That's worth dissecting. It defines the purpose: parties that trade with the most knowledge use the exchange to secure the value of that knowledge. It recognizes that the purpose of the exchange is to arbitrage out special information so that the prices of assets represent true economic value. Finally, by describing the exchange as a process, it focuses on the dynamics, not the floorboards.

However, it misses the central reason for the existence of a securities market – the pricing of assets and investment risk and thereby expected returns. A definition that includes this goal – and gets rid of that awkward "knowledge arbitrage profits" phrase – would read as:

A discovery and learning process that prices assets and investment risks and rewards the best informed participants with the greatest returns from research and risk bearing."

With that in mind, we can go back and consider some of the working parts that an exchange provides:

1. A forum, a place where buyers and sellers can come together. The forum may be physical or electronic.
2. A means for buyers and sellers to address that forum, either in person, through an agent, or self-representing electronic messages.
3. A means of discovering a price satisfactory to both buyer and seller.
4. A means of intermediating time so that buyer and seller who arrive at uncoordinated times and can find each other.
5. Dissemination of information about [1] prices and quantities of available merchandise, and [2] records of executed trade prices and size. This is advertising, plain and simple.
6. Rules for orderly conduct so that transactors are not taken advantage of by unscrupulous exchange insiders or outside parties. Investor confidence is essential to any market competing for business.
7. Efficient payment and delivery systems; a guarantee that counter parties will perform or the exchange will step in as guarantor of the trade.

Considering all of these factors together, we can see that investors and their agents have attained a new level of power over how their assets are treated when exposed to the flux of the market. The changes have been mostly positive, and have driven costs down remarkably.

The results have been more mixed for the brokerage and exchange communities. Large, capital rich, adroit brokers have thrived, as have the providers of facilities such as dark pools which have attained market acceptance. The exchanges are scrambling to redefine themselves. The old traditions are no longer valued. Most brokers are struggling with redefining their value proposition, as are the exchanges.

But the game is still in the opening quarter; the ultimate winners and losers are neither known nor predictable. It's too early to declare the ultimate winners, but talent, flexibility, innovation and dedication will carry the day.

The Decline and Fall of the NYSE Club

By John Aidan Byrne, Cloverhill Enterprise

The Dow Jones Industrial Average set another trading record on this strange, cloudy and sentimental day, as I once again sat foot on the floor of the New York Stock Exchange. It was a time of reflection, this visit to witness an institution dying on its feet, literally -- the once big and brave specialist system that has famously facilitated American capitalism for over two centuries. The old excitement and high fives were gone, and the crowd on the floor -- combat troops and optimists by nature -- were as downcast and gloomy as a speech by ex-Fed boss Alan Greenspan. That was on May of 2007. The last visit to the floor, about six years earlier, was a striking contrast to this death sentence moment. I don't recall the exact day, or what the Dow closed at six years before, but heck, it hardly mattered. By the trading day's end, the floor traders were playful and had energy to spare. It was the season of parties, and they never seemed to end. The parties are a distant memory. And that heavenly scene – like an over-the-top evangelical revival meeting – will never be repeated again. This is the final scene, and it is awful. The NYSE floor community is disappearing as advanced technology replaces human traders. This story is about the rise of the high-tech NYSE Euronext Empire, and the fall of the low-tech NYSE Club.

What was the Club? The Club was the name for the generations of traders who paced the floor of the Big Board in nylon jackets; stout-hearted generations of hyphenated Americans from the Irish, Italian and Jewish communities, great people, fun, intelligent, sharp with numbers, decent, scrappy people, who lived and died for the Club. These are the traders who today are packing their personal belongings -- each and every day – so that soon the venerable floor will become like the ghost town long predicted by experts on the technological changes sweeping trading. The changes include the NYSE Hybrid and Reg NMS from the Securities and Exchange Commission. The promise is better pricing anywhere – on the Big Board, the Amex, NASDAQ, the regionals, BATS Trading, Instinet, anywhere -- for investors; fairness, transparency, and speed of executions. The Club never had much of a hope with this long laundry list of goals. Some downcast traders from the Club, tossed onto the sidewalk like pathetic scraps of red meat for the dogs, have sought counseling from psychiatrists and psychologists. (Psychologist Ari Kiev, best-selling author of several books on the psychology of trading, recently confided to me that some NYSE pros have met him.)

The Club is as old as the exchange itself. And this is not the first time it was so intensely in the crosshairs of regulators, technology and big investors. The last time was in the late '60s and early '70s, in the days and months that preceded one of the last great shocks to Wall Street in modern financial history – 1975, the year that fixed commissions were finally abolished. Don't just take my word for it about the Club. The best authority, as I have so far discovered, is the esteemed Chris Welles, formerly of *Institutional Investor*, who penned the seminal book, *The Last Days of the Club*, back in the year – get this – 1975! (E.F. Dutton & Co., Inc, New York, 1975, 460 pages). Welles traced the origins of the Club to the Buttonwood Tree Agreement of May 17, 1792. This agreement had two significant rules – fixed commissions to non-members, and preferential treatment by members among themselves. Over time, these principles of business conduct were sanctioned by the government, according to Welles.

> *"Until not very long ago, members of the Club believed their good fortune in possessing an officially sanctioned natural monopoly guaranteed them prosperity. If the Exchange was not organized the way it is, they said, it would certainly collapse, a cataclysm that would do irreparable harm to the world's greatest economy and alter our way of life. So confident were Club members that they recognized only very belatedly two serious challenges to the privileges of their world, challenges unlike they had ever faced before."*[xxix]

Picture the floor these days, occupied now by about 1,500 trading professionals at full capacity – nobody can give an accurate count because it has declined precipitously, of course -- compared with 5,000 specialists, brokers and clerks only a few years ago. The massive job reductions had turned into a bit of a media feeding frenzy. Each blow on the chin was worth a biting headline. The New York Post broke the news that the floor was finally becoming a tourist attraction. I admit to writing that salty piece about John O'Shea, Chairman and CEO of Westminster Securities who, in mid-career, finally qualified as a floor broker – so that he could escort clients on tours of the floor! As I write now, it's the turn of LaBranche & Co., Inc., which was reportedly mulling a sale of itself as trading revenue plunged a staggering 59 percent in one recent quarter alone. Electronic trading encroaches every day on the role of human traders -- and more volume is being handled electronically. "The best-paid traders are lucky to take home

$200,000 a year. Back six years ago, some people were each pulling in $1 million a year," one floor pro told me. "Hybrid is a lie – there's no profitable role for human traders here." (Sorry, $200,000 is still a small fortune to many folks on Main Street, but there were other trading pros on the floor barely taking home what a hot dog vendor makes on Broad Street.)

The rise of NYSE Euronext formally began in March 2006 -- first under former Goldman Sachs' luminary, the soft-spoken CEO John Thain, and later under another ex-Goldman bigwig, Duncan Niederauer, known for his down-home style. It began with a daring bit of corporate and legal shuffling. It was slowly emerging before then, of course, with the convergence of certain events on Wall Street – which makes Welles' tome a page turner – and the startling ouster of former exchange chairman, Dick Grasso. Grasso protected the NYSE like a human pitbull. Say what you like, his departure is regarded by some old NYSE hands as a mixed blessing. Dick Grasso, the once indomitable boss of the NYSE from Queens, was the champion of the Club. But March 2006 was a watershed and by then Dick was gone (but not forgotten). The NYSE had become a publicly-traded company when it merged early in the month with Archipelago Holdings – NYSE's former arch enemy from the Chicago boonies. "Being a newly public company will create a cultural change," William Cline, a managing partner for global capital at Accenture, told a reporter. "Historically, it's been an insular culture made even more so by SIAC [NYSE's technology unit]." Welles wrote about the very same forces that were threatening the Club back in the early 1970s. The author, of course, made his call too early but he was surely right about the reasons for the Club's collapse, which were as relevant then as they clearly are today. He cited the role of large institutional investors, the elimination of fixed commissions – and modern technology.

> "New computer technology poses a second, ever more fundamental threat to the Exchange monopoly. If applied to the antediluvian, paper-ridden NYSE floor, it clearly has the potential to disrupt entrenched power relationships within the Exchange and put many members out of business. Technology's most severe disruptive potential, though, lies in its application to the over-the-counter market."[xxx]

Welles noted that until this time, the then OTC market – the market for non-exchange-listed stocks -- had never been able to compete with the Big Board. How could it? For one thing, it did not have the advantage of a central location like the exchange floor. For another, it also lacked the exchange's auction system, which so efficiently executed small orders. However, the emerging OTC market – NASDAQ – did have several advantages: it had competing dealers linked by a system which could evolve into a juggernaut, a juggernaut that combined an automated auction mechanism serving both retail and institutional investors. Welles saw the writing on the NYSE's neoclassical walls. But he could hardly have imagined the SEC-mandated order handling rules two decades later, rules that would initially hurt big NASDAQ traders, but ultimately propel the growth of electronic trading, including ECNs and ATSs. In case you missed that epochal moment, the SEC approved the creation of certain networked technologies in 1997 – Electronic Communications Networks, or ECNs -- that permitted NASDAQ's market makers to publicly display their customers' superior limit orders, limit orders that the SEC had accused these same market makers of hiding to protect their fat profits. It was a scandal worth another chapter. There are independent experts who swear the real scandal was in the government's case: The evidence of price collusion by dealers accused of artificially inflating the bid-ask spreads was scant. It rested, in part, on a study by two academics that purported to show a pattern of NASDAQ market making that could only be the work of the devil Yet, there was no convincing proof, only plenty of accusations of price fixing. (In fairness to the feds, all this regulatory attention, starting with the decision to abolish fixed commissions back in 1975, eventually led to an extraordinary reduction in the commissions charged institutional and retail investors. For instance, the move to decimal pricing in recent years would have made the original discount brokers of the late 1970s hot under the collar.)

In time, NASDAQ was also forced to transform itself into a defacto ECN in a painful and expensive process of acquisition. NASDAQ did become a formidable competitor that challenged the world domination of the NYSE. But despite the rhetoric and bluster, NASDAQ never overtook the NYSE. Welles was close.

> "The New York Stock Exchange may still be today's natural monopoly," Welles wrote in 1975, "but the new electronic OTC marketplace which is emerging will almost certainly be tomorrow's."

Today, market structure is at a crossroads. The coming months will inevitably produce more winners and losers as Reg NMS and Hybrid trading, as well as global consolidation among stock markets – this spurred by shareholders' demanding higher returns – claw at the soul of human trading. Although NASDAQ never delivered that knockout punch to the NYSE, it contributed in large measure to its modernization (for instance, the electronic delivery and execution of orders up to 10,000 shares on the NYSE DOT system). NASDAQ's example encouraged the growth of rival electronic venues – clones of NASDAQ that stole NASDAQ's lunch. And the combined forces of NASDAQ and its rivals and other NYSE competition, dramatically has reduced the NYSE's market share in the trading of its own stock. Of course, NYSE Euronext is not down. On the contrary, some analysts predict a bright future for this public company, but a future that does not include the floor trader.

As we stepped outside the exchange on this strange and sentimental day, the clouds above were heavy and the sky darkened. Then all of a sudden, a terrible storm started, the wind scattering garbage across Broad Street. It was a scene straight out of an Alfred Hitchcock movie. The streets were empty except for the occasional stray trader. I was with Jonathan "Nat" Niles, a veteran floor trader, and we took refuge in the nearest watering hole. He bantered along the way with a fellow broker, a cigar-chomping fellow of good nature with a mane of white hair and a wit that could cut slice salami. Niles confided that trading on the floor was not his original career choice. As a youngster, growing up on a farm in New Jersey, he had planned to work his life with horses but his life took a different turn, so instead of livestock it was stock securities. Niles predicted many more exchange floor jobs disappearing, unless the exchange itself honors its pledge that the human specialist system is important. Niles and his colleagues can forget the pledge, some analysts say. How do you argue with the NYSE Euronext now serving public shareholders, a worldwide company that owns Euronext in Europe and other colonial possessions? And it is really no longer just a stock exchange because it also trades derivatives.

Back in 1975, as Welles noted, institutional investors were calling for the NYSE's scalp – they demanded the exchange tear down its protected barriers. However, the NYSE had a monopoly in listed trading which was too big a fight for most, unless you were the reform-minded Donald Weeden. He's the same curmudgeon Donald Weeden of today's Weeden & Co. Today, this respected Greenwich gentleman is much less prone to rabble-rousing. Back in the old days, Weeden was pioneering the "third market," pressing sharply for reforms like some protestor on the streets in a land run by a mad despot. That despite the inherent risks to his professional reputation. Listed block trading was becoming bigger business, and pros like Weeden had found cost-effective ways to trade these blocks away from the exchange. "We didn't set out to destroy the New York Stock Exchange," he told Welles. "We just wanted to conduct a quiet business and compete with them. The way we saw it, it was live and let live. We didn't feel any antagonism toward them. But when they came along and used slander and illegal boycotts and economic pressure on our customers to perpetuate their monopoly and to try and put us out of business, well it just teed us off." Weeden used his bully pulpit, made speeches, bought advertisements in newspapers, spoke before the SEC and Congress. He never let up, constantly attacking the "monopoly power" of the NYSE and calling for a new, open-access marketplace.

Weeden wasn't alone. Former NYSE president, Robert Hack, delivered an unprecedented speech for a man of his professional public standing, a speech that pointed to the inevitability of the Club's demise, according to Welles. The date was November 17, 1970, and it was delivered at the tony Waldorf=Astoria in New York to members of the Economic Club, a group of influential business leaders. "If Mr. Haack had dropped a bomb on the trading floor," the *Wall Street Journal* reported afterwards, "he hardly could have caused more commotion." The speech began ordinarily enough, praising 178 years of NYSE service and tradition, high regulatory standards, close supervision of members and excellent disclosure rules.

> *"Yet...,"Haack said, pausing just an instant. Some of his friends in the audience observed that he seemed very nervous. His voice was cracking slightly and his hands were shaking, as he continued. "I am concerned lest we bask in the glory of the past, and in the process become obvious to the emerging trends." Paramount among the latter, he said, was the fact that an increasing amount of trading volume was being diverted from the Exchange to the regional stock exchanges and the third market....Even worse, he went on, were the conditions accompanying this "fragmentation" of the market, specifically a dense and often bizarre complex of reciprocal relationships and kickback schemes under which brokerage commissions are split among various parties...[xxxi]*

It was in this famous speech that the word "Club" was formally acknowledged and solidified by a ranking NYSE executive. Haack warned: "Whatever vestiges of a private-club atmosphere which remain at the New York Stock Exchange must be discarded." That speech, which sounds so familiar today, is coming up to four decades ago, when advanced technology and cut-throat competition was even then all the range. It was, surely, an intense bout of competition, a bout that preoccupied business writers who were writing off the Big Board as an anachronism. But it was just the warm-up act for the final curtain. Today, the exchange, fending off competition again from all and sundry, could very well succeed as a public company at the expense of human traders. The biggest differences today include the acceleration in the speed of trade executions – micro and millisecond executions are common occurrences -- the introduction of complex order routing technology, algorithms, dark pools, and the fulfillment of institutional demands for NYSE trading reforms. Most important, for better or worse, the regulators finally pulled the plug on the NYSE's trading monopoly. How else can you explain the inexorable rise of BATS Trading, which uses a bunch of cheap computer boxes to swipe volume from the NYSE? Now the floor community is getting hosed.

An usual event occurred on April Fools Day, 1968. The volume on the exchange climbed to a record 17,730,000 shares, which is small compared with the multi-billion share days that would follow many years later. Welles recalled how the Club was falling over itself with pure joy and shock. Commission dollars were pouring in so fast, that members hardly had time to catch their breath, or enjoy a cocktail. It was a jet-setting era of fabulous wealth, new homes and vacations, for members of the Club. But the policy wonks in Washington were about to spoil this fun. Little did NYSE members realize that on this same April Fools Day, the ink had dried on a damning 67-document that attorneys in the antitrust division of the Department of Justice, had submitted to the SEC. The document would unleash a round of public calls by the Congress and SEC for radical change at the NYSE, an outcry that led to the abolition of fix commissions in 1975. Rate fixing, Justice said, "is a product of history, not logic or necessity."

Today, by some accounts, we have witnessed the death of the NYSE Club. The NYSE is, in effect, an ECN like NASDAQ, albeit a bigger ECN than NASDAQ. By some estimates, only about 50 percent of orders – that might be generous -- in NYSE-listed stocks are posted these days on the specialists' book. Most are electronic and anonymous, broken up and processed by algorithms, so that the specialist does not know if a series of small orders actually are from the same customer. And this is the frightening scenario ahead: specialists are losing the kind of direct contact with customers which once was at the heart of their business. In this hellhole, how can specialists be successful in dampening volatility as intermediaries, and at offering critical, potentially market-moving information to the public companies they represent? Surely this is not the kind of market structure the SEC believes is in the best interest of investors?

One other reason to lament the demise of the NYSE Club is the kind of excitement and camaraderie only an institution like this can nurture. When I think of NYSE floor traders and pros, I sometimes think of highly compensated coal miners who come up in the afternoon from the bowels of the earth. Fine, I am getting ahead of myself. But think of the vanishing floor as a once lucrative cash cow – the Wall Street equivalent of a livestock mart. Niles had dreamed of horses, so it is not so far-fetched. The NYSE "miners" or "ranchers" had class. Computers are boring company. As we quaffed our second beverage on this windy afternoon, another trader from the NYSE floor came into the licensed premises, a guitar strung loosely across his shoulder. He could have been cast as one of the Clancy Brothers, that great Irish folk group made famous, legend has it, by an appearance on the Ed Sullivan Show on TV. He told us he was playing a gig later in the neighborhood, but would be pleased to join us for a moment of simple conviviality. The guitar-strumming trader had pen and paper in his jacket pocket and he didn't plan to write up some stock orders. That's right. He was working on a new song – a lament for the last and final days of the NYSE Club.

On the Rise of Machines:
US Equities and the Migration to Algorithmic Trading

Dan Mathisson, Managing Director - Head of Advanced Execution Services, Credit Suisse

In the 1984 movie "The Terminator", a disturbing future is revealed: Killing machines have taken over the Earth, their red eyes glowing as they march about methodically trying to defeat the remaining humans. Only a few determined rebels stand between the machines and their goal of total world domination.

In the markets of today, the image many have is similar: quant machines have taken over the financial world, their LCD screens glowing as they methodically capture market share from the remaining traders on the floors. But unlike the outcome in the movie, in this story the floor traders in the sparsely populated trading pits are not likely to stop the rise of the machines.

Just twenty years ago, massive trading floors were run on a diet of sandwiches and cigarettes, filled with ringing phones and the thunking of time clocks stamping carbon-copied trade tickets. Today's smaller floors are run instead on a steady diet of real-time data, the machines voraciously sucking in thousands of price quotes each second, chewing each one for a few milliseconds and occasionally spitting out a silent trade into the markets.

Money managers are now besieged with invitations to dozens of algorithmic trading conferences and seminars. Virtually all of the trading on the venerable New York Stock Exchange is now executed without any human intervention, while the exchange painfully shuts down the floor one room at a time.[xxxii] Trading desks are increasingly staffed by former academics with degrees in physics and computer science. An article in the New York Post summed up the situation nicely, the headline reading "Geeks Invade Wall Street."[xxxiii]

How did the markets get here? The story of the rise of the machines is a case study in how changes in regulations often have unintended consequences, and how seemingly small changes in rules or technology can lead to huge changes in the business world. This chapter will start by exploring the factors that led to the dominance of algorithmic trading in the US equity markets. Then we will look at the upcoming trends and regulatory changes in the US equity markets and speculate on what's likely to evolve in the near future.

Factor 1: the computers begin talking

As with most man vs. machine stories, our story begins with the increase in the capabilities of the machines. Of course Wall Street benefited from the same general increase in computer speed, memory, and stability that benefited almost every industry in the past 20 years. But perhaps more important than the increase in raw computer power was the fact that starting in the 90's, the computers on Wall Street learned to talk to each other.

Starting in 1992, a group of engineers working for mutual fund giant Fidelity Investments and brokerage firm Salomon Brothers began creating a new communication protocol. Called "FIX", which stands for Financial Information eXchange, the new protocol allowed these two firms to route US equity orders and fills to each other by computer. This didn't (yet) change the way decision-making was done – it was strictly for improving the process of communicating orders.

The way it was

Prior to FIX, even as recently as the mid-1990s, orders had to survive a marathon game of telephone to arrive at their execution destination intact.

An order would typically get phoned from the institutional client to the brokerage salesperson, who would yell it over to the brokerage block trader, who would phone it to the clerk on the floor of the NYSE, who would write it down on a scrap of paper and give it to a floor runner who would physically carry the paper to the floor broker, who would then discuss the trade with the crowd at the post and with the specialist. Then the specialist would fill a part of the order, and the chain of paper, phone calls, and shouts would begin again in reverse. And at each stop, the clerk, trader, or salesperson would have to fill out a paper ticket and clock it, which eventually would get passed to an assistant who since the 1970s would "key-punch" the details into a computer to allow the trade to clear and settle.

Somewhat miraculously, most trades did manage to settle without "breaking" the next morning, but only because traders invested a lot of effort, time, and pride into the art of passing orders and fills along correctly. The chain of phone calls and shouts employed thousands of highly paid people whose primary skill was the ability to pass along trade information with impressively low error rates. But as with many impressive skills that get made obsolete by technology, the Fidelity and Salomon FIX teams quietly working in 1992 spelled the beginning of the end of order-passing as a desired and highly compensated skill.

An industry standard is born

With FIX, orders get passed up this chain of people via computer, and then the fills automatically percolate back down, with the computers time-stamping and saving each fill. There are no tickets to write, no time-clocks to stamp, and virtually no chance of the computer passing along the wrong price or the wrong quantity.

Fidelity quickly saw the potential for FIX to improve their bottom line by making trading more efficient, and they began to push their huge list of brokers to accept the new FIX standard. It was quickly adopted by brokers, exchanges, other major mutual funds and asset managers. Within a few years of its creation, a clear industry standard had been established. [See Figure 1]

Figure 1: Adoption of FIX Connectivity as % of Total US Volume

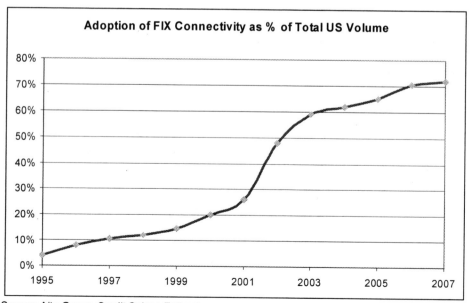

Source: Aite Group, Credit Suisse Estimates

Since the late 1980s the technology had existed to allow computers to read prices in real-time and make trading decisions, but mostly this resulted in a suggestion popping up on a trader's screen, who would then begin working the phones. But as it became possible in the mid '90s for orders and fills to fly around Wall Street without telephones, it became theoretically possible for a computer to bake the whole cake: dream up a trade, send it out for a fully automated execution, monitor the fills, and bank the profits. The only problem was that at the time, the machines still couldn't know what was really going on in the markets.

Factor 2: The Order Handling rules and the birth of ECNs

The way it was

Prior to 1997, Nasdaq was an unfair market. There were really two markets: the market that was publicly displayed to the world for mom-and-pop investors, and the real market for professionals, which mostly took place in an ancient-looking computer with blinking green numbers called an Instinet "box."

The public would trade with "market-makers", dealers who in theory were required to be willing to buy or sell at all times in the stocks in which they had agreed to play. For the market makers the game was easy – they would keep their quotes ¼ or ½ wide, always around the Instinet quote. In other words, if the Instinet market in Microsoft (MSFT) was 89 3/16 – 89 ¼ (which means a trader can either sell at 89 3/16, or can buy at 89 ¼,) the market makers would typically collude to quote 89 – 89 ½. So if a retail client wanted to buy 500 shares of MSFT, the market-maker that received the order would buy the shares on Instinet at 89 ¼, and immediately flip them to the client at the visible national best offer of 89 ½, pocketing the difference without having taken any risk.

So the published market read by computers and retail investors was not the real market. But a bigger problem was that the real market would not publish its quotes. At the time, the conventional wisdom on the Street was that broker-dealers needed to own the client's desktop to own the client's order flow. Instinet management thought that if computers could read and respond to the Instinet quotes, people would not need to look at the blinking green box anymore. They worried they would lose the valuable "real estate" Instinet had painfully acquired over more than 20 years of installing boxes throughout the world.

Instinet's decision meant that institutional clients that traded Nasdaq stocks needed living, breathing people to look at the Instinet box and determine where the real market was, and then either type the orders into Instinet, or pick up the phone and negotiate with a market-maker. As with trading in all dealer markets, getting good prices outside of "the box" was still very much a relationship game.

The market gets cleaned up

Surprisingly, it was an academic paper that ended the dual market system. In May of 1994, the Journal of Finance published an article by William Christie and Paul Schultz, entitled, "Why do Nasdaq market makers avoid odd eighths quotes?"[xxxiv] The professors found that quotes on the published market were almost always at prices ending in ¼, ½, ¾, or 0. Their suggestion as to why this was the case was that market-makers were colluding to hold spreads artificially wide.

Shortly after the paper was published, the Department of Justice launched an investigation which uncovered hours of somewhat humorous phone conversations of market-makers cajoling and berating each other to move off an "odd-eighth" quote. Market-makers referred to tight markets as "Chinese markets" and in the investigation many examples were found of market-makers calling each other to order chicken chow mein in a thick accent, which was apparently a favorite way to send a message to another market-maker that they were messing up the normally wide published spread.[xxxv]

The SEC responded to this breach of market integrity with a series of new rules over the next three years that would in time transform trading in Nasdaq-listed stocks from an unfair insider's market into a model of efficiency and fairness. The "Manning" rules (named after an arbitration case) required that market-makers publicly display limit orders sent to them. Manning was followed by the Order Handling Rules which went into effect in early 1997. The Order Handling Rules designated computerized trading platforms like Instinet as "ECNs" (electronic communications networks.) Under the new rules, ECNs would be essentially electronic market-makers; they would publish their quote on the publicly displayed markets, thus making the public market at least as tight as the Instinet market.

The dual markets had been killed off. Within a few years of the rule changes, more than 10 new ECNs plunged into the marketplace, competing with each other on speed, price, and reliability. Instinet lost its monopoly among professional traders, and suddenly found itself competing with aggressive newcomers like Archipelago and Island.[xxxvi] And clients trading Nasdaq-listed stocks finally had the ability to get a fast, cheap, and fair automated fill on their orders.

But while the Nasdaq was becoming more electronic by the day, the same was not true of the NYSE. The machines were still at a significant disadvantage to the floor brokers. This lasted until the SEC passed another change referred to as decimalization.

Factor 3: Decimalization decimates the old system

While the Nasdaq was going through radical changes in the late '90s, the NYSE continued motoring along, trading much the same way it had since it was founded in 1792 under the iconic buttonwood tree.

The NYSE had added plenty of technology over the years in the form of quote screens and computer systems to clear and settle trades, but the actual trading in the '90s still occurred as it had always. Each stock was assigned to a specialist who was charged with maintaining an orderly market. The specialists stood all day at their assigned posts, and floor brokers would walk over (there is a "no running" rule on the floor) and interact with the specialist or the "crowd." Added to the mix were DOT orders, which looked like electronic orders, but really were just orders electronically delivered to the specialist directly, who would then verbally represent them in the crowd.

The way it was

Since the 18th century, stocks had traded in 1/8th increments dating back to when the Spanish dollar was the currency of choice, and "pieces of eight" were its basic unit. This continued for more than 200 years until June of 1997, when the minimum increment on the NYSE dropped to 1/16th. Even after the switch, a sixteenth was still a big minimum spread in the more liquid stocks. On a typical $25 stock, a 6.25c increment amounts to a huge 25 basis points between the bid and the offer (a basis point = 1/100th of 1%.) The wide minimum spread discouraged electronic trading on the NYSE in several ways.

When the minimum spread in any market is larger than the spread would naturally be, a lot of shares tend to build up on both the bid and the offer. Let's say that Merck was 36 ¼ - 36 5/16 with 30,000 on the bid and 60,000 shares on the offer. A trader wants to sell 25,000 shares. The minimum 1/16 increment leaves him with a binary decision: either whack the bid, or join the offer. Offering somewhere in the middle is not an option. Regardless of the decision, an institutional trader was wise to use a human floor broker instead of the "electronic" DOT system.

If the trader decided to join the offer, a floor broker would typically perform much better than the DOT system. This was due to the way shares were allocated on the NYSE; an example will illustrate the system:

> Let's say the 36 5/16 offer in Merck mentioned above was made up of three floor broker orders of 10,000 shares each, plus another three offers over the DOT system also for 10,000 shares each. A market buy order of 10,000 shares then arrives at the post. Which of the six equal size sellers would have gotten the shares?

To allocate the shares, specialists typically used a "matching" system. Each floor broker that had a match in the crowd would get an even share, and the DOT system as a whole would get a share. So in the above example, each floor broker would sell 2,500 shares, and the DOT would get 2,500 shares which would go to the client who was there first. So all the clients represented by floor brokers would get something done, but only one of the three DOT clients would sell any stock.

If the trader decided to instead whack the 36 ¼ bid, he would still want to send in a floor broker rather than send the order down over DOT. This was less due to the actual rules and more due to the way DOT orders were often abused by the specialist.

> *Example: If the client sent in a 36 ¼ low on the 25,000 shares via DOT, the specialist would typically announce the offer to the crowd prior to executing it. The floor brokers in the crowd offering at 36 5/16ths then had the opportunity to jump ahead of the DOT order, or the specialist would sometimes even jump ahead of the DOT order himself.*

Years later, in 2004, the SEC working with the NYSE regulators reached a $245 million settlement with all seven specialist firms to account for years of violating the exchange's own rules.[xxxvii] In addition to the civil penalties, in 2006 several specialists pled guilty to securities fraud. Prosecutors devoted significant time to demonstrating how NYSE specialists systematically abused DOT orders during the "good ol' days."[xxxviii]

So the DOT system was of limited use, essentially relegated to being a tool for small orders while all the real action continued to go through floor brokers. And so the specialists' corruption held the machines at bay for a few more years.

Decimalization and Direct+ rock the boat

However, in 2000, the SEC blew away the high minimum spreads, ordering all US markets to be decimalized by April of 2001. They had several reasons for pursuing this, including simplification of quotes, compatibility with overseas markets, and reducing spreads for small investors.

In early 2001, the Nasdaq, the Amex, and the NYSE all moved to a minimum increment of 1c. Traders now had the option of dropping orders between the bid and the offer and the ability to choose 100 price points within each dollar where before they had been restricted to only 16.

So how did the professional traders like this new pricing flexibility? They despised it. While the tighter spreads were great for the proverbial "little guy" buying 200 shares of Disney, they made it much more difficult for an institutional trader trying to buy 500,000 shares of Disney. A problem known as "penny jumping" quickly became apparent to big traders. If a trader showed a large bid, for only a cost of a penny another buyer could step ahead of it. So if someone showed a 42.10 bid in Disney for 50,000 shares, within seconds someone would show a 42.11 bid for small size and "penny" them. As a result, traders quickly became wary of displaying large bids or offers, and displayed size plummeted. [see Figures 2 and 3 on next page]

To the NYSE's credit, the management had correctly anticipated that decimalization would lead to more prints and a need for more efficient tools. Simultaneous with the switch to decimalization in February of 2001, the exchange began rolling out a new feature called "Direct+", which was their first true electronic trading product. Direct+ allowed a member firm of the NYSE to trade up to 1,099 shares once every 30 seconds electronically, without giving the "crowd" an opportunity to get in front of the order.

The Direct+ initiative had been approved before decimalization was launched. It had been less controversial than might have been expected, since its maximum size was so small. Even though their livelihoods depended on manual trading, most members of the NYSE didn't see electronic orders of 1,000 shares making a dent in their earnings. Few realized that very small orders were about to become the preferred way to trade, to such an extent that by 2007, the average execution on the NYSE would plummet to just 280 shares.[xxxix]

In February 2001, when both decimalization and the initial phase of Direct+ simultaneously hit the NYSE, the DOT system suddenly became relevant and in some cases even preferable to using a floor broker. Traders who had formerly shunned DOT as worthless soon found that they could avoid getting "pennied" and avoid the specialist by carefully watching the real-time quotes while typing dozens of little orders into Direct+.

Figure 2: Average Trade Size in US Markets (1995 – 2006)

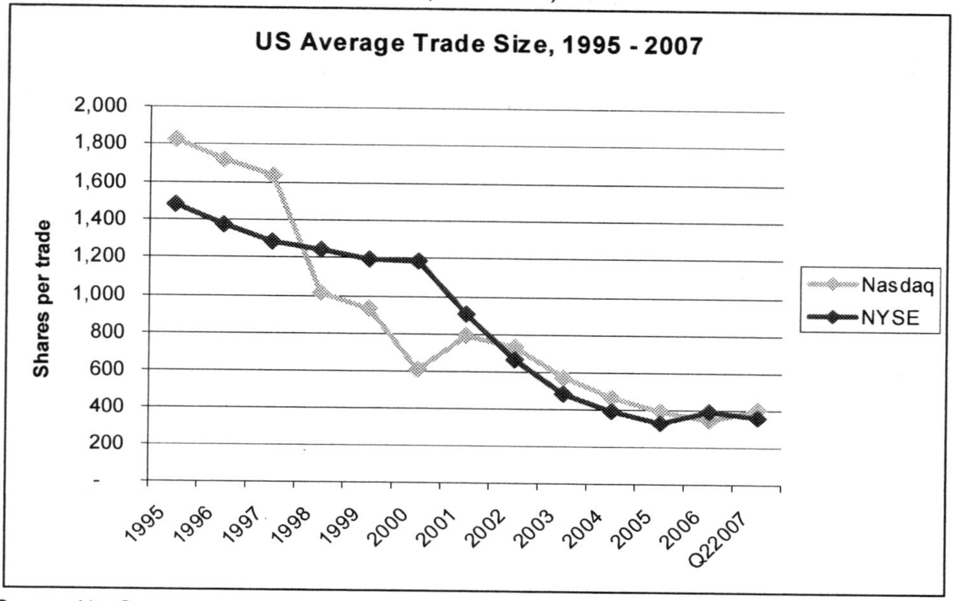

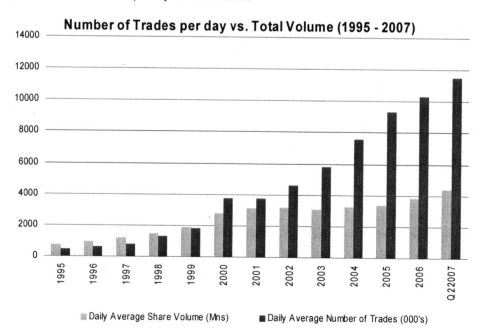

Source: Aite Group

Figure 3: Number of Trades per day vs. Total Volume

Source: Aite Group

In April 2001, the Nasdaq followed the NYSE in adopting decimalized pricing. The story was similar: spreads collapsed, displayed size dropped, and trading in small electronic pieces on the ECNs became more appealing.

But trading in smaller pieces was logistically difficult for larger trading desks across Wall Street. A trader for a big institution does not have time to work a 500,000 share order in hundreds of little pieces. As a result, sophisticated proprietary trading desks and a handful of quantitative hedge funds began to experiment with systems that would automatically "slice 'n dice" large orders. And soon Wall Street would package these tools into user-friendly systems and make them available to virtually every mutual fund, pension fund, asset manager, endowment, and hedge fund throughout the world.

The algorithmic trading desk is born

By mid-2001, all of the pieces were in place for a trading revolution in the US market. Most of the Street were sending orders and receiving fills via FIX connectivity. Fully-automated exchange-like entities called ECNs existed and were fast, cheap, and fair places to trade Nasdaq securities. The NYSE had a true electronic order type for the first time ever. And trading effectively in the decimalized markets often required slicing big orders into numerous small pieces, a job that can be done much more efficiently by a machine than by a roomful of people gradually giving themselves Carpal Tunnel Syndrome.

Necessity is said to be the mother of invention, and there was a clear need among institutional traders for a tool that would slice orders up into smaller pieces in a reasonably intelligent way. And if necessity is invention's mother, its father is probably desperation, and traditional Wall Street was definitely feeling some of that. Because in 2001, Wall Street was getting squeezed on all sides.

The internet-fueled bull market of the late 90's was deflating, and as investment performance declined, the mutual funds and big asset managers became serious about trimming transaction costs and squeezing every basis point out of their portfolios. Wall Street took it on the chin in this environment, with average commissions accelerating their long-term plummet. [See Figure 4 on next page]

On top of that, when decimalization rolled out, the Nasdaq market-making desks throughout the Street went overnight from being money-printing machines to being loss leaders. With the collapse of spreads in the liquid stocks from 6.25c down to 1c, market-makers that traditionally bought on the bid and sold on the offer were hit hard. Jersey City, once the epicenter of wholesale market-making, began emptying of its shouting minions as the number of big Nasdaq wholesalers dropped from five to one.[xl]

Figure 4: Average Commissions per

Average Commissions Per Share, US 1980-2006

Share, US 1980-2006
Source: SIA Database, Credit Suisse Research

With traditional commissions being squeezed and market-making desks no longer profitable, Wall Street was in need of a new way to add value to its clients. It was under this pressure that in late 2001 the first new type of equities desk was launched in the US since Program Trading desks were set up twenty years prior: the algorithmic trading desk.

The typical algorithmic trading desk differs from traditional desks in several ways:

1. Philosophy that trading is a science rather than an art
2. All trading decisions are made by a computer running an algorithm
3. All orders and fills are sent and received electronically
4. Marginal costs, and therefore commissions, are low

Philosophy that trading is a science rather than an art
On traditional desks, trading is a game of instinct and skill built up over many years of studying the markets. In other words, an art. Algorithmic desks approach trading as a science. There is an underlying assumption that most trading situations are not unique, and that optimal trading

methodologies can be developed over time through empirical analysis and monitored experimentation.

All trading decisions are done by a computer running an algorithm

The algorithms themselves are essentially a set of rules or procedures that tell the computer how to behave in different situations. The computers typically have access to real-time quotes across all publicly traded securities, historical trading patterns and descriptive statistics for each stock. More sophisticated offerings use complex inputs like covariance matrices that define how stocks tend to move with other stocks or other securities, news feeds with the latest headlines, and heat maps tracking which trading destinations are likely to have liquidity.

Most trading algorithms are set up as optimization problems; the algorithm attempts to mathematically maximize or minimize something subject to some set of constraints, i.e., buy 250,000 shares of Gillette while minimizing market impact, subject to being at least 5% of the volume during the course of the trade. The algorithm will then monitor trading activity in Gillette and make all decisions as to when to bid, where to bid, how much to bid for, etc., typically shooting a stream of small orders and cancels to the markets throughout the execution period.

All orders and fills are routed electronically

The computer doesn't just make the trading decisions and then display them as suggestions for people; the machines also execute the trades. Fully electronic trading with no human intervention leads to the speed, low error rates, confidentiality, and efficiency that are the hallmarks of algorithmic trading.

Marginal costs, and therefore commissions, are low

Algorithmic trading is a high fixed cost / low variable cost product. It costs a significant amount of money, expertise, and effort to build an algorithmic trading platform. However, once it's built, the cost of each incremental share that runs through the system is low. In this respect it's a very different business model than traditional trading which is a classic "high-touch" service model. High-touch services have high marginal costs and therefore require a relatively high commission to be profitable. Algorithmic trading is almost the opposite: once the intellectual property has been created, it is in the interests of management to run the machines near capacity, which results in lower commissions than traditional trading.

With greater efficiency, lower costs, and a methodology that worked effectively in decimalized markets, algorithmic trading very quickly became a fixture on Wall Street. [See Figure 5 on next page]

Figure 5: Electronic Trading as % of Total US Equity Volume (2000-2007)

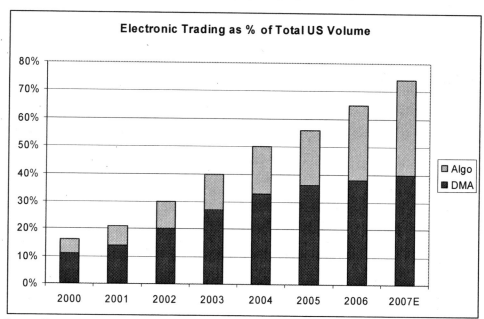

Source: Tower Group Estimates

Reg NMS and Hybrid Market sweep the floor

The latest major regulatory change to hit the US markets was "Regulation NMS (National Market System)". Passed by the SEC in 2005, Reg NMS was fully implemented in August of 2007. It was an ambitious attempt to electronically link the various exchanges and create one virtual electronic market. The key piece of the regulation required that exchanges handle electronic orders instantaneously, or otherwise be branded "slow" markets that can be legally ignored by other market participants. This put the NYSE, still mostly manual after all these years, at risk of being made irrelevant if it didn't automate in a hurry.

In response to this rule, the NYSE created a plan called "Hybrid Market", which was an attempt to allow it to qualify as an automated market center under the Reg NMS rules, while still preserving a role for human beings on the floor in some of the transactions. The NYSE completed the Hybrid roll-out in February of 2007.

The unique innovation behind Hybrid was the concept of 'LRPs' (Liquidity Replenishment Points). The idea was that the NYSE would function as an electronic market most of the time, but any sudden large price move would trigger an LRP, at which time the market would revert to a manual market and the human specialist would take over. Specialists were cast in the role of beach lifeguards: they were supposed to just sit there and watch everyone swimming when the water was calm, but when the water got rough they were to dive in and risk their own capital to save innocent public orders from the perils of volatility.

But while the NYSE executives preached the gospel of the new Hybrid market, the brokers and clerks in the trenches were not believers, and feared Hybrid would cost them their lucrative jobs. Ahead of the originally scheduled December 2006 roll-out, gallows humor began to prevail on the floor. Hybrid was widely joked to be an acronym for Have Your Bag Ready In December.

As it turned out, Hybrid was half successful in its twin goals of making the market electronic while keeping human traders around. While Hybrid did successfully turn the NYSE into a "fast" market under Reg NMS, it largely failed to preserve a meaningful role for the people who walked around all day on the creaky wooden floorboards of the exchange. The LRPs were rarely triggered and the NYSE quickly became viewed as an electronic destination. By spring of 2007, just a few months after Hybrid was fully deployed, most brokerage firms began massively reducing their floor staffs, laying off 75% or more of their floor employees.[xli] One newspaper article cited the specialist firm LaBranche as having dropped its floor staff from 330 to 80, and Bank of America as having dropped from 225 to 85. The article noted that firms throughout the NYSE floor were "dropping headcount as fast as they are losing money."[xlii]

Meanwhile, the NYSE's upstart competitors were investing in making their systems faster and cheaper. Reg NMS was viewed by the smaller regional exchanges as an opportunity to become relevant again. The regulation states that the major exchanges may not ignore or trade through the published inside quote on the minor exchanges. As a result, Boston, Philadelphia, National, Chicago, and others re-capitalized and launched electronic systems. Additionally new alternative trading systems began coming out of the woodwork. By mid-2007, the US market was awash in electronic trading destinations, with 10 functioning exchanges[xliii], 5 ECN's (Electronic Communication Networks), and over 30 ATS's (Alternative Trading Systems).

The NYSE gradually lost its monopoly in trading its own stocks and its market share dropped steadily in the new electronic environment [See Figure 6: NYSE mkt share drop]. Trading in the US became fragmented over dozens of electronic venues, making it difficult to trade without "smart order routing", which consists of high speed algorithms to make the decision about where to route orders. Algorithmic desks and smart order routers became a necessary step in the trading process and quickly gobbled up the order flow that previously had been executed manually by floor brokers and OTC market-makers. By December 2007, the situation on the NYSE floor has grown more dire, three of the five room that formerly made up the floor had been shut down, and two of the seven remaining specialist firms, Van der Moolen and Susquehanna, announced they were shutting down their long-standing floor operations.

Regulation NMS and the NYSE's Hybrid market had completed the process that began in 1992 with the birth of the FIX protocol. By mid-2007, the days of paper tickets and runners and shouting was quickly coming to an end, and the raucous applause that had greeted the bell each morning for 215 years was subdued. Much of that former applause had been replaced with the sounds of frustrated floor brokers booing the executives of the NYSE.[xliv]

Figure 6:

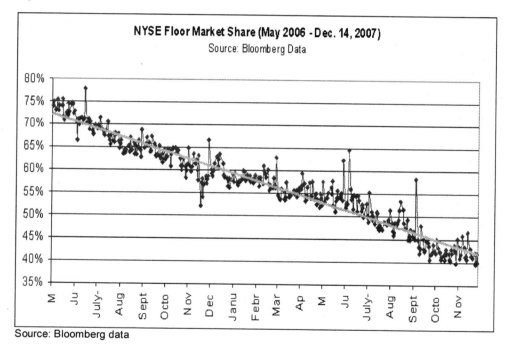

Source: Bloomberg data

See no evil, hear no evil, speak no evil

Traditional trading was largely a game of sniffing out the supply and demand in a particular stock and figuring out if it was likely to go up or down in the short term. The game involved talking to players in the markets, getting "looks" from the floor of the NYSE, constantly watching the tape, and attempting to keep track of who was doing what. If a client needed to buy an illiquid stock, a good trader knew "where the bodies were buried" and was sometimes able to quickly find the other side of the trade. If not, the trader may at least have had an opinion of whether the stock was on its way up or down based on tracking the buyers and sellers.

Experienced traders with good relationships and the biggest institutional clients used to have an edge in this game. For example, calls used to go out that a seller on the floor had pushed the price down, but was "cleaning up", meaning they were almost done selling. If the call was correct, it indicated a buying opportunity (although if incorrect, and the seller wasn't really done, the buyer risked getting "picked off", or worse "run over", or worse still, "carried out".)

Calls like this were a big part of the game. But a frequent complaint among experienced traders is that in an algorithm-dominated world, these calls have dried up. As most of the flow has moved to the electronic side, no one knows who's buying, who's selling, or how much size anyone has to trade in any name. Little prints hit the tape throughout the day and there's no central place remaining where an insider can find out the true picture.

But the lack of information flowing out of algorithms is not a negative side-effect; it is by design. Good algorithmic desks strive to emit no information. Orders are kept confidential, computer systems are locked down, and only dedicated employees of the algorithmic desk (who by definition don't trade themselves) have access to the clients' trading flows. Good algorithmic desks route slices to multiple trading venues whenever possible, and also route some random percentage of slices through third parties if forced to route repetitive orders to the NYSE or other venues that may disclose the "give-up" of the broker. The mixed routing is deliberately aimed at further obscuring the supply / demand picture and leaving the inside player clueless as to who is buying, how much they are buying, and when they will stop buying.

The result of all of this secrecy is that no one really knows what's going on in a stock anymore. And ironically, this state of confusion is likely to reduce transaction costs throughout the Street. When an employee pension fund begins buying Hormel Foods through a signal-reducing algorithm, the stock doesn't begin shooting up, because no traders are getting "the call" anymore. When a mutual fund sells US Steel through dark pools, the investors don't pay a toll to a floor broker that repeatedly steps a penny in front of their order. The new confidential electronic order types do not feed the experienced insiders, and as a result the playing field has become more level than ever before.

Guerrillas in our midst

A new term has entered the financial lexicon in the past few years. "Signaling Risk" is the risk of causing an adverse move in the price of a security by conveying trading intentions to other market participants.

Signals can consist of publicly displayed bids and offers, floor broker conversations, or broker IOIs ("indications of interest", these are phone calls or electronic messages that "ping" a client to reveal the broker has activity in a particular security.)   Signals can also include more nefarious exchanges, like in the "Squawk Box" scandal on Wall Street in 2005, when clerks at some firms were caught receiving kickbacks in return for leaking trade order information.[xlv] While most signals aren't illegal, all potentially adversely push the price of a stock and hurt the investor.

It's been common sense for centuries that if a broker walks into the crowd with a ticket on his forehead, the stock is going to move. But only in recent years has the quantitative community begun to study the effects of signaling risk.[xlvi] And algorithmic desks that are studying signaling are finding it is a far bigger cost than most traders think. In fact, damage caused by sending signals is probably the most expensive portion of typical transaction costs.

In response to these findings, a huge amount of effort has gone into figuring out new and creative ways to hide flow. Trading without signaling is a quandary: in order to trade at all, at some point you must reveal that you are a buyer to attract a seller, yet the moment you do that, you push the stock higher. So in the words of a trader, how can you "be there without being there?"

If there is money to be made by answering a question, you can be sure that Wall Street will rise to the challenge, and so it is currently in the process of responding. The Street has come up with various ways to reduce signals over the past three years, known as "hidden orders", "dark pools" of liquidity, and "guerrilla" trades.

The concept behind "hidden orders" is based on an order type developed in European markets called "iceberg" orders. "Icebergs," as their name implies, are orders that only publicly display a tiny piece, while most of the size sits unseen below the surface.   If someone hits the tiny bid showing, it immediately reloads with a fresh tiny bid. While this does reduce signaling significantly over showing the whole order, it still has a prominent signal: as soon as the bid refreshes, the market knows there is still a buyer lurking around.

"Hidden orders" take the iceberg concept a step further. There is an order lurking out there somewhere, yet nothing at all shows above the surface. The order is essentially a fishing net below the surface, waiting for the opposite side to swim past, as in the following example:

> *A trader places a hidden order to buy 10,000 shares of Heinz (HNZ) with a 42.35 top on the Peoria Stock Exchange. The Peoria exchange's computers accept the order, but do not*

> *display or publish it, so no one in the world other than the buyer knows that the buy order exists. Ten minutes later, another trader sends an order to the Peoria to sell 5,000 HNZ at the market. The bid/ask at the time is 42.27 x 42.29. Before the sell order can trade with the 42.27 bid, it is intercepted by the hidden buy order and it trades at 42.28.*

In the above example, the buyer bought 5,000 shares without having signaled anything to the other market participants. After the print, the market knows that there was a buyer, but the market does not know if the buyer is finished or if a bid remains out there. Several venues, known in Wall Street lingo as "dark pools," accept only hidden orders, which then interact with each other – the nets below the water seeking to catch other nets.

While hidden orders and dark pools are clearly effective at reducing signaling risk, they come at a cost of lower fill rates. Stretching a net over the Peoria exchange can only catch sell orders coming to Peoria; it won't catch orders sent to other venues. To maximize the "hit rate", brokers have begun creating algorithms that spray hidden orders into as many venues as possible, to increase the likelihood of being in the right venue to intercept the next opposite-side order.

Called by a variety of names, such as "Guerrilla" orders, these orders seek to trade without trumpeting intentions to the market. The client sends one electronic order to a broker's system, which then uses a variety of quantitative techniques and clever order placement to maximize hit rates while minimizing signaling risk.

Conversely, as more and more liquidity shifts to hidden orders on ECNs and regional exchanges, brokers are developing algorithms that probe multiple venues looking for hidden liquidity at better prices than what is publicly displayed. As these tools also rise in popularity, an entire ecosystem of hidden liquidity is forming: Guerrilla-style algorithms hide orders, and probing algorithms try to find them. Together the two types of orders are feeding on each other and have been spiraling upwards in use.

Where are the markets headed next?

The key algorithmic competition over the next several years will likely take place on a dark battlefield. Hidden orders on ECNs and regional exchanges will continue to rapidly gain in market share at the expense of traditional signaled orders. As the hidden market grows, we will return to a two-tiered market: a wide publicly displayed market, and a much narrower hidden market. For example, the displayed market might be 15.25 x 15.28, but there will be multiple hidden bids at 15.26, and multiple hidden offers at 15.27.

Typically the regulators try to create an environment that is transparent for all players, but handling this hidden order explosion will be tricky. While on the surface, a hidden market seems like less transparency, it's also a market with less information leakage, fewer signals, and dramatically fewer opportunities for insiders to make money at the expense of the outsiders.

When all the smoke clears, it is likely that dark orders will be available to all and will become the dominant way to trade, further reducing or even eliminating leaking of order information. And as signaling of information decreases, total execution costs will continue to drop, leading to a continued increase in trading volumes, with eventually tens of billions of shares traded daily in the US markets.

Although the machines appear to have won the battle on the exchange floors, the result is not a Terminator-like landscape of smoking ruins. The rise of the machines has resulted in less leaking of trade information, greater speed and efficiency, fewer errors, and fewer unfair advantages for insiders. The end result is a market that has less drama than the colorful trading pits and frantic shouting of the last century, but it is also a market that is faster, cheaper, and cleaner.

MONITOR OR PERISH:
"You Are Only As Fast As Your Slowest Component"

By James Leman, Westwater Coporation

Looking back in time to when the sell side of the business began to embrace paperless trading in a serious way an interesting but predictable scenario came to pass. I can say this because I saw it first hand at the large broker dealer firm I worked for in 1992. Equity traders were beginning to be weaned away from their paper tickets and order slips by the introduction of a paperless order management system very creatively called the Equity Desk Trading System or EDTS. The system took a year plus to build with sporadic participation from a group of block traders and sales traders on the listed equities desk. At first while the system went into production along with a touch screen technology in the booths on the NYSE floor, it was treated as a novelty, something to be dabbled with but not to be relied upon. In the words of one senior floor broker on the NYSE "this system could probably be great but if we really get busy, we'll have to go back to the paper system".

Needless to say that didn't really happen. What did happen was that, over not too long a period of time and capped by the first World Trade Center bombing, EDTS went from a novelty on the desk to an absolute necessity. The developers responsible saw a frightening but gratifying shift in perspective. It went from "ok I'll use it for a few trades" to "It can't go down, I can't handle the volume without the system". The linkage of the sales traders in New York and regional branch offices to the block traders in New York and onward to the booths on the perimeter of the NYSE floor along with access to the NYSE DOT system became critical in handling higher and higher levels of transaction volume with the same number of personnel and with fewer errors.

We know today that that scenario was played over and over again on Wall Street around the years surrounding the early 90s as paperless trading systems began to become commonplace and the need for monitoring capabilities were identified. Focused initially on the health of internal users at the main office and then branch offices serving institutional desks, the block business in listed and OTC securities, whether reliant on home grown or vendor provided order management software, knew it didn't want the system to go down during trading hours. It could bring on disastrous results. This potential for problems was compounded as access to the NYSE DOT system was included as a feature in most order management systems. Now the monitoring was for internal systems and those linked to exchanges where orders flowed and returned executed.

IT STARTED WITH PAPERLESS ORDER MANAGEMENT

The next step in the significance of monitoring of trading systems came with the empowerment of institutional clients to send order flow to brokers electronically for block trades from the buy side order management systems which were growing in number and being aggressively adopted by larger clients. Now when a system problem occurred it was very transparent to the client that something was not working. Having become accustomed to nearly immediate acknowledgement of orders sent electronically, the buy side trader came to rely on that electronic acceptance and did not confirm by phone. Brokers began to monitor not only their internal systems and connections to exchanges. They now began to realize they needed to monitor networks over which clients communicated. As direct market access by institutional clients picked up speed the transparency issue grew. Clients began to factor such performance into informal evaluation of broker performance.

With equities as the primary driver of connectivity needs, the equity departments or business units found that it fell to them to engage their technology organizations to establish appropriate infrastructure and processing capabilities to handle the growing levels of order traffic. This demand was initiated in the US market with the expansion of buy side OMS and later EMS platforms as well as through market data provisioning platforms, such as Bloomberg and others, which offered a straight forward order entry tool early in the growth of electronic trading. After several years of this growing process of clients becoming connected to their favorite brokers and brokers moving to get all of their primary clients connected, the need for connectivity to European and Asian clients for their US market order flow was growing in relevance. Beyond that the appetite for US based clients to reach European and later Asian markets was beginning to evidence itself.

THE FIX PROTOCOL OPENED PANDORA'S BOX

As the Fix protocol was introduced into the US market in 1995 after a 2 year start up phase the buy side and sell side used connectivity to send large and small order flow to brokers for cleaner handling. Right on the heels of this phenomenon the desire for direct market access (DMA) was born. With DMA the brokerage firm's sales trader did not have to touch the client launched order if it met certain criteria. The order would go through the client and then the broker's computer and on the exchange immediately. Upon execution the detailed execution reports would similarly flow directly back to the client. This became very attractive to many clients over time and created challenges for brokers where large numbers of orders could flow very rapidly to the market. This trend caused expanding demands for fix engine connection capability and for quick seamless connectivity and related monitoring capability to become a necessity. While the US clients embraced this form of trading, the non US domiciled investors began to require electronic order delivery as well into US markets. This fostered the expanding need for network connectivity. Fix engines and monitoring mechanisms needed to be available more rapidly than what US domiciled buy side firms required. It also required systems to be up and available and subject to active monitoring early in the morning as European clients who were 4 or 5 hours ahead of the US wanted to get orders across to brokers as early as possible.

As larger brokers sensed the appetites of their clients to trade more electronically on both an institutional and a retail level, it also became apparent that overseas interest in electronic order delivery on a cross border basis was growing. Given that the London Stock Exchange had experienced its "Big Bang" event and most developed European and Asian markets traded in an electronic and "floor-less" environment, the opportunity was ripe to apply standards and processes that were proving attractive in the US markets.

LINKING INVESTORS, BROKERS & MARKETS

The Fix committee sensed this opportunity and engaged Europe first in 1996, Japan in 1998 and the Asian markets in 2000. In each instance local regional Fix committees were established to suggest modifications to Fix to accommodate the unique needs of each new market so electronic order delivery between parties could be conducted. With the growth of investing in these overseas markets, the opportunity to apply technology to the process of order delivery, and the complexity of network connectivity, the need for monitoring capabilities on a round the clock basis became clear. Moreover, maintaining consistent performance standards became a much more complex undertaking. Now, rather than dealing in one country's markets and a base of clients operating in three time zones through one language; large, global brokers were overseeing around 12 to 16 marketplaces across 7 or 8 time zones for the US and Europe and were dealing with different languages and market conventions. This later shifted, as Japan and Asian markets began to participate actively, to a nearly 5 by 24 hour a day commitment, usually bridging several logical calendar days.

These challenges presented themselves to the buy side and their supporting vendors as well as the brokers. Placing orders in one time zone today for tomorrow's trading in another time zone and related issues proved taxing, especially as the larger buy side firms staffed 24 hour trading desks with three shifts of personnel so they could trade overseas markets "live". This placed challenging demands on the systems and networks serving these demanding users and the brokers they relied upon to make the connections production ready. Monitoring the flow of orders from originating systems and networks to other time zones and brokers on their way to foreign exchanges was a complex task requiring coordinated activities among many players spread across organizations and continents.

Throughout these years of expansion and growth, managing clients' experience so that problems experienced by one customer did not spill over to affect another was a distinct challenge. Ensuring that exposure to market risk was limited to only orders placed in an affected market and not any other market required constant oversight. Being able to effectively bring down one component of a malfunctioning process while keeping the other elements in production and then restoring the repaired element without causing substantial client distress was a challenge for many of the early players on the brokerage side. Enhancements were constantly being implemented to address issues very promptly so that as the transparency of problem occurrences became instantly visible everything possible was done to eliminate exceptions immediately.

THE NEED FOR SPEED

In the movie "Top Gun", actor Tom Cruise and his "rear "or navigation officer coined a famous line when they both said "I feel the need for speed". From its initial appearance in the mid to late 90's, the world of electronic trading quickly developed not only "the need for speed", it also developed as an unforeseen byproduct "the need for immediate problem detection and resolution" to keep clients satisfied. Connectivity fostered a reliance on technology that shortly became an absolute necessity. Transparency took on an entirely new meaning. Brokers, software vendors, developers and clients all quickly realized that all of their mistakes, blemishes and shortcomings were immediately apparent to their clients. Today's equivalent of this experience is the challenge high definition or HD television is placing on actors appearing in shows carried in HD.

With technology offering to instantly let institutional and retail clients send orders to their brokers in direct market access (DMA) offerings connected to the various market venues, a new obligation became immediately obvious. Monitoring of the health of client connectivity from end to end was a new necessary process. As many of the initial providers of electronic connectivity were larger broker/dealers with their own technology personnel, the need to monitor was addressed by the sell side technical or support teams. Traders and Sales/Traders did not get paid to watch such issues and address problems so it fell to the technical teams.

TRANSPARENCY – THE NEW REALITY

Given the growth of electronic trading, the variety of buy side vendor solutions, the number of DMA providers, the number of market side destinations and the increasing "need for speed", the problem took on a new level of intensity. The problem began to be recognized for what it had become – a situation where thousands of complex orders were arriving from a myriad of front end systems over a variety of networks which once accepted needed to pass through the brokers systems and on to the exchanges and ECNs at sub second rates of speed where a clog in any section of the pipe could create market risk, operational risk, monetary risk and reputation risk if the clog was not cured immediately.

The introduction of smart routing to meet the market's need to send OTC and later listed securities, to a selection of ECNs in the late 90's to seek liquidity, created the demand for greater speed for both client and proprietary trading activity. Each ECN had its own range of order types, and speed was an essential element in an effective trading strategy for many. The speed of order generation, order delivery by client systems to brokers and from brokers to the different venues was paramount. To be competitive, ECNs needed to be very cost competitive and fast. Speed was measured in milliseconds, and ECNs slower than 25 milliseconds could see order flow siphoned by other venues. Similarly, brokers who could not support at least this speed for their base of clients, whether for their market making desks or on an agency business, could suffer loss of business or unacceptable execution performance. Again monitoring activities became an issue. Constantly identifying how well the entire set of connections, networks, applications and marketplace servers were performing throughout the day was essential for adequate performance in the new world All of this was true before algorithmic trading showed its face and threw another series of challenges at the brokers and marketplace players.

ALGORITHMIC TRADING – A MAN MADE TSUNAMI

The emergence of algorithmic trading strategies added further complexity for several uniquely distinctive reasons. First, these algorithms were dependent on the timely receipt of price feed data and the ability to process and digest it very quickly. As a secondary event they, if nothing else, could generate a veritable blizzards of orders which needed to be sent to the market, often to be cancelled and replaced at different price points to reflect changing market conditions. The variety of algorithmic strategies mushroomed in each providing broker/dealer's shop, and the number of brokers offering them grew. Of course the brokers saw the provisioning of these algorithms as a competitive weapon in pursuing institutional order flow.

This then led to the need to enable the various third party and proprietary buy side order management and later execution management systems to be able to represent the 200 plus variety of algorithmic strategies to be initiated from the client's desk tops, with timely updates to be rapidly provided to the clients. This introduction of high volume market data, extremely higher levels of order generation and consumption of network bandwidth within brokerage systems demanded constant monitoring in order not to have thousands of orders get clogged up behind a narrow connection. This problem also stretched back to the initiating clients and forward to the exchange or liquidity destinations being accessed by the brokers. Consider the broker's plight. He or she has enabled hundreds of electronic connections to buy side clients across 20 different order management systems and perhaps 10 different networks. Some clients launch individual orders and others use program trading or list strategies. Now to remain competitive ,you introduce 10 to 15 different algorithmic trading strategies and invite clients to slice up orders into as many as 40 or 50 pieces, with each one launched periodically or within seconds depending on the flow of market data being collected and stored on your systems, and some that trade within 20 to 30 milliseconds of receipt. Beyond this reality, the most competitive brokers were compelled to offer personalized solutions to garner order flow from customers as gradually more complex algorithmic strategies were rolled out. This personalization called for distinct strategies to be tuned to the particular trading style of certain large demanding clients, with another consideration to be given to how quickly all the algorithmic strategies invoked could be launched and performance overseen. This was the state of the equity trading world prior to the implementation of Regulation NMS in the US market.

REG NMS IMPACT, ALTERNATE LIQUIDITY AND ELEVEN MARKETPLACES

Leading up to the implementation of Regulation NMS, we have witnessed the introduction of internalization activities by broker/dealers and the emergence of almost 40 different "dark pools" of liquidity as well as the reemergence of regional exchanges.

These pools of liquidity, which are called alternative trading services [systems] or ATS, do not publish quotes per se but most probably will generate "pinging" activity as those with orders seek to locate liquidity much as a submarine would use sonar to locate another submarine. These ATS offerings come in several varieties. Some use a mid point crossing system continuously operating. Others offer bi party negotiated operation while others offer periodic session based activity. Still others employ minimal order sizes or order types to differentiate themselves. The release of information from these facilities is a very dear commodity, so transparency is essentially non-existent. Moreover, the operator of the ATS can administer rules as they see fit as long as all parties receive most favored nation treatment.

Beyond the range of ATS access being offered, the desire to try to harness retail order flow on its way to the market so that it can possible interact with and cross against institutional order flow is a much sought after prize as it can yields several desirable results. It can reduce market impact; it can reduce fees brokers pay to an exchange or ATS. It can create the opportunity for price improvement and thereby hopefully attract more institutional flow. With Reg NMS in place, the 11 different exchanges or ECN choices have an obligation to route orders away to other marketplace entities where better prices are displayed. The decision then becomes more complex. Do I route orders to ATS players initially? How many do I interact with before sending orders off to marketplaces publishing quotes? How many marketplace quotes must I consume and evaluate? Will all 11 be necessary and must latency be an issue at a certain point? Will my smart router be quick enough to fulfill all of its tasks in an acceptable timeframe? These issues now compound the challenge of monitoring activities. Systems must now be monitored individually and as groups to determine how well each is performing based on the load they are under at any time during the trading day.

ENTER VOLATILITY IN A REG NMS WORLD

Shortly after the initial legs of Regulation NMS implementation were in place in 2007, the early effects of an 11 marketplace market structure combined with the algorithmically stoked order generation environment were felt when the sub prime events rumbled through the volatility components of the marketplace. Brokers were now faced with 40 alternative unpublished liquidity pool options. They now had 11 market destinations to choose to route to throughout the day and had to balance speed and customer service issues for each destination. Market data streams emanating from the exchanges and ECNs overwhelmed the vendors' and brokers' own data collection and support mechanisms with overwhelming numbers of data points and at speeds unprecedented in the marketplace. Best execution and transaction cost analysis conducted by clients on brokers or by brokers on their own performance promised to examine every aspect of order handling in excruciating detail, not to mention compliance and regulatory oversight interest. Lacking an industry wide testing exercise prior to implementation with adequate stress testing not undertaken, the markets experienced sporadic melt down conditions and the importance of aggressive monitoring systems, multilevel problem detection tools and remedial strategy solutions were brought home with a vengeance.

ELECTRONIC CROSS BORDER EQUITY DMA

While the situation for the US market is quite complex, the appetite for investing across borders into Europe and Asia as well as the Americas has also substantially grown and is contributing to monitoring issues as clients in other countries wish to use technology to send orders to the US, and US located clients wish to use technology to route orders to foreign markets around the world operating in different time zones. To address the challenges this complex scenario represents, it becomes essential to consider the variety of order origination points and discrete systems in play. Different order types, multiple exchanges in various countries, various holiday calendars and minimum order sizes and other conventions challenge both buy side and sell side alike. Orders entered today for trading tomorrow or orders entered today with no reporting to be achieved before the following day present all players involved with concerns regarding system and desk handoffs. As algorithmic strategies are adopted with greater frequency in overseas markets, the same need for aggressive monitoring of market data, all systems and networks involved and exchange or marketplace latency come into play, especially when problem resolution cannot be achieved before normal business day operations or cutoff times are exceeded. Beyond these dimensions, the sweeping implications of the MiFID regulatory changes enacted across the participating European Union countries promise to describe a comparably complex series of liquidity choices and regulatory oversight mechanisms for buy and sell side alike that will change roles and responsibilities for years to come. Again monitoring tools that identify and point out emerging problems in the systems utilized will go a long way to manage risk and quality of service available in the market place.

LISTED OPTIONS, LISTED FUTURES, FOREIGN EXCHANGE AND FIXED INCOME

Up to this point the impact of electronic trading and client connectivity has been focused primarily on equity securities. In recent years, and particularly as the community of hedge funds clients have grown and embraced electronic trading, the expansion of this type of trading has reached most other products generally handled by the larger broker dealers operating in the Us and foreign markets. As brokers acknowledged this shift in client appetites, they also observed that the majority of processes and tools implemented were focused on equity products. As other products embraced electronic trading the Fix engines, order management systems, support mechanisms and architectural elements of broker dealers needed to become multi product compatible, especially since the clients expected multi product support from their brokers. To effectively avoid a repeat of the very expensive separate silo approach followed for other legacy systems, a much more collaborative and complex approach was needed to support the products and deliver a more integrated client services experience. In preparing to deliver such a solution, an exhaustive review of the products brokers offer and how they are accessed within the broker/dealer premises is key. A comprehensive accounting of the various destinations orders can be sent to and how those destinations operate needs to also be undertaken. Along with this effort, a detailed network roadmap of external networks used on the way in and out of the broker/dealer must be created. All points of failure and all throughput capacities must be measured, and the consequences of delays, surges and outright failures must be assessed to begin to create a strategy to use in operating such complex systems and environments.

WHERE THE INDUSTRY IS TODAY

Admittedly, substantial work has been carried out to bring us to the point we are at today. A variety of home grown and or vendor provided products are present in the universe. Most of these address segments of the overall picture, with few covering the gamut of systems and processes necessary to do a comprehensive and consummate job, either for one country's markets or for a global collection of markets or different product sets.

However, the growth of DMA activity, algorithmic strategy use and the new world of dark pools, a hybrid NYSE model and an evolving Reg NMS adoption, warrant a fresh and comprehensive look at the facilities we expect to serve us well in the future. Moreover, as other areas like listed options and non equity product areas such as FX, listed futures and fixed income begin to embrace electronic trading more actively, we expect they will want to ride the same rails as equities have and clients will expect those synergies as well.

Monitoring will need to move way beyond whether systems are up or down. Intra day and dynamic data management load balancing must be pursued and tested against various scenarios. Adding clients must be balanced against existing system capacities and the expenses necessary to support different styles. They will need to be monitored comprehensively against standards identified by management that balance traffic levels against the economics of greater speed that may be competitively called for by clients and internal users alike. Millisecond response time is quickly becoming a bit slow and the need for ever faster calculation capabilities and integrated multi asset class concurrent strategies are moving forward at an increasing pace. With more available market data and the maturity of quantitatively assisted strategy models now available, feeling the "need for speed" is real. However, that demand must be balanced against the need to be able to cash the check that this emerging demand is writing.

Economic Value of a Trading Floor:
Evidence from the American Stock Exchange

By Puneet Handa, University of Iowa
Robert Schwartz, Professor of Finance and University Distinguished Professor,
Department of Economics & Finance, Zicklin School of Business, Baruch
College, CUNY & Ashish Tiwari, University of Iowa

We would like to thank the American Stock Exchange, especially Brett
Redfern and Russ Monahan, for making the necessary data available to us
and for providing technical assistance and information. We are also most
grateful to the referee for his or her helpful insights and suggestions. We
further thank Bill Christie, Hank Bessembinder, Tom George, Bill Lupien,
Deniz Ozenbas, Evan Schulman, George Sofianos, Dan Weaver and seminar
participants at Dartmouth College, the OPIM Seminar at the Wharton
School, University of Delaware, University of Missouri – Columbia,
University of Iowa and the 1999 WFA meetings for their comments and
suggestions. All errors remain ours.

Abstract

This paper provides evidence that floor brokers add value that helps offset
the higher cost of accessing the trading floor, making it a desirable venue for
orders requiring more careful handling. We compare execution costs of non-
block trades handled by Amex floor brokers with trades entered through its
automated Post Execution Reporting (PER) system. Essentially, because floor
traders can opportunistically seize liquidity without showing their hands too
quickly, using a floor broker is equivalent to placing a "smart" limit order."
Overall, floor trades have a lower realized half-spread than PER trades (-3.06
bps versus 4.43 bps). This finding holds for other measures of execution costs
as well and is consistent across all order-size categories. The light our
findings shed on the value of intermediation in security markets also has
implications for automated trading systems.

I. **Introduction**

In recent years, the trend in equity market structure has been away from floor based trading to automated floor-less trading systems. xlvii But the two national U.S. stock exchanges, the New York Stock Exchange and the American Stock Exchange, still have trading floors. Is this the result of technological inertia and vested interests, or does the floor have economic value? Our objective in this paper is to assess the economic *raision d'être* of a trading floor. To this end, we examine trades on the floor of the American Stock Exchange (Amex) and contrast them with trades on Amex's automated Post Execution Reporting (PER) system. We find evidence of intelligent order handling by floor traders which results in reduced execution costs that may offset the higher handling costs of floor trades.xlviii

Microstructure economists have in the past paid scant attention to the economic value of a trading floor. xlix Some have simply thought the floor archaic in an electronic environment where participants can work with a bank of computer screens far more easily on the upstairs desks than on the trading floor where space is at a premium.[1] Presumably, the computerization of information dissemination would give electronic trading a strong informational advantage vis-à-vis a floor. Nevertheless, Sofianos and Werner (1997), in their analysis of floor broker participation on the NYSE, find that floor brokers do contribute additional liquidity. Pagano and Röell (1992) point out a further advantage of a floor-based trading system: it gives participants "the opportunity to observe who trades what with whom, how urgently they seem to want to trade, etc." (p. 619). There are a number of other ways in which a floor trader may add value: (a) the trader might obtain knowledge of the presence of a contra party, mitigating price impact, (b) the trader could "round up" multiple counter parties, again cushioning the impact by trading in what may be viewed as a spontaneous call auction, (c) the trader could anticipate periods when liquidity is high and trade more often and in larger sizes during such periods, (d) the trader could avoid trading in periods when trading is low, and (e) the trader may possess superior ability to read momentum in the market and to time trades accordingly.

A potential drawback of trading via the floor is that handling costs are higher for orders worked on the floor than for orders delivered electronically through PER, and the fixed cost component may be appreciable.li Consequently, the floor may be an attractive venue for large, predominantly institutional participants who are concerned with controlling market impact. PER, on the other hand, may be attractive to small, predominantly retail participants whose orders are not large enough to have market impact or to justify the higher fixed cost component of floor-based order handling.

In this paper, we focus on comparing execution costs across the two venues (PER and the floor) for orders in the same stock matched by stock and trade characteristics such as execution price, order size and trade direction. We restrict ourselves to measuring implicit costs of execution such as realized spreads, quoted spreads and effective spreads.[lii] We employ a matched pair technique to control for the self-selection of trades submitted to the floor or to PER by investors, thereby allowing for a more meaningful comparison of execution costs across the two venues.

In our data set (October, 2001 Trade and Quote Data for 973 Amex stocks), 23.40% of the trading volume was initiated by floor brokers. Using the matched pair technique, we find that floor broker timed order handling generally results in lower execution costs. Overall, trades handled by floor brokers have a significantly smaller realized half-spread than do PER trades (-3.06 basis points versus 4.43 basis points). It is interesting to note that the realized half-spread for floor trades is actually negative. The contrast holds for all trade size categories in our sample. In addition, floor trades have a lower effective half-spread compared to PER trades (8.11 basis points versus 10.27 basis points). Finally, the quoted half-spread is also lower when floor orders initiate trades than when PER orders initiate trades (16.23 basis points versus 17.47 basis points). These differences are all statistically significant at the 1% level of significance and are economically meaningful.

Our finding of a lower realized spread for floor trades is robust to controls for the information content of a trade. In specific, we extend the matched pair technique to control for permanent price effects, and continue to find that execution costs are lower on the trading floor. We also examine execution costs for SPDRs (Standard and Poors Depository Receipts), a security that is not subject to information asymmetries. Our findings on SPDRs provide strong confirmation that the execution cost differentials are driven by the relative efficiency of order handling on the floor, rather than by information asymmetries.

We examine the determinants of trade initiation on the floor vs. PER using a probit analysis. Our findings are that the floor trading mechanism is preferred for larger sized trades, on occasions when the order flow is in the direction of the initiating trade (but not following a recent large price change) during morning and late afternoon hours, and for less liquid stocks. We further examine the determinants of execution costs on the trading floor by modeling a floor trader's decision to trade that accounts for the potential selectivity bias in the data.[liii] Our major findings are that the execution costs are lower for trades initiated in the direction of the order flow, but are higher for trades following large price changes. Together, these findings suggest that floor traders exhibit strategic behavior, becoming more aggressive in response to a thickening of the book on their own side, and becoming more patient following large pre-trade price changes. It thus appears that floor traders can opportunistically seize liquidity without showing their hands too quickly and that, consequently, using a floor broker is equivalent to placing a "smart" limit order." This implies a standard that electronic trading must meet in order to provide an environment that, from the point of view of institutional investors, is competitive with the trading floor. Currently, an increasing number of institutional investors have their own DOT machines and smart order handling systems, and are thereby able, to a limited extent, to handle their orders strategically from their upstairs desks, as they would be worked on the trading floor.[liv]

In the next section of this paper, we consider order handling mechanisms and price determination in an electronic continuous trading system vs. a floor based continuous market. In Section III, we describe the data and methodology used for the study. In Section IV, we present our empirical results. Section V contains our conclusions.

II Order handling and price formation

Standard limit and market orders are delivered to the Amex specialists through the Amex's Post Execution Reporting (PER) system. Market orders sent in electronically over PER typically trigger trades immediately. They are directly routed to the specialist who may execute them at the prevailing quote or at an improved price within the quote. Some large institutional investors have DOT machines on their trading desks and send in system orders that are market timed. Predominantly, however, this is not the case.

In contrast, an order may be given to a floor broker to be worked on a "not held" (NH) basis. The order is called "NH" because the broker is "not held" to the price existing at the time of the order's arrival if he or she eventually fills the order at a worse price. Price limits are commonly placed on NH orders. Within these limits, a floor broker has the discretion to market time an NH order. Large floor orders are commonly broken up and presented to the market in smaller tranches in the hope of obtaining more favorable market conditions and in an attempt to minimize price impact.

Having an NH order worked on the floor of an exchange may have important benefits for the investor. By responding to market events as they occur, a floor broker can better control two polar opposite implicit execution costs: (i) the market impact cost of trading a large order too aggressively, and (ii) the opportunity cost of trading it too patiently. One might also use a floor broker to gain access to, and to profit from, the agent's superior information about latent order flow.

Comprehensively viewed, the key service provided by floor traders is the timing, sizing, and pricing of the tranches of an order. We expect floor brokers to time NH orders according to current market conditions. This may, in fact, be an important reason why investors submit orders to the floor. In other words, it may be more difficult to work such orders away from the floor. The time an order is actually submitted is not observable from our data. Floor traders disclose neither the time an order is received nor the full size of the order. Our tests focus on the liquidity impact cost at the time when part or all of an order triggers a trade. It would be of some interest to examine the spreads prevailing in the market at the time an order is placed but, unfortunately, we are not able to do so. Because floor orders are commonly broken up and presented to the market in smaller tranches, the "full order" that was initially submitted is generally larger than the "tranche" that triggers a trade at any point in time. This is of no serious consequence for our analysis; we consider the initial order a package of smaller orders, and focus on the timing of the tranches as they are revealed to the market and turned into trades.

III. The Data and Test Design

A. Data

Our analysis uses October, 2001 non-block trade and quote data for 973 Amex stocks. For each stock (ticker symbol), for each day, we have: (i) *the quote file* (for each posted quote, the time of the posting, the posting exchange, the bid price posted, the size of the bid, the ask price posted, and the size of the ask); and (ii) *the trade file* (for each trade, the time the trade was reported executed, identification code for the buy account, the quantity purchased, identification code for the sell account and the quantity sold).

In order to classify trades, we first re-construct the National Best Bid and Offer (*NBBO*)[lv] from the quote file, which is updated each time a new quote is posted by an exchange. In re-constructing the *NBBO*, we adhere strictly to the Consolidated Tape Association's price, size and time priority rules. We follow tradition by using the Lee-Ready algorithm to infer the initiating party.[lvi] Hence, our master data file contains trades arranged in chronological order and identified as buyer or seller initiated, the source of the initiating order (floor versus PER), and the *NBBO* at the time of trade execution.

We are concerned about strategic order splitting by traders and its affect on our measure of execution cost. We measure market impact by the price adjustment that occurs after a trade. Because order splitting can impact prices after a floor trade *t*, it can bias our measure of the market impact of the order that triggered trade *t*. We have information on broker identification. Thus, we eliminate possibly split trades by using the following heuristic rule: for each trade *t*, we examine the fifteen trades immediately following it. If a trade during this fifteen-trade interval has the same clearing firm on the same side of the trade as trade *t*, it is identified as a "split" trade. If trade *t* has more than three "split" trades during the following fifteen-trade interval, we eliminate it from the sample. Our analysis is based on this reduced sample of trade observations.

B. Measuring Execution Costs

Consistent with previous studies [for example, Bessembinder and Kauffman (1997); Huang and Stoll (1996)], we measure the quoted half-spread and the effective half-spread for floor trades and PER trades. Consistent with standard practice, the quoted half-spread is defined as one-half of the ratio of the bid-ask spread to the prevailing midquote. The quoted half-spread is an appropriate measure of execution cost only if trades are assumed to occur at the posted quotes. However, it is not appropriate if trades occur away from the quotes.

The relevant measure in the latter case is the effective half-spread which is usually defined as the ratio of the difference between the execution price and the prevailing midquote, to the midquote. The effective half-spread is an accurate measure of the revenue realized by the liquidity provider (and hence, the cost incurred by the liquidity demander) if the value of the asset is unchanged following the trade. However, there is evidence in the literature that the asset value moves in the direction of the trade following the trade [Hasbrouck (1988), Huang and Stoll (1994)]. In other words, the price increases following a market buy and declines following a market sell. Accordingly, a more accurate measure of the execution cost is the realized half-spread, which is sometimes referred to as the temporary price impact.

Following Huang and Stoll (1996) and Bessembinder and Kaufman (1997), we define the realized half-spread for trade *t* for stock *i* as the negative of the logarithmic return from the transaction to the mid-quote at the time of the fifteenth trade after the transaction. [lvii]

C. Matched Pair Sampling Technique

Our objective is to compare execution costs across the two trading venues, floor and PER. There are, of course, exogenous factors such as stock specific characteristics, order size, trade direction (buy or sell), among others, that impact execution costs. To control for these factors we use a matched pair sampling technique. For each floor trade, we try to locate a matching PER trade. The matching criteria are: (1) trades must be in the same stock, (2) trades must be in the same direction (buy or sell), (3) the execution price of the PER trade must be within 20% of the price of the floor trade, and (4) the size of the PER trade must be within 20% of the size of the floor trade.[lviii] We present our empirical results by categorizing trades into four groups: trades less than 500 shares, trades between 500 and 999 shares, trades between 1000 and 1499 shares and trades between 1500 and 9999 shares.

D. Determinants of Trade Initiation on Floor vs. PER

Our hypothesis is that trades executed on the floor are strategically timed to account for order characteristics and to coincide with market conditions that reduce execution costs. We first focus on understanding the determinants of trade initiation on the two venues. Theoretical research on order submission strategies suggests two variables that may be of particular relevance to our study. The first explanatory variable, *order size*, is suggested by theoretical models such as Easley and O'Hara (1987). The second explanatory variable, *order imbalance*, is suggested by market microstructure models such as Kyle (1985) and Admati and Pfleiderer (1988). Glosten and Harris (1988), Madhavan, Richardson and Roomans (1997) and Huang and Stoll (1997) provide evidence that trade indicator variables (buyer-initiated and seller-initiated trades) also explain intra-day price movements.

To obtain a measure of order imbalance for a trade t, we begin by dividing each day into 15-minute intervals. Order imbalance for trade t is the aggregate trading volume triggered by orders on the same side of the market (as the order that triggered trade t) relative to total trading volume in the stock over the contemporaneous 15-minute interval.[lix] To ensure that the measure is not contaminated by a trader's own trading volume in that 15-minute interval, in computing the imbalance we eliminate all trades that the same trader participates in during that period. Hence, we define the order imbalance for trade t as

$$Imb_t = \frac{Own\text{-}side\ 15\text{-}minute\ trading\ volume}{Total\ 15\text{-}minute\ trading\ volume}$$

For trading intervals during which no trades are recorded for a stock we set Imb_t equal to 0.50.

It is possible to identify other variables that may affect the order submission strategy. For example, implementing a momentum strategy requires that one react more aggressively to price changes compared to a value strategy.[lx] Hence, recent price changes may be a relevant factor in our analysis. We capture this by incorporating the pre-trade price change as an explanatory variable in our model. Additionally, the time of day may influence order placement. In particular, as the afternoon progresses, we expect to see participants stepping forward to trade because they do not want to risk carrying unfilled orders into the overnight period. We control for the time of the day effect by dividing the trading day into three periods; an opening period (9:30 AM to 10:00 AM), a mid-day period (10:00 AM to 3:30 PM), and a closing period (3:30 PM to 4:00 PM).

We formally model the probability of a trade occurring on PER as follows:

$$\Pr(y_t = 0) = \Phi(\theta' z_t)$$

where $\theta' z_t = \theta_0 + \theta_1 q_{1t} + \theta_2 q_{2t} + \theta_3 q_{3t} + \theta_4 Imb_t + \theta_5 Preret_t + \theta_6 D_{1t} + \theta_7 D_{2t} + \theta_8 Vol_t$

The variable q_{1t} is a binary indicator variable that takes a value of 1 if the order size is between 500 and 999 shares and zero otherwise, q_{2t} takes a value of 1 if the order size is between 1000 and 1499 shares, and q_{3t} takes a value of 1 if the order size is between 1500 and 9999 shares. The variable Imb_t captures the trading imbalance in the market, taking a value closer to zero (one) when there is less (more) trading interest on the side of the initiating trade. The variable $Preret_t$ is defined as the absolute value of the return from the mid-quote prevailing fifteen trades prior to trade t, to trade t. The variable D_{1t} is a binary indicator variable that takes a value of 1 if the trade occurs between 9:30 AM and 10 AM and zero otherwise, and D_{2t} takes a value of 1 if the trade occurs between 3:30 PM and 4 PM and zero otherwise. The variable Vol_t is the logarithm of the average daily trading volume during October 2001 for the stock being traded.

E. Determinants of Execution Costs with Endogenous Trade Initiation by Floor Traders

We now turn to an analysis of the determinants of execution costs for floor trades when floor traders may time orders to minimize realized costs. To handle the potential selection bias in the data, we model the traders' decision to initiate trades, i.e., the decision to submit or withhold an order given the order characteristics and market conditions. Our model follows the standard treatment of cases involving selection bias with an endogenous event.[lxi] It is similar in spirit to Madhavan and Cheng (1997) who use an endogenous switching regression model to study the price impact of block trades across two venues, namely, the upstairs market and the downstairs market. Both models represent the treatment of cases where data are generated by the self-selection of traders, i.e., by the endogenous choices made by the traders. However, there are important differences. Madhavan and Cheng model the choice of the appropriate venue by an agent and use a two-stage procedure to estimate the model by using data on block trades executed on both venues. In contrast, we analyze the determinants of the realized half-spread for floor trades by modeling a floor trader's decision to execute trades selectively. Since we use data on executed floor trades, two-stage estimation methods are not appropriate in our context. Accordingly, we use the maximum likelihood method to estimate our model.

In our model, the floor trader's decision to initiate trades is dependent on the expected realized half-spread of a trade. Consider a trader who initiates trade t (for simplicity, let t also denote that trader) and who faces a realized half-spread r_t^f. We express the realized half-spread as:

$$r_t^f = \beta_0^f + \beta_{11}^f q_{1t} + \beta_{12}^f q_{2t} + \beta_{13}^f q_{3t} + \beta_2^f Imb_t + \beta_3^f Preret_t +$$
$$\beta_{41}^f D_{1t} + \beta_{42}^f D_{2t} + \beta_5^f Vol_t + \varepsilon_t^f$$

(2)

where ε_t^f is a stochastic error term with variance σ^2. The explanatory variables are as defined under equation 1. The order size indicator variables q_{it} control for the variations in realized half-spread related to the size of the order that the market has to absorb. The order imbalance variable Imbt controls for variations in execution costs relative to the costs of waiting. The variable Prerett controls for the impact of recent price changes on order placement. The time-of-day indicator variables D_{1t} and D_{2t} account for intra-day effects. The variable Volt is a proxy measure of the general level of liquidity of the stock and is expected to be an important determinant of the execution cost.[lxii]

Note that equation (2) could not be estimated using standard OLS procedures if floor traders endogenously time their trades. In this case, the data would be subject to a selectivity bias. Hence, the OLS procedure would yield inconsistent parameter estimates since the conditional means of the observed error terms in equation (2) would be non-zero.

We expect a floor trader to initiate a trade if and only if the expected realized half-spread is below a threshold level.[lxiii] We define the latent variable y_t^* as the expected difference between the realized half-spread for trader t and the threshold value c_t:

$$y_t^* = E\left[\left(r_t^f - c_t\right)\middle|\Omega_t\right] + \xi_t \quad (3)$$

where Ω_t is the information set for trader t and ξ_t denotes an error term with variance normalized to 1. We can write the above equation in compact form as:

$$y_t^* = \gamma' z_t + \xi_t \quad (4)$$

where z_t is the vector of explanatory variables outlined in equation (1), and γ is the vector of coefficients.[lxiv] Floor trader t chooses to step forward with an order if $y_t^* \leq 0$, otherwise the trader withholds the order. Let y_t represent a variable that takes the value 1 if the trader chooses to trade and takes the value 0 otherwise. Hence, the observable variable is:

$$y_t = \begin{cases} 1 & \text{if } y_t^* \leq 0 \\ 0 & \text{if } y_t^* > 0 \end{cases} \quad (5)$$

We assume that $\left(\varepsilon_t^f, \xi_t\right)$ are jointly normally distributed with means zero and covariance matrix Σ, where:

$$\Sigma = \begin{bmatrix} \sigma^2 & \rho\sigma \\ \rho\sigma & 1 \end{bmatrix} \quad (6)$$

Using the properties of the normal distribution, we can write the expected realized half-spread conditional on observing a floor trade as:[lxv]

$$E\left(r_t^f \mid y^* \leq 0\right) = \beta_0^f + \beta_{11}^f q_{1t} + \beta_{12}^f q_{2t} + \beta_{13}^f q_{3t} + \beta_2^f Imb_t + + \beta_3^f Preret_t +$$

$$\beta_{41}^f D_{1t} + \beta_{42}^f D_{2t} + \beta_5^f Vol_t + \rho\sigma\left[\frac{-\phi(\gamma'z_t)}{1 - \Phi(\gamma'z_t)}\right]$$

(7)

Re-writing equation (7) in compact notation, we get:

$$E\left(r_t^f \mid y^* \leq 0\right) = X_t\beta + \rho\sigma\left[\frac{-\phi(\gamma'z_t)}{1 - \Phi(\gamma'z_t)}\right] \quad (8)$$

where ϕ and Φ are, respectively, the density function and the cumulative distribution function of the standard normal (evaluated at $\gamma'z_t$) and ρ is the correlation between ε_t^f and ξ_t. Note that in the absence of self-selection of orders by the traders, ρ would be equal to zero. This allows us to test the null hypothesis that traders do not time their orders.

We use data on executed floor trades for our analysis. Equation (8) is estimated by maximizing the following likelihood function that takes into account the truncated nature of the data:[lxvi]

$$L = \prod_i [\Phi(-Z_i\gamma)]^{-1} \frac{1}{\sigma} \exp\left[-\frac{1}{2\sigma^2}(y_i - X_i\beta)^2\right] \times \Phi\left(\frac{-[Z_i\gamma - \rho(y_i - X_i\beta)/\sigma]}{(1 - \rho^2)^{1/2}}\right)$$

(9)

IV. Results

A. Characteristics of Trades Executed on the Amex

Table 1 presents descriptive statistics for the trades in the sample we have analyzed. Overall, the volume of trades initiated on the floor is 110,489,600, accounting for 23.40% of the total volume. Trading volume initiated on PER accounts for 361,739,540 shares traded, or 76.60% of total volume. In addition to the 23.40% trading volume reported in Table 1 that is initiated on the floor, there is an additional 10.39% trading volume in which the trading floor is a passive participant. It is clear that the trading floor is an attractive venue for many non-block trades. Henceforth, we refer to trades initiated on the floor as floor trades and those initiated on PER as PER trades. We classify trades into four categories according to the number of shares transacted at the trade: (i) less than 500 shares, (ii) between 500 and 999 shares, (iii) between 1000 and 1499 shares, and (iv) between 1500 and 9,999 shares.

For trades less than 500 shares, floor trades account for only 3.96 million shares (0.84% of total trading volume) and PER trades account for 58.54 million shares (12.40% of total trading volume). The average size of floor trades in this category is 283.76 shares. For PER trades, the average size is slightly smaller at 250.54 shares. As may be seen from the last panel of Table 1, the average time spanned by the thirty trades surrounding a typical trade of less than 500 shares is 30.54 minutes. For floor trades, this time span is marginally more than the time span for PER trades.

There are 73.47 million shares traded in the 500-999 trade size category. Floor trades account for 8.50 million shares (1.80% of the total trading volume) while PER trades account for the remainder 64.97 million shares (13.76% of total trading volume). The average size of floor trades is 905.19 shares. For PER trades, the average size is again slightly smaller at 882.46 shares. The average time spanned by the thirty trades surrounding a typical trade of between 500 shares and 999 shares is 26.07 minutes.

There are only 27.48 million shares traded in the 1000-1500 trade size category. Of these, floor trades account for 4.72 million shares (1.00% of total trading volume) while PER trades account for 22.77 million shares (4.82% of total trading volume). As in the other categories, PER trades are smaller-sized with an average of 1346.59 shares compared to floor trades (1358.08 shares). The average time spanned by the thirty trades surrounding a typical trade in this category is 27.74 minutes.

Finally, for the trades between 1500 and 9999 shares, floor trades account for 93.31 million shares (19.76% of total trading volume) and PER trades account for 215.46 million shares (45.63% of trading volume). The average size of floor trades of between 1500 shares and 9999 shares is 4038.46 shares. For PER trades, the average size is considerably smaller at 3366.31 shares. The average time spanned by the thirty trades surrounding a typical trade in this category is only 21.34 minutes.

B. Evidence on execution costs

Table 2 presents our measures of execution costs for a matched sample of floor and PER trades. Using the matching criteria discussed in Section III C, we were able to find a matching PER trade for 48,471 floor trades out of a total of 49,940 floor trades (i.e., 97.06%). The matching procedure led to a close match between the trade pairs. Namely, the mean difference in trade execution price between the pairs was 7.04% with a median difference of 5.26%, and the mean difference in trade size between the pairs was 7.09% with a median difference of 2.44%. We present evidence on the following measures of execution cost: the quoted half-spread, the effective half-spread and the realized half-spread. The trades are classified into four trade size categories: less than 500 shares, 500 - 999 shares, 1000 – 1499 shares and 1500 - 9999 shares.

Panel 1 of the table presents evidence on the quoted half-spread. Overall, the floor trade sample has an average quoted half-spread of 16.23 basis points as compared to 17.49 basis points for the matched PER trade sample. The difference of -1.24 basis points is significant at the 1% level of significance. In terms of trade size categories, the quoted half-spread is significantly lower for floor trades in all of the categories. The difference varies from -0.84 basis points for large trades to -2.56 basis points for the 1000-1499 shares category.

As stated earlier, the quoted half-spread reflects the true execution cost only if trades occur at the quotes. In panel 2, we present evidence on the effective half-spread. The effective half-spread is consistently lower for floor trades across all categories, and averages 8.11 basis points as compared to 10.27 basis points for a matched sample of PER trades. The difference of negative 2.16 basis points is significant at the 1% level of significance. It varies from - 1.57 basis points for large trades to -2.89 basis points for the 500-999 shares category. It is significant at the 1% level for all cases.

In panel 3, we present evidence on the realized half-spread. As discussed previously, the realized half-spread is the most appropriate measure of the compensation realized by a liquidity provider, and hence, the cost to a liquidity seeker. The realized half-spread is consistently lower for floor trades, averaging -3.06 basis points compared to 4.43 basis points for the matched sample of PER trades. The difference of -7.49 basis points is significant at the 1% level. This difference is negative and significant for each of the trade-size categories. It is interesting to note that the realized spread on floor orders is consistently negative for all trade categories. This suggests that, with effective order handling, trading gains may be realized instead of market impact costs being incurred.

At this stage it is worthwhile to ask whether the differences in execution costs across the two venues are economically meaningful. To assess this issue we can compare the difference in execution costs to the mean quoted half-spread of 16.85 bps in our matched sample. The differences in realized half-spreads reported in Panel 3 translate to between 36.38 percent and 57.63 percent of the mean quoted half-spread. This suggests that differential execution costs are appreciable, and that trading on the more expensive venue can aggregate into major dollar costs for investors. Alternatively stated, bringing orders to the floor can generate savings that justify the higher fees that floor access involves.

The evidence on realized half-spreads is consistent with the hypothesis that floor traders time their orders to minimize execution costs, by buying (selling) at times of rising (falling) stock prices. This would explain why, in equilibrium, some trades would be submitted to the trading floor in spite of higher access costs (that are not measured in this study). An alternative interpretation of these findings is that floor trades have higher information content. In the next section, we seek to distinguish between these two hypotheses.

C. Evidence on Execution Costs of Trades with Similar Information Content

We refine our matching technique to control for the information content of trades. Specifically, we expand the matching criteria to include a control for the Permanent Price Impact of a trade defined as:

$$Permanent\ Price\ Impact = D_{it} \cdot \left[\ln\left(\frac{M_{+15}}{M_{-15}} \right) \right]$$

where D_{it} is an indicator variable that is equal to $+1$ for buyer-initiated trades and is equal to -1 for seller-initiated trades, and M_{+15} (M_{-15}) refers to the mid-quote prevailing at the time of the fifteenth trade after (before) trade t. The permanent price impact is a measure of the information content of a trade (see, for example, Kraus and Stoll (1972), and Madhavan and Cheng (1997)).

In addition to the previous matching criteria, we now require the permanent price impact of PER trades to be within 20% of the permanent price impact of floor trades. With this constraint we obtain matching PER trades for 45,536 floor trades (i.e., 91.18% of all floor trades). The mean difference in the trade execution price between the pairs is 6.79% with a median difference of 5.69%. The mean difference in trade size between the pairs is 6.70% with a median difference of 0. Finally, the mean difference in permanent price impact between the pairs is 9.66% with a median difference of 9.64%.

We present measures of the execution cost for this reduced sample of matched trades in Table 3. The first panel in the table presents the quoted half-spreads for the matched sample of floor trades and PER trades classified by four trade size categories. The average quoted half-spread for floor trades is 14.53 basis points as compared to 15.38 basis points for PER trades. The difference of –0.85 basis points is significant at the 1% level. Additionally, floor trades have significantly lower quoted half-spreads for each of the four trade-size categories.

Results on effective half-spreads are presented in the second panel of the table. Similar to the results for the full sample in Section 3.2, effective half-spreads for floor trades average 7.13 basis points as compared to 8.94 basis points for the matched sample of PER trades. The difference of -1.81 basis points is significant at the 1% level of significance. Also, it is significantly negative for all the trade size categories, varying from -1.15 basis points for the large trade category to -2.64 basis points for the 500-999 share category.

In the third panel of the table, we present results on the realized half-spreads. Overall, realized half-spreads for floor trades average -4.21 basis points as compared to -0.09 basis points for PER trades. The difference of –4.12 basis points is significant at the 1% level of significance. The difference is significantly negative for individual trade size categories. Once again, realized spreads are negative for floor trades in all trade size categories, varying from -2.88 basis points for large trades to -6.68 basis points for the 1000-1499 share category. Also, the realized spread is negative for the PER small trades at -2.55 basis points.

Overall, the results for the sample where we control for the permanent price impact are similar to the results for the full sample. We note, however, that, with just one exception, for all three half-spread measures and four size categories for both floor and PER orders, the half-spread values are somewhat smaller when we control for the permanent price impact. A higher information content of floor trades could account for this. Nevertheless, all measures of execution costs shown in Table 3, including the quoted half-spread, the effective half-spread and the realized half-spread, are significantly lower for the floor trades. This suggests that we can rule out information differences as the main reason for the lower realized half-spreads for floor trades. We further test the information content hypothesis by focusing on SPDRs, a security for which we expect no meaningful informational asymmetries.

D. Evidence on Execution Costs of Trades for SPDRS

The Amex's SPDRs (Standard and Poors Depository Receipts) are an exchange traded fund (ETF), that is potentially subject to little or no information asymmetry.[lxvii] A SPDR represents an ownership interest in the SPDR trust that holds all of the S&P 500 composite stocks, and is a highly liquid alternative to the S&P index mutual funds. SPDRs offer us an opportunity to compare execution costs across the floor and PER in a setting that is largely devoid of private information. A finding that execution costs are different across the two venues for SPDR trades would further confirm the hypothesis that these cost differentials are driven by the relative efficiency of order handling in the two venues, rather than by informational asymmetries.

Table 4 presents the evidence on execution costs for SPDRS. The first panel in the table presents the quoted half-spreads for the matched sample of floor trades and PER trades classified by four trade size categories. The average quoted half-spread for floor trades is 3.93 basis points as compared to 4.01 basis points for PER trades. The difference of –0.08 basis points is not significant. Floor trades have lower quoted half-spreads for the larger trade size categories but a higher quoted spread for the less than 500 share trade size category. Even though the differences in these two categories are statistically significant, they do not appear to be economically meaningful. Results on effective half-spreads are presented in the second panel of the table. Effective half-spreads for floor trades average 0.95 basis points as compared to 2.23 basis points for the matched sample of PER trades. The difference of –1.27 basis points is significant at the 1% level. Also, it is significantly negative for each of the individual trade size categories.

In the third panel of the table, we present results on the realized half-spreads. Overall, realized half-spreads for floor trades average -0.09 basis points as compared to 2.06 basis points for PER trades. The difference of –2.16 basis points is negative and significant at the 1% level. Also, the difference is consistently negative and significant at the 1% level across all trade size categories. To benchmark these results, note that the mean quoted half-spread in our matched sample is 3.97 bps. Hence, the differences in realized half-spread that we report in Panel 3, range from 47.36 % to 70.03% of the mean quoted half-spread.

In contrast to our full sample of stocks, the quoted half-spreads and effective half-spreads for SPDRS are substantially smaller across the board. This is also true for the realized half-spread for SPDR PER trades (though not for floor trades). This finding is consistent with the absence of any meaningful informational asymmetries for SPDRs. Despite absence of information asymmetries, we observe differences between the execution costs of floor and PER trades reported in Table 4 that are consistent with our earlier findings.

This strongly suggests that the trading floor offers the advantage of lower execution costs through improved order handling.

E. Evidence on Determinants of Order Arrival on Floor vs. PER

We present below the probit estimates based on equation (1) (chi-square statistics are in parenthesis):

$$\theta'z_t = \begin{matrix} 0.9031 & - & 0.4037 \; q_{1t} & - & 0.6578 \; q_{2t} & - & 1.0240 \; q_{3t} & - & 0.2094 \; Imb_t \\ (3106.60) & & (3220.58) & & (3420.17) & & (26378.8) & & (662.25) \end{matrix}$$

$$\begin{matrix} + & 6.0362 \; Preret_t & -0.0093\, D_{1t} & -0.0207\, D_{2t} & + & 0.0864 \; Vol_t \\ & (280.20) & (1.14) & (5.39) & & (2795.18) \end{matrix}$$

Log Likelihood $= -140988.0619$

(10)

The coefficients on the three order size indicator variables are all significantly negative, indicating that larger sized orders have a lower probability of being executed on PER and, therefore, a greater probability of execution on the floor. The coefficient on the variable Imb_t is significantly negative, suggesting that, as own-side order imbalance increases, there is a lower probability of a PER trade and, correspondingly, a higher probability of a floor-based trade. The co-efficient on the variable $Preret_t$ is significantly positive, indicating that a PER trade is more likely following a large pre-trade price change. The findings on Imb_t and $Preret_t$ imply that floor traders observe and react to order imbalance and that floor trades are more likely when there is more interest on the side of the initiating trade. At the same time, floor traders appear to be relatively patient and to avoid trading after large pre-trade price changes. Later on we show that this behavior is consistent with minimizing execution costs. Conversely, PER traders appear more apt to chase price changes (i.e., to engage in momentum trading), which may explain our earlier findings of higher realized half-spreads for PER trades.[lxviii]

The morning time-of-day indicator variable (D_{1t}) has a negative but insignificant co-efficient, and the late afternoon time-of-day indicator variable (D_{2t}) has a significantly negative co-efficient. This indicates that, relative to mid-day, floor trades are more likely in the morning and afternoon. There are two factors at play here: (1) there is evidence that the markets are more liquid during the morning and afternoon hours than during mid-day [see, for example, Jain and Joh (1988)], and (2) floor traders who may be willing to be patient earlier in the trading day, are more apt to step forth and trade as the closing bell approaches so as to avoid carrying an open position into the overnight period.

Finally, the coefficient on average trading volume is significantly positive, implying that the probability of a PER trade increases with the average trading volume of the stock (that is a measure of the stock's liquidity). Conversely, for a given order size, a less liquid stock that requires more special order handling is more likely to be traded via the floor.

In sum, the probit estimates suggest that the floor trading mechanism is preferred for larger sized trades, on occasions when the book is thicker on the side of the trade initiating order (but not following a recent large price change), during the late afternoon hours and for less liquid stocks.

G. Evidence on Determinants of Execution Costs

The estimates of the trade initiation model given by equation (8) are presented below:

$$E\left(r_t^f \mid y^* \leq 0\right) = 0.00003^* + 0.00042^{***} q_{1t} + 0.00037^{**} q_{2t} + 0.00063^{***} q_{3t} - 0.00399^{***} Imb_t$$

$$+ .06184^{**} Preret_t - 0.00046^{***} D_{1t} + 0.00011 D_{2t} + 0.00014^{***} Vol_t + 0.08683\left[\frac{-\hat{\phi}(\gamma' Z_t)}{1 - \hat{\Phi}(\gamma' Z_t)}\right]$$

(11)

where

$$\gamma' Z_t = 0.60402 - 0.18755 q_{1t} + 0.50145^{***} q_{2t} + 0.79156^{***} q_{3t} + 0.72311^* Imb_t$$

$$+ 0.13271 Preret_t + 0.26139^{***} D_{1t} + 0.15004 D_{2t} + 1.48472^{**} Vol_t$$

(12)

***   indicates significance at the 1% level ;
**   indicates significance at the 5% level;
*   indicates significance at the 10% level.

In equation (11), the co-efficients corresponding to the second through the fourth terms (corresponding to the order-size indicator variables q_{1t}, q_{2t} and q_{3t}) are significantly positive, which indicates that the expected realized half-spread increases with order size. In contrast, the co-efficient of Imb_t in equation (11) is significantly negative, implying that the expected realized half-spread decreases with order imbalance. The co-efficient for $Preret_t$ in equation (11) is significantly positive, implying that the expected realized half-spread increases following recent price changes. The results on Imb_t and $Preret_t$ in conjunction with our earlier Probit results, suggest strategic behavior on the part of floor traders who become more aggressive in response to a thickening of the book on their own side, and who become patient following large pre-trade price changes.

The co-efficient of the morning dummy variable D_{1t} in equation (11) is significantly negative, implying that the expected realized half-spread is low in the morning hours, at a time when we expect market liquidity to be higher.

The co-efficient of the afternoon dummy variable D_{2t} is positive but insignificant. Given our earlier probit results that the probability of floor initiated trades is higher in the afternoons, it appears that, as the day wears on, the traders' patience wears thin and the desire to complete their orders increases. Finally, the co-efficient of average trading volume is positive and significant, which would suggest that the expected cost of trading via the floor is higher for larger volume stocks, and that the floor is a relatively more attractive venue for less liquid stocks. The last term of equation (11) is commonly referred to as the Inverse Mills ratio. The co-efficient of this term is insignificant, which indicates that selectivity bias may be absent in the data.[lxix]

Similarly, the results in equation (12) are economically insightful. The equation presents the relationship between the probability of a floor trade occurring (as opposed to a trade being withheld) and order size, order imbalance, recent price change, time of day and average trading volume for the stock. This probability increases with order size except for the small share category, for which the co-efficient is insignificant. The probability of a floor trade increases with order imbalance as well. With respect to price changes, the results are insignificant. With respect to the time-of-day, floor trades are more likely in the morning hours. The results are insignificant with respect to the late afternoon. The results are consistent with more liquidity being available in the morning. Finally, the probability of a floor trade increases with average trading volume, indicating that floor traders are more inclined to trade a stock with higher average trading volume quickly than they are to trade a stock with lower average trading volume. As one would expect, more strategic behavior is required for stocks with lower average trading volume.

V. Conclusion

For an expanding array of equity markets, including Toronto, Paris, Tokyo, Australia, Madrid, Stockholm, Switzerland, Frankfurt and London, floorless electronic trading systems have been the wave of the future. In this paper, we have focused on the value of a trading floor. Our analysis of non-block trades on the Amex, a floor-based market, suggests that the floor environment adds value through improved order handling. Consistent with this, we find that 23.40% of the trading volume in our sample is initiated on the trading floor and that, on the passive side, the floor participates in an additional 10.39% of the trading volume.

Using a matched pair technique, we find that floor broker timed order handling generally results in lower execution costs. Overall, trades handled by floor brokers have a significantly smaller realized half-spread than do PER trades (-3.06 basis points versus 4.43 basis points). This difference of

7.49 basis points is equivalent to a savings of 3.94 cents per share for an average priced stock on the Amex.[lxx]   Given the aggregate floor trading volume of 110,489,600 shares in October 2001, this translates to a total savings of $4.36 million for the month. In addition, floor trades have a lower effective half-spread compared to PER trades (8.11 basis points versus 10.27 basis points). The quoted half-spread is also lower when floor orders initiate trades than when PER orders initiate trades (16.23 basis points versus 17.47 basis points).

Our finding of a lower realized spread for floor trades is robust to controls for the information content of a trade. In specific, we examine execution costs for a restricted sample that further controls for the permanent price effect. We continue to find that execution costs are lower on the trading floor.
Our evidence on SPDRs, a security that is not subject to information asymmetries, further reinforces the above findings. We find that execution costs continue to be lower on the floor despite absence of information differentials for matched trades compared across the two venues.

Our findings on SPDRs strongly suggest that the trading floor offers the advantage of reduced execution costs through improved order handling.

We have examined the determinants of trade initiation on the floor vs. PER. Our findings are that the floor trading mechanism is preferred for larger sized trades, on occasions when the order flow is in the direction of the initiating trade (but not following a recent large price change), during morning and late afternoon hours, and for less liquid stocks. Our findings on the determinants of execution costs on the trading floor are that the execution costs are lower for trades initiated in the direction of the order flow, but higher for trades that are preceded by large price changes.

Together, these findings suggest that floor traders exhibit strategic behavior, becoming more aggressive in response to a thickening of the book on their own side, and becoming more patient following large pre-trade price changes. In contrast, PER traders are more apt to chase recent price changes. This helps explain why floor orders incur lower (and even negative) execution costs and sheds light on the role of floor brokers and the value of intermediation in an equity market.

It is important to point out, however, that, to some extent at least, the functions of a floor trader can be carried out in an electronic environment, and that the strategic timing of trades does not necessarily require verbal order entry by human intermediaries. A growing number of institutional investors now have DOT machines and smart order handling systems that give them some ability to work their orders strategically from their upstairs desks. The ECNs show orders away from the best bid and offer (as the New

York Stock Exchange now does through its Open Book), and some of the ECNs have reserve book functionality. While this may not yet be enough for buyside traders working their own smart limit orders to compete with floor traders handling not held orders,[lxxi] with improvements in the technology for order routing and handling and the development of superior market design, one might expect the future to lie with electronic trading.

Observing that trading costs can be controlled by proper trade initiation underscores the need to design an environment that best presents the relevant information on market conditions to participants. Our analysis suggests a standard that the electronic platforms must meet, especially with regard to institutional order flow.

[*] Robert L. Jensen Fellow in Finance, Henry B. Tippie College of Business, University of Iowa
[**]Marvin M. Speiser Professor of Finance and University Distinguished Professor, Zicklin School of Business, Baruch College, CUNY
[***]Henry B. Tippie, Assistant Professor, College of Business, University of Iowa

REFERENCES

Admati, A., and Pfleiderer, P., 1988, "A theory of intraday patterns: volume and price variability," *Review of Financial Studies* 1, 3-40.

Amihud, Yakov and Haim Mendelson, 1986, "Asset pricing and the bid-ask spread," Journal of Financial Economics 17, 223-249.

Amihud, Yakov, Haim Mendelson and Beni Lauterbach, 1997, "Market microstructure and securities values: Evidence from the Tel Aviv Stock Exchange," *Journal of Financial Economics* 45, 365-390.

Bessembinder, H. and H.M. Kaufman, 1997, "A cross-exchange comparison of execution costs and information flow for NYSE-listed stocks," *Journal of Financial Economics* 46, 293-319.

Brennan, M. and A. Subrahmanyam, 1996, "Market microstructure and asset pricing: on the compensation for illiquidity in stock returns," *Journal of Financial Economics* 41, 441-464.

Conrad, Jennifer, Kevin M. Johnson and Sunil Wahal, 2001, Alternative Trading Systems, Working Paper, Emory University.

Easley, David and Maureen O'Hara, 1987, "Price, trade size and information in securities markets." *Journal of Financial Economics* 19, 69-90.

Glosten, L. and L. Harris, 1988, "Estimating the components of the bid/ask spread," *Journal of Financial Economics* 21, 123-142.

Huang, Roger D. and Hans R. Stoll, 1994, "Market microstructure and stock return predictions" A paired comparison of execution costs on NASDAQ and the NYSE," *Review of Financial Studies,* 7, 179-213.

Huang, Roger D. and Hans R. Stoll, 1996, "Dealer versus auction markets: A paired comparison of execution costs on NASDAQ and the NYSE," *Journal of Financial Economics* 41, 313-357.

Huang, Roger D. and Hans R. Stoll, 1997, "The components of the bid-ask spread: a general approach," *Review of Financial Studies,* 10, 995-1034.

Jain, Prem and Gun-Ho Joh, 1988, "The dependence between hourly prices and trading volume," *Journal of Financial and Quantitative Analysis,* 23, 269-284.

Keim, D. B., and A. Madhavan, 1995, "The Anatomy of the Trading Process," *Journal of Financial Economics,* 37, 391–398.

Keim, Donald B. and Ananth Madhavan, 1996. "The upstairs market for large-block transactions: analysis and measurement of price effects," *Review of Financial Studies,* 9, 1-36.

Kraus, A. and H. Stoll, 1972, "Price impacts of block trading on the New York Stock Exchange," *Journal of Finance* 27, 569-588.

Kyle, A., 1985, "Continuous auctions and insider trading," *Econometrica* 53, 1315-1335.

Lee, Charles and Mark Ready, 1991, "Inferring trade direction from intraday data," *Journal of Finance* 46, 733-746.

Maddala, G.S., 1983, Limited dependent and qualitative variables in econometrics (Cambridge University Press, New York).

Maddala, G.S., 1996, "Applications of the limited dependent variable models in finance," In G.S. Maddala and C.R. Rao (eds.), *Handbook of Statistics,* Vol 14, 553-566 (Elsevier Science B.V.)

Madhavan, Ananth and M. Cheng, 1997, "In search of liquidity: block trades in the upstairs and downstairs markets," *Review of Financial Studies* 10, 175-204.

Madhavan, Ananth, M. Richardson and M. Roomans, 1997, "Why do security prices change? A transaction-level analysis of NYSE stocks," *Review of Financial Studies* 10, 1035-1064.

Pagano, Marco and Ailsa Röell, 1992, "Auction and dealership markets: what is the difference?," *European Economic Review* 36, 613-623.

Sofianos, George and Ingrid M. Werner, 1997, "The trades of NYSE floor brokers, Working Paper," New York Stock Exchange.

Venkataraman, Kumar, 2001, "Automated versus floor trading: An analysis of execution costs on the Paris and New York exchanges," *Journal of Finance* 56, 1445-1485.

Sample Statistics

Share volume, percent of volume, trade size and time between trades for the four trade size categories at the American Stock Exchange during October 2001.

We classify both floor initiated and PER initiated trades into four categories: less than 500 shares, between 500 and 999 shares, between 1000 and 1499 shares, and between 1500 and 9999 shares. Number of trades, Percent of Trades (%), Trade size (shares), and Time between Trades −15 to +15 (in minutes) is reported in the four panels below.

Share Volume

	Less than 500 shares	500 – 999 shares	1000 – 1499 shares	1500 - 9999	Total
Floor	3,964,700	8,499,700	4,716,600	93,308,600	110,489,600
PER	58,542,440	64,967,400	22,765,400	215,464,300	361,739,540
All Trades	62,507,140	73,467,100	27,482,000	308,772,900	472,229,140

Percent of Total Volume (%)

	Less than 500 shares	500 – 999 shares	1000 – 1499 shares	1500 - 9999	Average order size
Floor	0.84	1.80	1.00	19.76	23.40
PER	12.40	13.76	4.82	45.63	76.60
All Trades	13.24	15.56	5.82	65.39	100.00

Table 1

Trade Size (shares)

	Less than 500 shares	500 – 999 shares	1000 – 1499 shares	1500 - 9999	Average order size
Floor	283.76	905.19	1358.08	4038.46	2212.45
PER	250.54	882.46	1346.59	3366.31	931.85
All Trades	252.42	885.03	1348.55	3544.59	1077.82

Time between trades -15 and +15 (in minutes)

	Less than 500 shares	500 – 999 shares	1000 – 1499 shares	1500 - 9999	Average order size
Floor	32.19	27.04	26.28	23.17	26.64
PER	30.44	25.95	28.04	20.68	27.87
All Trades	30.54	26.07	27.74	21.34	27.73

Table 2

Matched Sample Results, All Trades: Quoted half-spread, effective half-spread and realized half-spread, reported in basis points, for matched pairs of floor and PER initiated trades classified by the four trade size categories at the American Stock Exchange during October 2001. The quoted half-spread is defined as $Quoted\ Half-Spread = (Ask - Bid)/(Bid + Ask)$. The effective half-spread is $Effective\ Half-Spread = D_{it} \cdot \{[P_0 - (Bid + Ask)/2]/[(Bid + Ask)/2]\}$ where P_0 is the transaction price and D_{it} is an indicator variable that is equal to $+1$ for buyer-initiated trades and is equal to -1 for seller-initiated trades. The realized half-spread for trade t for stock i is the negative of the logarithmic return from the transaction (with the trade price denoted by P_0) to the mid-quote at the time of the fifteenth trade after the transaction denoted by M_{+15}, i.e., $Realized\ Half-Spread = D_{it} \cdot [\ln(P_0/M_{+15})]$. The matching is achieved as follows. For each floor trade, we try to locate a matching PER trade. The matching criteria are: (1) trades must be in the same stock, (2) trades must be in the same direction, buy or sell, (3) the execution price of the PER trade must be within 20% of the price of the floor trade, and (4) the size of the PER trade must be within 20% of the size of the floor trade.

Quoted Half-Spread (in basis points)

	Less than 500 shares	500 - 999 shares	1000 - 1499 shares	1500 - 9999 shares	Average
Floor	17.02	16.78	16.77	15.39	16.23
PER	18.18	18.60	19.33	16.23	17.47
Difference	*-1.16**	*-1.82**	*-2.56**	*-0.84**	*-1.24**

Effective Half-Spread (in basis points)

	Less than 500 shares	500 - 999 shares	1000 - 1499 shares	1500 - 9999 shares	Average
Floor	7.26	8.08	9.38	8.47	8.11
PER	9.69	10.97	12.16	10.04	10.27
Difference	*-2.44**	*-2.89**	*-2.78**	*-1.57**	*-2.16**

Realized Half-Spread (in basis points)

	Less than 500 shares	500 - 999 shares	1000 - 1499 shares	1500 - 9999 shares	Average
Floor	-7.20	-3.03	-3.47	-0.33	-3.06
PER	2.51	3.10	3.94	6.33	4.43
Difference	*-9.71**	*-6.13**	*-7.41**	*-6.67**	*-7.49**

** Denotes significance at the 1% level

Table 3

Matched Sample Results, Trades with Similar Information Content: Quoted half-spread, effective half-spread and realized half-spread, reported in basis points, for matched pairs of floor and PER initiated trades classified by the four trade size categories at the American Stock Exchange during October 2001.The quoted half-spread is defined as $Quoted\ Half - Spread = (Ask - Bid)/(Bid + Ask)$. The effective half-spread is $Effective\ Half - Spread = D_{it} \cdot \{[P_0 - (Bid + Ask)/2]/[(Bid + Ask)/2]\}$ where P_0 is the transaction price and D_{it} is an indicator variable that is equal to +1 for buyer-initiated trades and is equal to -1 for seller-initiated trades. The realized half-spread for trade t for stock i is the negative of the logarithmic return from the transaction (with the trade price denoted by P_0) to the mid-quote at the time of the fifteenth trade after the transaction denoted by

M_{+15}, i.e., *Realized Half-Spread* $= D_{it} \cdot [\ln(P_0/M_{+15})]$. The matching is achieved as follows. For each floor trade, we try to locate a matching PER trade. The matching criteria are: (1) trades must be in the same stock, (2) trades must be in the same direction, buy or sell, (3) the execution price of the PER trade must be within 20% of the price of the floor trade, and (4) the size of the PER trade must be within 20% of the size of the floor trade. Additionally, the permanent price impact, defined as *Permanent Price Impact* $= D_{it} \cdot [\ln(M_{+15}/M_{-15})]$, of the PER trade must be within 20% of that of the floor trade.

Quoted Half-Spread (in basis points)

	Less than 500 shares	500 - 999 shares	1000 – 1499 shares	1500 - 9999 shares	Average
Floor	15.81	15.85	14.96	12.96	14.53
PER	16.66	16.95	16.76	13.54	15.38
Difference	-0.85*	-1.10*	-1.80*	-0.58*	-0.85*

Effective Half-Spread (in basis points)

	Less than 500 shares	500 - 999 shares	1000 – 1499 shares	1500 - 9999 shares	Average
Floor	6.83	7.52	7.94	7.02	7.13
PER	8.89	10.16	10.34	8.17	8.94
Difference	-2.06*	-2.64*	-2.40*	-1.15*	-1.81**

Realized Half-Spread (in basis points)

	Less than 500 shares	500 - 999 shares	1000 – 1499 shares	1500 - 9999 shares	Average
Floor	-7.14	-4.61	-5.81	-1.72	-4.21
PER	-2.55	0.53	0.87	1.17	-0.09
Difference	-4.60*	-5.14*	-6.68*	-2.88*	-4.12*

* Denotes significance at the 5% level
** Denotes significance at the 1% level

Table 4
Matched Sample Results for SPDRS: Quoted half-spread, effective half-spread and realized half-spread, reported in basis points, for matched pairs of

floor and PER initiated trades classified by the four trade size categories at the American Stock Exchange during October 2001.

The quoted half-spread is defined as $Quoted\ Half-Spread = (Ask - Bid)/(Bid + Ask)$. The effective half-spread is $Effective\ Half-Spread = D_{it} \cdot \{[P_0 - (Bid + Ask)/2]/[(Bid + Ask)/2]\}$ where P_0 is the transaction price and D_{it} is an indicator variable that is equal to +1 for buyer-initiated trades and is equal to -1 for seller-initiated trades. The realized half-spread for trade t for stock i is the negative of the logarithmic return from the transaction (with the trade price denoted by P_0) to the mid-quote at the time of the fifteenth trade after the transaction denoted by M_{+15}, i.e., $Realized\ Half\text{-}Spread = D_{it} \cdot [\ln(P_0/M_{+15})]$. The matching is achieved as follows. For each floor trade, we try to locate a matching PER trade. The matching criteria are: (1) trades must be in the same direction, buy or sell, (2) the execution price of the PER trade must be within 20% of the price of the floor trade, and (3) the size of the PER trade must be within 20% of the size of the floor trade.

Quoted Half-Spread (in basis points)

	Less than 500 shares	500 - 999 shares	1000 - 1499 shares	1500 - 9999 shares	Average
Floor	4.01	3.91	3.94	3.92	3.93
PER	3.90	4.00	4.04	4.04	4.01
Difference	0.11**	-0.09	-0.11	-0.12*	-0.08

Effective Half-Spread (in basis points)

	Less than 500 shares	500 - 999 shares	1000 - 1499 shares	1500 - 9999 shares	Average
Floor	0.13	0.91	0.70	1.23	0.95
PER	1.84	2.15	2.37	2.34	2.23
Difference	-1.70*	-1.23*	-1.66*	-1.11**	-1.27*

Realized Half-Spread (in basis points)

	Less than 500 shares	500 -- 999 shares	1000 - 1499 shares	1500 - 9999 shares	Average
Floor	-0.43	-0.73	0.03	0.14	-0.09
PER	2.11	2.05	2.32	2.02	2.06
Difference	-2.54*	-2.78*	-2.29*	-1.88*	-2.16*

** Denotes significance at the 1% level

This chapter was originally published in the Journal of Business.

The Evolution of Automated Trading Systems: New Requirements for an Increasingly Complex Marketplace

By Ary Kahtchikian, Portware and Harrell Smith, Portware

Over the past several years, the global capital markets have undergone major structural and regulatory upheavals. Driven in part by the inexorable advance of technology, these changes have forced firms to constantly address new business requirements – while simultaneously providing firms with new opportunities for growth.

Nowhere has this trend been more apparent than in the adoption of electronic trading. Beginning with basic order management systems and continuing on through the introduction of DMA, broker-front ends, and early execution management systems, the market for electronic trading solutions has developed in response to the needs of an increasingly sophisticated client base. Today, firms are seeking a combination of increased efficiency, flexibility, multi-asset support and an integrated solution with which to create and deploy proprietary trading strategies. At the same time, more and more of these firms realize that they can no longer rely on their legacy trading systems to meet these requirements – or the requirements of a future marketplace that promises to be even more challenging than today's. While these platforms may have adequately addressed many firms' early trading needs, the markets' rapid development, combined with the demand for more powerful and scalable trading architecture, is forcing firms to adopt advanced systems that can support their businesses today and, more importantly, tomorrow.

Early Market Structure and the OMS Model

During the mid 1980's, the global equity markets relied almost exclusively on an open-outcry model. Communications between brokers and clients were handled by phone and by fax. The NYSE, whose current tech infrastructure can handle over 64,000 messages per second (mps), could only handle 95 mps in 1987. The exchange landscape as a whole was "connected" by the Intermarket Trading System (ITS), ostensibly to ensure that orders were routed to appropriate market destinations for best execution. In reality, however, "trade throughs" were the norm and execution speed was often measured in minutes. The same held true for other markets as well. Options, futures, FX, fixed income – all were either traded in the pit, on the floor, or over the phone.

It was during this period that the first order management systems (OMS) came to market. Their purpose was to bring accounting, compliance, reporting, and other similar functions under one umbrella. Given that only established asset management firms needed (or could afford) such a solution, OMS vendors focused squarely on the largest buy-side and sell-side institutions. With this market in mind, OMS vendors adopted an "everything but the kitchen sink model," rolling out products that were heavy, complex – and expensive, both from an integration and customization standpoint. As OMS's became deeply entrenched in firms' technology infrastructure, attached to a web of back and mid office applications (many of which were proprietary), client firms found themselves beholden to their OMS vendors for technology upgrades, consulting services, product enhancements, etc. The cost of ripping out and replacing an OMS was prohibitive for most firms, and as such their OMSs gradually became part of their legacy infrastructure.

Given OMSs' stated business model as internal workflow applications, combined with the market environment that prevailed during their initial rollout, it is not surprising that early OMSs lacked any trading functionality whatsoever. In addition, other economic factors helped stall the development of OMS trading order management technology. Twenty years ago, buy-side institutions focused far less on trading costs than they do today. The prevailing attitude was that buy-side trading desks were little more than a collection of order clerks. As a result, firms paid little attention to their trading infrastructure. Traders relied on numerous back- and middle-office personnel to manually book trades, reconcile positions, and facilitate communications between the trading desk and brokers. These factors, combined with pre-decimalization spreads and less stringent regulatory oversight, provided little incentive for OMS vendors to focus on trade workflow processes.

As the market underwent significant changes, particularly with respect to the growth of electronic trading, OMS vendors' attitudes towards automated trading technology remained essentially the same. Indeed, it was not until the early to mid 2000s, when brokers began aggressively pushing their algorithmic strategies that OMSs focused on rolling out order execution functionality. By that point, legacy technology and rigid system architectures left OMS vendors unable to deploy anything approaching advanced trading functionality. Traders using OMSs for electronic execution could send orders to brokers' electronic destinations, receive confirmations, cancel and re-send, and, in certain cases, employ the most basic DMA functions. That, however, was the extent of OMSs' trading capabilities, a model that persists to this day.

The Birth of Electronic Trading

It was not until the mid 1990's that real electronic trading platforms began to emerge, signaling the beginning of an evolution that would eventually lead to execution management systems as we know them today. It was during this period that structural, economic, technological and regulatory forces began to reshape the US equities landscape in earnest. NASDAQ came into its own, creating an environment for the development of the electronic order book model. That in turn led to increased market fragmentation, as new ECNs and ATSs joined the fray. Decimalization propelled average trade sizes downward; combined with a net increase in share volumes, the number of orders skyrocketed. Electronic communication protocols, such as FIX, became more standardized. Improvements to the technology infrastructures and networks that supported electronic execution venues facilitated faster delivery of orders and market data. These forces, combined with sweeping new regulatory initiatives, (notably, RegNMS) would eventually push equity trading almost completely into the electronic medium.

At the same time, buy-side attitudes about execution quality began to shift. While the soft-dollar requirements that underpinned most order flow decisions remained intact, a new focus on minimizing trading costs began influencing the buy-side's trading decisions, forcing institutions to focus on operational efficiencies to a greater extent than ever before. The end result was that buy-side firms were suddenly forced to take greater responsibility for their order flow. Given the increasingly complex, technology-driven marketplace discussed above, firms needed new tools to efficiently navigate – and exploit – this new trading environment.

The Firs Broker Front Ends

The result was the creation of the first generation of direct market access (DMA) platforms. Although the business models that supported these systems varied, their key functional capabilities were more or less identical: a consolidated view of numerous order books (exchanges and ECNs); Level II market data/depth of book; single ticket order entry supporting user-defined parameters (i.e. order type, destination, limit prices, displayed quantity, etc.), and basic charting and blotter functionality. Early providers of DMA platforms included a mix of vendors and specialty agency brokers, such as ITG, Lava, UNX, Sonic, Neovest and FutureTrade.

While these and other systems were gaining traction in the marketplace, dealers were undergoing wrenching changes to their traditional brokerage businesses. Commissions were coming under increased downward pressure. Basic equity execution, particularly for liquid securities, had become commoditized, forcing firms to reevaluate the role of the traditional sales trader and focus on automating low-touch client trades. Compounding these problems were the aforementioned tech focused agency broker platforms, as well as a host of new crossing networks, who had managed to secure a sizable portion of the buy-side's daily order flow.

In response, the broker dealer community adopted a two pronged strategy. First, brokers who had long used algorithms to automate low touch trades began pushing these solutions out to their clients. Starting with rules based algorithms such as VWAP and TWAP, brokers soon jumped on the algorithmic bandwagon, developing a host of new and more exotic sounding algorithms from which their clients could choose. Marketed as cost effective strategies that were appropriate for a variety of different trading styles and scenarios, algorithms became essential components of any broker's suite of execution services.

Unfortunately, as the dealer community collectively rolled out these new algorithms, their clients were left with the impression that there was little, if any, difference between brokers' various execution services. All of these services were accessible via FIX and every broker had created essentially the same suite of algorithms. Few clients grasped the relative strengths and weaknesses of brokers' offerings, and fewer still engaged in comprehensive post-trade transaction cost analyses to compare their brokers' performance. How, then, could dealers separate themselves from the pack?

For many brokers, the answer lay on the client desktop. If they could provide clients with a DMA platform like Goldman's RediPLUS or Morgan Stanley's Passport, they could establish desktop preeminence and essentially become clients' default execution destination. Presumably, traders who just wanted to get an easy 100,000 share VWAP order done would be more likely than not to use the system in front of them.

Of course, there was another reason that firms across the street were looking jealously at Goldman's and Morgan Stanley's front ends. The business of prime brokerage was booming. The huge influx of capital into the hedge fund community brought with it a surge in prime brokerage fees, and brokers, facing sharp declines in their traditional brokerage businesses, wanted in. Goldman and Morgan Stanley were the two biggest players in the market, and for many brokers, having a front-end trading system like Redi that could be easily dropped onto clients' desktops was viewed as an essential piece of the prime brokerage puzzle. And, with multi-asset trading having become the newest industry buzzword, these front-ends would allow clients to execute not only equities electronically, but also FX, futures, options and other instruments from a single platform.

The inevitable result was a slew of acquisitions. Citigroup was one of the first to strike, purchasing Lava in 2004, followed by Bank of New York (Sonic) JP Morgan (Neovest) and Lehman Brothers (RealTick) in 2005. Today, virtually every major broker dealer and agency broker has a front-end of one kind or another. Those that don't have established pages on Bloomberg, or white label other firms' solutions.

Collectively, these various broker-provided front-ends/portals came to be known as execution management systems. Beginning with basic single ticket order entry and DMA, EMS's gradually became more sophisticated. Integrated transaction cost analysis (TCA), portfolio-level trading and multi-asset capabilities were some of the technological improvements to broker EMS's, providing traders with more sophisticated real-time control over their orders. New execution strategies were added, such as access to brokers' in house crossing networks, which were created to help recapture at least some of the order flow lost to independent crossing networks like Liquidnet, Pipeline and Posit.

For many firms, broker platforms were an adequate solution. Saddled with OMSs that provided little in the way of trading functionality, EMS's represented a giant leap forward. However, in an evolving and increasingly sophisticated marketplace, the limitations of the broker-EMS model soon became clear. It was the aforementioned surge in the number of hedge funds, coupled with increasingly sophisticated buy-side trading strategies, which brought this issue to light and forced firms to reevaluate their core trade management technology requirements.

The Emergence of True Execution Management Solutions

In the early 2000's, the topic of quantitative trading – developing and running proprietary algorithms for alpha generation – began receiving greater attention than ever before. Soaring trade volumes spoke to a significant increase in high frequency, model driven equity execution strategies, and it was not just institutional stat arb desks and a few established quant shops that were responsible for this flow. The number of firms involved in quant trading was growing rapidly, as were the variety of asset classes these firms were looking to trade. While equities still attracted the greatest attention, firms were increasingly turning to the FX and listed derivative markets as fertile grounds for the development of proprietary execution models.

What these new market entrants realized was that the core technology requirements for setting up advanced trading operations had decreased significantly over the past several years. Deploying and running proprietary high-frequency algorithmic strategies used to require a massive investment in technology infrastructure. In this respect, institutional stat arb desks enjoyed a competitive advantage, as did larger quant shops. Now, however, the rules were changing. Marching in lockstep with Moore's Law, the performance and cost of computing power continued to rise and plummet, respectively. Firms looking to set up their own prop trading operations could do so for a fraction of what it cost just a few years earlier. With capital pouring into the hedge fund sector, firms took advantage of the new economic realities of quant trading and jumped into the market.

Yet while the direct costs of algorithmic trading infrastructure had decreased, the actual process of setting up a high-frequency algorithmic trading solution remained extremely complex. Firms had to piece together their trading solutions using a variety of different components. This meant that firms still had to spend a significant amount of time and resources integrating various proprietary and third-party applications, creating and managing links to external data feeds and execution venues (some of which relied on standardized communication protocols, while others did not), managing network interfaces, and deploying an integrated trade workflow that included various front-end trade and position management applications, servers, gateways, etc. Purchasing, deploying, customizing and maintaining these various applications and trade workflow processes was an extremely complicated undertaking. The market clearly needed a complete, integrated trading solution that could be quickly deployed and easily maintained, allowing firms to focus on the pursuit of alpha as opposed to the piecemeal construction of a proprietary trading environment.

At the same time that new quant funds were grappling with the above challenges, traditional buy-side institutions found themselves facing new technology challenges as well. By the mid 2000's, more and more firms realized that their OMSs could not adequately support their trading needs and had turned to a variety of broker EMS's, taking advantage of what were, by comparison, relatively advanced trade execution and analytics platforms. As noted earlier, some of the newer enhancements to these systems included access to firms' internal crossing networks, more advanced charting and analytics, portfolio level TCA and execution, as well as support for additional asset classes such as FX, future, and options.

In spite of these enhancements, however, the limitations of the broker EMS model soon became apparent. First and foremost, they were all operated by brokers. As such, traders who used Redi could only route orders to Goldman, while those who used Passport were tied to Morgan Stanley. Other dealer strategies, crossing networks or specialized agency broker destinations were essentially off limits. The alternative, of course, was to simply open up another broker's EMS or order entry portal, yet this "swivel chair" approach introduced a host of workflow inefficiencies and only compounded desktop real-estate issues.

Another problem facing users was a lack of flexibility. Beyond basic integration with OMSs, broker EMSs were, and remain, essentially closed systems. Windows could be configured to a certain degree, basic preferences and default order types set, but beyond that, users could do very little in the way of customization. Those who used these systems were more or less at the mercy of their brokers in terms of functional capabilities, product coverage, access to market destinations, market data, speed of execution, etc.

Third, many broker systems simply could not handle the increased order flow and market data that accompanied periods of high volatility. Constrained by legacy architecture, these platforms were not designed to handle the kind of high frequency trading that many of their clients demanded. And because these systems were closed, there was little that client firms could do to improve the situation, other than wait for a promised upgrade that was often months away.

Finally, the promise of single platform multi-asset trading was often left unfulfilled. While many broker EMSs offered some version of multi-asset trading, more often than not, these additional asset classes were supported by technology that had been tacked onto what was primarily an equities trading platform. Clients may have been able to open separate FX trading windows, or trade listed futures and options via an additional portal, but because of these platforms were closed, firms could not engage in more complex cross-asset trading strategies, such as automatically hedging FX exposure, or engaging in arbitrage strategies that involved derivatives and the underlying cash components. Of course, it was not just the technical challenge of offering such a system that prevented brokers from offering true cross asset trading capabilities. Brokers still operated in silos, and support for each asset class came from different divisions, each of which maintained their own technology infrastructure – and managed their own technology budget. As such, it was virtually impossible for brokers to bring the technical and financial resources of these different groups together to support a common initiative.

In short, the very term EMS was something of a misnomer when it came to broker trading systems. Simply put, traders could not really manage their executions if they were using closed, inflexible trading systems. All buy-side firms – hedge funds and institutions alike – needed an integrated toolset with which they could manage increasingly complex order types, trade multiple assets, monitor workflow, connect to any broker, ECN, ATS, crossing network or market destination, and integrate with any part of their existing trade management workflow infrastructure. Nor could broker EMSs fulfill the needs of firms looking to create proprietary algorithmic trading strategies, or run strategies that had been developed on their behalf. These firms needed everything noted above, plus the ability to easily deploy those strategies in a system that combined all of the elements of a high-frequency prop trading solution under one roof: hyper-fast streaming data analysis and trade execution, fully integrated market data feed handlers, complete state management, and pre-certified connections to any and all market destinations.

The market today: meeting the demands of a dynamic trading environment
Today, market participants have the tools with which to meet all of the above challenges. Hedge funds and traditional buy-side firms can now quickly and easily deploy a complete, broker neutral execution management solution that provides the kind of flexibility and ease of integration they demand. But the benefits of such a solution are not limited to the buy-side alone. Like the quant shops and stat arb desks discussed earlier, dealers who want to develop and make available to their clients full-fledged algorithmic trading services no longer have to create a host of proprietary trading systems and workflow applications. Rather, they can deploy a single solution that brings all the required elements of an automated trading system together in one package.

However, the value of such a system extends far beyond its ability to operate in today's market environment. Having the flexibility to tackle future structural and regulatory challenges is just as important, if not more so. With legacy platforms ill equipped to address these challenges, more and more firms are turning to advanced EMSs to address new and emerging business requirements.

One example of this trend is the extent to which firms are employing new tools to help monitor trading costs and comply with new best execution initiatives. However, broker TCA solutions on which these firms rely were previously available only on a stand-alone basis. That is, a firm's traders and PMs would have to login to individual broker websites, or employ tools that are tightly integrated with broker-owned execution management systems. The end result was that firms using a broker-provided EMS who wanted tight TCA/EMS integration were essentially wedded to that broker's particular all-in-one solution. Accessing additional brokers' TCA resources involved opening several different applications simultaneously, leading to inevitable desktop real-estate problems and making the overall trade process less efficient. Separate modules also made identifying and analyzing deviations in broker TCA data a highly manual process.

Today, however, firms have the ability to aggregate all of their TCA resources into a single broker-neutral trade management system. Using direct broker feeds, firms can seamlessly incorporate brokers' TCA resources into their trade workflow, viewing multiple sets of data in a single screen. The types of analyses that traders once had to perform manually can now be automated. For example, firms can customize their pending orders view to include a consolidated pre-trade analysis of which trades will be easy to execute and which will be more difficult, based on the expected trading costs. Traders could set up rules to execute all easy-to-trade orders automatically, and hold for further analysis all others that are expected to be more difficult, or those where the standard deviation between brokers' TCA estimates differ by more than a certain amount. In short, aggregating TCA data into a multi-destination, broker neutral front-end allows firms to seamlessly move from trade analysis to trade execution without have to switch applications. The end result is an enormous increase in trading efficiency.

The benefits of TCA aggregation extend to compliance and trade monitoring initiatives as well. Aggregating TCA resources inside a firm's trade management platform means that the flow of information – from analytics to actual trade execution – is contained in a single system. Firms can easily view the entire trade lifecycle from beginning to end, assuaging regulators and allowing PMs to analyze their traders' decision making processes.

Another major issue that firms are dealing with is the enormous growth in trade volumes, which is only expected to increase. Indeed, for many firms, August of 2007 provided an unpleasant view of the future. During what is traditionally a quiet trading month, volatility surged as the markets responded to an emerging credit crisis. August trade volumes on the New York Stock Exchange were 43% higher than the previous seven month average. At the same time, the average number of shares per trade declined by 23% to just 275, versus 340 from January through July. For most firms, the sheer volume of orders and market data either crippled or significantly slowed their legacy order management and single dealer execution management systems. The underlying technology on which these systems were built simply could not keep up with the message traffic associated with the huge upswing in market activity. And while things gradually returned to normal, many firms were left to contemplate a future in which such volumes were the rule, not the exception.

After the dust settled, many firms began to seriously reevaluate their existing trade management architecture. Simply put, the systems on which they were relying had not been designed to handle high throughput messaging. As such, many firms that previously relied on legacy software installations are now turning to advanced EMSs to address the inevitable increase in trade volumes. Advanced EMSs have the kind of flexible architecture and leading edge technology design to handle whatever the market can throw at them. Given that these platforms were often deployed as the backbone of proprietary in-house algorithmic trading solutions, it came as no surprise that firms using advanced EMSs were able to trade during periods of extremely high volatility with no degradation of service.

A third major challenge facing firms today is how to harness liquidity from numerous FX liquidity providers. Traders today can execute against numerous dealers and on several different ECNs via their respective front ends. To take full advantage of these various liquidity pools, however, firms must be able to bypass dealer and ECN front ends and execute directly against their respective quotes. This model provides numerous advantages in terms of speed of execution and operational efficiencies, and allows firms to act against a single, consolidated "order book" of commingled liquidity. This, in turn, opens the door to the creation of advanced automated trading strategies. For example, firms can run alpha-generating algorithms in a single trading environment, or deploy auto-hedging strategies that monitor and adjust the FX exposure of numerous portfolios simultaneously.

The key challenge to implementing this type of trading solution, however, is aggregation. All dealers' and ECNs' feeds are different. Some rely on FIX, while others rely on proprietary messaging technology. For those that have proprietary feeds, incoming message traffic and outgoing orders must be handled by customized APIs and routing engines, respectively. Certifying, maintaining and aggregating all of these different quote feeds is a major undertaking for individual firms. Of course, aggregation is only part of the battle. Once these feeds have been aggregated, firms must still integrate them with their algorithmic engines, and/or connect to a front end so that traders can see a consolidated view of all liquidity at various price levels. This requires significant customization of an existing front end, or the creation of an entirely new GUI. Neither option is particularly attractive however, given the lack of flexibility inherent in legacy trading architecture and the inefficiencies and costs associated with creating or purchasing an entirely new FX trading interface (which may or may not integrate with a firm's existing trade workflow applications and will certainly inhibit the creation of true cross-asset trading strategies).

Today, however, firms can deploy a complete trading solution that incorporates an FX aggregator as well as a fully customizable GUI, all as part of a single multi-asset execution platform. As such, firms can deploy and run cross-asset algorithmic trading and auto-hedging strategies from within a single trading environment, negating the latency and integration headaches associated with multi-application solutions. Traders can focus on creating proprietary strategies as opposed to managing intractable workflow problems.

A final example of the kind of challenges facing firms today is how to actually deploy those strategies efficiently while minimizing the amount of proprietary integration work involved. Indeed, the extent to which software becomes part of a firm's legacy infrastructure can be traced to how much customized work is involved in getting that system up and running. To the extent that they can, firms always want to minimize custom integration work involved in piecing together numerous, individual components of their trade processes. Nowhere is this issue more prevalent today than in how firms employ event processing engines.

Firms today are facing with a dizzying array of so-called complex event processing engines, or CEPs. Marketed as high frequency, low latency analytical engines that can process data in real-time and form the backbone of firms' trading systems, CEPs have gained attention recently as firms seek to deploy customized algorithmic trading solutions. Through numerous "bake-offs," CEP vendors tout their ability to receive and process an ever increasing number of messages per second.

These solutions, however, are severely limited in their ability to provide firms with a true algorithmic trading engine. Indeed, beyond basic event processing, CEPs offer little else. Simply put, they only provide a single component of a firms' automated trading infrastructure. Everything else must be customized by the client firm. This includes the market data handlers that connect the platform to various feed providers and normalize all incoming data; connections to a front end (since no stand-alone CEP provides a front end); state management; and certified connections to all electronic market centers, ATSs, ECNs, exchanges, crossing networks, and broker destinations. In addition, the language on which these engines are built is proprietary. As a result, client firms must invest time and resources to learn how to write algorithms to their CEP of choice, or how to integrate a standalone CEP into their overall trade workflow.

Take, for example, the problem of state management. For an algorithmic trading engine to operate properly, it must be able to maintain and act on a complete, real-time view of a trade's lifecycle. Is it a single ticket entry? Is it a "child order," a small part of a larger order that might itself be part of a larger basket level strategy? Has the order been accepted? If so, is it subject to cancel/replace? Was there already a partial fill that would affect one's position? All of these issues can affect how an order should be handled. Furthermore, the messaging logic that brokers and other market centers use to convey this execution information is far from consistent. As such, users of basic CEPs have to spend a tremendous amount of time and energy ensuring that their system can handle and normalize these various messaging protocols.

On the other hand, using an advanced, fully integrated EMS solution allows firms to deploy algorithms to a hyper-fast engine that can handle massive amounts of streaming data and comes pre-equipped with integrated solutions to handle not just state/position management, but all of the other requirements listed above. Just as important, firms can use these solutions without having to learn any type of proprietary code, as they are based on industry standard messaging and language protocols. And, given their flexibility and open architecture, these platforms can handle any and all changes to the global capital market landscape, including the development of new products and execution destinations; the incorporation of emerging messaging standards; the aforementioned increased in trade volumes and associated message traffic; and any single- or multi-asset proprietary algorithm that firms can devise.

Ready for the Future?

The history of electronic trading illustrates the limits of early platforms, while the requirements of today and tomorrow speak to firms' growing need to move away from these platforms and adopt significantly more advanced technology solutions. Yet the previous examples only scratch the surface of what traders will need from their systems over the next few years. The markets are constantly evolving, and all participants – hedge funds, institutions, brokers, etc. – will find their business and technology requirements changing just as fast.

It's impossible to predict the future, but it is for that very reason that firms are now abandoning their legacy trading technology. Firms realize that such systems are ill-equipped to handle not only the challenges of today's marketplace, but whatever challenges the future may bring as well. As firms' needs change and traders seek out new opportunities in electronic trading, the ability to scale without additional resources will be a major competitive differentiator. As such, companies must be extremely wary of adopting rigid systems that cannot grow alongside their emerging business requirements. In the end, the extent to which firms' underlying trade architecture allows them to tailor solutions that meet their specific needs will determine how well they adapt to an increasingly complex and dynamic global marketplace.

Branding Sand

by Steve Wunsch, ISE

The reform-induced breakup of the stock market network discussed in the last *Auction Countdown* is undermining more than liquidity and price discovery. It is also dissolving the potential to exploit network effects on which the business models of most exchanges, brokers and dealers depend. As the membership structures that held the network in place disintegrate, continuous markets are losing their capacity to support brandable services related to their operation. While the rapid rise of ECNs and e-brokers appears to herald a durable business opportunity for the winners, in fact these shifting shares are just the beginning of what will become a relentless process of commoditization from which none are safe. Powerful old continuous trading brands – NYSE, Nasdaq, Merrill Lynch, Instinet – may indeed disperse to the winds under the onslaught of their new competitors. But the newcomers will not celebrate long, for they will soon realize that the same regulatory policy that created their apparent opportunity will permanently prevent profits.

Call Markets May Provide Some Relief

Two points need to be remembered from the last *Auction Countdown* (5/1/99) in order to follow the thread into this one. Both contradict conventional wisdom. The first is that it is regulatory reform – not technology – that is driving the whirlwind of changes to our market structure. ECNs, day trading and demutualization are *creatures of* the reforms, not spontaneous responses to new technology. While regulators and their academic supporters like to portray such changes as the result of the inevitable march of technological progress, to which they must respond quickly with academically supportable regulatory adjustments, in fact it is the march of regulation itself to which they are responding. The second point is that, while the reforms are consistent with the antitrust tradition of breaking up network industries, breaking up the stock market network is disrupting its most important functions, such as liquidity and price discovery. Stock markets traditionally organized around membership structures do, indeed, appear to violate antitrust principles. It is, therefore, not surprising that reforms are pressuring them to demutualize. But I see this as evidence that *antitrust* should be re-examined, not stock market structure.

This *Commentary* will focus on how reforms, by breaking up the stock market's network, are also neutralizing the value of its *network effects*, such as those which drive trading to larger exchanges and away from smaller ones as investors seek liquidity. This powerful force for centralization, which also provided the basis for profitable intermediation, is being fragmented by reforms. One consequence for intermediaries is that the loss of the potential to exploit network effects is rapidly undermining the business models of almost all exchanges and broker-dealers. Where they used to generate value and brand recognition by offering unique pockets of liquidity to customers, they are now being forced to share their liquidity with everyone – including their competitors. As a result, ECNs can now launch new businesses without any liquidity of their own by being mere "front ends" to the public liquidity. This situation will not lead to the generally predicted consolidation, but rather to *more* ECNs and *more* exchanges. Few, if any, however, will find this role profitable, a predicament we will trace to the missing network effects.

Call markets, which operate at fixed points in time, rather than continuously, could provide some relief from these problems. That is because continuous markets need membership organizations to create networks and network effects, while call markets do not. While reforms pressure membership organizations to demutualize, call markets – because they do not need those now verboten anti-competitive organizing methods – can restore some lost functionality to the markets by, in effect, reconnecting the network. Along the way, they may also help shore up some important business models. Being different in kind from the commoditizing continuous pool, they naturally distinguish themselves from the pack. Those continuous market vendors who specialize also in call market access may do so as well. Unfortunately, this will take time. Meanwhile, since almost all markets are now continuous, the disintegration of membership organizations will remain a big problem affecting the liquidity and stability of the markets, and the viability of Wall Street's businesses.

Organizing Markets

First let's see how membership structures create network effects, positive feedback, and monopolies. As *Auction Countdown* readers know, I do not use the word "monopoly" pejoratively, as long as such business forms are the natural result of competition, not Government protection. True natural monopolies are essential, in my view, to the proper functioning of stock markets, among other things. And, as we shall see here, they are also needed to support durable differentiation and profitable brands for markets and members. Whether they form without deliberate cartelization and market division, as they do in call markets, or by use of those traditional (and now illegal) organizing techniques, as they do in continuous markets, monopolies are essential to centralization, liquidity, price discovery – and profitable intermediation.

Traditional market organization is virtually synonymous with cartelization: it always involves some form of loyalty oath. A strong form of such an oath might say "We members agree to only trade stocks listed on our exchange and only with its members and to refrain from trading with the members of or dealing in the listed securities of any other exchange, or from engaging in any business whatsoever with those who do." While modern descendents of such rules – of which NYSE Rule 390 is the best known example – are never so strongly worded, every traditional exchange still has at least tacit prohibitions and inducements designed to prevent its members and the exchange itself from supporting competitors. Such practices promote "tipping." Any competition among two or more exchanges for members or listings will quickly tip in favor of the first or biggest. The bigger it gets, the more untenable all alternative exchanges become, as their prospective members and listed companies are effectively ostracized from the relevant community.

Such membership tipping is a positive feedback loop that is normally strongly reinforced by a similar liquidity loop, which drives trading to larger and more liquid exchanges. These two positive feedback loops work powerfully in tandem to winnow the weaker and smaller exchanges until only one is left standing. But exchanges should never assume that establishing a monopoly position means they will keep it forever. In particular, exchanges should not fall into the trap of believing that, having won the day, they can rely henceforward on the liquidity loop alone and abandon those uncomfortably "anti-competitive" features of the politically incorrect loyalty loop. If the lack – or loss through regulatory prohibition – of effective loyalty provisions allows non-members or other exchanges to free-ride off the prices being determined on an exchange, even very large liquidity advantages can turn to sand.

This is roughly the situation faced today by most of the world's largest exchanges, including the NYSE and Nasdaq. Not only have their property rights in trading information been undermined by mandated public tape and quotation systems, but the latest order handling rules mandate direct access to trading opportunities, too. Thus, retail customers of e-brokers and ECNs in Nasdaq stocks have direct terminal access to trading on an equal basis with the professional members of that market. Because the rules require that all ECNs be allowed to free-ride on each other's and the general market's liquidity through Selectnet, the concept of proprietary liquidity on a market whose members are loyal to it is already out the window in the Nasdaq market. Once ECNs become exchanges, as several plan to do, this situation will also apply in NYSE-listed stocks.

Collapsing Categories

While the press often portrays these ECN applications to become "full-fledged" exchanges as if they were moving up to a higher level of regulation, in fact exchange regulation is defining itself down to them. There is no practical difference between ECNs linked through Selectnet for the trading of Nasdaq stocks, and those same entities linked through ITS (Intermarket Trading System) for the trading of Listed stocks. The fact that in order to do the latter they need to register as exchanges under new Rule ATS does nothing to change their basic structure or business model. And Rule ATS will also allow old markets, such as NYSE and Nasdaq, to become demutualized, for-profit "exchanges," effectively to compete as ECNs, too.

In the end, merging definitions under the new regulatory reforms will force competitors to converge on a business structure similar to what ECNs trading Nasdaq stocks look like now, and all competing entities – the NYSE, Nasdaq, all current and new exchanges, ECNs, and brokers – will adopt that form. Whether through merger, alliance, association, multiple registrations, or other means, all continuing competitors will have to be all things to all people. In order to get tape revenues and full access to trading Listed stocks – including an ITS link and a pass on NYSE Rule 390 – all ECNs will become (or associate with) an "exchange." In order to compete at electronic access with ECNs in Nasdaq stocks, all exchanges will demutualize and become or sponsor ECNs. All these ECNs/exchanges (probably under some new name or acronym, since the categories will have formally merged) will free-ride off each others' and the general market's liquidity via Selectnet, ITS or successor systems. And they will all provide customers with direct electronic access to all information and trading facilities.

One doesn't need to follow this line of thinking very far to see that even the most fundamental and familiar distinctions in the market could soon disappear. With the NYSE planning to launch an ECN to trade Nasdaq stocks and Nasdaq planning to register as an exchange to trade Listed stocks, and both of them planning to demutualize their members out of any say in whether their systems become fully electronic, before long there may be no difference between auction markets and dealer markets, NYSE and Nasdaq.

They will, for all intents and purposes, be the same market using the same system to trade the same merged list.

Dancing Definitions

It is a matter of no small irony that the regulatory juggernaut leveling categories and distinctions all around has been fueled for several decades of National Market System reform by an effort to legally define the *difference* between exchanges and brokers. This effort was not necessary in the first place and has utterly failed. Fraught with perilous competitive issues and beset by vested interests on all sides, regulators went through the Institutional Investor Study in the 'Sixties, NMS hearings in the 'Seventies, the Delta case in the 'Eighties, and Market 2000, Order Handling, and ATS in the 'Nineties – only to arrive at ever more incomprehensible "exchange" definitions that moved progressively away from accomplishing their distinguishing task. The first irony is that there is no longer any practical difference between exchanges and brokers, as tacitly recognized by Rule ATS, which gives them a choice of how to register. The double irony is that the obvious answer all along has been that a stock exchange is a membership organization for the trading of stocks – a definition never considered by modern regulators.

The triple irony is that this is not too far from the original definition in the Securities Exchange Act of 1934, whose authors apparently considered what an exchange was to be so obvious that they dispensed with the matter in circular fashion, essentially saying an exchange is an exchange "as that term is commonly understood." While the rest of the '34 Act definition could apply to both exchanges and brokers, does anyone really believe that the Congress of 1934 was unaware of the difference? To imagine that all the subsequent re-defining was necessary, one has to imagine that Congress was both ignorant of the obvious differences between exchanges and brokers *and* willing to let the SEC defy the law by requiring exchange registration of membership exchanges only and never of brokers. Since neither of these assumptions is conceivably justified, much less both of them, one is left to conclude that the entire NMS exercise that has led to the currently collapsing categories was, at best, unnecessary – an argument over how many angels can dance on the head of a pin.

As unnecessary as NMS has been, its result – that exchanges and brokers must compete with each other as if there were no difference between them – is consistent with antitrust principles. Market division is an antitrust evil, along with cartelization, and the first purpose of traditional market organization was to divide the role of the exchange itself from that of its members. This first act of market division then provided the backdrop for the further differentiation of the businesses of the members, a sort of tacit market division enabling each member to develop a unique and, therefore, profitable niche (more on this below). Members were profit-seeking businesses who chose to organize their exchange so it could maintain a favored environment for their pursuit of profit. Exchanges were non-profits because their only purpose was to maintain that profitable environment for their members and never, under any circumstances, to compete with them. How things have changed.

Many observers of the demutualization trend have concluded naively that it is being driven by technology. It is not. While the presumed need to rapidly insert technology into the market provided the nominal justification for NMS – as if modernization would not happen without Government intervention to force it – the real reason that exchanges are demutualizing is that NMS trust-busting has made the exchange role, with all its market division and cartelization, untenable. In other words, it is reforms – not technology – which are forcing exchanges to demutualize. Technology is only delivering the coup de grace.

The regulatory consequences of having never considered the obvious – that exchanges are membership organizations whose first purpose is to divide the roles of markets and members – are many. Having ejected the membership structure from its official definition even as the SEC's entire registration and regulation methods were based on it, the Commission is now facing several dilemmas. How do you accomplish the registration of electronic brokers (ECNs) as exchanges, when their structure as brokers is fundamentally inconsistent with exchange structure? The answer appears to be – a la ATS – that you alter the regulation regime for exchanges to allow non-membership, for-profit brokers to fit into it. If you do that, however, fairness dictates that you let the old membership exchanges out of *their* regulation regimes by letting them become for-profit, non-membership entities, too.

Although such dilemmas will continue to perplex regulators, their practical import for competitors is that reforms will push markets rapidly toward a situation in which stock market intermediation becomes a commodity and essentially disappears. Such "democratization" is understandably popular with the e-crowd, especially day traders. But it is bad news for the exchanges and their members, because it erodes the exclusivity value of membership, with all its cartelization and market division benefits. Although seat prices may stay aloft as long as members expect the cash out value of their seats in an IPO or merger to reflect the strength of their exchanges' powerful brand names and critical mass of trading, conversion to for-profit status will in reality be accompanied by loss of the foundation on which the brands were built and consequent rapid dispersal of their critical mass advantage. With reforms effectively mandating direct public access to all its facilities, for example, it is difficult to imagine what the residual value of "permanent" access for members in the NYSE's reported IPO plan is. Not only will the public have equivalent access without needing to be members, but – without brand-building and brand-protecting loyalty provisions – the world's largest exchange will become just another ECN competing with those created by its erstwhile loyal members.

Worse, the exchange will have to allow its competitors to free-ride – read "feed" – off its critical mass via NMS linkages like ITS. Taken to extremes – where we are clearly headed – all markets and former members will be relegated to roles of being mere windows on the "public" market, front-ends to a system designed and effectively run by the SEC and its academic advisors. With the loyalty loop dead by law and the liquidity loop transformed into a public utility, such once differentiable competitors as NYSE and Nasdaq, Instinet and Merrill Lynch – even newcomers like E-Trade and Archipelago – could all become mere six-of-one-half-a-dozen-of-another access points, differentiable by little more than their screens' color schemes.

Perfect Competition

Some economists have noted that what antitrust theory calls "perfect competition" is, in the end, a profitless condition. That condition is upon the stock market now. As hard as it is to imagine that such a traditionally profitable industry as securities trading could suddenly become profitless, the threat is real. To understand why, we need to look first at how things used to work. Until recently, each member was able to develop a distinct book of customers and a distinct set of procedures backed by a distinct mix of agency order matching and capital commitment, such that the combination for each firm was a distinct liquidity pool, different from its competitors. Salomon's brand of liquidity was different from Goldman's, which was different from Merrill's, Schwab's or Instinet's. And upstairs discussions about order flow – the kind that were banned by the antitrust settlements – enabled the discovery of good prices given those flows, thereby facilitating order matching and capital commitment.

How? In the pre-electronic, pre-anonymous days, the unique personal relationships of each firm's individual traders with customers and other dealers put a high reputational premium on honesty and integrity. Buy-side traders were reluctant to mislead dealers about their orders' true sizes, because a burned dealer would not commit capital for them again. Moreover, because traders do talk among themselves, the dissembling buy-side trader could get such a reputation that no dealers would deal with him. Similarly, sell-side traders were careful to avoid harming a valued customer through whatever upstairs discussions resulted in arranging a large trade. Failure to do so – in the non-anonymous environment – would result in the dealer losing that customer. And, again, because traders do talk among themselves, a front-running dealer would probably lose many more customers than the one whose trust he abused.

Such detailed and unique counter-party auditing in the pre-anonymous days enabled the liquidity and price discovery network to function very effectively. Considerations ranging from the P&L to individual career prospects to a firm's standing in the industry all hinged upon – and enforced – honest communication of accurate information about order flows. Importantly, the depth and strength of this reputation-based information network increased with size. In another example of increasing returns in a positive feedback loop, the larger institutions sought out the largest and most honest dealers, and the larger dealers sought out the largest and most honest institutions so they could service their liquidity needs – and see their flows. For institutions, the bigger they got, the more their size could command the best liquidity servicing by the largest dealers. For dealers, the bigger they got from servicing the larger institutions, the easier it was to credibly sell their liquidity services to them – and, therefore, the bigger they got.

This positive feedback loop enhancing size and concentration is important, because the larger the institution, the larger the orders, and the larger the orders, the more price discovery import they would have. Thus, "size talking to size" led to an information pyramid or hierarchy in which the largest and most important flows were handled by the largest dealers, who would work as needed with peers or down the chain to smaller dealers to complete a trade. With so much capital and reputation on the line, these ad hoc syndicates had to discover accurate prices – and they had the order flow information to do so.

In yet another positive feedback loop, the more size-talking-to-size enabled accurate prices and liquidity based on them, the more viable the businesses of ever larger institutions became, which, in turn, enabled the further aggregation of meaningful order flow and better price discovery. The one word that best captures this size aggregation process is "institutionalization." But, while many have debated the pros and cons of aggregating individual interests in the hands of large institutions, the debate has turned almost entirely on the populist question of whether bigness is bad per se. Neither side in the debate – from the time the SEC's Institutional Investor Study kicked it off – seems to have noted the potentially critical connection between institutionalization and price discovery, much less the fact that, if such a connection exists, de-institutionalizing the market could be highly destabilizing.

In any case, regulatory reform has suddenly turned the institutionalization process upside down. By banning as anti-competitive such personal relationship-based practices as holding non-disclosed orders in the crowd at the specialist's post and engaging in upstairs dealer discussions about customer orders, reforms have destroyed the reputational infrastructure which constituted the price discovery network. And by fostering electronic trading as a replacement, reforms have inadvertently encouraged participants to drop their old honest ways and anonymously engage in a variety of at least misleading and sometimes manipulative order placement practices. As a result, price discovery has turned into a crap shoot, making dealing in size at any one of those fleeting prices too dangerous for both institutions and dealers, and forcing even the largest of them to contemplate emulating the day traders they complain about, even though their average trade size is less than 1/1000th the size of the average institutional order.

The academic pipe dream underlying NMS is that connecting all traders to an electronic system in which everyone has exactly the same information is itself a full liquidity and price discovery network. The problem is that neither viewing the continuous tape of small trades nor the quotes of traders' willingness to trade in such small sizes conveys any of the meaningful information that characterized the old network. Moreover, expecting thousands of day trading truck drivers, hair dressers and dentists to make up for the liquidity lost when NMS prevents professionals from doing their job is an academic conceit of gargantuan proportions. The playing field may be level now, but the old players are gone and the new ones can't do the job.

While it is not inconceivable for the old network to form again in spite of the presence of the black box, that is unlikely. The volatility engendered by the black box renders disclosure of real information about size far more dangerous than before. Moreover, with the regulatory environment so strongly biased against private information, all the legal departments of the large firms are simply advising their traders to stop complaining, stop talking – and just use the black box. The reality is that the old methods were a complex and detailed ecosystem. Expecting it to regrow after NMS's black box mandates would be like expecting the arctic tundra to redevelop if all of it were covered by a massive oil spill.

The transformation of the market from one in which a relative handful of dealers at the top of an information hierarchy did the heavy lifting in price discovery and liquidity provision to one in which that role has been dispersed among thousands of individual on-line traders is perhaps the world's best example to date of what antitrust critics call "atomization." Competition is now so "perfect" that there is no longer any chance of collusion – tacit or otherwise. There is also no differentiation and no pricing power. Reforms have turned the only naturally differentiable aspect of the Wall Street value proposition – the organization and packaging of liquidity – into the equivalent of a public utility run by regulators. Instead of providing liquidity itself – a differentiable and brandable activity – competitors today can only provide access to the common liquidity pool. Both access and the common pool are inherently undifferentiable commodities.

In an increasingly desperate bid to retain some relevance in this Brave New World, virtually all brokers now offer or plan to offer the on-line service that is turning customers into competitors. While this would seem to validate the position of the e-brokers riding the new paradigm, there will be few opportunities to durably differentiate them either and, thus, precious little pricing power for anyone. Going forward, the e-competitors will not only include all new and old brokers, but ECNs and exchanges, too, all vying to provide their brand of access to the same public liquidity.

The old broker brands naturally differentiated themselves by virtue of their trading reputations, which were almost impossible to precisely copy once a firm began riding the increasing returns to size in its personalized niche. Moreover, those trading reputation-based brands did not need much in the way of expensive advertising, because word of mouth was so efficient at reaching the key decision-makers at the firms you wanted to do business with. Most important, your brand was not just an image trumped up in an ad, it was a unique reality that, in the truest sense of the term, advertised itself.

In contrast, few if any of the new elements of broker brands offer either increasing returns to size or unique niche-building potential of any kind. Moreover, because the audience has changed from a few key decision-makers easily reachable by word of mouth – and each one personally loyal to the person who services him – to millions of individuals your traders will never know, any successful brand can and will be copied. The best broker that is also a financial portal? Copyable. The best discount broker, period? Copyable. The best broker that projects an image of fast day trading? Or the best that encourages a responsible approach? Both easily copyable. Research? Entertainment? Real time account updates? Level II? Psychological counseling for compulsive traders? While all of these seem potentially brandable, efforts to build brands around them will be characterized by old-fashioned diminishing returns, not the increasing returns that naturally protect brands. So every success can and will be copied and commoditized. The situation will require ever escalating advertising costs to keep the brand fresh, ever-escalating development costs to keep the product up-to-date, and continuous price discounting to stay in the game.

Heads in the Sand

That almost all competitors in the stock market business are likely to face grave difficulties soon is not generally recognized. This lack of recognition stems largely from the view also held by regulators and academics that change is just the result of the inevitable march of technology, rather than radical regulatory reform. This view allows its holders to assume that, after a few difficult years of transition, new structures and competitors will establish themselves – better and stronger than the old ones – and we will all happily say good riddance to those antiquated, anti-competitive membership exchanges. Typically, those who hold this view seem to focus only on the liquidity-begets-liquidity phenomenon, apparently having forgotten the traditionally tight relationship between success generated by an exchange's liquidity and that generated by its loyalty oath features. The oversight has led to confident predictions from leading figures at exchanges and ECNs – as well as from prominent regulators and academics – that will almost certainly prove wrong.

Their predictions appear to be based on the presumption that, once the anti-competitive loyalty oaths are dissolved, the network effects will again reassert themselves, allowing positive feedback in the liquidity loop to re-centralize trading and bestow incumbent monopoly status on a new winner. Thus, the heads of several ECNs predict that all the new ECNs and exchanges will consolidate soon into only one or two trading venues (presumably including the speaker's own). What they are missing is that, without loyalty provisions, any liquidity advantage (in a continuous market, anyway) can and will be dissipated by free-riding. In that the reforms as much as mandate free-riding forever, none of the brokers, ECNs or exchanges that expect to gain, ride or keep a liquidity advantage will be able to do so.

A scenario more consistent with current regulatory reality would see continued fragmentation, indeed, accelerating proliferation of trading systems, as more and more firms realize that the reforms encourage free-riding on the liquidity and prices of the incumbents who are now powerless to prevent it through loyalty oaths. Going forward, the National Market System reforms will play out in either weak form or strong form. Weak form NMS is essentially what we have now: linked trading venues in which the linkage is imperfect enough that different liquidity pools can maintain some semblance of uniqueness and independent liquidity, but not so imperfect as to enable one or two of them to dominate. Strong form NMS is a "hard" CLOB (consolidated limit order book), to which every system is connected so perfectly by CLOB-wide price and time order handling priorities that it makes no difference whatsoever what system you come in through: the liquidity is identical.

If liquidity anywhere becomes liquidity everywhere in the National Market System, then it no longer matters whether you are big or small; you can get into the game even if you have no liquidity to offer, and you can't be knocked out by competitors who have more. This environment will breed more, not fewer, "exchanges," and more, not fewer, ECNs. Although the names of the categories could certainly change again, the number of entities providing official access will probably continue to include not only all of the current entrants, but perhaps many others in related businesses, too.

The H&R Block purchase of Olde and the CNBC purchase of a piece of Archipelago made clear that the definition of "related businesses" is becoming increasingly attenuated. In addition to all the brokers, ECNs and exchanges, who will be better able to compete in their category if they also own, associate with or register as the other category, some in even less related businesses will be sucked in by that calculus. More TV stations and tax preparers may enter the "exchange" game. Eventually, newspapers and magazines, entertainment companies and Internet portals, e-commerce behemoths like Microsoft, Amazon and eBay – perhaps even the Wall Street Deli – will discover they can better attract customers to their main product by also being an exchange, an official window on the National Market System. When Microsoft gives away free browsers or ISP access to turn you into a more loyal Windows customer, such actions put pressure on the prices Netscape or AOL can charge. Similarly, if you are in the business of trying to sell stock market access against many competitors selling exactly the same thing – some of whom view your core business as a loss leader – you are not likely to have much pricing power.

One implication of all this is that the announcement-a-day consolidation craze is chasing the wrong rabbit. Big old firms, and giant new e-brokers, are all frantically trying to buy into the right system or coalition, so as to be part of the new central market when it finally forms. Many of them are buying into multiple ECNs and multiple coalitions, just to make sure they have the winning ticket in their pocket. Since, by regulatory design, none of them will be able to consolidate liquidity, none of these coalitions or systems – nor all of them together – will "win." The fancy prices being paid for these portfolios of lottery tickets could perhaps be reduced, therefore, by starting negotiations with the Wall Street Deli. Mandatory public access means that almost any old firm will do the trick to be part of the new NMS. In fact, by the time all the categories finish crumbling, many of the firms ponying up for multiple tickets now may find they had a perfectly serviceable one in their pocket all along.

Holding the Line

Since fixed time call markets are in many ways the opposite of continuous markets, it may not be surprising that call market providers are not generally subject to the problems now facing purveyors of continuous trading. There are two basic reasons for this. First, calls do not need membership organizations or loyalty oaths to prevent free-riding and are not, therefore, targets of the current antitrust-based reforms. Second, because calls centralize trading in the temporal dimension, their liquidity pools are naturally distinct from any others, whether they be other calls or continuous trading venues. This means that – while calls cannot free-ride their way into existence the way ECNs can – once established, others cannot free-ride on them either. Both the uniqueness and the independence of call markets enable their providers to naturally differentiate what they do from the crowd providing access to the homogenized continuous pool.

Continuous trading naturally encourages free-riding, because it is basically a free-riding process itself. Without temporal aggregation of interest, every trade keys off old trades – the last print, the close, the VWAP etc. Since theoretical equilibrium is an unknown, both parties essentially accept – i.e., free-ride on – the reference price, give or take a spread and/or a commission. This natural free-riding on continuous prices forms the basis for such practices as payment for order flow or other forms of dealer guaranteed liquidity, block trades, crossing networks and principal program trades. It also is the basis for all the linked markets in the NMS, particularly the Selectnet and ITS systems.

This natural tendency toward free-riding in continuous trading was countered by membership exchanges in two ways. The first line of defense was their loyalty oath features, which originally simply prohibited non-members or other exchanges from seeing their prices. Reinforcing the loyalty oath was the fact that, by promoting the development of a strong reputation-based order flow information network, membership exchanges made customers want to come to them rather than help competitors free-ride off them. With *size talking to size*, the network was able to discern meaningful order flow well enough to discover good prices, which emboldened members to provide sizable liquidity at those prices. While membership exchanges, loyalty oaths and upstairs information networks worked very well at providing good price discovery, good liquidity and protection against free-riding, reforms are extinguishing all of them. In the absence of the membership organization, I know of no other way to prevent free-riding in continuous markets.

Even a CLOB could not do it, because, as mentioned, continuous trading is itself a free-riding process. Forcing all trading through one continuous CLOB would only accelerate the process of spreading trading out temporally, thereby putting an even greater premium on getting the prices that everyone else is getting – say VWAP. By increasing the number of trades and decreasing their relative size, a CLOB would push you to shrink and spread out your own trades so that they do not stand out against all the others. And, because you are shrinking your size to free-ride off them, others will shrink theirs to free-ride off you.

Call markets do not have the free-riding problem. Because they centralize all trading interest into a point in time, they discover true equilibrium very directly and accurately. Moreover, anyone who wants in on that price can do so *only* by participating in the call. There is no incentive to free-ride, and those who try will risk missing the consensus price they could have easily had. For example, since no one knows precisely what the price is going to be until the call ends at its appointed time, attempts to free-ride on it prior to its conclusion would risk missing the real price. Similarly, attempts to free-ride off its price by waiting until it is over would risk not finding counter-parties willing to trade at it anymore.

The fact that a call naturally defines its own liquidity opportunity, and, thus, naturally defends itself against free-riding, is not just the source of its price discovery power. It is also a natural protection against commoditization. Two calls at the same time cannot exist for long as businesses. Just as membership exchange competition would tip in favor of one exchange – the one with the most members and liquidity – the competition between two or more markets running competing calls at the same time would quickly tip in favor of the biggest. The winning call would not only be able to easily differentiate *itself* in the crowd. At least some of those continuous markets and brokers described earlier, who are now so hard pressed to differentiate themselves, could, by offering that call periodically to customers, stand out, too.

The Big Mo

Some might argue that the theories and terms bandied about here – path dependence, positive feedback, increasing returns, tipping, lock-in – are awfully esoteric to use to criticize such settled doctrines as antitrust, the National Market System, electronic trading and transparency. And how could the loss of network effects they never heard of so severely threaten the livelihoods of experienced stock market hands? Wouldn't the academics and regulators have warned them if such a threat existed?

The answer is that it is the academics and regulators – in a sort of mutual admiration society – who have spun theories that don't hold water. Settled doctrine or not, it makes no sense to turn the stock market into a testing laboratory for anyone's theories. But the fact is that, after all the tinkering, the academics and regulators have become the chief designers of the stock market today. This fact alone should make us question their theories. But, blind to their errors – and perhaps enjoying the power and recognition – academics and regulators keep egging each other on to the next level of intervention and experimentation, as if each policy disaster (fragmentation, day trading, demutualization) justifies more meddling to fix it. The latest example is the increasingly shrill cries for a CLOB as the only way to fix the fragmentation that somehow sprang up in the wake of the order handling rules. Long since banished from the debate is whether their theories made any sense in the first place. This, of course, precludes consideration of whether the actions they have already taken based on those theories may be the cause of the problems they are now trying to fix.

The public is not so gullible. They understand network effects and related concepts instinctively – although perhaps in less esoteric terms – because they are based on plain old common sense. Voters in the real democracy, for example, would not fall for any phony "democratization" schemes claiming to use "modern telecommunications technology" to put them "on an equal footing" with the "bosses in the smoke-filled rooms." Voters understand why we prohibit reporting election results prior to the time polls have closed. They recognize that West Coast voters are disadvantaged if East Coast returns – or even news stations' reports of their exit polls – are made available before they finish voting. They can see that early reports of winners would build their credibility and discourage opposing voters (displaying increasing returns). They see that early success is dependent on who votes first (displaying path dependence), and that continuous transparency would build momentum (positive feedback), perhaps delivering (tipping) elections to early favorites, even if a simultaneous or non-transparent vote would produce a different consensus and winner.

Transparency? How absurd. That would require a running tally so that each voter could see the "tape" of how voting was going prior to casting his ballot. Many voters are even aware of problems in primary voting due precisely to what amounts to continuous transparency. With each state voting separately in a set sequence – so there is plenty of time to transparently report the results prior to the next primary – there is considerable path dependence, increasing returns, positive feedback and tipping. Former President George Bush called it "The Big Mo" (for "momentum"), by which early success in Iowa or New Hampshire becomes a self-fulfilling prophecy (exhibits positive feedback) convincing later primary voters to consider a candidate viable and, therefore, worthy of their consideration. His son, it is said, became the early frontrunner for the Republican 2000 nomination by topping early polls when many of those polled accidentally confused him with his father. Riding increasing returns since then – and long after those careless (devious?) pollsters had corrected their error – Governor Bush appears to have sewn up (locked in) the nomination.

The primary process itself is one of the world's best examples of lock-in. No candidate or party can risk challenging it or the sequence of primaries for fear of alienating the very states most needed to gain that initial spark. But these are not esoteric or difficult concepts. Ordinary Americans can easily understand how this locked in process of continuously visible voting can lead to distortions relative to the true will of the electorate. How else to explain the disproportionate number of presidential candidates who express support for ethanol subsidies (to get through Iowa) and sign a pledge to not raise taxes (to get through New Hampshire)? Regardless of the merits of these policies, the fact that these states come first gives their voters disproportionate influence on candidates' views. These states also seem to have more than their share of voter manipulation incidents, such as the use of "push polling," in which candidates ask leading questions in "polls" of far more voters than necessary to sample their views, with the intent of smearing their opponents. And early primary states are also home to various questionable tactics to create the appearance of more support than candidates actually have, such as paying "supporters" to attend rallies or busing them in from nearby states.

The point here is that the theoretical factors that might improve or harm electoral process are not so esoteric that voters cannot understand them. Investors, too, can understand such matters as the potential importance of privacy in the interactions between large institutions and dealers. Investors, too, can understand that there might be some natural order or value in a system of membership exchanges where the individual does not trade "on a level playing field" with Salomon Brothers. And investors would certainly understand that, just as Hertz probably gets cars at better prices than individual buyers do, mutual funds might get quantity discounts, too.

Network effect theory is not rocket science. It is common sense. A brief look at either would convince any reasonable person that the settled NMS doctrine of continuous electronic transparency is bound to produce non-consensus prices, distorted valuations, volatility and manipulation in markets. Not that there is anything wrong with any piece of that doctrine taken separately. Continuous trading, electronic trading, and transparent trading all have very powerful and valuable uses. Electronic and transparent even combine very nicely in call markets. Putting all three together, however, is a formula for the disaster that is unfolding now as a disintegrating stock market structure.

But rare is the academic or regulator who does not feel that intervention to improve "fairness" is always good. And what could be more popular, populist and "fair" than combining those three key playing field levelers to benefit the small investor? The resulting screams of intermediaries only seemed to confirm that these populist academics and regulators were, indeed, doing good. And there is no question that the SEC's populist attack on the status quo struck a chord with many – Utopian schemes always do. But it is also clear that even average investors can see that their ultimate interest does not lie in egalitarian redistributions of the assets of intermediaries, but in a stock market that works properly. The populism behind regulators' and academics' radical reforms not only enables them to ignore all these obvious points, but also to avoid acknowledging any potentially valid theories that might call into question the wisdom of their massive interventions. This populist ethos, for example, appears to make regulators and academics studiously unaware that it is the reforms that are the principal cause of the day trading phenomenon.

An article in a recent Barron's defended day trading as nothing more than the modern electronic version of what professional traders have always done. That's true, to a degree, but beside the point. You can't do what professionals did electronically, at least not the size talking to size part. In effect, the SEC gave day traders a license to steal from Nasdaq's dealers by free-riding off their prices. Happy to play Robin Hood helping the SOES bandits break through Nasdaq's loyalty oath, the SEC launched the day trading profession, never giving a thought to the possibility that enabling truck drivers to play Wall Street professionals might have consequences beyond simply giving both the opportunity to change careers. The irony is that now regulators are treating day trading like some plague of locusts that blew in by chance on their watch. These are not investors, or even speculators – they are gamblers, say regulators in their highest moral dudgeon. They need counseling, and the firms that house them are violating suitability, capital adequacy and margin lending laws. There is no admission that day trading is a phenomenon 100% created by the SEC's desire to "level the playing field." The real tragedy of this Frankenstein from the NMS Labs is not that it exists, but that the rest of the market's most important functions and businesses had to be sacrificed to give it life. Like price discovery.

If It Ain't Broke, Don't Fix It

To promote the democratization that is giving day traders their opening, all the underpinnings of good price discovery in continuous markets are being pushed aside. Membership organizations are demutualizing, dealers no longer talk to each other about order flow, and trade size is breaking down into a thin stream of meaningless prices all free-riding off each other, none of which can be trusted to support a sizable trade. No wonder tech and Internet stocks are so high that Microsoft president Steve Ballmer calls the whole industry overpriced. No wonder some subsidiaries of listed stocks are trading for free or less, according to a recent Wall Street Journal article. And no wonder it's so easy to promote "pump and dump" schemes on the Internet that regulatory roundups are reported seemingly every other day, reflecting a virtual explosion of fraud. The core problem giving simultaneous rise to "irrational exuberance," "irrational indifference," and a rich playground for crooks is the loss of reliable price discovery. Yet so sure are regulators and their academic supporters that their egalitarian theories are correct that they have, again, never considered the possibility that the policies based on them are causing the problems they are now trying to solve with more of the same.

Democracies, it is said, are stable because their governments reflect the consensus of the governed – no need for revolution. But it should be clear by now that electoral process can promote or inhibit the formation of that consensus. Amending the original thought to reflect this, one would say: Democracies are stable in the degree to which their governments reflect the consensus of the governed. Similarly, stock markets are stable in the degree to which their prices reflect the consensus of investors. At accurately determined prices, great volumes of transactions can be confidently done, allowing assets to change hands and capital to flow to productive enterprise. But stock markets, like elections, are dependent on the effectiveness of the process used to discover consensus. If prices are very inaccurate, crashes can happen – just as revolutions to change non-consensus governments can happen. If the price discovery process is built on a poor theoretical foundation, the market is unstable. Worse, if very large markets had developed naturally on top of a relatively correct theoretical foundation – but suddenly had that foundation pulled out from under them – the result could be disastrous instability.

In that several decades of flawed theory are now pulling the rug out from under continuous markets, it is time to consider how fixed time call markets can solve the problems investors and intermediaries face. Call markets produce a consensus price; so they have a stabilizing effect on the market. They can stop a crash in its tracks, being natural circuit breakers that don't even need to shut the market down in order to work their wonders. They can alleviate the danger that mutual fund liquidations will cause the market to "melt down" or "seize up" with illiquidity. They can also do more mundane tasks, like opening or closing markets without the accustomed volatility, manipulation and sense of unfairness. They can allow stocks to be added to or deleted from the S&P500 without disruption. Because call markets allow many people to trade at once – and at one price – they have deep liquidity at very low cost for institutions and a feeling of true "empowerment" for individuals. Neither the largest institutional orders nor the wildest packs of day traders whipping up momentum can upset them.

In terms of how calls may provide business opportunities for intermediaries, because calls' liquidity pools are naturally distinct, intermediaries associated with their introduction and operation will differentiate themselves from the competition. And, because call markets cannot be free-ridden on, they need no loyalty oaths, market division or other anti-competitive agreements to become effective. This means that calls will not present the antitrust targets that continuous markets did. Even antitrust hawks acknowledge that it is not illegal to be a monopoly; it is only illegal to engage in anti-competitive practices to become, defend or extend one. Because call markets can rely on liquidity alone to create, defend and extend their position, they will have no need to engage in questionable practices. Those intermediaries who build the call market will, therefore, build an asset for themselves that is durable even in today's commoditizing technological and treacherous regulatory environment. Most important, call markets will spring up naturally to solve the market's price discovery and other problems. There is no need for studies, regulation, legislation or other interventions to implement them.

(Originally Issued October 1, 1999)

Hitting the Button: The Birthday of Automated Trading

By Richard A. Holway, CEO, Capital Enterprises International

"I swear to God I'm going to kill somebody at NY Bell Hell," Al Haley screamed. He banged his phone's handset on the desk and dragged a forearm across his long forehead. He leaned back in the captain's chair and stared up at the chintzy stained ceiling tiles. "#$%*."

"What's the problem now?" Head Trader Tom Light asked coolly, looking up over the half glasses he wore on the tip of his nose whenever he reviewed the P & S runs. Tom never lost his composure no matter how bad things got on the trading desk. It was a trait Al admired as he himself tended to be high-strung and overly emotional.

After months of development and untold late and frustrating nights testing with SIAC, the first list based trading system to go electronically port-to-port to the central message switch at the NYSE had been launched successfully and now had been in production at Bankers for months...Sort of.

It wasn't perfect by a long shot and Al was always uneasy about that. This list processing business could be dangerous. And Al was the frontline guy for it on the desk. No one else wanted anything to do with it.

Senior Trader Big Jim Beamer had to weigh in. He stood up and jimmied his pants up his Buddha belly as he spoke. "I always said.... mixing trading with frickin' computers is a BAD idea. Bad. Bad. BAD! ...BIG frickin' mistake. Just look at what happened over at Witter."

In fact, when Bankers Reliance went live Al knew that Dean Witter was the closest competitor on their tail. Recently he'd heard about a young trader over there that had to hit their button for the 1st time, the same situation Al had been in the first time they'd tried it at BR.

Witter was doing their first live electronic list and this poor bastard trader was apparently so nervous that he hit the button...and then hit the button again just to be sure. He launched two full index programs back to back. It cost Dean Witter millions. They fired him on the spot and shut the project down.

"I told you the freakin' thing would be nothing but a royal pain in the ass." Chris Wilson, the slight, wisecracking Senior Trader, shouted from the other side of the turret. "What do you expect?" he added, sawing an index finger across his mustache. "Those geeks couldn't even speak the language."

Which was true. The developers were from Taiwan and communicating with them was a chore...actually communication was accomplished with only the older one. The younger one hardly ever spoke and almost no English at all.

Al had spent months trying to translate what they wanted into terms these guys could understand. It was often a combination of hand waving, picture drawing and what must have sounded like pig Latin. But they were talented programmers and understood these new computers.

What they custom coded ended up being an early execution management system with a pretty slick front-end for list processing. It gave BR a huge advantage in '86 and '87 and helped them make gobs of money doing index arbitrage.

"Yeah and Hey" Chris jumped up next to Jimmy waving his hands, his diatribe punctuated by his infectious laugh. "Al, AL, remember the first time you asked the geeks what they liked for lunch and the guy says: ANYTHING and when you came back and gave them tuna fish sandwiches, they threw them right in the trash. And you ask him why and he goes 'no like tuna'... 'member that, Al?" Chris finished with such a rolling laugh of glee that even Tommy let go his back laugh snicker.

"Yeah. I remember." Al answered automatically but despite smiling, he was distracted by his current problem. "They've got me on perma-hold again." Al moaned cradling the phone on his shoulder as he banged on the enter key of the receiving PC. "Still nothing. Crap!"

"Did you escalate?" Tom asked.

"Yeah. Four times." Al replied, "And now I'm talking to some guy under a manhole cover on Water Street...."

"Get AH-TA here." Tom snorted in his Long Island drawl. "Are you kidding me?"

"Ohhhh...now that's good, huh?" Chris said, contorting his face into a sardonic grin. "Tell him to twist the red wire from midtown with the red one to the exchange." Chris chortled. Jimbo guffawed.

"No. I'm not kidding...I just talked to this guy. He told me he's under the street fixing the wires. This is just unbelievable...I've got a live list somewhere in space and I'm talking to a guy in the freaking' sewer." Chris was still laughing at his own joke.

"Hello? Yeah. OK. Thanks." Al slammed the phone down, jumped up and ran around to the back of the special horseshoe-shaped desk he specially built for "The Machine" and reset the incoming mux. The printer on the reporting PC jumped to life and started banging out reports as Al announced the obvious. "We're back up."

"Yeah? For how long you figure this time?" Chris asked.

All the Bankers Reliance brass, and these were the Big Boys, had trooped over to the ratty 5th Ave location from the fancy HQ on Park to witness the first live list trade. Al was in the hot seat. He was the one who had to hit the button.

He was a Junior Trader and was as nervous as a cat in a room full of rockers. What young Al was afraid of was a trading train wreck. A screw up so bad that he would lose his job. A job he really liked.

Al had always loved Wall Street. He'd read every book he could find on the subject and fancied himself a kind of historian of the business. Al was working at a little boiler room placement firm on Broadway just south of Wall and the prick of an owner was stiffing him out of his money. That's when Al decided it was time to go to "The Street."

He was placing people at E.F. Hutton, Salomon Bros., and J.P. Morgan and saw what they did and made and he had buddies in the business, too, who were coaxing him to get involved. Al decided that Sales/Trading was the way to go.

He found out that Bankers Reliance was in the process of starting a brokerage operation from Little Norm Lisle, BR's new floor clerk. Little Norm wasn't little at all but he wasn't as big as his old man.

Big Norm was known as "The Moose" on the floor. He was a veteran $2 dollar broker who stood as big as a mountain in the crowd. He was 6' 8", 280 pounds of hard drinking fun. They got Al onto the floor and let him hang around Moose's booth in the garage while he tried to get in.

Each had given Al their version of trading 101. He got some schooling from the specialists, too. Moose snuck him inside the "blue line" when it was slow. He was awed the first time one brought down and showed him "the book". He had read about all this, dreamed about it and here he was, right in the middle of it.

He learned the difference between a bid and an offer and how things basically worked on the floor of the Big Board. He started practicing giving and taking quotes, mumbling to himself: 40 a quarter; 3/8ths, 10 by 20. 2 an 1/8th a quarter, 100 up, so much that his new wife asked him to knock it off around her.

Little Norm made Al promise that he didn't hear it from him before he passed the number for Head Trader Tom Light on. And for good reason: Al called Tom every day – sometimes twice a day – all through the summer of '85, begging for a chance to get upstairs on the desk.

Finally, Tom agreed to meet for a quick beer after the close but he made Al swear he'd never call him again thereafter. Al knew this was his shot and a long shot at that.

They were to meet at a classic Irish pub off Fifth. 4:30 – Sharp. Al got there early.
It was a narrow room with high ceilings, a classic bar and rail. It was not very crowded. Al grabbed a stool near the door and started practicing his quoting on a napkin, mumbling to himself as he kept an eye on the door.

Al knew what Tom looked like from Little Norm's description and he assessed each new person passing through the door. The appointed time passed and then some. Al threw the scribbled napkins away and started wondering if he'd been blown off.

And then he got the recognition jolt, a meticulously dressed guy in a gray pinstriped suit, red tie and highly polished wingtips, of average height with sharp features and a shock of thick jet-black hair combed straight back strolled in. He looked like Mr. Wall Street himself. Al waved and Tom nodded and walked over.

He appeared deadly serious. Tom declined to sit down so Al got up off the stool and they exchanged the preliminary niceties and ordered. As soon as the longneck Bud Tom had ordered hit the bar, he looked Al right in the eye and got to the point: "You're not going to call me anymore after this, right?"

Al agreed. "OK. What the hell can you do that makes you think you can trade?"

Tom took a sip of beer without looking away. Al was prepared. He grabbed a fresh bar napkin and grabbed the pen from his pocket. He proudly started to show Tom that he knew how to record a 4-way quote. Tom cut him off. "A monkey can do that. What can you do that makes you think you can trade?"

Al's ace in the hole fluttered to the floor. He went to his back up plan which he considered pretty flimsy but his dreams were evaporating and in desperation he blurted: "I'm a carpenter and can do math in my head real fast in 1/8th's and ¼'s." which was true.

"What's 20 and 7/8th's plus a quarter?" Tom asked immediately.

"21 and an1/8th." Al responded.

"33 5/8th's less 7/8th's?"

"32 and ¾'s."

Tom pulled his wallet out and threw a bill on the bar, took a short swig and set his still near full bottle down on the $10 spot and smiled for the first time. "Best answer I've ever heard. You start next Monday. Be there at 7:00 -- Sharp.
I gotta catch a train." Tom headed for the door. Al mumbled "Bye. Thanks...", gave a little wave, but was in shock and wondering if this wasn't some sort of a joke. Wall St. lore is full of such pranks.

"You get one shot at passing the 7." Tom shouted back over his shoulder pointing at Al as he bolted out the door. The Series 7, yes, of course. It sunk in: He was in.

Tom had given Al a chance in a million. Mostly luck. Al got the seat of "Wing Nut" who had just been fired for being an error magnet. Tom gave Al a 3" binder full of his predecessor's error reports on the 1st day and said read these and learn what not to do in this job.

Al passed his exams, he had been on the desk for months now and was a bonafide institutional Sales/Trader. A dream comes true.

When the portfolio guys asked for someone on the desk that understood computers, all the senior guys pointed at Al. So being involved in this new computerized trading thing was not really voluntary.

"The List Machine" was actually two 286 IBM PCs linked together with the original Novell network and an impressive array of muxes and modems and switches all blinking lights and stacked up on shelves above the twin monitors. The traders called it the Starship Enterprise. And they called tall gangly Al with his erratic auburn hair: the mad scientist.

The Enterprise had its own special horseshoe desk set off to the side with a captain's chair tucked in between the wings facing dual screens and keyboards. Only the tangled morass of cables and wires leading out the back and snaking under duct tape across the worn carpet to the communications closet belied its impressive futuristic look.

Al had literally put the machine together piece by piece. He had spent so much time testing and configuring it that he knew it inside and out. He knew how to reset every piece of communications equipment, resynchronize the reporting, download the execution file from the VAX via KERMIT and hand parse it in Lotus and upload it into the Enterprise, transmit the execution reports over to ADP for booking, everything. He had hit the button that made it all go hundreds of times… in simulation. But never live…until today.

The idea for the system was the brainchild of a couple of young portfolio managers on the passive side of Bankers: Paul Brooks and Lloyd Beckman. Bankers ran the world's largest pool of indexed money mostly on the S&P 500.

Al was putting in 14-hour days getting this thing put together. He and Lloyd had had a lot of dinners across the street at the only restaurant open that late: an authentic Sushi joint. Al was surprised that he actually liked sushi. The Tsingtaos and Sakes he and Lloyd shared over dinner probably helped.

And he was thankful because Lloyd and Paul taught him about how the arb worked theoretically from the portfolio side. But today, Al wasn't too thankful at all. He was worried. This wasn't theory anymore.

When he hit that button, hundreds upon hundreds of live orders would be released in to a live market for execution in an instant. There was no turning back, no way to explain a mistake, no margin for error. This was his reality.

Access to DOT, the nickname for the Designated Order Turn-around system on the NYSE, which was a semi-automated order delivery system to the post, was rudimentary for single order entry. The best systems at the time were no more than dumb terminal emulators.

To enter an order electronically, a trader had to enter a very specific format required by the NYSE central message switch, by hand, typically on a drab black and green display. Someone had to manually type in gibberish that looked something like this: C_TS; Buy; 5,000; IBM; MKT; DAY and then hit the button & off it went.

Orders entered this way printed out behind the counter at the post. The specialist clerk sitting behind the counter ripped them off the printer or pulled the card and shouted them out to the specialist who was usually out in front of the post, who shouted back the fill price.

The clerk would then manually enter the execution details into the system and the execution report would be electronically transmitted back to the sender. In addition, an exchange reporter standing by the post would manually stroke a print form and put that into a separate reader by the post and the trade would be printed to the tape.

DOT was designed for single order entry of small orders and therefore had size constraints on what you could send down in this manner. DOT had a controversial introduction to the NYSE floor. Ostensibly, the 1st DOT box on the floor was found with a fire ax through it the morning after its installation.

Al knew all of this and felt like there was a fire ax lurking behind him right now if all didn't go as planned. He also knew that -- even though he had been testing with SIAC for months -- DOT wasn't really designed to handle what he was about to unleash

A huge list of orders representing the listed side of the S&P 500 that Al had loaded up into the Enterprise were now sitting there ready to go. The system automatically formatted each order so it could be read and routed by the Central Message Switch on the exchange. It acted like a battalion of traders typing in: C_TS...and hitting the enter button...all at the same time.

The Enterprise was ready to fire. Even though, he had done this a hundred times while testing, Al felt the pressure building sitting in that damn chair. Now it was for real. No one else had ever even tried to do this live before. It was the very first time. One mistake anywhere along the line could cost millions in an instant.

The bank mukluks stood at that weird respectful distance people give the condemned, all dressed for the part, too, standing behind Al in their dark funereal director suits. Anticipation was in the air. They had come to watch the new fangled technology in action. And Al was the one who had to hit THE button.

The call came from Lloyd a few minutes after the planned time. The arb was good enough to go for it. "What the hell." Al thought. He took a deep breath and hit the button.

The orders scrolled down the screen so fast you couldn't read them. And they were gone. The 1st live S&P 500 list processed trade ever attempted was launched. "OK." Al thought, "so far so good."

A tidal wave of orders was on their way, hurtling downtown, approaching the NYSE at the speed of light through the telephone wires about to electronically assault the exchange. When these orders hit their printers, the Specialists later described it as like having 50 machine guns all starting to fire at once.

Al looked at the dot-matrix printer on his left. The one connected to PC #2 for receiving executions back. It was silent. He glanced back to the sending screen, which showed the orders had been successfully transmitted as a list with no problems. So, where were the reports?

The reports screen was unchanging, its printer inanimate. During testing it had always responded immediately. Al stared hopefully at it. He wanted to smack it with his phone but the audience behind him curbed that impulse. The screen remained blank...the printer eerily silent. "C'mon, c'mon..." Al coaxed in his head, his stomach starting to knot up. .

The boys on the desk who had been pretending non-interest were now shifting uncomfortably in their chairs. Chris called Tom on the inside just to do something. Jimbo started his nervous tic: tap-tap-tapping his pen on the desk.

The undertakers began clearing their throats one right after the other. Al saw them peripherally behind him shifting from foot to foot. Their muffled, unintelligible communications definitely taking on a rising tone of concern. His mouth was dry and he was experiencing a strange déjà vu of impending doom.
Still nothing. Janet Roche was standing back with the officer corps. She was a bean counter who had the personality of same, a middle manager in the bank given charge of the brokerage operation. She thought she knew the business. She didn't. Janet took a step forward and commanded that Al explain what was going on.

Al heard her but remained motionless, running through everything in his mind. Where's the problem? What could've gone wrong? Comms good...blinking green...orders out: OK...systems good. Where the hell are the execution reports?

"Um..." Al started to temporize, as he had no answer at all. The volume of the bankers' voices was rising in consternation. Although perfectly still, Al was suddenly overwhelmed with a spinning sensation.

The hardest part of putting on an Index Arbitrage trade was getting the cash equity leg done. Hundreds and hundreds of individual stock orders had to get distributed to the right post for execution...the faster the better because the dislocation of cash value versus the index future that made the trade work was fleeting.

The big institutional brokerage houses had runners on staff specifically for their sprinting speed and explicitly for the Index Arb business. These runners would literally dash to the NYSE and AMEX floors with shoeboxes full of order tickets representing the underlying index, usually the S&P 500.

When Al hit the button, this whole process was automated. No more need for sprinters breathlessly delivering boxes of orders arranged by post location. At least that was the intent. "Why were there no reports?" he thought desperately, "Where the hell were the reports?" The whole situation had become surreal.

Janet repeated her request for an explanation with greater emphasis and bite. Al jumped and started, reality again: "Um..." God, he felt like puking. "Maybe it takes longer to process REAL trades." Tom averred. Al looked over to him in thanks...

Suddenly, a racket Al found so annoying during those endless nights of testing broke the uneasy quiet: the dot-matrix printer to his left started hammering the familiar staccato of execution reports rolling in.

He had been praying to hear that sound. But now he was shaking. Were the reports pairing off? Were they matching up against the orders sent? What if it was a disaster? Would he get fired? How would he react to that? He thought about how he had cried when he got fired from his summer job at the Coca-Cola plant...but he was a kid then.

Al was aware that his emotions were teetering tenuously now -- just like then. He was choking up but determined that he would not let it show...no matter what.

He ripped the first reports sheets with wobbly hands hoping for the best, preparing for the worst. What if the list was on the wrong side? What if the share counts were off? He was mentally exhausted. He took a deep breath, checked and double-checked. No one spoke.

Finally, Al exhaled loudly. He pushed away from the desk. He swiveled slowly around in the captain's chair his emotions amok. The recent college grad looked out at the leaders of Bankers Reliance without making eye contact. He mutely gave the thumbs up. The damn thing had worked.

Al didn't realize it but he was part of history being made. The cash equity side of a full index trade had just been completed electronically for the first time ever and what soon became known – and later derided -- as Program Trading, was born.

The executives smiled, nodded approvingly, slapped each other on the back and engaged in upbeat conversations as they shuffled off the trading floor and probably went for a 2-martini victory lunch. Al ran to the bathroom and his lunch was now part of the history.

Section II –
Electronic Trading
Applications & Practices

Algorithmic Trading in Financial Markets:
The Evolving Palette of Techniques

by Bruce Weber, London Business School

Algorithmic trading relies on live market data and rule-driven software to automatically place and execute orders. Trading based on algorithms is changing the landscape of financial markets. A tremendous variety of algorithms is in use, and their application across different asset classes and investing strategies will continue to expand. This chapter will outline the rationale for algorithmic trading, and outline the types of algorithms in use. Algorithms can be generic, and supplied by vendors or brokers to trading clients, or they can be proprietary and developed in-house by money managers. The broad use of algorithms today is evidence that trading takes place in a non-random walk environment, and that the supply of trading liquidity is limited and costly. Algorithmic trading is an optimal response to the problems of illiquidity and poor quantity discovery observable in today's markets. As imperfect market structures are improved and better trading designs appear, however, some of the reasons for algorithmic trading will disappear.

Introduction

One vision of professional investment management in the future involves traders, their computers, and their dogs. The computers run the trading operations, and the money managers keep the dogs fed and happy. The role of the canine companions is to keep the managers away from the computers, lest the humans mistakenly think their intuitions can match the emotionless efficiency of the trading software.

I have yet to see dogs going in and out of trading offices in London and New York, but the use of algorithms has become pervasive. Algorithmic trading is driven by a specific set of rules, and it is sometimes referred to as rules-based trading. Estimates are that 20 to 40 percent of trades in the major global equity exchanges originate from software-based trading algorithms. Yet algorithms lack a simple, common description. They come in many shapes and flavors, and are used for a broad range of investment purposes.

Despite their growing presence, many questions about algorithms remain. – What is the economic logic for trading with algorithms? What is an algorithmic trading platform? What are the types of trading algorithms employed and what are their objectives? What impact does algorithmic trading have on other market participants? And, finally, what will the market look like as trading becomes predominantly or entirely algorithm-driven?

Economic Rationale for Algorithms

Recall from your Finance 101 class that in a frictionless, perfectly efficient market, asset prices will follow a random walk. Early statistical tests of random walk by financial economists using day-to-day price movements were largely supportive of the weak form of the Efficient Markets Hypothesis (EMH). That is, day-to-day price patterns provided no basis for reliable forecasts, and no consistent excess returns. More recent analyses of intraday tick-by-tick data however show contradictory results (Lo and MacKinlay, 1999). Short-term returns are statistically predictable in violation of the EMH.

A related empirical fact is that transactions costs in financial market are positive and significant. The mere attempt to trade leads to costs that are subtracted from investors' returns. The Plexus Group's estimate of transactions costs for large cap U.S. stocks in 2004 was $0.23 per share, or 0.71%. Less liquid, small cap stocks impose even higher costs. Trading costs are made up of commissions, market impact, trade execution delays, and missed trades, which are transactions foregone as a result of costs and market conditions. Standard models in capital markets theory and portfolio theory assume zero transactions costs. Frictions in trading however are real and important. Winning investment ideas will not "beat the market" unless these trading costs are controlled.

In a random walk world without trading costs, algorithmic trading would be largely unnecessary. Software for automated trading would be useful as a labor saving tool only. Yet today's money managers, in their quest for outperformance or "alpha" from their investment ideas, use algorithms extensively.

The value of algorithmic trading lies in the intricacies and imperfections of price and quantity discovery (Schwartz, Francioni, and Weber, 2006). Non-random price behavior and real frictions and costs in trading are the two main economic reasons for algorithms' growing popularity. As the following sections will detail, algorithms are used to time the release of orders into the market to capitalize on price and volume patterns. They are also used to manage trading costs by tracking price benchmarks, such as volume-weighted average trade price (VWAP), and placing orders to minimize the performance shortfalls from a valid reference price.

Defining Algorithmic Trading

Defining what constitutes algorithmic trading is not simple. Experts have offered the follow descriptions:

Algorithmic trading is the automated, computer-based execution of equity orders via direct market-access channels, usually with the goal of meeting a particular benchmark. — Ian Domowitz and Henry Yegerman, ITG

Algorithmic trading covers automated trading in which large orders are broken up and sent into the marketplace according to predetermined quantitative rules. These rules could be based on a number of historical volume patterns, the current day's price and volume activity, as well as other trading systems. — Nina Mehta, Traders Magazine

Market participants often refer to *algorithmic trading platforms*. An algorithmic trading platform is a system that receives live market data, and runs it through rule-based software which automatically place and execute orders according to trading conditions. Some of the leading commercial platforms for algorithmic trading are detailed in Figure 1.

Figure 1: Companies and their algorithmic trading platforms

Provider	Product / Product Suite	Firm type
Bear Stearns	Smart Order Router (SOR): SOR Stealth, SOR Post, SOR Reserve, and SOR Cloak	Brokerage firm
Citigroup Global Markets	Lava electronic execution	Brokerage firm
Credit Suisse	Advanced Execution Services (AES)	Brokerage firm
EdgeTrade	Covert, FAN (smart order execution strategy)	Agency-only broker
Fidessa	BlueBox	IT vendor
4th Story	4S	IT vendor
Goldman Sachs	Goldman Sachs Algorithmic Trading (GSAT)	Brokerage firm
Instinet	Sidewinder	Agency broker subsidiary of Nomura (Japan)

Orc Software	Orc Liquidator, Orc Liquidator Hosted	IT vendor
UBS Investment Bank	Tap and TapNow , Comm-PASS (Commodities Portfolio Algorithmic Strategy System)	Brokerage firm

Example algorithmic trading platform

It is helpful to look in detail at one leading firm's algorithmic trading platform. Investment Technology Group (ITG) has provided IT support for trading since its founding in 1986. It has always had strong ties with quantitative investors, and now offers five general algorithmic trading strategies, which are summarized below:

Dark: a liquidity-seeking strategy that probes for liquidity in displayed and hidden execution venues, but avoids exposing its orders. It also splits order submissions among various alternative trading systems, including ITG's own POSIT crossing and order matching system.

Active: supplies liquidity and places some of its orders as limit orders to earn the bid-ask spread, and removes liquidity with market orders at opportune times.

Volume Participation (VP): participates in no more than a user-specified percentage of printed trading volume (POV), to avoid distorting the market.

VWAP: a volume-weighted average price (VWAP) strategy that executes orders over chosen time window, and distributes trading based on past volume patterns to achieve an overall price equal to or better than VWAP.

Implementation Shortfall (IS): sends orders to minimize execution costs relative to an IS benchmark, which is based on arrival price when the trading instruction is first received. Client-specified urgency levels determine the aggressiveness of the strategy.

Selection Criteria for Algorithmic Trading Platforms

Client users of algorithmic trading platforms have differing needs. The most popular features and their usefulness are:

- Flexible – enable users to seek to generate returns in a range of ways, including automated strategies for both long and short position taking, and allow for defined parameters to be modified on-the fly by users

- Venue customization – allow users to seek liquidity from user selected liquidity sources such as brokers' internal pools, alternative trading systems and dark pools, traditional exchanges, and displayed markets
- Time-sensitivity – offer urgency options that control how fast an order is exposed or filled, and how much of the order can interact with displayed markets rather than dark pools
- Balanced execution – minimize the risks of negative selection, which occurs when algorithmic orders are "cherry-picked" to execute, leaving many difficult, expensive trades uncompleted
- Asset class neutral – treat equity, fixed, and derivatives instruments the same so that all analytics and scenarios are available in multiple domains
- Avoid gaming – hide or mix the order release tactics to "not give the strategy away."
- Rapid development – able to develop and deploy new algorithms quickly
- Volume-dependence – adjust order sizes and participation rate as a stock's price moves relative to a benchmark. Gives advantages from "value" or "momentum" situations as they arise in markets
- In-house and industry-standard strategies – apply generic strategies along with frameworks for building in-house proprietary models
- Portfolio-based algorithms – handle portfolio strategies that seek to buy or sell a set of stock simultaneously. Enabling, for example, a basket or portfolio to be sold based on the price movement of a single trigger instrument or index.
- Compatible with FIX Algorithmic Trading Definition Language – FIXATDL will enable users to specify algorithmic order types in an XML format and reduce the effort required to roll out new algorithmic order types.
- Robust – at critical high-volume, high-traffic times, traders need platform to be reliable. Outages or latencies undermine the purpose of having algorithmic platforms.

Robustness is an important consideration. Algorithmic trading platforms depend on data feeds from multiple vendors and exchanges. On high volume, high volatility days, many brokerage firms' smart order routers have not been able to keep up with incoming data traffic. In these cases, traders and clients had to fall back on less sophisticated systems. In some cases, the source of algorithmic trading problems is delayed market data feeds from vendors as exchanges occasionally have problems delivering timely data. High volumes of market data, and the possibility of some data being delayed, both affect any underlying algorithm's ability to function. Since Regulation NMS went into effect in 2006 in the U.S., delays of more than one second in responding to an incoming order are deemed too long, and brokers have the right to exclude the slow exchange from its venue selection process for orders. Major Algorithm Types.

Broadly speaking, five types of algorithms are in wide use. These are:

- Trading-strategy algorithms
- Order execution algorithms
- Smart routing algorithms
- Information algorithms
- Future algorithms

Matching the algorithm type to the investor, and then customizing it to their needs, requires consideration of a number of factors. Investor and fund characteristics that should influence the decision of what trading algorithms to use include:

- Assets traded and number of positions
- Investment strategy
- Frequency of trades
- Time horizon (how long positions are held) and turnover
- Size of trades
- Speed of response to news or price actions
- Frequency of inflows and outflows to the fund

An algorithm type that provides significant value for an active, momentum-driven small cap trader may not meet the needs of a quantitatively managed value fund. Kissell (2007) presents a useful statistical framework for comparing the performance of alternative algorithms.

The first type of algorithm, **trading-strategy** algorithms are developed for short-term, proprietary opportunity investing based on historic data relationships, and use real-time analysis of data flows. Trading strategy or quantitative algorithms scan for opportunities to buy or sell profitably based on some pattern or relationship that is expected to hold in the market. To profit from small, short-term opportunities, strategy algorithms depend on high frequency data and rapid order entry. Strategies can include quantitative trading with automated programs that implement any of the approaches below:

- High level strategy rules that provide automated market making, placing both buy and sell orders in a market, and seeking to earn the spread between them

- Event-driven and news-driven trading that responds to announcements to capture profit from price moves
- Tactically-triggered trading, such as buying or selling on moving average cross-overs, such as when a 30-day moving average falls below a 120-day moving average
- Risk arbitrage-based trading that uses takeover and mergers activity to buy target companies and sell buying companies
- Statistical arbitrage looking for pairs and spread trading opportunities, such as selling GM stock and buying Ford when GM appears too highly valued.
- Index arbitrage generated orders to buy and sell index products, such as exchange traded funds (ETF) or index futures, against the underlying securities in the index
- Conversion arbitrage: including American Depository Receipts (ADRs), Global Depository Receipts (GDRs), and convertible debt
- Spot-forward: bond and currencies
- Predatory trading exploits forced liquidations, when, for instance, a short seller needs to cover a position, or a margin call creates a price-moving demand for immediate liquidity

A second group of algorithms is **order execution** algorithms. Unlike trading strategy algorithms, these do not use the algorithm to generate orders, but rather take the orders as given, and seek to execute them as efficiently as possible.

The objective of an order execution algorithm is to achieve the best possible *result* for the investor. Notice the best price or an immediate trade may not be the best result A good result means timely completion and achieving a fair price for the entire quantity bought or sold. A challenge arises, because impatient trading can impact the market price adversely, while trying to get the best price may mean the order goes largely unfilled. Willingness to accept some price concessions enables the trade to be completed.

The illustration in Figure 2 shows a stylized depiction of how a large sell instruction might incur "slippage" costs as it is sliced into smaller orders that are released into the market. In this case, there is a small pre-trade cost as some of the money manager's negative opinion about the security's value becomes evident in the price. The price decline accelerates as the sell orders hit the market, leading to lower bid and ask quotes. Money managers generating trading instructions typically face an expected base-price move (why else would they be buying or selling?), which is a permanent price change after a trading decision is made. Algorithms are used to minimize the expected liquidity impact, which is the short-term, generally temporary, price move needed to entice the other side of the market to trade.

Figure 2: Trading costs for a large sell instruction that is executed in three trades broken into temporary market impact and permanent market impact.

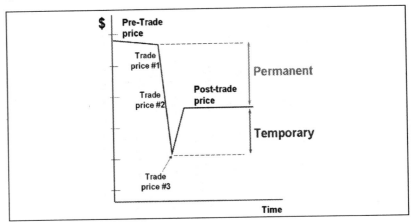

Although market impact is difficult to forecast pre-trade, permanent impact is the unavoidable revaluation in the market due to the new information (negative for a large sell order). Order execution algorithms are fine-tuned to seek to trade as much as possible before the entire permanent impact is realized, and to keep any temporary impact to a minimum.

Order execution algorithms in wide use include:

- Enhanced automated execution – These often rely on Direct Market Access (DMA) systems to reduce market impact on buy and sell orders. This may entail timing and routing of orders, volume slicing, sweep orders, iceberg orders, pegging orders to an index, or bid-ask spread capture orders. Example functions are:
  - Issue single large orders into the market if liquidity is good, or issue them as a series of smaller slices if liquidity is poor
  - Decide on the threshold of liquidity when introducing slicing, for instance an absolute 20 percent slice, or incrementally as liquidity deteriorates the slices decrease from 20% to 10% to 5%.
- Benchmark-guided – These use benchmark reference prices, and submit orders to match or beat the reference price. The possible benchmarks to reference are:
  - Volume-weighted or time-weighted average price (VWAP, TWAP). A sell instruction, for example, will be managed to achieve an average execution price greater than VWAP in the relevant period of time, such as a day.
  - Arrival price – Used in Implementation Shortfall (IS) approaches that seek to keep a large buy or sell instruction from moving the market against the client. The mid-quote price when the order is

first entered is a common IS reference. Then, IS is the pre-trade cost added to the market impact.

- – Open-High-Low-Close prices – Combinations of these prices are applied in rules to ensure attractive trade prices
- – Participation limits – Percentage or cap orders that ensure the client's trading is no more than a certain proportion of total volume to avoid destabilizing the market
- Portfolio trading – These handle a list of stocks whose order submissions are simultaneously managed with dynamic controls as the orders begin to execute. A control, for example, will seek to ensure that buy and sell orders execute in balance in order to avoid surplus cash (too many sell orders filled) or a cash deficit (too many buy orders execute).
- Liquidity-providing – These attempt to enhance returns by placing passive, "resting" orders into the market in order to buy at the bid, and sell at the higher ask price. These orders can be sent to a broker, placed in a crossing network, or routed to an exchange or ECN.
- Finally FX currency pricing can be an input to algorithms to manage orders in cross-currency equities so that strategies can operate across countries.

An example order execution strategy is illustrated below. In all algorithmic trading, it is essential to avoid predictable schedules and behavior that could be detected. Prior to the algorithm submitting orders, the system or user sets parameters such as the maximum percent volume to join in so as not to affect the price of the security. The following are logical descriptions of the rules a trading algorithm would apply:

- Example 1: Buy 1.6 million shares of ORCL to match the morning (9:30-12 noon) VWAP. Price limit = Prior Day's Low ($17). Remain at or below 10 percent of consolidated volume in each 5 minute period the order is being "worked."

Order execution algorithms must balance getting the trade done with limiting market impact. Another example that aims for price improvements is below:

- Example 2: Buy 100,000 BRCM with a $28.98 top as quickly as possible but without causing market impact. Track momentum, and attempt to differentiate "noise" from genuine momentum. Post on the bid while price changes are noise. If prices start to move up, convert to aggressive buys at offer.

Smart routing algorithms use real time market data to select the best market to send an order based on predefined rules created by the trader. This approach consolidates prices for the same security in a single display, using screen real estate efficiently. Routing destinations may include exchanges, electronic communication networks (ECN), alterative trading systems, brokers with liquidity-providing desks, or dark liquidity pools (e.g., Posit, Liquidnet, Pipeline). SOR also ensures the best priced market generally receives the order. Example applications of SOR include:

- Simultaneously trading Eurodollar futures on Chicago Mercantile Exchange (CME) and LIFFE from a single display
- Basis trading the U.S. Treasury futures on CBOT against the underlying cash on E-Speed or BrokerTec
- Trading multiply-listed equity options on the six U.S. options exchanges (Figure 3)
- Trading a liquid U.S. equity such as Cisco using the Nasdaq Market Center or the ECN with the best current quote (Figure 4)

Figure 3: Consolidated display for IBM Call options with $75 strike. Smart order router will determine the best market from among six available based on price, order size, and speed.

Last Exch	Bid	Size	Exch	Ask	Size
8.80 BOX	6.50	127	BOX	6.70	142
0.00 PCX	6.50	92	PCX	6.70	17
0.00 PHLX	6.50	79	ISE	6.70	11
6.60 ISE	6.50	71	PHLX	6.70	11
6.60 CBOE	6.50	61	CBOE	6.70	11
8.00 AMEX	6.50	10	AMEX	6.80	10

Figure 4: Reuters Xtra's Nasdaq Level 2 display for Cisco shares. Smart order router will determine the best order execution venue based on user-selected preferences and displayed prices and sizes.

Smart routing algorithms can streamline compliance with "Best Execution" regulations. The best execution destination, however, may not always be the market with the best displayed quote. In some cases, speed of execution, the desire for anonymity, the chance for price improvement, or the need for greater size may lead to a different destination for an order.

Information algorithms are a fourth type of order execution algorithm. They typically search and filter information and news flow, using text information to find securities whose prices are likely to change. Historic market data flows are often related to news releases to set algorithm triggers for buying and selling when news text appears to be sufficiently positive or negative. Certain news releases can initiate alarms that alert human traders, or they can be "search and strike" algorithms with auto-executions from live news events.

Order management behavior will differ depending on how the information is interpreted by the algorithm. After news, orders may be re-priced or cancelled if it is not filled within a given time. Clipping or iceberging a single order into smaller slices, and placing more aggressive order sizes if the market conditions are good, or utilizing random factors to mask the size and period between orders will be a part of the user's input to this algorithm.

Future algorithms are applications that are in development and not yet in wide use. These include cutting edge strategies for dynamic portfolio trading with tilting, multi-asset algorithms that handle orders simultaneously among equities, commodities, and currencies. Genetic and neuro algorithms are currently finding more applications using biologically-inspired rules development such as adaptation and evolution. Algorithms are also gaining favor for pre-trade cost analysis. These provide a transactions cost forecast, which is then used to direct order management tactics subsequently used in trading.

Risk Management for Algorithmic Trading

The trend toward real-time algorithmic trading has allowed money managers and traders to become more responsive and competitive, but has led to strains on risk management systems. Risk systems typically run end-of-day, but trading is becoming increasingly based on intra-day movements and position-taking, which may not be monitored. This mismatch must be improved to give firms an intra-day view of positions and the associated risk. Key indicators for risk management of algorithmic trading are position information, short-term value-at-risk calculations, and trades as well as market data to determine what hedging strategy should be applied.

Conclusions

Algorithmic trading is revolutionizing markets and how traders operate in them. Trading algorithms rely on live market data and rule-driven software to automatically place and execute orders. A variety of algorithms are in use, and their applications continue to expand. Because of the speed and non-random walk environment of today's markets and illiquidity costs, algorithmic trading is an optimal response. Investors can manage more orders with greater consistency, which helps to address the problems of illiquidity and reduce slippage observable in today's markets. Yet evidence suggests market structures are improving, and that better trading intelligence is being built into basic order management software. As a result, the marginal value of developing trading algorithms may decrease in the future. For now, however, the benefits of well-designed trading algorithms more than justify the presence of the proverbial "trading room dog", who entertains the traders and allows the software to do the hard work.

References

Kissell, Robert (2007) "Statistical Methods to Compare Algorithmic Performance", The Journal of Trading, Vol. 2, No. 2, pp. 53-62

Lo, Andrew W. and A. Craig MacKinlay (1999), "A Non-Random Walk Down Wall Street", Princeton University Press.

Schwartz, R.A., R. Francioni, and B.W. Weber (2006) "The Equity Trader Course", John Wiley & Sons.

The Changing Paradigms of Trading Institutional-Sized Orders

By Pavan Sahgal, Editor-in-Chief, Global Investment Technology

After years of whittling down their trades into smaller and smaller pieces to reduce market impact or to interact with liquidity in ECNs and alternative trading systems, institutional investors may soon experience a resurgence in their ability to execute block trades across a broadening spectrum of liquidity pools.

Block trading is alive and well, investment managers say, and ready to make a strong comeback in a different form, in spite of, or maybe even because of, the emergence of fragmented pools of liquidity. Top-tier investment management firms share a perspective that block trading is coming into prominence again, albeit in a new incarnation. Heads of trading desks report that their firms are taking "appropriate steps to make sure we can take advantage" of new ways to accomplish the execution of large-block trades. To do so, they are building or buying trading technologies that can deliver low-latency, millisecond access to liquidity wherever it may dot the securities trading landscape. In short, they are thinking outside the box and accomplishing the trading of large blocks of securities, although not in the manner they may have transacted 20 years ago.

Buy-side traders are discovering that trading algorithms can help them create an increasing stream of event-specific liquidity that can be tapped throughout the day. They are harnessing these continuous streams alongside closed venues such as Liquidnet, which limit who can participate within the system and enable negotiated trades; crossing engines such as ITG's POSIT; and forums such as Pipeline Trading that are open to both buy- and sell-side participants, among a plethora of liquidity pools, including undisclosed liquidity – the so-called 'dark pools.'

The changed outlook for the buy-side's ability to execute large block orders emerges less than two years after market participants expressed alarm that regulatory changes such as Reg NMS could lead to trading practices that support oligopolies. Fears that an exchange duopoly essentially controlled by The New York Stock Exchange and The Nasdaq Stock Market turn out to have been a catalyst for boosting the viability of many alternative trading venues.

Those fears led to the formation of dozens of electronically accessed pools of non-displayed, off-exchange liquidity, with institutional investors willingly exposing their order flow to them, sometimes just for a few milliseconds using advanced trading algorithms. Some buy-side traders have tended to see that as detrimental to large block trading.

In their view, as the information evaporates, with the elimination of trading floors and sell-side intermediaries, it is harder to make a trading decision. Consequently, buy-side traders are forced to cut back on the size of their orders. Eliminate the broker from the process and it becomes increasingly difficult to put large block trades together in the ways it used to be done, they contend.

A trader needs to be able to assess the supply and demand, and that is very difficult to do if he or she must look at four, five or six venues all at once, they point out. Therefore, most money managers are merely along for the ride with a lot of the price movements whether it is 15, 16, or 18 cents.

Others clearly see such views as very 'old school.' Yes, there may be some truth in them, but the coupling of algorithms and electronic access sets the scene for block trading, too, to undergo a metamorphosis. Think differently, they say, and suddenly you experience how an upswing and proliferation of block trading becomes possible. The resurgence of ECNs and the dark pools of liquidity do not pose a threat, but present a trading opportunity to be seized. Certainly, for those staying a step ahead with state-of-the-art technological tools and advanced connectivity, the emergence of a couple of new dark pools a day is a key factor recreating the block trading franchise that existed in the past. Of course, while it is being recreated, it is taking on a much different shape.

The key enabler of the latest trading paradigm is a powerful mix of trading savvy, stronger business relationships, particularly with agency brokerages, and sophisticated algorithmic trading tools. Buy-side traders are leveraging these algorithms, many of which are supplied by broker-dealer firms, to sweep the electronically connected pools of non-displayed liquidity, popularly dubbed dark pools, which continue to mushroom.

Together, these factors are rekindling an awakening among buy-side traders of the inherent value of trading large blocks of stocks rapidly, without registering any significant price movement in the marketplace. But there is also a sense of paranoia among some buy-side traders that advanced algorithms could be reverse engineered by their providers to yield valuable clues about trading strategies. These concerns add a new electronic twist to age-old fears about institutional trading producing an undesired market impact that could lead to disadvantageous price moves. Many major money management firms say they are already looking to write their own proprietary algorithms. At the same time, they are also seeking ways to benchmark the effectiveness of broker-supplied algorithms.

Buy-side traders say that they certainly will continue to find value in the so-called upstairs market, industry jargon for the network of trading desks of brokerage firms and institutional investors who communicate over the telephone or via computer screens to negotiate and execute block trades. They also see a continuing important role for the displayed liquidity on exchanges to enable their trading goals.

Indeed, electronic trading does not make the sell side extinct. To be sure, almost every head of trading on the buy side insists that the partnership with the sell side will remain invaluable, despite the advance of technology. But there is a catch. There will be fewer sell side firms that the buy side will seek out as partners. One deciding factor may be how quickly and effectively sell side firms, too, reinvent their services for buy-side institutions.

While "really good coverage that a good broker provides will always remain valuable," the electronic layer that is growing very rapidly between the broker and investment manager will continue to gain greater acceptance and importance. Agency brokers such as ITG, Inc., a pioneer in electronic trading solutions, and newly re-constituted BNY ConvergEx, recognize this unfolding change and are leading the charge against the traditional, bulge-bracket broker-dealers. Buy-side traders point out that upstairs marketplaces are often turning into systematic internalizers by offering attractive trading alternatives to capture flows they wouldn't otherwise have. One of the first to do that was ITG's POSIT electronic crossing system.

More changes are manifesting with the Markets in Financial Instruments Directive (MiFID), which took effect in the EU on November 1, 2007, enabling pseudo-exchanges, multi-lateral trading facilities (MTFs), and trade-reporting facilities to take shape. In the United States, a deeper understanding of all the nuances of Reg NMS may give an added boost to alternative trading venues that help support a rise in block trading. For now, Reg NMS has been taken as the regulatory nod of approval for dark pools to cross trades at the mid-point of the bid-ask spread or the National Best Bid and Offer (NBBO).

Like a painless injection given by a nimble nurse, the leveled playing field created by Reg NMS has been so swift that many call the regulatory change a non-event. Many in the industry appear to think Reg NMS is all about trading within the bid-ask spread, but that is really not the case. There is a lot more to come. For instance, Reg NMS for the first time in the history of securities trading, in its own obtuse way, formalizes a process for sell-side firms to offer institutional investors, say, a discount bid. While MiFID, without defining anything, sets the stage for the industry itself to determine what's best execution.

In that way, these regulatory changes may come to support the notion that best execution could be about a *process*, and meeting an investment objective, more than anything else.

In time, North American and European markets' experience of Reg NMS and MiFID will likely converge toward common practices. If MiFID clearly underscores the importance of best execution, on closer scrutiny, Reg NMS yields the intuition that market participants may do block trades outside the bid-ask spread, as long as they have satisfied the top of book. Such subtleties underlying regulatory changes, and the windows of opportunity they open along the entire securities trading value chain, as well as related technology challenges, have been probed at several recent meetings of the *Global Investment Technology **Leadership Roundtable***. The membership forum, whose deliberations are private, comprises a cross-section of the complete investment value chain, starting with asset owners, thereby yielding penetrating insights on market structure shifts and business-model transformations shaping the future of pension funds, money managers, hedge funds, securities firms, exchanges and intermediaries, as well as the clearance and settlement infrastructure that support them.

Reg NMS, it appears, will eventually be seen as formalizing and institutionalizing off-market block trades, as long as the transaction satisfies the best, displayed bid. As long as a trade satisfies the top of the book, it may be printed as a block trade away from the bid-ask. In time, this aspect of Reg NMS may come to be seen as fostering and encouraging active price discovery by the buy side. It could prove to be beneficial for the market, especially if it leads more institutional investors towards negotiated trades. Electronic trading platforms – perhaps owned by buy- and sell-side consortia – that enable these negotiated transactions could be the next big innovation to foster better price discovery in the 21st century.

To be sure, the crowd has starkly thinned, if not wholly disappeared, from the NYSE. Some on the buy side consider this an indication that they are not operating at an information disadvantage anymore. They don't need to peer into a crowd or "deal with a bucket brigade of people" to get to the result of their trading activity. In fact, they're taking back control of the order flow. Regulatory changes have lifted the barriers that shielded exchanges from competitors.

Buy-side participants are now price makers, not price takers, concur those familiar with block trading and its demands. The buy side used to rely on the broker-dealer to step in whenever there was a problem in the aftermarket, but not anymore. Today, the buy side trader can manage portfolios in a far more sophisticated manner with the help of direct market access (DMA), custom algorithms, and advanced tools. The buy-side trader can control market impact, manage transaction costs, and meet best-execution requirements. These advances signal a death knell for the traditional role of intermediaries, calling into question the role of traditional sales traders and forcing the sell side to augment or reinvent their skill sets.

Some buy-side traders are also experiencing a new sense of empowerment by acknowledging that broker-dealers are no longer the sole source of insights on where the price equilibrium might lie in a trading strategy. Electronic markets are leveling the playing field between the buy- and sell-side, while making the game more complex. More and more, pre-trade analytics and market-access tools and technologies, including liquidity-aggregating algorithms, will be recognized as conferring distinct advantages. Ironically, institutional investors will be polarized into the haves and the have-nots.

Buy-side traders themselves may be the ones firing the next salvo in the marketplace by becoming more proactive in negotiating trades, providing an added boost to block transactions and making exchanges truly the venue of last resort in securities trading. Currently, order management systems (OMSs) on the buy side do not reflect the true supply and demand picture in securities trading. The reason for this is that order management systems are being routinely swept by order-capture technologies that take those orders and put them into the market.

Buy-side traders often choose to keep the true extent of their supply and demand details outside their OMSs and dribble out order flow as they see fit when the doors are opened to a liquidity provider. Order segregation and playing close to the vest strongly suggests the existence of latent or hidden liquidity that extends beyond the liquidity available at the bid-ask spread for any stock. Consider the ramifications of buy side traders widening the liquidity at the bid-ask spread to, say, 20 cents above and 20 cents below, and how much that might expand the liquidity horizon incrementally?

A platform where institutional investors might more proactively stimulate price discovery could certainly uncork some of the bottled up liquidity. Could institutional investors find natural, non-reactive participants in a system run by a traditional exchange? NYSE Euronext hopes so as it launches it MatchPoint, in January 2008 to enable the exchange to offer pre-scheduled matching events, from as few as a single match a day to as many as 500. Transparency and price discovery go hand in hand, but so do opacity and quantity discovery, goes the reasoning at the exchange. In November 2007, NYSE Euronet became the 13th investor in BIDS Holdings LP, which was originally formed in 2006 by six leading broker dealers to operate BIDS Trading. BIDS will become the access point for trading block liquidity on the NYSE. The idea is to re-aggregate blocks that certainly are being broken down to trade. Perhaps there is a promising future for an electronic call market at the exchange.

Meanwhile, The Nasdaq Stock Market, Inc. has fired its own salvo with the launch of a comprehensive suite of crossing products, among them Nasdaq Intraday Cross and Post-Close Cross, to complement its successful Opening and Closing Crosses. Nasdaq plans to launch a Continuous Cross, subject to SEC approval in 2008. The goal is to help institutional-sized orders find liquidity anonymously and with greater efficiency, not to mention siphoning away business in NYSE-listed and American Stock Exchange securities.

Buy-side traders remain open to all possibilities. The days of picking up a phone and calling in an order are as quaint as the ticker tapes of yesteryears. The key to success now rests not just in leveraging advanced trading technologies, but also in recognizing people and firms who are thought leaders in their field and partnering with them. Those partners could be brokerage firms, or software and systems vendors, connectivity and infrastructure services providers, or who knows, even a custodial bank with the gumption to think outside the box.

Pavan Sahgal is Editor in Chief of *Global Investment Technology*, a bi-weekly publication offering strategic coverage of securities trading and operations in an electronic marketplace, and the *Global Investment Technology **Leadership Roundtable**,* a members-only, live forum that meets every six months. For more information, visit *www.globalinv.com*

The Importance of Being Earnest

By Evan Schulman, Founder, Tykhe, LLC &
Charles Polk, Founder, The Martian Trust

Markets that trade continuously, such as the NYSE, the London Stock Exchange, and NASDAQ, are so structured that they inadequately meet the trading needs of large investors, in particular institutional investors[lxxii]. Richard Roll calculated that some 27% of daily variance in stock prices is due to the trading system itself[lxxiii]. In fact he notes that markets that trade continuously had the worst performance in the market debacle of October 1987[lxxiv].

For exposition, and perhaps entertainment, we can define three types of traders in a market: wolves, sheep and hyenas. Wolves are information players. They have information about a company that will shortly be revealed. They must trade before that information becomes public; they prey on other traders. Sheep are liquidity traders; they are putting cash flow to work, or they are selling securities to replenish their cash reserves. Sheep also include portfolio managers who are restructuring client portfolios in order to have a more appropriate exposure to risk or underlying economic factors. Hyenas are day-traders and the like who see trading patterns generated by the other two and try to front-run those orders.

Of course we also need a shepherd who attempts to protect the sheep so that they can graze in peace. In this case the shepherd stands for the market operator whose duty is to see that traders can execute trades in a market that imposes minimum costs to their business. This means designing markets to protect liquidity traders from the ravages of wolves and hyenas.

The Basic Problem

When a portfolio manager restructures a portfolio it is necessary to sell some securities in order to invest in others. The manager thinks in terms of swapping '*this*' security for '*that*': or more likely, '*these*' securities for '*those*' securities. However, the NYSE and other exchanges are designed as single security markets; as a result the trading desk, the executing broker and other participants all focus on the sell and buy order(s) as separate items: - the sell order for Avid Technologies, - the buy order for Cree Inc. If the portfolios being restructured are large, then leaks, deductions and rumors about the size and intent of orders act like bait for the hyenas and wolves. The result, prices will be pushed apart. Continuing with the metaphor, since the shepherd (market operator) has not implemented a structure that allows liquidity traders to execute combinations of orders as single trades (portfolio trades), the sheep (liquidity traders) must spend time and effort, over and above their portfolio management duties, devising strategies to protect themselves.

Devising and executing strategies to defend against the failings of the market structure are direct costs to the sheep in that scarce resources are removed from the portfolio management process. Money managers establish and staff trading desks, the mandate of which is to execute trades without divulging the manager's intentions – lying takes effort. These strategies impact the orders that sheep submit. This imposes costs to the whole market system if the result is decreased trade volume and/or inefficient prices. Because the sheep cannot act in earnest, they hurt themselves and the system suffers overall. The necessity to pursue strategies that are devised to mitigate shortcomings in the market process indicates a need to improve or change the market process used. Examples of mitigating strategies employed by sheep are:

Mitigating Strategy #1, Limit Orders

In the good old days when the minimum spread between the bid and ask was 1/8th or ¼ of a dollar, institutions used limit orders to reduce the price impact of their orders. Given that the markets enforced 'price/time' priority, traders needed to improve the price by at least an 1/8th or a ¼ to move ahead of an existing order, otherwise new orders moved to the back of the queue. If a trader did improve the price in order to move ahead and the price of subsequent trades did not move in the appropriate direction, the loss involved in unwinding the trade could be substantial.

Nowadays, with spreads of one or two cents, the strategy of using a limit order to avoid market impact is basically a loser's game. Others can place their orders a penny or so in front of a large order. If the trader with the limit order has information, or just becomes impatient and wants to get the order executed, s/he will become more aggressive, thus moving the price and generating trading profits for those who traded ahead. If not, the front-running trader can unwind the order for the cost of a penny or so a share, an order of magnitude or so less than under the previous regime.

Thus, limit orders are no longer a viable mitigating strategy – by allowing smaller spreads, the shepherd opened the gates to the hyenas.

Mitigating Strategy #2, Partial Executions

To execute without limits and yet control impact, trading desks now slice pieces of an order to the market using a number of different timing and order size strategies. The result is that an inventory of unexecuted and unsatisfied orders builds up on the trading desk. It is rumored that large investment managers each have several days' average trading volume of orders sitting on their desks. These firms try to keep this information confidential because street knowledge of the pending orders would move the price of the securities in anticipation of the orders coming to market. However, keeping the orders hidden means they are not available for execution and, as the desk continues to parse the orders to market, astute traders note the flow and move the prices anyway.

Indeed, it is hard to keep information about a large order quiet: rumors that Fidelity is buying "X" or equivalent are constantly surfacing and, if buttressed by order flow, that security will soon have the *scent* of one or more institutions attached to it.

Years ago, an institutional money manager where one of the authors worked was involved in a large portfolio restructuring program. They attempted to measure this *scent* effect. The buy and sell programs were divided into sections. Each of the buy sections and each of the sell sections were as comparable as they could make them in terms of market capitalization, sector exposure, percentage of the average day's volume, volatility, etc.

After a few days of operating with one section of the restructuring program they would cancel all the orders and replace them with the orders from another, equivalent section. They then measured the price impact both when they initiated a section and when they stopped trading. On average the prices of the securities moved against them when they commenced trading: that is those securities that they wanted to purchase rose relative to the market, those they wanted to sell, fell. When they stopped trading, the relative prices retreated back, but not the whole way.

If we label the relative price move observed as a trading alpha then, on average, the securities would shed roughly ½ their trading alpha once they stopped trading in those securities. Those stocks had the institution's *scent*; traders expected them to return to buy (or sell) more of these because, given their size, they clearly had not executed sufficient to meet their needs.

Markets Should Let the Sheep Work in Earnest

As alluded to above and noted in more detail below, there are infrastructure and personnel costs involved in implementing these and other[lxxv] mitigation strategies. Such effort removes resources from the portfolio management function (managers work under a budget) and further reduces the efficiency of the market because of the withheld orders. Is there another trading regime, another shepherd, which would allow the sheep to do their job in earnest?

The first step along the path to identifying a better shepherd is to review the basic single-price call market, an old market concept that is still used, if sparingly. Debt auctions by the U.S. Treasury are single-price call auctions, and the open at the NYSE is a single price call market executed in parallel on a security-by-security basis.

A call market has two phases, order accumulation followed by order matching. After orders have been allowed to accumulate, without their bid or ask prices having been made public, the accumulation phase is closed at a pre-announced time – the market is *called*. Orders are then ranked by aggressiveness of price (highest to lowest for purchases, lowest to highest for sales): see Table 1.

Table 1

Price	Purchase Orders	Sell Orders
10.10		500
10.09		1,700
10.08	300	800
10.07	1,000	900
10.06	500	600
10.05	1,500	
10.04	200	
10.03		

At the call, the market maker, specialist or clerk executes orders that "cross"; that is buys with an equal or higher bid are matched to sales with an equal or lower offer. In the above case there are orders to purchase 300 shares at $10.08 or lower and 1,000 shares at a price of $10.07 or lower. Matching these are orders to sell 900 shares at a price of $10.07 or higher and 600 shares at $10.06 or higher. In a non-price discriminatory, or single-price call market, the reported trade would be for 1,300 shares at a price of $10.07, leaving the best bid of $10.06 for 500 shares and the best offer of $10.07 for the remaining 200 shares of the 900 shares originally offered at that price.

Notice that the traders who placed more aggressive orders are not charged any penalty for having been more aggressive: the purchase order for 300 shares at $10.08 and the sell order for 600 shares at $10.06 both get executed at an improved price of $10.07. The orders at the margin set the price, orders that are priced more aggressively get filled with price improvement, orders that are not sufficiently competitive remain as orders instead of becoming trades. In a single-price call market, the only strategic consideration faced by a trader is the probability that he or she will end up as a marginal trader – a probability that decreases rapidly as the number of traders in the market increases.[lxxvi] With a number of hours between calls, a trader who needs to move volume dare not overweigh the risk of being at the margin, lest he or she end up not trading at all. Thus, for a sheep who believes there will be other sheep on his or her side of a market, earnestness is the best strategy. The wolves and hyenas will play to define the margin in such a call market and may occasionally nip a bit of value from a marginal sheep, but that is a far cry from their impact in a continuous market.

If the time between calls is reasonable, say a trading day, those trying to front-run institutional orders will be placed at a serious disadvantage. Also the attractiveness of such markets is greatly reduced for those trading on short-term information. The longer they wait, the more likely their information will become public. Thus, for the sheep, the chances of trading with wolves and hyenas decrease and the chances of a "crossed" market increase.

Enhancing the Call Market to address the Basic Problem

The classic call market frees liquidity traders from the need to concoct and implement trading strategies to combat the behavior of other traders; however, the classic call market is a security-by-security process and so does not address the Basic Problem of portfolio management. To meet the needs of portfolio managers, we need a shepherd who will not only provide an environment in which earnestness is best but also allow combination orders. The combinatoric call market is such a shepherd – newly arrived due to the creative application of mathematics and modern computational resources –

that employs two cross-security conditions, AND and OR, in an order language that speaks to the Basic Problem[lxxvii].

The AND Condition

The order that a portfolio manager would like to send to market is something like "I have '*these*' securities to sell in order to buy '*those*', **AND** I have a budget of so many dollars to spend in (or take from) this transaction". In a well designed call market it is not necessary to have one natural counter party to fill the order. The contra side can be filled from many different orders, making best use of existing liquidity and ensuring that at least some of the contra orders will be initiated by "sheep". Wolves will still trade in these markets if they determine that the information they have has not yet become public. Wolves will bid aggressively in terms of price in order to trade. They are unlikely to be the marginal order and thus will not directly be the traders setting prices (see the description of Table 1.).

There is an interesting aspect to such orders; the binding limit is really just the cash or budget constraint. In the order above selling, say, 1 million shares of AVID[lxxviii] to purchase 1.3 million shares of CREE, **AND** requiring that the trade generate at least $1,575,000 in cash for the portfolio gives the trading exchange/program flexibility. More flexibility can be added if the manager can accept a partial fill of the order, as long as it is prorated. If the trade meets the order's budget constraint, (i.e. generates $1,575,000. or more, prorated) and the budget constraint is realistic given current prices, the exchange/program can adjust prices to make the trade happen[lxxix]. The trader or portfolio manager may wish to further constrain the order by adding price limits, but it is not necessary; in fact such limits act as additional constraints on the order's execution.

The use of **AND** can be broadened, of course, such as sell 1 million shares of AVID to purchase 670,000 million shares of CREE, **AND** 712,000 shares of INTC **AND** generate $1,575,000 in cash. Here the proceeds of any sale would be invested proportionately into CREE and INTC.

The OR Condition

Many portfolio managers trade securities to achieve specific industry or factor exposures for their portfolios. They are not wedded to a particular stock. For readers who find this an anathema I suggest ranking the top 3 or 4 securities in an industry or sector. Do this for several industries/sectors. Wait a couple of months and check the performance of those securities since the original ranking. I always find the experience humbling and am thus receptive to the idea of substitutions or alternative vehicles to help position the portfolio's industry, factor or risk exposures.

Given the last paragraph, at least some portfolio managers could use the **OR** operative when expressing an order. Thus the above order could be restated as follows: sell 1 million shares of AVID to purchase 1.3 million shares of CREE, **OR** 3,012,000 shares of Taiwan Semiconductor Manufacturing Ltd (TSM) **OR** 1,467,000 shares of Intel (INTC). **AND** generate $1,575,000 in cash: - **AND** if the order cannot be completed, prorate. The result may include purchases of some or all the purchase candidates.

Compelling Evidence in favor of the new Shepherd

Peter Bossaerts at Caltech tried to validate the Capital Asset Pricing Model using MBA students at Stanford and Yale as traders. The environment met all the CAPM assumptions: All participants had the same time horizon and the same knowledge of the securities. The market contained a riskless security and two securities whose return distributions were known. All the available assets were tradable and held by the investors, and so on.[lxxx] The students' initial portfolios were all different, thus creating a need for trades to rebalance their portfolios. In our language, all the students were sheep. Based on the CAPM theory Bossaerts expected the students to trade their portfolios to attain the highest Sharpe ratio, set to be that of the capitalization weighted market. He assumed the students would drive their portfolios to the zero line, as shown in Figure 1.

The students traded in continuous market mechanisms like those used by the NYSE, NASDAQ, and London's SETS. When there were very many traders, more than 60 traders for the two securities, the asset markets equilibrated as predicted by the CAPM theory. However, even with as many as 40 traders, the results were far from the line. Indeed, the students, who were well versed in finance, left potentially profitable arbitrage opportunities on the table because, when trading one security for another, they could not be certain of filling the second part of the trade at an advantageous price. The result of only partially completing the trade might leave their portfolios further from equilibrium than their current position. The result was that portfolios failed to reach the zero line as in panel 1 of Figure 1: "Conventional vs. Combined Value Trading".

Realizing that the risk of not completing the legs of swaps was creating inefficiencies when standard markets were used, Bossaerts, Fine, and Ledyard[lxxxi] ran exactly the same experiment with the same securities but now using conditional orders in a call market format (operands **AND** and **OR**). In these situations relatively few traders (only 12 - read thin markets), were able to drive their portfolios to equilibrium very quickly. See panel 2 of Figure 1. Call markets allow conditional orders to make the best of existing liquidity and are ideal for thin markets. We note that because of their size, institutions habitually face thin markets.

Transitioning to a Better Market Structure

It seems clear to us that if we are in earnest about establishing and using appropriate market structures, we will transition to a trading infrastructure that allows investors to trade in non-price discriminatory call markets that support conditional orders.

Why the Transition has not happened

1. Everybody on all sides of this game is deeply familiar with the mechanics of the existing system and has a vested interest in maintaining their skills therein. There is a cost of changing which must be more than covered by the benefits of changing.

2. If all the sheep knew that there was a better shepherd just over the next hill (the effort to get over the hill representing the cost just mentioned), but that the new shepherd had no flock at present, then the Sheep would stay put until enough other sheep had already jumped shepherds; this is especially true for the large sheep. While a combinatoric call market makes the best of what liquidity it has, there is still some critical number of traders needed before it can perform as well as a continuous market that has many more traders.

3. Until the era of "negotiated rates" the *Sell side* was interested in agency trades and the corresponding flow of commission revenues. Now that competition has cut the commission rates per share by some 90% the *Sell side* concentrates on investment banking, proprietary trading (wolves) and cost cutting[lxxxii].

    In restructuring their operations the *Sell side* invested in infrastructure that allows institutional investors to service themselves: - direct electronic access to the markets including sophisticated algorithms to parse orders to the market over the trading day. They will resist developing another system that needs none of this infrastructure, is inimical to their role as wolves and will cannibalize their current order flow.

    This is the sunk cost argument and, while sunk costs are indeed sunk, it will clearly hinder introduction of combinatoric call markets. However there is more to it: individual *Sell side* firms will have little with which to differentiate themselves if such markets are embraced by the *Buy side*. There will be no need for *Sell side* trading expertise, order flow will not be divulged to them and the *Buy side* may settle directly through their custodians as opposed to using the broker as the middleman.

Why the Transition will Happen

1. The technology and mathematical algorithms are available now. These are relatively cheap to implement and operate compared to the computing power, infrastructure and personnel costs required to keep a continuous market up and running.

2. The *Sell side* will experience even lower marginal costs than under their current self-service, do-it-yourself, offerings because the new self-service regime would apply to even 'difficult' orders that institutions still funnel through the *Sell side* trading desks.

3. The *Buy side* will enjoy better throughput in terms of executed orders. To manage the immense accumulation of institutional assets now held by many money managers they must solve the bottleneck in trading. If the *Sell side* will not service its clients by exploiting existing and relevant technology, then the *Buy side* can form a cooperative or pressure its custodian banks to provide the service. After all, such markets boast low fixed costs and insignificant marginal costs. The only barrier to entry seems to be getting critical mass, which the cooperative model, if honored, would solve[lxxxiii].

Forecast:

Our forecast is that if and when such an infrastructure is available, institutions will trade primarily in such call markets. These markets will be called no more than twice daily; - the open and close[lxxxiv]. Continuous electronic markets will be there to service the retail investor who may, to avoid uncertainty, need an immediate execution. Liquidity providing limit orders in the continuous markets will be submitted by speculators and dealers trying to profit by accepting the risk of moving orders from the continuous market to a subsequent call market. Institutions might want to be liquidity providers to continuous markets, but to make it worth their while, and move meaningful quantities of stock against the retail flow; they would likely tip their hand to astute observers.

The Gestalts of Open Outcry and Electronic Trading

By John Lothian, John J. Lothian & Company, Inc.

The difference between open outcry trading and electronic trading is not just the means by which the trades are physically transacted, but it is also the difference of two cultures, their values and goals. One of those cultures is the presumed eventual winner in this ongoing struggle, but yet I believe the values and goals of the other are worth saving and seeing preserved in some manner.

Each culture in a sense has it own particular gestalt, or image and sense of the market as a whole and how that is perceived. And therein lies the conflict, one gestalt battling with the other.

Open outcry markets have more sensory input than electronic markets for those actually executing the trades. The trader in the pit, or even standing outside the pit at a trading desk, is constantly exposed to a variety of stimuli that the electronic trader does not receive. Thus, for the open outcry trader, the trading pit becomes a living, breathing organism with sights, sounds, smells, and rhythm.

There are also sights, sounds and a rhythm to electronic trading, but they are different than those of open outcry trading. The dinging of a bell on a PC to report an electronic fill does not replace the adrenaline rush of shouting sold across a crowded and rowdy trading pit. The physical activity of trading in a pit and the endurance necessary relative to electronic trading are enough to release entirely different chemical and hormonal reactions in the human body. It could be argued that the physical activity of trading in a pit is a good way to release the inherent stress of trading. And it is no coincidence that former athletes or those athletically inclined are among those attracted to life in the trading pits.

There is a very important social component of life in the pits that is a piece of the open outcry gestalt. The solitude of electronic trading can be a negative factor for some electronic traders just like the organized chaos of the trading pit can overwhelm some pit traders. It is not a surprise then that one form of electronic trading is the trading arcade. Why travel to the city to sit in front of a bank of computers when you could have the same set up and connectivity in your den? One reason is because of the important social element of trading.

Many electronic traders seek the virtual companionship of other traders in Internet chat rooms, trading related forums and discussion lists. Like the traders in the pit, the electronic trader is seeking insight into the thoughts and actions of other traders by staking out such mediums. But they are also seeking the comfort of a community of people interested in like subjects. The social needs of traders are a significant factor in both gestalts, though they take different forms.

There is even a sexual sub-component of the social element of open outcry and electronic trading. It is not a coincidence that male traders will hire beautiful girls and women to work for them on the trading floor. The desire to surround one self with attractive members of the opposite sex is a basic human drive. The trading floor is no different and in the macho world of the pits some traders will compete with each other for who can hire the most attractive clerks.

One time at a previous firm I worked for we had a very attractive young woman working as a trading floor runner for us. She was cute, smart and had an attractive disposition and presence, but very little market experience. After about 2 months with us she was hired away by some traders from the CBOT financial floor. It should be obvious, but these traders were guys. They asked her how much she made and she said $500. The trader who hired her said they would pay her $550 a week and try to get her a raise in a couple weeks. The $500 she mentioned was her bi-weekly check amount, not weekly pay rate. Thus, she more than doubled her pay in that move. She lasted 3 months. I believe she fell prey to this one-upmanship of who has the hottest trading floor babes working for them.

On the other hand, the environment of electronic trading leaves the solitary trader or community of traders with a world of sexual images at their fingertips. This can lead some to various levels of harmless voyeurism or outright debauchery as traders fill idle market time by surfing the World Wide Web for images or video to fulfill their perceived needs.

There is an important visual component to open outcry trading that is masked by the digital anonymity of electronic trading. Where else but in the trading pits, rings and stations can you see all your direct competition face to face? Where else can you see what they are doing? Where else can you monitor with whom they are trading?

This multilateral transparency is a critical factor to the fairness and integrity of the markets. This multi-faceted market transparency is important for many pit traders and how they look at the markets. All the traders can potentially see the price and volume of the trade being made in the pit. There is a level of market transparency in open outcry trading that is just not reproduced in electronic trading (at this time). However, the electronic trader has a greater view of the number of bids and offers below and above the market, though the electronic trader does not know who is bidding or offering.

And those who hold to the gestalt of electronic trading, they value the anonymity of electronic trading. They value being able to move into and out of the markets without any of their competitors knowing who is doing the trading. Ultimately some of this information comes out in the trade clearing, but that is post trade information to be retrieved, organized and analyzed. This is not real time trade information like in the open outcry-trading pit.

The information flow from the trading floor to the outside world is important in the decision making of many traders. Today we have television market reporters giving us market commentary with the buzz of the market in the background. These TV, radio and wire service reporters have direct face-to-face contact with many of their sources by visiting them on the trading floor. With electronic trading the anonymity of the trade makes it more difficult to track down the players and their potential motivations.

While some market commentary from the floor may be more filling time or space rather than actual reporting, the very realization of the irrelevancy and/or repetitiveness of the market commentary itself becomes a market factor. It may be the electronic trader who has greater access to this news media stimulus, but without the open outcry environment being present the information would not be the same.

The open outcry traders can hear the cadence and emotion of the other trader's voices, as well as the prices and amounts being bid and offered. The electronic trader can see the depth of the market, volume of the trade and the speed of the trading, but hears nothing but the pings and rings of the computer settings. This aural sensation gives many traders a feel for the market. It is important to how they trade the market. It is important to their gestalt.

In the trading pit you can see the other guy sweat. You can see the stress that the market movement and their market position are putting on them. You can see the panic when the 10-lot trader starts frantically trading larger size. You can smell the fear.

The electronic trader does not have this benefit. To the open outcry trader, the market has a human face. To the electronic trader the imagery of the market is different. It is more computer oriented.

The open outcry trader values the honor and integrity of the other traders in the trading pit. The electronic trader worries about the reliability of their hardware, connectivity and software. When the reliability of a pit trader comes in question, the open outcry trader trades with someone else and avoids trading with the questionable party. When electronic trading platforms perform questionably, the electronic trader switches to another system, line or computer if possible.

The open outcry trader values the integrity of the markets inherent in a multilateral transparent environment. The transparency the electronic trader appreciates is more narrowly focused.

The open outcry trader values finding one trading counter-party to trade with to increase speed, diminish market impact, reduce recording keeping time and eliminate potential out-trades. The electronic trader does not need a single counter-party to get off a size trade. The size of the cumulative bid(s) or offer(s) is all the electronic trader seeks. The electronic trader can hit multiple and numerous traders in a single mouse click or keystroke. The open outcry trader must complete a trade with one fellow trader at a time, thus giving other traders in the pit the opportunity to drop their bids or offers. The open outcry trader may also find their completing a trade has brought on competing bids or offers joining theirs.

In the open outcry pit traders can sometimes tell what type of buying and selling is coming into the market by which brokers are filling the orders. Is it a broker who fills orders for large commercial interests, or commodity funds? Or is it a broker who handles the small lot retail trade? Is it a broker filling a spread bidding up a certain month? The electronic trader does not receive this qualitative market information because there is no filling broker.

In paper order driven markets, as opposed to markets where orders are flashed in with hand signals or delivered to an electronic terminal in the pit, sometimes there are buy and sell brokers. One broker handles the buys and sell stops and the other broker handles the sells and buy stops. It does not take a rocket scientist to figure out the market is going to go up when the open outcry traders see a stack of order bearing runners trying to get into the buy broker. The electronic trader has no way of seeing equivalent directional market interest.

The open outcry trader will join the bid and lean on a large order identified as resting in the pit. If the open outcry trader sees the large order being filled they can quickly hit the big order to scratch any trades they have taken on while leaning on an order. The electronic trader trading a first in first out matching engine scheme can see the size of the bid and other offer, but goes to the back of the queue in a First in First Out matching algorithm if they seek to join the bid or offer. Thus, the utility of a very popular open outcry trading technique is essentially nullified in a FIFO electronic trading world.

The electronic trader values the surety of trading on an electronic matching engine. The open outcry trader comes in the next morning after trading the previous day to check for out-trades.

For the open outcry trader hugely volatile and chaotic markets create tremendous profit opportunities, but also increased out-trade risk. For the electronic trader, hugely volatile and chaotic markets could mean trades are busted or negated by the exchange, leaving the trader in an exposed and uncertain market position.

As you can see from my comparisons there are inherent differences between open outcry trading and electronic trading. This leads to the different gestalts I spoke of. The traders in each of these camps simply look at the market differently. They hold different values. They have different experiences from which they construct their view of the market.

The above comparisons include many generalities and is not meant to be a comprehensive essay on the differences between the two types of trading and cultures. Certainly there are those who can move freely from open outcry to electronic trading and back, seemingly unaffected by the differences in culture. Certainly there are analytical pit traders who care nothing about the stimulus of the trading floor in their decision making, but are still exposed to it. And certainly there are those talented computer savvy electronic traders who can create excessive amounts of market related stimulus of sound and sight, enough to make the head of an experienced pit trader spin.

The growth in electronic trading over the last few years certainly indicates that the culture of electronic trading is finding more and more recruits. Some are coming from the memberships of the open outcry exchanges and many more are coming from an increasingly wired world. And more will come from the outside as the numerical constraints of exchange membership and are replaced by open memberships of the new electronic exchanges. In the world of electronic trading it does no matter who you are, as long as you have a clearing firm guaranteeing your trade and you pass their due diligence checks.

In the world of open outcry trading, it does matter who you are. It matters who you trade for. It matters that you trust the other traders and they trust you. It matters that everyone else can see what you are trading, should they choose to watch. And it matters that the open outcry market is self-policing.

The automation of electronic trading makes many of those functions obsolete and improves the efficiency of the order flow dramatically.

I confess I believe it is only a matter of time for electronic trading to overwhelm open outcry trading. But if it does that without bringing along some of the values of open outcry trading like increased market transparency and integrity of the transactions, then we may not be as better off as we could have been. And as for the physical element, I am designing a stationary bicycle electronic trading station that generates its own electricity for the computers.

From the Pits to the Screens:
The Migration of U.S. Commodity Trading from Open Outcry to Electronic Platforms – An Introductory Description and Analysis

*By Jay Gottlieb, Commodities and Energy Economist &
Hua Zhu, Applied Financial Mathematics, University of Connecticut*

The Change

For well over a hundred years, commodity trading in the United States has been the most exciting, physical financial activity the world has ever experienced. The most active markets opened, closed and moved with the roar of hundreds of traders and their clerks and runners. More essential than the drama and adrenaline rushes, open outcry provided unparalleled liquidity and market efficiency. Also, with one slow sweep of the head, any one on the trading floor could consider an amazing array of information from the flow of orders from brokerage desks to the price movements in the pits and up to the price boards displaying all commodity and financial market activities. Two dimensional screens cannot replace that depth of information.

In the last five years, the roars have been hushed. The long heralded and feared usurpation of open outcry by electronic trading has arrived. While electronic trading platforms were initially developed to meet the need for overnight trading when the pits were closed, all the exchanges have moved to place electronic trading side by side with open outcry. The results have been conclusive, open outcry is all but finished and the screen dominates.

This chapter provides the first comparative snapshot of the pace of migration from the pits to the screens at the major exchanges, CME, CBOT and NYMEX.[lxxxv] Only future developments will show whether relegation of open outcry to at best a minor role in commodity trading is a loss only to those who made their living in the pits, or whether aspects of market liquidity and efficiency, especially in times of market crisis and liquidity crunches, as a whole have been damaged. We also list some of the questions that future developments will answer as to whether moving from the pits has been an unqualified positive for users of commodity markets.

How Quickly

Recent changes were the most rapid and dramatic. They occurred in the energy and metals markets at NYMEX and COMEX, which became fully open for trading on the CME's Globex platform on September 5, 2006.

Gold trading at COMEX instantaneously left the floor and went electronic on the first day of side by side trading, December 4, 2006 (see Chart 1). This was due in large part to the stiff competition from the electronic gold trading contracts at CBOT.

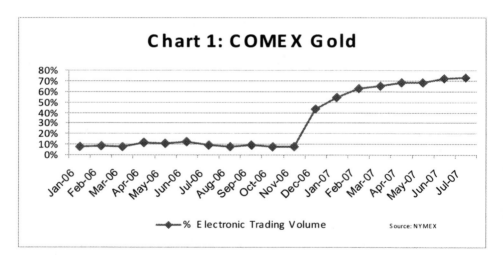

Petroleum trading, facing competition from the ICE, also moved rapidly as shown in the following charts. When full side by side trading started in the NYMEX petroleum complex on September 5, 2006, electronic trading quickly moved from 34% to over 50% in 2 months and was up to 71% by end of July 2007.

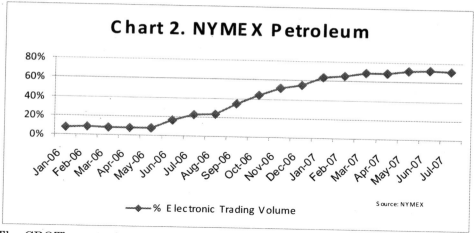

The CBOT's agricultural complex moved over a longer period from the launch of side by side trading on August 1, 2006. It took 10 months to go from 5 percent to over 50 percent.

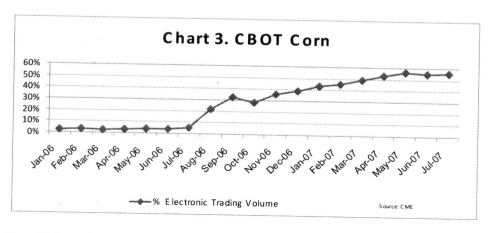

The CBOT's financial complex moved even more slowly. This process began on August 28, 2001. Unfortunately, neither the CBOT nor the CME could provide data with the breakdown between open outcry and side-by-side electronic trading prior to January 2004.

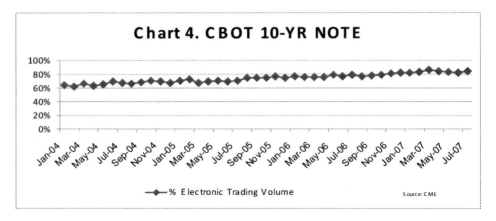

The following chart illustrates an example of migration from open-outcry to electronic trading platform in CME, also limited by the unavailability of relevant data prior to January 2004.

Currency Future:

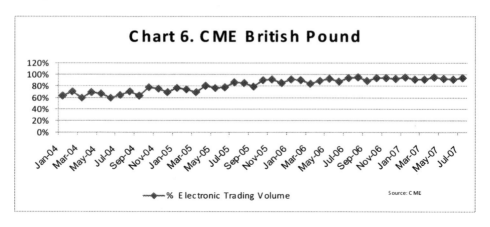

How well will the markets be served in the future?

These are the open questions going forward. Certainly the transaction costs for market participation have gone down as the legions of floor traders and their staffs no longer make a living. However, it still remains to be seen how much liquidity, flexibility and market depth will be lost in times of crisis. I submit that it is possible that there will be times when open outcry is missed for its essential market functions. Clearly, the excitement of the pits is missed by all.

Organizational Change and Transformation in Fixed Income Trading[lxxxvi]

By Janet Rovenpor, Manhattan College and David Bauman, Integrated Wealth Services, LLC, A Rockefeller Company

The purpose of this chapter is to provide the reader with an overview of different management approaches to planned organizational change and a description of the types of transformations that are occurring within fixed income trading groups of financial service companies, to a great extent because of the growth of electronic trading. In the chapter, we will provide some definitions and discuss several attributes of planned organizational change; describe three popular methods used by companies to implement change, Business Process Reengineering (BPR), Total Quality Management (TQM) and the development of learning organizations; and relate the experiences of a company that has successfully implemented a technological change which streamlined its fixed income portfolio management and trading workflow, in the process moving it closer to true straight through processin. The chapter is divided into the following main sections:

1. Planned Organizational Change and Transformation: Basic Concepts
2. Three Popular Approaches to Planned Organizational Change
3. Transformation in the Fixed Income Securities Market
4. Technology Initiatives in the Fixed Income Securities Market
5. Organizational Change at Ridge Capital LP
6. Benefits of Ridge's New Fixed Income Portfolio Management System
7. Lessons Learned from the Experiences at Ridge LP
8. Future Technological Challenges for Fixed Income Trading Groups
9. Summary

Planned Organizational Change and Transformation: Basic Concepts

In its most rudimentary form, planned organizational change involves a conscious and deliberate effort made by a firm's top management to take the firm, or its subunit, from its current state at time one to a new, improved state at time two. According to Kanter, Stein and Jick (1992, p. 375), organizational change typically involves a three-part process that "takes the flawed organization, moves it through an arduous transition stage, and deposits it at the end in the enriched, desired stage." In the first step, members of the organization wake up to a new reality, realizing that they must disengage from the past because the future requires new ways of operating. Current standard operating procedures are no longer appropriate. In the second step, organizational members create and embrace a new vision of the future and establish mechanisms for achieving that vision. A new strategic plan, a modified organizational structure, and better employee motivational techniques are designed to make sure the vision is both reachable and sustainable. In the third step, new attitudes, practices, and policies are put into place and are solidified.

The impetus for change can come from either external or internal forces. External forces include government legislation, threat of a takeover, a lawsuit, an economic recession, a shortage of raw materials, labor market fluctuations, or moves made by competitors. Internal forces include the death of a CEO, low employee morale, inefficiencies, a breach of ethics, or simply a feeling of uneasiness among a company's key executives. Many companies strive to remake themselves even though they are enjoying current levels of success. Managers are encouraged to create a "mini crisis" in order to stimulate proactive thinking and to ward off a sense of complacency.

Planned organizational change is accomplished through a series of transformational events and activities that are directed at the firm when it is in its initial state (e.g., hiring a new CEO, implementing a new technology, revising a firm's mission). It is the accumulation of these events and activities that lead to the change we witness at the end. The transformation process can occur in either a revolutionary fashion or in an incremental one. Revolutionary change forces a firm to adopt a radically new approach to how the company operates and how it achieves its goals. It takes place suddenly and requires that the organization completely break away from its past. Incremental change comes in the form of small, continual improvements that build over time. It requires relatively minor adjustments or shifts as the firm attempts to better align its strategy, structure, culture and processes. Three popular approaches to planned organizational change will be reviewed in the next section.

Three Popular Approaches to Planned Organizational Change

Dervitsiotis (1998) identified three of the most popular sets of techniques for implementing wide-scale organizational change. These are: Total Quality Management (TQM), Business Process Reengineering (BPR) and the development of learning organizations. TQM had its origins more than 50 years ago in a series of lectures on product quality given by W. Edwards

Deming and Joseph M. Juran. Although there are many definitions of TQM, one definition that is acceptable to many and was endorsed by the CEOs of nine major corporations, deans and professors of well-known universities and reputable consultants, appears in Bounds, Dobbins and Fowler (1995, p. 63). It reads as follows:

> Total Quality (TQ) is a people-focused management system that aims at continual increase in customer satisfaction at continually lower cost. TQ is a total system approach (not a separate area or program) and an integral part of high-level strategy. It works horizontally across functions and departments, involving all employees, top to bottom, and extends backwards and forwards to include the supply chain and the customer chain. TQ stresses learning and adaptation to continual changes as keys to organizational success.

> The foundation of Total Quality is the scientific method. TQ includes systems, methods, and tools. The systems permit change; the philosophy stays the same. TQ is anchored in values and the power of community action. This definition of "Total Quality" suggests that customer satisfaction -- even customer delight -- is a useful definition of "quality."

TQM, therefore, is a management philosophy for the entire organization, requiring that employees fulfill two roles: they are responsible for performing every day tasks and activities as defined by their formal job descriptions and are expected to step aside and reflect on ways to improve what they are doing, the process by which they are doing it, and the nature of their relations with other coworkers. Total customer satisfaction is an overarching goal but the firm should also focus on costs, delivery times, product development cycles, business processes, and changes in the market place. Companies must strive for continuous improvements in quality. They should make use of: (a) the seven tools of quality (e.g., Pareto charts and scatterplots), (b) the seven management tools (e.g., affinity diagrams, tree diagrams and matrix diagrams), and (c) the seven product planning tools (e.g., group interviews and questionnaire surveys). To be successful, TQM projects must have the support and commitment of a firm's top managers.

Business Process Reengineering (BPR) is a technique that was first popularized by Michael Hammer in a 1990 *Harvard Business Review* article entitled, "Reengineering Work: Don't Automate, Obliterate." BPR encourages executives to adopt a new set of principles regarding how businesses should be organized and managed. Work should be organized according to "processes," not according to "functions" or "tasks." Processes, defined as sequences and combinations of activities that deliver value to a customer, cut across hierarchy. Inefficiencies result when work is handed from one specialist to the next, from one department to the next. It becomes necessary, therefore, to eliminate barriers, delays and obstacles encountered as work makes its way through the organization.

A company is advised to start its reengineering efforts with a blank sheet. It should then identify a number of core business processes -- e.g., product development, order fulfillment, sales generation -- that are crucial to success. Next, qualified employees are pulled from their functional departments and put into case teams with one team responsible for an entire process. Measures by which performance is evaluated are created; compensation systems are modified to reward teams based on their abilities to create value for the customer. Finally, employee values and beliefs are shaped to be consistent with the new requirements of "speed," "quality," and "accuracy."

There are several characteristics that typify reengineered processes. As a result of BPR (Hammer & Champy, 1993):

- Several jobs, that were formerly considered distinct, are combined into one;
- Workers make decisions by themselves and do not have to ask their superiors for solutions to problems;
- Many steps in a process that were once performed in a linear sequence can now be completed simultaneously;
- Multiple versions of processes are created so that special, complex or large orders are handled separately from simple, routine and small orders;
- Work is performed where it makes the most sense via outsourcing certain functions or allowing functional managers to bypass formal authority to get what they need;
- Checks and controls are conducted periodically when needed and not as every single activity is completed;
- The need to reconcile purchase orders and invoices or incoming goods and outgoing goods, is reduced because there are fewer hand-offs;
- Customer service representatives have all the information they need at their fingertips to handle customer requests, orders, or complaints; and
- Information technology enables the home office to define acceptable parameters that allows it to remain competitive (e.g., the lowest price, the fastest delivery time) while giving the field representative greater autonomy to complete the sale by himself, without calling in for a quote or waiting for approval.

The phrase, the "learning organization," was coined during the 1980's. It refers to the recognition by an increasing number of managers at such companies as Xerox, 3M and British Airways, that in order to bring rapid and dramatic change to their organizations, they needed to continually enhance and utilize the skills and aptitudes of their employees. In today's turbulent environment, the only sustainable competitive advantage is being able to learn more quickly than one's industry rivals. A major proponent of the concept of learning organizations and its application to the business world is Peter Senge from Massachusetts Institute of Technology. According to Senge (1990, p. 3), learning organizations are organizations where "people continually expand their capacity to create the results they truly desire, where new and expansive patterns of thinking are nurtured, where collective aspiration is set free, and where people are continually learning how to learn together." Senge believes that today's organizations are a reflection of how we think and how we interact with one another. Only by changing how we think, can we change the policies and practices which are so deeply embedded in our organizations. Changing patterns of thinking and interacting, however, is difficult, disorienting and frightening. It can only occur within a community of learners.

Senge suggests that there are five components, or "disciplines" that are required to transform organizations into learning organizations:

(1) Systems thinking: Organizations are systems with interrelated parts. A change made to one part of the system can have unanticipated repercussions on the other parts. If, for example, a company adopts a flatter organizational structure, the change will have implications for work methods, communication patterns and decision making procedures. More work will be done is teams; horizontal communication will replace vertical communication; a greater number of employees will be involved in decision making. Systems thinking helps managers view their organization as a whole. They must identify those parts of the system that can be easily changed to bring about maximum change to the other parts of the system for the ultimate benefit of the entire enterprise.

(2) Personal mastery: Employees should be encouraged to continually clarify and deepen their personal vision, focus their energies, develop patience and see reality objectively. Individuals with a high level of personal mastery are able to consistently realize the results that matter most deeply to them. Personal mastery means being able to focus on what one truly wants, on one's intrinsic desires.

(3) Mental models: Individuals must uncover, analyze and discuss their most deeply ingrained assumptions, generalizations, or images of the world. These become the source for all subsequent actions. Mental models are simplifications of reality and become dangerous when we are unaware of them and when the world changes but are models do not. In the 1970's, U. S. automobile manufacturers lost their competitive edge to the Japanese because they neglected quality and reliability. They operated on the outdated

assumption that cars were status symbols and that consumers only cared about styling.

(4) Building a shared vision: Managers should work with employees to build a shared vision. Companies cannot be successful without goals, values, and a sense of the future. The leader must be able to translate his/her personal vision into a shared one. When people truly share a vision they are connected and bound together by a common aspiration. They feel a sense of commitment to the vision which, in turn, helps them focus and direct their energies. In many organizations, however, individuals merely comply with a vision imposed on them by top management.

(5) Team building: Teams, not individuals, are the fundamental unit in most organizations. Companies can benefit tremendously when teams learn how to tap the potential of many minds which can be more intelligent than one mind, when teams develop innovative ideas which are implemented through coordinated action and when the practices and skills of a successful team effort are shared more widely with other teams in the organization. For this to happen, teams must recognize early on what the barriers to learning in teams are (e.g., pressures operating on individuals to conform to group norms). They must engage in a true dialogue, which includes both talking and listening, so that complex ideas can be explored freely and creatively.

What can managers of fixed income trading groups learn from the three approaches to change? Each approach has its advantages and disadvantages. TQM, for example, has been criticized for being too complex to implement (Hermel, 1997) and for not caring enough about employees (Connor, 1997). According to Dervitsiotis (1998), TQM is less demanding intellectually compared to the development of learning organizations and, therefore, can be implemented in shorter time spans. Employees can more easily participate in group problem solving. TQM methods, such as cause-and-effect diagrams, seem to be most appropriate for plant or front-office operating problems.

The radical change advocated by BPR may be too traumatic for employees (Hemp, 1992) and may encourage managers to use information technology as a quick fix to the firm's problems (Coulson-Thomas, 1995). It may be most appropriate when an organization wants to achieve impressive results quickly in order to give employees a boost in morale. The effort should be followed up with a continuous improvement and culture change program so that the effects of BPR will be more long-lasting. When the need for change is not urgent, the learning organization approach is useful. It requires organizations to train employees and managers in the basic disciplines of systems thinking, personal mastery, mental models, building a shared vision and team learning. This takes time. Systems thinking and issues analysis are most helpful for an organization's strategic and global problems (Dervitsiotis, 1998).

A number of organizations have combined the best elements in each approach to change. Hermel (1997) reported that a European company, Lipha, developed a strategic plan which included a total quality program and a re-engineering program. Managers seem to be realizing that it is important to first reconstruct all management processes, figure out which ones need to be improved to increase value to customers, use information technology to automate routine procedures, and to focus on deliverables -- e.g., quality and customer satisfaction. Throughout, managers can use systems thinking, team learning, and vision shaping to help employees focus on worthy goals and to identify and solve problems related to work processes. Personal mastery will encourage individuals to think creatively about what they would really like to see happen in their work units. Finally, making implicit assumptions explicit and critically evaluating them will help the organization engage in the process of continuous improvement.

Transformation in the Fixed Income Securities Market

Over the years, the fixed income securities market has undergone a number of dramatic changes. First, there has been a proliferation of new, innovative products. These include mortgage-backed securities, asset-backed securities, high-yield or so-called "junk" bonds, and interest rate swaps. There has even been talk about a new life settlement-backed security, often referred to as a "death bond" (Goldstein, 2007). Americans, who may find that paying high premiums for their life insurance policies have become a financial burden, can sell their policies to investors. Investors continue to pay the premiums until the policy holders die; they then collect the payouts. Soon, Wall Street firms may buy life-insurance policies, put them in a pool, divide the pool into bonds and sell the bonds to pension funds, college endowments, and other professional investors (Goldstein, 2007). Bond markets have also become riskier as witnessed by the adverse impact that defaults on subprime mortgages have had on mortgage-backed securities, causing tremendous losses and the removal of heads of fixed income groups at financial institutions like Merrill Lynch and Bear Stearns. According to Peter Knez, head of fixed income at Barclays Global Investors, "Fixed-income markets are starting to look more like equities with the use of shorting, leveraging, and also higher fees. The momentum is even greater than we anticipated" (quoted in Brewster, 2007, p. 21).

Second, bond markets are greatly affected by the recent volatility in interest rates. When interest rates rise, bond prices fall and yields rise. Investors end up with a bond they bought for $1,000 with a yield of 5% while a newly issued bond might sell for $500 with a yield of 10%. High interest rates encourage investors to put their money in bank savings accounts instead of bonds.

Certain types of bonds are more sensitive to changes in interest rates than others.

Third, new opportunities have opened up in financial markets overseas. In Europe, for example, the introduction of a single currency in 1999 created a large, attractive capital market in which multinational corporations could raise funds by issuing bonds. With the help of JP Morgan, Deutsche Bank, USB and others, AT&T, for example, took advantage of favorable market conditions to issue dual tranche bonds in the euro and sterling markets -- all in one eventful day on March 9, 2007. In the past six years, international capital markets have doubled in size in terms of bond issuance (Oakley & Tett, 2007).

Fourth, the internet has made it possible for individual investors to buy bonds on their own with no need to contact a broker. Charles Schwab clients, for example, can buy newly issued Treasuries online for free; they can buy corporate bonds, municipal bonds and government-issued bonds online for a flat fee of $1 per bond (Kim, 2007). Clients are given the tools to build a diversified portfolio of bonds with different investment grades, maturities and yields ("Fixed Income Investors," 2006). Schwab's BondSource matrix allows investors to see all types of fixed income products on a single page (see http://www.schwab.com/bondsource_preview). According to Kim, "Better technology is helping to lower the bar to buying bonds. In the past, buying most bonds typically required contacting a broker, who would have to first check his own firm's inventory to find a bond, then with other dealers elsewhere. Now, many firms are using electronic platforms that consolidate prices from various dealers' inventories" (Kim, 2007).

All these changes have made the job of the fixed income portfolio manager more complex. According to Bill Gross, CEO of Pacific Investment Management Company (as quoted in Mintz, Dakin & Willison, 1998, p. 144), "A top-notch bond manager must now be one-third economist, who knows -- or thinks he or she knows -- when interest rates are going up or down; one-third mathematician, because bonds are mathematical creatures; and one-third horse trader, because there is a buyer and a seller in every transaction, and there are always people at the other end of the telephone line who want to take your money." Now, the manager must be computer literate as well. New information technologies, especially electronic trading platforms, data management and risk analysis software, and the automation of back-office functions can greatly improve the quality of advice given to clients and the accuracy and speed with which transactions are completed. Tools are available to provide on-line order entry, trade execution, display of firm bids and offers, automated and anonymous matching, and fixed income data. In this chapter, we will focus on the trend towards greater automation and electronic trading. We will review some of the systems that are currently available to make the job of portfolio managers and traders easier.

Technology Initiatives in the Fixed Income Securities Market

Most bond trading, which is done in the over-the-counter (OTC) market, is still conducted the old fashioned way. In the US, there are approximately 4 million bond issues compared to 10,000 stocks available for buying and selling (Braham, 2006). The OTC market consists of thousands of brokers/dealers dispersed throughout the country who use the telephone to negotiate buy/sell orders. When a client calls a brokerage firm with an order, the broker/dealer can handle the request if the firm makes a market in that security. If the firm does not have the security in its inventory, the broker/dealer has two choices: he/she can short the security by selling it now and buying it later or he/she can contact another firm that is a market maker in that security and complete the trade on behalf of the client. Successful trading often boils down to who you know, how good your sources of information are and how quickly you can close the deal. As Zipf (1997, p. 143) remarked, "for all bond traders ...the best source of information consists of their contacts in the business. Who among other firms' traders has a certain type of bond in inventory? Which of them owes a favor, and to whom? Who quoted a favorable price on a certain bond just this morning? Who is trying to sell off a weak issue? ...Information like this is so specialized and often so fleeting that not even a highly automated quotation system like NASDAQ can capture it."

Nonetheless, Sang Lee, a managing partner at the consulting firm, Aite Group LLC, estimates that more than 60% of bond trading will be done electronically by 2008, compared with 35% in 2004 and 2.6% in 1998 (Crawford, 2005). A breakdown by fixed-income asset type revealed that, in 2004, 68% of US treasuries were traded electronically, 30% of mortgage-backed securities were traded electronically and 9% of corporate bonds were traded electronically (Opiela, 2007).

Electronic trading platforms are important because they "act as an intermediary between asset managers and fixed income dealers. Instead of phoning dealers to try to find the best price on a bond, asset managers can send a one-off request to the platform and receive the best quotes back within 45 seconds. It can take a buy-side asset manager five minutes to collect the data from five or six dealers by phone. Some asset managers could try 300 to 400 transactions a day. Saving three minutes on each of these transactions adds up to 900 minutes" ("Trading Platforms," 2006, p.1). Simple trades get done quickly and efficiently enabling fixed-income portfolio managers and traders to spend more time on complex trades. David Vuchinich, a senior portfolio manager at ING, likes electronic trading because it allows him to handle a large number of small-lot trades in a short period of time freeing him up to work on large and more difficult orders (Crawford, 2005).

To take advantage of new technologies, managers of fixed-income groups have two important decisions to make. They must choose among the 70 or so different electronic bond-trading platforms that have been introduced into the market since 2001 and they must try to solve back office problems by building automated systems to provide straight through processing (STP). STP is defined by Tom Girard, a managing director at Weiss, Peck and Greer, as "the ability to trade on an electronic system, allocate the trade into an account and send the trade to the back office, which would link to the counter party's back office for settlement" (quoted in Schmerken, 2004, p. 34).

Unfortunately, there is no single electronic trading platform that enables traders to conduct transactions across all fixed-income asset types (Opiela, 2007). Firms, therefore, may need to subscribe to more than one service. According to the Securities Industry and Financial Markets Association (SIFMA) in its 2006 review of electronic transaction systems, there are 74 different platform vendors offering four different types of electronic execution venues (Decker, Davidson, Vieira, et al., 2006). There are:

- 26 inter-dealer platforms, referred to as B2B, which allow dealers to execute transactions electronically with other dealers (e.g., Automated Bond System, BondDesk Group and eSpeed, Inc.).
- 26 multiple dealer-to-customer platforms, referred to as B2C, which provide customers with consolidated orders from two or more dealers and with the ability to execute from among multiple quotes (e.g., Blackbird, BondVision, Eurex and MarketAxess). The customers are usually institutional investors but some platforms also cater to retail investors.
- 7 single dealer-to-customer platforms, also referred to as B2C, which allow investors to execute transactions directly with a specific dealer of choice, with the dealer acting as principal in each transaction (e.g., Autobahn, Bondpage.com, and LehmanLive). The customers are usually institutional investors but some platforms also cater to retail investors.
- 9 new issue platforms that support sales of new bond issues to either broker-dealers or institutional investors or both (e.g., Axon and Grant Street Group) [lxxxvii]
-

The market is still fragmented and there is overlap among fixed-income trading platforms. Tom Price, senior analyst in the Securities & Capital Markets practice at TowerGroup, hopes that the major players will work towards common communication protocols and standards in order to better leverage the efficiencies of electronic trading (Opiela, 2007).

For full benefits, electronic trading platforms should be linked STP systems. It has been said that the average portfolio manager has about three feet of research to go through every day (David Culbertson, vice president and general manager of First Call BondCall as quoted in Iyer, 1997, p. 9). It is well worth using an integrated system to not only access the data electronically but also to analyze them, perform simulations, complete trades, send transaction details automatically to the back office for clearance and settlement, and update client portfolio holdings. 18 trading platform vendors report that they provide users with electronic research delivery, 24 offer pre-trade analytics, and 34 enable direct access to trade clearance and settlement systems (Decker, Davidson, Vieira, et al., 2006). The following case study will demonstrate in greater detail how technological change can be successfully implemented in a fixed income securities trading firm.

Organizational Change at Ridge Capital LP [lxxxviii]

"There has to be a better way!" exclaimed Alex Fineman for the third time that afternoon. Alex is a fixed income portfolio manager with ten years experience who takes his job very seriously. For the past few months, Alex has worked for Ridge Capital LP, a moderately sized institutional investment advisory firm with an asset base of approximately $15 billion in fixed income securities. He knows he still has to prove himself. It was the first Tuesday of the month and in three more days the government would issue its unemployment report. This meant that Alex had to finish figuring out how to modify the portfolio holdings of the accounts for which he was responsible based on three possible scenarios that might unfold that coming Friday: unemployment rates were up, were down or stayed the same.

When Alex arrived at work at 8:30 a.m. that Tuesday morning, he had found dozens of computer printouts on his desk awaiting his attention. The printouts contained updated information on the accounts he managed. Every evening, at the close of business, Ridge's computer automatically generates reports with current information on the portfolio holdings in his clients' accounts based on that day's transactions and pricing information. The information is downloaded from the fixed income group's portfolio accounting system and includes new holdings, prices, costs, total market values, unrealized gains/losses, durations, yields, and so forth.

Alex's next step was to access the Microsoft Excel spreadsheet templates that he maintained on an ongoing basis. These templates provided basic client information such as account name, percentage of account that was allocated to fixed income investments, holdings, duration, yield and other analytical data. This information, of course, was historical in nature and did not include the account's most recent transactions and the current market values. This information was only to be found on last night's printouts. Alex was now in the middle of a tedious, manual process in which he had to manually enter information from the printouts on the new portfolio holdings of his accounts to the spreadsheets that were open on the screen of his personal computer. Only after he entered the necessary data into his spreadsheet, would he be able to generate his "what if" scenarios. These would help him determine which securities to buy or sell if Friday's unemployment figures were favorable, unfavorable or indifferent to bond market trading. He had about 5 more spreadsheets to update (each spreadsheet contains accounts with different scenarios which are to be managed in a similar way).

As Alex's frustration level mounted, he was reminded of an article he had read a few days ago when he was traveling on a homeward bound Metro North commuter train. The article, from *Wall Street and Technology*, reported that the Information Technology (IT) department of Summit Capital Management (a competitor of Ridge) had just received a $13 million budget from its managing partner and founder. The IT department planned to spend a portion of its budget on installing a LandMark equities trading system available from the Long View group, a firm that specialized in systems for the back office of buy-side firms. Benefits from LandMark were said to include the ability to create electronic tickets, reporting modules, and pre-trade compliance modules. It also had an electronic blotter and rebalancer, together which would enable portfolio managers to project "What if" scenarios and to automatically create orders which would adjust account holdings to a desired percentage.

Alex's group at Ridge needed something like that. Were there no similar systems for fixed income securities trading? Alex estimated that it would cost only a fraction of $13 million to design, test and install a more sophisticated fixed income electronic trading system at Ridge. He made a mental note to himself to speak to his boss about the possibilities at the next monthly meeting. For, now, however, he had to finish updating the information on his spreadsheets.

Alex Fineman eventually got support from Ridge's Vice President and Manager of Investment Systems to explore ways of developing an integrated fixed income portfolio management system that would enable bond managers to model, analyze, review and manipulate portfolio holdings and trade information, bond analytic data and client account restrictions and requirements. Not happy with "off-the-shelf" fixed income portfolio management systems available from vendors, Ridge decided to hire a financial technology consulting firm to custom design and develop a system that would both meet the needs of the group's portfolio managers and could be easily integrated into its current system. Alex was to assume a leading role in the development of the new system.

The New Fixed Income Portfolio Management System at Ridge

As we saw in the description of a typical work day for Alex Fineman, the original process of generating trades at Ridge was inefficient, error-prone, and paper and manually intensive. Typically, a portfolio manager would begin his work with a certain objective in mind. He might, for example, want to improve the quality of the securities in his accounts by swapping one bond for another or to extend the duration of some portfolios by buying securities with later maturities from the proceeds of securities that have matured. For purposes of illustration, let's assume that the portfolio manager would like to rebalance ten of his portfolios so that 4 percent of every account is made up of the City of Norwich municipal bonds.

The manager would group together accounts with the same investment objectives (e.g., to derive a low risk, steady income flow from tax exempt securities) by tapping into the group's client information data base. He would also learn whether or not there were restrictions to the accounts (some clients may not want to invest in securities being offered by tobacco companies). The manager would print out crucial information about these accounts, such as their current holdings and total market values. He would then access pricing information and analytics on the municipal bonds and enter the information into a Microsoft Excel spreadsheet. Data, including a security's cusip, rating/quality, sector, coupon rate, price, maturity date, duration, convexity and yield, were downloaded daily from CMS/BondEdge's bulletin board. The manager would run simulations to determine how much of the municipal bond to buy or sell for each account and what impact the trades would have on the portfolios. When he was satisfied with the results, he would use another system to send the orders to the trader.

The trader would print out copies of the orders from all the portfolio managers in the fixed income group and would get real-time prices for the bonds by logging onto Bloomberg, one of the most trusted sources for price data, historical information, and complex analytical functions in the industry. She would then call a few dealers on the telephone to try to get the best price possible for the bonds before the market changes. When the orders were finally executed, she would write a paper ticket and fax the tickets to the back office. Key punch operators would type the trades of the day into the portfolio accounting system.

Most fixed income portfolio managers at Ridge followed these procedures. There was, however, one exception. Andrew Stone, an old-timer at Ridge, had his own unique way of managing his portfolios. He liked to keep track of a select group of offerings that were made available by seven or eight big-name issuers, such as IBM. He would always manage his accounts towards these offerings. He saw no need for a new portfolio management system and had to be convinced of its benefits.

Ridge's new fixed income portfolio management system was designed, tested and installed within 9 months. It enables a portfolio manager to click an "account selection" function on his computer screen to automatically select accounts which have the same investment objectives. He can then add or delete accounts manually to and from the original grouping. He proceeds by opening a simulation screen and choosing, for example, the "security optimizer" option which will ensure that a certain percentage of a bond will be in each account. Other simulation techniques can be selected at this point. One simulation will show a manager how a portfolio might look if he/she were to buy, modify or sell a certain security and another will calculate the impact that a swap of one security for another will have on the portfolio's duration.

When selecting the "security optimizer" option the portfolio manager adds in the bond's cusip and the percentage he wants. Now he is able to run the simulation with another click of the mouse. A screen appears which shows what each account's current holdings are and how much of the bond he needs to buy/sell to meet his objectives. If the manager is happy with the way his portfolios look, he creates orders by clicking on an icon that reads "save as open orders." This sends an e-mail message to the trader. The trader looks into her "open orders" file and sees all the orders that have been forwarded to her by the various fixed income portfolio managers in the group. This allows her to consolidate orders on her screen so that she can execute orders for the same securities together at the same time, even though the orders were placed by different managers. The trader determines what the price is for the issue by accessing Bloomberg On-line and then follows up with several calls to dealers to find out how much of the issue is available and at what price. Checking issue prices with multiple sources is part of her fiduciary responsibility to her clients.

When the order is executed at a certain price, the trader enters the execution details into the new fixed income portfolio management system and clicks on a button to notify the back office. An accountant in the back office reviews the trade. Upon receipt of the official notification of the trade from the dealer, she compares details of the transaction with what was entered into the system to check for any discrepancies. Finally, the trade is typed manually into the portfolio accounting system. The next step, one that Ridge has not yet taken, would be to add in the capability to automatically route execution details to the portfolio accounting system. New transactions could be posted electronically to the clients' accounts and entered into their portfolio holdings.

Benefits of Ridge's New Fixed Income Portfolio Management System

The most tangible benefit attributed to Ridge's new portfolio management system was an increase in trade volume. The new system was fully operational in January, 1997. Average monthly fixed income trade volume increased 35% in the 12 month period between January, 1997 and December, 1998 compared to the 18 month period between July, 1996 and December, 1997. Because fixed income managers can now easily select groups of accounts to participate in trades, generate orders, analyze the impact of orders on their portfolios and electronically send orders to the trading desk, minimal time is spent on the administrative task of creating orders. In addition, smaller accounts can now participate in the same trading programs and receive similar attention as larger accounts. Accounts can be monitored more closely and re-balanced regularly. Fixed income managers can spend more time studying the market and reacting to macroeconomic and political events. A consultant who worked on subsequent enhancements to the Ridge system summarized the benefits as follows: "Sophisticated tools help when the bond manager has decided the market is going to move one way or the other. He can, with lightening speed, go in and figure out exactly what he wants to do to get his portfolios the way he wants them. He can fire the orders off and have it done as opposed to spending hours or maybe days figuring out what he wants to do with his accounts." Traders also benefited from the new system. They can now receive and execute orders without writing paper trade tickets and can notify the managers and operations staff electronically when a trade has been completed.

Lessons Learned from the Experiences at Ridge LP

The Ridge case provides some important lessons regarding how technological change can be successfully implemented in firms trading in fixed income securities. First, technological change can begin anywhere in the organization. Ideas for change can originate high up in the organization, when top managers develop strategic plans for their company's future or down in the trenches, with those individuals who are directly involved in carrying out financial transactions for a company's clients. At Ridge, the new portfolio management system was really the "brain child" of one aggressive manager who had a vision of how work processes could be improved. The key lies in identifying who these individuals are, encouraging their creativity, and supporting their initiatives. As Kirk Kramer, vice president of Mercer Management Consultants pointed out, "There is a critical 20% of an organization that drives 80% of change" (as cited in Murdoch, 1998). These change agents need to be empowered.

Second, small scale changes which address one system at a time and build upon a well understood technology can be more successful than large scale change that is overly ambitious, ahead of its time, and potentially disruptive to the organization. One should follow the advice provided by Geoffrey (1997): "Don't go where no IT group has gone before." In the Ridge case, managers of the fixed income group knew exactly what they wanted and the consulting firm was able to accommodate every request perfectly. Ridge's original request for proposal (RFP) was 49 pages long and included 23 exhibits. It spelled out everything from what types of reports the new fixed income portfolio management system must be able to generate, to which operating system and server should be used, to who would have ownership of the source code for the fixed income portfolio management system. One rarely sees such level of specificity in a client RFP. The outside consulting firm was able to establish an excellent working relationship with Ridge partly because it too operates on the belief that it is desirable, when appropriate, to utilize tools that are familiar to the client.

Third, it is important to create a "win win" situation for everyone and to maintain regular contact with the end users of the new system. Geoffey (1997, p. 86) believes that "keeping end users involved in the design, implementation, and testing of a new system is one of the best ways to guarantee project success. When end users are fully engaged, they feel more ownership for project success and will work more closely with IT to resolve glitches and problems. That can go a long way toward making certain that a project doesn't degenerate into finger pointing, name calling, and confusion."
As mentioned previously, it took some amount of persuading to get one of Ridge's fixed income portfolio managers, Andrew Stone, committed to the change. He was, to a degree, set in his ways and skeptical about new information technologies. His suspicions were only confirmed when a demonstration of the new system crashed before his eyes just as the consultant was trying to point out its benefits. Andrew was, however, happy in the end. The consultant accommodated Andrew's needs by adding functionality to one of the simulation screens in the new system. Andrew could now use the system to develop models based on issuers rather than issues and to type in an order directly without having to use the "What if" simulations. This enhancement had the added benefit of enabling other types of orders (e.g., for short-term securities, for verbal orders from a client to buy/sell a specific security, or for other securities that were hard to model) to be typed in and sent automatically to the trader. Thus, the system offered one point of entry for all types of trades.

Fourth, new change agents are needed to maintain the momentum for continued technological progress in a firm. It is nice when an IT project that was successful in one group can be rolled out to another group that is in need of more sophisticated systems. In the Ridge case, another new portfolio management system, one that could be modeled after the one developed for the fixed income group, could be designed rather easily for the firm's equities business. The company, however, was subsequently acquired by another buyside firm and such projects were probably temporarily put on hold.

Future Technological Challenges for Fixed Income Trading Groups
Transformation in fixed income markets is likely to continue. As Tom Price, senior analyst at TowerGroup, reports, "Some firms have remained hesitant to embrace electronification for fear of losing control over lucrative fixed-

income franchises and their 'high touch' approach to the market. Yet ultimately the benefits of automation are too potent to ignore, given that it provides for greater control of risk and facilitates best execution - two factors of paramount importance to regulators" (Price, 2007). More can always been done in terms of process improvements. The ideal would be, according to Joseph Rosen, President of RKA Inc., to provide an electronic auction system at the very beginning of the trading process when the issuer makes the decision to raise funds in the capital markets.[lxxxix] A municipality, for example, thinks of a new issue and approaches various underwriters by communicating with them electronically. Various bids are received and the municipality chooses an underwriter to underwrite the municipal security. The underwriter distributes it to its syndicate members. Perhaps the underwriter has an asset management arm and may buy some of the securities for its clients. The underwriter has access to an analytical system which helps its managers do their modeling. A trade ticket is generated electronically so that the trader can execute it. The trade then flows into clearance and settlement systems and into the custodian bank's ERISA account.

Dexter Senft, head of fixed-income e-commerce at Lehman Brothers was asked to predict which new advances in information technology would have the greatest impact on fixed income trading in the future (as interviewed by Kite, 2004, p. 22). He believes that: (a) breakthroughs in voice recognition and synthesis will enable traders to communicate with one another verbally so that software will even translate conversations being held between parties who speak different languages; (b) computing power will grow so that traders can analyze complex products and risk management scenarios; (c) errors and costs will be reduced because STP systems will have automated the post-trade process so that "the back offices of both buy-side and sell-side can be transformed from places that process the business to places that monitor the processing of business" (as quoted in Kite, 2004, p. 24).

Summary

This chapter has provided readers with an overview of three popular approaches to planned organizational change. It has discussed recent technological developments in fixed income markets and how various companies are responding to the new opportunities. Based on a case study, some of the key factors that can lead to successful organizational change were identified. The chapter ends with a discussion of some of the future challenges facing organizations in the fixed income sector of the financial services industry.

References

Bounds, G. M., Dobbins, G. H., & Fowler, O. S. (1995). *Management: A total quality perspective.* Cincinnati: South Western College Publishing.

Braham, Lewis (2006, November 13). Fixed income at your fingertips, *Business Week,* 124.

Brewster, D. (2007, April 2). New strategies shake up bond markets. *Financial Times,* 21.

Connor, P. E. (1997, Nov./Dec.). Total quality management: A selective commentary on its human dimensions with special reference to its downside. *Public Administration Review, 57* (6): 501-509.

Crawford, G. (2005, August 8). More managers using electronic trading platforms to make the most of advantages offered by systems. *Pensions & Investments, 33* (16): 11-12.

Coulson-Thomas, C. J. (1995). Re-engineering in practice. In *The Financial Times Handbook of Management.* (S. Crainer, editor). London: Pitman Publishing.

Dervitsiotis, K. N. (1998, February). The challenge of managing organizational change: Exploring the relationship of re-engineering, developing learning organizations and total quality management. *Total Quality Management, 9* (1): 109-120.

Decker, M., Davidson, S.C., Vieira, N., Coln, T., Gross, B., & Bateman, M. (2006, December). eCommerce in the Fixed-Income Markets. Securities Industry and Financial Markets Association, http://www.sifma.org/research/pdf/2006 eCommerceSurveyFinal120606.pdf

Fixed income investors get expanded trading hours, access to extensive inventory, more research and improved screening tools on Schwab.com, (2006, December 20), *PR Newswire.*

Geoffrey, J. (1997, November). IT fiascoes . . . and how to avoid them. *Datamation, 43* (11): 83-88.

Goldstein, M. (2007, July 30). Profiting from mortality; death bonds may be the most `macabre investment scheme ever devised by Wall Street, *Business Week,* issue 4044, 4.

Hammer, M. (1990, July-August). Reengineering work: Don't automate, obliterate. *Harvard Business Review, 90* (4): 104-112.

Hammer, M., & Champy, J. (1993). *Reengineering the corporation: A manifesto for business revolution.* NY: Harper Collins Publishers.

Hemp. P. (1992, June 30). Preaching the gospel. *The Boston Globe:* 35.

Hermel, P. (1997, August). The new faces of total quality in Europe and the U.S. *Total Quality Management, 8* (4): 131-143.

Iyer, S. (1997, March 13). First Call launches electronic research source on Internet for large fixed income investors. *Fixed Income Daily, II* (48): 1, 9.

Kanter, R. M.; Stein, B. A.; Jick, T. D. (1992). *The challenge of organizational change: How companies experience it and leaders guide it.* NY: The Free Press.

Kim, J. J. (2007, June 12). Brokers made bonds easier; more transparency helps lower bar for small investors, *Wall Street Journal,* p. D4.

Kite, S. (2004, February 2). When cometh the next era in fixed-income technology? *Securities Industry News,* 22, 24.

Mintz, S. L.; Dakin, D.; & Willison, T. (1998). *Beyond Wall Street: The Art of Investing.* NY: Wiley.

Murdoch, A. (1998, March). Human re-engineering. *Management Today,* 66-70.

Oakley, D., & Tett, G. (2007, January 15). Euro displaces dollar in bond markets. *FT.com,* 1.

Opiela, N. (2007, July-August). The electric slide. *CFA Magazine,* 58-59.

Price, T. (2007, May 2). 'Electronification' of fixed income drives new products and geographies, despite lack of standards and other challenges. Retrieved October 25, 2007, from the World Wide Web: http://www.towergroup.com/research/news/ news.htm?newsId=2500

Schmerken, I. (2004, January). Favorite few rule e-bond trading, *Wall Street &Technology,* p. 34.

Senge, P. M. (1990). *The fifth discipline: The art and practice of the learning organization.* NY: Doubleday.

Trading platforms -- How to get out of a FIX. (2006, September 13). *Mandate,* 1.

Zipf, R. (1997). *How the bond market works.* Second edition. NY: New York Institute of Finance.

The Nasdaq Stock Market:
Current State of Play and Plans for the Future

Frank Hatheway, The NASDAQ Stock Market

Since its founding in 1971, the Nasdaq Stock Market ("NASDAQ®") has always been a pioneer in the electronic trading of stocks. Its early history played out during a period when floor-based manual exchanges were the norm and commonly viewed as the superior model as the benefits of electronic trading were yet to be established. NASDAQ was designed as a market of many dealers, not a sole specialist, linked electronically to provide benefits from competition, transparency, flexibility, and efficiency.

As technology improved, however, so did NASDAQ's electronic marketplace and the superiority of its operating philosophy became more apparent. Globally, other national exchanges, including the London Stock Exchange and Paris Borse in 1986 and Frankfurt Borse in 1991, embraced electronic platforms for their primary market system. Eventually, by the time of the approval of the Security and Exchange Commission's ("SEC") Regulation NMS, the electronic market was formally endorsed as the superior model in the U.S. This article begins with the background of the current state of electronic trading in U.S. equities. It then describes three current NASDAQ initiatives intended to extend the role of electronic trading into new arenas.

Current Trading Landscape

The current competitive landscape of trading in U.S. cash equities has its origins in events announced during a three-month span in the spring of 2005. During the same remarkable week in April 2005, both the acquisition of the ArcaEx exchange by the NYSE and the acquisition of the INET ECN by NASDAQ were announced. This was followed in June by the SEC's approval of Regulation NMS. These events collectively established the predominance of the electronic market structure as the future of equity trading in the U.S., and triggered the abandonment of the traditional trading floor and opening a new round of competition among U.S. markets.

Trading of NASDAQ-listed Stocks

The world of trading NASDAQ-listed stocks has always been characterized by a single salient characteristic: competition. Originally, competition played out between market makers with the electronic market providing only an average quote in each security. A series of changes through the 1980s and 1990s added the inside quotes, real time last sale, automatic execution of small orders, and large numbers of additional stocks to the system as well as expanding NASDAQ style trading into exchange-listed securities. Also during this period the first viable electronic order book, Instinet, emerged as a major trading system. Collectively, these changes increased transparency in NASDAQ stocks and underscored the flexibility of electronic systems. Beginning with the Order Handling Rules of 1997, competition expanded into a new arena that of electronic order books, now termed ECNs. While NASDAQ always had provided a basic regulatory and trade reporting infrastructure, its trading systems (the quote montage, SOES and SelectNet) had been used to support systems provided by ECNs and market makers. In response to the new environment created in 1997, NASDAQ announced in 1999 plans to upgrade its trading system to compete directly with ECNs. After numerous delays, created mostly by regulators' competitive concerns, the new system was introduced in 2002, and colloquially called SuperMontage.

Also in 2002, a new dimension of competition emerged, as the largest ECNs left the NASD/NASDAQ regulatory ambit for other exchanges. Island became, technically, a specialist at the National Stock Exchange (formerly known as the Cincinnati Stock Exchange). Archipelago became a facility of the Pacific Exchange. Instinet quoted and traded outside of SuperMontage, on the NASD's Alternative Display Facility. BRUT quoted on SuperMontage, but reported its trades to the Boston Stock Exchange.

This fierce level of competition provided the catalyst for a remarkable period of product enhancements and fee reductions. Among the product enhancements was the creation of electronic trading algorithms, such as orders that would automatically track the national best bid and offer, or hold reserve size that would refresh the displayed quote with randomly selected size. These new algorithms initially sought to mimic the behavior of human traders but quickly provided complex logic that traditional traders could not match. A new pricing model also took hold, by which the posters of non-marketable orders received a rebate for an execution, rather than a charge. Creative ways were found to transfer Tape revenue received by NASDAQ and the exchanges to the users of the ECNs. The net effect of the dynamism created by the competitive environment arguably made the NASDAQ-listed world far more interesting, innovative, efficient, and customer focused than the NYSE-listed world.

The initial proliferation of ECNs in the late 1990s was followed by a period of consolidation. Examples of significant mergers include those between BRUT and Strike (2000) Archipelago and RediBook (2002), and Island and Instinet (2002), which formed the INET ECN. NASDAQ acquired BRUT in 2004. The 2005 NYSE and NASDAQ deals referred to above initially appeared to form the capstone of the consolidation trend. Largely in response to these deals, however, a major proprietary trading firm, Tradebot, announced its intention to build a new ECN, BATS. By early 2006, seven months after its announcement, BATS was operational. The BATS experience demonstrates the lack of barriers to entry that is characteristic of the competition among electronic markets.

The INET/NASDAQ deal closed in December 2005. At that point, an effort was made to consolidate NASDAQ's three books, SuperMontage, BRUT and INET, into a single platform. Of the three trading systems, the INET technology was deemed the best. Stemming from the original Island system designed to meet the needs of daytraders, INET offered the fastest trade turnaround of any competing system. The three NASDAQ books were therefore consolidated onto a single book largely based on INET technology. This single book became operational in October 2006.

A final development warranting mention is the formal registration in August 2006 of NASDAQ as a registered securities exchange, making it independent of the NASD. As part of the exchange agreement with the SEC, trades by dealers off NASDAQ's book would be reported to the new NASDAQ Trade Reporting Facility (TRF), which would remain under the authority of the NASD (now called FINRA).

At present, NASDAQ's dealer market legacy notwithstanding, dealer volume reported to the TRF only accounts for about a quarter of total NASDAQ-listed volume. The remaining three quarters is done on competing price/time limit order books. Currently NASDAQ's book is the most active, followed at a significant margin by Arca and BATS. The FINRA ADF, itself comprised of three ECNs, is in fourth place. In addition, there are five other market centers trading NASDAQ-listed stocks. Noteworthy among these are the ISE and CBOE, the two largest options exchanges, which have both used their exchange licenses and trading technology to expand their operations into cash equities. The level of competition in the NASDAQ-listed sphere of trading remains fierce.

Regulation NMS and the Remaking of the NYSE

The NYSE/ArcaEx deal marked two major turning points in the history of the NYSE. First, it provided an NYSE acknowledgement of the importance of electronic trading. There was an element of irony in the new combination as Arca had, in its marketing campaigns, been quite vocal in its criticism of the NYSE and the specialist system. The merger allowed NYSE an expanded product offering to complement the traditional floor model. NYSE CEO John Thain even went so far as to remark that some stocks, particularly the more active ones, could likely trade successfully on a purely electronic platform without specialist intervention. The second aspect of the deal was that it ended the NYSE's traditional member-based corporate structure.

It was the SEC's Regulation NMS, however, that arguably had the biggest impact on the NYSE. The central debate during the Reg NMS hearings dealt with the so-called trade-through rule. During the public hearings, various commentators argued persuasively that quotes from manual (slow) markets should not be granted trade-through protection. To protect such quotes could seriously disadvantage traders as they would be forced to wait for slow markets to respond, while electronic markets would continue to move. The final rule as adopted by the SEC provided that only "fast" automated quotes would receive trade-through protection. Further, as if to underscore the point, the SEC adopted another rule that would award data revenue for quotations only when those quotations were automated. In effect, with Reg NMS the SEC rendered the traditional NYSE market structure practically untenable as a viable business model.

The trading of NYSE-listed issues becomes far more competitive during Reg NMS debate and implementation. Traditional NYSE market share throughout the 1990s and into the 2000s hovered in the low to mid 80 percent range. Non-NYSE volume was done by regional exchanges and off-Board dealers whose business models were primarily oriented towards matching the quotes of the NYSE. Beginning roughly in 2003, this market share began to fall. Particularly noteworthy was the growth in trading on electronic markets such as INET and Arca, markets in which independent price discovery could occur. Seeing the opportunity created by Reg NMS, NASDAQ became a member of the NYSE and other exchanges through its BRUT subsidiary in 2005.

The NYSE's response to Reg NMS was the Hybrid market, rolled out during the fourth quarter of 2006. In concept, the Hybrid aimed to reframe the NYSE specialist system within an electronic model. For example, the system features an API intended to give the specialist electronic abilities similar to the manual market and a circuit-breaker that suspends automatic execution when prices move beyond a certain band within a short time period. During these slow-market periods the market lapses into a traditional and manual auction modality. In practice, however, these features have proven to be very rarely used and other features of the Hybrid have proven detrimental to the specialists. The Hybrid has to date, therefore, turned out to be essentially another electronic limit order book, albeit one that is much slower and less feature-laden than more advanced books such as NASDAQ. NYSE market share has fallen continuously to the point at which by the summer of 2007, it was routinely less than 45%. The primary beneficiary of the shift in trading has been NASDAQ, both in trading done on its book as well as trading done by dealers and reported to the FINRA/NASDAQ TRF. Furthermore, NASDAQ is currently the most active member of the NSYE. The Arca book has also gained share. Arca's gains have not offset the NYSE's losses.

The current competitive landscape in NYSE-listed issues has come to look much like that for NASDAQ issues. In both worlds, there is a primary market, the market that performs the listing function. Neither commands more than 50% of the trading volume, however. The NYSE has had to face unprecedented pricing pressure in this new environment. In the NYSE-listed world, NASDAQ and Arca are major second and third-place electronic competitors, while in the NASDAQ-listed world Arca and BATS serve these roles. In both worlds, dealerized trading sums to between one-quarter and one-fifth of total volume. Finally, in both worlds, a small but not insignificant group of markets provide a competitive fringe. These markets consist of the American Stock Exchange, regional exchanges, ECNs trading on FINRA's ADF, and the two options exchanges, CBOE and ISE.

Arguably, the distinction between NASDAQ- and NYSE-listed issues is declining in importance. Trading of U.S. cash equities is becoming, in effect, a single, large, linked, electronic, marketplace, with virtually all markets trading all securities. Furthermore, competition between exchanges is becoming increasingly international while financially challenging for exchange operators, the transformation of cash equity trading to a world of competing electronic markets has yielded great benefits to the trading community in terms of lower prices and better service.

NASDAQ's Plans for the Future

Operating in a highly competitive environment, NASDAQ is currently the largest U.S. equities exchange in terms of matched share volume. It is also pursuing a number of new initiatives outside its traditional lines of business. Three such initiatives that involve the expansion of electronic trading are Options Trading, Exchange Globalization, and the PORTAL marketplace.

Move into Options

There are two proximate reasons for NASDAQ's entry into options. First, as automated options trading increased following the 2000 launch of the ISE, options trading has been growing more rapidly than stocks trading. Share volume in NASDAQ-listed issues has been effectively flat during the last five years, while options volume has been growing at about 25% per year during the same time period. Given the near perfect substitutability of cash equity and options trading strategies, particularly for active traders, it makes sense for NASDAQ to move towards servicing the growing segments of the securities markets.

A second clear reason for NASDAQ's expansion into options is the opportunity to leverage the INET platform and extend NASDAQ's operating philosophy to options. The same system used to trade equities can be used, at comparatively low incremental cost, to trade other securities. Indeed, the leverage argument was put forward by CBOE and ISE as their rationale for entering the equity markets.

There are currently six U.S. options exchanges. What value would a seventh offer? The Nasdaq Options Market intends to offer a new market structure to the options world. Traditional floor-based options exchanges have had market structures heavily oriented towards specialist-style intermediaries (specialists, designated primary market makers, etc.). The absence of an off-exchange dealer market has also led to the creation of rules governing directed order flow creating essentially on-exchange dealer internalization. The extensive involvement of trading professionals in turn has required, as a public policy matter, complex priority rules to ensure that public investors receive proper treatment. This general specialist-centric approach to market structure can be, and has been, moved to wholly electronic platforms, as in the case of the ISE and the BOX. Formerly floor-based exchanges have also grafted electronic systems onto their existing market structures much as the NYSE did with the Hybrid.

More fundamentally, there is a change coming to the options arena in terms of a reduction in the trading tick size. Currently, options under $3 trade in nickels, while those above $3 trade in dimes. Starting January 2007, at the urging of the SEC, all the options exchanges initiated the options "penny pilot," in which the tick sizes moved to a penny for options under $3, a nickel for those above $3. This pilot was applied to 13 options classes. As expected, spreads fell in the pilot stocks, albeit with declining quoted depth. It is anticipated that the SEC will view the pilot as a success for investors (particularly retail), and that all options classes will ultimately be traded in finer increments than is the case currently. (At this writing, the established options exchanges are preparing for the expansion of the penny pilot.)

The move to penny tick sizes occurred in the equity markets in 2001 with profound impact on the way the markets functioned. The role of dealers was particularly impacted as retail spreads narrowed dramatically. As noted above, only about a quarter of NASDAQ-listed volume is done via dealers post decimalization. In the electronic limit order books, an important new type of trader emerged to take the place of the traditional dealer. This trader type, sometimes referred to as "e-market maker," trades proprietarily on the books, generally posting passive, liquidity-supplying orders. This type of trading currently represents a very large fraction of trading on the NASDAQ book. Success in this business depends on the ability to quickly post and cancel orders, to avoid being "picked off." The posting and cancelling of orders is all done by computers using sophisticated models that react instantly to changing market conditions. The INET technology with the ability to trade in sub-milliseconds and quickly cancel orders is ideally suited to this type of trader.

The NASDAQ strategy, then, is to bring this type of transparent and competitive trading to the options world using the proven INET technology. In place of complex priority rules and designated liquidity providers, the NASDAQ options market will provide a relatively flat market structure, based on essentially the same price/time principles used in the equity business. NASDAQ hopes that the availability of a high performance platform will not only increase the size of the options pie, but also win market share from other exchanges that are not as well suited to trading in the new penny-tick environment.

Global Linkages

As is well known, stock exchanges in recent years have begun to reach outside national borders to form alliances with each other. There are two different forms of alliances, a corporate alliance and a technological alliance. A corporate alliance of exchanges under a single holding company can be either an alliance of equals or an alliance of smaller markets around a dominant central market. The corporate structure seeks to benefit the exchange's dealer and investor customers by providing a common technology and regulatory infrastructure for accessing a larger pool of securities than the national exchanges offered independently. A technological alliance also seeks to offer a common technology infrastructure but benefits for brokers and investors from the technology alliance are not as significant as for the corporate alliance because local practice and regulation often limit the extent of common technology that can be offered.

Europe currently has two existing corporate alliances. OMX Group owns and operates markets in Denmark, Finland, Iceland and Sweden (the Nordic Exchange) and Estonia, Latvia, and Lithuania (the Baltic Exchange). While each market is a separate legal entity with its own national regulator and rule book, both exchanges have a common technology infrastructure and many rules in common. For the most part, OMX's two exchange groups consist of similar sized exchanges from countries with similar economies and benefits issuers by increasing liquidity and establishing a shared identity and brand for the listed companies. Euronext is a consortium of markets in Belgium, France, the Netherlands, Portugal, and the UK (Liffe), originally formed in 2000. While each national market retained its separate legal and regulatory identity, in 2004 the markets began operating on a common, integrated IT platform for trading and clearing. Derivatives and equities trading on Euronext centers around Liffe and Euronext Paris, respectively.

OMX and ATOS/Euronext are the world leaders in technological alliances. Leveraging its development of exchange trading software, OMX provides IT services to 60 exchanges around the world, including large, active markets such as the ISE in the U.S. and the Australian Securities Exchange. ATOS Euronext is the technology provider to 25 exchanges including some of the largest derivatives exchanges in Europe and North America. Besides the liquidity benefits from improved technology, there is little significant benefit from regulatory efficiencies or brand identity.

The year 2006 marked a major turning point in global consolidation of exchanges, as the NYSE and Euronext announced their intent to merge and NASDAQ began to acquire shares in the London Stock Exchange (LSE) as part of an ultimately unsuccessful takeover attempt. The wave of transatlantic alliances continued with the announcement in April 2007 of the acquisition of ISE by Eurex, followed in the next month by the announced merger between NASDAQ and OMX. In addition to transatlantic alliances, mention of alliances with Asian markets in Japan, China and India frequently arises in the media.

The central question thus emerges as to the future and structure of global exchanges. NASDAQ's general approach to this question can be outlined as follows. Unlike the case with floor-based exchanges, in a world of electronic markets, trading technology is highly portable. Furthermore in an electronic environment the locus of trading becomes ill-defined. Consequently there is no shield from international competition in the provision of trading technology services. Incumbency matters little, if at all. Rather, emerging from a competitive international landscape, the best trading technologies can be identified, and deployed around the world. Success as a global exchange means competing globally as an electronic market.

It is not at all clear, in fact is probably doubtful, that within the immediate horizon there will emerge a single or small set of dominant global equity markets. While investors should, and in fact do diversify their portfolios by investing in companies outside their own national borders, there remains substantial home country bias in investing. There also remain substantial regulatory barriers to borderless trading, some due to legitimate concerns, others likely due to simple inertia or protectionism. There is a long way to go, for example, before a security registered in Eastern Europe is allowed to be listed and traded in the U.S. without that security being vetted and approved by the U.S. SEC. (The projected 2008 launch of MiFID will provide an interesting test case to see whether countries in the European Union, largely united by history and geography, will be able to transcend national borders to create a seamless European market system.)

A more likely model is a world of increasingly linked but still separate national or regional markets. There is no anticipation that 24-hour trading will emerge for more than perhaps a handful of equity securities. Various world-wide markets would retain their own identities, but look to global technology providers to build or operate electronic exchanges. The electronic platforms would probably look more alike than different, being variations on the price/time electronic limit order book. With the advance of time and as circumstances warrant, increasing levels of integration or harmonization between markets could take place, all facilitated by common underlying technology.

In this environment, NASDAQ hopes to be able to be a leader in providing the technology for the world's increasingly competitive and demanding capital markets. NASDAQ pioneered electronic trading in a dealer market and has continued to innovate over the last thirty years and now has the fastest, most efficient trading platform in the world. The combined company's multiple liquidity pools, sophisticated and flexible market structure, advanced speed of execution and integrated cross-border trading capabilities would provide investors and issuers with increased visibility and access to global markets.

PORTAL, an Institutional Market

Much is being said currently about the challenges facing public issuers in the U.S. The Sarbanes-Oxley legislation and excessive litigation risk are frequently-cited culprits. Foreign issuers seem to becoming increasingly skittish about raising public capital in the U.S. There is, however, an alternative to public markets. Increasingly, both domestic and foreign issuers are turning to the 144A market. SEC rule 144A provides a safe harbor from many of the usual registration and disclosure requirements applied to public securities. In turn, this market is available only to qualified institutional buyers (QIBs). Generally, QIBs are banks, large institutions with $100 million or more in assets, and broker-dealers. NASDAQ currently operates the PORTAL system to designate securities as 144A eligible— during 2006 about 2700 securities were designated as 144A eligible using

PORTAL. This designation process allows a security to be assigned a CUSIP number and be eligible for clearance and settlement through DTC.

Due to a lack of uniform international disclosure standards, it is difficult to precisely gauge the size of the 144A private placement market. One way to get a general idea of the potential, however, is to look at the size of capital-raising efforts in which some part of the deal involved a 144A tranche. For example, in 2002, $457 billion in global debt and equity capital was raised in deals in which at least some of the money came from a 144A placement. In 2006, the same number was $1,531 billion, an increase of a factor of 3.4. This growth is likely due both to increased levels of capital raising generally as well as increased use of 144A. The aforementioned figures represent debt instruments as well as equity, with debt representing the large majority. Considering equity only, in 2002 $32 billion in equity was raised globally in deals in which some portion had a 144A placement. In 2006 the same figure was $162 billion, a factor of 5 increase. Another way of viewing the $162 billion is to note that during 2006 total equity capital raised on the NYSE, Amex and NASDAQ together summed to $154 billion. Again, an unknown fraction of the $162 billion actually went into 144A placements, but the growth of the number suggests that both awareness of the 144A market and the size of the potential 144A pool are rapidly expanding.

In light of the current growth potential of 144A placements, NASDAQ plans to add to its PORTAL system an electronic marketplace for the secondary trading of these securities. The trading platform will provide PORTAL participants with the opportunity to post quotes, negotiate trades, and report trades. The platform will be Internet based, and by design open only to qualified subscribers. In addition to the trading platform, PORTAL provides enhanced online tools for the designation of the securities as being eligible for 144A trading, as well as a new procedure for the certification of QIBs.

A particular advantage for NASDAQ is the way in which PORTAL, as its name implies, can act as a gateway to issuers to U.S. capital. Particularly for foreign issuers, a PORTAL listing can be a first step, testing the institutional market. If future plans warrant, the issuer can take the next step into a full-blown public listing, preferably on NASDAQ. In PORTAL NASDAQ sees itself coming full circle in linking electronically a market of many dealers to provide benefits from competition, transparency, flexibility, and efficiency.

Conclusion

Thirty-four years after its founding NASDAQ's electronic market was embraced as the model for U.S. equity markets by the Securities and Exchange Commission, a final validation to similar decisions made by market operators and regulators around the globe. However gratifying those decisions have been, NASDAQ recognizes that its success was based on serving dealers, investors, and issues with a steady succession of marketplace enhancements designed to provide mutual benefits to all our customers and constituents. Going forward we will be guided by the same principles in continuing to provide innovations to the financial markets.

Global Securities Exchanges:
The Beginning of a Beautiful Friendship?

By Udayan Goyal, Managing Director, Global Banking, Deutsche Bank.

Historical Overview

The history of stock exchanges can be traced to 12th century France, when the first brokers are believed to have developed, trading in debt and government securities. Unofficial stock markets existed across Europe through the 1600s, where brokers would meet outside or in coffee houses to make trades. The origins of the term "bourse" are widely disputed amongst commentators. Some believe it comes from the Latin bursa meaning a bag because, in 13th century Bruges, the sign of a purse (or perhaps three purses), hung on the front of the house where merchants met. It is more likely that in the late 13th century commodity traders in Bruges gathered inside the house of a man called Van der Burse, and in 1309 they institutionalized this until now informal meeting and became the "Bruges Bourse"[xc]. The idea spread quickly around Flanders and neighboring counties and "Bourses" soon opened in Ghent and Amsterdam. The Dutch later started joint stock companies, which let shareholders invest in business ventures and get a share of their profits - or losses. The Amsterdam Stock Exchange, created in 1602, became the first official stock exchange when it began trading shares of the Dutch East India Company. These were the first company shares ever issued. In 1688, the trading of stocks began on a stock exchange in London.

Since these early days of exchanges, things have come a long way. Today, the exchange industry is a $200bn+ market segment in its own right with some of the strongest growth characteristics of any sub-sector within financials. This article seeks to explore some of the underlying trends shaping the exchange space and what the future may have in store for this dynamic segment.

Major Trends Shaping Global Exchanges

There have been a number of major trends that have shaped and continue to shape the exchange landscape over the last few years. Perhaps the first starting point has been the change in ownership structure from mutually owned organizations to corporations which have ultimately become publicly owned. In 1993, the Stockholm Exchange became the first exchange to demutualize (see Table 1). This was followed by a raft of other exchanges doing the same with the next step being a public listing of these exchanges. The main factors that lead to this structural change was the dramatic change in the operating environment of exchanges, in particular the advent of global competition and the significant developments in technology. Whereas in previous years, exchanges operated on a near virtual monopoly in their home markets, as capital markets became increasingly liquid and global, issuers had the option to raise capital in other countries and their exchanges. As a result, for the first time, real competition started to develop which entailed significant changes in the way exchanges operated, these changes were ultimately facilitated by a shift away from mutually owned organizations.

Table 1: Exchanges privatization/demutualization

Demutualized exchanges	Year	Demutualized exchanges	Year	Demutualized exchanges	Year
Stockholm Stock Exchange	1993	Athens Stock Exchange	1999	Chicago Mercantile Exchange	2002
Helsinki Stock Exchange	1995	Stock Exchange of Singapore	2000	Chicago Board of Trade	2005
Copenhagen Stock Exchange	1996	Hong Kong Stock Exchange	2000	NYMEX	2006
Amsterdam Stock Exchange	1997	Toronto Stock Exchange	2000		
Borsa Italiana	1997	London Stock Exchange	2000		
Australian Stock Exchange	1998	Deutsche Börse	2000		
Iceland Stock Exchange	1999	Euronext	2000		
Simex	1999	The Nasdaq Stock Market	2000		

As exchanges moved into the domain of shareholder entities, so did the pressing need to become more efficient. It is interesting to see that the margin improvement of exchanges following their newly acquired public company status has been impressive (see Chart 1).

Chart 1: Margin improvements of exchanges (04 – 08E)

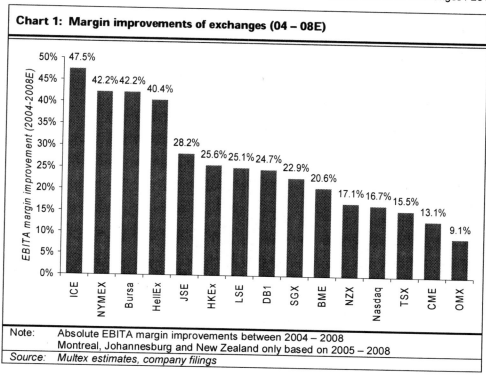

Note: Absolute EBITA margin improvements between 2004 – 2008
Montreal, Johannesburg and New Zealand only based on 2005 – 2008
Source: Multex estimates, company filings

Along with demutualization came the electronification of exchanges. The traditional floor based exchanges often suffered as their limited space and seats, combined with the need for a physical presence on the floor, limited the access of investors to the exchange through largely local intermediaries. As electronic communication networks (ECNs) began to drive competition, exchanges began their process of demutualization and started to shift to the electronic trading model. The distinct advantage of this model was the ability to allow remote members to connect and trade on the exchange thereby increasing the relevance of the exchange to a much wider audience and become truly leveraged from an operational and financial perspective. At the same time the rise of the hedge funds (see Chart 2 on next page) changed the way securities were traded.

The old "long only" style of trading where asset manager would buy and hold securities started to shift in favor of algorithmic trading strategies driven by the "black box" hedge funds. Even conventional "long only" asset managers discovered that breaking up their trades into smaller sizes and using algorithmic trading engines to execute the trades on electronic platforms would significantly enhance the overall cost of the trade by minimizing the market impact a larger trade would have. As a result of this, trading velocity

on exchanges sharply increased (see Chart 3 and Chart 4 on next page) with
the size of the average trade dropping.

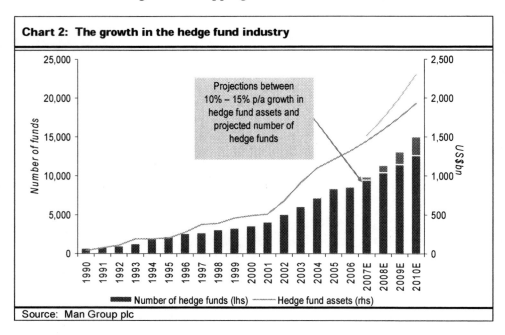

Chart 2: The growth in the hedge fund industry

Projections between 10% – 15% p/a growth in hedge fund assets and projected number of hedge funds

Number of hedge funds (lhs) —— Hedge fund assets (rhs)

Source: Man Group plc

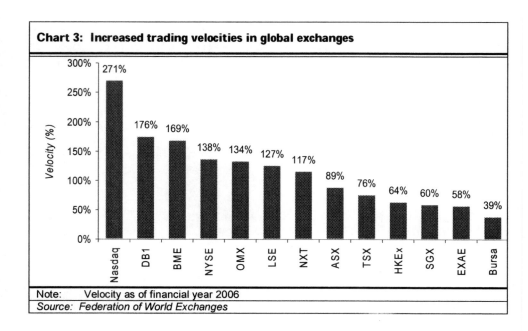

Chart 3: Increased trading velocities in global exchanges

271% (Nasdaq), 176% (DB1), 169% (BME), 138% (NYSE), 134% (OMX), 127% (LSE), 117% (NXT), 89% (ASX), 76% (TSX), 64% (HKEx), 60% (SGX), 58% (EXAE), 39% (Bursa)

Note: Velocity as of financial year 2006

Source: Federation of World Exchanges

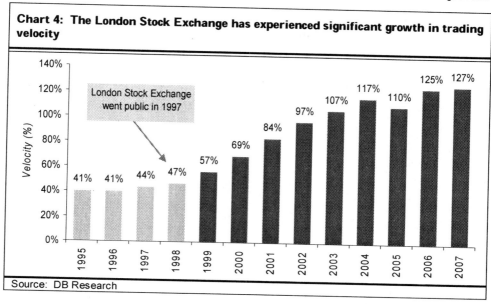

Chart 4: The London Stock Exchange has experienced significant growth in trading velocity

Source: DB Research

Exchanges, who operated on a transaction based pricing model, were suddenly under pressure from these funds and the sell side to change their pricing models in favor of volume based pricing. In addition, today there is significant pressure on exchanges to become more efficient from a technology perspective in order to decrease the latency on trades as markets continue to become more efficient and the speed of executing a trade becomes even more critical.

In addition to the pressure to become more efficient by rationalizing cost structures and becoming technologically advanced, exchanges, for the first time, found the need to develop new products in order to grow their top line revenues in the face of increased competition on their incumbent products and the cyclical nature of equity markets (see Chart 5 on next page).

At the same time, with the growth of the hedge fund community, the increased appetite for risk mitigation through financial instruments and the use of derivatives as a proxy for cash itself, the demand for derivatives soared driving the phenomenal growth of exchange trade derivative products (see Chart 6 on next page) which make up a fraction of the overall derivatives traded globally (see Chart 7 and Chart 8 following the next page).

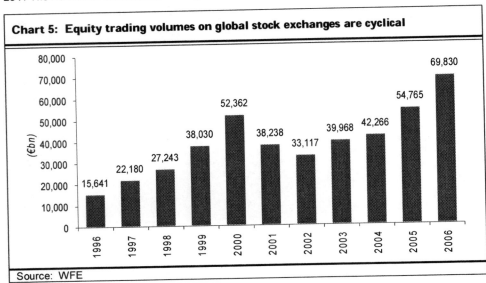

Chart 5: Equity trading volumes on global stock exchanges are cyclical

Source: WFE

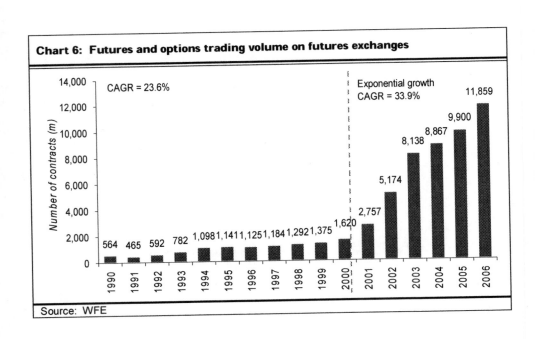

Chart 6: Futures and options trading volume on futures exchanges

Source: WFE

Chart 7: Global OTC and exchange traded derivative volumes

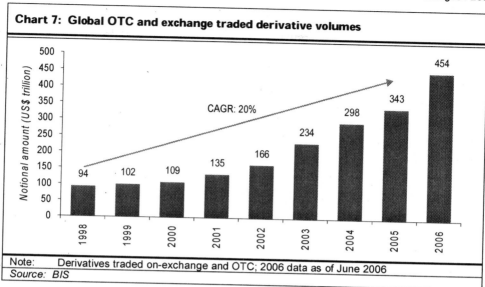

Note: Derivatives traded on-exchange and OTC; 2006 data as of June 2006
Source: BIS

Chart 8: Exchanges have significant room for channelling OTC flows on-exchange
(US$ in trillions)

	OTC(a)	As %	Exchange traded futures(b)	As %	Exchange traded options(b)	As %	Total
FX	40.1	7.8%	30.2	5.9%	56.0	10.9%	126.3
Interest rate	292.0	57.0%	0.2	0.0%	0.1	0.0%	292.3
Equity-linked	7.5	1.5%	1.3	0.3%	8.9	1.7%	17.7
Other	75.6	14.8%	n/a	0.0%	n/a	0.0%	75.6
Total	**415.2**	**81.1%**	**31.7**	**6.2%**	**65.0**	**12.7%**	**511.8**

(a) Source BIS December 2006
(b) June 2007
Source: BIS Quarterly September 2007

In addition, there was significant growth in commodity products (see Chart 9 and Chart 10) as well as other asset classes such as credit derivatives (see Chart 11 on the following pages).

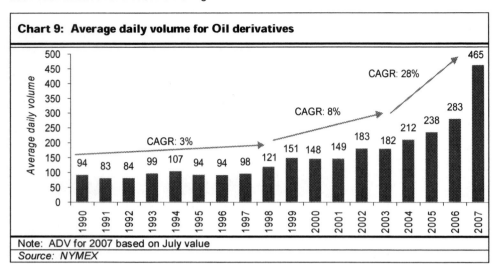

Chart 9: Average daily volume for Oil derivatives

Note: ADV for 2007 based on July value
Source: NYMEX

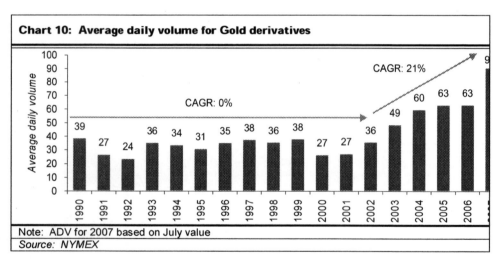

Chart 10: Average daily volume for Gold derivatives

Note: ADV for 2007 based on July value
Source: NYMEX

Unfortunately for the exchanges, organic growth initiatives were less than successful. As can be seen in Table 2, a number of initiatives in the equities space in Europe to create competition ultimately resulted in failure. This trend repeated itself when exchanges attempted to enter each other's markets (see Table 3).

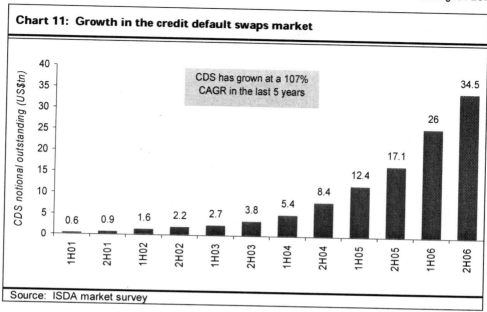

Chart 11: Growth in the credit default swaps market

CDS notional outstanding (US$tn)

CDS has grown at a 107% CAGR in the last 5 years

1H01	2H01	1H02	2H02	1H03	2H03	1H04	2H04	1H05	2H05	1H06	2H06
0.6	0.9	1.6	2.2	2.7	3.8	5.4	8.4	12.4	17.1	26	34.5

Source: ISDA market survey

In hindsight, it was clear that not having the sell side community's specific buy-in and involvement in these initiatives was the ultimate downfall of these attempts. Interestingly enough, similar initiatives in the US equity options space such as PHLX were more successful as they had the explicit support of the sell side banks (see later for a fuller discussion on recent sell side initiatives). Hence, for many exchanges, the next logical step was to look for other exchanges to buy, something that was made possible through the earlier demutualization and listing of exchanges around the world.

And thus began the first wave of consolidation (see Table 4) where exchanges were either integrating across geographies ("horizontal integration"), across the value chain ("vertical integration"), or across products ("diversification") – see Table 5.

With the first wave of consolidation over, exchanges looked increasingly outside their own regions to acquire exchanges in order to create even larger pools of integrated capital, which has brought us to the current second wave of consolidation (see Chart 12).

Table 2: Organic growth initiatives by regulated exchanges in Europe have failed

Name of firm or venture	Established	Customer sponsorship	Post-trade infrastructure provider	Characteristics of the offer and differentiation from incumbent	Incumbent's response	Status to date
Tradepoint/ virt-x	1995 in London/ Relaunched as virt-x in 2000	Customer sponsored. SWX took complete ownership in 2003	LCH, CRESTCo and SIS X-Clear	Tradepoint: electronic trading virt-x: European blue chips under a single rule book, regulatory regime and post trade infrastructure	Contributed to LSE introducing electronic trading	In operation: minimal trading volume on non-Swiss equities
EASDAQ/ NASDAQ Europe	1996 in Brussels/ relaunched as NASDAQ Europe in 2001	Customer sponsored with a minority stake held by NASDAQ	EuroCCP[(a)] for Clearing, Euroclear and Clearstream ICSD to settle trades	EASDAQ: European high-growth companies NASDAQ Europe: US and European technology companies traded at European trading hours		Stopped operating in 2003
Jiway	2000 in London	Joint venture by OM Group and customer Morgan Stanley Dean Witter (MSDW). OM acquired MSDW stake in 2001	Trading and post-trading infrastructure provided by OM	Cross-border trading, clearing and settlement of over 2,500 European and US equities		Stopped operating in 2002
NASDAQ Deutschland	2003 in Bremen/ Berlin	Customer sponsored. NASDAQ as stakeholder	Clearstream	User netting (which DBAG did not offer at that time)		Stopped operating in August 2003
Xetra Stars (DBAG)	2003 in Frankfurt	'Encouraged' by customers	Eurex clearing and link to Euroclear Nederland	No significant differentiation		In operation: minimal trading volume
DTS-Eurosets (LSE)	2004 in London	'Encouraged' by customers	LCH, Clearnet, Euroclear CRESTCo	Lower fees, better service, better reliability	Euronext cut fee by up to 50%	In operation: minimal trading volume
Project Tiger (Euronext)	2004 in London	Detailed discussions with customers	–	Lower fees	–	Never went into operation

(a) European Central Counterparty Limited (EuroCCP) is a wholly owned subsidiary of DTCC, which was created to provide post-trade services for NASDAQ Europe

Table 3: Competitors directly entering each others' markets have also failed		
	Market entry	**Result**
Deutsche Börse	■ DB1 offers treasury futures trading (Feb-04)	■ Deutsche Börse captures ~1% of Treasury futures trades by Jan-05
vs		
Chicago Board of Trade	■ CBOT announces plan to list German Bund futures contracts (Feb-04)	■ CBOT Bund initiative had 'sunk without a trace' by Mar-05
London STOCK EXCHANGE	■ LSE launches trading of Dutch equities at fees 40% below Euronext (May-04)	■ LSE captures ~2% of Dutch equities trading volume by Nov-04
vs		
euronext	■ Euronext announces plan to trade FTSE 100 stocks	■ Euronext announces in Mar-05 that it has dropped plans to trade FTSE 100 stocks

(a) Financial Times, 15 March 2005

Obviously, the reasons for consolidation are compelling, including:

- Economies of scale/ technology – trading via electronic trading platforms have high fixed costs but very little marginal costs
- Economies of scale/ liquidity – the virtuous cycle of large and liquid markets attracting new liquidity (trading volumes) and listings
- Expansion of investor audience
- Reduction of user costs – eliminates duplicate connectivity and exchange fees
- Follows user needs – users increasingly want the ability to trade in multiple asset classes on a global basis

Of course there will always be significant barriers to consolidation including differences in regulatory regimes, IT platforms, and user resistance to transition costs, competition concerns and reconciling the horizontal integration versus vertical integration debate.

Table 4: The first wave of exchange consolidation

	2000	2001	2002	2003	2004	2005
DB1	■ Merger of DB1 Clearing and Cedel Intl to Clearstream Intl ■ LOI on merger with to create iX (withdrawn)	■ IPO ■ Acquisition of entory AG (IT)	■ Acquisition of 50% of Clearstream from Cedel, DBAG now owns 100% in Clearstream ■ Acquisition of 50% of Infobolsa (realtime information)	■ Eurex co-operation with SWX prolonged till 2014 with adjusted profit sharing (85% DBAG)		■ Offer for LSE (withdrawn) ■ Share buy-back-programme ■ Disposal of entory AG (IT)
LSE	■ Commencement of trading ■ Rejection of approach by OM	■ IPO on Main Market ■ Approach to LIFFE regarding potential offer	■ Creation of EDX in co-operation with OM			■ Takeover offers by DB1 (withdrawn) and Euronext (pending)
Euronext	■ Exchanges of Amsterdam, Brussels and Paris merge to form Euronext NV	■ Cash offer for LIFFE	■ Merges with the Portuguese exchange BVLP ■ Acquisition of LIFFE completed	■ Disposal of stakes in LCH and Clearnet to LCH.Clearnet in exchange of shares in LCH.Clearnet		■ Takeover offer for LSE (pending)
OMX	■ Merger approach rejected by LSE ■ Subsequent hostile offer failed			■ Merger between OM and HEX	■ Merger of OMX AB with Copenhagen Stock Exchange A/S ■ Merger of VPC AB and Finish OMX-owned CSD (APK), and the Swedish VPC	
BME				■ Capital increase of €65.4m to acquire the remaining 39.7% of Spanish settlement house Iberclear		■ IPO planned for end 2005/early 2006 (30% to be placed)
Borsa Italiana						■ Borsa Italiana and Euronext partner-up for the acquisition of 51% in Italian bond trading platform MTS ■ Plans for IPO in early stage

Source: Company information

Table 5: Consolidation trends in the exchange sector

Horizontal integration

11/2004	Acquisition of Copenhagen Stock Exchange by OMX
04/2005	Acquisition of Archipelago by NYSE
06/2006	Acquisition of Euronext by NYSE
09/2006	Acquisition of NYBOT by ICE
04/2007	Acquisition of ISE by Deutsche Börse
06/2007	Acquisition of Winnipeg Commodities Exchange by ICE
07/2007	Acquisition of CBOT by CME
07/2007	Merger between Borsa Italiana and LSE
08/2007	Acquisition of OMX by Nasdaq and Borse Dubai

Vertical integration

06/1999	Acquisition of Austraclear by SFE
03/2002	Acquisition of Clearstream by Deutsche Börse
07/2002	Acquisition of Monte Titoli by Borsa Italiana

Minority acquisitions

02/2007	Acquisition of minority stake in Bombay Stock Exchange by Deutsche Börse (5%)
03/2007	Acquisition of minority stake in Bombay Stock Exchange by SGX (5%)
06/2007	Acquisition of minority stake in SGX by Tokyo Stock Exchange (4.9%)

Diversification

10/1996	Merger between HKE and HK Futures Exchange
12/1999	Formation of SGX out of the Stock Exchange of Singapore and the Singapore International Monetary Exchange
10/2001	Acquisition of LIFFE by Euronext
03/2001	Acquisition of Natural Gas Exchange by TSX
03/2006	Acquisition of SFE by ASX
04/2007	Acquisition of ISE by Deutsche Börse

As discussed, the main value drivers of this spectacular performance include:

- Trading volumes have grown exponentially across all geographies
- Consolidation within the sector has generated value through both combinations and bid speculation (i.e. LSE, Euronext, CBOT)
- Visibility of the exchange space through high-profile mergers (NYSE Euronext) or market listings (NYMEX) have increased the investor appetite
- Demutualization, rationalization and a change to a "For-profit" business model are improving efficiencies (ie NYSE)
- Whilst cash has performed well in 2006, the real growth opportunity seems to be in exchange traded derivatives

As it relates to the last point above, there is a clear relative valuation bifurcation between the derivative exchanges and the other exchanges (cash and universal) as can be seen in Chart 15:

Chart 12: Unprecedented M&A activity in the exchange space

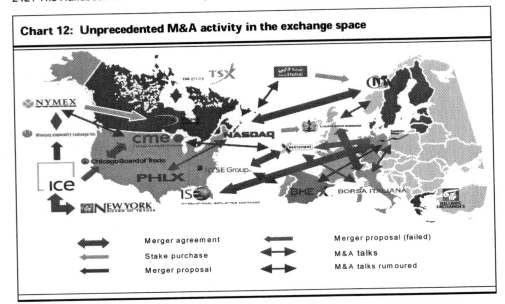

Legend	
⟷ Merger agreement	⟵ Merger proposal (failed)
⟵ Stake purchase	⟷ M&A talks
⟵ Merger proposal	⟷ M&A talks rumoured

Market Performance of Public Exchanges

All of this activity, as already intimated, has led to a sub-sector that has delivered stellar performance and outperformed all financial sub segments (see Chart 13) with the current valuation being higher on a relative basis as well (see Chart 14).

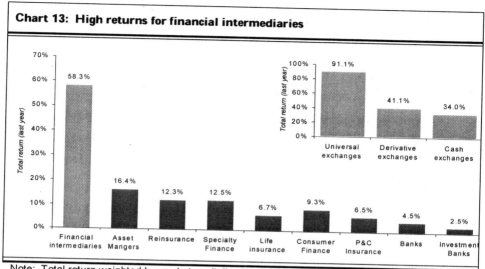

Chart 13: High returns for financial intermediaries

Note: Total return weighted by market capitalization
Source: Datastream as of 15 October 2007

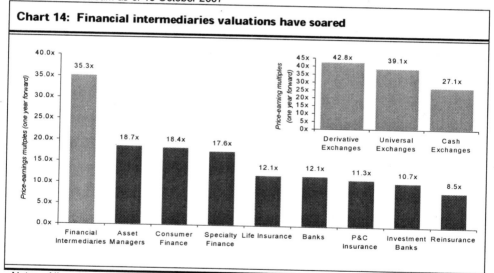

Chart 14: Financial intermediaries valuations have soared

Note: All multiples of global peergroups calculated on an average weighted basis. Financial
Intermediaries based on normal mean
Source: Datastream as of 15 October 2007

Cash equity markets

- Dramatic increase in trading volume, in particular in the Emerging markets

- Regulatory pressure in North America and Europe force cash exchanges to consolidate their platforms and reduce their pricing structures
- Increased pressure from new competitors such as BATS (US), Project Turquoise (Europe) or New Zealand Exchange (Australia)
- New listings have been primarily attracted by London and Hong Kong with New York losing its competitive position slowly

Derivative markets

- Trading volumes increase tremendously due to electronic trading
- Innovation of the OTC market spills over to exchange traded markets as traded products become commoditized
- Option exchanges face increased competition as technological leadership is no longer a differentiator between market participants
- With derivatives being non-fungible, exchanges drive to capture new markets to establish new liquidity pools (CDS, Real estate, weather, dry freight)

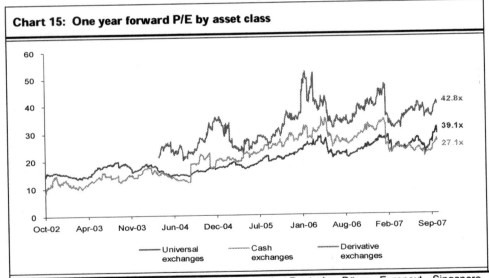

Chart 15: One year forward P/E by asset class

Note: Universal Exchanges: ASX, Bursa Malaysia, Deutsche Börse, Euronext, Singapore Exchange, Hong Kong Exchanges & Clearing Cash Exchanges: BME, Hellenic Exchanges, London Stock Exchange, NASDAQ, NYSE, OMX, TSX Derivative Exchanges: CME Group and Intercontinental Exchange
Source: Datastream as of 15 October 2007

North America

- Transition from floor to electronic trading models increase efficiencies in the sector (NYSE, NYMEX)
- Ongoing consolidation and synergy expectations have built-in substantial M&A premium into its valuations
- The Americas continue to be attractive relative to other regions as they transition their business models towards fully electronic exchanges

At a geographical level, there is also a clear difference between the growth in Asia versus both the US and Europe (see Chart 16):

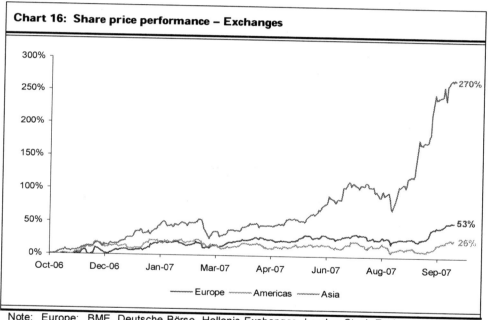

Chart 16: Share price performance – Exchanges

Note: Europe: BME, Deutsche Börse, Hellenic Exchanges, London Stock Exchange and OMX
America: CME Group, Intercontinental Exchange, NASDAQ, NYMEX, NYSE and TSX
Asia: ASX, Bursa Malaysia, Hong Kong Exchanges & Clearing Cash Exchanges and Singapore Exchange
Source: Datastream as of 15 October 2007

Europe

- Regulations and the threat of project Turquoise has lead to reductions in pricing fees. However, trading volumes remain robust as velocity increases
- The European exchanges remain robust through their diversified business models which provide a natural cyclical hedge

- Asia
- Strict regulations limit consolidation to stake building in regional exchanges
- Exchanges driven by outstanding macroeconomic conditions
- Vertical business models enable exchanges to capture the entire value chain
- Asia, particularly China and India, continues to be the most fundamentally attractive market

Given all the various factors above which seem to have a direct bearing on the way exchanges are valued by the public markets, one area that investors have not (yet) had to consider is the susceptibility of the exchange model to be adversely affected in a downturn scenario. Perhaps the most important aspect of this is the overall diversification of the exchange from a revenue perspective. In Chart 17, the revenue mix of each publicly traded exchange has been plotted on a proportional basis. In addition, a diversification index has been created to reflect the level of revenue diversification of each exchange. What is clear from the analysis is that those exchanges with lower diversification indices are likely to be more resilient if particular market segments are affected (e.g. if there is an equity market downturn). Critically, it is interesting to note that the least volatile and vulnerable exchanges from a takeover perspective were those which were vertically integrated and had some element of geographical (horizontal) diversification. Even those exchanges who have previously eschewed the vertically integrated model such as the London Stock Exchange, are now actively embracing it in some form or the other (in this case through the linkage of Monte Titoli from the Borsa Italiana acquisition to the LSE London market) as it is seen as a critical part of building a well diversified and stable revenue base.

Chart 17: Business mix by revenue (2006) Diversification Index

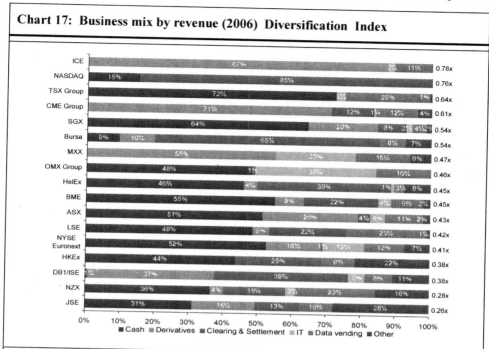

Note: The diversification index awards rankings to companies based on an ideal revenue split of 16.7% per segment, with highest rank starting at a multiple of 0.00x

Source: Company data, DB Research

Even though it is always worth discussing potential downside scenarios, it is encouraging that even after the significant historically observed gains, the buy side analyst community continues to remain positive on the sector (see Chart 18).

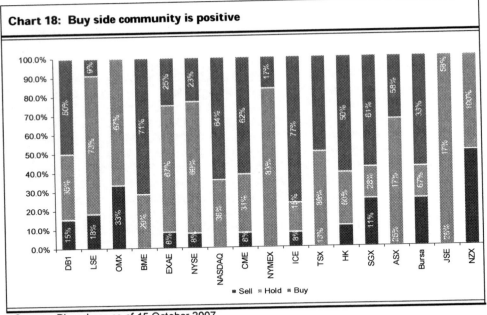

Chart 18: Buy side community is positive

Source: Bloomberg as of 15 October 2007

One area that has not been discussed here but is ultimately beyond the scope of this article is the rise of centralized clearing and the demand from end users to net and effectively manage collateral. The upcoming adoption of Basle II is going to fundamentally change the way sell side institutions set aside capital for trading. The need to set aside capital for operational risk is going to make any form of bilateral trading significantly more expensive than it is currently. As a result there continues to be pressure to create straight through processing (STP) settlement on a T+0 basis with credit disintermediation through a central counter party (CCP). Ultimately users would like collateral to be fungible between different CCPs and also have the ability to net positions between asset classes in order to reduce margin and therefore overall capital. This is clearly a challenge the exchanges and clearing houses are currently dealing with and is set to be one of the major issues that will need to be resolved in the next few years.

The Rise of Competition with the Sell Side

The Buttonwood Agreement, which took place on May 17, 1792, started the New York Stock & Exchange Board (now called the NYSE). This agreement was signed by twenty-four stock brokers outside of 68 Wall Street in New York under a buttonwood tree. The agreement had main two provisions: the brokers were to deal only with each other, thereby eliminating the auctioneers; and the commissions were to be 0.25%. It read as follows "We the Subscribers, Brokers for the Purchase and Sale of the Public Stock, do hereby solemnly promise and pledge ourselves to each other, that we will not buy or sell from this day for any person whatsoever, any kind of Public Stock, at less than one quarter of one percent Commission on the Specie value and that we will give preference to each other in our Negotiations."[xci] Thus was born the first vestiges of the formalization of disintermediation between the buy side and exchanges via the sell side.

Things have moved on since those early days, and the hitherto ubiquitous clubs that prevented the end user from accessing the market directly have started to break down. Perhaps the biggest cause of this change had been the advent of the demutualization of the big exchanges whereby their control passed from their biggest customers to outside investors. The breakdown in this ownership relation has resulted in a disconnect between the objectives of an exchange as a for-profit entity and as a type of "club" for its former owners.

As exchanges seek to deliver shareholder value in the form of superior returns, they do it at the cost of their former owners who also happen to be their biggest customers. This has lead to the reasoning, that it is the sell side investment banks and brokers themselves, who control the liquidity in certain markets and therefore can effectively club together the trade with each other by disintermediating the exchanges. At the same time, exchanges are looking at ways to disintermediate their former owners by accessing the buy side directly. The combination of these two factors has now resulted in a situation where the exchanges have begun to compete head on head with their former masters, aided by the recent changes in legislation such as Regulation NMS and MiFID.

Late last year, a group of Europe's largest investment banks announced plans for a rival to the region's stock exchanges, Project Turquoise, aimed at providing low-cost trading and access to hidden pools of liquidity that are often off-exchange. In the US, alternative electronic trading platforms (ECN's) have been around for quite some time. In that market, things went full circle with the NYSE and Nasdaq, having to buy them in order to regain their lost liquidity. Even after this, a number of regional exchanges have been set up, backed by the banks that are their customers, precisely with the intention of challenging the duopoly. For example, BATS Trading, now accounts for 8-10 per cent of total US equities turn-over.

The club mentality continues to manifest itself in many ways. When MTS, the European electronic bond trading platform, proposed offering direct access to hedge funds, it caused an outcry amongst the dealer community. Following this, more recently, the same banks have bought back into a dealer to customer platform that they had originally sold to Thompson called

Tradeweb at an implied valuation three times what they had originally sold it for. The idea is that the banks will work alongside Thomson and re-invest in the business to create a global multi-asset class execution venue for clients. So, the banks (read "sell side community") are finding other ways to compete with incumbent exchanges as they realize that disintermediation for them is becoming a reality. It is only a matter of time before the big exchanges start to openly access the end-user customer as competition becomes more intense.

The one impediment to direct access of the buy side to exchanges is the need for banking and risk control functions that allows the clearing of trades. Often such clearing and settlement are accompanied by the need to lend cash and securities in order to either finance a particular trade or to make it more efficient. It is very unlikely that regulators would allow anyone but the most sophisticated buy side investors to manage such functions themselves without the help of a qualified intermediary. The half way house on this particular issue has been the rise of broker agnostic direct market access (DMA) platform, which allow the buy side direct electronic access to exchanges whilst directing the clearing and settlement of trades to their nominated prime brokers. This gives the advantage of low latency on a trade, particularly for the algorithmic traders, whilst maintaining the traditional back office infrastructure from a risk and operational perspective.

The Road Ahead

As discussed above, the global exchange environment has become a sub-asset class in its own right. As a consequence of the move from being predominantly mutually owned to shareholder corporations, the industry has been forced to evolve and become more competitive. What the industry was not prepared for was the intense competition from the sell side community who ultimately controlled liquidity in most financial products and came full circle with the consortia approach of pooling their liquidity in order to compete with the incumbents. What happens next is the billion dollar question. History has shown that the sell side community is only too ready to monetize consortia structures in attractive valuation environments. Given the level of the loss of control the last time round, one could argue that the sell side community will be more cautious before selling off the crown jewels, but one should never rule out the sometimes irrational behavior when large sums of money are involved!

Obviously the one piece in the puzzle which may ultimately tip the balance in favor of the eventual winner is the attitude of the buy side community. Increasingly, the larger investment managers and funds are getting concerned with the role of the sell side community in the trading environment and the potential for positional information to cross the Chinese wall between their agency businesses and their proprietary businesses. What may happen is that the buy side community itself may either push for direct access to trading venues (as discussed above) or form "clubs" of their own to trade with each other. To a certain extent, we are already starting to see a manifestation of this trend through the so called dark pool trading venues (e.g. Liquidnet) which essentially act as clearing houses for the buy side to trade equity blocks off the traditional marketplaces. Whether this will extend to other asset classes and products remains to be seen and would also be subject to regulatory consent.

Whatever the outcome, it looks like it is going to be an interesting ride ahead on a winding, precarious and sometimes dangerous road for all concerned.

Market Makers Here to Stay

By Michael Wojcik, Selero

Ever since Reg NMS was announced several years ago, there has been debate over the future of Market Makers, and industry opinions have swung from the belief that they were destined for extinction to the belief that they were here to stay. We explain here why the need to provide a fair and orderly market that gave rise to Market Makers in the first place will still exist under Reg NMS. It highlights recent actions taken by regulators to keep them in place, and it describes the kind of systems Market Makers will need under Reg NMS both to give the market what it needs and to maximize their own profitability in the process.

Who's Who

Exchanges as Regulators: The SEC is the governing body responsible for the oversight of the US equities markets. As the hierarchy goes, Exchanges are at the tier under the SEC, as they are considered Self-Regulating Organizations, or "SROs". Their primary function is to regulate trading activity on their respective Exchanges, providing a fair and orderly marketplace.

Market Makers: Providing a fair and orderly market is accomplished through several different business models. Agency brokerage is an operation that acts as a conduit or vehicle for public customer orders to purchase and sell securities, representing the orders in the market as well as clearing and settling the transaction. Specifically, customer orders are meant to interact with other customer orders, but often illiquid stocks do not generate enough customer interest. If there are no sell orders for buy orders to interact with, or vice versa, the volatility of the stock price may not truly reflect the valuation of the underlying security. That is where Market Makers have historically provided a market or supplied liquidity where customer orders didn't exist.

<u>Exchanges as "For Profit" Entities</u>: As a natural characteristic of a free market, customer orders are routed to Exchange destinations where the "best execution" will occur. To protect the general public, the SEC enforces standards for "best execution" as well as "order handling rules". As SROs, Exchanges monitor member trading practices to ensure compliance with the SEC guidelines. Naturally, this offers an opportunity for Exchanges to compete with each other for business. As a result, the Exchanges' primary function of regulation has become intertwined with the opportunity to compete for business, and both objectives fall under the directive of a CEO. Historically, the CEOs of Exchanges have been controlled and compensated by a Board of Directors comprised of the heads of member organizations.

History

Governmental agencies are created in the name of protecting the general public and to expose abuses in business practices across regulated industries. In the securities industry, the SEC typically provides very broad guidelines that must be met, leaving the onus of compliance in the hands of the regulated entities themselves and using periodic examinations to monitor compliance.

Shortly after the turn of the century, it was determined that Market Makers were not only providing markets when needed but they were also participating to the disadvantage of the public customer. Consequently, the Regulators at the SROs were found to be negligent in their surveillance of their members' behavior and to be too liberal in their interpretation of SEC guidelines, because the fines charged by the SEC were nominal compared to the profits made. As soon as the government realized the guidelines weren't working, change was in the air.

At the same time that the need for change became clear, there was mounting evidence that electronic marketplaces offered customers superior efficiency. Electronic Communications Networks, or ECNs, grew in popularity in the late 90's because they used computers to match customer orders in a strict price/time priority, delivering fair and equal treatment in trade execution as well as a fast, low cost processing.

As Exchanges lost market share to the ECNs, Market Makers tried to fight back by using statistics to show that, in fact, the fair and orderly market often provided price improvement and overall better execution to customers. However, additional evidence showed that Market Maker operations sometimes earned billions at the expense of the public customer.

In light of these revelations, the SEC deemed that something needed to be done to address unfair Market Maker trading practices and the inability of regulators to effectively maintain order. As a result, they directed all Exchanges to examine every customer execution for 7 years to identify each and every case of customer disadvantage as well as the associated dollar amount. The SEC then used this data to fine the Exchanges, their CEOs, and their member firms. They also determined that the National Market System needed to be restructured, and Regulation NMS was born.

Reg NMS would employ modern technology to deliver efficient trade execution while simultaneously removing SRO authority to monitor member firm trading practices. Orders transacted on an Exchange under Reg NMS would be directly exposed to a new systems architecture, forcing strict price/time priority and resulting in compliance with rules that had been in place all along, such as the "trade through" rule. Systems auditing in this new world would be the regulatory "name of the game" at Exchanges.

After the initial publication of the 300 page market structure document, public comment and debate ensued. Now, several years later, we're nearing full implementation of the new market structure for which Exchanges have rewritten their own internal rules and have adopted new corporate governance guidelines, such as creating the position of Chief Regulatory Officer, reporting directly to the Board of Directors. The Boards of Directors have also had to change, to minimize membership control and to maximize the influence of "public" directors from both inside and outside the industry.

Market Restructuring

Ever since Reg NMS was unveiled, Exchanges have been restructuring and watching each other change, beginning with the merger of the Pacific Stock Exchange with one of the ECNs (Archipelago) to create the first, strict price/time priority market. Other Exchanges contemplated similar alliances at the same time, in light of the obvious efficiencies of ECNs not to mention their growth in market share. Since the ECNs were not official Exchanges, they still needed a place to transact business and a way to comply with quoting obligations (Limit Order Display Rule). Therefore, many found refuge at regional Exchanges, using them as print facilities while claiming the lion's share of the market data revenue earned by the respective Exchanges.

NASDAQ was not an Exchange, at this point, but they were filing for an Exchange license. In addition, many of the ECN's originated their businesses on the NASDAQ, reporting transactions to the Securities Information Processor (SIP) component of the NASDAQ infrastructure. NASDAQ viewed ECNs as competitors, so they tried to put the ECNs out of business by charging fees for quotes and trades reported to the SIP, with the goal of having all ECN traffic transact on NASDAQ systems. That is why they created SuperMontage, a system on which all NASDAQ business would be consolidated.

Further, when Reg NMS forced Exchanges to automate, the NYSE demutualized. They became the NYSE Group, and they acquired Archipelago/PSE. Immediately following the announcement by NYSE Group, NASDAQ purchased their market share back, by acquiring Brut, followed by INET (the former Island ECN), and they began the long road of integrating systems to create the SingleBook.

The mergers and acquisitions of the NASDAQ and the NYSE positioned each of them to compete with the other in an automated, Reg NMS compliant environment. The systems of ARCA, INET and Brut made both Exchanges strict price time priority marketplaces and made them more alike than different. In addition, each of them was positioned to trade the other's instruments (NASDAQ Securities & NYSE/AMEX Listed securities). While historically NASDAQ had had higher daily share volumes because of the high level of participation in the automatic marketplace, the market capitalization of NYSE Listed Stocks was 3 to 4 times greater than that of NASDAQ's securities. Now, share volumes were poised to grow exponentially as the two giants attempted to dominate each other.

Finally, as NASDAQ's Exchange license became imminent, they needed to separate the strict price/time priority Exchange from the rest of their business, and the same was true of the NYSE Group. Although NYSE had long been separated from its SIP (Securities Industry Automation Corporation or SIAC), under the NYSE Group, a hybrid system was developed to integrate the NYSE trading floor into the modern world. NASDAQ was already a publicly held company, so a little reorganization was needed to fit the mold. NASDAQ separated the SIP from the rest of the business and put it under the control of a committee of participants, although it would still be operated under the NASDAQ umbrella, along with the NASD regulatory body.

As for the Regional Exchanges, they were left to figure out how they were going to compete with the duopoly of NYSE Group and NASDAQ.

The Continued Need for Market Makers

Now that the market structure had been formulated, the trading community began to ask "what will become of us?" For as long as there have been marketplaces, there have been professionals dedicated to contributing liquidity to ensure there was an orderly market. This concept of liquidity providing also expanded over the years to include bulge bracket firms who were attracted by the lucrative nature of the business. Today, many large firms internalize a portion of their customer order flow, so they can give faster and better execution to clients, while also participating on the other side of the transaction. These Capital Markets divisions, as they are frequently called, are profit centers unto themselves. They also save their parent companies execution costs, although they still need to have access to Exchanges in order to report transactions done under this business model.

Many Exchanges thought at first that this business model was obsolete, and that it had no place in the era of strict price/time priority and algorithmic trading. The reality is that there will always be a percentage of the market generated from public customers. Without them, professional traders would continue to feed on one another, with faster technology winning out. The fact is that customer investments are also drivers of the market for equities trading. There will be times when public participation is high. There will be times when public participation is low, but many private investors still believe in the general principal of investing in stocks. It is the differences of opinion regarding the best time to buy or sell a stock that create investment opportunities and that lead to fluctuation in market participation.

Therefore, liquidity in a security is correlated to interest level, and even when public interest is low, a security still holds value – whether it is calculated by P/E ratios or market capitalization divided by the number of shares. Further, when the interest to execute trades is not equal on both sides of the market, investors still need to have a place to buy and sell securities. This is where Market Makers enter the equation, providing liquidity at an accurate price for customers to buy or sell securities at will. In the model where technology makes Market Makers obsolete, there is no place for this transaction to take place other than a professional trader entering his "market" on one of the Exchange platforms, hoping to buy and sell enough shares to make it worth his while. Instead of providing a marketplace for customer buyers and sellers, he exposes himself to the world of algorithmic trading in sub-second decision making, where he can't possibly compete with a processor capable of handling millions of data elements, making multiple decisions, simultaneously. But in a stock where there is no available liquidity, Market Makers are needed to provide it.

Market making has existed on the NASDAQ since its inception, eventually reaching 30% of its daily volume of shares traded and representing a significant component of its market share. So, the investors in NASDAQ demanded the Market Maker model continue to exist. They also placed bets on the regional Exchanges, investing in their respective futures and charging each Exchange with trying to figure out how its internalization model would fit in the new world, so investors could continue generating profits from internalized order flow.

The final piece of the puzzle fell into place when the NASDAQ proposed spinning off its market making business in a way that would allow the strict price/time priority business in order to become an Exchange and to allow them to retain the revenue generated by market making. Along those lines, the NASD had long been a separate entity under the NASDAQ umbrella, responsible for regulating all trading done in NASDAQ securities. Now, the NASDAQ proposed to the SEC that the NASD become the "super-regulator" for all transactional business not suited to the strict price time priority model. That would extend the existing NASD Alternative Display Facility (or ADF) for quoting to include trading under what is known as the Trade Reporting Facility (or TRF), and the transactions would still occur on NASDAQ systems. The difference was they would now be reported as NASD trades with an Exchange code "D" as opposed to the NASDAQ's "T". This joint venture between NASDAQ and NASD opened the door for other Exchanges to form ventures that would allow them to retain business and market share too, while separating that activity from the Exchange business.

As a result of these changes, transactions done on TRFs are all regulated by the NASD and regulatory conflicts have been eliminated. The Exchanges have also been freed from the regulatory burden that caused them trouble, while still being able to participate in the revenue generated from Market Maker transactions. Finally, given the relationship between the NASD and the NASDAQ, the TRF trades reported to the tape add to the volume of the NASDAQ overall, giving the impression of increased market share.

Now that there is a place for internalized transactions to occur, many firms are interested in printing transactions on TRFs. Trades reported to TRFs are a direct result of some internalization mechanism, or alternative execution venue. Although industry participants clearly see that there is nothing they can contribute (from a liquidity perspective) to a highly liquid stock, there is tremendous opportunity to add value in stocks that are less liquid.

It is important to note that the reason SEC accepted NASDAQ's proposal for the NASD was that market making plays an important role for investors, traders, and Exchanges, and in particular, the repositioning of the NASD eliminated one of the major hurdles standing in the way of Market Makers under Reg NMS. The SEC's decision demonstrated the industry's commitment to keeping market making in place as an important contributor to continued balance and order in the marketplace.

Short Term Challenges

While the continued need for Market Makers is clear, there are so many changes under way in the industry right now, that the path to Market Maker profitability is not, and everyone is watching to see how trade execution will actually play out.

For example, not only are all of the Exchanges operating new systems architected for Reg NMS compliance, but the Reg NMS Order Handling Rules require Exchanges to connect directly to one another via participant agreements or memberships in order to pass order flow between them, making the Intermarket Trading System (or ITS) obsolete. These changes in turn are creating new opportunities for Exchanges to generate revenue, and they plan on taking advantage of them, such as the opportunity to charge for outbound order routing. Further, as more consolidation is on the horizon for Exchanges, many in the trading community fear that less competition among Exchanges will mean higher execution fees. On the flip side, the proliferation of low cost dark pools serving overlapping but distinct market segments is also producing industry fragmentation which could mean lower execution fees. In addition, Market Makers are seeing the mix of orders flowing to them shift away from a fairly even split between limit orders and market orders to fewer limit orders (typically profit opportunities) and more market orders (prone to produce losses). So many of the constants of the past are now in flux, and the dynamics of trade execution under Reg NMS are impossible to predict before Reg NMS goes into effect.

That said, there are also processes and business models that are not in flux, such as the economics of providing / taking liquidity, and the requirement that all trades get executed at the best price available nationwide, or better. These relatively predictable components of trade execution give traders clues about when, where, and how they will want to execute trades under the Regulation. Therefore, given the dynamics of trade execution under Reg NMS include both elements that are predictable and elements that are not, the best systems for market participants up and down the equities trading supply chain will offer traders both pre-built functionality aimed at managing what is known and the flexibility to adjust their tactics based on hands-on experience with Reg NMS.

Arming Market Makers for Success

The need to respond quickly to the lessons learned in the Reg NMS world is particularly acute for Market Makers. First, Transaction Cost Analysis tools provide rapid and granular insight into the sources of profits and losses, but they do not provide the capabilities required to react to that insight. At the same time, the squeeze on profits caused by decimalization leaves little margin or time to spend on process optimization. Finally, Rule 605 exposes their performance relative to their peers, and their customers in turn are obligated to seek out the best execution available regardless of the well established working relationships they may have with their Market Makers.

Therefore, Market Makers need trade execution and smart order routing systems that will allow them to drive and tune pre-built, automated strategies based on the "knowns" of the Reg NMS world through direct, real-time, control over critical parameters. The systems must also allow traders to add and control new decision elements to their operation. For example, the execution strategies of price improvement, automatically linking orders to primary Exchanges, primary trade protection, shred detection, and automatic identification of orders suited to manual handling will be relevant under Reg NMS just as they are today. The need for new routing strategies has also become clear, strategies such as sweep and post, sweep and cancel for market orders, sweep and cancel for limit orders, and sweep and cross. Beyond these recognized needs, market making systems need to be readily extensible. They must be capable of easily incorporating home grown or third party systems like algo engines into their operation, and they must be capable of including new decision rules like exchange latency in their order routing. In other words, the best systems for Market Makers will offer pre-built functionality to fulfill needs that can be anticipated and they will have the flexibility to be tuned and extended in light of needs that can't.

In Summary

The U.S. National Market System needs Market Makers to provide balance and order to the marketplace, so a business model that works for customers and service providers will certainly be negotiated in the event the current one falls short. At the same time, the securities industry is also notoriously intolerant of inefficiency. That means system selection and trader expertise will continue to determine the winners and losers under Reg NMS. With the right systems in their hands, skilled Market Makers can be in compliance for regulators, deliver high quality execution for their customers, and maximize profits for themselves for years to come.

The Decline and Fall of Displayed Markets???

By Joe Gawronski, Rosenblatt Securities

With the constant stream of new dark pools being announced and the limited resources most firms have to sort through the confusing array of information about them--never mind actually connect to them--we thought we'd take a moment to highlight some of the new entrants that have been gaining some traction, which will also hopefully help with prioritization. ITG's Posit and Liquidnet have been the clear leaders in the crossing network space the past several years, with Pipeline a safe third, but the picture has been getting a bit muddier this year, so let us try to shed some light on recent volume trends and the reasons behind them at the various non-displayed venues. In addition, it is very much worth noting that in terms of overall trends not only are the number of venues on the rise, but the usage and market share of the crossing networks and all forms of non-displayed liquidity is generally on the rise. In fact, Goldman reportedly now executes 20 percent of its electronic customer order flow algorithmically through dark order types, while Credit Suisse claims about 25% of its customer algorithmic flow is executed in dark pools of various sorts. We'll leave a detailed analysis of the reasons behind that for another time, but let's just say that Reg NMS' attempts to encourage the posting of limit orders to display liquidity by changing the market data formula to reward quotes and to protect quotes via an expanded trade-through protection regime have been insufficient to counteract the perceived need of institutions to hide their order flow. The demand to be hidden has even pervaded the traditionally displayed markets with non-displayed order types seemingly all the rage.

There is some hype surrounding dark pools that needs to be addressed, however. First, the current size of the market is often exaggerated.For instance, Aite Group's recent report"Rise of Dark Pools and Rebirth of ECNs" estimated that the current market share for single broker-owned dark pools (10%) and independent dark pools (5%) was about 15% of the market's overall average daily volume (ADV). While the report is still worth a read for relative and overall market share trends, background, etc., we think those dark pool volume estimates are high by a factor of two because most of the dark pools double-count their volume, counting both the buy and the sell for each trade towards total volume, whereas the large displayed markets typically do not.Second, the recent rapid rise of some of the newer entrants has not merely been additive to the overall market share of dark pools, but in part has come at the expense of the veterans.September saw volume dips virtually across the board at all of the dark pool players (after record volumes for most of them in August like the industry in general), but noticeably there have been dips or slowing growth rates at some of the more established players for several months now.In part, this reflects much lower pricing at some of the new entrants that encourage algo providers, smart order routers and desks in general to place these new venues higher on their routing tables and let them have the "first look" order flow. is particularly true for the sell-side who formed some of these consortiums undoubtedly to have lower-priced alternatives to venues such as Posit and a playground that they weren't excluded from in the case of Liquidnet.That said, the importance of the pools cannot be underestimated as a tool for the trading desk and we believe that they will continue to grow in importance as Aite Group predicts.In fact, our own firm's use of the various flavors of dark pools is far in excess of (corrected) industry averages, and we execute about 10% of our single-stock order flow in them and up to one-third of certain types of program trades we receive.

Let us take a brief look at what we consider the top five stories about relative newcomers to the market and also use each example to illustrate a more general point about the trends. Before we do though, here is a chart for your convenience that captures recent volume trends among major non-displayed (and part non-displayed) venues.

	Sept	Aug	Overall 3Q	Overall 2Q	Record Day	Record Date
BIDS Trading	15.35	14.13	15.47	3.8	64	25-Sep
CBX (Instinet)	22.5	35	28	14.8	69	09-Aug
Direct Edge*	358.8	330.4	323.3	169.2	629	25-Oct
ISE**	92.3	43.8	50	5.6	115.7	-Sep
LeveL	21	33.7	28.7	10.8	87	13-Aug
Liquidnet	52.8	67.5	60.9	54.9	113.5	08-Aug
NYFIX Millennium	46	46	49	54	96	27-Jul
Pipeline	24	29	28	31	49.1	-Jul
Posit (ITG)***	~40 - 45	~45-50	~45 - 50	53.3	159	8-Aug
SigmaX (Goldman)	102	110	~109	61.1	197	26-Jul

Figure 1— Non-displayed liquidity pool volumes (in millions)
Monthly and quarterly figures represent average daily volume, or ADV

* DirectEdge is comprised of two separate systems: EDGX and EDGA. A combined 20 to 40 million shares a day is being routed to dark pools on average from the two systems, while the rest is executed via the more typical ECN model.

** ISE does not break out its dark Midpoint Match product from its displayed market, so it is important to note that the bulk of the volume is believed to be from the displayed market, which received a big boost recently when BATS started quoting on the ISE instead of exclusively on the NSX.

*** All figures in the chart above were provided by the company itself or are available publicly, except for the Posit figures, which are merely estimates. As a public company, ITG cannot release 3Q Posit figures until it reports its quarter on November 1. That said, we are confident of the negative trend from 2Q to 3Q and that a dip was experienced from August to September.

LeveL ATS

Perhaps the most notable story in the dark pool space has been the meteoric rise of the LeveL ATS. LeveL is the ATS that grew out of the Boston Equities Exchange and its partners include Citigroup, Credit Suisse, Fidelity Brokerage, Lehman and Merrill. These partners are among the mere twenty-one sell-side firms LeveL counts as customers (including us!) today. There are not yet any buy-side customers hooked up and, because this is a sell-side friendly product by design (and ownership) all buy-siders will have to be sponsored by a sell-side firm, unlike models like Liquidnet, Posit and Pipeline that do allow direct relationships with the buy-side. Yet, after completing its first trades just in January of this year, it reached its first 20 million share day on June 6th, then 60 million shares on July 26th, 75 million shares the following day and a one-day record of 87 million shares on August 13th, which is record growth for an ATS we believe. The averages smooth out those spikes of course and LeveL averaged 28.7 million shares per day in the third quarter. These figures do need to be discounted by somewhere between 10 and 20% because as the name LeveL implies there are different levels of matching within the system, with Level 1 essentially being an internalization engine for a sell-side user's own order flow and Level 2 a true matching engine to interact with external parties. That said, the numbers are still impressive.

Reaching these milestones this rapidly begs the question of what is accounting for the success of LeveL? It is not clear to us how much Fidelity, one of the initial sponsors (granted the brokerage unit, technically), is instrumental to the success thus far, considering it has always been a supporter of the exchange in Boston. So outside of that, what's the core reason? Simply put, pricing. While we have argued in the past and certainly still believe that any venue's success is dependent on a multitude of factors and that one-trick pony venues can't survive in the long-term (see our prior

Trading Talk *Pricing and Product and Speed, Oh My!*
http://www.rblt.com/documents/TradingTalkPricingandproductandspeed11-15-06.pdf),
in this case we think the pricing differential is so significant that it has
driven volume.

LeveL's pricing is orders of magnitude cheaper than its competitor ATSs.
With no charge for adding liquidity and only a 5 cents a hundred shares
charge for taking liquidity vs. the historic 2 cents a share charge from the
veterans of the crossing network space like Liquidnet and Pipeline and 50
cents a hundred from some of the newer entrants, LeveL has priced its
product as a utility. In addition, there is a small per ticket clearing charge of
15 cents a ticket per side or 50 cents a ticket per side compressed. By pricing
this as a true utility, competitive in pricing with exchanges and ECNs rather
than crossing networks (in fact, the NYSE's pricing as of October 1st is 8
cents a hundred for taking and nothing for adding liquidty, or 8 cents a
hundred net per trade, and ECNs net anywhere from 2 to 10 cents a hundred
in total from the two sides of a trade, making LeveL even cheaper than the
many of the displayed markets at 5 cents a hundred earned for two sides of a
trade!), LeveL has made this a compelling stop for its broker dealer partners.
Brokers can avoid the steep charges of the crossing networks and yet get the
benefits of interacting in a non-displayed market such as avoidance of paying
the full spread and perhaps less information leakage and market impact.
This incentive is then helping create a real pool of liquidity which builds on
itself. Of course, this success also has implications for pricing at ATSs more
generally. We have predicted before that ATSs would suffer pricing pressure
from the competition of all these new entrants, some of whom had suggested
they would aggressively price themselves as utilities. This is now becoming a
reality. After all, when crossing networks first arrived on the scene, 2 cents a
share was a discounted commission in comparison to the typical 5 or 6 cents a
share full service brokerage commission. The high-end has come down,
making 2 cents look a bit rich now for an electronic execution. Stay tuned for
crossing network adjustments on the pricing front over the next year or so
and any impact that could have on the possible Liquidnet IPO in 2008...

While no venue can grow at this pace indefinitely, and LeveL suffered the dip
in volume that most destinations did from August to September as volatility
waned and overall market volumes trailed off as if September were actually
ushering in the summer (going from ADV of 33.7 million shares in August to
21 million a day in September) there is no reason to expect LeveL's explosive
growth to level off (ha ha) for good. The queue to be connected to LeveL is
long and remember that the buy-side has yet to enter into the picture yet.
Simply getting connected as a destination from all the major order
management systems (OMSs) and execution management systems (EMSs) is
no easy task and it will take time for LeveL to build this out. In fact, with so
many new venues being created these days, the backlog to be added as

destination to most OMSs and EMSs is long, so a new form of "payola" has entered into the landscape with the new destinations agreeing to pay the OMSs and EMSs who have the keys either an upfront fixed fee for FIX development integration work or a variable per share charge (or both) to move up the list.

NYFIX Millennium

NYFIX Millennium, since it has been around for a lot longer than LeveL and started from a much stronger base, can't be spoken about as a phenomenon, it is nevertheless a hot story over the past year or so as its growth has been on fire until a recent slight dip. While Pipeline, the clearly emerging number three crossing network in 2006 that seemed like it could eventually mount a challenge to the incumbents Posit and Liquidnet, has continued to experience growth over the past year or so, e.g., growing from about 22 million shares a day executed in the fourth quarter of 2006 to about 28 million a day in the third quarter of this year, NYFIX Millennium's has leapfrogged past it. From 29 million shares a day back in the fourth quarter of 2006, Millennium averaged 49 million shares a day for the third quarter of this year. It is worth noting that Millennium actually averaged 54 million shares a day in the second quarter though, so it has suffered a bit of a setback of late. We attribute this pause to the arrival on the scene of LeveL and BIDS, who are both algo-friendly and offered broker-dealers who have traditionally been the core users of Millennium a cheaper alternative for their dark orders, not to mention potentially enhancing the value of their equity investments in the systems in many cases. Thus, while in the second quarter, it was a three-way horse race for the top independent non-displayed liquidity pool, with ADV figures of 54.9 million, 54 million and 53.3 million, respectively, for Liquidnet, NYFIX Millennium and Posit (including not only PositMatch and PositNow, but also BlockAlert, a joint venture between ITG and Merrill that helped revitalize Posit; incidentally, because of its success, it would not surprise us if ITG and Merrill invited another large BD or two into BlockAlert), for the moment NYFIX Millennium and Posit have fallen out of the race. Their business models were simply more susceptible to LeveL and BIDS' adoption by the broker-dealer community because of their greater dependence on BD flow. Liquidnet increased its ADV to 60.9 million shares in the 3rd quarter while Millennium suffered the dip to 49 million ADV and Posit experienced a quarter to quarter dip we believe. (Goldman's Sigma X, as elaborated below, appears to have wrested the overall title from the independents).

To what do we attribute the fast pace of growth of NYFIX Millennium? The two primary factors that we would point to are Millennium's being algorithm-friendly and its renewed focus on the buy-side. Let us explain. First, Millennium's original pass-through business model made it one of the most algorithmic-friendly designed systems in a period in which algorithm usage has exploded and each of the other three leading crossing networks were curtailing algorithm usage of their systems in some way. Pipeline, which is designed specifically to be a block trading system, employs minimum order sizes of 10, 25 and 100 thousand shares (depending on ADV of the particular stock) to discourage gaming and non-productive pinging of the system, which makes it very difficult for participation-type algorithms (e.g., VWAP) to use the system successfully to begin with, and then earlier this year Pipeline banned algorithmic vendor access to its crossing network altogether. While this has made Pipeline one of the most attractive venues for true block orders and has resulted in an average execution size of over 38,000 shares and both a hit rate and fill rate of 20%—both impressive stats and much higher than typical dark pools—it has left it largely out of one of the fastest growing segments of the market. ITG, likely for competitive reasons and negotiating leverage, also banned a number of algorithmic providers (not including ITG's own algorithms of course) from Posit earlier this year. Liquidnet, by design a buy-side only, blotter-driven product, historically was not a liquidity pool that algorithms could access. While all three firms have attempted to become more algo-friendly in their own ways since then (Pipeline via a new product called the Algorithm Switching Engine; ITG reversing course to some extent and letting certain algorithms back in, e.g., its deal with UBS in mid-July; and Liquidnet acquiring Miletus, an agency algorithm provider, launching its Supernatural product which can interact with the displayed markets when no match is found, and making a real push for its H20 product, which allows nineteen streaming liquidity partner broker/dealers (BDs), including ourselves, to electronically access at least part of the core Liquidnet liquidity pool), there was a long period of time when Millennium was the most established player of the algo-friendly non-displayed liquidity pools. ISE Mid-point Match, LeveL and BIDS have all also benefited from being algo-friendly, but arguably Millennium has benefited the most as it had much more liquidity than those upstarts out of the gate when algorithmic usage started to explode. Millennium also seems to have benefited from its breadth of symbols, particularly on the NYSE-listed side, with over 6700 symbols in the system daily.

The second factor we would emphasize for Millennium's success is its attempt over the past year or so to really focus on including the buy-side in the system. In somewhat of a mirror image of Liquidnet's business model, which was originally buy-side only, Millennium grew out of the strong installed base of NYFIX terminals (aka the old Trinitech terminals) that NYFIX had on the major BDs listed block trading desks. The pitch was simple. Pass-through Millennium on your way down to DOT (Nasdaq trading was added later, but has lagged because it did not have the same installed user base, and to this day only comprises about 15% of NYFIX Millennium executed volume) and you might get price or volume improvement. If you didn't, no harm, no foul. Convincing the sell-side and more recently the buy-side to put conditional orders that rest in the system and serve as the catcher's mitt for any pass-through flow has been crucial to the success of Millennium. Hiring a professional, dedicated buy-side sales force recently and focusing on this was key to driving penetration and liquidity. With great traction and an investment of $75 million from financial services savvy private equity firm Warburg Pincus in the last year, we would suspect growth in volumes will return at some point as the indigestion it is experiencing from the new entrants coming on the scene fades and NYFIX devotes the substantial resources it now has in growth initiatives and innovations, including focus on the buy-side and trading Nasdaq symbols where it had historically been weak.

BIDS Trading ("BIDS")

BIDS, like LeveL, is taking a broker consortium[lxcii] utility approach and like NYFIX Millennium it is algo-friendly. Between the fact that it was a little later out of the gate than LeveL (its first trade was not until March 23, 2007) and its pricing is not quite as aggressive as LeveL (though still cheap for a crossing network, especially after the recent revision of its pricing schedule, which is structured in such a way to reward the very largest orders with the lowest fees around), BIDS is trailing LeveL in terms of average daily volume executed thus far. Nevertheless, volume averaged almost 15 million shares a day in the third quarter and a one-day record of 64 million shares was achieved on September 25th. Eleven of its twelve investors now connected to BIDS. That said, many of these firms have been making multiple bets in the electronic trading space (including overlap with the LeveL shareholder base!), so we don't believe there is the same potential for committed order flow like we believe we're seeing in some of the recent investments in the ECN space (see DirectEdge and BATS comments later). Nevertheless, we believe they, like LeveL, are hooking up customers at a rapid pace after very carefully limiting the initial roll-out to the BD investors (we know that for a fact as we tried to get involved earlier and at first were told to just be patient, but now are finally connected!). In fact, in mid-August, BIDS announced that the EMSs three of its investors, Goldman, Morgan Stanley and JP Morgan, give buy-side customers—Redi, Passport and Neovest, respectively—would now offer connectivity and sponsored access to BIDS for their institutional clientele so the buy-side is now using BIDS through this sponsorship model. We expect the announcement in the near-future of additional EMSs and sell-side algos being able to access BIDS, which will allow BIDS to gain some momentum on the buy-side.

Another potential issue is Larry Leibowitz' recent move from UBS to a high post at the NYSE as he seemed to be taking the lead among the founding firms and could have been the glue that held things together on the shareholder front and certainly was experienced in the electronic trading space. That said, one could also speculate that as the NYSE explores "getting dark" again— which we think is something they need to do desperately, but for which there are indeed some fairly easy solutions— BIDS could be a target if the NYSE seeks an independent, bolt-on solution rather than the integrated approach we favor.

Besides its low pricing and potential help from its consortium members, BIDS has two other advantages that may prove useful over time. First, the system is more flexible than most of the other ATSs available which typically follow exclusively either an auto-execution approach (e.g., midpoint of the NBBO like Posit and for the most part Pipeline) or a negotiation approach (a la Liquidnet). While reportedly so far the BD customers have only used BIDS' auto-ex functionality, over time the negotiation features, which brokers are somewhat unaccustomed to using in an automated system as they have been excluded from Liquidnet (other than the H20 product which is a different animal and auto-ex in nature also), will undoubtedly be used by the buy-side and as the sell-side perhaps gets used to it. Second, having a CEO like Tim Mahoney, a long-time veteran of Merrill Lynch Investment Management, should assist in growing beyond the initial BD user base considering his extensive buy-side experience.

Goldman's Sigma X

When pundits throw out numbers like 40+ "dark pools" in the market, the truth is the vast bulk of them are not really new non-displayed markets at all but rather electronic versions of the old upstairs phone market made necessary by the rise of algorithm and DMA use by the buy-side—in other words block desks under a different guise. Without an electronic way for the customer flow to interact in many cases ships would be passing through the night and brokers would miss out on the opportunity to cross stock of their customers as well as the opportunity to have that customer flow interact with the proprietary flow of the broker's desk. Enter single-BD dark pools.

That brings me to Goldman's Sigma X product, which so far has clearly been the greatest success story among the broker dark pools. The pace of growth is worth noting as a streak of adding 20 million shares a month was only recently broken with September ADV at 102 million shares and August at 110 million, but prior to that , April at 40 million, May at 60 million, June at 82 million and July averaging more than 100 million shares a day. In addition, SigmaX crossed 197 million shares on July 26th. While most of the other major broker dark pools don't trumpet their numbers so we can't be certain about their volumes, we think one of the primary reasons for their relative silence is the more subdued growth of their dark pools. We believe that in the late spring Goldman's Sigma X started to pull away from the pack of BD dark pools and we would guess that even the more established of the competitor single-BD operated dark pools like UBS PIN and CSFB Crossfinder (who both benefit from popular algorithmic offerings that naturally lead to more crossing opportunities in a dark pool) likely remain stuck at less than half of SigmaX's ADV. While Instinet's CBX dark pool offering is only about one-quarter of the size of SigmaX based on third quarter numbers (28 million vs. about 109 million a day), it is also an interesting one to watch on the single BD-operated dark pool side of things because of its agency approach, long history in the crossing space (most notably for its end-of-day cross, which is still offered, but also for its VWAP cross), and its embrace, like Goldman as elaborated below, of a strategy of routing to other dark pools as well, including a reciprocal deal with CSFB.

Besides its own undoubtedly large pool of liquidity from both proprietary and customer flow, Goldman (perhaps having learned a valuable lesson as an early investor in Arca, whose success was largely built on a route-out strategy) has been one of the most active BDs in connecting its dark pool to other non-displayed pools as well, so that the "crossing" can take place either within the pool itself or with outside venues. While Goldman's reach is not comprehensive, it is already connected to six other venues (or external liquidity providers—XLPs—in the Goldman parlance), including Liquidnet H20, Knight, ATD and NYFIX Millennium, and more are in the queue. This hub approach seems to have proven very successful thus far, with 15-20% of the volume executed at XLPs in August and September. It should be noted that this XLP volume is only single-counted by Sigma X as it only has half the trade, while like other dark pools the rest of the volume is double-counted with each side counted. It is also worth noting that Sigma X does give the user the choice of interacting with Goldman's proprietary flow or not. As a pure agent who prides itself on a no-conflicts approach, and actually built our business in part on the tendency of the bulge bracket firms to abuse their customers through their principal trading activities, we certainly had a healthy degree of skepticism when considering that choice personally. That said, in our own use of Sigma X at times we have opted in for interacting with Goldman's prop flow with positive results.

DirectEdge

So with all of our talk about the explosive growth of some of these non-displayed venues, do we think the displayed markets are dead or dying as asked in the title of this piece? Hardly. That said, we do think the displayed markets will continue to take on a "If you can't beat 'em, join 'em" posture and push out more non-displayed alternatives. DirectEdge is one of the pioneers in this approach— a displayed market that appreciates the appeal of dark liquidity— but before we look at the specifics let's take a look at some of the background of displayed markets and their approach to non-displayed liquidity. To begin with, Nasdaq already claims that about 18% of its executed liquidity is non-displayed. And this number is only likely to grow as Nasdaq rolls out the Continuous Cross soon and as its intraday crossing product starts to gain some traction (it has had a slow start and volume figures that are likely too low to publish). NYSE Matchpoint is planning a launch of a re-vamped version of the current after-hours NYSE crosses that will be more portfolio-friendly. That is planned for November now after slipping from a hoped for September launch, but could be earlier if accelerated SEC approval is granted (which offers a great example of one the difficulties of exchanges competing in the dark pool space as rule change approvals are typically much more onerous than for non-exchange dark pools). Within four to six weeks of going live with that, the plan seems to be to launch intra-day call market crosses. It's our personal opinion that because the battered but not beaten NYSE is still the deepest pool of liquidity around (still maintaining a 40-45% share in its own listings) it has the potential to reclaim some of the block business it has lost and can and should do so with continuous, non-displayed crossing products that are fully integrated into the current auction rather than resorting to point-in-time crosses. In other words, the NYSE needs to get dark and quick. After all, floor brokers in many ways used to be the "human reserve" and the NYSE was de facto the largest dark pool in the world. That ability to "go dark" has largely been destroyed in the current incarnation of the NYSE Hybrid, but there are ways to bring that back and the NYSE is indeed working on some initiatives. More on that another time...

The reasons we think that displayed markets are not going the way of the dinosaur any time soon are manifold. First, the regulators want them for their price discovery function and also to make sure retail flow isn't too disadvantaged. They will step in and re-shape the markets if the market starts to get too opaque. Second, displayed markets of course actually do serve a useful function, in terms of price discovery and the institutional need to use quotes as tactical advertisements of potential liquidity to attract the contra side of a trade. Third, and perhaps the point that is most overlooked, limit orders visible on order books are comprised not just of retail limit orders and tactical advertisements of potential liquidity to draw out the contra side, but also rebate-driven orders, which have become a huge driver of the current market structure and a source of tremendous liquidity. At 20 cents a hundred and greater rebates have created business models in which firms post a few hundred shares on both sides of the market in liquid stocks all day long hoping to stay flat on the trades but earn the rebates. In the process of creating these businesses, these players have literally transformed our markets. The impact of this type of order flow can't be underestimated. We have heard estimates that it now represents upwards of 40% of all volume. If confirmation is needed about how dramatic the change has been, check out Nasdaq's official list of the top ten market makers in NYSE and Nasdaq securities for August in Figure 2 on the next page. We'd venture to guess that the complete absence of a firms like Bear Stearns and JP Morgan on the list and the inconsistent ranking of the other bulge bracket firms is as surprising to some as the inclusion of firms like Wedbush Morgan (who are believed to clear for Getco and Tradebot), Citadel, Lime Brokerage and Biremis. These rebate-driven players aren't going away (note General Atlantic's reported $300 million investment in Getco and Citi's acquisition of ATD for nearly $700 million dollars) and have a real incentive to support healthy displayed markets.

Rank	MPID	Firm
\multicolumn{3}{|c|}{**Top Liquidity Providers in NYSE-Listed Securities**}		
Rank	MPID	Firm
1	MSCO	Morgan Stanley & Co., Inc.
2	WEDB	Wedbush Morgan Securities Inc.
3	LIME	Lime Brokerage, LLC
4	CORG	Citadel Derivatives Group, LLC
5	INCS	Instinet Corporation
6	UBSS	UBS Securities, LLC
7	LEHM	Lehman Brothers, LLC
8	MLCO	Merrill Lynch, Pierce, Fenner & Smith Inc.
9	SBSH	Citigroup Global Markets Inc.
10	AUTO	Automated Trading
\multicolumn{3}{|c|}{**Top Liquidity Providers in NASDAQ-Listed Securities**}		
Rank	MPID	Firm
1	WEDB	Wedbush Morgan Securities Inc.
2	MSCO	Morgan Stanley & Co., Inc.
3	GSCO	Goldman, Sachs & Co.
4	LEHM	Lehman Brothers, LLC
5	UBSS	UBS Securities, LLC
6	MLCO	Merrill Lynch, Pierce, Fenner & Smith Inc.
7	FBCO	Credit Suisse Securities (USA) LLC
8	FOMA	TD Ameritrade, Inc.
9	ECUT	BNY ConvergEx Group
10	CORG	Citadel Derivatives Group, LLC

Figure 2— Nasdaq Top Liquidity Providers Month of September 2007

With that background, it is now worth turning to the most recent primarily displayed market to gain traction— DirectEdge, the old Attain ECN that was acquired by Knight in mid-2005. Until recently, DirectEdge had been the ugly sister to the belle of the ball BATS Trading, but by taking a page out of BATS play book in mid-July and selling a stake to Citadel, one of the largest electronic market makers and retail flow consolidators, and then a few weeks later another stake to Goldman (led by the Redi electronic trading unit we believe, which by its nature has more centralized control over routing tables and directing order flow than a typical desk comprised of many individual traders), DirectEdge is starting to come on strong. Why?

Despite all the hype about BATS' speed and its great pricing, including the January effect promotion in which BATS was willing to lose money for every trade it completed in order to build market share followed by a similar loss-leading strategy to build listed market share in September, the primary reason behind BATS' success in our opinion has been a shareholder base comprised of the most active quote-posting, new breed of rebate-seeking firms like Getco, Tradebot and Lime Brokerage. By supporting BATS by posting aggressive limit orders on the platform, these firms forced contra parties to trade there if they wanted the best price (interestingly, during the January effect and September promotions while BATS was losing money the shareholder users were getting higher rebates for their limit orders, making that easier to bear!). BATS rapid march of market share gains, which saw it reach 300 million shares on January 26, 2007, 400 million shares on June 27th, the 500 million milestone less than a month later on July 24th and 751 million shares just a few days later, is now being followed by Direct Edge which broke through the 300 and 400 million share marks in July, then the 500 and 600 million share milestones in October. While volatility and generally high volume days undoubtedly played a part too, we believe that the addition of Citadel and then Goldman as minority investors had a lot to do with it. While Knight is an old school market maker that has successfully made the transition to the world of electronic market making, it is after all only one firm. The support it could give to its internal ECN DirectEdge paled in comparison to what the Getcos and Limes of the world could deliver to BATS. Adding Citadel and Goldman to the shareholder registry, assuming the support is there which it seems to be at first blush,[2] evens the score a bit. Remember, earlier in the year, when BATS had gotten so aggressive with its pricing with great fanfare and success, DirectEdge had also gotten aggressive and simply did not see the volume gains of BATS. We think that was in part due to a shareholder base of one powerful player as opposed to several powerful firms.

A second reason for DirectEdge's continued growth relates to the fact that it recently hired William O'Brien as CEO. Bill is an industry veteran despite only being 36 years old and most recently ran the listings business for Nasdaq. Prior to that though, he was the COO of Brut before it was acquired by Nasdaq and was one of the architects of the very clever and successful Brut/Nasdaq free DOT offering that helped catapult Nasdaq's market share in NYSE-listed securities. Interestingly, the strategy was rooted in an understanding of the importance of routing out to another market center, which is central to DirectEdge's strategy.

So now let's take a moment to discuss DirectEdge's somewhat unique strategy among displayed markets, which is the third reason we believe it has met with success. To begin with, DirectEdge is the only displayed venue integrated into multiple dark pools of liquidity (the displayed market run by the ISE does route to the ISE Midpoint Match but does not route to other dark pools). While the displayed market components still account for the bulk of its volume (323.3 million shares average daily volume in the third quarter), it is now doing anywhere from about 20 to 40 million shares per day in total with its half-dozen enhanced liquidity providers (ELPs), the name it gives to the dark pools of liquidity to which it routes, including Liquidnet H2O, the only venue which it has publicly disclosed. DirectEdge is also one of the few venues that seems to truly understand the need to integrate multiple types of market participants, catering to retail, wholesalers, and the buy-side (the latter seems to be more of a work in progress).

DirectEdge does this by essentially running two different systems, one called EDGX with pricing at 26 cents a hundred to take liquidity and 26 cents a hundred rebate to post liquidity, netting no fee, but a 26 cents a hundred fee when routing to other market centers, and another called EDGA, which charges nothing to add liquidity and nothing to take liquidity, but again 26 cents a hundred to route to other market centers. EDGX typically represents approximately three-quarters of DirectEdge's daily volume and EDGA the other one-quarter. Taking a page from the NYX Group's bifurcated pricing model which allows the NYSE to offer one of the cheapest take rates in the industry to encourage users to make the NYSE the first stop when taking liquidity and at the same time have Arca offer one of the most aggressive rebates in the industry (which is a strategy we almost certainly will see Nasdaq adopt soon too in light of its recent acquisition of the Boston Stock Exchange, since the deal was in part motivated to allow it this flexibility in pricing), DirectEdge's pricing model offers a way to appeal to different constituencies with different pricing. EDGX offers fairly competitive take rates and route-out fees, but offers the highest rebate in the industry to encourage the rebate-driven electronic market makers (that have become so crucial to the overall market structure as discussed earlier) to post aggressively there, which in turn attracts orders taking liquidity in a Reg NMS world where best price wins. EDGA, on the other hand, offers a "free-free" pricing model that aims to make it the first choice on the routing tables of extremely fee sensitive order flow providers like large retail brokers who can sweep through EDGA's book and if they are successful pay no fee at all and have a significant chance for price and volume improvement from the ELPs to boot. On the other hand, while those posting liquidity in EDGA get no rebate, which is a negative, what they do get is a chance to interact with "first look" order flow from retail and other market participants, which can be much more valuable than the sub-penny rebate foregone. EDGA's approach seems to be working and garnering a greater percentage of DirectEdge's order flow over time.

DirectEdge is the perfect venue with which to end this article as it is representative of the new market structure we live in, one in which dark pools and non-displayed order types are of increasing importance and one in which even displayed markets may leverage them to strengthen their offerings and help them continue to thrive rather than bury their heads in the sand and ignore them. That said, just like in real life, the "dark" needs to be approached with caution. The order types and rules of the dark pools and how they can potentially be gamed or how they can leak information must be seriously considered in before diving in and risking injury. They are not a cure–all and can also be very inappropriate for certain types of order flow. Similarly, the solutions out there to help deal with the fragmentation of dark pools need to be approached with a grain of salt. The "dark algos" being offered by the Street are not all created equal. In practice, they make varying degrees of effort to actually access the dark pools they say they are accessing because many of the dark pools have expensive fees. Paying a penny a share to a dark pool when one is only charging a penny for the algorithm to the customer is something some brokers try to avoid with margin considerations being put ahead of the customer's interests. Demand your execution reports/statistics from your brokers as you are entitled by regulation to know the venues at which executions take place if you make the request. And note that some purveyors of dark algos provide this information proactively. Compare the results. Caveat emptor.

Trading Talk

1. In fact, long before Nasdaq announced its stake in the LSE (and even before the speculation began about Nasdaq's desire to acquire the LSE), John Thain had issued public statements about wanting the NYSE Group to be one of the leaders in the global consolidation of the exchange space.
2. See Jim Cramer's May 26th editorial rant in the WSJ as he explains this rationale in a much more amusing and direct way than we ever could.
3. While there seems to be quite a bit of confusion over the value of Deutsche Börse's offer (particularly because of the 3-month look back formula) vis -a- vis that of the NYSE, Euronext management will have very little ability to get through anything that is not at least in the ballpark of a comparable deal, especially with hedge funds being such a large component of the shareholder base. While stock prices

fluctuate and an acquirer can always decide to leverage itself more or give up more of itself if it really wants the asset, we do give an edge to the NYSE on this front because of the greater cash component it has initially offered, the higher multiples US exchanges sport relative to European ones, and its intangible brand name value.

4. A few weeks ago at STA's annual Washington, DC conference we actually asked Commissioner Campos, the lone Commissioner left who voted in favor of NMS, whether with implementation costs now becoming a reality and most observers thinking that if Reg NMS were voted on again today, the vote would be 3-2 against, there is any possibility that the Reg NMS would be revisited. Not surprisingly, his basic answer was of course not, but what else could he say?

This chapter was originally published in the Journal of Trading.

MiFID and Its Impact

Robert Barnes, FSI, Managing Director, Equities, UBS Investment Bank
Chairman, Securities Trading Committee, London Investment Banking
Association

Expect more. Expect more competition, more complexity and more change with opportunities for those delivering the highest standards. Why?

MiFID will impact 3 relationships:

1. How buy-side firms interact with their clients
2. How sell-side firms interact with their buy-side clients
3. Exchange and broker relationships

Changes to these relationships will lead to the following consequences:

Competition will reduce Exchange and Central Counter Party (CCP) fees starting with Cash Equities. Why does this matter? Because lower Exchange fees increase liquidity, help reduce market impact, and ultimately improve investment performance, and these are good for the market.

The market landscape will become more complex. With competitive new entry, there will be more choice of execution venues and related entities which will require more sophisticated tools and methods to manage.

Buy-side firms embracing change and building on unbundling trends can become more efficient. As buy-side firms have new best execution obligations to their clients, the potential for added importance derives from how effectively buy-side firms exercise their responsibilities in justifying their choices among executing brokers using MiFID criteria that excludes research, while separately rewarding value-added research, for example, through Commission Sharing Agreements (CSAs).

Conclusions about the impact of MiFID revolve around how the landscape will change. Volumes will grow due to lower Exchange fees and upgrades to faster matching engines. Smart-order-routing will arrive in Europe to pool in a virtual manner the multiple physical liquidity puddles resulting from competitive new entry. Order flow and new business will concentrate to those most capable in an increasingly fierce technological and commercial arms race.

MiFID sets the regulatory framework encouraging competitive new entry and entrepreneurial opportunity. Realising this opportunity arises from understanding and embracing impending change to market structures.

What Do We Mean by Market Structures?

MARKET STRUCTURES comprise the rules and institutions that determine competition among trading platforms. This definition encompasses the framework for interaction, including Exchange fees, which ultimately shape order execution strategies. The focus includes external factors that impact business and operating models driving opportunities to grow revenues and to reduce costs.

COMPETITION Enabled by MiFID and Encouraged by the Regulators

There is a symbiotic relationship that exists between Exchanges and their members, including brokers. One can see the brokers as a free sales and distribution arm for Exchanges, for example piping orderflow onto Exchange orderbooks as brokers sign Direct Execution clients or when brokers hedge blocks in smaller pieces on-orderbook.

As trading flows increase, through competitive broker automation for example, and Exchange internal unit costs fall as is the positive expectation of Exchanges as fixed cost platform providers, Exchange members have a reasonable case for Exchange tariffs to improve. Competition can lead to lower frictional costs.

Figure 1 shows the size of the market. According to the World Federation of Exchanges, the value of Cash Equities traded around the world in the most recent year 2006 was equivalent to USD 70 trillion with more than half represented by Americas. The lower level of value traded in Europe presents an interesting opportunity as economists indicate that the American and European economies are similar. Reducing frictional costs of trading, i.e. reducing Exchange and post-trade Central Counterparty (CCP) fees, may stimulate more liquidity in Europe.

Figure 1

$70tn+Cash Equities traded in 2006, up 37%+

Source: WFE single counted

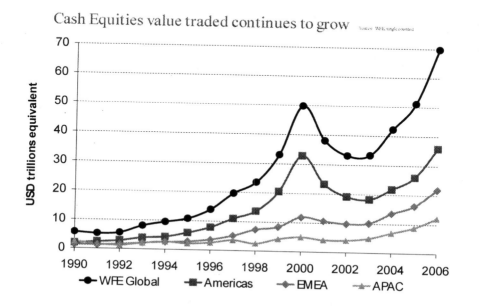

AMERICAS	$35,908,566m +38%	EMEA	$21,824,356m +34%	APAC	$12,099,937m +37%
American SE	$601,188m	Athens Exchange	$107,879m	Australian SE	$860,663m
Bermuda SE	$157m	BME Spanish Exchanges	$1,941,227m	Bombay SE	$215,010m
		Borsa Italiana	$1,596,199m	Bursa Malaysia	$75,487m
Buenos Aires SE	$5,281m	Budapest SE	$31,000m	Colombo SE	$1,004m
		Deutsche Börse	$2,741,608m	Hong Kong Exchanges	$832,386m
Colombia SE	$15,000m	Euronext	$3,805,260m	Jakarta SE	$48,844m
Lima SE	$5,492m	Irish SE	$81,786m	Korea Exchange	$1,339,638m
		Istanbul SE	$224,610m	National Stock Exchange India	$424,251m
Mexican Exchange	$96,320m	JSE	$312,296m	New Zealand Exchange	$22,185m
		Ljubljana SE	$2,059m	Osaka SE	$262,954m
Nasdaq	$11,807,491m	London SE	$7,583,762m	Philippine SE	$11,252m
		Luxembourg SE	$263m	Shanghai SE	$738,859m
NYSE	$21,789,392m	Malta SE	$255m	Shenzhen SE	$423,699m
		OMX Exchanges	$1,332,732m		
Santiago SE	$29,691m	Oslo Bors	$406,469m	Singapore Exchange	$180,440m
Sao Paulo SE	$267,076m	Swiss Exchange & virt-x	$1,395,567m	Taiwan SE Corp.	$737,742m
		Tehran SE	$4,886m		
TSX Group	$1,282,478m	Tel Aviv SE	$65,538m	Thailand Stock Exchange	$100,654m
		Warsaw SE	$56,061m	Tokyo Stock Exchange	$5,824,867m
		Wiener Börse	$82,245m		

Figure 2

Cash Equities value traded continues to grow

Source: WFE single counted

USD trillions equivalent

(graph showing values from 1990 to 2006, y-axis 0 to 70)

● WFE Global ■ Americas ◆ EMEA ▲ APAC

Figure 2 shows 17 years of data from the World Federation of Exchanges with the top right point highlighting the USD 70 trillion total value of Cash Equities traded in 2006 from Figure 1. While there is a relative peak in 2000 just before the bursting of the "internet bubble", the overwhelming trend of the data is that values trading on Exchanges are increasing.

Brokers directing this flow to Exchanges operate in an increasingly competitive environment. To compete at the top, brokers must innovate.

Fast technology is the enabler, algorithms the logic, and automation by brokers speeds the process. Clients benefit from brokers offering faster execution, potential price improvement and better service. The positive result is increased market activity.

A focus area for order execution strategies is minimising market impact, for example by slicing orders into ever-smaller sizes before deploying them, intelligently, onto Exchange orderbooks. The consequence for Exchange orderbooks is a trend of increasing number of bargains and smaller average size per trade as shown clearly in the next table.

Figure 3

Consequences for Orderbooks: bargains up + order size down

Source: www.londonstockexchange.com Factsheets and News

	Order book average size (£)	Order book number of bargains
2006	19,362	78,246,367
2005	20,463	51,415,546
2004	21,472	40,771,163
2003	21,739	32,897,427
2002	28,126	23,839,550
2001	41,283	15,750,253
2000	61,749	8,594,471
1999	63,020	5,374,520
1998	58,508	3,583,128

Figure 3 summarizes data from the London Stock Exchange (LSE). The trend is one of increasing number of bargains and lower average bargain size. This trend is broadly similar for all Exchanges with electronic orderbooks processing activity from brokers competing with other brokers in a fiercely challenging environment.

The timetable displayed coincides with brokers deploying increasingly sophisticated order execution engines. In 1999, the "internet bubble" neared its peak, and approximately 5 million bargains by number matched on LSE's orderbook across all members. By 2006, orderbook trades had grown to more than 78 million. Looking only at the growth in number of bargains, one never would have guessed there had been a "bear" market occurring 2000 to 2003. The table shows for 1999-2006 the average bargain size falling from GBP 63 thousand to less than GBP 20 thousand.

By multiplying the average size by number of bargains, one can see the overall value traded grew from 1999 to 2006 by almost 5 times and the number of trades by approximately 15 times. Exchanges benefit from these trends as they charge tariffs on a combination of number and value variables for processing trades through what are broadly fixed cost platforms.

As a fixed cost platform processes more activity, the internal unit cost of production falls which is good for the Exchange as it is good for its profitability. The benefits of economies of scale lead to more internal efficiencies at the Exchange, and this is shown clearly in the example provided by Deutsche Boerse summarized in Figure 4.

Figure 4

Deutsche Boerse 2002 annual report, page 24

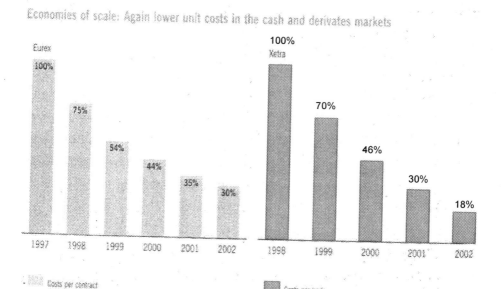

In Figure 4, Deutsche Boerse shows how its internal unit costs of processing a trade on Xetra, its Exchange orderbook, positively falls from a nomalised 100% in 1998 to 18% by 2002. This trend of reducing internal unit costs is broadly true for Exchanges with electronic orderbooks over the last few years. Although the chart stops at 2002, one would expect the reduction in unit costs to continue as orderbook activity has grown dramatically since then.

Meanwhile, Exchange fees to members of Exchanges have not reflected these economies of scales. In fact, the public statements from some of the Exchanges attempting a transformational merger with the London Stock Exchange, for example, suggested intentions not to raise Exchange fees [Macquarie, Nasdaq] or in some cases the potential sharing of synergy benefits with Users to the tune of approximately 10% cut in Exchange fees [Deutsche Boerse, Euronext]. LSE in January 2007, still independent, itself announced a selection of tariff cuts that will eventually be worth approximately 10%. Such offers, while welcome in principle, are underwhelming in context.

With the introduction of Cash Equities Central Counterparties (CCPs) to European markets in recent years, a new layer of frictional costs have appeared on top of Exchange fees for matching trades. So even where functionalities, such as netting, physically reduce the number of settlements, the current European Exchange and CCP tariff structures mean that Exchange and CCP fees for processing business have increased, contrary to expectations. This suggests a compelling need to review tariff structures.

Some European Exchanges and CCPs have engaged positively with the User community, for example through their own established User advisory groups or via the industry's representatives at the London Investment Banking Association (LIBA). This has led to new tariff structures which do yield lower marginal and average unit costs in some cases. The magnitude of the overall trend, however, of increasing number of bargains and lower average bargain size mean that the frictional costs of trading remain significant, and Exchange and CCP tariffs are material variable costs to brokers which becomes increasingly important to the market as business scales.

There is widespread belief in the market that additional value for money has not increased commensurately with Exchange volumes and revenues. The industry view, originally expressed through LIBA and increasingly widely supported by other trade associations, therefore, is that Exchanges and CCPs should address three issues regarding tariffs: headline cuts (to reflect the significant contributions already by members to the platforms), incentives for incremental flow (such as volume discounts, caps on aggregate fees, plus other creative mathematical ideas), and simplification of invoices.

What is the context for these consistent requests? Exchange members, including brokers, start with goodwill towards Exchanges and recognise the positive symbiotic relationship between Exchanges and Exchange members. Ideally, the way to grow business further is to work together with the incumbent Exchanges and CCPs in a spirit of entrepreneurialism and partnership. The motivation for reduction in frictional costs, particularly European Exchange and CCP fees, is to increase liquidity, lower market impact of pro-competitive broker order execution strategies, and ultimately increase investment performance for buy-side clients.

The reality today is that brokers have little influence with most Exchanges and post-trade providers such as CCPs, beyond the goodwill the Exchanges and post-trade providers offer, and this is particularly true in Europe. Given the current landscape and activity trends, one can understand why the incumbent Exchanges and post-trade providers prefer to preserve their privileged positions and yields from current tariff structures.

The free market alternative for addressing frictional costs is competitive new entry. Helpfully, there is regulatory support and encouragement for this.

MiFID Sets a Framework Enabling and Encouraging Competitive New Entry

There are three areas ripe for competitive new entry in Europe enabled by MiFID

1. Trade reporting and market data
2. Trade execution
3. Cash Equities clearing by CCP

Trade Reporting and Market Data – Project Boat

Post-MiFID, there will be more transparency obligations and therefore more market data. Firms, however, will no longer be obliged to report only to Exchanges. As long as the data format is easily accessible to other market participants and available on a reasonable commercial basis, then firms may direct reports to a choice of destinations, including Exchanges as well as other destinations such as the offices of a third party or proprietary arrangements. The industry already is responding to this MiFID-enabled opportunity.

On 19 September 2006, nine firms, including UBS Investment Bank, announced Project BOAT, the intention to embrace the opportunity created by MiFID to pool trading transparency information across Europe to create a trade data and market data dissemination platform. BOAT will be inclusive and welcome contributions from other market participants. The ideal consequences will be improved efficiency, reduced reporting fees and pro-competitive challenge to the economic paradigm of market data. On 22 January 2007, the BOAT consortium announced its selection of technology and business partners.

Trade Execution – Pan European MTF / Project Turquoise

MiFID removes domestic Exchange concentration rules and recognises three trading destinations: Regulated Markets (RMs), Multi-lateral Trading Facilities (MTFs), and Systematic Internalisers (SIs). Everything else is Over-The-Counter (OTC).

RMs and MTFs are similar in that both require market surveillance. RMs and MTFs will have non-discretionary rules and bring together multiple third party buyers and sellers. Beyond an MTF, RMs verify that issuers comply with disclosure obligations. MTFs can admit to trading a stock name without issuer consent. SIs are firms dealing on own account that also are executing on an organised, frequent and systematic basis outside an RM or MTF. SIs have SI-specific market-wide transparency rules and some protection for firms operating as SIs by limiting to that firm's clients access to that firm's capital.

MiFID thus sets a framework for competitive trade execution. The industry already is responding to this MiFID-enabled opportunity.

With internalisation, MiFID encourages the competitive behaviour of queue-jumping, which can enable immediacy of execution, by allowing the ability to 'trade-through' a similar price elsewhere historically protected by 'price-time' priority. In February 2007, Euronext announced its intention to offer internalisation within its infrastructure and effectively recognise a shift to 'price-member-time' (PMT) priority for this functionality.

Interestingly, MiFID and the regulators anticipate that MTFs will be set up by RMs or firms. Already, there have been multiple announcements of intentions to offer alternative trading destinations. For example, a firm, Instinet, announced MTF Chi-X, and an Exchange, EASDAQ, announced its plan to launch Equiduct (it may become an RM).

On 15 November 2006, seven firms, including UBS Investment Bank, announced the intention to create a pan-European Equities trading platform followed by a statement on 18 April 2007 of the choice of clearing and settlement provider. Aligned with the spirit and letter of the impending MiFID regulations promoting competition, the driver for this MTF is to reduce frictional costs of trading, i.e. Exchange orderbook fees, and potentially innovate, e.g. with some smart anonymous block auctioning to minimize trading impact. This functionality may be analogous to that of BIDS, which stands for Block Interest Discovery Service, another consortium announced on 27 September 2006 by six banks including UBS Investment Bank to establish pro-competitive block trading in America (there followed on 1 March 2007 a statement of the joining by another six financial firms).

Similar to BOAT, the pan-European MTF, also referred to as Project Turquoise, plans to be inclusive and be open to all qualifying participants that wish to be members. A company with independent management will operate the MTF separately from the banks, and there is no intention to force client flow onto the platform.

The proposed MTF will therefore be just one more parallel venue, so the success of this MTF will depend on the attractiveness of its own fees and functionality. Helpfully, key regulators have expressed views supporting this pro-competitive initiative by the banks (see Appendix).

Cash Equities Clearing by CCP

MiFID access provisions regarding CCP, clearing and settlement arrangements complemented by the European Code of Conduct signed on 7 November 2006 by European Exchanges, CCPs, and Settlement entities, encourage competitive new entry and provide the regulatory tools for Users to escalate concerns to European regulators for "adult supervision" if an incumbent attempts to frustrate pro-competitive new entry. The industry already is responding to this MiFID-enabled opportunity.

In consultation with Users, including UBS Investment Bank, LSE and SIS x-clear announced on 24 May 2006 the intention to provide member firms with a choice of clearing provider in addition to LCH.Clearnet for UK equity trades processed by LSE from the latter part of 2007. This coincided with publication of a paper by the EU Commission Competition DG entitled, "Competition in EU securities trading and post-trading Issues Paper" which stated in the Executive Summary on page 2, "CCP services could - and probably should - operate in a competitive environment provided issues of interoperability are overcome."

For some years, a working interoperability precedent has existed facilitating User choice of CCP for Swiss blue-chips as part of the virt-x post-trade market model. Like most offerings by virt-x, this was a result of consultation with Users. Interestingly, Users, including platform-neutral pro-competition UBS Investment Bank, suggested ahead of the original virt-x CCP launch that SIS x-clear should not be the only CCP for virt-x as LCH was such an important service provider to the international markets. The record shows subsequently that SIS x-clear operating in a competitive environment won additional clearing business, including that moved to SIS x-clear by UBS Investment Bank, on objective merit via its compelling commercial and functional offerings. Such achievement sends a strong signal that competition works.

Extension of initiatives such as SIS x-clear to the UK market will give further credibility to rolling out similar competitive initiatives to other European markets that have incumbent CCPs. The elegance of the proposed competitive CCP model open to all is that only members that believe they will benefit commercially and functionally from migrating clearing from the incumbent need switch. The rest stay with the incumbent if they wish. N.B. Users also can choose between LCH.Clearnet and CC&G in Italy for Fixed Income trades matched on the MTS platform.

With Competitive New Entry Comes More Choice and Therefore COMPLEXITY

Competition will reduce Exchange and CCP fees leading to increased liquidity. Competitive new entry also means more entities and thus more fragmentation. Brokers will need more technology to manage this new complexity, and this will require significant technological investment. Two innovations likely to arrive in Europe will include intelligent or Smart-Order-Routing (SOR) and dark pools of liquidity.

Smart-Order-Routing (SOR)

Many will recall previous attempts at competitive new entry for orderbook trading, including pan-European initiatives from Tradepoint, Jiway, Easdaq, virt-x, Nasdaq Europe, Borsa Italiana's MTA International, and the more targeted challenges vs Euronext of Deutsche Boerse's Dutch initiative and LSE's Eurosets Dutch Trading Service. Aside from SWX successfully growing its global market share of its core Swiss blue chip trading by pro-actively moving its liquidity pool to its London-based virt-x Recognised Investment Exchange (UK RIE), all previous orderbook attempts to compete with incumbent platforms have yet to gain meaningful market share. This is due to neither lack of good ideas nor lack of resources. One key missing structural component is the lack of SOR mass deployment in Europe.

Because of the overriding importance to participants of liquidity, the current market structure encourages Exchange members to continue to direct "at-market" orders (which take offers and hit bids on electronic orderbooks) to the domestic pool of liquidity, and "limit" orders (the actual bids and offers that fill the order-book) to where those limit orders are most likely to be 'hit' by at-market orders (i.e. again, the domestic market). Unless Users have comfort that other market participants can both recognise and seamlessly interact with limit orders placed on alternative platforms, the status quo will remain.

SOR pools puddles. Via intelligent electronic links to multiple platforms, SOR enables seamless recognition and interaction with orders across these physically fragmented platforms as if they belong to one virtual pool of liquidity. Like the fax machine, internet and mobile phone, SOR becomes meaningful with mass deployment.

Why is meaningful deployment of SOR in Europe more probable now than before? Firstly, MiFID as a regulatory imperative means firms are all preparing for the same start date, November 2007. This means all are, legitimately, looking at the same issues at the same time, and all are, in parallel, upgrading systems as relevant. Secondly, SOR is available, and many are familiar with SOR methods that have existed within the USA market structure for years. In fact, brokers not deploying SOR in Europe may find themselves at a competitive disadvantage.

How Might the Incumbents Respond to These Competitive Challenges?

1. Downplay potential competition and maintain that the status quo will continue.
2. Slow progress of a competitive new entrant by initiating a regulatory complaint with the resulting bureaucratic process. Such a tactic seems less likely given the awareness and positive comments in the public domain from key regulators supporting the announced pro-competitive initiatives (see Appendix).
3. Pro-actively reduce fees. This is starting, welcome but small in scale.
4. Perhaps the most interesting is that incumbents may leverage their existing or announce new competitive offerings. Mass deployment of SOR will increase the success probability of the pro-competitive MTF announced on 15 November 2006 as well as that of the earlier Exchange initiatives listed above. One way or another competition will reduce Exchange fees.
5. Volunteer to participate in market initiatives. There are also some examples of this.

Dark Pools of Liquidity

Where SOR pools puddles, dark pools aim to reduce information leakage while finding anonymous liquidity. Dark pools, an increasingly used buzz word, exist where firm orders are not yet executed nor displayed to the market. This is hardly novel. Consider the hidden components of iceberg orders. For example, if one has 100 to trade, shows 10 and hides 90 through an iceberg order-type, this is classic functionality that exists on many Exchanges. Similarly, the traditional matching by brokers of buy and sell orders on the way to the market is another example of accessing dark liquidity.

Dark pools effectively augment traditional broker skills of finding the other side of a trade and automate the process with electronic pipes. More recent examples include alternative crossing systems, such as Liquidnet or BIDS. There are also likely to be improved broker blind crossing of institutional flow and broker blind crossing of institutional with retail flow.

The Challenge to Manage More Complexity

The challenge is to source liquidity in an increasingly fragmented landscape. This is therefore not only about technology, it is about improving process.

MiFID itself provides an example with Best Execution. Best Execution in many jurisdictions today emphasises price. MiFID redefines Best Execution as a "Process to deliver Best Possible Result."

Under MiFID, firms (both buy-side and sell-side) have new Best Execution obligations which are broadly to have an Execution policy to take all reasonable steps to achieve the best possible result for their respective clients and to be able to demonstrate on request from clients or regulators they have executed orders in accordance with their policies.

Research is no longer a criterion for choice of executing broker. Building on the trends of unbundling legislation adopted since 2006 in the UK, buy-side clients have freedom to direct orders to the destination that gives Best Execution. Separately, buy-side clients have the power to reward value-added Research, for example, via Commission Sharing Agreements (CSAs).

The result will be more competition among firms in an increasingly fierce commercial and technical arms race. Order flow and business should concentrate to those most capable.

What skills will clients increasingly demand? Skills will include crossing, pro-active liquidity finding, and competence deploying quality technology.

On what criteria will brokers seek to differentiate themselves? Market share and the quality of internal liquidity access will be critical to a broker's crossing performance. The logic for buy-side clients will be to direct order flow to the brokers with larger market share and better internal liquidity since this will increase the probability of crossing and therefore the probability of potential price improvement leading to better investment performance.

Connecting only to an Exchange's orderbook will miss all the potential dark liquidity of the leading broker. Pro-active liquidity finding is all about the traditional brokerage ability of confidentially finding the other side of the trade. Confidentiality and minimising information leakage will highlight the increasingly important need to interact with a broker that stands by a policy in public, for example, of "No pre-hedging ahead of client orders."

Technology competence will include connection of Smart-Order-Routing to a meaningful number and range of multiple venues, algorithmic trading for minimising market impact on deployment of order execution strategies, and a structured process for monitoring and evaluation. Order flow will concentrate to those most capable.

CHANGE is a Dynamic Process

Buy-side clients embracing change can have more importance if they more effectively exercise their responsibilities to understand, explain, monitor, decide, and justify their choice of executing broker. This may require some buy-side clients to make new efforts to learn about the state-of-the-art services of their sell-side execution brokers, including, for example, how algorithms work and how directing orderflow to the best executing brokers help the buy-side client better compete with other buy-side peers through benchmark outperformance. The process to deliver best possible result by brokers will increasingly extend to include sales/trading complementing highest consistent execution quality with calls of relevance and insight.

The Impact of MiFID

MiFID creates opportunities for those delivering the highest standards and duty of care.

MiFID will increase competition, lower Exchange and CCP fees, and increase liquidity. MiFID will increase choice and therefore complexity, and Europe will see Smart Order Routing deployed. MiFID will increase change adding importance to those buy-side clients building on unbundling trends and exercising their new responsibilities to understand, explain, monitor, decide, and justify their choice of executing broker on MiFID criteria that excludes research, while separately rewarding value-added research, for example, through Commission Sharing Agreements (CSAs).

Ultimately, MiFID sets a framework where orderflow and new business can concentrate to those most capable in an increasingly fierce commercial and technical arms race.

Appendix: Regulators Encourage Competition Through MiFID

Views from Regulators support the pro-competitive initiative by banks

"Because I am convinced that competition drives competitiveness, growth and productivity, **I am encouraged by the news that a group of banks is considering launching a new trading platform**...I trust that, if needs be, it will be able to seamlessly plug into the existing post-trade infrastructure on a non-discriminatory basis...The same applies for some other platform providers."
Neelie Kroes
European Minister for Competition Policy
30 November 2006, City & Financial/ICMA conference, Brussels:
"Securities markets – the post-trading Code of Conduct and competition"
http://europa.eu.int/rapid/pressReleasesAction.do?reference=SPEECH/06/764&format=HTML&a
ged=0&language=EN&guiLanguage=en

"The overall purpose of [MiFID] is to broaden and deepen competition in the field of investment services, to stimulate competition between stock exchanges and alternative trading platforms across Europe and to enhance the overall efficiency of the pan-European investment services industry. Already we are beginning to see positive impacts: Last week Project Turquoise was announced – a project initiated by seven global investment banks to establish a new trading platform for equities to compete with the established European exchanges. It is expected to be up and running in 2008- shortly after the MIFID takes full legal effect. **This is good news for competition and will I hope bring down the cost of trading.**"
Charlie McCreevy
European Commissioner for Internal Market and Services
24 November 2006, Institute of European Affairs, Dublin:
"Fulfilling the Promise of Europe's Asset Management Industry"
http://europa.eu/rapid/pressReleasesAction.do?reference=SPEECH/06/745&format=HTML&aged=0&
language=EN&guiLanguage=en

"The MiFID standard is intended to drive orders to those venues that deliver the best possible result for clients. It is interesting to see that the marketplace is already changing to compete against this standard. We have noted with interest the recent announcement by a group of major banks that they intend to establish a bank-driven European trading platform. **We anticipate that MiFID will continue to stimulate competition and that this will drive down the cost of dealing across Europe.**"
Hector Sants
Managing Director, Wholesale Markets Division, FSA
23 November 2006, MiFID Trade Tech Conference:
"Implementing Best Execution Requirements in Different Markets for Different Clients"
http://www.fsa.gov.uk/pages/Library/Communication/Speeches/2006/1123_hs.shtml

Ed Balls suggested that **the recent move by leading banks to create a virtual exchange to challenge established forces was a triumph for MiFID.** "We were right when we said this was going to open up markets and make financial services more competitive"
Ed Balls
Economic Secretary to the UK Treasury and City Minister
22 November 2006, Financial Times, page 2

Dark Matters

By Howard Edelstein, Nyfix

The New York Stock Exchange traces its foundations to brokers who traded under a Buttonwood tree on Wall Street. If we were to extend the trading into contemporary times, we might see them move behind the tree, into its darkest shadows, and trading only when no one could see enough detail to identify the traders.

Exchanges have become the venues of last resort for a trade because all the current strategies imply that you don't want your trading intentions to become known. Paradoxically, exchanges were set up to provide information, and now exchanges are a place where you can't get things done because everybody knows what you want to do.

Trading has been moving off exchanges to ECNs and, increasingly, dark pools and crossing nets. The US has approximately 29 dark pools or crossing nets in or near production; the numbers fluctuate and brokerages consider or create new entrants relatively quickly, drawing on their internal order flow to provide immediate liquidity.

Unlike ECNs, which were set up to display limit orders, dark pools are completely non-transparent and thus offer a compelling combination of liquidity and anonymity – not only are the players anonymous but their orders are invisible until they are triggered by a match on the opposite side. The mysterious nature of dark liquidity accounts both for its rapid growth and some recent regulatory interest.

A little historical background

The changing role of the exchanges follows one of the oldest, and least predictable, rules of life – the law of unintended consequences. The United States had relatively few off-exchange venues, such as POSIT and Instinet, before Congressional direction to the SEC led to regulatory changes that spawned ECNs. Until then, most trades in NYSE and AMEX stocks were conducted through specialists whose job was to maintain an orderly and confidential market, goals which were largely achieved most of the time.

The shift to ECNs, and the fast-growing number of them, was largely responsible for the rapid electronification of trading in American equity capital markets. The move to decimalization and the resulting spreads counted in pennies further encouraged electronic trading; involving human traders drove costs into the red.

But the predictable effect of multiple ECNs and thin, narrow markets was much greater difficulty in finding liquidity – it was spread across venues and across a range of prices, only the top of them identifiable. If you are trying to move a large amount of a stock which doesn't trade in volume, it is hard to find the liquidity and it is hard to consummate the trade without significant market impact.

Now that the major sell-side houses are making a substantial share of their earnings from proprietary trading, buy-side institutions are reluctant to turn to them to handle block trades, concerned that they might be easy pickings for the prop desk.

Algorithmic trading is one solution. Traders chop up their blocks and hit the market with numerous small orders at a specific price, cancelling those that don't fill. As a strategy, this approaches the law of diminishing returns. Shares per trade on the NYSE today run around 300, approaching retail levels. Disposing of a large block of stock can require hundreds of separate orders that need to be managed, and even trading in small batches risks alerting the market that someone is trying to move a large position, just through the sheer volume of orders.

Enter Dark Pools

Though off-exchange crossing networks like Posit and Instinet have existed for decades, NYFIX Millennium, launched in 2001, was the first real-time continuous pool of non-displayed liquidity, and hence represented a significant innovation in the dark pool space. Millennium has been followed by a growing number of pools of non-displayed liquidity, or crossing networks, as institutions have become more comfortable with the concept and recognized them as a legitimate source of liquidity.

In general, the pools fall into two general categories – the independent entities such as Millennium, Pipeline, and LiquidNet -- and a longer list of alternative trading systems that have been registered by brokers. Many of these are motivated by brokers' desire to internalize trades. So where brokers formerly crossed a buyer and seller on the desk, the firm has put into place an electronic market that can execute the trade and produce records to demonstrate best price.

About half the existing crossing networks are broker internalization engines and fulfill an important function for the brokerage. They won't be quick to consolidate, as long as they fulfill their goal, but the industry will probably see consolidation among the standalone ATS services.

Although they still haven't gained widespread recognition amongst the general public, most of which still thinks the bell ringing on the NYSE is somehow important, dark pools are taking a steadily increasing share of electronic trading.

Exponentially Growing Volumes

As institutions have become more comfortable with the dark pool concept, Millennium's volumes have risen consistently and rapidly. With this success, the competitive landscape has become very crowded. As of this writing there are more than 30 dark pools or crossing networks in or near production. According to recent research from The Tabb Group, these dark liquidity centers account for nearly 10 percent of the market's total equity volumes. While most of these are currently operating within the US market, Europe too is beginning to experience a similar explosion fueled primarily by MiFID requirements.

NYFIX Millennium is unique in that it was built to leverage NYFIX's robust FIX-based trading community, the NYFIX Marketplace. The Marketplace consists of 330 buy side firms, 120 brokers and connectivity with more than 30 third-party networks, providing Millennium participants access to a huge swath of the market. As a key component of the Marketplace, Millennium clients directly benefit from the ability to quickly and seamlessly take any order and either expose it or deliver it to the matching engine. Participation in the NYFIX Marketplace also yields an extreme level of flexibility, providing users the ability to get orders into the system in an efficient, turnkey manner.

NYFIX Millennium also distinguishes itself from this crowded field in a number of ways. For one, Millennium takes great pride in being non-exclusionary and more open than other systems. This 'openness' extends to both the participants and types of order flow present in the system — buy side, sell side, algorithmic, block, etc. — to the manner in which orders are executed within Millennium. By exposing participants to such a diverse range of order types and market players, Millennium users' freedom of choice is maximized.

Millennium is also open in its approach to how orders get executed. NYFIX does not discriminate based on size nor confine orders to only execute at the midpoint. This allows for a tremendous level of both scalability and flexibility, enabling the trader or algorithm to use Millennium as a tool to source liquidity in a variety of different ways. For example, if a trader only wants to execute 100,000 shares at the midpoint they can do that, but if in a different symbol they are willing to soak up as much liquidity as possible when the spread is 2 cents or less, they can easily do that as well.

These characteristics have led to what is perhaps the most compelling aspect of NYFIX Millennium, its sheer volume. By providing a venue for an extremely diverse range of order flow interaction and by providing users a flexible means of execution, NYFIX Millennium has attained impressive and steadily increasing volume figures. By the end of 2006, Millennium was touching more than a billion shares per day. Matched shares in Millennium now average more than 45 million daily. In May of 2007, the system set a single-day volume record by matching more than 80 million shares.

Buy-side firms tell research analysts that they are already sending up to 50 percent of their orders to crossing networks, while only 12 to 20 percent gets matched. Both buy-side and sell-side expect their trading volumes on crossing networks to increase over the next two years, although they are hesitant to estimate how much. Still, with over 30 dark pools already out there and more on the horizon, market fragmentation is beginning to become a concern.

Algorithms are one way to avoid fragmentation of the marketplace.   But there are others as well. A new NYFIX innovation called Millennium PLUS draws in liquidity from other dark pools and streaming liquidity providers by generating "liquidity alerts" that indicate a block of shares is available. Matching rates for users of Millennium PLUS orders have increased 40-50% over their previous levels. The Millennium PLUS Liquidity Alerts operate purely at the market infrastructure level – there are no IOIs generated that an alert trader could act on or position against.   This minimizes market impact as well as fragmentation.

Next Stop: Europe

Changes being introduced by the European Commission aimed at creating a single capital market across the 31 countries of the EEA (European Economic Area) are proving a significant catalyst for change in the nature of trading. This is driving competition among participants seeking to operate and provide services to this emerging single market.   Principal among the regulatory change is the Markets in Financial Instrument Directive (MiFID) which came into force in November 2007. MiFID will eliminate national financial boundaries creating opportunity for market participants to operate on a truly pan-European basis.

Electronic trading is also on the increase. Buy-side, Hedge Fund and sell-side firms are all driving more and more trading electronic in an effort to provide efficiency, achieve true STP and ultimately drive down the cost of trading. This is true across all instruments across all markets.

There are currently 40 Equity Markets spread across 29 European countries. This number includes a small number of dark pools like ITG POSIT and Liquidnet. In some countries, such as France and Spain, such pools were not permitted pre-MiFID, thanks to 1993 legislation under the Financial Investment Services Directive (ISD). The ISD contained legislation that allowed national exchanges to compel members to execute trades ONLY on the exchange in securities listed on that exchange. Some markets, like the UK and Germany never went as far as adopting this legislation and therefore do not have a so-called "concentration" rule in place.

It is within these markets that dark pools currently operate. In Germany, as much as 40% of the daily turnover in equity volume is done off exchange, even though there are no formal crossing facilities. Since 2000, approximately 10 ATS trading systems have been launched in the UK alone. While adoption of these systems has been slow, by the end of 2006 the five remaining platforms claimed a market share estimated to be about 1% of the LSE trading volumes. Because of the changing market conditions this is expected to change rapidly in 2007 and beyond.

Liquidnet, which has been active in Europe since the end of 2002, is widely viewed as the largest player in that region among the dark pools. ITG's POSIT is another significant player, largely in UK small and mid-cap names. With the introduction of MiFID, other leading US players, including NYFIX Millennium, have announced plans to enter the market as well. This should dramatically alter the competitive landscape in 2008 and beyond.

Future Models

As we can see from the slow rate of adoption outside the US, dark pools are still in their early phases and will continue to evolve. Consolidation is likely, as is specialization. Eventually, as sell-side trading systems are increasingly commoditized, we could see the emergence of competing commercial order matching utilities within the industry, similar to what has emerged in the pre- and post-trade space. Such a utility would allow the sell-side to focus on serving the buy-side without having to worry about being disintermediated.

On its face, outsourcing the trade itself may sound like a bridge too far, even in a world that is changing as rapidly as ours. To get there will require a fresh view of technology and customer value propositions throughout the industry. But who would have predicted 10 years ago that the market that started under the canopy of the Buttonwood tree would eventually drift off into the shadows once again.

Is It Time For a New Generation of Trading Systems?

By Bijan Monassebian, Ordex Systems

Abstract

Eighty percent of buy-side traders are dissatisfied with their order management systems, according to a study by TABB Group[xciii]. In addition, 33 percent of advancedtrading.com readers named challenges with their OMSs and EMSs as their biggest overall challenge[1]. OMS and EMS vendors are responding to this challenge by enhancing and upgrading their systems.

This article reviews these challenges and outlines the new underlying software architecture needed to make it easier and more efficient to meet the existing and new business requirements of the industry.

The author, Bijan Monassebian, is an industry veteran who has managed, built, and installed many trading and order management systems for financial services organizations[xciv]. [this should be in bio as should the footnote]

Introduction

Capital Markets participants are constantly faced with industry dynamics that require changes and enhancement to the way business is conducted. These dynamics, including competitive pressures, regulatory changes, increasing transaction rates and business innovation considerations, almost always impact the trading systems utilized by these organizations.

The architecture for a new generation of trade (order and execution) management systems must enable the user organizations to respond and adapt to these required changes and enhancements efficiently and quickly in order to avoid both opportunity costs and higher cost of software ownership.

Challenges

Much has been written by industry professionals and analysts outlining the many challenges that traders, particularly on the buy-side, face in their normal day-to-day trading activities. To establish a point of reference, we summarize below some of these issues[xcv]:

- While the functionality and complexity of software applications such as order management systems (OMS) and execution management systems (EMS) that traders use are increasing, it is not unusual to find screens from multiple brokers and vendors on traders' desktops. Various industry studies show that a large number of buy-side firms utilize more than one trading platform on their desktops to satisfy their needs. It is not uncommon for information entered in one system not to appear in the other, causing expensive errors.
- Many buy-side traders have an OMS that performs functions such as allocations, position management, and communication between portfolio managers and traders. The issues facing traders in this scenario are –
- Do I also need an EMS?
- If so, how do I integrate my OMS with the EMS system?
- How do I avoid duplication of functions and data?
- How do I ensure that my multiple systems are always in sync?
- OMS systems were designed to manage the buy-side's workflow and help control operational expenses. Most of these systems were not originally designed to handle complex trading functions. On the other hand, EMS platforms were specifically designed to manage automated trading across multiple venues. True seamless integration between an EMS and OMS is not an easy task.
- In some OMS systems, a great deal of transaction processing is performed in the user workstation (client tier). This approach necessitates transmitting large number of transactions from the server to the client resulting in processing delays and backups, particularly during high volume periods, a problem that can only grow worse as the average order size continues to shrink.
- Some firms that utilize both OMS and EMS find it necessary to enter certain transactions twice, once in each system.
- There are many existing and emerging specialty function providers such as advanced algorithmic trading, pre and post trade compliance, Reg. NMS smart routing, sophisticated optimization techniques that help buy-side traders manage their orders across dark pools, and

transaction cost accounting. It is not always possible or easy for traders to take advantage of these offerings by integrating their existing OMS or EMS platforms with these service providers.

- Traders and trading managers need to be able to conduct their business from remote locations away from their offices via the Internet.

Putting Issues in Perspective

It is clear from the above, that the trading community has issues with existing OMS and EMS platforms. They expect solutions in addition to assurances that the future needs of the industry are accommodated by the vendors. In order to address them methodically, the issues can be categorized as follows:

- Number of different EMS platforms a trader has to use to get the job done
- Integration of OMS and EMS platforms
- Ability to handle transaction peaks without delay
- Ability to seamlessly utilize services provided by third parties
- Secured access to all trading functions through Internet

New software technologies have become commercially viable in the last 2-3 years that make it feasible and cost effective to address the above issues. First, a review of the issues:

Number of Different EMS Platforms a Trader Has to Use to Get The Job Done

Trading system providers offer a wide variety of features and services. In addition, many of the features and functions provided have their own unique twists that make them attractive to certain users. Switching from one vendor to another in order to satisfy the firms' evolving business requirements is very costly. As the result, many trading firms find it necessary to utilize more than one trading system, in particular EMS, to address the needs of their trading desks.

As discussed in the next section of this article, the long-term solution to this problem is the new and evolving design approach in complementing one's own trading system functions by also utilizing 'best-of-breed' services provided by third parties to address the overall needs of trading desks.

Integration of OMS and EMS platforms

There have been many articles written outlining the issues and challenges in integrating existing OMS and EMS systems. While this pseudo integration can be accomplished by some sort of messaging or API (Application Programming Interface), it generally results in duplication of data, duplication of functions, synchronization issues between two or more systems, and overhead of dealing with multiple and different systems.

Available technology today along with possible architectural approaches make it very feasible to build a new generation of trading systems that can accommodate user needs by 'plugging in' specific functions and seamlessly integrate with third party service providers.

The divide between OMS and EMS functionally results from the evolution of these systems over a number of years based on the user requirements in each area and the available technology at the time. There are absolutely no technical or business reasons today why the new generation of integrated OMS/EMS systems, when designed properly from ground-up, cannot enable users to choose the functionality that they need in one comprehensive trading platform. These systems will be "service bus" oriented as to where to process a transaction or a user request;, the appropriate functions are invoked as necessary.

The new generation trading systems must also employ comprehensive scalability (discussed in detail later) features to accommodate growth. It should be clear to the reader that one of the problems in some of the existing systems is the lack of this upgrade capability. For example, in a typical client/server design approach, the client computer, generally a PC, may receive a significant number of transactions during peak market periods. Since the architecture of the PC is generally a single computer and only capable of one-for-one upgrade, the users need to constantly upgrade to a more powerful computer and if not feasible, live with the delays in processing.

The typical client/server design has been an excellent choice to enable us to provide the users with "rich" user interfaces (GUI's). However, this design approach limits the choices available for upgrading the user computer (PC).

Ability to Handle Transaction Peaks Without Delay

We can see from the above issues that there exists a common thread across all of them. If we design a system that is capable of providing the necessary level of scalability, these problems can be dealt with and overcome. This platform will then enable support for integrated OMS and EMS functionality.

A later section outlines the architectural and design considerations that must be taken into account to ensure a high level of scalability. Proper design for high scalability also solves the issues related to processing speeds and the notion that OMS systems cannot be expected to have the same speeds as EMS systems.

Ability to Seamlessly Utilize Services Provided by Third Parties

There are many services that are provided by firms who specialize in a particular field and offer "best-of-breed" services such as:

- Advanced algorithmic trading
- Pre and post trade compliance
- Reg. NMS smart routing
- Sophisticated optimization techniques that help buy-side traders manage their orders across dark pools
- Transaction cost accounting
- Market data

It is neither practical nor cost effective to build and maintain the above services in-house or expect a vendor to be able to excel in every area and provide the needed services. Systems that are SOA (Service Oriented Architecture) enabled offer the opportunity to interact and utilize the services offered by other SOA enabled service providers. A more detailed discussion of SOA appears later.

Secured Access To All trading Functions Through The Internet

As mentioned earlier, the typical client/server design provides users with "rich" user interfaces (GUI's). However, it limits the portability of the trading systems by not allowing the users to access the trading system from any remote location without the need for some portion of the application software residing on the PC.

A totally server-based application will allow the authorized users of the system access to it from remote locations. PC workstations do not need to install any application modules and they are not tightly coupled with the server for processing of transactions. PC workstations' only responsibility is to support interactions with the server utilizing standard Web browser capabilities.

In addition, a server-based-only application makes it easier to provide load balancing, fault-tolerance, and database replication.

How to Address the Above Issues

In systems that require high performance and high availability, the issues that are outlined above interact and determine the over-all satisfaction level of the users. It can be demonstrated that most if not all of these issues can be addressed by two key concepts if built into the architecture of the new generation of trading systems. These two concepts, while easy to describe are difficult and complex to incorporate into the design of an application system. The concepts are:

- Scalability
- Service oriented design

These two concepts can be simply described as: 1) for an application to do what is demanded of it, it needs sufficient computer processing power, and 2) given sufficient computer processing power, the application must be capable of utilizing this power to get the job done speedily and efficiently.

Scalability

Scalability is a key pre-requisite for a trading system to be viable. Scalability of applications refers to the ability to upgrade the computer hardware configuration in order to accommodate higher processing demands on the hardware resources resulting from additional users, increased transaction rates, and other processing demands such as new software features.
Scalability can be achieved in two ways -- *scaling up* and *scaling out*.

- *Scaling up* does not require any special software features or capabilities. It simply involves replacing the existing server with a more powerful version and to optimize the software to accommodate additional transactions or users. This approach generally is not cost effective since it requires a complete change of a server. It is also limited by the resources of the most powerful computer available to do the job.
- *Scaling out* allows the addition of servers without disturbing the operation of the software. Under this type of configuration multiple servers work in tandem and additional servers can be added as required. A pre-requisite for this approach to work is the design of the software to be able to operate seamlessly on multiple servers.

It can be seen from the above two design approaches that the *scaling out* design offers the most flexibility in addressing future growth requirements of a business. It is a key factor to consider when designing a trading application or evaluating vendor provided trading systems. This approach is server-based and is recommended for maximum flexibility and growth potential. The typical Client/server design that utilizes what is commonly referred to as "thick client", limits the ability of the system to scale out as discussed earlier. Scalability is accompanied by other requirements such as availability, maintainability, and reliability as briefly described below:

Availability

Availability, or more precisely high availability refers to what percentage of the time the application is up and running. It is measured over a time period and in trading environments this number is expected to be 99.999% or better.

Maintainability

An application is considered maintainable if it can cater easily to the changing needs of the business and users over its lifetime. Maintainability includes the ability to:

- Change/enhance existing functions as well as the addition of new functions
- Increase the number of users as needed
- Upgrade server (scale up) or incrementally add new server(s) as needed (scale out)
- Easily train new maintenance programmers, as required

Other factors that affect maintainability include third party components that are used by the application. Applications that are not tightly connected to third party components offer more flexibility in choosing the most appropriate components such as operating systems, database management systems, and other application middleware components as the business needs dictate over time.

Reliability

Downtime of an application due to bugs in the software is called the unreliability factor. It is readily obvious that reliability has a direct impact on availability of the application.

Service oriented design

The basic objective of a "service oriented design" approach is the separation of application functions. It is the process of modularizing and breaking out a software application into distinct features and functions; a process that ensures minimum overlap in functionality among modules. Service oriented design encompasses two implementation approaches:

- Internal services provided by application
- External services provided by service providers

These design approaches require a significant amount of time and space to discuss fully. For the purposes of this document, we simplify the discussion, and limit it to basic reasons why they are critical considerations in a trading application.

Internal Services Provided by Application

Internal services can be provided by software components to other software components. These services also include those provided by the any middleware utilized by the application. In this software architecture, referred to as "enterprise service bus", service requests are event driven and are invoked utilizing well defined interfaces and "service contracts". The significance here is in the benefits that this design model offers. Along with scaling out (distributed processing) and proper multi-threading design, it enables application systems to successfully cope with high business processing demands without delays and with speed.

External Services Provided by Service Providers

External services can be invoked by utilizing SOA (Service Oriented Architecture). SOA is a business concept or approach. It defines how Information Technology can be used to plan and deliver services for specific business needs. SOA is not a tool in itself but a conceptual architecture that can be utilized by business partners to provide and consume services.

Order Management Systems Vs. Execution Management Systems

By Patrick Keough

The recent explosion in popularity of Execution Management Systems (EMS) with the Buy Side over the last 5 years has brought unexpected competition for the market leading vendors of Order Management Systems (OMS). As both EMS and OMS vendors continue to innovate and evolve to meet market demand they continue to encroach on what was originally considered separate and differentiating core functionality. Although the lines between EMS and OMS systems are increasingly becoming blurry, there are still significant differences between the two types of systems and the functionality they provide to a prospective asset management client.

In order to better understand the differences and the ever increasing similarities between the two types of systems it is important to understand the history and evolution of the major vendors of both types of systems. It is also important to look forward to the future plans of these vendors, as they currently race to fill the ever increasingly sophisticated needs of their clients.

Order Management Systems

We will start by examining the key components and functionality of the older sibling, the OMS. Most buy-side firms are very comfortable with the traditional role that the OMS plays in their front office workflows. Over the last 15 years several software vendors have become very well established in this space. Several of the vendors started off with portfolio and pre-trade compliance systems which morphed into multi-asset trading systems. They have continued to evolve in an attempt to capture more and more of the buy side systems spend budget. One example of this functionality expansion is the OMS vendors' establishment of proprietary integrated FIX networks to seamlessly connect their trading systems to the sell-side broker desks. This has put considerable pressure on established FIX network providers such as

NYFIX and Thompsons ATR. Another example of this OMS vendor functionality expansion is the move to connect to multiple liquidity pools and integrate access to broker algorithms, effectively competing against EMS products' strengths.

There are several ways to determine which OMS vendors are among the United States market leaders. One could measure a company's success by installed client base, current OMS and FIX network yearly revenue, or the percentage of new client contracts signed per year. By any of these measures there are still relatively few OMS vendors who complete strongly across most of the major asset classes, including domestic and international equity, fixed income, including structured securities, currency, and derivatives. These are listed in the table below

Vendor	Product
Charles River Development	CR IMS
LatentZero	Capstone Suite
Macgregor	XIP/XEC
Linedata	Longview Trading
Bloomberg	POMS

This is not to say that these systems are the only game in town, as several other OMS venders have a very strong following in certain asset management areas. For example Eze Castle's Traders Console is a full multi-asset class OMS product which is a favorite with hedge fund managers due to its real-time Profit and Loss capabilities. Eze Castle also has recently increased EMS like functionality within their offering by leveraging the EMS expertise of the BNY ConvergEx Group.

It is important to understand the functionality domains of OMS products and the depth of their coverage in these areas. Traditionally an OMS system will consist of either a single piece of software or several tightly integrated pieces of software which will provide asset managers with the following functionality:

- Order Generation
- Compliance
- Order Execution
- Settlements support
- Integration to multiple data sources and down-stream systems

Order Generation

A key component of an OMS product is its ability to facilitate order generation for users. We will later see how this is both a strong positive characteristic of an OMS but also a significant limiting factor for OMS vendors as they try to remain as nimble and quick moving as their EMS counterparts. Among many other scenarios, order generation includes targeting a specific security weighting versus a portfolio value such as market value, portfolio review against benchmarks and models allowing for quick rebalancing of portfolios, as well as allowing users to quickly invest or divest cash across a portfolio based on the current weightings of its holdings. OMS systems also allow for more sophisticated order generation techniques such as dynamic composite modeling, duration neutral swaps, contingent orders or order generation based on derivative exposure. OMS systems will also allow portfolio managers to review tax implications of transactions and allow for optimal lot relief when generating sell transactions.

For an OMS to provide this level of order generation capability it is important for the OMS to maintain full detailed current portfolio holdings and tax lots as well as robust security and account information to ensure proper portfolio compliance. An OMS must also provide users the ability to create, load and maintain models, benchmarks and composites for use when generating orders.

Compliance

A natural compliment to order generation is pre-trade compliance. This allows a portfolio manager to quickly measure the impact of the newly generated orders against a myriad of legal, regulatory and client restrictions to ensure that the results of the transactions will still allow the involved portfolios to remain fully compliant prior to sending the trades to the trading desk to be executed. OMS products will also evaluate portfolio position verse compliance restrictions at the close of market to ensure that market valuation changes have not shifted the portfolios out of compliance. The need for robust compliance functionality has been a main catalyst for the acceptance and success of OMS products by asset managers. Many large institutional clients and smaller private wealth clients alike will require prospective money managers to demonstrate that they have proper controls in place to properly manage their money while ensuring complete adherence to legal and client mandated compliance restrictions. This area is a differentiator of the OMS versus the EMS. For obvious reasons it is again important for the OMS to maintain full detailed current portfolio holdings as well as robust security and account information to ensure proper portfolio compliance.

Order Execution

As one might expect, order execution is ground zero of the functionality battle between the OMS and EMS products. OMS offerings have been steadily evolving toward a more dynamic approach to order execution spurred forward by the popularity of the EMS products. In their simplest form, OMS products allow the user to provide a centralized and auditable environment for ticket capture and routing. Most OMS users leverage their system for considerably more than this though. Certainly on both the domestic and international equity front clients will use the OMS as the gateway, via FIX protocol, to electronic communication with the sell-side broker desks as well as Electronic Communications Networks (ECNs) such as Lava, BATS, and Bloomberg Tradebook and Alternative Trading Systems (ATSs) such a ITG Posit, Liquidnet, or Pipeline. Access to broker algorithms and more robust program trading capabilities are also hallmarks of the evolving OMS platforms.

This connectivity to multiple trading venues has become a key OMS strength and provides a competitive advantage to equity asset management firms executing through these venues. Although some of the leading OMS products have expanded the use of the FIX protocol to provide connectivity to fixed income trading venues such as MarketAxess and TradeWeb, as well as foreign exchange trading venues such as FXAll and FX Connect we will see when discussing the strengths of the EMS products that the EMS products certainly maintain a dominance in non-equity execution functionality.

Embedded real-time pricing information is another key component to assist traders in quickly identifying trading opportunities in fast paced markets. OMS vendors have made a series of product enhancements to incorporate real-time market information such as Level II quote information including bid, ask, last, and volume information into a centralized location. Although a good start for the OMS vendors, the true EMS products still hold a measurable lead in the depth and flexibility of real-time market data including full depth of book information (exceeding top five bids and asks), including Market Maker ID and the ever important time adjusted data elements. A trader's performance will often be benchmarked versus time adjusted market analytics such as Volume Weighted Average Price (VWAP). It isn't sufficient for a trader to know the current day's VWAP for a security. A trader needs to be able to view the security's VWAP based on market transactions from the time to order was received on the trading desk which can occur anytime throughout the day. Time adjusted analytics can be used to determine if a trader is too aggressive or too passive on a trade. These values are used throughout the day to give the trader a real-time look into realized and unrealized Profit and Loss calculations, and when captured along with the execution information of the trade, can be an effective tool for Transaction Cost Analysis (TCA).

Settlement Support

OMS products attempt to incorporate as much trade date order life cycle functionality as possible. There are numerous interfaces in these products to facilitate exporting trades to accounting systems and data warehouses, broker confirmation and allocation notification, custodial trade notification, trade matching and ticket routing. OASYS, CTM, ISITC and SWIFT messaging are among the interfaces provided by these products to allow trade support to quickly and efficiently begin the settlements process from the central location of the OMS product on trade date.

Many OMS vendors will maintain the interface between their system and the settlement systems. This frees the client from needing to create and maintain the interfaces to adapt to systems changes. Although these integrated interfaces are an important strength of the OMS products, it is not hard to see how this makes an OMS install a very involved process. The OMS sits at the starting point of the order life cycle and has interfaces to many of a money manager's most critical systems. Any upgrade of OMS software is therefore necessarily complicated by the multiple integration points and regression testing will normally involve multiple other systems and groups that use those systems. This causes the upgrade cycle of the OMS to be considerably more involved than the EMS which is tightly used by just the trading desk.

Integration to multiple data sources and down-stream systems

In order to support the complicated functionality of Order Generation, Compliance, Execution, and Settlements, the OMS products must be flexible enough to receive multiple data feeds for account information, security master file definition, positions, tax lots, corporate actions, broker direction, commission calculation, settlement instructions and tracking as well as any real-time market data updates.

Often it is the case that the information held in the OMS is not necessary for the actual execution of the transaction but is necessary to complete one of the other core functions of the OMS such as Compliance or Order Generation. Some examples of this type of non-trading critical data are:

- Proper portfolio modeling may require that a fixed income security must have an accurate duration or convexity. This will often require a load from a third party application such as Salomon's Yield Book or Lehman Point.
- In order to satisfy a pre-trade compliance test the security may need multiple security ratings such as a Moody or S&P rating.
- Often asset classes not traded on the OMS, such as real property or exotic derivatives, must be loaded into the OMS at the position level in order to appropriately calculate exposure for compliance testing.

The blessing of the OMS is that it is a single, central system that allows users to manage an order from inception through to settlement, but this is also among its biggest challenges, as it necessitates a complexity of interfaces and dependencies which the EMS products need not contend with. This complexity has lead the major OMS vendors to take very different tracks when adding EMS-like functionality. These different tracks are examined below in the section 'The Future of OMS Products'. The degree in which the OMS vendors integrate EMS-like functionality into the already complex dependencies of their products may very well be the deciding factor in their success or failure in competing with both their EMS and OMS rivals.

Execution Management Systems

The EMS product space is a fast moving and ever changing space. Implementations are relatively quick and easy compared to OMS products and new vendors with innovative functionality can rise to prominence quite quickly. Any list of top vendors in this space is bound to be dated before very long. This is a partial list of established multi-asset class vendors and products.

Vendor	Product
Portware	Portware Professional
Flex Trade	FlexTrader, FlexFX, FlexFutures, FlexOpt
Inforeach	TMS
Fidessa	Workstation

To be sure, there are many other vendors in this space and many have particular strengths in certain areas and there are many up and coming vendors showing great promise, Aegis Software's AthenaTrader and Tethys Technology's Exacta just to mention two. We intentionally excluded the broker owned EMS products, such as Goldman Sachs' REDIPlus, Citigroup's Lava Trading, and Lehman Brothers' Realtick, to focus on the true 'Broker Neutral' EMS offerings from ISVs (independent software vendors).

As with the OMS products, it is important to understand the functionality of EMS products and the depth of their coverage in these areas. We caution against too tightly defining the characteristics of an EMS, as they are quickly evolving. However the main characteristics of EMS products focus on order execution. Some of the main order execution characteristics are:

- Packaged and customizable trading strategies/algorithms
- Full depth of book real-time market data
- Pre and Post Trade Cost Analysis
- Flexible and customizable blotter and order handling
- Real-time event handling to trigger strategies/algorithms
- Real-time profit and loss calculations based on definable analytics
- Supports real-time risk management and exposure constrained trade execution
- Built for speed and volume (1000+ transactions per second in some cases)
- For Foreign Exchange trades Direct Liquidity Access – Banks, Dealers, ECNs, Exchanges
- Net orders, split orders, internally crossed and manual orders & executions
- For Futures and Options trades incorporated pricing models including custom, real-time Greek analytics calculations (delta, gamma, theta and vega)

There are many loose definitions of what bare qualifications a system must have to be considered an EMS. For the most part these qualifications grossly underestimate the flexibility, configurability and performance of workflows provided by EMS products. Most of these 'low bar' qualifications tend to focus on domestic equity trading which is where the EMS products started, but they have grown into much more since they first came to market.

The Tower Group defines an EMS as the following:

"A software-based platform that facilitates and manages the execution of securities orders, typically through the FIX protocol. An EMS has four key features: a trading blotter, connectivity, multiple destinations, and real-time market data."

Often the attribute of incorporating broker algorithms will be added to the above definition.

This definition, or one very similar, is touted often by the OMS vendors for the obvious reason that they compare quite favorably to EMS products when they are defined in this limited way. As we reviewed above, OMS products have a trading blotter, allow access to broker algorithms, provide connectivity to multiple destinations and can incorporate real-time market data.

If that is really all an EMS is, then why is there some much focus on how to determine where an OMS leaves off and an EMS begins? The answer is simple: First, an EMS is much more than this limited definition. Secondly, the configurability, adaptability and nimbleness of functional enhancements (as defined by time to market) of the EMS products compared to current OMS products are significantly different.

When looking at the differences between an OMS and an EMS product, it is less critical to compare which broad functionality areas are covered by each product than it is to compare precisely how that functionality is deployed from a technology and user's perspective.

Order Execution

One main misconception I see repeated by OMS marketing is that they often limit the scope of EMS functionality to the equity markets and primarily domestic markets at that. The EMS vendors have been in an arms race with each other to provide the best of breed solution across all asset classes including equity, fixed income, foreign exchange and derivatives. The true flexibility and lightning quick functionality enhancements can really show through on these more obscure and difficult to manage asset classes. Most integrated offerings by OMS vendors to date have been focused on EMS-like functionality for equity trading only.

The following is a slightly complicated, but extremely telling example of how EMS functionality differences run much deeper.

Presently one EMS vendor responding to client needs will soon offer foreign exchange traders the ability to quickly disassemble currency pairs into risk baskets and then trade those risk baskets against the most liquid currency pairs to achieve the best execution (defined as tightest bid/ask spread). The EMS will then reassemble the orders to their original currency pairs for settlement.

To better illustrate this let's examine a typical foreign exchange order a trader may receive.

An order is received on the trader's desk to sell Swiss Franc and purchase Mexican Peso. The currency pair Swiss Franc to Mexican Peso is not heavily traded therefore it has a wide bid/ask spread which will lead to poor execution. The EMS will allow the trader to quickly decouple the currencies and view the bid/ask spreads against all currencies and allow the trader to determine the best currency to triangulate the order for execution. In this case, the trader may decide to sell the Swiss Franc to purchase United States Dollar then use the United Stated Dollar to purchase Mexican Peso. The United States Dollar is more liquid to both the Swiss Franc and the Mexican Peso, thereby providing tighter bid/ask spreads for both legs of the transaction thus allowing for better execution. The EMS would then reassemble the Swiss Franc to Mexican Peso order based on the triangulated execution price to allow for settlement.

Now extrapolate this example to a foreign exchange trader that receives 100 or 1,000 currency trades at the same time, with wide variety of currency pairs. The EMS allows the trader to do the identical workflow across all the orders simultaneously ensuring the tightest spread execution for all transactions.

This example illustrates how the flexibility, customizability and agility of the EMS products have far outgrown the simple definition of "connectivity, multiple destinations, and real-time market data" as defined above. As mentioned prior, it has become less about the category of the functionality of an OMS versus an EMS than it is about the flexibility of how that functionality is implemented.

Performance

Performance is a hallmark of any EMS product. User interaction response times and minimal connectivity latency are a prime focus of these systems. EMS systems focus on the display of streaming real-time data, allowing traders to interact with a large number of orders, sending orders out to execution venues and retrieving fill information as close to instantaneously as possible. The advantages EMS systems have in the performance arena are that they are in general much lighter applications than OMS systems, and traders do not have to share limited system resources with all the different groups within their organization which typically use an OMS. This frees the trader from being constrained by a system that is slower to respond because it is built to do much more than order execution. The strength of the OMS system is its ability to facilitate order generation, compliance, order execution, settlements and system integration. By cutting such a broad path there is necessarily a performance overhead and system complexity which hamstrings an OMS from focusing solely on what is best for only order execution. At any given time, an OMS product on a trader's desktop may be recalculating the cash and position balances for every account allocation on an order, testing compliance limits, querying the database for settlement status, performing allocations on partial fills and competing for finite database and network resources with portfolio managers, compliance, settlements and data maintenance users. EMS products are not burdened by any of this performance overhead .

An EMS benchmark for performance is to be able to process over 1,000 database transactions per second while streaming real time data. Dealing with large quantities of orders, 1,000s at a time, without showing slowness or latency for streaming data, order placements and fill receipt is a must for an EMS.

Adaptability

Another key strength for EMS products is their adaptability and response time for integrating and deploying new functionality to keep pace with changing market conditions. This goes far beyond simply adding new strategies, execution venues or algorithms to an existing workflow. It includes designing creative new workflows like the foreign exchange triangulation example detailed previously. The ability for this fast and flexible functionality deployment is something that the EMS owes again to its simpler and more focused client application. It is not atypical for an EMS vendor to add significant functionality to their product and complete all tasks from design, through testing, delivery and implementation at a client site in a matter of weeks to a couple of months.

Because of the size and the complexity of an OMS, these products do not enjoy the luxury of quickness to market that an EMS product does. For OMS vendors, major functionality changes are time consuming from a design and development perspective because they must tie into all aspects of the system. For example, an OMS vendor cannot add trading functionality for a certain complex derivative type until they also provide support for order generation, compliance, settlements and exports for that same instrument. OMS vendors must view all functionality enhancements for order execution as a small part of a much larger picture. EMS vendors have the luxury of focusing solely on the order execution tasks. On top of the design and development complexity the implementation effort for a client to install an OMS upgrade is significantly greater (not to mention more expensive) due again to the overall size and complexity of the product. Multiple groups within the asset management firm must be involved, performing significant regression testing to ensure all processes that the OMS touches are working properly. For OMS vendors it is not atypical for a major product release to be measured in months to even years from time of design to implementation at a client. That last part is worth repeating, it is not atypical for OMS users to wait a year or longer to receive significant new trade execution functionality from their vendors, compared to weeks to months for EMS products.

Additional Functionality

We've focused a lot up to this point on what an OMS does and how OMS products have taken on many characteristics of EMS product but we have mentioned very little about EMS products taking on characteristics of OMS products. This was not an oversight, but rather intentional. The reason for this lack of attention is that although some EMS vendors have begun to create offerings in areas of order generation, compliance and settlements, these efforts have tended to be functionality-light when compared to OMS products. To change EMS products to be more competitive across all the functionality areas that OMS products dominate would be to dramatically change what an EMS is; an ultra-fast, adaptive system focused on the best possible order execution. Facilitating order generation means loading accurate cash, positions, tax lots and maintaining models and benchmarks. Integrating full compliance for all asset classes and supporting global regulatory rules is extremely complicated and ever changing. Were an EMS vendor to build this functionality into their product, it would necessarily reduce the benefits and nimbleness that these products enjoy today because of their narrow focus.

The one area that looks to be a true battle ground for EMS vendors when competing with OMS vendors is trade settlements. This is a logical extension of the EMS as all execution details are known to the system and settlements can occur separately and externally to executions. Providing settlements for multiple asset classes across global markets is not a trivial matter to be sure, so we expect most EMS vendors to partner significantly in this area with established settlements firms.

Future of OMS Products

There is no doubt that the major OMS players intend to integrate as much EMS functionality into their products as possible. The interesting thing is that many of them have chosen completely different paths to do so. It will be interesting to see which of these vendors' product teams will have taken the best approach. We will have to wait several years to measure these efforts, and to determine each vendor's ability to adapt to new trade execution functionality.

For now all we can do is look at some of the first steps these vendors have taken, as well as near term plans to enhance their offerings. We chose LatentZero, Charles River Development and Macgregor as three examples, not because of the OMS or EMS offerings themselves, but because of the differences in the direction they've chosen to implement their EMS-like functionality.

LatentZero

We begin with LatentZero because they were the first OMS vendor to incorporate true EMS-like functionality into a production ready release of their product. To be sure their first offering must be considered EMS-Light as it does not begin to broach the full functionality of an EMS market leading product like Flex Trade or Portware. LatentZero's offering focuses mainly on venue connectivity and streaming Level II data. It does a better job than a standard OMS of allowing a trader to use strategies and algorithms while providing aggregate liquidity directly from the OMS blotter. The system's Level II data streaming is a significant advantage as it displays the top five bids and asks including size and Market Maker ID.

More interesting than the added functionality is the approach LatentZero has taken in deploying the application. LatentZero was careful in its decision not to integrate the new functionality directly into their trading application Minerva. Instead, the EMS offering is a separate tightly integrated application that interacts with Minerva. In theory this will provide LatentZero with the ability to add EMS functionality and allow clients to implement it without having to upgrade their entire OMS. It will be interesting to see if this theory holds up in practice. As the OMS blotter and the EMS product interact, trader workflows will cross between the two products. Only new or changing workflows not dependent on changes to the OMS blotter will be able to be quickly added and released to clients without the client needing to undertake a large scale OMS upgrade.

One main advantage of integrating EMS-like functionality into the OMS is eliminating the need to stage orders in the OMS only to be sent via FIX or API to a separate EMS. Some view this process as time consuming and error prone. The consideration here is that with all other concerns being equal, the less an order needs to be passed from system to system the better.

Another wildcard for LatentZero is that they have been recently acquired by Fidessa. Fidessa Workstation (formerly royalblue) is a leading full functionality EMS. The direction Fidessa is taking with melding LatentZero into a cross functional product is clear in their marketing efforts as they have rebranded the LatentZero OMS product as an OEMS.

Although LatentZero's OMS was an early adopter of EMS-like functionality, the most interesting story will be what impact the EMS expertise of new parent Fidessa will have on future product direction.

Charles River Development (CRD)
Arguably the current market leader in the OMS space, CRD has a major EMS product initiative in the works. CRD's current offering, CR IMS V8 has limited EMS-like components; connectivity to multiple trading venues via FIX, access to broker algorithms and limited real time data. Currently the real-time data is not Level II, as you can only display the information on the top bid and ask and cannot display Market Maker information.

Current CR IMS EMS-like functionality will soon take a back seat to the radically redesigned CR IMS V9. CR IMS V9 is a markedly different user experience than V8. As mentioned prior, OMS vendors' major initiatives can often be marked in terms of years, and CR IMS V9 is a great example of that, as it has been in the works since the V8 production release in April of 2006, and its delivery to clients has yet to be determined.

What makes CR IMS V9 so different? CRD's move to a full C## and .Net application has opened up its ability to greatly increase performance and functionality. The order blotter has undergone radical changes, adding significant display flexibility and true event driven functionality. Some examples of this functionality are placing orders at execution venues via drag and drop, integrating news sources into the blotter that filter based on selected orders, and dynamically changing execution strategies based on market conditions.

CR IMS V9 EMS-like functionality is again focused on the global equity markets, but the functionality offered for this asset class should compare respectably with true full-featured EMS products.

The most interesting aspect of CRD's future offering is that all the EMS-like functionality is fully integrated into the OMS. Unlike LatentZero's effort to tightly integrate two separate applications, CRD took the approach of integrating all functionality into a single application. Tight integration has some benefits from a system cohesion standpoint, but it also means that many workflow enhancements may require clients to upgrade their entire OMS. CRD took many steps to alleviate this requirement, for example new broker algorithms can be added simply without an upgrade but it remains to be seen how quickly CRD can adapt to changing market needs in the EMS space when complicated enhancements may take a full upgrade cycle.

Like LatentZero, CRD's approach has the advantage of eliminating the need to stage orders in the OMS only to be sent via FIX or API to a separate EMS.

Macgregor
Like LatentZero, Macgregor has recently been acquired. ITG purchased Macgregor in July of 2005. ITG already offers a myriad of products to connect buy side firms to execution venues; POSIT, Triton, and ITG Channel in particular. Macgregor and ITG currently have ambitious plans to integrate Macgregor's OMS offering, (XIP) with ITG's execution systems into a new product called Triton X.

The goal is to leverage all of ITG's execution management expertise with XIP's OMS workflows. This integration will be a looser integration than that of LatentZero or Charles River Development. The end result is that ITG's EMS portion will be available to integrate with any OMS via FIX protocol. This would require staging or auto routing orders via FIX from another vendor's OMS to Triton X to take advantage of Triton X's execution abilities.

This is obviously a radically different approach than other OMS vendors, but it makes perfect sense based on ITG's mature line of systems that facilitate execution today. By opening up to other vendor's OMS products they are not narrowing their EMS client base to just XIP users.

Other advantages of loosely integrating the two platforms are that they can grow and add functionality independently. As we have seen, EMS products need to be much more reactive to market needs, and be quick to add and change functionality, whereas OMS systems are burdened with slower upgrade cycles.

Future of EMS Products
Since EMS products are newer and change much more rapidly than OMS products, major initiatives and market leaders are harder to track and stay on top of, as major changes can occur in just weeks or several months.

To be sure, there are some major trends that apply across all EMS vendors that are worth watching. One is the adoption and addition of OMS-like functionality. This has only occurred in small steps at this time, but the interesting area here will be to see if EMS vendors will start to offer full global settlement services. This is the mostly likely area for EMS vendors to compete with their OMS counterparts.

The second change we are waiting to see in the EMS space is a move to greater flexibility in their pricing models. Right now EMS systems can be a big expense for buy side shops. This limits their adoption to larger asset managers who have the trading volume to justify the additional cost of the systems. EMS vendors are loathe at this point in time to reduce prices for clients who wish to use limited functionality of their products. Right sizing the price tag to the functionality demands of a client will open the door to many new buy side firms. An analogy is often made about EMS product's functionality being comparable to a Ferrari, which is a great compliment, but when a buy side shop is only looking to use functionality relative to a Honda, they are still being required to pay the Ferrari price tag.

Possible client adoption
Looking towards the future it is difficult to see how buy side firms will react to all these changes. The big question of course is will there come a time when one product, OMS or EMS, will win out and become the single system of choice of asset managers.

The adoption of OMS and EMS products will be directly related to client needs and vendor pricing. OMS systems are slow to adapt to market changes and provide little to no EMS-like functionality to non-equity asset classes. Therefore it is hard to envision how OMS products will replace EMS products at high end, multi-asset class shops in the near term. Although we doubt that EMS products will ever take over the order generation and compliance functions owned by the OMS products today, there is room for them to be the main trading system for certain asset managers.

Client Approach

Large asset managers, loosely defined as managers with 100+ billion in assets under management, have large enough trading volumes and budgets to justify multiple trading systems. These managers have the luxury of determining which approach to OMS and EMS systems they wish to take when procuring trading systems. Shops of this size can potentially take a best of breed approach when deciding on OMS systems and EMS systems.

The real battleground between OMS and EMS vendors will be for the middle sized asset managers with approximately 50 to 100 billion in assets under management. They are necessarily more cost sensitive, not only to the license fees associated with using multiple vendor systems, but also the cost in hardware and personnel to support the separate products. This is a golden opportunity for the OMS vendors. Because of the OMS product's order generation and compliance functions, having an OMS system is a necessity for this sized shop. If that same OMS product can offer some EMS-like functionality, even if not full functionality, it would be a great boon to the mid-sized shop. They may be very happy living with a single OMS system which meets all of their OMS needs and gives them core EMS functionality. This will most certainly force the EMS vendors to seriously consider right sizing the cost of their products; as OMS products offer more EMS-like functionality, cost constrained shops will likely be willing to live with less than full EMS functionality rather than double their trading system expenses.

Smaller shops, 10 to 50 billion assets under management, may have little choice as they may not have the budget or resources to support an OMS and an EMS, but could look to EMS-like functionality as a key determinate when selecting an OMS.

Not to be out done, EMS systems have a great opportunity to replace OMS products in certain asset management shops as well. One type of money manager uniquely vulnerable to foregoing the use of an OMS for an EMS is the quantitative asset manager. Quantitative shops will often rely on a third kind of system to accomplish some of the typical OMS tasks. These systems are known as Optimizers. Optimizers are systems that hold all the parameters of the proprietary quantitative models which mathematically determine which securities to buy and sell for the asset managers. These systems often perform the tasks of order generation and compliance, therefore removing the need to utilize that functionality in an OMS. If EMS products can provide integrated global settlements it is entirely possible that we will soon see some quantitative shops relinquishing the OMS systems and moving to an EMS only model.

The only thing that is certain is that there will be no one size fits all vendor solution coming from either the OMS or EMS vendors in the near term. Both systems have fundamental workflow and technology differences that give them strengths that are hard to fully compete against. The real interesting action in the next few years will be the battle ground areas for OMS and EMS vendors of the medium size asset managers and quantitative shops. Also it will take several years to determine which OMS vendor has picked the optimal strategy for integrating EMS functionality into their products. This is a competition that may not have a clear winner for some time.

Syndicated Commercial Loan Trading

By Randy Schafer

Introduction

While bank loans are perhaps the oldest financial instrument in existence, the recent evolution in commercial lending has been quite dramatic. Once largely the province of commercial banks in a buy-and-hold strategy, as an asset class, loans have become part of the institutional investment landscape.

The settlement of corporate bonds has been fairly well-standardized and automated. By contrast, bank loans remain one of the most inefficient to settle and service – at a time when their appeal has dramatically broadened to a wide range of institutional investors. This, in part, has been fueled by the recent surge in privatizations, which are financed in large measure with "bank debt" – syndicated commercial loans.

This chapter will explore the issues related to loan trading and settlement, and to a lesser extent, loan servicing. It should be noted that as this article is being written, industry efforts, led largely by a consortium of large agent banks under the sponsorship of the US-based Loan Syndication & Trading Association (LSTA), are underway to bring process improvements to a market in need of such. It must also be noted that this chapter was written before the September 2008 upheaval in the financial markets really came to the fore. Even so, throughout this chapter's drafting, a number of changes were taking place in the market which run counter to the trends noted in this paper. This chapter takes the view that a one-year trend should not indicate a fundamental change to market trends playing out over a 10-20 years.

What is a syndicated loan?

A syndicated loan is a credit arrangement between a borrower and a group of lenders. A group of lead banks structures a credit agreement with the borrower, which could be a corporate or government entity. Once the credit agreement is in place, the loan is then divided into smaller pieces in order to diversify the lender base (much as in the debt markets), and to ensure that funding comes from the most efficient pools of money available – institutional investors, which carry neither capital nor reserve requirements.

By their very nature, loans are a specific form of private placement. They do not trade publicly, and not every potential investor is suitable (to hold the asset) nor acceptable (to the borrower). They are far more complex than traditional debt instruments, both in terms of documentation and process. The great attraction to borrowers is very much tied to this complexity – the flexibility in how loans are structured and restructured as needed. A single credit agreement between borrower and lenders can allow for multiple borrowing "facilities" or "tranches". Within a given facility, loans can be drawn and continuously restructured in different "contracts"[xcvi] All of this is in sharp contrast with the traditional debt markets where securities are not restructured and where limitations on who may "lend" are not imposed by the borrower. For a variety of reasons, loan market participants go to great lengths to avoid creating appearances of the loan asset class even looking like a security.

Unique to the loan market, loans can be categorized along two dimensions in terms of market appetite and trade settlement:

- Leveraged vs. Non-leveraged. A variety of interrelated criteria are used to establish if a loan is leveraged. One article establishes that a loan issued by a company rating of BB, BB/B and B or lower, or with higher spreads, is deemed to be leveraged[xcvii]. Others in the loan market indicate that the balance sheet of the borrowing entity after the borrowing can also push a loan into a "leveraged" status. Leveraged loans, because of their higher levels of volatility and yield, tend to draw the interest of institutional investors. These are also the loans which have been behind most of the recent (and in the past six months significantly dampened) privatization efforts – companies bought on leverage. A loan is known to be leveraged at the time of its issuance; this information can easily be gleaned from the loan documentation prepared as part of the underwriting.

- Par vs. Distressed. Whereas a loan is known to be leveraged or not at the time of its issuance, a loan's performance as measured in the price range in which it trades determines if it is "par" or "distressed".

Par loans usually trade at "95"[xcviii] or above; loans that do not meet that trading range are usually deemed to be "distressed". As another indication of the current environment, using the "95" standard, in today's market condition, virtually all loans would categorized as distressed – something obviously not the case.

The significance of this has to do with the time, effort and cost to settle trades. Distressed loans undergo a greater level of due diligence by the buyer, largely to ensure that it understands preexisting liabilities to previous lenders from past missed income payments. The claims to the loans are thoroughly traced back to the point of issuance.

The Loan Market Structure, and How it Compares With Debt Securities

It is easier, and more appropriate, to first identify the similarities of the loan and debt securities asset classes. Commonalities include:

- The role of the fund manager in the institutional market. Setting aside the individual investor, syndicated loan investment decisions are made in much the same way as those for debt securities: the plan sponsor will allocate assets to one or more fund managers based upon their specific expertise; these fund managers will make specific investment decisions. As with other asset classes, there are a number of firms that have a boutique business in managing portfolios of loans, including creating pools of loans (discussed below).
- The role of the custodian. As in the other asset classes, the custodian has an important role in the institutional market. The custodian tracks positions, manages cash flows and provides reports to the plan sponsors and their governing bodies. The custodian, however, is not maintaining an official record of customer ownership in loan positions as it does with securities with which it has a depository position; for loans, the only official record of ownership sits with the loan's "agent bank". And as will be outlined below, the mechanics of this role are distinctly different from those of securities.
- Sizeable transactions. As with bond underwritings, there have been some very sizeable loan underwritings, especially given their role in financing large private equity transactions. In fact, in Q1 2007, leveraged loan issuance for non-investment grade companies totaled $216 billion, up 65% from the same period in 2006. By contrast, companies sold "only" $39 billion of high-yield bonds.[xcix] Further insight can be gained by looking at a sample of six large privatization deals in the pipeline at the time of this writing: total deal value of $202 billion; exactly half of which will be financed by bank loans.

Another 25% will be financed by bonds and bridge loans.[c] Of course, in the recent nine months, the long-term growth trend has reversed; loan market issuance has actually declined for the last three quarters – the first such decline in a number of years.

- Pooled investments. Loans, like other fixed income instruments, often end up as part of pooled investment vehicles. 40 Act mutual funds are obviously one type of investor in fixed income vehicles; most mutual fund complexes offer one or more bond funds, with each fund typically having a specific type of focus (e.g., corporate debt, municipal debt or sovereign debt). Similarly, 40 Act mutual funds can invest in loans, but their consumption of loans representing a very low share of loan purchase. Instead, a very high proportion of loans, particularly leveraged loans, are used to create Collateralized Loan Obligations (CLOs), which are complex, structured financial instruments. CLOs are more aggressively funded (via leverage) and managed (e.g., trading the underlying assets). CLO pools are typically several hundred million dollars, and typically hold over 100 different loans at any given time. Another trend that has reversed – loan market participants debate for how long – is the significance of CLOs as consumers as loans. A recent shift has seen banks come back to the market as a larger source of lending.

- Block traded. As with debt securities, loans are often traded on behalf of more than one investor[ci], with the fund manager providing the formal allocations after the trade is executed but before settlement is completed.

The differences between loans and debt securities are far more numerous and important than their similarities. Aside from the definitional and regulatory aspects covered above, the loan asset class has a number of other distinctions from the debt securities, including:

- **Registration.** In the US, at least, securities must be registered with the SEC. As private placements, loans have no such requirements. By extension, just before their issuance, securities are assigned public identifiers (CUSIPs in the US); loans are moving towards CUSIPs to facilitate long-needed "straight-thru processing" (STP).

- **Flexibility.** Syndicated loans can be put to many purposes – financing inventory on a seasonal basis, project financing, etc. In recent times, however, the significant growth of the asset class has been driven by the recent upsurge in privatization deals. The attraction of loan financing is that the asset class offers greater levels of flexibility in terms of calling in loans, restructuring loans, etc. than would be found with traditional bonds.

- **Trading without interest.** Bonds trade with accrued interest, which means that the buyer of a bond is paying the seller for the right to the income which has accrued since the last interest payment. This cash will be coming to the buyer of the bond when interest is next paid, and the custodian no longer need to track the seller. Loans, by contrast, typically do not behave this way[cii]. As a result, the many parties to a loan – the agent bank, custodian and fund manager – must all maintain and mirror the records of investors who have exited loans mid-period, and participate in the income distribution process at period-end.

- **Size of market traded.** Despite rapid growth – several major dealing rooms report loan trading has doubled in H1 2007, putting it on pace for annual trading approach $500 billion for the entire year – the market is approximately $2 billion per day. As will be shown later in the chapter, bond trading is on another order of magnitude. In spite of general market trends in the loan market, trading volume does not appear to be a casualty of the recent upheavals.

- **Borrower approval.** Given the private nature of syndicated loans, borrowers – or their agent bank acting as surrogate – may need to approve the lenders in the funding group. While not as common today as has been in the past, and not as onerous as it might seem, it is a curious difference. Most dealers will trade on the assumption that the borrower or agent will approve (if they retain that right, and later deal with the consequences of this not happening[ciii].

- **Supporting Market Infrastructures.** In some markets – the US, for example – most debt securities trades are matched for confirmation and netted down via clearinghouses, and then subsequently settled via depositories (industry-owned or via for-profit companies serving in the role of an industry utility).

- Loan trades, by contrast, have been manually confirmed with the middle or back office of a dealer and the fund manager phoning or e-mailing each other to agree on the details of the trade. Once this has been done, settlement dates are agreed – for each allocation, and settlement instructions exchanged as well. Instead of settling thru a central utility which confirms settlement on a DvP / RvP basis, the buyer of a loan pays the seller of a loan on "assignment date" – the date the agent bank records the change in ownership. As with securities, the fund manager will direct payment to or from the custodian bank.

- Historically, this has been a highly manual, paper-intensive process. In recent years, however, at least two "settlement platforms"[civ], both US-based, have emerged to bring ecommerce capabilities to this process, including support for trade matching[cv], generation of appropriate documents to complete the transfer and exchange of settlement instructions Both companies are for-profit entities. They support primary issuance as well as secondary trading. Some level of manual intervention is needed to shepherd the trades to settlement – no doubt a reflection of traditional industry practices including the lack of complete standardization of terms, processes, documents, etc. in the industry. A number of industry participants have indicated it will take some time for standardization to reach a point where this process can flow more seamlessly.

- **Contractual settlement.** As noted in the prior point, loans do not have a formal contractual settlement period[cvi] as is found in the typical security. Instead, during the period when the trading counterparties are confirming the trade, a settlement date is negotiated for each allocation – which need not be the same. Many factors can drive targeted settlement date including deal complexity (which impacts the review time needed by the legal teams), liquidity of the buyer or an insufficient position on the part of the seller ... which leads to the next difference.

- **Short trading.** Whereas short trading is clearly a strategy in the securities markets, the same is not true in loans[cvii]. While this once may have been a desirable trading strategy limited by the mechanics and tradition of the loan market, from a practical perspective today, there are other ways to achieve the same effect, most notably, derivatives such as Credit Default Swaps (CDS), Loan CDSs and Total Return Swaps[cviii].

- **Market Reference Data.** As the loan industry looks to streamline its processes under initiatives sponsored first by the LSTA and now by the London-based Loan Marketing Association (LMA), it has also come to realize that the appropriate reference data is not yet in place to drive STP. Specifically missing is the widespread use of standard industry identifiers for both the loans and the investors.

Loan identification through the use of CUSIPs is a relatively recent initiative, started by the LSTA in collaboration with S&P. The use of CUSIPs is far from universal at this point, and when used, never go down to the level of the loan contract – important for loan servicing, and often don't even reach the level of the credit facility, which is critical for loan trading and settlement. A number of firms still use proprietary numbering in their internal operations, even where CUSIPs have been made available at the time of the underwriting. Outside the US, use of CUSIPs or alternative industry-standard numbering schemas is far less prevalent.

Participant identification, most notably, lender of record, is a very new concept to the loan market. Agent banks do not keep records of internal account numbers used by fund managers and custodians. Hence, the processing of loan trades (and more significantly, the extensive level of asset servicing) requires manual look-up on an alphabetic basis – inhibiting STP and increasing risk and cost. The loan industry is looking to find a solution to this problem by creating universal identifiers for institutional accounts which invest in loans, which will ultimately require all market participants to build this type of cross-referencing into their systems. How many lender numbering schemes will gain traction in the market remains to be seen, but clearly the fewer the better.

In many respects, the loan market is a unique asset class – with characteristics that blend aspects of traditional cash market instruments with those of the OTC derivatives market. These characteristics are shown on the following page:

Similarities to Cash Market

- Tangible "investment" in the balance sheet of a corporate entity
- Opportunity for capital gain
- Generation of interest income
- Asset servicing events on the asset itself

Similarities to OTC Derivatives

- Contract-based instruments
- No contractual settlement on the trade
- No formal regulated market infrastructures to "novate" or "assign" trades[cix], and maintain depository positions[cx]
- Recent efforts to standardize documentation and reference data

Implications on trading volumes

Trading in syndicated loans is dwarfed by all other fixed income cash market asset classes, as illustrated below[cxi]:

Instrument Average Daily Volume, 2006

a) Treasury and Agency MBS $779 billion

b) Federal Agencies $74 billion

c) Corporate Bonds $22.7 billion

d) Municipals $22.5 billion

e) Loans ~$1 billion

Many reasons would explain this:

- Relative newness to institutional markets. As a measure, in 1991, only $8 billion in loans were traded. The appetite by both lenders and borrowers to explore this channel simply was not there.
- Qualified Institutional Buyer-like nature of investors. As private placements, the universe of possible investors is going to be far narrower. Furthermore, the numbers of intermediaries equipped to deal in these instruments with their clients is quite narrow as well.
- No "contractual settlement." Given the mechanics of settlement, loans are not as simple to get in and get out of. The process has gotten far better, for sure, but there is no predictable 1- or 3-day settlement period as with securities.
- Complicated documentation. Loan agreements are very long, complex documents. Whereas a brokerage firm will settle a security trade in a very routine way, lawyers are usually involved in the loan settlement process.
- Governance covenants for institutional investors. The covenants which govern pools of institutional money often place restrictions on the types of assets the fund can invest in. One of the factors giving rise to CLOs, no doubt, is the desire to invest in loans through a more diversified, liquid and professionally managed class of assets. The institutional investor is not investing directly in loans, but in securities or private placements that are tied to the loans in the CLO. Furthermore, the CLO allows investors to participate in specific tranches, each of which carries its own risk (rating) and return (yield).
- Recent growth of alternatives to loan assets. The bond markets had a long history before alternative investments – derivatives – came along to create or hedge exposures to credit risk. By contrast, as the loan market has been institutionalizing, a cashless alternative to loans has also arisen – the Loan Credit Default Swap, which behaves similarly to the traditional credit default swap, but is tied to loan credits.
- Onerous administrative responsibilities. Access to loan data must be filtered by a dedicated staff to ensure private loan information is not shared with traders in public securities. Additionally, the loan must be continuously monitored for unanticipated servicing requirements such as a borrower's wish to restructure, draw funds or repay principal which is not anticipated in the loan's amortization schedule. These administrative challenges are compounded by the fact that the loan market has not had a standardized approach to messaging in regard to both post-trade settlement and loan servicing. Faxes have

been the order of the day, supplemented by e-mails and telephone and/or voice mails).

In spite of this, and the recent swings in the loan market arising in liquidity issues stemming from the "sub-prime" mortgage problems of the summer of 2007, syndicated loans do offer two advantages vis-à-vis other forms of debt.

- **Greater transparency.** Credit agreements generally provide far more transparency than can be found in the prospectus for a bond offering. In addition, when problems arise, the lending group engages in very close consultations with the borrower. In this sense, they have a far better sense of what is really going on.

- **Default is not the same as bankruptcy.** Loans are ahead of corporate bonds and of course equity in the creditor line. As has been observed by one industry participant, there is a large difference between a default and a bankruptcy, and there are many cases where borrowers in default continue to pay interest as due.

Automation and Trading – Likely Directions

What does all of this mean for the future of automation? For one thing, there are no loan trading systems which are the equivalent to a TradeWeb in the Treasury market, or an Archipelago in the equities arena. Nor are any likely to arise in the near future – at least until simplified trading and settlement, and deeper market demand is realized. As long as loan instruments have complicated terms which can be negotiated, a human element will always be part of the execution process. If some portion of the loan market can be simplified in terms of the mechanics – be it in the loan structure or in the terms that dealers are willing to offer their counterparties, some form of electronic trading can take place – perhaps initially against the largest dealers' desk, and eventually through infrastructures shared by dealers – the TradeWeb model.

To the extent that the terms which are negotiated by people can be codified, trade settlement can move to more automated forms of matching.

But on the immediate horizon, it is easiest to see automation achieving great benefit in two areas: the post-match settlement processes and loan servicing.

On the post-confirmation processing front, many elements of automation are in place today. Trade settlement platforms can produce many of the settlement-related documents, and can bring the agent bank into the settlement process as well. But there is room for more automation, and the industry has come together to chart a way forward.

Most immediate on the industry's road map are two key initiatives.

1. Tools by which agent banks and lenders can reconcile positions, being sponsored by industry infrastructures DTCC and Euroclear. This will help eliminate many of the breaks related to cash flows that typically happen at month- and quarter-end.

2. The automation of loan servicing messaging. FpML-based message standards are currently being defined by an industry working group; these messages will be capable of replacing most the estimated 15-20 million loan servicing faxes sent each year by agent banks. SWIFT (one of my clients) is working with the industry infrastructures, vendors and market participants to help bring about electronic delivery of these standardized messages.

In short, the loan market would appear to follow the model of many other asset classes – automation starting from the settlement and asset servicing, back out to the post-trade "clearing" (matching, and subsequently novation and netting) and eventually to the trading process itself.

In Summary

The opportunities for improved processing in the loan market primarily relate to trade settlement and asset servicing. Keys to realizing this improvement are:

- Continued standardization and simplification of loan documentation and business process coordinated by industry groups such as LSTA and LMA

- Creation of standardized industry reference data representing both assets and investors, which will remove ambiguity from messages between market participants

- The creation and take-up of standardized industry messaging by the largest market participants in the market, regardless of the role(s) they play (i.e., agent bank, dealer, fund manager, trustee or custodian)

- The adoption and improvement of the trade settlement platforms in existence and integration with evolving industry messaging standards

Interdealer Brokers in the Fixed Income Markets

By SIFMA

Introduction

Broker/dealers and other financial institutions utilize the secondary fixed income markets to execute their customers' orders, trade for a profit and manage their exposure to risk, including credit, interest rate and exchange rate risks. There is no centralized exchange in the fixed income market. As a result, financial institutions need a way to find information, liquidity and anonymity for their trading activity. This need created a demand for the services of perhaps the least known and understood market participants, interdealer brokers (IDBs).

IDBs in the secondary government, agencies, corporate and other debt markets — also known as "Municipal Securities Broker's Brokers" in the municipal bond markets— are specialized securities companies who act as intermediaries working to facilitate transactions between broker/dealers and dealer banks in these markets. IDBs are sometimes described as providing a "Petri dish" of liquidity in the bond markets. That is, they provide a "nurturing environment" wherein market participants can ascertain information about a given market, thereby eventually facilitating a trade between buyers and sellers.

That IDBs are crucial to the functioning of the markets has been repeatedly highlighted in times of market stress. In times like these, dealers are often the only parties willing to buy bonds they believe are undervalued, and to hold them until a market imbalance is righted. Because IDBs are global and trade on a 24/7 basis, their ability to identify dealers and arrange trades is regarded as key to keeping the financial markets open in such highly stressful times as the aftermath of the attacks of September 11, 2001.

The Markets

The IDB community distributes information and facilitates transactions in the secondary, or wholesale, financial debt markets between dealers and dealer banks around the world. Although market participants often refer colloquially to a single "bond market," there are actually quite separate markets, which include: (1) high grade sovereigns, including the U.S. government and G-10 foreign governments, (2) U.S. federal agencies and government sponsored enterprises ("GSEs", and, collectively with federal agencies, "Agencies"), (3) corporate debt, (4) Agency and non-Agency mortgage backed securities (MBS) and asset-backed securities ("ABS"), including collateralized debt obligations ("CDO"), (5) high yield securities, such as high yield corporate debt, distressed debt and emerging markets debt, including emerging markets sovereigns, (6) municipal securities, and (7) interest rate, credit and other derivative products. Some of these debt markets utilize IDBs more than others. Typically, markets which make extensive use of IDBs include the corporate bond, fixed income derivatives, U.S. Government and Agency, municipal securities and emerging markets.

Overall, the markets that IDBs are active in can be characterized as single-price auctions. Unlike exchanges, trades in these markets tend to occur sporadically. They are characterized by "evaporative" liquidity, as participants are either ready to transact at given prices, or out of the market entirely. As a result, dealers seek out IDBs with expertise in the securities they seek to trade in, so that they can test trade ideas against what may be possible in the market at any given time. This is in contrast, for example, to an open-outcry system (such as a futures pit or other exchange) wherein many market participants provide bids and offers on many trades in a public environment.

The Role of Interdealer Brokers

Interdealer brokers play varying roles in each of the fixed income markets and have become instrumental to their effectiveness and efficiency. IDBs draw together buyers and sellers so that trades can be executed by market participants.

Some IDBs are licensed as broker/dealers; others are not. Whether or not an IDB is licensed depends on the security or instrument being brokered. For example, whereas brokering credit rate default swaps does not require a license, performing the same services for U.S. Treasury notes does.

IDBs provide potential buyers and sellers with the critical market information they need to trade. This information includes the narrowness of bid and offer quotes, for example, and follows a strict protocol regarding identification of sellers. In general, dealers with an order to buy or sell a bond (on behalf of a customer or themselves) must ascertain the best price available in the interdealer market. In their search, they can contact an IDB directly via telephone or obtain an aggregated quotation from an IDB's electronic screen. An IDB may also act as the dealer's independent intermediary, thereby protecting the dealer's identity and level of trading interest. This is to guard against the possibility that revelation of this information to the market could negatively impact the price at which the dealer is willing to buy or sell the security.

Municipal Securities Broker's Brokers

In the municipal securities markets, a municipal securities broker's broker ("MSBB") intermediates in the interdealer segment of the secondary market (made up of dealers and dealer banks). There are several aspects of the municipal bond market and its regulatory structure that set MSBBs apart from IDBs in other markets. First, as a consequence of this market's size, complexity and lack of homogeneity, MSBBs tend to specialize in subsections of the municipal bond markets, either by region, issuer or type of security. Second, unlike IDBs in other markets, MSBBs do not normally present traders with "live" or "tradeable" prices via electronic platforms. Rather, business is primarily conducted through voice communication. Third, MSBBs use a method for finding prices for securities which is unique to that market. This method is referred to as "Bids Wanted", where a dealer asks an MSBB to gather bids from the interdealer market on a specific security so the dealer or ultimate owner (customer) may make a sell or hold decision on their position.

It is important to note that under the Securities Exchange Commission net capital rules, MSBBs are prohibited from maintaining customer accounts, and are further specifically restricted from maintaining an inventory of securities for their own accounts (ie proprietary inventory). Thus, all transactions that an MSBB undertakes must be equally-matched buys and sells. Registered broker/dealers and dealer banks are their clients, including (a) dealers seeking liquidity on behalf of a customer, retail or institutional, or (b) dealers seeking to distribute a new issue or adjust an inventory position.

All MSBB executions must have a dealer or dealer bank as the contra-party. MSBBs may provide information to non-dealers; however, they may not execute transactions directly with customers.

Earning Transaction Fees

IDBs earn transaction fees when acting as intermediaries. This transaction fee is customarily known to all parties prior to a trade. By virtue of their business model, IDBs do not receive remuneration for posting prices which they receive from buyers and sellers, although this practice in fact represents the vast majority of their daily activity. The way they earn a transaction fee is if the seller and buyer agree to execute the trade. An IDB's transaction fee is earned at the point of sale. IDBs almost never know what the execution price will be and they necessarily must work to find the best acceptable price to the buyer and seller, in the hope of earning the right to facilitate that trade.

Interdealer Brokers' Value to the Debt Markets In general terms, IDBs add value to the markets by:

- Enhancing price discovery and transparency (Via communicating dealer interests and transactions)
- Providing anonymity and confidentiality (Via their position in the "middle" of trades)
- Facilitating information flow (Via acting as a central information point)
- Facilitating enhanced liquidity (Via their broad range of contacts)
- Improving market efficiency (Via their rapid access to liquidity)
- Lowering costs (Via their provision of prices to traders without incurring staffing costs)

Enhancing Price Discovery and Transparency

In connection with their facilitation of transactions, IDBs provide pre-trade price discovery in their markets. Prior to execution, an IDB distributes its dealer quotes, in the form of bona fide bids and offers for securities through a variety of methods ranging from custom-designed trading platforms to voice and e-mail communications. The IDB has received this information from dealers who have the same or similar market interests.

The IDB usually aggregates quote information in order to show its dealer clients the "best" quotes available in the market place. In the municipal bond markets, for example, an MSBB will select the highest bid and lowest offer available — otherwise known as "reflecting a market" — to show to dealers who are interested in trading. Dealers use this information to trade for their own account and to facilitate customer transactions. In this way, IDBs provide analogous services for the fixed income markets as the consolidated quotation system provides for the equities markets.

IDBs also provide information to dealers about the depth of the market, for example providing different quotes based on the par value of a particular security being bid or offered. Regardless of the market, however, IDBs who use electronic screens will distribute best prices to all participants, not only to those who might be interested in trading. In contrast, for efficiency's sake off-screen brokers may only call traders who they believe may have an interest in trading these particular bonds. Overall, IDBs publish the best bid and offer available to the markets in an effort to improve price discovery and with the ultimate goal of bringing buyers and sellers together at one price.

Providing Anonymity and Confidentiality

Pursuant to industry practice and regulation, the relationship between a dealer and an IDB is a confidential relationship. An IDB maintains participant anonymity with regards to broker/dealers and dealer banks during the price discovery process in the sale and purchase of bonds. This is in order to prevent competing dealers from discerning each other's strategies by monitoring the market activities of their competitors.

During price discovery, dealer interactions with IDBs mask their identity from the marketplace. This anonymity reduces the market impact costs associated with the value to the market of the knowledge that a particular dealer is seeking to buy or sell a specific quantity of bonds. For example, a large bank or dealer may be looking to acquire or sell a large amount of inventory. If done directly, such massive trades may well affect market levels, with consequent negative impact on the dealer's trading strategy. By transacting their business through an IDB, the initiator of trading activity remains anonymous. And the large quantity of bonds can be sold in smaller lots, thus maintaining a stable market and uniform price throughout the transactions.

For students of human nature, it will be apparent that another important reason anonymity is highly valued by traders is what former Fed chairman Alan Greenspan recently described as the "gregarious nature" of this business. While traders have a natural impulse to publicize their accomplishments, it does not benefit them to have the marketplace as a whole know their identity as a participant in any given trade. This, plus the fact that disclosing a participant's identity does not enhance liquidity, is the reason why IDBs do not typically disclose the identity of their dealer clients. The marketplace receives the information that is needed — that is, the price and the amount of bonds traded — in order to come to a deeper understanding of the market and of where liquidity is available, without needing to know the identity of the participants in the deal.

Facilitating Information Flow

IDBs' significant role in facilitating the flow of information between dealers is a critical service which both enhances liquidity and results in improved prices for market participants.

Pre-trade, IDBs facilitate market information (prices on securities, interest in buying and selling securities and transactions in securities) flow in several ways. First, in many markets, IDBs post and disseminate market information through an electronic system to their dealer clients. This information typically includes the bond issue description, the bids and offers in the bond, and the associated size of the bids and offers. Second, in providing anonymity to their dealer clients, IDBs thereby encourage dealers to supply the IDB with market information, typically in the form of calls received seeking bonds or from those looking for a buyer of their bonds. Finally, by aggregating quotations, IDBs provide participants with valuable information that reflects the buying and selling interest in the bonds among dealers.

This information, of course, has its limits. Depending on the market, participants must post a security's availability in order to obtain a market price. Too, some systems may only disseminate requests for bids. In all cases, the disseminated information does not attribute the willingness to buy or sell to any given broker-dealer.

IDBs also facilitate post-execution price transparency. For example, after a municipal bid-wanted trade is executed, an MSBB may provide a dealer with information about the "cover" bid, i.e., the next best bid after the level at which the bond traded or whether the bonds are re-offered and at what price. This is important information for dealers to have in assessing the depth of the market and the risk involved in bidding or offering bonds at particular levels. This information permits dealers to quote markets with better certainty, and presumably at lower spreads, increasing secondary market liquidity and the ability for investors to sell their bonds.

It's important to note here that the benefits of market data distribution that the IDBs have long championed have been institutionalized by regulators in some markets. In corporate bonds, all transactions are reported on the NASD TRACE system (National Association of Securities Dealers' Trade Reporting and Compliance Engine) system. In the municipal bond world, all MSBB trades in municipal securities are reported to the Municipal Securities Rulemaking Board's Real-Time Transaction Reporting System.

Whether pre- or post-trade, IDBs' dissemination of information reduces market participants' costs associated with searching for buyers and sellers and levels (ie prices) in a decentralized marketplace and provides them with access to the current market price for a specific bond.

Enhancing Liquidity

Regardless of the particular financial market, several factors affect market liquidity: issuer's name, issuer's credit rating, outstanding size of the particular issue and the total
size of other issues outstanding from the same issuer. Traders are more willing to buy and sell bonds that are from a recognized issuer and part of large issues. Such bonds are also likely to be more liquid or easier for an investor to sell back into the market at a competitive price. Other things being equal, traders or dealers, then, face less price risk with bonds from large recognizable issuers than with bonds from smaller issuers. In addition, bonds with a variable or floating interest rates are more liquid than those with a fixed coupon, since their prices are less volatile.

In their roles as agents, IDBs provide dealers with quotes from other dealers, thereby enhancing the information available to the market and the market's overall efficiency. In addition, an IDB may participate in certain marketplaces by posting quotations for its own account and by acting as principal on unmatched trades to facilitate transactions, add liquidity, increase revenue opportunities and attract additional order flow. Thus, IDBs facilitate trades and ensure a more liquid market. Too, the fact of market competition among IDBs means that overall liquidity is further enhanced because there are competing, decentralized pools of liquidity which traders can access.

Finally, traders' multiple responsibilities often include managing their firm's risk, dealing with customers in addition to investigating new market opportunities. As a result, they often look to IDBs to support them on the market side with their specialist knowledge.

As one example of this, an MSBB can be said to provide liquidity because they have specific knowledge of a state or region or specialty bond. As such they act as an information clearinghouse for municipal bonds of a certain type. Their expertise, in effect, eliminates the need for a desk-to-desk search on the part of potential buyers and sellers of that security. The fact that there are competing MSBBs with specialist knowledge also means that there is more liquidity for traders to access.

Improving Market E fficiency

IDBs save their dealer clients time. For traders, time is of the essence, because trading activity does not typically occur with regularity. As a result, traders enhance their profitability by making the greatest possible number of bond trades per day. Regardless of the market, when a trader is looking to participate in a given market, time is critical. As it is the IDBs' special concern to have up-to-the-minute knowledge of market participants' activity, this must be available to dealer/ traders at a moment's notice. For traders, the timesaving element of working with IDBs may easily make the difference between executing or missing a trade.

Lowering Costs

By collecting information from dealers on an independent basis, inter-dealer brokers "gather" the liquidity available for a particular bond series. This function serves to make available a market value for often illiquid securities and also serves to lower search costs for broker-dealers. Without IDBs, brokers and/or dealers would be in the position of having to expose their identity to the marketplace as they search for liquidity. This would only serve to impair their bargaining position and raise their costs, as inevitably the information would be used against them in the marketplace.

IDBs also bring together and execute transactions for buyers and sellers of bonds. The transactions may be effected on an agency basis. IDBs use their knowledge of market "color" to assist in the price negotiation process and to bring together buyers and sellers. This service brings the market together and provides broker-dealers with efficient
matching.

How Interdealer Brokers Execute Trades

Other than in those circumstances when an IDB acts for its own account, all IDBs transact in one of three ways: (1) In markets where the IDB maintains the dealers' anonymity, the IDB — like all market participants — trades as agent for one side and executes the trade as a riskless principal, and shares in the risk of clearing and settlement through a central Registered Clearing Agency, such as the Depository Trust Clearing Corporation (DTCC). (2) In a "name give-up" transaction, the IDB "steps out" of the transaction at the point of sale, leaving the buyer and seller to clear and settle through the appropriate market mechanism. (3) In exchange-traded products such as futures contracts, the IDB also steps out of the transaction at the point of sale, thereby allowing the counterparties to notify, clear and settle through the exchange. (Please note that in the second and third cases, where the IDB is acting only to facilitate the trade, it is important to note that it is the buyer and seller who assume the risk and therefore utilize the appropriate mechanism for their respective markets to clear and settle the trade.)

The Future For Interdealer Brokers

Many observers cite the tremendous growth in the secondary fixed income markets as the major factor driving several other trading trends. These include a plethora of new products, volatility in interest rates, increased allocation of capital for trading by banks and hedge funds, demand for significant deficit financing in many of the G7 countries, increased new issuance in the corporate bond and MBS markets of securities, shifts in the foreign exchange markets as well as significant changes in the supply and demand for commodities such as oil, coal and gas. As the need for specialized knowledge proliferates with these growing markets, so does the demand for IDBs' services. In addition, as volume has grown, so has the need for transparency and the sophisticated trading systems IDBs employ to provide more and better information to market participants.

Generally speaking, as rapidly evolving trading technologies make more information available to market participants, products tend to become commoditized. As this occurs, trading opportunities tend to decrease. Participants such as IDBs who earn fees by facilitating trades therefore tend to move away from trading in these products, often toward more esoteric products and the voice-facilitated brokerage that support them.

In markets where trading opportunities are fleeting, IDBs have historically demonstrated their capability to facilitate liquidity and maximize their participation. For example, as most regulated institutions (especially banks, brokerdealers and pension and insurance companies) now use the bond markets to hedge their exposure to interest rate and credit risk, IDBs increasingly play an integral role in this growing market. In markets such as fixed income derivatives and emerging markets debt, IDBs have over the last fifteen years continued to innovate to respond to market needs for effective price dissemination and market knowledge.

As marketplaces evolve, IDBs will continue to closely track market needs, providing information, liquidity, anonymity and a centralized place to execute trades. This ability continues to reflect the respect and reliance placed in them by the fixed income markets globally.

Leadership and Liquidity:
Innovation at Financial Exchanges

By Piet Van de Velde, IBM

Executive Summary

This brief presents a short exploration of the challenges facing financial exchanges as they respond to competitive pressures and strive to affirm their position as cornerstones of the world's capital markets. The vital question of the day for exchanges is how to capitalize on proven business and technology innovations to set new standards in cost efficiency and to promote innovative service enhancements.

Financial exchanges are going through an unprecedented time of competition and rapid market evolution. They face major challenges, including:

- Significant increases in trading volume and overall data transmission requirements
- New commercial and regulatory requirements that add to data volume and the need for improved connectivity
- Loss of order flow to internalized trading by both buy- and sell-side participants and to OTC markets
- Convergence of cash and derivatives trading
- Increasing price pressure and the need to reduce trading costs for both buy and sell-side participants.

Exchanges are being tested to exploit the economic opportunities available to them when they do not control transaction volume, and can no longer set prices. The solution involves managing technology and operations costs to the lowest practical level while seeking ways to increase transaction loads at minimal incremental cost. Competitive advantages may arise from attracting liquidity from competitors, by increasing performance and decreasing costs, or demonstrating business innovation.

Attracting Liquidity

The possibility exists today for exchanges to gain the flexibility they need to capitalize on innovations in the marketplace. Advances in business modeling and architecture can increase profitability for exchanges by streamlining their operations and increasing the efficiency of providing their core services. Those that take the lead in supporting strategic goals with a revitalized infrastructure can achieve market leadership through:

- Reducing latency in trade matching and preparing for dramatic growth in transaction volumes
- Simplifying transaction processing and data access for market participants
- Designing for flexibility to accommodate the fast rollout of new products or services and response to new and complex trading rules and regulations
- Planning for greater integration of cash and derivatives markets
- Improving services to intermediaries to retain liquidity on the exchanges and recover lost liquidity
- Providing improved access for institutional investors to ensure their liquidity stays with the exchange
- Creating alliances and partnerships with market participants, creating specific market structures to attract liquidity back to market centers – taking vantage of challenges to the buy and sell sides.

Diversification of Exchange Services

Leadership among financial exchanges will come to those that position themselves as service organizations working actively to open new channels of business. There is a chance to broaden the customer base in a way that brings new forms of trading activity to the exchange. The opportunity exists because of potential improvements in quality of access that exchanges could offer to investors and market professionals alike.

Modern exchanges may be seen as hubs connecting a universe of liquidity providers and investors. Their central position in the market structure provides two potential key competitive advantages: counterparty risk management and extensive connectivity. As consolidation points for diverse pools of liquidity, powered by widespread low latency connectivity, exchanges can position themselves as primary distribution channels for assets currently traded through diverse, unconnected networks. The onus is not necessarily on exchanges to create new products, but to facilitate the interaction of market makers and investors. A new range of structured products or packaged investment vehicles could be distributed in this way. Today, a variety of such investments are offered directly to the investor, but they are not readily tradable. An exchange environment could bring new liquidity to products such as bank-issued warrants on third-party assets and equity-linked deposits.

A natural extension of the model is to have the financial exchange act as a network through which the buyside could dynamically define the profile of a desired investment and source an appropriate counterparty. Likewise, the sell-side could use the exchange infrastructure to offer new vehicles. Baskets of shares, commodity price-linked deposits, synthetic convertible bonds – there is literally no limit to the number of structures that could be created and distributed through an exchange. The requirements would be well-defined products that are regulator-approved and subject to an appropriate risk management regime. The key prerequisites are enhanced connectivity to the exchange and low latency messaging with extreme reliability.

The Tools to Lead

To make the move will take a new vision of strategically aligning business needs with leading technologies. Traditional linear approaches to business planning (such as business process reengineering) may yield optimized routines but fail to generate an effective structure across the enterprise. Financial exchanges can apply business and infrastructure models now delivering powerful results in other transaction-intensive industries, like banking and insurance. At the core is component-based planning and service-oriented architecture. Leveraging this framework, exchanges can build a true on demand business model, integrated end-to-end with key partners and customers.

Component Business Modeling (CBM), for example, simplifies the way firms look at their operations and integrates resources to focus on the fundamental value drivers of the business. The results are increased cost efficiency and the flexibility to thrive in a constantly changing business environment. Effective implementation of the strategic business model demands a service-oriented reference architecture tailored specifically to the industry and enterprise.

Several exchanges are now experimenting with open systems-based technologies and general-purpose computing platforms to build new trading engines. These trading engines are designed to be far more adaptable and flexible, while just as robust and dependable as any proprietary one.

This is the way of the future. It's the way for exchanges to achieve market leadership today.

The Changing Marketplace

Opportunity: Meet Rising Transaction Volume and Data Requirements

In recent years, the overall volume of data passing through exchanges has ballooned. Algorithmic-driven transaction volume has risen significantly, particularly in the U.S. After decimalization in mid-2001, the market depth of the best bid and offer shrank as did the average trade size, while the number of trades per day rose significantly. More recently, there has been another upsurge as more institutional investors adopt direct access and algorithmic trading.

Algorithmic trading firms typically have continuously running models that demand constant data at low latency. The parameters of algorithmic models are tuned using real-time data. The effect on exchanges is not just in order management and trade matching, but connectivity and dissemination of market data. Many exchanges have not optimized their market data applications for operating in real time. This represents a fundamental weakness in the current infrastructure. Today new models are needed to support very low latency trading, by reliably delivering a greater depth of information with maximum immediacy.

Options markets are also responsible for large increases in market data volume. Worldwide growth in exchange traded single stock options over the last few years has exceeded 50%; equity index options are even more popular. The array of strike prices available for a given option series means that a single tick change in an underlying product may lead to staggering data volume. In the U.S., the Options Price Reporting Authority (OPRA) is projecting consolidated data volumes of 110,000 messages per second (MPS) by July of 2005, 130,000 MPS by January 2006 and 149,000 MPS by July of 2006.[cxii]

Exchanges must address the twin problems of handling quote traffic and protecting option market makers from arbitrageurs' exploitation of any latency that causes underlying price changes and option quotes to diverge. Options markets demand low latency from exchanges to prevent widening spreads and quotes – in case this is not difficult enough, low latency leads to higher quote volumes, and the exchanges don't recover costs on quote services.

Opportunity: Respond faster to changes in market regulation

Regulators continue to impose higher standards of fairness and transparency on market participants. Exchanges that can bear more of this burden will have a competitive advantage.

In the U.S., new regulations to be implemented soon (including Reg NMS) are intended to maintain a level playing field by enacting rules to address market distortions that may favor certain investors. The impacts will be:

1. The strict order of transactions is preserved. The customer is assured that his order will not be bypassed in favor of another customer's.
2. The best price is always available. Through the interconnection of market centers, pools of liquidity are consolidated and the customer has access to the best price across markets.

In Europe, similar directives will affect trading by market participants in almost all asset classes. The goal is to create greater market transparency and to ensure "best execution" for investors whether trading occurs on-exchange or off-exchange. Investment firms, exchanges, trading platforms and market data vendors will all have to adapt their business processes and their IT systems in order to comply with new regulations.

New rules will require sophisticated and very fast routing of orders to the appropriate markets. Low latency and improved connectivity with cost control are the issues facing exchanges in adapting to new regulations.

Opportunity: Compete on Cost

Each exchange is unique, but all share the common characteristic of having to operate in an environment of increased competition from other exchanges and their own customers. The core service of a central order book and matching engine has become a commodity business. Exchanges can differentiate themselves with other services, but the greatest perceived value for the participant is in low-cost trade execution. The lowest cost provider will capture order flow, assuming a certain level of trading engine performance and reliability. Exchanges need to offer new services and market models to suit the shifting balance between market participants such as the shift of power between the buy and sell-sides in the U.S. A high cost to introduce a new way of trading can be as deadly as a high cost of transaction processing.

Competing on cost means lowest total cost of execution; a narrow bid/offer spread may be more important than trading fees in determining price efficiency. Liquidity is therefore paramount. Even exchanges that have a domestic liquidity advantage may face price pressure, particularly in smaller markets where order flow is concentrated among a relatively small number of large participants. And derivatives markets are more exposed to competition than the underlying markets. Competitors may simply create new derivative contracts operating under new business models that are more in tune with customer demand.

Competition occurs among exchanges, particularly where central clearing organizations exist. But it also comes from the traditional customers of exchanges such as brokers and the investment banking arms of major financial institutions. These participants may either internalize order flow or may form consortia to set up their own alternative trading systems (also known in the U.S. as electronic communications networks "ECNs" and in Europe as multilateral trading facilities "MTFs"). Such networks have an advantage in lower costs related to regulatory requirements.

Derivatives markets are particularly vulnerable to competition from intermediaries. OTC markets can duplicate exchange-traded offerings. In Europe, banks and brokers already operate their own platforms for trading many kinds of OTC derivatives products. Contracts-for-difference (CFDs) are heavily traded off-exchange by these firms, where clients access the "market" through Web portals. By some estimates, OTC transactions are as much as 5 times the value of what is traded on an exchange.

Exchanges can only maintain competitiveness by cutting costs and improving service. Both types of initiatives involve the deployment of cost-reducing, value-enhancing technology in new ways.

Opportunity: Speed The Flow of Data With Standardization

A proprietary gateway to the market is now a competitive disadvantage for a financial exchange. The goal of improving connectivity and end-to-end trade efficiency has given rise to a standard for electronic communication of trade-related messages, the Financial Information eXchange ("FIX") Protocol. FIX is an open and free specification that has been widely adopted by both the buy-side and sell-side and by many large exchanges and ECNs. Work is currently underway to streamline the FIX protocol to reduce network usage.

As investors demand greater scope of information, financial exchanges can add value by acting as information clearinghouses and providing data such as company information.

In this regard, an important standard to consider is the XBRL "eXtensible Business Reporting Language" protocol that is also free and open. Investment in an XBRL database and reporting system may generate a new source of revenue for the exchange that takes the lead in offering such a service.

By employing standards-based approaches, an exchange can reduce the cost of new products to its customers and promote their rapid and widespread adoption.

Opportunity: Innovate and Attract Liquidity Through Integration and Diversification

Many exchanges host cash and derivatives trading under the same roof. None, however, actually trades cash products and their derivatives products under the same system architecture, although several have plans to do so. Significant cost savings, liquidity enhancement, regulatory efficiencies and opportunities for product innovation can be achieved by integrating cash and derivative markets. In addition to the obvious benefit of avoiding dual systems, integration facilitates multi-legged trades dependent on simultaneous positions in derivatives and underlying assets, such as arbitrage strategies. An integrated platform reduces the risk to the customer of failing to get all aspects of a complex trade completed. The greater security of a "one stop shop" promotes liquidity.

To date, the pace of innovation at exchanges has been slow and the focus has been on traditional activities. New product development boosts order flow, resulting in commissions for member brokers and trading profits for locals and market makers. In addition to these traditional benefits, new products may assist financial exchanges in broadening their customer bases. Innovation by exchanges in the areas of ETFs, credit derivatives, securitized and structured products – to name just a few – offers the potential to capture liquidity from the OTC markets, or to put it another way, bring transparency to the OTC markets.

Opportunities for diversification arise when exchanges position themselves as information hubs providing central connectivity for diverse and currently fragmented pools of liquidity. The exchange's central position in the market structure provides two key competitive advantages: counter-party risk management and extensive connectivity.

As consolidation points of liquidity, powered by broad low-latency connectivity, exchanges can position themselves as a primary distribution channel for assets currently traded through unconnected networks. The onus is not necessarily on exchanges to create new products, but to facilitate the interaction of market makers and investors.

A multitude of structured or packaged investments could be distributed in this way. Today, a variety of such investments are offered directly to the investor, but they are not readily tradable. For example, banks in Europe offer trading platforms that allow investors to trade bonds, CFDs on equities and stock indexes, mutual funds etc. on-line through a common portal. An exchange environment could bring new liquidity to products such as bank-issued warrants on third-party assets and equity-linked deposits.

Thinking one step ahead, the model might be extended to see financial exchanges acting as central intermediary and furnishing the network through which the buy- and sell-sides interact. The investor could dynamically define the profile of a desired investment and source an appropriate counterparty. Likewise, the market maker could use the exchange infrastructure to offer new vehicles. Baskets of shares, commodity price-linked deposits, synthetic convertible bonds and other structures currently traded outside the exchange could be created and distributed through an exchange. Bringing such new liquidity into the exchange would require fungible, well-defined products subject to regulator approval and sophisticated risk management.

The key requirements for such initiatives are flexible and scalable technology that minimizes time-to-market; connectivity standards that reduce the cost of adoption for market participants; and extreme reliability of information flow and data integrity.

Technological Trends and Challenges

The chief role of the exchange is to provide a secure, reliable, continuously available, and high-performance network to match orders at a low cost. The functionality of today's financial exchange systems is not fundamentally different from what was offered 10 years ago. Yet today's marketplace is vastly different. Therein lies the challenge.

Exchange systems have evolved from proprietary systems/APIs and multiple single-purpose technologies. These have been time-consuming to build, expensive to maintain and unresponsive to market innovation and demand for scalability.

The process of increasing system functionality over many years has resulted in making even trivial modifications costly to implement. Reluctance to accept the task of updating infrastructure has prevented some exchanges from benefiting from advances in the performance, cost, and reliability of architecture available to the general computing market.

More recent advances in general-purpose computing platforms and open systems software technology are able to provide the continuous availability and reliability required in electronic markets. Using fault isolation, detection and correction technology, redundancy and software- and hardware-based high-availability capabilities, online systems based on "open" platforms are now operating at extremely high levels of reliability. Much of this is due to basic hardware and network engineering advances and improved operational and management tools, as well as architectures and design techniques proven in the development of high-volume e-commerce applications.

The Need for High-Speed, Low-Latency Trading

The significant increase in trading through direct market access and algorithmic/model-driven trading by institutional traders, hedge funds and proprietary traders is driving increased trading volumes at exchanges and the demand for very high-speed, low-latency trading. The automated models employed by these traders react immediately to changing market conditions and changing risk profiles, creating a stream of orders and cancellation requests. This order activity is significantly changing U.S. and European markets and is putting pressure on exchanges to provide immediate feedback to traders, particularly under high-volume and high-volatility conditions. Turnaround speed on orders is critical to these automated trading models – forcing exchanges not only to increase system and network capacity, but also to eliminate latencies from their networks, order routing systems, execution systems and market data reporting systems. Acceptable latency times are 10 milliseconds or less, and the target threshold is being pushed toward low single-digit response times.

The need to manage high volumes

The goal is not just low latency, but minimal latency at high throughput rates. Equity trading systems must accommodate volumes of 8,000 to 10,000 trades per symbol per second, with up to 100,000 matches across the field. Derivatives trading will, before long, drive rates to one million market data ticks per second. In order to deal with peak volumes, exchanges generally size capacity to handle 2 to 5 times the average historical messaging volume.

A key to minimizing costs is moving to a flexible, variable-cost technology pricing structure that can accommodate spikes in demand, such as occur at the open and close of markets, rather than making a massive fixed asset investment for peak configurations that remain under-utilized most of the time.

The Need for Extreme Reliability and Data Integrity

Through the trading cycle, data integrity and continuous system availability are paramount. Integrity comprises: losing no transactions, maintaining the strict order of transactions, and ensuring recoverability to whatever limit legislation and customer service level agreements require. Advances in software now make it possible to ensure extreme reliability in the application and take the burden of integrity away from older fault-tolerant hardware technology.

For example, the NYSE has taken advantage of this new technology to improve dramatically the efficiency, extensibility and scalability of its order management systems while meeting extreme standards for messaging reliability. The exchange has introduced new features and an improved interface for the customer in its TradeWorks system, which replaces a 10-

year-old application. The new system, based on IBM WebSphere® and DB2® technologies, offers more intelligence to traders at unprecedented speed. As a result, the exchange benefits by taking a major step forward in implementing its future hybrid trading strategy.

The Opportunity for Market ILeadership

The cost of departing from old ways can be high. It makes sense to base new models on tested and proven techniques now being successfully used by leaders in other transaction-intensive industries. Financial exchanges can leverage innovations in business planning, in combination with the best available technology, to become cost efficiency champions and effective market leaders.

The road to operating efficiency and cost control is built on two core principles: simplification and integration. Simplification of infrastructure enables efficient network management. It provides a single, consolidated, logical view of resources across the enterprise and streamlined access to management tools. A simpler infrastructure is more maneuverable. Resources can be shifted easily and new capabilities added quickly to increase flexibility and the ability to innovate.

Likewise, integration of people, processes and information, both within the enterprise and beyond, makes businesses of any size faster, more flexible and better positioned to respond to events in the business environment. Whether it's a surge in customer demand, an unexpected development in the markets or a new initiative from the competition, integration makes an enterprise more sensitive and responsive to change. Such an organization can operate on demand in an environment of continuous and unpredictable change.

Solving the simplification challenge: Component-Based Business Modeling

Prior to making technology choices, exchanges need a strategic vision of their business, an overall view of their portfolio of services. For this design work, a powerful analytical toolset is needed. Rather than bottom-up engineering of numerous processes based on deliverables, it demands a top-down method of recognizing commonalities across diverse processes. The goal: a simplified and holistic view of operations that identifies true sources of value in the enterprise. The need: an analytical toolset that generates a focused, enterprise-wide view of operations and the fundamental value drivers of the business.

Component Business Modeling (CBM) is such an analytical method.

In brief, CBM defines components that are clearly bounded groups of tightly linked business activities. The defining attribute of a component is the service it provides rather than the position it occupies along a fixed sequence of steps. Instead of stages in a process, components function as discrete nodes in a configurable value network.

Components have well-defined interfaces: each receives inputs, adds value and outputs the results to other components. Standardized interfaces, such as a publish-and-subscribe messaging bus, between components make it easy to configure services and introduce new ones. With components, there is no need to untangle organizational wiring or solder it into a new shape.

The use of CBM promotes the highest levels of operational efficiency and process optimization. Metrics derived from CBM analysis expose the true cost, processing effectiveness and output quality of the firm's constituent services. Armed with these measurements, each component can be evaluated to decide if it is differentiating for the firm; if it can or should be outsourced; and, whether to invest in transforming the component as needed.

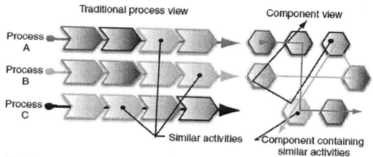

Figure 1: Grouping activities by process leaves similarities undiscovered. Grouping activities by component can reduce redundancy

Solving the integration challenge: A new reference architecture for financial exchanges

A reference architecture (RA) includes both functional and operational aspects of an IT system. The functional aspect is concerned with collaborating software components, the operational aspect with the distribution of components across the organization to achieve the required service levels. The RA specifies the software architecture, but also defines structures for the placement of software on hardware nodes and for hardware connectivity. Service-Oriented Architecture (SOA), now emerging as the way of the future, is an architectural style for developing software applications that use services available in a network such as the Web. It promotes loose coupling between software components so they can be easily reused.

IBM has developed a Securities Exchange Reference Architecture (SX RA) that targets the challenges facing financial exchanges while leveraging SOA principles. The SX RA first defines the business model of a specific exchange:

its operating environment, the services it offers, the processes it depends on and their resiliency, and the volume of transactions it must handle. Next, the SX RA outlines the IT environment and describes in detail how systems components work together to meet the business requirements.

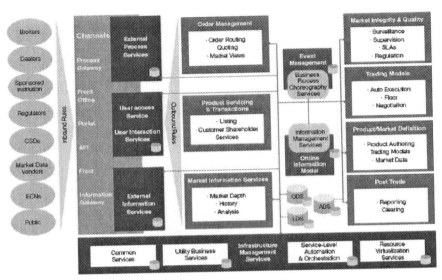

Figure 2: SXRA's Service Portfolio

The SX RA is built on standard and proven elements. The IBM On Demand Operating Environment and Component Business Model, for example, were used to create the IBM Financial Services Architecture – a set of models specific to the financial services industries. The SX RA is an industry model based on these broader frameworks and architectures, specifically tailored to exchanges. It provides a set of guidelines that collectively act as a multi-layer blueprint for an exchange's activity:

- Business Solutions Framework
- Business Architecture
- Application Architecture
- Data Architecture
- Technical Architecture

The SX RA therefore guides the creation of a migration path to the target environment, proving key milestones for an exchange to transform itself step-by-logical-step into a fully on demand business.

Benefits of the solution:

- Increased transaction-processing capacity; cannot only handle more transactions at existing trade levels, but can handle expanded volumes as the transaction load increases
- Increased customer satisfaction and responsiveness to customer needs
- Increased profitability and improved competitive posture.

Conclusion

Financial exchanges are being challenged to maintain profitability in the face of increased competition, price pressure and staggering increases in data volume. The need to increase operational efficiency and cut costs has never been greater. The most liquid and well-regulated exchanges will win the lion's share of order flow.

Exchanges must keep pace with product innovations in financial markets and offer widespread connectivity to attract a diverse global customer base with varied requirements. Leadership will come from exchanges that position themselves as a conduit linking investors to the issuers and market makers for a broader range of trading and information services.

Successful exchanges will function as hubs in the financial network, hosting and integrating cash, derivatives and new products to facilitate increasingly sophisticated trading in real time. The exchange will act as a central distribution center and will naturally attract liquidity by functioning as a key intermediary and locus of connectivity for disparate market participants.

Preparation for the changing role of leading exchanges will come from strategic modeling of business lines, integration of resources, and simplification of core processes. This analytical process supports rapid systems development and cost effective infrastructure. Component Business Modeling and Service-Oriented Architecture offer proven tools that have allowed businesses in a number of evolving industries to reduce costs, increase operational efficiency and maintain flexibility for the future.

Tactical Market Access:
Beyond DMA

By Michael Rosen, UNX

Direct Market Access (DMA) was a radical innovation that allows active traders the ability to directly interact with liquidity without the intervention of a broker. The beginning of this decade witnessed the rapid expansion in the number of DMA firms and within the past two years an equally fast consolidation and acquisition of these firms by larger full service brokers until only a handful of players remain. The question that we address in this chapter is, Now that DMA has entered the mainstream of trading tools what tools will be needed to allow active traders the next level of control?

Forces Driving the Market that require hands on access

This question, of course, assumes that there are forces in play in the market in 2007 that did not exist in the earlier part of the decade. The drivers that we will focus on are:
Reg NMS and the reactions to it; and the proliferation of Algorithms.

Reg NMS
Reg NMS, and in particular the Order Protection Rule, is having several far reaching consequences. We will not spend much time on the rule since it has also been covered elsewhere in this book. Rather, we highlight the major consequences of Reg NMS. The Order Protection Rule requires brokers to send orders to Electronic Marketplaces that have protected quotes. If brokers decide to execute for their client at a price better than the protected quote, they are required to take the protected quote out prior to executing their order. In addition Reg NMS creates a new order type called an Intermarket Sweep Order (ISO) that allows a broker to send orders simultaneously to several venues, even if the price on the order is inferior to the protected quote, since the ISO informs that venue that the broker has attempted to clear out the protected quote at the other venues, therefore maintaining the primacy of the protected quote.

The immediate consequences of Reg NMS have been:

- Increased fragmentation in the marketplace as venues strive to innovate and create incentives for brokers to drive the volume to them.
- Further deterioration of the NYSE and NASDAQ's duopoly as the strict differentiation between listed and OTC marketplaces disappear and other marketplaces compete directly for the order flow
- NYSE creation of the Hybrid market to allow it to compete as an electronic venue.
- Driving of volume into hidden and reserve orders on the electronic venues as participants try to hide their volume and take advantage of Reg NMS opportunities
- Proliferation of "dark" pools which trade away from the protected marketplace as brokers try to create alternative liquidity away from the visible marketplace to allow larger blocks to cross.

The net result of these trends is a marketplace that is much more complex than it was just one year ago and that threatens to become increasingly more complex. In addition to these trends we have seen a return of volatility in the past few months. It is not unusual to see the markets move over the course of a day ½ to one percentage point and then swing in the other direction. Whether this is a response to Reg NMS or simply a secular trend that is now re-emerging is impossible to tell. But, nonetheless, it adds to the difficulty of managing one's trading.

Proliferation of Algorithms

A second trend that makes the management of one's trades more difficult is the proliferation of Algorithms. It is estimated that Algorithms today account for roughly 21% of the market volume and it is anticipated that this will grow over the next two years to 24%. [cxiii] The driver behind the Algorithms has been to allow institutions to manage block size trades so that the trade volume slips into the normal flow of the day's volume without causing any untoward price slippage. The graphs below make the argument that this objective has, largely, been met.[cxiv]

The graphs show the normalized volume curve over the course of a day for two representative stocks for the month of May, 2007, MSFT and BDK. The first graph in each series shows the average volume distribution in five minute intervals. The second graph shows the clustering of block trades, defined as execution over 10,000 shares. The final graph shows the price volatility of the stock. It is immediately noticeable that the blocks are sparse and far between, even for the liquid stock MSFT. This would support the argument that the Algorithms have displaced block trades as the mechanism of choice of executing large quantities. The volatility charts show that the trading of these implicitly large blocks parceled out in small chunks throughout the day does not seem to have an adverse affect on volatility. The most extreme movements are at the open and close. This may also indirectly answer the question of why Algorithms have not increased performance significantly. The answer is that they have largely succeeded in their goal of fitting the block trades into the volume curve and as such have not caused negative slippage.

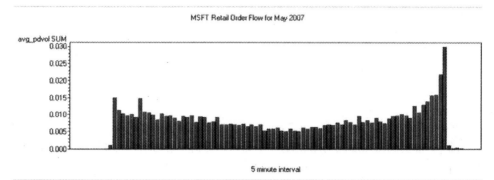

MSFT Retail Order Flow for May 2007

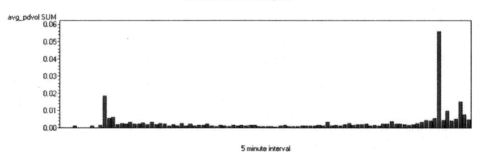

MSFT Block Order Flow for May 2007

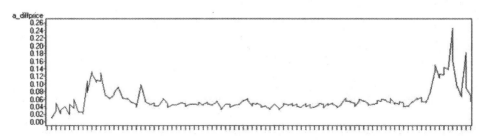

MSFT Volatility DiffPrice for May 2007

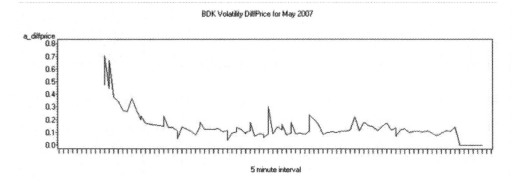

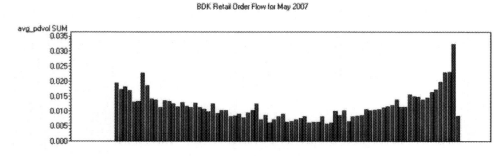

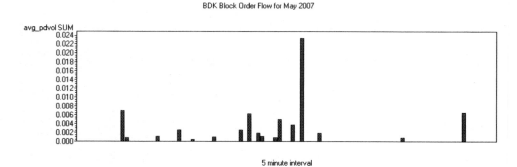

The challenge then that the algorithm's success brings to the trader is the paradox, now that we have succeeded in learning how to morph block trades into "retail size" tickets and thus gotten average retail performance, is there a way to regain alpha in the trading of these tickets?

The answer lies in moving to the next generation of algorithms. An approach which is now being considered is the use of Bayesian techniques to refine the working of the algorithm in direct response to current market conditions[cxv]. In the past the algorithms were based upon statistical models that predicted optimal market behavior. The problem with this approach is that if the actual market behavior does not correspond exactly to the model, then performance will deviate from expected performance. The solution to this problem is to allow the algorithm to adjust in real time to market conditions.

This is the theory. The problem is how to implement a flexible structure that allows rapid implementation of the optimal strategy at any one time? More importantly, how does one then go about measuring the algorithm to determine which particular branch that encapsulated a distinct strategy worked best?

At UNX we have built our algorithms from the "bottom up" so that we can more easily measure each component. We decouple the two algorithmic problems from one another and treat them as two separate problems. The first problem is optimizing the slices in terms of size and trading horizon. The second problem is optimizing the execution characteristics of each slice. In this area we bring a unique approach. We have constructed our tactical algorithms in such a manner that they can be easily strung together in a framework we call "Blueprints" that allow us to build multiple execution strategies into a single algorithm and allow the one(s) that are most effective to rise to the top and carry out the implementation of that slice's order.

Equally important, we can analyze via Transaction Cost Analysis at the tactical level to determine which of the execution strategies worked best and then use that in a feedback loop to further refine the model. Thus we can turn around an execution level algorithm that is optimized to the client's objectives in days rather than the timeframe of others which is measured in weeks.

Why DMA is no longer enough

The market evolution since the early part of this decade argues for a tool that is more powerful than simply DMA. DMA assumes that the trader can keep on top of the information and react to the market quickly as the trader handles each order or list. DMA gives the trader the instant response to the markets. Unfortunately, the introduction of Reg NMS combined with the growing need to execute via algorithms and the changes to market behavior that algorithms have caused means that the trader needs more than a fast pipe to move orders. The trader needs to have a tool that supplies what we call Algorithmic Market Access (AMA).

Algorithmic Market Access is defined by UNX as a total trading solution that supplies the trader with a set of tools that allow direct access and control of the underlying components of the algorithms. This allows the trader, together with the broker, to tweak them to produce the desired trading results.

It is not simply enough to create new trading tactics and algorithms in anticipation of Reg NMS and in reaction to market structure changes. Creating tactics and algorithms that are static and "hard coded" into the client's execution fabric is an approach that will not optimize trading performance. Clients must be provided with Bayesian tools that use an instant feedback from execution success. This allows the client to adjust not only the aggressiveness lever or time span of the trade but also the actual components that make up a trading algorithm so that the use of these tools are simply a part of the traders every day tools. The trader needs to have a means of experimentation on the individual component basis of the algorithm.

The structure and behavior of the market is shifting so rapidly that many times the trader would like nothing more than to "try it out" and see what happens. Our experience in designing these tactical algorithms with the trader is that new ideas emerge from the actual versus expected behavior that take the algorithm down paths that may not have been originally contemplated.

A few examples of the problems that the trader faces may help move this discussion from the theoretical to the practical. The examples are taken from real world solutions UNX offers to our clients to optimize performance in a post-Reg NMS world. The issues that drove UNX to develop these solutions were the changing structure of the market and the need to allow a trader maximum flexibility to decide on a trade by trade basis how to best achieve best execution objectives.

Sweeping Markets in an NMS World

UNX has created a new sweep mechanism to optimize behavior in a Reg NMS world. Our previous generation of sweepers simply swept the market in a sequential manner. When STORM was first introduced it was a revolutionary approach. Its objective was to go out to the market as quickly as possible and take out as much liquidity as it could. Under Reg NMS this approach is no longer optimal. If the approach to sweeping is a "set it and forget it" approach, you will be sweeping markets that are not at the protected quote. Hence precious time will be lost to rejected orders from the non-protected venues. As a result UNX developed IntelliSweep.

IntelliSweep takes into account the trader's objective. If the trader is interested in maximizing fill rate at the cost of speed, then it will sweep all the markets. If the trader wants to bypass manual markets, then it will only sweep electronic markets. In addition IntelliSweep takes a snapshot of the market before each sweep to determine the current protected markets and those with the highest likelihood of successful execution.

Posting to Markets in an NMS World

UNX has also reconsidered the traditional approach to posting. In the past, a simple DMA solution of passively posting to the marketplaces was sufficient. In a Reg NMS world several possible strategies make sense depending upon the objectives of the trader. One possible strategy is to post at those markets that are protected quotes. But simply posting without actively querying the market to see how the protected quote is shifting runs the risk of having the market topography change either in respect to the number of protected quotes or the actual price and being left behind. Thus IntelliPost is constantly querying the market to optimize the placement of posted orders to those venues that have the most liquidity.

A second strategy is a contrarian one that seeks a market that is not within the protected quote and posts a quote equal to the protected quote there. The strategy here would be that the potential contra side would seek out a protected quote that is thin and not risk being at the end of the line and possibly losing an execution opportunity at a more crowded marketplace.

Why DMA without AMA extension is not sufficient

The dilemma faced by the trader is that these new tools in combination with the existing tools present the trader with a overwhelming variety of choice. If the DMA framework is not made more flexible for the trader then the trader is faced with the alternatives of having to manually monitor each trade to see which approach is currently working. AMA allows the trader to set up a hierarchy of trading strategies and then work through them automatically using an iterative approach based upon fill rate or time span to determine when a particular approach is not working and either a strategy should be abandoned in favor of another, or that same strategy should continue to be used but possibly with a different level of aggressiveness. Trying to do this on a traditional DMA platform is difficult if not impossible.

Algorithmic Market Access Represent a Unified Approach

The AMA approach represents the next level in trading. It requires a teamwork approach between the customer trading and the brokerage firm. The broker must supply the trader with both the mechanical tools to allow market access and the tools to analyze trading performance on both the macro level of how the order was divided and traded throughout the day as well as how each individual slice was worked and which specific trading strategies and order types were most useful in meeting the trading objectives.

This data cannot be the traditional Transaction Cost Analysis that looks at total orders over a given time period. While that is important for understanding total performance, it is at too high a level to get to the granularity of the individual order. The analysis of the most granular components needs to be done. This means that the trader needs to be able to see how a specific order type and trading tactic worked in particular market conditions. Only in this way the can trader best determine the proper tools to use to best effect trading strategy. This, in turn, completes the toolkit that the trader uses to come to a trading hypothesis, an algorithm that incorporates specific trading tactics and order types to execute discrete slices, and finally a post analysis Transaction Cost Analysis tool to examine at the most basic levels, how effective each step of the algorithm functioned.

The Bionic Trader:
AMS – The Next Generation

By Phil Slavin, Fidessa

> *"Steve Austin: astronaut. A man barely alive. Gentlemen, we can rebuild him. We have the technology. We have the capability to make the world's first bionic man. Steve Austin will be that man. Better than he was before. Better...stronger...faster."*

This was the opening narration to a hit American TV show during the mid 1970s chronicling the adventures of Steve Austin, a cybernetically enhanced astronaut turned secret agent. Following an accident and after an infamous $6m operation to replace his legs, an arm and one eye with cybernetic implants, he became known as the 'bionic man' who used his enhanced strength, speed and vision to fight a host of villains in over 100 episodes on prime time TV. His success relied on his machine—assisted skills giving him superhuman abilities to foil his adversaries.

Fast forward 30 years and we find another type of bionic man. Not one that uses enhanced physical skills to beat his opponents but one that uses a highly sophisticated order management system (OMS) and an arsenal of other technical/computerized weapons to make him smarter, faster and, at the end of the day, more profitable than the rest. Say hello to today's traders who have at their disposal a plethora of tools to receive and analyze vast quantities of data and make and execute trading decisions in milliseconds.

In fact in a growing number of trading situations machines do all of the work and there is no need for any human intervention at all. In recent years, this explosive growth in automated trading has caused the debate about the future of the traditional trader to rage. The Man vs. Machine argument has polarized the trading community from those that believe the trader is now redundant to those that feel that he is now more important than ever.

Those who are betting on the machines say that black box trading systems have the edge in a number of ways. They are able to analyze and correlate market data to identify short term trends in the markets or react to pricing anomalies a hundred times faster than a human to profit from tiny price discrepancies or inefficiencies in the market.

They are able to mine vast quantities of historic market data to identify historic trading patterns for stocks to minimize market impact as they trade towards specific pricing benchmarks or in accordance with the investor's specified risk profile.

The incredible speed with which computers make decisions is now paralleled with very fast execution speeds. Proximity service providers are now allowing black boxes to be located in the same data centers as the exchanges to cut network latency down to a minimum. And it won't be too long before the algorithms are built into computer chips to reduce processing time to a minimum.

To build the models that these systems use, the traditional trader has been replaced by the quantitative analyst and the computer programmer. Between them they hope to work out optimal trading strategies and build them into self—sufficient algorithms that feed off low latency real time market data and huge quantities of historic tick data.

Recent trends have seen the more astute (some may say covert) model designers scouring the market data for trading patterns or signals left by human traders or other algorithms and reverse engineer the logic to trade against them for profit. This in turn has lead the original model designers to increase the randomness of their trading decisions or send spoof orders into the market to create confusion and hide their true intent.

Whilst computers never tire and, with the right models, will happily 'follow—the—sun' with trading strategies across all the global markets that it can access, the ultimate goal for searching out 'alpha' is proving ever more elusive and investors are now looking further—a—field to maintain profit margins. As they stray from the well-trodden path of public exchanges and highly liquid instruments the lack of historic and real-time market data starves the algorithm of its vital lifeblood making it less efficient and useful, i.e., profitable. Significant efforts are now being invested to evolve and adapt these models to operate in illiquid conditions and even dark markets as well as to understand the interaction between different asset classes including derivatives, foreign exchange and fixed income. Overlay on top of all this the changes in market structure in the US and Europe, and opportunities for regulatory arbitrage are also now emerging.

Against all this compelling evidence it would seem that the extinction of the trader is inevitable and those betting on machines would be safe. Nevertheless, there is a large contingent that says computers are still a long way from being able to act on the instinct that makes a good trader. Yet, all would agree that, when used correctly, computers can take away the routine and straightforward orders and free the trader for concentrating on the value added services that bring in the higher margin business.

However the argument has a middle ground where Man and Machine can survive in harmony, compensating for each other's weaknesses, and in turn create something greater than the individual parts. By combining the trader's intelligence and cunning—and model creation/testing skills—with the algorithmic engine's data crunching and execution capabilities, it is possible to create profitable trading opportunities in even the harshest trading environments. This requires the evolution of the traditional OMS, melding more tightly with the black box, to create the next generation of trading systems that seamlessly integrates the critical features and functions of both types of system to support the next generation of trader. These innovative new applications, Algorithmic Management Systems (AMS), represent the perfect alliance of man and machine creating, if you like, bionic traders.

Simply joining an order management system to a black box, however, does not create the most harmonious environment for this new trading style. Black boxes are usually designed to take full ownership of the orders under their control, and rarely allow traders to interact with them once they have started other than to stop the engine to change the model parameters before having to restart it again. Everything that happens in between is typically invisible to the trader, and as such leaves them feeling vulnerable. This lack of visibility and control is resolved by an AMS, which embraces the black box and brings it closer into the OMS environment than ever before. By representing the black box as a virtual trader, an AMS is able to share ownership of the order with the human trader whilst it is being managed by the engine. In fact, not only is the parent order visible to the trader but so are all the active market orders associated with it. Consequently a trader can track key performance indicators in real—time and step in to alter parameters on the fly, slow down or speed up trading, or pause or stop the algorithm to react to changing market conditions.

There is no arguing the fact whilst computers are extremely good at crunching vast amounts of data, traders can assimilate the impact of data from an enormously diverse range of information sources. With an AMS the impact of all this information can be used to optimize the parameters of the model without interrupting the engine. Traders can use sophisticated pre- and intra—trade analytics to evaluate performance and mitigate risk while the algorithm monitors the market. Giving the trader the ability to not only see what the model is up to but also to play alongside it means that they no longer feel helpless and redundant. Whilst this may seem like a 'nice to have' —when it comes to automated trading it is actually vital to its success as the greatest hurdle to the adoption of algorithmic trading is user confidence. Finding a way to build confidence in models quickly increases their speed of adoption, which in turn attracts greater order flow.

It is worth noting that, as a consequence of this symbiotic relationship, models that are built to work with AMSs are subtly different to those that work alone within traditional back boxes. They have to include additional logic to prevent the traders trying to perform maneuvers that the model itself cannot tolerate. For example, a trader would be prevented from accelerating an order if it breached the specified participation rate.

When an experienced model builder creates a new algorithm they will expend enormous effort back testing it to make sure that is operates in a controlled and predictable fashion, especially in unusual market conditions. Despite all this, when a new model is launched it will only be used tentatively until it has a proven track record in the live trading environment. This is especially true when the community looking to adopt the model is removed from the original model designers.

So, for those algorithmic traders that live and breathe the model through its design, build and testing there is little to worry them about the robustness of the model. However, these represent only a small number of the actual target community that could access and use the model once it has become mainstream. This larger audience finds that an AMS allows them to familiarize themselves with the model in a controlled—but still more open— way, and helps them to adopt it more rapidly.

It is easy to see that a trader will be far more open to the idea of using a new model if they can interact with it through their AMS and take control if they feel the model has misinterpreted a trading signal or some market anomaly has occurred that the model has not been designed to accommodate. There are many examples of rogue traders managing to build up incredible loses over a period of time, so it is not surprising that everyone is wary of the possibility of a rogue model doing the same thing but in a matter of seconds. Giving the trader the ability to gradually relinquish control of the order significantly reduces the time by which they eventually feel confident enough to leave the model to trade entirely by itself – but still under the 'supervision' of a human trader. This is key to the successful uptake of a model within the larger trading community

So as we can see, irrespective of which trading platform and black box combination you use, how essential it is that models can be built, tested, and promoted into the live trading environment in as fast and controlled a fashion as possible. AMSs are specifically engineered to support algorithmic trading and, as such, have a number of additional features that make the development and release of models a seamless process.

Firstly they come with specific algorithmic development environments that have been engineered to remove any dependence on the existing trading platform and make the building of models as intuitive as possible. This means that the model writer only needs to focus on the model logic itself and not complex issues like 'order state' models. Secondly, they provide specific draw—on—demand technology that allows the parameter dialogues for a new model to become available for traders to use as soon as the files are promoted to the live environment. This removes the need for a potentially long and complex upgrade process to the entire trading platform that severely impacts the timeframes for launching any new or enhanced model. This is especially useful for models that have been built to exploit a new opportunity in the market that is trying to profit from first mover advantage and may not be successful in a few months time. For the model builders working in this space the ability to rapidly deploy the new model is likely to be the key to its success

In addition to these technical features and the confidence created through visibility, ownership and control of orders, an AMS provides additional benefits derived from its evolution out of an OMS in that it supports the full order lifecycle. As a result, all the OMS workflows, from the electronic receipt over FIX and returning execution notifications, through to the completion and booking of the orders, creation of confirmations and back office interfaces can be reused. In addition, the complex issues around trade and regulatory reporting are accounted for, which will come as a welcome relief to any compliance office involved in 'signing off' on any automated trading system. Similarly, when you have to be able to prove to your client that for any order and at any point in time you used best efforts to obtain the best price it is essential that you have a comprehensive audit trail for supporting and documenting your best execution policy.

Another area that is often overlooked but one that has an enormous impact is data. Data can be divided into three categories: reference, transactional and market data.

An AMS will inherit its instrument and client universe as well as all other relevant reference data from its OMS ancestor, which ensures that the onerous task of maintaining data integrity is made as easy as possible. This is vitally important, as an AMS will also leverage the existing connectivity and conformance to all upstream and downstream systems, including settlements and risk management systems, where the issues of data integrity and instrument symbology are even harder to resolve.

In regards to transactional data, the AMS has access to all the different order and trade record structures that support a fully functional OMS. This means that several different business models can be offered as part of the algorithmic service including pure agency, principal, riskless principal and guaranteed order flows as well as the full suite of trade types from direct member to non—member and OTC. It should also not be forgotten that the trade and order data model, which has been designed and optimized over the lifetime of the OMS for the parent—child relationship, is an integral part of any automated trading system's control logic.

Last, but by no means least, is the provision for market data. An AMS is able to not only offer aggregated market data for the trader to view but also low latency feeds directly into the engine itself for use in computational decisions. This market data, along with the trade data of the firm, is then stored in huge instant access data archives for later use in model analytics, risk management and by back testing harnesses. Along with market data, an AMS will offer to its traders integrated news feeds. These are now being provided in a tokenized format that can be 'read' and interpreted by algorithms as part of the trading decision.

There are a few other functional gems that an AMS can provide that really start to make a difference as algorithmic trading is adopted across the entire business. Since it evolved from an OMS that centralized all the agency, program and principal order flow onto a single trading platform, the resulting pool of natural internal liquidity can be accessed by the AMS's algorithms to maximize off-market trading thus minimizing market impact and execution costs. Another source of liquidity can be exposed through the intelligent use of Indications of Interest (IOIs), which is yet another standard function within the suite of integrated AMS products.

Finally, an OMS supports the trading of multiple asset classes either through direct low latency market gateways or via DMA brokers for those firms that are not market members. Consequently AMS model builders are able to leverage this capability to create true cross-asset algorithms that combine instruments and prices from different asset classes into synthetic products for trading.

Returning to the Man Vs Machine argument, we can now see why although machines have a very valuable and increasingly significant role in the trading environment, they should be used to supplement and enhance the skills already used by—and not to replace—the trader. By putting all of the above together within a single integrated trading environment, an Algorithmic Management system offers the best for both the model builder and the model user. By developing the trader's abilities and giving him the confidence to embrace new automated trading services, an AMS solution should lead to greater productivity and profitability for the business.

> *"Gentlemen, we have the technology to make the world's first bionic trader. Better than he was before. Better...smarter... faster."*

From Fragmentation to FAN:
Intersection of Reg NMS/MiFID, Dark Pools and Charting a Clear Path to Actionable Liquidity

By Joseph Wald, Managing Director, Knight Capital.&
Kyle Zasky, Managing Director, Knight Capital

The U.S. securities trading market is in a period of unprecedented fragmentation among trading venues and sources of liquidity. Numerous macroeconomic and regulatory factors have caused liquidity to extend from the traditional exchange and appear in varying quantities among publicly displayed and non-public trading venues. Some might see this as a crisis – traders must learn to execute large block trades efficiently across multiple venues without giving up vital information – but it is also an opportunity. The opportunity comes from using the right tools to gain access to these venues – tools that hunt for available liquidity while strategically protecting the order from interference – and aggressively acting on this liquidity once it is discovered. This paper will show you how to navigate the new paradigm of fragmentation – and leverage unprecedented liquidity opportunities.

Market Fragmentation

Although it is commonly presented as a new phenomenon, fragmentation has always existed in the U.S. stock market. Any trader worth his/her salt knows it's worth checking "upstairs": seeking shares that may be withheld by brokers from the exchange floor, in order to find the best price. What has changed in the past ten years is the degree to which share volume, both "upstairs" and on the exchanges, has gone electronic.

"Fragmentation", as is generally described today, is an outgrowth of a regulatory change that lowered quote sizes and made information more widely available. The Securities and Exchange Commission (SEC) enacted new order handling rules (OHR) for Nasdaq-listed securities in 1997, which stipulated that the general public, usually expressed as customer orders coming through electronic communications networks (ECNs), could display quotes alongside market makers responsible for maintaining liquidity, as long as these quotes were as good or better than the National Best Bid and Offer (NBBO). [cxvi]

These changes were followed by a reduction in the minimum tick size from $1/8 to $1/16, and in 2000 a change to $0.01 increments for all equities. The effect of these changes was that market makers and specialists working on the Nasdaq and New York Stock Exchange (NYSE) increased quotation activity, offered a deeper view of liquidity at more price points, and their ability to charge wide spreads diminished. Meanwhile, as matching-engine technology improved, new trading ECNs such as Island, Brut and Archipelago developed to cross shares off the exchanges entirely. Soon, it became necessary for buy-side traders to split up the execution of large block orders across multiple venues, rather than simply send them to the exchange floor. After all, liquidity was no longer concentrated on the exchange floor and new electronic venues offered quick matches at tighter spreads, with a lower likelihood of order exposure.

To split these orders effectively, brokers and vendors developed the first generation of algorithms – smart order routing technology (SORT). These algorithms partially automated the execution process by finding quotes, sending orders and moving on to the next venue until the order was filled, often splitting the main order into smaller sizes that were more likely to be executed in these venues. SORT's highly linear approach worked reasonably well in the ECNs and on the exchanges that offered immediate electronic executions for a select number of order types.

However, fragmentation continued. Further to the goal of protecting large institutional orders, several crossing networks developed, touting anonymity and an ability to cross larger volumes at once, when compared to the ECNs. Some crossing networks have special rules that prohibit brokers from the marketplace entirely, so that buy-side traders will feel more comfortable sending large orders there. Despite the appeal of these platforms conceptually, they do not consistently attract enough volume to make ignoring other venues an option – less than 10 percent of their volume ever crosses[cxvii]

The latest development in the fragmented markets is the advent of so-called "dark pools," or non-displayed liquidity. Increasingly, individual brokers and consortia of brokers alike are creating trading venues that either cross natural counterparty orders between their clients, cross client flow with proprietary flow or some combination of the two. What makes these venues "dark" is the fact that they do not display quotes in the public market. Therefore, larger transactions can take place with a degree of order protection – at least from parties other than the client and broker. There are as many as 40 dark pools "in play" or in the works – often the aforementioned crossing networks are grouped with broker-operated dark pools – comprising about 10 percent of the equity market's liquidity. TABB Group estimates that volume traded at dark and crossing venues will supersede trading volume on exchanges by 2010[cxviii].

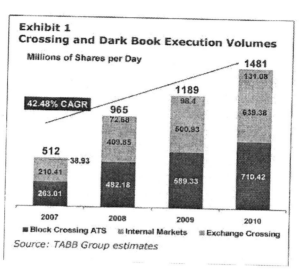

Exhibit 1
Crossing and Dark Book Execution Volumes

Millions of Shares per Day

The multitude of venues we see today make the operation of SORT ineffective, as these algorithms rely on quotes in order to make decisions, nor were they designed to quickly obtain best execution in an intensely fragmented marketplace. A new type of algorithm based on the concept of smart order execution (SOE), a phrase coined by EdgeTrade in 2005, must be deployed to effectively compete for liquidity and best execution in the electronic markets. SOE algorithms use a combination of live and historical data, and respond in real time to changing conditions while bridging information gaps.

Regulation NMS

Order routing and trading execution will become a complicated proposition as Regulation National Market System (Reg NMS) fully takes over. The regulation, an attempt to acknowledge changes wrought by technological advancements over the past ten years, will affect everyone in the trading community. Under the order protection rule (611), the most significant provision of Reg NMS, displayed quotes from any market are protected; in other words, each market must always route an order to wherever the best price resides, and, with few exceptions, may not "trade through" – execute at an inferior price – whether it is an exchange, displayed or non-displayed trading system. Since the rule stipulates that a quotation must be immediately and automatically accessible, it virtually mandates that all trading centers operate electronically. This is why the NYSE and AMEX have moved to create "hybrid" markets, regional exchanges have moved to more automated, ECN-like models, and numerous ECNs have been acquired by exchanges and broker consortia.[cxix]

As straightforward a goal as this may be, Rule 611 will have a tremendous impact on order routing practices currently in place. The complexities are several.

The regulation does not explicitly require, but sets the conditions for a network of private linkages between venues to replace the Intermarket Trading System (ITS), which has connected exchanges since the mid-1970s. Exchanges will be obligated to "route out" to venues they have not previously accessed directly. Traders will need to be assured that their service providers and brokers can reach all of the venues and that their trading technology can, through some variation of smart order execution tactics, intelligently and rapidly – often simultaneously – execute orders across all appropriate venues.

Rule 611 also exposes differences between the technological capabilities and vested business interests of each venue. In other words, it would be a hazardous strategy to simply hand an order to a chosen broker under the assumption that, because all quotes are technically "protected," no significant disadvantages will befall the order. For example, although the SEC refers to "fast" markets, the fact remains that some venues are faster than others; in a market where milliseconds count, it is important that data about transaction speed be incorporated into one's trading scheme. Additionally, some venues have internal policies, such as searching for liquidity within their own dark pool or internal crossing network before passing the order on to the general market, which could cost the order precious milliseconds. These factors could result in missed opportunities and disadvantage the trade. To succeed under this new paradigm, the trader must be armed with tools that will proactively adapt to such factors in real time.

All Dark Pools are not Equal

While it is generally accepted all trading venues that do not publicly display liquidity can be classified as "dark pools," there are major conceptual differences between them, and within each sub-category many have differing methodologies and ownership structures.

Scheduled crossing networks run single-priced, double-sided auctions at set intervals. Trading is not continuous and all executions occur simultaneously. Negotiated crossing networks (e.g. Liquidnet) rely on providing indications of trade potential (not quotes), and attracting large block trades by selectively providing information. In Liquidnet's case, the system actively queries the participants' order-management systems (OMS) and sends an indication of interest to each side, which initiates negotiation.

Most dark pools fall into the continuous blind-crossing or internal-crossing category, wherein orders are posted, participants can be notified when there is trade potential, immediate-or-cancel order types are supported, and an order can be passed on to another venue. The most user-friendly and "safe" pools allow the trader to specify whether they are interacting with resident or transient orders. However, with this model, there is a danger that proprietary traders could be lurking behind small market or "transient" orders, which appear to be retail orders but may actually represent the efforts of a proprietary trader to glean knowledge from institutional activity[cxx].

This phenomenon is sometimes called "toxicity," and it illustrates the importance of employing a trading partner that has zero vested interest in its execution strategy and related technology, particularly as dark pools grow to an estimated 15% of the U.S. equity market by 2010.[cxxi] Although dark pools in many ways represent a boon for institutional investors, because there is more anonymity and possibly higher-quality executions than can be found in the open market, there is also some potential for proprietary traders to move against buy-side traders. Also, brokers benefit from internal order crossing since they can often collect commissions from both sides of the trade.[cxxii] The motivation is there to do so: TABB Group predicts a 31.37% compound annual growth rate (CAGR) in equities proprietary trading profits, from $28.06 billion in 2004 to $63.62 billion in 2007.

There are too many variations on these categories to specify within the bounds of this paper; these examples are illustrative but not exhaustive. The point is simply that a trader in search of best execution must know that not all dark books are created equal, proprietary trading is still growing, and a knowledgeable guide to this new landscape is essential.

Exhibit 3
Profits from Equities Prop Trading Activities

Source: TABB Group

Liquidity: An Unprecedented Bonanza

The electronic trading world of the present and future is festooned with opportunity, lurking in unexpected corners – it simply requires intelligent, impartial guidance to navigate it successfully.

Currently, dark pool match rates are languishing around 6%-10% cxxiii -- just enough to make them essential stopping points on the road to liquidity. It's important to realize, however, that many dark pools represent liquidity that would have been even more difficult to reach before algorithmic and electronic trading cut a clear path through the woods. It was routine for orders to sit on the broker's desk for the better part of a day while the traders phoned each other and attempted to find a natural buyer or seller. The process of doing so also ran the risk of moving the market against the trade. Now, these orders are candidates for instant execution. We are entering a period where electronic trading is, paradoxically, both the cause and the cure for fragmentation – a proliferation of venues has splintered the market, but the illuminating effects and efficacy associated with electronic trading means that the "connective tissue" between the disparate venues is stronger and more reliable. As the Bank of International Settlements has noted, "consolidation and fragmentation effects can operate in parallel."cxxiv The key is to capitalize on the benefits of both.

Smart Order Execution

Today's equities marketplace requires algorithms to adopt as much of a live trader's resourcefulness and intuition as possible; it will no longer be efficient to simply load an order into a black box and let it "fire away." This concept of dynamic adaptation to real-time events infuses EdgeTrade's concept, "Smart Order Execution." Whereas SORT algorithms were primarily concerned with a linear approach to choosing a destination and splitting up an order to avoid moving the market in its constituent shares, SOE algorithms carry the greater goal of best execution in their logic. By constantly evaluating market conditions and processing historical and proprietary analytics throughout the life of a trade, SOE algorithms can change course instantaneously as conditions warrant. The smart-order execution concept goes hand-in-hand with the concept of "active order placement." Active order placement means that each market venue is treated objectively and aggressively with best execution always driving the action. By merely handing an order over to one venue or market participant and expecting that entity to achieve best execution on behalf of the client, the trader is only pursuing "passive order placement." In today's fast-moving market, traders and their tools must be actively responsive to changes in liquidity quality and availability, independent of the agendas of any one venue.

FAN ("Find and Nail"):
The Connective Tissue and Aggregator of Displayed and Dark Liquidity

EdgeTrade Inc. developed the FAN ("Find and Nail") algorithm in response to these dynamics. This SOE algorithm was created to systematically and proactively seek and access liquidity in both displayed and non-displayed markets. FAN acts as an aggregator of disparate liquidity pools and as connective tissue in the marketplace. Rather than serially passing from one venue to the next until the order is completed, as early SORT algorithms did, FAN instead employs quantitative techniques in its logic and learns from each execution, by evaluating the performance of venues against historical and real-time trade data and adapting to present conditions. In real time, FAN actively seeks out locations in the marketplace where the most trading is occurring in given shares, moves the balance of the order in that direction and repeats this process relentlessly over a matter of milliseconds until the fill is complete. Furthermore, it has the ability to act in multiple venues simultaneously, feeding back information on fills so that no double executions occur, which gives it the facility to change course in a millisecond.

To achieve this capability, FAN must be able to receive as much as 10 times the volume of message traffic as a typical SORT algorithm. Many algorithms hit only publicly displayed quotes; FAN investigates both dark and displayed liquidity using two different methodologies simultaneously. To access dark pools, where quotes are not displayed, test trades must be made. If there is a cursory response – a "nibble," or small-volume trade executed in a dark pool – then a judgment must be made as to whether more hidden liquidity exists behind that small trade. Drawing from its database of historical data and proprietary analytics, FAN assesses that likelihood in a split-second and decides whether to trade further, while constantly maintaining contact between all parent and child orders working in other venues. Few algorithmic offerings currently possess the capability to learn from prior experience, balance multiple strategies, and make intuitive decisions and adjustments on the fly. FAN also possesses the intelligence to route itself around venues that are experiencing technical difficulties, thus reducing wasted time. The differentiating characteristic of FAN is that it mimics the behavior and intuition of a live trader, while juggling information at rates far beyond a human's comprehension, and the capabilities of its competing offerings. The results of this aggressive investment in quantitative trading technology have been borne out in the marketplace: compared to average dark-pool match rates that hover between 6% and 10%, FAN has recorded match rates as high as 28.9% in the dark on an average daily basis.

Covert – Playing in the Dark

Buy-side and sell-side traders globally have aggressively adopted FAN since its introduction in September 2006, and it soon became clear that there was demand for an algorithm that operates exclusively in dark pools. Thus, Covert was introduced in June 2007. This algorithm follows the same principles as FAN, but is intended for market participants to whom preventing information leakage is of paramount importance. Covert lives up to its name by applying the logic of FAN solely in dark pools. As more traffic flows through dark pools, it is likely that demand for these types of solutions will rise.

Best Execution in Absolute Terms

"Best execution" is a term used liberally and very loosely by market participants and vendors when attempting to describe all manner of positive trading results. It can be understood as a process, as opposed to an agglomeration of benchmarks. According to the Chartered Financial Analyst (CFA) Institute's trade-management guidelines, best execution is defined "as the trading process firms apply that seeks to maximize the value of a client's portfolio within the client's stated investment objectives and constraints."[cxxv] Regulators evaluating the fiduciary responsibilities and executions of traders are looking for this process. Some traders evaluate performance against benchmarks such as implementation shortfall, arrival price, and volume-weighted average price (VWAP). Others evaluate trade quality by placing priority on speed, or on absolute price improvement, or on the percentage of successful (filled) executions. Costs such as commissions and market impact must also be incorporated in the analysis. Best execution and effective transaction cost analysis (TCA) incorporates all of the above; these are not one-dimensional metrics, but instead are dependent on contextual data that shows accurately the circumstances of each execution.

In the December 2006 Institutional Investor magazine annual listing of top execution performance providers (benchmarked against volume weighted average price), EdgeTrade ranked among the top ten brokerage firms in both NYSE and Nasdaq trading over a 12 month period.

A Global Issue

Conditions described in this paper are not limited to the U.S. domestic equities market. In fact, despite "concentration rules" that focus trading activity on exchanges, off-exchange electronic trading has become highly prevalent in Europe -- averaging about 56% in Germany from 2003 to 2005, for example[cxxvi] -- where many exchanges have ceased floor-based trading altogether. The reasons for this seem to parallel those in the U.S.: a survey of 70 buy-side equity traders revealed that finding liquidity and avoiding market impact were the two biggest challenges facing the trading desk in Europe. The same survey found that fragmentation would be the most profound factor influencing buy-side trading desk decisions in Europe, once the Markets in Financial Instruments Directive (MiFID) is implemented in November 2007. MiFID is a much broader framework than Reg NMS, which simply ratified a change already underway – the move to electronic markets. But it does contain similar provisions, such as a requirement to seek best execution and to display limit orders in the public markets, which are likely to have similar impacts to those stemming from Reg NMS.

There are already signs that multi-lateral dark pools may become the vogue of early 21st-century European financial trading: seven major global investment banks established Project Turquoise this year, as a dark-pool trading system that also allows exchange trading. ITG recently opened Posit Now, a continuous matching platform, which seems to indicate that speed is just as important a factor in the nascent European conception of best execution as is price.

It would be overreaching to suggest that the European market will turn out exactly like that of the U.S. – but it seems certain that the combination of a new regulatory regime and a burgeoning electronic trading market will mean more choices for buy-siders to make in terms of finding liquidity and sourcing executions, and they will need to make those choices at algorithmic speed and with precision, aided by an expert guide.

The Agency-Only Trading Firm

It's no secret that bulge bracket firms have racked up record profits over the past several years. Much of this windfall is unequivocally attributed to proprietary trading – trading the firm's capital for its own accounts. Sometimes this proprietary flow is traded against customer (retail and institutional) flow, or customer flow activity is observed by proprietary traders and the information is used to move the markets in the proprietary traders' favor – which often means the market moves against the customer order. Sell-side profits have reflected this – see the chart previously introduced on page 364.

Historically, the buy-side has tolerated this model because brokers had exclusionary control of information and capital, and it was common practice to pay for other valuable services, such as company research, through trading commissions paid to the broker – paying in "soft dollars" instead of explicitly paying for each service. Directing specific trades to a certain broker to fulfill research commitments runs counter to the goal of best execution. The SEC passed legislation last year to try to limit the types of software and services that could be offered on a soft-dollar basis[12]. Debate on this hotly contested topic ensues.

These practices are being challenged by the increasing availability of real-time price information, the regulatory move toward unbundling the so-called "soft dollar" arrangements, and rise of the agency broker. The main attraction of using a full-service broker is its capital commitment to ensure a customer can complete key transactions. However, the increased availability of electronic trading venues and sophisticated technology for reaching those venues makes this a less compelling incentive than in the past. Running a trade through a sales desk remains almost four times as expensive an option as using an algorithm[13].

An agency-only broker is exclusively employed in trading on behalf of the customer. There is no proprietary trading conducted by the firm that could disadvantage the customer. Services, such as execution, trading technology such as algorithms, back-office, research and commission recapture, are available on an a-la-carte basis, in a transparent and open environment. There is no incentive for the agency broker to direct trades to a certain venue before others, which could disadvantage the customer for whom speed of execution is a priority. The buy side appears to be responding to this, listing agency brokerage as the single most important service offered by a broker.

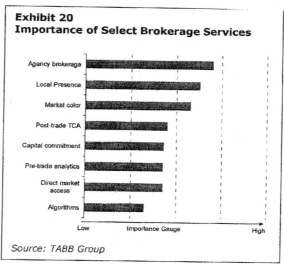

Exhibit 20
Importance of Select Brokerage Services

Source: TABB Group

That being said, EdgeTrade draws a line in the sand about what an agency-only trading firm should deliver to clients in the way of unconflicted services and technology. For instance, a buy-side trader deliberately avoiding bulge-bracket algorithms to curtail information leakage would be surprised to learn their order flow may be going through them indirectly via an agency broker. Ask your agency trading firm if they're a re-seller of bulge-bracket algorithms. EdgeTrade's organically developed algorithms and anonymous execution services are purely agency-only. The principles of EdgeTrade's unconflicted, agency-only model also translate into a collaboration with buy-side traders that is essential for openly consulting on their trading strategy and employing an algorithmic solution that meets a stated objective. These are highly sensitive discussions the buy-side is normally uneasy participating in with just any broker that has execution motives outside of their clients' trading objectives.

The Empowered Buy-Side Trader

The 21st century is the buy-side trader's century, if he/she chooses to accept it. Increasingly, sophisticated tools that were only available to the big Wall Street brokers are now in the hands of buy-side traders. Regulators and institutional customers such as pension funds are applying increased pressure on portfolio managers to fulfill fiduciary obligations and achieve best execution, which of course filters directly to the trader. The convergence of these trends obligates the trader to assume greater control, and make intelligent use of the liquidity options available. With impartial advice and the right tools for navigation, the empowered buy-side trader will discover advantages that come from choice of: strategy, technology and venue. The ability to toggle seamlessly between passive and active strategies several times a day will become increasingly important as liquidity moves around the expanding trading universe. Possessing the right technological tools in terms of speed and comprehensiveness can make the critical difference between pulling ahead in the game and being left in the dust.

Sell-Side on the Sidelines: Reinvent or Relinquish?

Just as the buy-side trader must adapt to this changing environment, so too must the broker. As more tools, such as algorithms and direct market access (DMA) become available to the buy-side trader directly, the sell-side firm must stay one step ahead of the game or risk irrelevance. The sell-side firm of the 21st century must become an educated leader in state-of-the-art trading technology and the new market landscape, and offer this technology to its clients in conjunction with all the other valuable services it has historically provided. The days of accepting an order for a 6-cent-per-share commission and phoning around the Street for a price have passed. Equity commission rates fell from 6 to 4 cents per share between 2000 and 2003, and sell-side revenue dropped 16.2% over the same period, largely because sell-side sales desks were competing with new electronic trading venues. The addition of algorithmic trading offerings and transaction cost analysis (TCA) technology has helped revenues improve at sell-side brokers more recently[14]. Still, firms lacking these capabilities or resources to stay competitive will continue to lose order flow, executions, commissions and even client relationships to other brokers.

Increasingly, brokerage firms must confront the "build or buy" decision with regards to trading technology. They face the choice of attempting to keep pace with changes and improvements in the technology, as well as evolutions in market structure and the regulatory environment. Their response, if any, would likely include either investing heavily in developing, maintaining and distributing proprietary systems, or outsourcing the task to experienced providers. Broker-dealers with a competitive edge are firms that can access multiple pools of liquidity automatically, and not only provide the best price but prove it to investors and regulators. Some sell-side firms are at a standstill, and one must look no further than the demise of research, sales and trading at Prudential Securities to understand the fate that befalls those that do not take a forward-looking view of market trends. The firm did not react quickly to the rise of Internet-based specialty research firms, and eventually lost the game of catch-up and was forced to close its research division. It also found itself unable to fund its research division because stock-trading commissions had declined[15].

EdgeTrade offers an alternative to the deep-pockets and historically risky (failed) proprietary technology build – the Quantitative Service Bureau™.

Leveraged by a broad range of firms, from global banks to minority owned broker-dealers, EdgeTrade's QSB™ offers sell-side firms all the benefits of an agency-only and anonymous algorithmic trading infrastructure.

Conclusion

If traders expect to survive in the 21st century, they must learn to adapt to changes that are occurring at an unforgiving pace. We are exiting an era of customers paying brokers wide spreads, only to find the market has moved against them and to the advantage of their brokers. The new era is marked by high-speed transactions, market fragmentation and flickering pools of liquidity, that require tenacity and up-to-the-millisecond information, in order to navigate and to deliver best execution for investors. The best partner to serve as a guide through a new landscape is an unconflicted, technologically adept software and execution services provider whose only interest is its clients' success. Equally important to addressing the here and now is aligning with a strategically sensible partner offering the infrastructure, expertise and long-term vision necessary for adapting to rapid market changes.

What is Smart Order Routing?

Thomas Steinthal, BSG Alliance and David Lustig, BSG Alliance

Overview

Electronic trading firms and algorithmic trading groups at the major Wall Street investment banks often talk about their Smart Order Routing technology (or their Smart Order Router itself). Most of the Wall Street firms and the technology vendors believe their Smart Order Routers give them a competitive advantage. Given the market fragmentation in the global Equities markets, utilizing Smart Order Routing technology is a day-to-day necessity for market participants. Furthermore, as markets in other asset classes become more electronic, Smart Order Routing techniques will likely become prevalent with traders in those markets. However, the term is over used and often misunderstood. What is "*Smart Order Routing*"? What makes it "*Smart*"? Is it just a marketing term? How does Smart Order Routing work?

In this chapter, we explore these questions as we discuss various Smart Order Routing techniques that are used in practice around Wall Street. We will start with a simple definition of Smart Order Routing, introduce the concepts around Smart Order Routing with simple examples of a 100 share order, and expand on this example to discuss order types such as Spray, Sweep, Drip, Post, Probe, and Snipe. Along the way, we will discuss Regulation NMS and how the order protection rules within Regulation NMS all but require the use of Smart Order Routing technology. We will conclude by looking at Algorithmic Trading Engines and explain why they are not Smart Order Routers, but rather that they use Smart Order Routers.

A Simple Definition

Smart Order Routing is the systematic distribution of pieces of an entire securities order to one or more sources of liquidity in order to efficiently achieve a specific execution objective not otherwise normally achievable through order destination techniques provided by a firm's various trading systems.

The level of sophistication of Smart Order Routers (SOR's) varies depending on the specific objectives the trading firm expects to attain. In this chapter, we explain the basic *"smart"* operation of *"simple"* SOR's, then layer on examples of additional capability and complexity provided by *"smarter"* SOR's.

Simple Case – 100 Share Marketable Order

When understanding Smart Order Routing techniques, it is helpful to look first at how to route a 100 share market order, an order for one round lot of trading that is tradable immediately at the best market price available. The techniques for trading one round lot differ from those for larger orders, and the techniques for market orders are different than those of limit orders. An SOR usually sits between a firm's various order generating systems and external order destinations. Smart Order Routers use limit orders to ensure price certainty at execution, but to start we will still look at market orders. As we will show later, larger orders can be split to several smaller orders, so for now we will ignore that complexity and focus on the simple case of a single round lot market order.

Simple Smart Order Routers utilize current Level II market data to determine where to route orders. These SOR's subscribe to a full Level II feed which contains the depth of book for all market makers, ECN's, and exchanges and cache the data in memory to enable fast access to this information when needed. When the order arrives into the SOR for routing, the SOR queries its internal cache to see which destination is at the top of the book, and then routes the order to that destination. For example, assume the top of book (or best prices) Level II market data for a U.S. equity security is as shown on the following page.

In this example, if the customer wants to buy 100 shares of Oracle at the market, the order would be routed to the market participant (i.e., market making firm, ECN, ATS, or Exchange) that is offering the stock at the lowest price. In this case, the firm is EDGX which is offering 800 shares of ORCL at $20.39 (the share display above is in 100's so the 8 under the Size column is 800 shares). The Smart Order router maintains in cache memory the current state of the Level II market data, so it knows the pricing above, and it immediately routes an order to buy 100 shares to EDGX. Assuming no other buyer comes in to EDGX to complete their 800 shares displayed, the customer's order will be filled. If EDGX's shares are all exhausted, the market order will be filled at the best possible price in the market that is prevailing, which is likely 20.40 as that is the next best price where stock is offered at this time, and there are ample shares offered to fill a 100 share order.

(Image property of Fidessa, used with permission)

Now, if we change the order to be routed by the Smart Order Router to be a 100 share limit order with a specified price, the example above would change slightly. Using the same example market data above, if the customer wants to buy 100 shares at a limit of $20.39, the order would still be routed to the market participant offering the stock at the lowest price. In this case, the firm is EDGX which is offering 800 shares of ORCL at $20.39. Assuming no other buyer comes in to EDGX to complete their 800 shares displayed, the customer's order will be filled. If EDGX's shares are all exhausted, the limit order will not be filled. If the limit order is configured to be Immediate or Cancel (IOC) (as is typically done), then the order will be cancelled back to the sending firm, and nothing will be executed at this time. Alternatively, if the limit order is configured to post if not executed, the customer's order will then be represented in the Level II montage with a bid price equal to the limit price of $20.39 that was on the order.

Routing when Prices are Equal

Consider the 100 share order with the following example:

(Image property of Fidessa, used with permission)

As the customer's 100 share buy order arrives at the Smart Order Router, which market participant should the SOR choose to send the order? ARCX? ETRD? NSDQ? INSE? EDGA? EDGX? CINN? There is no hard or fast rule that SOR's use. Should it preference market makers? Should it preference ECN's? Should it preference Exchanges? Does it matter what fees these various participants charge to access their quotes? SOR's differentiate themselves on how they answer these questions, and how they support the answers. Some will allow limited configuration options at a macro level, e.g., always preference market makers first, then exchanges, and then ECN's. Some will allow different configuration for different securities, e.g., for example, follow the previous rule for liquid securities, but first preference ECN's, then exchanges, and then market makers for illiquid securities.

In the above examples, the order that is sent by the Simple Smart Order Router to the destination is then forgotten by the SOR. These SOR's are fire-and-forget engines. SOR's that use this technique are designed to minimize the time an order stays in the router, and compete on speed. If the destination does not grant a fill back to the SOR, it typically does not care. It is the order source system's responsibility to decide whether to send another order to market.

Additional Options to Consider

Even in the simple case of a market order or a marketable limit order for 100 shares, there are configuration choices with which the author of the Smart Order Router has to contend. Should the order be sent with the IOC flag set? Should the order post into the Level II montage if not immediately executed? Should the order interact with only market makers, with only ECN's, or with only exchanges? If there are multiple market participants at the inside market, what rule will the Smart Order Router follow to decide to whom to route the order?

While we studied the 100 share order cases above, it can be debated how valuable Smart Order Routing is for these standard 100 share orders. Is using an SOR for a 100 share order a bit like using a sledgehammer to drive a nail? While an SOR can be used for 100 share orders, SOR's are better suited for larger orders.

More Complex Cases – Larger Orders

How then should Smart Order Routing be used to handle larger orders of say 500 shares, 1,000 shares, 10,000 shares, etc...? There are several methods for attacking the problem of larger orders, and these methods can be generally characterized as Spray, Sweep, Drip, Post, and Snipe. Spray orders take the larger order (which we can call the parent order) and generate several child orders which are simultaneously sent into the market to multiple destinations. Sweep orders work by sending orders to exhaust all available liquidity through a specified price level. Drip orders slowly send smaller child orders into the market in order to reduce market impact. Post orders place orders into the public marketplace to allow other market participates to trade with you. Snipe orders sit in the background and wait for an order to be posted in the public marketplace, and then fire child orders to grab that liquidity before anyone else can interact with it. In this section, we will discuss Spray and Sweep orders in some detail, and in the next section on Routers that Trade an Order, we will discuss Drip, Post, and Snipe orders.

Before we discuss Spray and Sweep orders, it is important to highlight some details about the Level II display and to discuss how Regulation NMS impacts Smart Order Routers. The Level II display contains quotes and orders from market participants. Quotes are by definition two sided in that the market maker displaying that quote must show a bid, a price at which they are willing to buy the stock, and an offer (or ask), a price at which they are willing to sell the stock. Their bid and offer must both contain a quantity of shares for which they are willing to transact at that bid or offer price. Optionally, bids and offers can have reserve shares with the exchange or ECN which is holding the quote. These shares are not publicly displayed like their quote size is displayed, but rather are held in reserve. As executions are given against this quote, the reserve size is depleted before the publicly displayed shares are depleted. In addition to quotes, ECN's and exchanges also support orders to be placed into their book and displayed side-by-side with the quotes. These orders have all of the same attributes as a quote including price, displayed quantity, and reserve quantity. Smart Order Routers that use Spray, Sweep, and Snipe techniques often have logic built into them to attempt to interact with reserve quantities.

Regulation NMS and How it Impacts Smart Order Routing

In the U.S. markets, Regulation NMS also affects the construction of Smart Order Routers because of the new requirements not to trade through the top of book on any protected venues (ECN's, ATS's, or exchanges). Prior to Regulation NMS, some SOR's looked to bypass a venue with a price if they could fill an order with certainty and only give up $0.01 on price. With Regulation NMS, the top of book at all venues must be respected when using Spray, Sweep, and Snipe techniques. Also, as Smart Order Routers are making the routing decisions, SOR's always flag outbound orders with the attribute DO NOT SHIP set. By setting this attribute on outbound orders, the receiving destination is allowed to trade with the order it receives even if another venue has a better price. The SOR itself ensures compliance with Regulation NMS, so the receiving destination is not required to ensure compliance.

Spray orders are used to quickly access liquidity at one or more price levels. To see two examples of Spray orders, imagine a Level II display is showing the following on the next page.

If we wanted to use a Spray order to sell 24,000 shares, there are several ways to accomplish this given the Microsoft market display above. There is 186,600 shares available at bid side of the inside market between the six market participants. The SOR could send one order to NSDQ, ARCX, INSE, or EDGX as they have ample shares to cover the whole order. Alternatively, the SOR could spray six orders for 4,000 shares each to all of the participants. Another choice would be to spray 5,000 share orders to all of the participants except NFSC as that one participant is only bidding for 6,600 shares, and there is a chance some of their shares may be exhausted by other orders coming into them. By sending the Spray to the less than the displayed liquidity, the Smart Order Router is increasing the chances it will receive fills from the various venues to which the orders were sent.

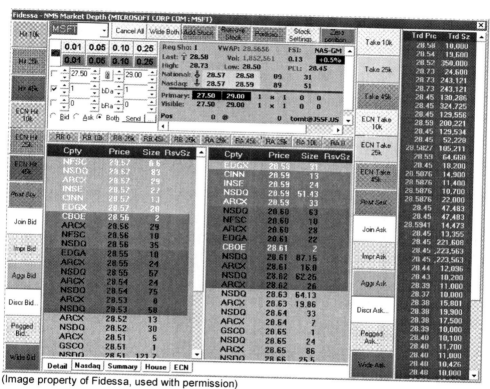

(Image property of Fidessa, used with permission)

Using the same Microsoft market, if you wanted to buy 20,000 shares and price was not an issue, with an oversized Spray order, it is possible to receive fills at prices no worse than $28.58 or $28.59. The SOR could start by sending 20,000 to EDGX at $28.58 to see if they have 16,900 in reserves that are not displayed. Alternatively, the SOR could send oversized orders to EDGX at $28.58 and oversized orders to CINN, INSE, NSDQ, and ARCX at $28.59 to see if it gets additional shares back from those venues. By sending oversized orders, there is a chance that the Spray will find there was reserve size not displayed. If any shares are executed against reserve shares, the Spray will get a better price than Sprays that solely accessed the displayed size. Simple Spray orders as described here are another example of fire and forget orders. Smart Order Routers send the Spray into the market, and they are not guaranteed to get all of the shares requested.

Sweep orders are similar to Spray orders, but are more systematic in the approach to sweeping up all available liquidity. Some venues such as Nasdaq support Sweep orders natively, and the Smart Order Router can be optimized to use these orders.

Considering the example above for Spray orders using the same Microsoft market, if you wanted to buy 20,000 shares and price was not an issue, the SOR could take the displayed liquidity with a sweep on the sell side and get done with no worse than $28.61 or $28.62 for some of the fills. The SOR could send NSDQ (Nasdaq) a sweep order for 20,000 with a limit of $28.61 with external routing from Nasdaq turned on. Nasdaq will fill what it can from its book, and will sweep up all of the shares available at other market participants. Alternatively, the SOR could send orders to all market participants at their displayed size, or send oversized orders to all market participants to attempt to sweep up all available sizes. In this example, the Sweep is done and the orders are sent and then forgotten by the Smart Order Router.

Smarter Order Routers that Trade an Order

Some Sweeps are done by Smart Order Routers that keep track of the requested quantity to be done, and resend additional orders if that quantity is not completed with the first set of orders. There is one key difference between "Smarter" Order Routers that Trade an Order and the simple Smart Order Routers. Smarter Order Routers need to keep track of state. They cannot fire and forget about the orders. These SOR's have a goal to accomplish, and keep working until they accomplish that goal. In addition, the system that sends orders to these Smarter Order Routers can assume that the SOR will be working on its behalf until it accomplishes the goal of the parent order.

Using this Google Market as an example, if you wanted to by 5,000 at a price of no worse than $513.10 through the use of a Sweep order, you should send orders to NSDQ, INSE, CINN, ARCX, and PERT for 1,000 each at 513.10 or better. This will try to sweep up all of the shares. If the SOR is a Smarter Order Router that can track the resultant fills, it might find that only 3,400 were executed. It could reassess the market, and send additional Sweep orders until the full 5,000 shares are executed.

(Image property of Fidessa, used with permission)

Posting orders to the market is generally described as a "passive" way to have Smart Order Routers configured. Posted orders only get executed if another market participant interacts with the order that is posted. In all of our previous examples, the orders sent by the SOR aggressively seek out liquidity and try to execute against existing market participants. Posted orders passively wait until someone else seeks you out. There are some very good reasons SOR's are configured for passive trading. First, many trading venues charge people who aggressively take liquidity from their venue, while paying people who provide the liquidity that was removed. For example, a venue may charge $0.30 to remove a 100 share order from their book, while paying the provider of that liquidity $0.25 for the same 100 shares. This liquidity rebate may seem small, and for 100 shares it is, but Smart Order Routers may post millions of shares in a given trading day, and now the $0.0025 per share credit starts adding up quickly. Second, if you post and are traded with, you are buying at the bid instead of buying at the offer, and therefore you have improved the price you have received for this order. Third, by using a Post order with reserve behind it, you may hide your true intent to move a large block of stock in a more effective way than a Sweep or a Spray. Fourth, Posts are often done in concert with a Sweep or a Spray. For example, if you have 10,000 shares to buy, you may Post 5,000 shares at the bid size to try to get price improvement, while using Sweeping or Spraying techniques on the balance.

Like a sniper on a rooftop in a spy movie, a Snipe order lurks in the background and fires off its orders when a triggering condition is met. A popular Snipe order looks for shares to be bid at a specific price, and when that price is met, it fires off an order immediately to try to access that liquidity. By having the actual order message locked and loaded, the user of the Snipe technique is hoping to beat all other market participants to that liquidity. A variant of the Snipe is the Probe order, an order which Probes the price points between the bid and offer to see if there is hidden liquidity non-displayed at better than the publicly displayed prices. Probes can be done as part of a Sweep to try to access liquidity at improved prices.

Even Smarter Smart Order Routers

The trading technologists at the major banks and the major trading software vendors are continually looking to improve their Smart Order Routers to make them even smarter. Some things that have been done include two-phased orders, self-learning routers, and routers that leverage history.

A two-phased order can be thought of as a Probe order that is combined with Snipe. Two-phased orders are staged as two orders in the Even Smarter Order Router. The first order will be the Probe, and it is probing for non-displayed liquidity by sending an order for 100 more than the displayed size of the order. If the result fill from the first order completes this order, then the trading partner has non-displayed liquidity of some unknown amount. Accordingly, the SOR will fire off the second order for the full size desired. This technique can be combined further with a Spray as follows. Assume you have 50,000 to buy at current market prices, and there are four market participants and they are displaying a total of 700 shares (100, 100, 200, and 300 are displayed). The SOR would Spray four Probe orders for 200, 200, 300, and 400 respectively (or 11,000 of the 50,000), while at the same time readying a Snipe order for 39,000 that will be sent to the first destination that responds with a complete fill of the oversized order. These types of strategies are used by advanced trading engines looking to mask the complete picture of what is being done.

Some Even Smarter Order Routers look at the exhaust of their trading activity in order to predict where to transact at specific time intervals. One venue might never answer at market open, while it may be the fastest to answer during lunch time. An SOR that knows these tendencies can adjust the routing preferences intraday to reflect where they may more likely get fills. Another way to use the exhaust is to mine it to see which market participant tends to have reserves non-displayed at given times in the day.

Probes can be adjusted to focus on the venues where the liquidity tends to be resident. Further, routers can monitor the speed it takes to place an order to a given venue, and receive a fill from that venue. With this knowledge, the router can adjust where it might place the next order. Finally, SOR's can look at the fill rates provided by venues in specific securities, and can preference the venue with the higher fill rate for a given security.

Technologically oriented traders, quantitative analysts, and savvy technology professionals are looking to be innovative with their Smart Order Routers, so the techniques described here in the chapter are not intended to be a comprehensive list. Our intention is to explain common parts of various Smart Order Routers, and how and when these parts are used in practice. As Wall Street firms and vendors look to innovate with their Smart Order Routing technology, there are two races that are on-going: (1) to reduce the amount of time it takes to get an order to market, and (2) to add new and different trading "smarts". Firms have been able to get some advantage over their competition at times, but these two races do not show signs of letting up any time soon.

Smart Order Routers vs. Algorithmic Trading Engines

Algorithmic Trading Engines take larger orders (parent orders) and utilize quantitative methods to determine (a) how many child orders to slice off the parent order and (b) when to place the client orders into the market. Algorithmic Trading Engines generally contain a Smart Order Routing component, either internal to the engine or external to the engine, to take the child order slices and route them to the market as described above.

How does the Algorithmic Engine work? That is best answered in a separate document discussing Algorithmic Trading at length. In simple terms, the Algorithmic Engine is a black box that uses a combination of historical information, current market data, heuristics, and internal rules to continually evaluate the parent orders to generate the child slices. Some of the data that an Algorithmic engine might use to make its decision are: (a) information about current trading, such as fill rates on child orders, (b) deviation from the average price achieved so far on the parent order to a specific benchmark, (c) historical volume for a given time interval, (d) whether this is a normal trading day, or a special trading day (i.e., expiration days), and (e) deviation from generally seen market pattern in current activity. In summary, Algorithmic Engines are black box order slicers that use SOR's for order routing once the decision is made to actually place an order into the market.

Conclusion

While the term Smart Order Routing is overused around Wall Street, and much of what they do is kept a mystery by the algorithmic or electronic trading groups, the general characteristics of Smart Order Routers are straightforward. Having a Smart Order Router is not just a marketing gimmick. The smarts of the SOR take an order and determine where to place it in order to rapidly find the best price available across the entire market place – a critical necessity in today's increasing fragmented markets. Firms cannot stop being innovative in their approach to Smart Order Routing, or they will immediately fall behind their competition in terms of speed to market and in terms of functionality.

The Choice of Execution Algorithm: VWAP or Shortfall?

By Dmitry Rakhlin & George Sofianos[cxxvii], Goldman, Sachs & Co.

Abstract

In this article, we use execution data from the Goldman Sachs algorithmic trading desk to compare the performance of VWAP and shortfall algorithms. Our analysis shows that the two algorithms work as intended: shortfall performs better than VWAP when short-term alpha is high, helping traders to reduce alpha loss. The shortfall algorithm also delivers lower execution risk. We also find, however, that the average trader does not optimally allocate orders between the VWAP and shortfall algorithms. Our findings suggest that providers should better educate users on the relative merits of VWAP and shortfall algorithms and better quantify the trade-offs. If users cannot easily differentiate between high and low short-term alpha orders, a practical alternative is to choose the one algorithm that best fits the overall characteristics of their order flow.

The Choice of Execution Algorithm: VWAP or Shortfall?

In this article, we use execution data from the Goldman Sachs algorithmic trading desk (GSAT) to compare the performance of VWAP and shortfall algorithms. VWAP algorithms passively execute in proportion to the historical volume profile of a stock over the execution horizon. Shortfall algorithms allow users to speed-up and possibly front-load executions, reducing short-term alpha loss and execution risk. Our analysis of the GSAT data shows that:

- The two algorithms work as intended. The GSAT shortfall algorithm (called 4Cast) performs better than the VWAP algorithm when short-term (ST) alpha is high, reducing ST alpha loss. 4Cast also delivers lower execution risk;

- The average trader, however, does not optimally allocate orders between VWAP and 4Cast based on ST alpha. Users, on average, send the same type orders to the two algorithms.

Our findings suggest that:

- Providers should better educate users on the relative merits of VWAP and shortfall algorithms;
- Providers and users should better quantify the trade-offs: execution risk, liquidity impact, ST-alpha loss;
- If users cannot easily differentiate between high and low ST-alpha orders, a practical alternative is to choose the one algorithm that best fits the overall characteristics of their order flow.

In the next section we introduce our terminology and summarize the relative merits of VWAP and shortfall algorithms. In section two we discuss our data and in section three we present the empirical results. We conclude with our recommendations.

1. ST Alpha and The Choice Between VWAP and Shortfall Algorithms

Exhibit 1 introduces our terminology. We evaluate execution quality using a pre-trade benchmark (strike price):[cxxviii] the midquote when GSAT receives the order. For buy orders, we define execution shortfall as the execution price minus the strike price. Measured relative to the strike price, the execution shortfall in Exhibit 1 is 48 bps. For buy orders, we define ST alpha as the price increase over the execution horizon, *aside from the liquidity impact of the trade itself.*[cxxix] Again measured relative to the strike price, the ST alpha in Exhibit 1 is 120 bps.[cxxx]

In Exhibit 1 we decompose the 48 bps shortfall into liquidity impact and ST-alpha loss. We assumed the order arrived at 12:00 and executed one hour later. The ST alpha from 12:00 to 16:00 is 120 bps, so an easy way to estimate the ST-alpha loss is to allocate this four-hour ST-alpha in proportion to the execution horizon (one hour in our example): the ST-alpha loss is 30 bps. We can then back-out the liquidity impact (shortfall minus ST-alpha loss): 18 bps.

Exhibit 1. Short-term (ST) alpha and the components of execution shortfall

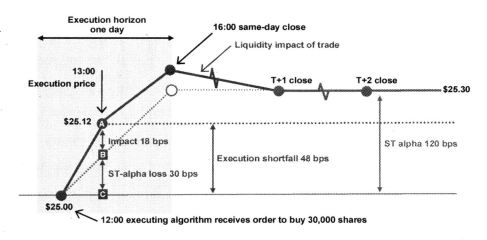

The diagram is not in scale.

We use the framework in Exhibit 1 to discuss the choice between VWAP and shortfall algorithms. The GSAT VWAP algorithm is a coded representation of a VWAP execution strategy. The user specifies the quantity to buy or sell and the execution horizon (start and end time). The algorithm then slices up the order and executes in proportion to the historical volume pattern over the user-specified horizon.[cxxxi] For example, if the execution horizon is from 12:00 to 16:00 and over this period the stock usually trades 30% of its volume from 12:00 to 14:00 and 70% from 14:00 to 16:00, the VWAP algorithm will also execute 30% of the order from 12:00 to 14:00 and 70% from 14:00 to 16:00.

The GSAT 4Cast algorithm is a coded representation of a shortfall execution strategy. In addition to quantity and execution horizon, the user specifies a level of aggressiveness from 1 to 10. The algorithm uses the aggressiveness level to derive the optimum execution schedule by balancing estimated impact cost against execution risk and expected ST alpha.[cxxxii] For high aggressiveness levels, 4Cast speed up the execution in two ways: (a) it chooses an earlier expected completion time than the user-specified maximum, and (b) within the shortened execution horizon may take advantage of available liquidity to front-load the executions. In our example, a high aggressiveness 4Cast may execute 70% of the order from 12:00 to 14:00 (instead of 30% VWAP) and 30% from 14:00 to 16:00 (instead of 70% VWAP).

The optimum choice between VWAP and the various 4Cast aggressiveness levels depends on execution risk and expected ST-alpha. Execution risk depends on stock price volatility: prices are equally likely to go up or down over the execution horizon and volatility increases with time to execution. Traders can use the 4Cast algorithm to speed up their executions and reduce execution risk.

Exhibit 2 illustrates the importance of expected ST alpha in choosing between VWAP and 4Cast executions. We assume the trader wants to buy 500,000 HPQ beginning at 12:00 and we compare a VWAP execution from 12:00 to 16:00 with a 4Cast execution, aggressiveness level 4. The 4Cast execution also begins at 12:00 but has an expected execution horizon of 2-hours. From the Goldman Sachs t-cost model, the estimated liquidity impact is 8 bps for the VWAP execution and 11 bps for the 4Cast execution.[cxxxiii]

Exhibit 2. ST alpha and the choice of algorithm: VWAP or shortfall?

Order to buy 500,000 shares HPQ beginning at 12:00						
	ST alpha 0 bps		ST alpha 12 bps		ST alpha 40 bps	
	4-hour VWAP	2-hour 4Cast[c]	4-hour VWAP	2-hour 4Cast	4-hour VWAP	2-hour 4Cast
Estimated liquidity impact[a]	8 bps	11 bps	8 bps	11 bps	8 bps	11 bps
Estimated ST-alpha loss[b]	0 bps	0 bps	6 bps	3 bps	20 bps	10 bps
Total execution shortfall	8 bps	11 bps	14 bps	14 bps	28 bps	21 bps

a. From Goldman Sachs t-cost model; estimation date December 28, 2005. HPQ price was $30 and the 500,000 shares were 5% of ADV, 8% participation over the 4-hour and 22% participation over the 2-hour execution horizon. The model gives a shortfall estimate. About a third of this shortfall estimate reflects the average ST alpha embedded in the t-cost model. Our impact estimate is 2/3rds of the model shortfall estimate.

b. Assumes executions are distributed uniformly over the 4-hour and 2-hour execution intervals.

c. The Goldman Sachs shortfall algorithm, aggressiveness level 4.

We compare three scenarios: ST alpha from 12:00 to 16:00 equals zero, 12 bps, and 40 bps. The liquidity impact of the VWAP and 4Cast executions does not depend on ST alpha, and is therefore the same in the three scenarios.

With expected ST alpha zero, the only cost of the VWAP and 4Cast executions is liquidity impact: 8 bps for VWAP and 11 bps for 4Cast. VWAP is the better choice. With expected ST alpha 40 bps, the expected cost of each strategy has both an impact and an alpha-loss component. Assuming uniform executions over the execution horizon, the expected ST-alpha loss is 20 bps for VWAP and 10 bps for 4Cast.[cxxxiv] The total shortfall, therefore, is 28 bps for the VWAP and 21 bps for 4Cast: 4Cast is the better choice.

With expected ST alpha 12 bps, the total shortfall of the VWAP and 4Cast algorithms is the same: 14 bps. ST alpha of 12 bps, therefore, is the threshold value for these two strategies: for expected ST alpha less than 12 bps VWAP is better and for ST alpha more than 12 bps 4Cast is better.

2. The Data Sample

Our data consist of GSAT parent-order executions over the 3-month period September 15 to December 15, 2005. GSAT offers several algorithms, in our analysis we focus on the VWAP and 4Cast algorithms. We drop limit orders from our sample and orders less than 0.5% of ADV. In the Appendix we explain the construction of our final sample.

We estimate ST alpha using same-day closing prices (alpha-to-close): for buy orders, for example, alpha-to-close is the same-day closing price minus the midquote at order arrival. One problem with this approach is that the executions liquidity impact may affect the closing price itself as in our example in Exhibit 1. If this were the case, using same-day closing prices will overstate the true ST alpha. To reduce the likelihood of this we drop large orders (more than 10% of ADV) from our sample.[cxxxv]

Exhibit 3 summarizes our final sample: 28,000 VWAP and 5,000 4Cast orders. The large number of VWAP orders reflects the continued popularity of VWAP algorithms. Shortfall algorithms are relatively new but their usage is increasing. Average order size is 3% of ADV (21,000 shares), average order arrival time 11:48 and average price $33. The average estimated liquidity impact is 12 bps. This pre-trade estimate assumes the execution starts at order arrival and ends two hours later.[cxxxvi]

In constructing the final sample, our biggest challenge was to ensure apples-to-apples comparisons between VWAP and 4Cast orders. Ideally the VWAP and 4Cast orders should be similar in all respects, except ST alpha. Comparing the VWAP and 4Cast samples in Exhibit 3 confirms we have matched samples. The order across the two algorithms is similar in size, strike price and estimated impact.[cxxxvii] Estimated impact, in addition to order size, depends on stock capitalization, volatility, quoted spreads and on whether the stock is NASDAQ or NYSE-listed. The similarity in estimated impact, therefore, suggests that VWAP and 4Cast orders are similar across all these dimensions.

3. The Empirical Evidence

Our analysis in Section 1 suggests that, all else equal, 4Cast should perform better than VWAP for high ST alpha orders and VWAP should perform better than 4Cast for low ST alpha orders. Exhibit 4 confirms this hypothesis. In Exhibit 4 we examine two types of orders: (a) orders that, looking back, had high ST alpha (greater than 40 bps), and (b) orders that had low ST alpha (less than 10 bps). These two types of orders are similar in all respects, except their ex-post ST alpha.[cxxxviii] By design (since we dropped limit orders), fill rates are close to 100%, so we ignore the opportunity cost of non-filled orders.[cxxxix]

Exhibit 3. Pre-trade characteristics of orders in sample: Matched samples

	# of orders	% of ADV[a]	shares per order	arrival time[b]	strike price[c]	est. impact two-hours (bps)[d]
VWAP & 4Cast algorithms	33,055	3.0%	21,005	11:48	$33	11.7
VWAP algorithm	28,022	3.1%	21,280	11:44	$33	11.9
4Cast (shortfall) algorithm	5,033	2.4%	19,021	12:06	$35	10.8

a. Order $ value received as percent of median consolidated daily $ trading value, regular trading hours (9:30 – 16:00), over previous 21 trading days.
b. $ value-weighted average arrival time.
c. Average price at order arrival.
d. From Goldman Sachs t-cost model assuming the execution starts at order arrival and ends two hours later or to the close, whichever comes first. $ value-weighted.

For both VWAP and 4Cast, the average ST-alpha of the high-alpha orders is 120 bps. The actual shortfall of the 4Cast orders, however, is only 33 bps compared to 61 bps for VWAP. For high ST alpha, therefore, 4Cast performs better than VWAP. 4Cast performs better because it executes faster: its average completion time is 60 minutes compared to 219 minutes for VWAP. The 4Cast participation rate over the execution horizon is an aggressive 23% compared to a leisurely 9% for VWAP.

The aggressiveness of the 4Cast algorithm results in higher liquidity impact. In Exhibit 4 we use the Goldman Sachs t-cost model to estimate this higher impact over *the actual execution horizon* of each order. For the 4Cast orders the average estimated impact is 15 bps while for the VWAP orders it is 12 bps. The additional 3 bps of 4Cast impact are worthwhile because the faster 4Cast executions allow traders to reduce ST-alpha loss.[cxl]

The aggressiveness of the 4Cast algorithm results in higher liquidity impact. In Exhibit 4 we use the Goldman Sachs t-cost model to estimate this higher impact over *the actual execution horizon* of each order. For the 4Cast orders the average estimated impact is 15 bps while for the VWAP orders it is 12 bps. The additional 3 bps of 4Cast impact are worthwhile because the faster 4Cast executions allow traders to reduce ST-alpha loss.[cxli]

Exhibit 4: The 4Cast (shortfall) and VWAP algorithms are performing as they should[a]

| | # of orders | % fill[b] | est. impact (bps)[c] | | % part.[d] | actual[e] shortfall (bps) | short-term alpha[f] (bps) | time to complete[g] (min) |
			two hours	actual horizon				
High ST alpha orders (>40 bps)								
VWAP algorithm	9,988	95%	12.5	12.0	9%	61 (1.5)	117 (1.9)	219
4Cast algorithm	1,755	94%	11.3	15.2	23%	33 (2.5)	122 (4.4)	60
Low ST alpha orders (<10 bps)								
VWAP algorithm	14,170	94%	11.5	11.1	10%	-26 (1.1)	-68 (1.6)	197
4Cast algorithm	2,632	96%	10.7	14.0	22%	2 (1.4)	-66 (3.3)	61

a. Standard errors in brackets below the estimates.
b. $ value filled as % of $ value received (includes filled part of partial fills).
c. From Goldman Sachs t-cost model; (a) assuming execution starts at order arrival and ends two hours later or to the close, whichever comes first, and (b) over actual execution horizon. Averages are $-value weighted.
d. $ value filled as % of total $ value traded over execution horizon. If numerator exceeds denominator we add numerator to denominator.
e. For buys: execution price minus strike price as % of strike. For sells: Strike price minus execution price as % of strike.
f. For buys: same-day close minus strike price as % of strike. For sells: strike price minus same-day close as % of strike.
g. $ value-weighted (in case of multiple executions) time to execution in minutes.

For the low-alpha orders in Exhibit 4, the average ST-alpha is *negative* 70bps: traders on average are buying in a falling market or selling in a rising market. For these orders, VWAP performs better than 4Cast. The relatively slow VWAP executions in a falling market (197 minutes on average) allow traders to buy 26 bps lower (negative shortfall) than the strike price. The aggressive 61-minute 4Cast executions, however, show an average positive shortfall of 2 bps.

The analysis in Section 2 also suggests that if traders optimally allocate orders between VWAP and 4Cast, all else equal, 4Cast orders should on average have higher ST alpha than VWAP orders. Exhibit 5 shows the average ST-alpha and post-trade execution quality for all the VWAP and 4Cast orders in our sample. Contrary to our hypothesis, the average ST alpha of the VWAP and 4Cast orders is similar.[cxlii] In Exhibit 3 we showed that the VWAP and 4Cast orders are also similar in all other respects (size, order arrival, etc.). Exhibits 3 and 5, therefore, suggest that the average user of the VWAP and 4Cast algorithms does not optimally route orders to each algorithm: this fictitious trader is randomly allocating orders to the two algorithms.

Because of the sub-optimal allocation of orders, 4Cast on average performs worse than VWAP. The average shortfall is 12 bps for VWAP orders and 15 bps for 4Cast orders. 4Cast performs worse than VWAP because even though the average ST alpha is the same for VWAP and 4Cast orders, the 4Cast executions are more aggressive. The average duration of 4Cast executions is 59 minutes compared to 201 minutes for VWAP; the 4Cast participation rate is 22% compared to 10% for VWAP.

Exhibit 5. Sub-optimal distribution of orders across 4Cast (shortfall) and VWAP algorithms[a]

	# of orders	% fill[b]	est. impact (bps)[c]		% part.[d]	actual[e] shortfall (bps)	short-term alpha[f] (bps)	time to complete[g] (min)	exec. risk ratio[h]
			two hours	actual horizon					
All orders in the sample									
VWAP & 4Cast	33,055	95%	11.7	12.6	12%	13 *(0.9)*	14 *(1.5)*	179	55%
VWAP algorithm	28,022	95%	11.9	11.5	10%	12 *(1.0)*	14 *(1.7)*	201	58%
4Cast algorithm	5,033	95%	10.8	14.2	22%	15 *(1.2)*	12 *(3.6)*	59	35%

a. Standard errors in brackets below the estimates.
b. $ value filled as % of $ value received (includes filled part of partial fills).
c. From Goldman Sachs t-cost model assuming the execution starts at order arrival and ends two hours later or to the close, whichever comes first. $ value-weighted.
d. $ value filled as % of total $ value executed in the market over the execution horizon. If numerator exceeds denominator we add numerator to denominator.
e. For buys: volume-weighted execution price minus strike price as percent of strike price. For sells: Strike price minus volume-weighted execution price as percent of strike price.
f. For buys: same-day official close minus strike price as % of strike price. For sells: strike price minus same-day official close as % of strike price.
g. $ value-weighted (in case of multiple executions) time to execution in minutes.
h. Standard deviation of actual shortfall as % of standard deviation of short-term alpha.

The relatively aggressive 4Cast executions have one advantage over the VWAP executions: lower execution risk. In Exhibit 5 we measure execution risk as the ratio of standard deviation of actual shortfall to standard deviation of ST alpha.[cxliii] The execution risk ratio is 58% for the VWAP executions, but only 35% for the 4Cast executions.

4. Recommendations

Exhibit 5 suggests that the average trader does not optimally allocate orders to VWAP and shortfall algorithms. One reason for this may be poor understanding of the relative merits of the two algorithms. If this were the case, the solution is better education and this is one of the purposes of this article. The optimum choice between passive VWAP and aggressive shortfall involves trade-offs: execution risk, liquidity impact, ST-alpha loss. Better education, therefore, should include quantification of these trade-offs. Exhibits 2, 4 and 5 present our attempt to quantify these trade-offs.[cxliv]
Traders may also make sub-optimal choices because they cannot easily predict ST alpha. ST-alpha has both a market and a stock-specific component, so if the execution strategy is not market neutral the trader must predict both.[cxlv] The stock-specific component is influenced by both the underlying investment strategy and short-term flow pressures. Traders can use three sources of information to better predict ST alpha:

- The portfolio manager's input on the underlying investment strategy, passive or active, and if active what is the size and duration of the buy or sell signal.
- The traders "feel for the market:" is the stock experiencing unusual liquidity pressure? Buy-side traders, sell-side traders and, for NYSE stocks, floor traders, can provide valuable information on short term liquidity pressure.
- Analysis of past-executions. Large-sample statistical analysis of past executions can help traders quantify their past average ST alpha. Traders can then use this historical average ST alpha as one input in selecting an execution strategy.

ST-alpha, however, is fundamentally difficult to predict, especially order-by-order. If traders cannot easily differentiate between high and low ST-alpha orders, a more practical approach is to choose the one algorithm that best fits the *overall* characteristics of their order flow. Suppose, for example, based on an analysis of past data, average ST alpha is only 10 bps. Then Exhibits 2 and 4 suggest that the best single algorithm is VWAP or 4Cast with a low aggressiveness level (less than 3). If on the other hand the overall ST alpha is 40 bps, then medium-aggressiveness 4Cast (levels 3 to 5) may be best. Intermediate approaches are also possible. Traders, for example, may aggregate orders by portfolio manager (or investment strategy), and choose the algorithm that is best suited to each portfolio manager's orders.

APPENDIX: Construction of final sample

Our data consist of GSAT parent-order executions over the 3-month period September 15 to December 15, 2005. In this appendix we explain how we constructed our final sample.

3. 1. Since our purpose is to compare VWAP and shortfall execution strategies, we focus on the two GSAT algorithms that best represent these two strategies: VWAP and 4cast.

4. 2. We dropped limit orders. Users of the GSAT VWAP and 4Cast algorithms can specify a limit price. A limit VWAP order, for example, may say: buy 100,000 shares at VWAP between 10:30 and 16:00 but never buy above $20. Almost 20% of the VWAP and 4Cast orders in our sample include a limit price. The use of limit orders is yet another execution choice: conditional on being filled the user will get a better price but the order may not fill. To evaluate limit orders, therefore, we must include the opportunity cost of non-fills. Since our focus is on the choice between VWAP and shortfall strategies, we excluded limit orders from our analysis.

5. 3. We dropped small orders. Almost 70% of the orders in our sample are small, less than 0.5% of average daily volume. These small orders typically have execution horizons of a few minutes. The large number of small orders with short execution horizons suggests that many traders use algorithms as a quick and anonymous source of liquidity rather than for the coded VWAP or shortfall execution strategy. Since our purpose is to evaluate the VWAP and shortfall strategies, we excluded orders less than 0.5% of ADV from our analysis.

6. 4. We dropped large orders. In our empirical analysis we estimate ST alpha using same-day closing prices. One problem with this approach is that the executions may affect the closing price itself. To reduce the likelihood that the closing price is affected by the executions, we exclude orders that exceed 10% of ADV from our analysis. These large orders account for less than 2% of our original sample.

Limiting order size between 0.5% and 10% of ADV has the additional advantage of standardizing the average size across the two algorithms: in general, VWAP orders are larger than 4Cast orders.

REFERENCES

Bacidore, Jeff & George Sofianos, 2002, "Evaluating execution quality for large orders," *Goldman Sachs Trading and Market Structure*, October 24.
Bacidore, Jeff & Sharon Su, 2004, "VWAP Algorithms," *Goldman Sachs GSAT Insight reports*, Issue 1, September.
Bacidore, Jeff & Sharon Su, 2004, "Implementation Shortfall Algorithms," *Goldman Sachs GSAT Insight reports*, Issue 2, December.
Perold, Andre, 1988, "The implementation shortfall: paper versus reality," *Journal of Portfolio Management*, Spring 1988, pp. 4-9.
Sofianos, George, 2005, "Estimating and capturing trading alpha," *Goldman Sachs Street Smart reports*, Issue 23, March 31.
Sofianos, George, 2006, "The choice of execution benchmark: VWAP or pre-trade price," *Journal of Trading*, Issue 1, pages ???.
Rodella, Elena, 2005, "Introducing Cost Wizard: Comparing two-hour and all-day executions," *Goldman Sachs Cost Wizard reports*, Issue 1, May 12.

Note: This article originally appeared in Journal of Trading, Issue 1, January 2006

Cross-Asset Algorithmic Trading

By Eric Karpman, BNY Mellon Asset Management

Algorithmic Trading in Equities Market

Currently, almost 70 percent of US equity trades are communicated electronically. Many of these trades are done algorithmically. There are many mature algorithms available from the broker-dealers, OMS and other software vendors as well as the custom solutions developed in house by the buy-side institutions using the FIX protocol. A whole spectrum of algorithmic types exists: VWAP, TWAP and Time Slicing, Shortfall, Pegging and Smart Order Routing, Shortfall and Market on Close. All of these algorithms take into account the real-time market conditions and will automatically find the optimal order execution path.

The only reason that this concept works is because of available liquidity that exists in the electronic markets ready for simultaneous execution as soon as the desired conditions are met.

There are a number of factors whose combined result is the prevalence of algorithmic trading in the equities market. The equities market is extremely liquid, consisting of many market places where the securities are exchanged. There are well established traditional exchanges that have been receiving electronic orders from the street for the past 20 years or so. In the past decade, those exchanges have been augmented by a number of exclusively electronic exchanges, such as ISE, Nasdaq, Arca, etc. Finally, many crossing-networks/execution mechanisms provide similar services to market participants. All of this is happening electronically.

The technology has advanced as trading venues multiplied. Millisecond executions of tens of thousands of orders is a reality. As the spreads shrunk, brokers have found an opportunity via electronic trading to execute orders more cheaply, and get a better price for their clients.

The regulations, especially Reg NMS, have forced broker-dealers to analyze all available pools of liquidity more carefully to guarantee the best price for clients.

As the size of orders have increased, more buy-side firms started looking at proprietary desks of large broker dealers to realize the savings without the price degradation that exist on the traditional exchanges where the intentions and identities of players are hard to hide.

Algorithmic Trading: Components and Whole

Algorithmic trading is a complex process that requires a lot of data to make intelligent decisions. All of the components are critical to obtain the full benefits . Timely and accurate market data, robust price algorithms, risk management framework, compliance rules, connectivity and performance are all necessary to make algorithmic trading a success.

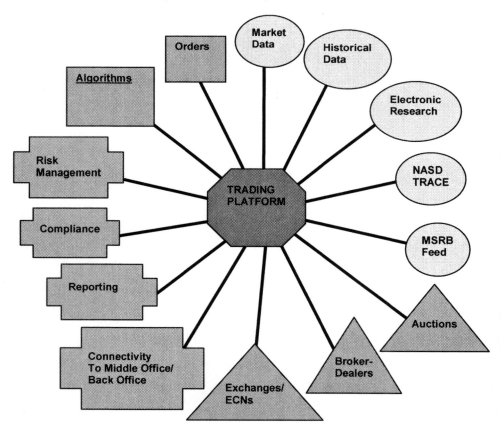

Unification of Standards and Protocols

In the past 5 to 7 years, we have seen a market place standardizing on a protocol that is used within the different securities market segments. Proprietary protocols maintained by either exchanges or specific broker-dealers are disappearing. The new reality is an industry-acceptable protocol, such as FIX or SWIFT. This integration results in the overall Straight Through Processing improvements, cost savings, reduced ambiguity as well as providing the framework to trade electronically across multiple asset classes.

FIX became the universally accepted protocol for automating pre-trade and trade functions, while SWIFT is still the main protocol on the back-office, clearance and settlement side.

Starting with Version 4, FIX has been supporting non-equity products. It was extended to cover equity derivatives in 1998, followed by foreign exchange in 2000 and fixed income in 2001. Currently, with version 5.0, FIX supports most asset classes.

SWIFT has been adopted by most financial institutions for their post-trade transactions. However, in the last five years, SWIFT has moved aggressively into the trade side with their 3xx and 5xx message types. SWIFT was also able to organize the industry groups and large financial organizations into creating a new XML-based standard, called ISO 20022, which is able to support all of the asset types while being independent of the parent organizational structure.

Current Securities Market Structure Changes

NYSE/ARCA, NASDAQ/INET, and Regional Exchanges: As more traditional exchanges are looking to simulate electronic-only marketplaces, more liquidity becomes available to the players connected to either market. These exchanges are also looking at the success of dark pools and are trying to launch similar venues (i.e. ISE Midpoint Match and NYSE MatchPoint. The use of algorithmic trading strategies grows as a result of such increased liquidity.

Uniform Security Identifier System: Since more securities are being assigned CUSIPs, SEDOLs and ISINs, it is easier for all participants to trade these securities electronically. Derivatives, fixed income and structured products are described universally across multiple electronic marketplaces creating various opportunities for algorithmic traders world-wide.

In addition to other structural changes, the last four years were marked by many securities regulations that have transformed the industry and fostered the move to electronic trading and algorithmic trading. We briefly outline below a number of regulations and their impact on algorithmic trading.

Regulation NMS: In order to guarantee the best price to investors, the SEC created this regulation to force market players to route orders to the venues that offer the best price (assuming they are 'fast markets', i.e., they provide a fast, automatic execution electronically for marketable orders). As a result, most of the sell-side as well some of the buy-side firms moved quicker to connecting to various electronic exchanges and marketplaces for better evaluating the best price available on the street. Once such connections were established, buy-side firms decided to create benefits for themselves by executing their orders algorithmically regardless of the order size through customized trading strategies.

SEC Risk Management Guidance, Risk-based Capital Framework: This guidance places more burdens on companies to analyze the risk associated with the transactions. With a fully-integrated algorithmic system, the internal compliance rules are validated electronically taking into consideration the complete cross-asset order.

SEC 10b-10 Requirements, NASD Uniform Practices Code, MSRB Rule G-15: These requirements protect investors' interests by dictating the content of trade confirmation messages sent by broker-dealer firms. FIX fully supports all required confirmation message fields. As a result, all orders placed using the algorithmic systems – if they are FIX-compliant - should conform to these requirements.

OATS: NASD rules designed to enhance trade execution transparency to both the investors and auditors. Since all of the algorithmic trades are executed electronically, the execution reports are generated instantaneously.

MiFID: A comprehensive framework introduced by the European Commission to guarantee best price execution, regardless of the asset type and greater transparency in the trading process. Algorithmic trades are fully compatible with MiFID regulations. By nature of algorithms, the executed trades find the best price available among many pools of liquidity and create a record of where and why the trades had been sent to for execution.

15-minute Reporting (TRACE, MSRB): All trades have to be sent to DTCC for confirmation within 15 minutes. These trades are distributed to any participant right after the 15 minute deadline to make sure these markets are completely transparent. For fixed income algorithms, the TRACE and

MSRB trade data become another source of determining the value of each security and to tune the fixed income algorithms.

Electronic Confirms for CDS: As Credit Default Swaps are becoming more and more important in the fixed income trading universe to hedge credit risk, there is more push from the regulators to standardize the contract templates for such products as well as automate its trading and clearance. Once the major electronic exchanges allowed trading in these derivative instruments and offered a straight-through processing of the trades via DTCC Deriv/SERV, many quantitative buy-side firms started generating more volume in this market. In addition, Markit and other data and price providers offer real-time services to the buy-side, whereby they can tune their algorithms to find arbitrage opportunities and perform advanced analysis of these complex instruments instantaneously.

Straight Through Processing (STP) and Electronic Trading in Non-Equities Markets

After the successful implementation of electronic trading in the Equities market, the non-equities markets started to pick up as well. There are a few reasons for that. First, some new electronic exchanges, or ECNs, have been established with the help of large broker-dealers to automate the order placements among them. Bloomberg, TradeWeb and MarketAccess are good examples of such venues. There is a hierarchy of securities as to how ready they are for electronic trading, illustrated below:

Tier 1	Equities Equity Derivatives
Tier 2	Foreign Exchange Government Bonds Credit Derivatives TBA-MBS Exchange-traded Funds Commodities
Tier 3	Corporate Bonds Municipal Bonds Structured Finance Securities Other Funds Exotics

Below we briefly describe the tiers and specific issues dealing with automation of these security types.

Tier 1: Equities and Equity Derivatives

Automating Equities is a reality. More than 40 percent of equities orders are executed via the FIX protocol. Electronic and algorithmic trading of options has been increasing nearly 40% in the past two years. Most of the bulge bracket dealers are offering algo solutions that incorporate both the equities and equity derivatives. This is partly due to the fact that many order management systems available to the buy-side traders are algorithms-capable. Sell side firms find competitive advantage in offering algorithmic trading strategies to the buy-side. Finally, the buy-side institutions have gotten more involved in quantitative trading and algorithms is one of the essential tools they utilize in their strategies.

Tier 2: Foreign Exchange, Government Bonds, Credit Derivatives

As various ECNs started offering forex, treasury bonds and credit derivatives, the liquidity in these markets increases. Also, since these products, for the main part, are traded electronically among the counterparts, they are good candidates for algorithmic trading.

Tier 3: Corporate and Muni Bonds, Structured Products, etc.

The securities listed in this tier are the hardest to automate and trade electronically. All of these securities have unique characteristics and lack either a centralized market place (such as the case with equities) or independent electronic exchanges (such as credit default swaps or foreign exchange). Even though some of the traditional exchanges move into the direction of offering corporate bonds on the exchanges, the liquidity available to the participants is not large enough to utilize algorithms. However, since the real-time data is available, some buy-side firms utilize the quantitative algorithmic framework for valuation and analysis of these instruments.

1. Handling Fixed Income Securities

There are several reasons why the fixed income market has not adopted algorithmic trading to the extent that the equities market has. Some of the reasons are:

- Complexity of the market and product characteristics;
- Problematic identification of various instruments;
- Lack of uniform communication standard;
- High need for market data for product pricing;
- Absence of uniform pricing methods;
- Few electronic exchanges;
- Reluctance of the sell-side to promote electronic execution

However, there are several fixed income instruments that are similar to the equities market in terms of their liquidity and the established electronic venues to trade them, e.g., U.S. government securities. The algorithms used to trade equities could be easily modified to accommodate electronic trading of such securities.

2. Handling Foreign Exchange

Algorithmic trading is growing rapidly in foreign exchange. Many equity algorithmic transactions have to do with multi-currency trades. As a result, there was always a need to integrate foreign exchange with algorithmic trading. Most of the algorithmic trades performed today are done via FIX. Since foreign exchange trade formats were developed by FIX Protocol right after the Equities formats, many large firms were already using the same formats. It was a natural progression for them to bundle forex trades with equities trades for simultaneous algorithmic execution.

Many vendors are offering algorithms that address this issue.

There are, however, specific issues with foreign exchange trading that limit the acceptance of algorithmic trading in this area.

- Existing automated trading with dealer-specific formats;
- Trade execution delay due to different formats (i.e., quote shopping);
- Reluctance of market participants to forego trading based on business relationships;
- No centralized exchange for all OTC foreign exchange products;
- Unique allocation requirements of the counterparties.

3. Handling Derivatives

Derivatives, especially non-equity derivatives, have always been considered difficult for algorithmic trading. Reasons include:

- Complex trading requirements for a variety of derivatives based on different equity, fixed income, FX and commodities products;
- Many contractual options;
- Various templates;
- Exchange vs. OTC derivatives trading;
- More market data needed to analyze derivatives;
- More benchmarks necessary for pricing of the derivative at the exact time of execution;
- Need for advanced analytics to calculate hedge ratios;
- Difference in algorithms to price derivatives between market participants (e.g. CDS: JPMorgan vs. Hull-White models);

- Manual Confirms for CDS and other more exotic derivatives;
- Bilateral settlement agreements: T+X.

However, the market realizes that in certain markets there are more derivative products than the primary underlying products. Also, some governments have encouraged the broker dealers to automate the execution and settlement of certain fixed income derivative products. Additionally, the derivative industry associations came up with templates of uniform standard contracts to trade derivative products. As a result, with the growth of electronic trading of such instruments and simultaneous pricing, the market participants have started utilizing algorithms to trade these instruments.

4. Handling Commodities, Private Placements and Exotic Securities

As the names suggest, it is quite difficult to trade automatically these instrument types. Here are some of the problems dealing with these securities.

- No universal identifiers;
- No standardization;
- Relatively small inter-dealer market;
- A lot of information to keep track of;
- Some of the assets trade so infrequently, hard to price;
- Many exchanges are not automated and "not-for-profit";
- No real automation in the market place;
- Possibilities for fraud.

However, these problems are currently being resolved. As a result, over time we will see a growing use of algorithms for trading these instruments.

Multi Asset Class Electronic Trading

When firms talk about algorithmic trading in the non-equities markets, they typically refer to automatic decisions and analytics to support these decisions that exist within the frameworks of their trading platforms. Because of the issues we have mentioned in other sections of this chapter, the traders need to have a say in whether the trades will be done electronically after the algorithm finds the best path or manually via the broker-dealer. As a result, many buy-side firms invest heavily into multi-asset class electronic trading systems with capabilities to trade using custom algorithms as well as the ability to generate signals for further manual execution.

Executing Balanced Transactions Electronically

Years ago, buy side firms had a clear distinction between equities and fixed income portfolios. The realities today are shifting. New asset allocation models as well as more advanced analytics available to the buy-side traders and portfolio managers today resulted in the popularity of balanced portfolios.

New risk frameworks and compliance requirements also helped with the creation of balanced portfolios. Because of various levels of correlation between different asset classes, the overall risk level is minimized if different assets are bundled together into one portfolio. The hedges which are now more important than ever to lessen risk are bundled together into similar strategies with the underlying products. The execution of one leg of such portfolios would not give the best result when considering the portfolio return as a whole. As a result, more buy-side traders are looking into the simultaneous algorithmic execution of all parts of their portfolios. The vendors, as well as the broker–dealers, are addressing these issues.

What's Next

Algorithmic trading is a still developing concept and tool. More and more buy-side firms are looking to use to gain the advantage over the competition. The sell-side and the software vendors also see algorithmic trading as a way to differentiate themselves when offering services to the investment management community. After the success of algorithmic trading in the equities market, more efforts are now being put into providing similar capabilities in the fixed income, derivatives, and foreign exchange and commodities markets. It is just a matter of time before we end up with true cross-asset trading systems, with full capabilities offering algorithmic trading across all of the supported asset classes.

Additionally, as algorithms for various asset classes become more affordable, many smaller players will enter the market for electronic trading. For example, smaller arbitrage based hedge funds will benefit from the instantaneous buy and sell orders to take advantage of price arbitrage opportunities in multiple markets across asset classes.

Section III –
Technology & Electronic Trading

The Fix Protocol:
The Silent Facilitator of Global Electronic Trading

By Courtney Doyle, Jordan & Jordan and Daniella Baker, Jordan & Jordan

The electronic trading environment is evolving. Algorithmic trading is on the rise, regulatory pressures are growing, market data volumes are skyrocketing, the pressure to reduce costs is ever-present, and automated trading is no longer just something performed by the folks over in Equities. Maintaining a competitive edge and staying in control of the technology budget within this changing landscape is proving increasingly difficult.

Most firms in the industry utilize the Financial Information eXchange ("FIX") Protocol to help them maintain their competitive edge while dealing with the ever changing world of Electronic Trading. The FIX Protocol is often viewed as fundamental to effective electronic trading; it is not a piece of software or a trading system but a series of freely available messaging specifications for the electronic communication of trade-related messages.

How does a messaging specification impact the multi-billion dollar business of global electronic trading? The fact that virtually every major stock exchange and investment bank uses FIX, as do the world's largest mutual funds and money managers, and thousands of smaller investment firms explains how FIX has and will continue to have a significant impact within the electronic trading arena.

The FIX Protocol does not just provide support for Equities. While its origins are in this space, FIX has come a long way since its inception in 1992 as a bilateral communications framework for equity trading between Fidelity Investments and Salomon Brothers. FIX has become not only the *de facto* messaging standard for pre-trade and trade communication globally within the Equity markets, the Protocol is now experiencing rapid horizontal expansion across the asset classes including the Foreign Exchange, Fixed Income and Derivative Markets and vertical growth throughout the trade lifecycle, supporting Straight-Through-Processing (STP) from Indication-of-Interest (IOI) to Allocations and Confirmations.

Figure 1 on the following page demonstrates the breadth and depth of FIX support for each asset class across the trade process. As shown in the table, the FIX Protocol rarely remains *in situ* for very long, and since 1996 its functionality has increased significantly. The very nature of the fast moving electronic trading environment means that if the product rested on its laurels for any period of time, it would soon become outdated. As a result, it is continuously developed to ensure it can meet the industry's ever expanding requirements, making the freely available protocol a primary example of open source technology at its very best.

The FIX Protocol is owned and maintained by the not-for-profit organization, FIX Protocol Limited (FPL). Development work on the Protocol is conducted not by a team of highly paid programmers locked away in a dark basement, but but rather by a group of incredibly energized volunteers based all over the globe. These volunteers are employees of FPL member firms who dedicate their time to help achieve the organization's mission, "To improve the global trading process by defining, managing, and promoting an open protocol for real-time, electronic communication between industry participants, while complementing industry standards". Why do they dedicate this time? The answer is simple: These individuals are exposed to the many challenges faced by the trading environment every day, and as a result, they recognize the huge value that the FIX standard provides to the industry and they want to see this value extended.

As an organization, FPL has witnessed significant growth over recent years, with membership numbers increasing four-fold since 2002. It now includes almost 200 member firms from across the global financial services sector with active participants within the Americas, Europe, Middle East and Africa (EMEA), Japanese and Asia Pacific regions. Without the support of these firms, the continued development of the Protocol would not be possible. Figure 2 demonstrates the growth of FPL over recent years which climbed steeply in 2003, mainly due to a policy change which allowed vendors to also join the organization.

Adoption of the FIX Protocol has also spread geographically at a rapid pace over recent years. Use of the Protocol is no longer a benefit reaped just by the world's largest and most advanced trading centers such as New York or London; it is now gaining significant momentum in additional global markets. A key example of this is the South African market where a significant growth in the use and adoption levels of FIX is evident, as this market continues to progress and adapt to international standards. This is a trend that has been driven by a variety of factors, including recent changes to the competitive landscape and the emergence of international regulations- factors that have in turn impacted local business practices.

Figure 1. FIX Functionality Matrix

Message Support	FIX 4.0 [Jan '96]	FIX 4.1 [Apr '98]	FIX 4.2 [Mar '00]	FIX 4.3 [Aug '01]	FIX 4.4 [Apr '03]	FIX 5.0 [Jan '07]
Equities						
Basic Order Flow						
IOIs and Advertisements						
Quotes						
Market Data						
Allocations						
Confirms / Affirms						
Trade Reporting						
Program Trading						
Algorithmic Trading						
Futures & Options						
Basic Order Flow						
Multi-leg Order Flow						
IOIs and Advertisements						
Quotes						
Market Data						
Allocations						
Confirms / Affirms						
Trade Reporting						
Security and Position Reporting						
Collateral Management (Listed derivatives)						
Fixed Income						
Basic Order Flow						
Multi-leg Order Flow (Repos, swaps/switches/ rolls)						
IOIs (offerings)						
Quotes						
Allocations						
Confirms / Affirms						
Trade Reporting						
Collateral Management						
Foreign Exchange						
Basic Order Flow (spots,forwards)						
Basic Order Flow (swaps)						
Quotes (spots, outright forwards, FX swaps)						
Market Data (executable streaming prices)						
Allocations						
Confirms / Affirms						
Trade Reporting						
General						
News						
Email						
Transport Independence Framework						
Regulatory Compliance						

Legend:	▮ No Support	Some Support	▦ Good Support	▨ Not Applicable

At the FPL Southern Africa Electronic Trading Conference, held in Cape Town in April 2007, the results from the recent FSmetrics survey were revealed. The survey of Buy-side firms was undertaken to highlight the similarities between the South African marketplace and other global markets and revealed that the South African survey respondents ranked the increased use of FIX as one of the biggest opportunities for improving operational performance in the industry in the next 12 months.

Figure 2. FPL Membership Growth

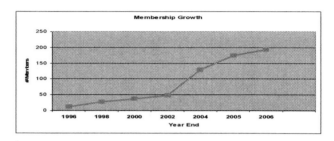

Additional progress has also been demonstrated in the Japanese market where the FIX Protocol was once viewed by many as a "foreign standard." This attitude, however, appears to be changing as leading market players are ramping up their support of the Protocol. A true testament to the level of FIX adoption was revealed at the October 2006 FPL Japan Electronic Trading Summit, which attracted almost 600 market participants from across the financial services sector. A live survey conducted at the event revealed that 72% of survey participants represented firms that traded electronically using FIX.

Figure 3. Survey responses received at the FPL Japan Electronic Trading Conference.

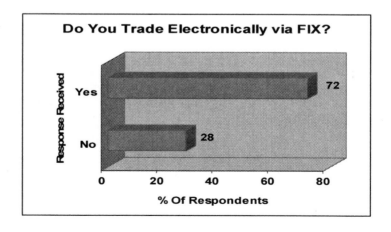

Why Choose FIX?

So why is it that the industry is voting with its technology dollars and choosing FIX? FIX has been described as "the html of Wall Street" due to its ubiquitous association with electronic trading. How did it achieve this status in a market still populated by a plethora of proprietary protocols each offering the ability to facilitate transparent automated trading?

The answers to these questions are based on a number of fundamental points:

Product Attributes: As the demand for FIX interfaces increase, the switching costs traditionally associated with proprietary interfaces are minimized, which in turn encourages competition as customers are granted greater freedom of movement within the industry.

The FIX Protocol itself is a specification of what and how to communicate. Market participants have the freedom to choose how they implement the software and the network aspects of connectivity, and they have the ability to upgrade or replace components as driven by their business needs.

As a result, by choosing to trade electronically with FIX, adopters reap the benefits of easy access to additional liquidity sources, greater cost efficiency, and Straight-Through Processing, factors imperative to achieving success in the current trading environment.

Market Positioning: The FIX Protocol is an open specification, which is available free of charge from the FPL website. By positioning FIX in this manner, adopters are provided with a cost efficient method of market entry. FPL member firms are keen to spread FIX adoption as they appreciate the benefits this delivers to the FIX community. Each time a new market place or market participant becomes FIX enabled, a potential trading partner is identified and an overall increase in the "network effect" is achieved.

The FPL Organization: A principal benefit of utilizing the FIX Protocol is that it is an industry-driven messaging standard. It was created by market participants to solve specific business needs and has continued to evolve in that same manner. Changes to the Protocol are suggested by volunteer market participants who identify needs; those same participants are responsible for maintaining and promoting the specification, and ultimately using those agreed upon enhancements within their businesses. As such, the FIX organization and process is very pragmatic; it is focused on meeting "real world" needs in an efficient, community-driven model.

The following section will explain how the FIX Protocol may be applied to assist firms as they seek to meet and address some of the key global trends surfacing within this industry.

Increased Regulatory Pressures

The FPL organization believes that by encouraging investment firms to leverage FIX these firms will benefit as the costs associated with regulatory compliance will be reduced. The goals of new regulatory initiatives generally require highly complex technical solutions. The regulatory goals would be made more achievable if all required participants exchanged data using the same technical language; that language is FIX. Such a recommendation reduces uncertainty, minimizes the cost of regulatory compliance, and increases the likelihood of a successful implementation upon release of a new regulation. The latest release of the FIX Protocol, version 5.0, provides support for new trading regulations such as Regulation NMS, OATS Phase 3 and MiFID.

Regulation NMS: Regulation National Market System (Reg NMS) became effective for Exchanges in March 2007, and in July 2007, it began impacting the broker-dealer community. This regulation is an initiative undertaken by the United States Securities and Exchange Commission (SEC), and will have a considerable impact on all participants and processes within the US Equity markets. According to the SEC, "Regulation NMS includes new substantive rules that are designed to modernize and strengthen the regulatory structure of the U.S. equity markets."

Reg NMS is a set of market-structure changes that compel brokers and exchanges to guarantee investors the best available price that is automatically executable. Market centers have to display an automated quotation that is both electronically accessible and immediately executable, or they will risk having their prices ignored by other market centers.

Reg NMS mandates that market centers route orders to the venue that offers the best price. This fundamental shift in the way equities are traded requires significant system changes and investments in technology by all market participants.

The Reg NMS extension in FIX 5.0 includes enhancements to the FIX specification that supports the identifiers required to assist broker-dealers and trading centers in complying with the Order Protection Rule (Rule 611) and the Sub-Penny Rule (Rule 612).

MiFID: As of November 1 2007, Markets in Financial Instruments Directive (MiFID) will be in effect and the European trading landscape is expected to begin an evolutionary process that will significantly change the current market structure. MiFID will impact the EU securities market significantly, including: pre-trade transparency, order handling, best execution, post-trade transparency and transaction reporting. MiFID will also present a number of new opportunities to market participants as it provides a single market in financial services, allowing firms to offer products and services across the European Union based on a single set of rules. It will also open up a new area of competition between regulated stock exchanges and investment banks by letting the banks offer their own trading platforms.

In complying with MiFID, a participant's decision to use FIX reduces uncertainty, lowers cost, eliminates the risk of multiple systems being used either throughout the lifecycle or across geographic zones and increases the likelihood of a successful MiFID implementation.

Through developments to the Protocol, FIX is now MiFID compliant. By encouraging firms to implement the recent enhancements, they will benefit by achieving a cost efficient method of compliance. Encouraging other existing trading infrastructures, particularly exchanges, to adopt the use of FIX rather than each continuing to use their own proprietary messaging protocol, will help investment firms across the European Economic Area (EEA) to reduce their costs of doing business. Reducing the cost of using exchanges would also encourage investment firms in other EEA states to become users of those exchanges, thereby facilitating the flow of capital throughout the EEA.

Changing Market Structure

During the 1990's, the exchange sector started moving toward more electronic trading practices, a trend which gained initial popularity with European and Asian participants and then developed a foothold in the United States.

The Exchange marketplace is one that has seen significant change in recent years and many indicators imply this pattern will continue. Globalization has played a huge role in changing the world's market structure. Over recent years trading boundaries have been removed, and the harmonization of trading rules and regulations is happening.

Another factor that has influenced this sector is demutualization, with exchanges all over the world moving toward this structure. Exchanges, whether demutualized or not, face pressures from a variety of sources including changing regulatory requirements, issuers and other market participants. However, a demutualized, for-profit exchange also faces additional pressure from its shareholders to deliver dividends, profits and cost efficiency. Successfully meeting the needs of such a diverse range of interested parties can prove very challenging. Additional external pressure on European exchanges will occur as they prepare for MiFID, which will not only generate further pressure on their technology budgets, but will also lead to increased competition in traditional territories. Both of these factors could significantly impact the bottom line of these recently demutualized organizations.

The pressures presented to this community are not limited to the business. The impact of MiFiD and demutualization will be equally felt by the technical teams that are charged with helping to achieve these goals. Over recent years, FPL has been focused on developing a stronger understanding of the challenges faced by this market sector. This goal led to the re-establishment of the FPL Exchanges/ECNs Working Group which is centered on providing additional FIX messaging functionality to this sector and the development and continued improvement of the FAST Protocol[SM].

The FPL Exchanges and ECNs Working Group was re-established in 2006 to enable and promote the harmonized usage of FIX by Exchanges and ECNs across asset classes. Over 35 Exchanges and ECNs are members of this working group and a key area of focus is exchange interface standardization. Exchanges operate by offering a single interface to their users, however, each user connects to multiple trading venues and as a result the user community is keen to see these interfaces standardized to reduce the costs associated with connecting to each location. The group is actively working to help achieve this goal.

Additionally, this group has benefited significantly from participation by OMX and their assistance in the delivery of a number of enhancements in the recently released FIX version 5.0. These enhancements were included to aid the implementation process of firms wishing to adopt FIX and to 'fill in the gaps' present in previous versions of the Protocol, enabling exchanges/ECNs to use a single API. These enhancements include the following:

- Additional fields to deliver improved support for Hit/Take markets and call auctions
- The submission of a parties block to a set of messages to support business level authorization rules
- A totally new set of workflows for the reporting of privately negotiated trades and the relaying of confirmed trades from an exchange

A major reason why FIX was not traditionally heavily utilized by this market sector was due to performance. The Protocol was criticized for being too verbose and just not an effective means to communicate the sky rocketing volumes of financial data experienced by this market in a quick and efficient manner. This view was especially prevalent with respect to the distribution of market data. In 2005, FPL set up the Market Data Optimization Working Group to address this issue and the resultant FAST (FIX Adapted for Streaming) Protocol^SM was born.

The FAST Protocol^SM offers a data compaction methodology that optimizes communication in the electronic exchange of financial data. FAST eliminates the descriptive information from financial messages, by converting numeric ASCII data to binary, and by sending repetitive data within a single network message only once. FAST works best with large quantities of data that share similarities in content and structure, presenting significant opportunities for the global capital markets. In proof of concept tests, the FAST Protocol^SM demonstrated the ability to radically reduce message size and bandwidth utilization, compressing FIX feeds by up to 90% without negatively impacting latency.

The FAST Protocol^SM has many uses. In addition to presenting a solution within the market data arena, it may also be applied to other areas demanding high compression and low latency communication such as high frequency trading, Direct Market Access and Exchange interfaces. With regards to its success, FAST has received significant support from the industry, and a number of prominent participants have announced interest in FAST, including the Archipelago Exchange (now NYSE Arca), the Chicago Mercantile Exchange (CME), the London Stock Exchange (LSE), OMX and the International Securities Exchange (ISE). The significant momentum behind FAST demonstrates its value and acceptance as an industry standard.

The Growing Popularity of Automated Trading Beyond Equities

Automated trading using the FIX Protocol has achieved broad industry adoption within the Equities space and as firms continue to realize the competitive edge that may be achieved by leveraging this technology, FIX usage is now starting to spread across the asset classes.

Through development and enhancements to the Protocol, FIX has enabled firms to expand their use of the Protocol across the Fixed Income, Derivative and Foreign Exchange markets and throughout the trade lifecycle, covering a multitude of functions including Allocations, Confirmations and Reporting. As the financial services market continues to evolve, FPL believes that the use of the FIX Protocol will also grow across all asset classes and trading processes. The industry no longer works in silos; firms are becoming more global in nature and trading is moving towards a multi-asset class environment, as investors seek to invest across a range of asset classes to deliver more profitable returns. By leveraging their automated trading and FIX investments across additional asset classes, firms profit from the ability to more effectively meet client needs.

The take-up of FIX has varied by asset class and is very much dependent upon market needs and levels of maturity within the electronic trading space. Fixed Income is an example of an asset class where market structure has created the need for a common protocol and a number of firms have chosen FIX. The Fixed Income market is segmented due to geography and as such the use of a common protocol can prove highly beneficial. Without taking this approach, a firm may easily find itself supporting a multitude of protocols globally which significantly limit STP and margin potential.

The speed at which automated trading and the FIX Protocol will penetrate the additional asset classes is a question that is not easily answered. However, when you consider the recent progress in Derivatives and Foreign Exchange, it is unlikely to be too far off.

Advancements in the Search for Dark Liquidity

The growing search for pools of dark liquidity has become the modern trader's Holy Grail. The ability to trade in significant size without arousing unwanted interest and undue market impact presents clear benefit to the trade participants. The concept of executing a trade in this fashion is not new. In the past, this activity frequently involved much discrete manual searching. However, the key difference today is that the industry is now seeking to achieve the same anonymity within a more fragmented marketplace, in an automated manner.

Participants want to source dark liquidity at the speed technology has enabled them to become accustomed to, with the added benefit of reduced manual input. Consistent with FPL's traditional responsiveness to customer and market needs, we are now starting to see changes in FIX that help facilitate this process. In January 2007, FPL launched the latest version of the Protocol, FIX 5.0. The specification includes a number of innovations that reflect the user community's desire to interact with dark pools of liquidity. A key example of this is the improved support that FIX 5.0 offers for more complex order types such as reserve, peg and trigger orders. Additionally, a standardized method for expressing algorithmic order types is being developed. FIX 5.0 also includes a number of new features that are designed to support the use of FIX outside of Equities, including tighter integration with the Financial products Mark-up Language (FpML) which is an XML messaging standard for the OTC Derivatives industry. In this manner, FIX and associated standards are penetrating more deeply into complex instruments and their OTC trading models.

Growing Popularity of Algorithmic Trading

Algorithmic trading is rapidly becoming main stream. This phenomenon began in the 1990's in response to two major market shifts, the SEC's "Reg ATS" in 1996, which created electronic crossing networks and generated greater fragmentation of liquidity, and the decimalization rules of 2001. These rules aimed to promote price competition in smaller increments and reduced bid-ask spreads. These factors led to a need to trade in smaller amounts so as to minimize market impact, and in turn, created the need for an effective trading approach to meet these goals. Having started in the US, algorithmic trading is now a global phenomenon, and it appears that as the market continues to evolve, a greater number of factors are influencing its adoption within the buy-side, sell side and exchange community.

Algorithmic trading strategies have emerged in many formats. Some aim to exploit trends in price movement to generate profit, where others focus more strongly on execution and cost. The manner in which the industry is using algorithms is also changing, and the buy-side is stepping up their use of algorithmic trading. Buy-side firms are increasingly leveraging the use of algorithmic trading strategies to decrease transaction costs and increase investment return. They are moving from basic algorithms and are keen to explore more advanced offerings and take greater control, expressing a stronger desire to monitor and manage the algorithms themselves. This is yet another factor that, at least in certain parts of the world, has been fueled by regulatory initiatives. In the UK, the FSA (Financial Services Authority) is paying increased attention to the unbundling of commissions, requiring fund managers to provide greater transparency to clients with regards to spending on trading and research. This has encouraged the buy-side to take a closer look at algorithmic trading, reinforcing their desire to take greater control. Sell-side firms are now competing for clients based on the performance of their algorithmic trading strategies.

Within FPL, an Algorithmic Trading Working Group has been formed, comprised of sell-side, buy-side and financial technology providers, to address algorithmic trading integration issues.

The current areas of focus are:

- Proposing algorithmic trading extensions to FIX messages to support unlimited algorithmic parameters in a standardized manner
- Addressing vendors' and clients' needs to represent new features on their front ends

The FIX Protocol has provided support for algorithmic trading since version 4.4 through a combination of three strategies related tags: TargetsStrategy (tag 847), TargetStrategyParamters (tag 848) and ParticipationRate (tag 849). Support was then enhanced through the recent release of FIX version 5.0 which significantly improved messaging functionality in this space.

These efforts will offer significant benefit to the community of algorithmic trading providers and users in the following ways:

- Allowing for more customization of broker algorithms
- Shortening the time-to-market by reducing integration development work required by the OMS vendor or client
- Making real-time 'on the fly' integration of new/modified algorithms possible in any OMS
- Permitting web-based deployment of new algorithms directly from brokers to their clients

With so much activity within this space over recent years, algorithmic trading has become an integral part of the industry's structure and it is a trend likely to grow and evolve. Innovative market players are using algorithms in asset classes not previously exposed to such trading strategies such as Derivatives, Foreign Exchange and Fixed Income. With the ongoing search for more ingenious methods of achieving alpha, algorithmic trading is likely to continue growing in popularity.

The FIX Protocol Today

As mentioned previously, since its inception the FIX Protocol has been continuously updated and improved, and with FIX 5.0, takes a massive step forward from previous iterations. FIX 5.0 includes 24 separate extension packs which together significantly enhance messaging capabilities across the board.

To help support the trend of applying electronic trading practices laterally across asset classes and vertically throughout the trade life cycle, FIX 5.0 provides significantly improved functionality for post-trade processing in the listed derivatives space. It also provides extensive enhancements to support foreign exchange trading in relation to requests for quotes, streaming executable prices, swaps, spots, forwards and vanilla foreign exchange spot options.

Other enhancements within FIX 5.0 include:

- Enriched support for order routing, trade capture, and external routing in an exchange environment

- A new Execution Acknowledgement message that allows the order initiating firm to explicitly acknowledge the receipt of an execution report
- Chinese STEP 1.0 support required by the Chinese exchange markets to aid FIX adoption in the region

Additionally, FIX 5.0 includes a Transport Independence framework which separates the FIX session layer from the application layer, enabling different message versions to be used within the same FIX session. For example, if a firm is happy with their FIX 4.2 order management and execution process but wants to be able to use the 4.4 allocation process without throwing away their 4.2 investment, transport independence will allow them to achieve this. From a business perspective, this significantly reduces the financial investment required to support new releases whilst allowing FIX to be used with a wider audience of participants from the most demanding low latency users to those requiring massive scalability.

The FIX Protocol and the support it provides for the industry has had an enormous impact on the financial services market. The launch of FIX 5.0 is just the latest in a series of initiatives delivered by FPL, encouraging great efficiency, increased transparency and cost reductions. The organization is constantly exploring further ways in which it can help move the industry forward and many projects are underway. To find out more about the FPL organization and the ways in which it is helping the industry move forward, please visit www.fixprotocol.org.

Complex Event Processing:
Essential Technology for Staying Ahead As the Pace of Trading Accelerates

By Don DeLoach, CEO, Aleri Inc.
Jeff Wootton, Vice President, Product Strategy, Aleri Inc.

Complex Event Processing is a new class of technology that addresses the need to analyze streaming data in real-time to provide insight and enable instantaneous response. The emergence of this technology has been driven by increasing data volumes, increasing message rates, and a competitive environment that measures an "immediate" response in milliseconds. Examples where this is being used in trading applications includes:

- Pricing engines
- Market liquidity aggregation and analysis
- Identifying trading opportunities
- Routing orders
- Monitoring orders/trades

Traditional tools for data manipulation and analysis cannot deliver immediate results across data sets that are constantly changing. While the capital markets have been doing "event processing" for years, just without calling it that, it's been done via hard-coded applications that perform a specific task. Today's markets demand more agility than hard-wired applications can provide.

In this chapter we will explore the concepts behind complex event processing and how it can be deployed in the trading environment to address the needs to automate, add intelligence, and at the same time improve speed and agility. We will go on to explore some specific examples of ways that event processing is being deployed today. Finally, we will touch on some ideas for the practical implementation of event processing technology within the financial enterprise.

The Accelerated Pace of Trading

There are a few unmistakable trends in the capital markets over the past few years. One of the most striking is the transition to electronic markets. A casual walk through the pits at the Chicago Board of Trade will testify to this. The "wild west" days of market action driven by open outcry have given way to what some of the seasoned pit traders affectionately refer to as the "iPod kids", who spend their days staring at a computer screen as if it were a video game. Off the exchanges, trading floors have gotten smaller as more low-value trades are automated using algorithms and human traders are reserved for high value trades.

The impact of this shift to electronic trading is far reaching. One major impact is that it has resulted in the acceleration of the markets. With manual trading, the speed of execution is limited by human processing power: market data feeds eyeballs and the incoming data is processed by the trader's brain to make a trading decision. Trades made over the phone add even more communication time. With electronic trading, the middle "man" is eliminated and the trade is communicated at near the speed of light, and where the decision to trade is automated it can be made in milliseconds. The average human response time is on the order of 250 milliseconds. Thus, when trading was done by humans, no one worried about latency down in the sub-500 millisecond range. Now every millisecond counts. Opportunities appear and disappear in milliseconds. Some traders are in and out of a position in less than half a second.

Another aspect to acceleration is the amount of data and the rate at which it arrives. Algorithmic trading (combined with penny pricing) has resulted in the average trade size dropping dramatically and the number of trades increasing. Market fragmentation has resulted in market data from more sources, and auto-quoting has caused an absolute explosion in the ratio of quotes to trades. The net effect is that traders are drowning in market data at the same time that they have to reduce latency to stay competitive.

Market Complexity

In parallel with the accelerating pace we have seen an increase in market complexity. Changes in market regulations have opened the door to increased competition among exchanges and alternative trading venues. Now there are multiple venues for many instruments, so the underlying trading systems have the need to simultaneously understand the status of multiple venues at any given point in time in order to ensure the maximum effectiveness of their trades. Then there is the mingling of asset classes, where trading and trade strategies are no longer confined to a single asset class. Not only are traders executing strategies across multiple asset classes, but the venues themselves are expanding their offerings across asset classes.

Recently, additional regulations have added complexity in the form of RegNMS in the US and MiFID in the EU. Both affect the rules on order routing among different execution venues; i.e. in the US with the order protection rule and in the EU with "best execution" policies. Not only do these add complexity to the order routing process, but they add the need to collect data to monitor and demonstrate compliance, and they are examples of a constantly changing market landscape that require agility and flexibility in the underlying trading systems.

Managing Risk

As markets have become increasingly interconnected, risk has increased. At the same time, the accelerating pace of the markets makes it more challenging to manage risk, increasing exposure both within firms as well as systemic exposure across the market. There are just many more positions to track with many more interrelationships between the positions. With the high profile collapse of certain hedge funds and increased bank exposure, there is a growing demand to better manage risk, requiring additional infrastructure to first determine the positions and relationships and then analyze those positions to determine the resulting exposure of the firm.

Stressing Existing Tools and Infrastructure

All of this has led to a significant increase in the demands placed on the technology infrastructure and the tools used to build applications. The trends are unmistakable and show no sign of slowing.

The relational database technology and transaction processing systems which worked well in a pre-electronic trading world are collapsing under the weight of this increased demand. In a sense, it would be like taking the population of Tokyo and dropping it into Chicago, expecting the infrastructure to work. The roads would come to a standstill, the trains and busses would be inadequate, the water, electricity, housing stock, and all related infrastructure would simply not support the load. That's the dilemma that is driving the demand for complex event processing technology. Simply put, it's an issue of scale and efficiency: the ability to process huge volumes of information moving at high rates with minimal latency.

This dilemma was first observed in 1998 in the context of the Sunrise project at Bell Labs, the first commercial implementation of an event processing platform. They observed that:

> *"For the most part, the performance needs of real-time applications are met by custom-designed information systems. Such custom solutions work well, but they make it impossible to amortize the cost of a system over a large number of applications. As the number of applications has grown, the custom-solution approach has become economically untenable." [Baulier]*

Just as the Bell Labs team observed in the context of telecommunications, when it comes to processing real-time data streams, the capital markets have been doing event processing for years – they just haven't had a name for it. The difference is that they also didn't have tools for it, so the event processing was always hard-coded within an application designed to carry out a specific task. When data rates were at a more manageable level, latency of a half a second was acceptable in slower moving markets, and change occurred at a stately pace, this was an acceptable approach. But now put everything on fast forward and custom applications built from scratch become an operational and competitive drag. Consider that:

- Custom applications built from scratch are expensive and time consuming to build and deploy; the cost of development must be absorbed by a single application

- The processing logic is typically "hard coded" and intrinsically linked to the data structures, making it difficult to adapt the processing rules to changing requirements

- Typical programmers don't have the training or experience to implement highly efficient code designed for high speed performance under heavy loads

This has led to the desire for new tools. Tools that can provide:

- Scalable capacity to keep up with growing data volumes and increasing message rates

- High-level authoring that allow for rapid implementation and deployment of business rules and provide flexibility to quickly alter the rules to improve competitiveness and respond to changes in the market

- A means of addressing complexity without sacrificing performance, applying complex logic in real-time, combining data from different sources, mixing asset classes and automating the response

The Emergence of Complex Event Processing Technology

Event Processing initially emerged as a body of research in the mid-1990's, with projects undertaken in parallel at a number of universities in the US and the UK and at Bell Labs (the Sunrise project mentioned in the previous section). While different projects focused on achieving different goals - some focused on detecting complex patterns of events [Luckam], while others focused more on high speed aggregation and continuous computation - the common thread was to provide high level "authoring" tools in the form of an event processing language or interactive environment that would allow a user to specify a set of business logic or "rules" to be applied to incoming data that carried information about events, along with an underlying processing engine that could apply the logic to the data as it arrived, producing results in real-time – in some cases at very high rates and with minimal latency. It was not until 2005, however, that general-purpose commercial complex event processing technology became available in the market and, not surprisingly, the capital markets participants have been some of the early adopters of this new technology. In 2007 we are now seeing widespread interest in this technology from the capital markets and increasing recognition of the benefits it can deliver.

What is an Event?

Quite simply, an event is something that happens. It could be a financial transaction, an airplane landing, an earthquake or a phone call. Major or minor, if it happens, it's an event. Some events have significance, and most events that have significance either produce data or cause data to be produced on their behalf. This data that contains information about an event, when transmitted in a computer network, could be considered an "event message" or "event object" or something similar. Typically, however, this simply is referred to as an "event" even though it is not the event itself but is a packet of data containing information about an event.

In an event-driven system or Event Driven Architecture (EDA), data about the event is transmitted or becomes available as soon as the event happens (or as soon as the event is detected in some cases). Other systems or applications wait for events (event messages) to arrive, and act on them when they do. Complex Event Processing is a technology that can be used within an event driven architecture to apply a set of logic or rules to incoming events to perform an operation.

Complex Event Processing:
Analyze and Act on Fast Moving Data

The purpose of complex event processing is to analyze events as they occur, in the context of other events, in order to determine and initiate an appropriate response and/or to provide insight that enables an appropriate response to be taken. In other words, to analyze data as it arrives, continuously updating the analysis as new data arrives, and responding (or enabling a response) based on the conclusions drawn from the data.

Complex event processing (CEP) operates on groups of events, creating high level "virtual" events from underlying patterns or aggregations of low-level events. Commercial complex event processing technology provides the means of easily defining the logic to be applied across sets of event data to produce useful information in the form of high level "abstract' events or summary information.

The relational database has been the traditional tool for data analysis for many years. CEP provides similar data analysis tools – correlation, aggregation, filtering – but in an event driven architecture. While a traditional database query is applied to a static set of data to select records matching a criteria, join them to other related records, and then group related records to compute statistics for the group, a CEP engine applies this logic to data sets that are constantly changing as new events arrive, updating the results in real-time with minimal latency. The Sunrise team at Bell Labs observed the limitations of traditional database technology for performing event-driven data analysis:

> *"To meet the real-time requirements of [the application], the service time [...] must not exceed a few milliseconds. In conventional database technology, however, the costs of invoking a structured query language (SQL) operation over a client-server interface, or the costs of a single access to secondary storage, can already account for hundreds of milliseconds. As a consequence, performance goals on the order of a few milliseconds may be unattainable even before the costs of the transaction's logic are taken into account"* [Baulier]

To meet the needs of demanding environments such as a trading application, high performance event processors are designed to do this at very high data rates and to produce results with minimal latency – where latency is the time lag from the arrival of the event to the response to the event.

Another term that is often used in describing a type of event processing is Event Stream Processing (ESP). Event stream processing is a form of Complex Event Processing that is specifically designed to operate very efficiently on continuous streams of event data rather than just isolated events. Event stream processing and complex event processing are not mutually exclusive: most commercial event stream processing technologies do complex event processing. Event stream processing can therefore be thought of as complex event processing that has been optimized for efficient handling of event streams.

What does it mean to Analyze and Act?

Moving beyond definitions, just what is meant by "analyze and act"? Posing the question "what is meant by acting on information" is fairly self evident. But "analyze" is a vague word so let's get specific. Event processing technology is designed to:

- Combine data from multiple sources to produce one or more data streams that are "derived" from the inputs

- Compute new values from combinations of the input data. This can range from computations on individual events to computations across groups of events to produce statistics such as moving averages

- Watch for specific conditions or patterns that represent a problem or an opportunity and trigger an instantaneous response (or deliver the information to enable a response)

Consider the following situations...

- An automated trading application that scans massive amounts of incoming market data to spot trading opportunities, where reaction has to be instantaneous or the opportunity is missed.

- A market making application that has to adjust internal or published rates in response to market movements – where delays either mean lost business or lost profit.

- A risk management application that continuously updates aggregate position and risk information, combining data from multiple systems to provide a single consolidated view that is always current.

These are just a few examples of the types of applications that can benefit from event processing technology. The common feature among these applications is that they share the need to continuously collect, process, and analyze data in *real-time*, producing results *instantly*, even when the data arrives at very high rates. The next section will take a closer look at some specific examples where event processing is being used today to facilitate electronic trading.

Applying Event Processing to Electronic Trading

Electronic trading involves many different applications that are linked to form the end-to-end process. While each of these applications perform a specific task, one thing they all have in common is the need to process incoming data in real-time, and perform their task with minimal latency. They also tend to operate on common data elements such as market quotes and price data, orders, order books and trades.

In the past, each of these applications would be built from scratch, designed to receive data and operate on the data to carry out their particular function. While relational databases could be used for some data management tasks that weren't latency-sensitive, most of the data handling was hard coded.

Event processing technology provides an alternative approach, with a reusable platform that implements all of the underlying data handling, in a high-performance real-time architecture. The business logic that implements the specific trading task can be quickly implemented using high level languages or authoring tools.

The benefits of this approach are:

- Rapid implementation and deployment: much faster than building an application from scratch, even when implementing complex logic and rules
- Performance and scalability: high-performance EP technology is designed to deliver low latency results under heavy loads. The application developer can focus on the logic rather than how to achieve performance and scalability.
- Flexibility: since the processing rules are written in a high-level event processing language, the logic can be changed easily and quickly in response to changes in the market or to implement improved algorithms

So, let's take a look at some of the applications that are being implemented using complex event processing technology:

Liquidity Aggregation: Consolidate and Analyze Market Depth

Changes in market regulations, starting with the creation of ECNs in the US in the 1990s and continuing with RegNMS in the US and MiFID in the EU, have paved the way for fragmented liquidity pools by opening up national exchanges to competition from other exchanges, alternative trading systems, and firms that do their own off-exchange matching. This can make trading more of a challenge since the liquidity in a given security is spread across multiple market centers; assessing the order book in a single center does not provide a complete view of the market. Traders need to re-assemble the market to see it as a whole, making trading decisions based on an understanding of the full depth of the market. Automated trading and order routing applications need to be able to act on the basis of liquidity in the market and determine where liquidity exists within desired price bands.

Using a programmable event processor, the logic to normalize, consolidate, and aggregate multiple pools of liquidity is very simple – particularly if the technology supports updates and deletes (which not all event processors support). Rules can control how the data is consolidated, perform any "de-duplication", and can dynamically control which centers contribute to the consolidated market. From there, the most powerful benefit comes from the ability to process an order in the context of the consolidated order book. So rather than simply displaying a consolidated order book to inform a human trader, the event processor can process an order, according to a set of rules that are applied to the full depth of the market.

Market Data Enrichment

As firms seek to reduce latency in their market data they are moving increasingly to direct feeds that take data direct from the source rather than through a consolidator. One of the by-products of this is data that is confined to basic trade and quote data without many of the value-added fields that traders and trading applications rely on. An event processor can be used to normalize/transform market data and compute value-added fields, whether they are commonly calculated fields or proprietary formulas to produce custom measures. Value-added fields can be computed on individual records, across groups of records for the same instrument, or across groups of records that span multiple instruments or entire markets.

In addition to computing and adding value-added fields to market data records, an event processor can be used to combine data from multiple sources. It can even be set up to combine data from multiple sources according to dynamic rules such that the input source may vary according to time of day, current data quality measures, or other computed indicators.

Market Making (Auto Quoting)

Trading Desk heads are being challenged, as the markets become increasingly electronic, to react fast enough to get the orders and maintain margins. This requires low-latency auto-quoting that can continuously adjust rates based on movements in the market combined with input from traders. Off-the-shelf auto-quoting applications exist but typically as part of a larger trading system that requires a much bigger commitment to implement and typically limits the amount of flexibility and control the user has over the pricing algorithms. This has forced firms to build their own auto-quoting applications from scratch. While this approach may work in the beginning, down the road they usually find that the custom-built quoting application lacks the ability to scale and/or the pricing algorithms are 'hard wired'.

Implementing pricing algorithms on an event processing platform is the natural evolution of these applications. The platform provides scalability and performance (minimizing latency between market movements and updates to the firm's quote) and high level tools for easily implementing the firm's proprietary pricing algorithms. An auto-quoting application built on an event processing platform can be implemented and deployed in a matter of weeks, and the pricing algorithms can easily be adjusted or replaced over time as improved algorithms are developed. The algorithms can include cleansing and validation rules to prevent any erroneous or suspicious market rates from being factored into the price. Traders can control parameters that feed into the pricing algorithms, controlling things like size of spread and skew to reflect anticipated market direction.

Order Validation

While validating an incoming order tends to be a fairly simple task, there are two important elements: the validation rules must be flexible and easily changed, and the checking must happen quickly so as to not slow the order down. An event processor can be used to apply any number of validation rules to incoming orders to check for errors before the order is processed, including checks against live market data, checks against margin and position limits, and checks against pre-set or dynamic thresholds.

Algorithmic Trading: Strategy Trading

Watching the market for pricing movements that represent opportunities requires a system that can process all the incoming market data, spot the opportunities, and react to the opportunities with minimal latency. Latency is absolutely critical since many of these opportunities are extremely short lived – a delay of 100 milliseconds or more and the opportunity may have disappeared. It also requires a system that can be easily adapted to apply new rules, since the efficiency of the markets is such that a particular strategy will have a finite lifespan. As traders seek out new ways of identifying market opportunities, they are also crossing the traditional boundaries of asset classes and geography.

As traders run up against the limits of existing applications and tools, whether those limits are performance limits, flexibility constraints, or the time required to implement and deploy, they are turning to event processing technology as a foundation on which to implement new strategies. Market data – either direct from source or via an in-house market data environment – can be fed into the event processor. Each incoming price tick can be fed through the range of strategies that are running. When the criteria for a particular strategy are met, a trading signal or an order is generated as the output from the event processing. The power of the event processor comes from allowing the user to define the rules underlying each strategy using high level authoring tools, and then to execute those rules on a platform designed for high throughput with minimal latency. As the strategies change, the data models that implement the rules can be changed, adding new rules, deleting or suspending others, or changing the mathematical formulas being used. The ability of an event processor to combine data from different sources enables strategies that cross markets, asset classes and currencies.

Algorithmic Trading: Order Execution

Execution algorithms – automating the process of breaking a large order into multiple trades to optimize yield – have been receiving a great deal of attention in the past two years. When it comes to large sell-side institutions implementing an algorithm for use by all of their clients, the cost of hard-coding an algorithm from scratch can be justified. As smaller institutions and buy-side firms seek to take more control and implement their own execution algorithms, tools that reduce the time and cost to implement and deploy an algorithm become more important. Many firms have been using event processors to collect the historic tick data needed to develop and power execution algorithms, and increasingly firms are beginning to implement new algorithms on top of event processing platforms.

Smart Order Routing

Several recent trends have increased the level of interest in so called "smart order routing" – i.e. automatically routing an order based on complex rules applied to the current state of the market. Among them are the increasing fragmentation of the markets into multiple pools of liquidity, Reg NMS in the US with its Order Protection Rule, and the MiFID directive in the EU that puts forth requirements for Best Execution. These new regulations change the "rules" that need to be applied when handling orders, determining where and how to trade. Existing order routing systems will need to be updated or replaced. All sell-side firms and execution venues will need to be able to demonstrate compliance, including the collection of data for reporting purposes. In the US, while a firm can look to the exchange to ensure compliance, firms are seeing that there is an opportunity in routing direct to the exchange of choice, but this requires that compliant routing mechanisms are in place.

Event Processing can be used as the basis of quickly implementing a smart order routing application that takes in market data from all execution venues, accesses customer data and reference data as necessary, and then processes each order according to the rules that have been defined to determine how to route the order. In the process, the inputs to and results of the routing algorithm can be captured and saved to a historical database to provide for compliance monitoring and reporting. Since the event processor is programmable, the order routing algorithms can be changed as the markets and regulations evolve, without the need to replace any of the underlying components.

Managing Positions, Real-time Risk, Real-time P&L

This application of event processing takes a somewhat different form that the ones described above. It is less latency sensitive but draws on the ability of an event processor to collect, normalize, combine, and aggregate large amounts of data in real-time.

Risk Officers, Fund Managers, and Trading Heads are all concerned about managing risk at the highest possible level. One of the main challenges they face is that data on positions and exposures is typically contained within many different operational "silos" where it is not shared across the systems and is not available in a common form. Traditional data warehouse and ETL tools are often used to consolidate data on a nightly basis, but waiting until the next day for the information is increasingly "just not good enough".

Event Processing can be used to consolidate data across these different systems in real-time, as well as to compute aggregate values across the consolidated data. Transaction streams can be fed into the event processor from any number of different systems. These streams don't need to share a common message structure or even conform to a common data model. The data model running on the event processor can normalize the data into a common format, consolidate the data across sources, and aggregate then compute aggregate values across different dimensions such as asset class, currency, customer, counter party or account. It can even apply a stream of market prices to continuously mark-to-market, re-computing limits, exposures, portfolio values, as well as gains and losses. Because the data normalization is done by the event processor, individual trading systems, risk management systems and position keeping systems don't need to be replaced. The event processor can be deployed as an overlay, as long as there is a way to access the data contained in those individual systems.

The Anatomy of an Event Processor

While event processors vary from product to product, they all generally consist of the following four components or attributes:

1. An authoring language or other tool(s) for defining the event processing logic to be applied
2. The event processing "engine" itself that will receive the incoming events, process them according the logic that has been defined, and produce the results
3. An interface for getting event data into the event processor
4. An interface for receiving results from the event processor

Beyond those four aspects that are present in all event processors, there may be other capabilities such as:

- a "command and control" interface for managing the event processor
- a monitoring interface to monitor the status of the event processor
- security components for authentication, access control and encryption
- adapters for integrating the event processor with common producers and consumers of event data as well as common messaging environments for delivering event data

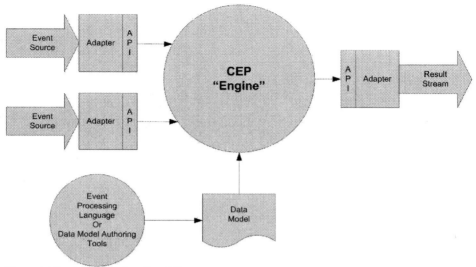

Figure 1. The Anatomy of an Event Processor

Authoring: Event Processing Languages

The value of an event processor is the ability to easily define complex processing logic using high level tools. These tools let the application developer focus on the business logic to be applied, rather than dealing with the underlying data handling. It also relieves the application developer of the need to worry about how to achieve scalability and high performance.

Commercial event processors may offer a language and/or an interactive development environment (IDE). The IDE may include tools for visualizing the data flow and for defining the processing logic by creating objects, connecting them to direct data flow, and defining their properties.

When it comes to languages, there are two general approaches being taken in the current generation of event processors: those that implement a proprietary "rule oriented" language and those that support a variant of SQL. The rules-oriented languages allow the programmer to define individual discrete rules that each take the general form of: "when this set of conditions is true, do this". Event processors that support an SQL-based event processing language use the concept of a "continuous query". This is looks like a traditional SQL query, but rather than being applied to a set of static data, the query is defined in advance and the result set is continually updated as the input data changes.

To use SQL with streaming event data, extensions must be added to define event windows. Thus an event stream can be thought of as a table, where incoming events either add rows to a table or update rows in a table. Since the table is changing over time as new events arrive, mechanisms to define "windows" are typically defined as proprietary extensions to standard SQL. The size of the window can typically be defined as a specific time period or a specific number of rows.

This "relational" approach to event processing therefore takes the form of one or more input streams that pass through a set of continuous queries to product one or more derived streams as shown in figure 2 on the next page.

Figure 2. Example of data flow in a CEP data model

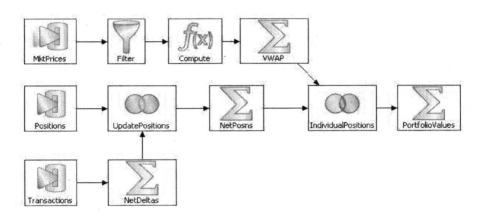

The Steps to Deploying Complex Event Processing in the Trading Environment

Complex Event Processing technology provides a platform for rapid implementation of applications that need to process and respond to streaming event data. As a platform for application development, deployment of a complete application involves a number of steps. This section describes the typical process of implementing and deploying a complete application based on event processing technology.

1. Have a Plan

First, make sure that the function of the application to be implemented is well understood. What is the objective? The desired outcome? Then:

- Define the data inputs. What event data will be processed? What other data will be required in the processing? What are the sources for the data? What are the needed results? How will the results be used? Where will they be sent?

- Once the sources of input data are identified, gather information on how the data will be accessed and the format of the data
- Define the business logic that will be applied, in terms of the high level data flow – this will serve as the "blueprint" when you begin authoring the data model
- Define the data outputs. How and where will the results be used? What form do they need to be in? What data fields do they need to contain?

2. Create the data model - Authoring

Use the authoring language or tools provided with the event processing technology you are using to define the data model. The data model will consist of two things: (1) the definitions of the fields and data types in incoming events (i.e the data schema) and any other external data that will be used, and (2) the operators and rules to be applied to the data to produce the desired results. The results will typically be streamed out, in the form of one or more streams of complex events – i.e. events that are produced as a result of processing the input events. These results can be used to trigger a response, alert someone to the need for a response, or to update an external data set. If your event processing technology allows retained data to be queried, the results may be held within the event processor for access by applications when needed.

All commercial event processors support a range of data types, a set of standard math operators, and a built-in function library of common functions. Some products also support user defined functions with an interface that allows functions in external libraries to be invoked during the event processing. Consider whether the available functions and operators will be sufficient or if they will have to be supplemented.

3. System Integration: getting the data in and out

Deployments will typically use adapters to stream data into and out of the event processor. Input adapters will be able to connect to the source of the data to receive or retrieve the data to be loaded or streamed into the event processor. The input adapter will then pass the information to the event processor, typically using an API. Thus the adapter is simply the "glue" that bridges the interface of the data source to the API of the event processor.

The output adapter does the same thing but in reverse: it will receive data from the event processor via the event processor's API and will then format the data as necessary and pass the data to the desired destination.

Most suppliers of commercial event processing technology also provide adapters for common messaging environments, databases, Microsoft Excel® and in some cases even market data sources. Additional adapters can be built by the user or commissioned from the vendor or from a third party.

Another consideration for getting data out of the event processor is by using an on-demand query capability. The ability to process on-demand queries against event data exists in some of the products available today. The idea is that users can query collected event data by sending SQL queries to the event processor through an ODBC or JDBC interface. This capability is useful in applications where a user wants to have immediate access to data sets that are always current, but does not want to have to continually monitor the changing data. Without an on-demand query interface, an external application will have to receive the streaming results from the event processor and maintain a current view of the data for access by users when needed.

4. User Interfaces

Depending on the application, user interfaces may be needed to allow users to input data and/or to allow users to view results.

User inputs may come within existing applications, in which case the approach is to integrate the application with the event processor using an adapter. There may be a need for a stand-alone tool for sending data into the event processor. Simple ways of doing this could use Microsoft Excel® or by building a simple Java or VB app that gives the user the needed input fields and/or controls.

There are a number of ways of displaying results for end users. These could range from a sophisticated real-time "dashboard" displaying current values, to displaying streaming data in Microsoft Excel®, or streaming data to a browser. Some vendors of event processing technology provide dashboard capabilities and there are also dashboard tools available from third parties.

5. Security

Needless to say given the nature of the many of the uses of event processing, security is often a critical consideration in the deployment of this technology. Security options will typically include things like authentication, access control and the option of encrypting input and/or output streams. You will need to define what the security aspects of the deployment will be.

The Keys to Successful Deployment of Event Processing Technology

Pick a Suitable Target as a Starting Point

If your organization has no experience with event processing, you should start out with a basic application which can be quickly and easily implemented. This is not to say that the long term vision of the specific application is limited, but rather that it can be limited in terns of the initial scope. For instance, you may want to implement real-time position management. While the long term goal might be aggregation of positions and transactions across many systems and asset classes, different currencies, and incorporation of market data for real-time profit/loss computation, it would be better to start small by defining three constituent systems where you are absorbing a transaction stream from each system in order to maintain a single consolidated view of net positions. Then, over time, you could add in other inputs and expand on the range of computations and analysis being performed. The idea is to begin with a small win, and further develop that application, or other applications based on incremental success and experience. Most EP technology is well suited for such an approach. They can be deployed as an overlay to existing systems, integrated non-intrusively, or the functionality can be rolled out incrementally. Bottom line: avoid big bang deployments that involve massive re-tooling.

Select the Technology

Take a close look at the technology options being considered. How similar or different are the products under consideration? Is each product equally well suited for the task at hand and for future applications that you are likely to undertake? See the final section in this chapter ("What to look for...") for a product selection checklist.

Extend the Benefits of a Service Oriented Architecture

Service oriented architectures (SOA) have been widely embraced because they allow firms to respond more quickly and efficiently to the changing needs of the business. Adding event processing can take SOA to the next level by moving from loosely coupled services to decoupled services that generate and respond to events. As long as services within the architecture are capable of producing event data, then event processing can be deployed as an overlay to process and respond to that event data as it is received. This can streamline deployment of new applications even beyond conventional SOA implementations since existing services don't even have to be aware of the event-driven services that respond to the events that they produce.

Leverage the Expertise of your Vendor

Make sure that your suppliers understand how your organization operates, both formally and culturally. Involve them to get the full benefit of their experience and expertise. Take advantage of any training that is available, ensuring that all staff involved in the project understand how to efficiently select and use the best tools for the job. Finally, maintain open lines of communication. Make sure your suppliers understand what you expect from them and what your dependencies are; let them know when you are having problems – they may be in a better position to solve them or offer advice, having seen similar situations in the past.

Assemble and Train the Project Team

Identify all the groups that will be affected and need to be involved; identify the skills sets needed to implement the full project. These may include:

- end users or representatives of the business function that will use or benefit from the application
- development staff that will be responsible for implementing the application
- system integration staff that will be responsible for integration with existing systems, applications, and components
- operations staff that will be responsible for the ongoing operation, management, and monitoring of the application once it is deployed
- support staff who will be responsible for supporting the application

Once the team is assembled, identify the training needs of the team. Ensure that each team member is trained on the tools that they will need to use.

Project approach and management

Create a project plan. This may seem obvious, but even small projects have dependencies and many moving parts. All too often a project fails or ends up seriously behind schedule because a dependency is overlooked or falls behind and no one notices.

What to Look for when Selecting Complex Event Processing Technology

The term "event processing" is actually very broad, simply meaning to process events [in real-time]. "Real-time" is in brackets because while not precisely a requirement, it's generally accepted that when people talk about event processing they are referring to real-time event processing.

With that said, event processors take a variety of forms and target many different aspects of event processing. Two different products that both do event processing may be designed for entirely different purposes and have completely different feature sets and characteristics. Therefore, when selecting the best event processing technology to deploy, here are some things to consider:

1. Performance: Throughput and Latency
    Does the technology provide the throughput (messages per second) and latency (time lag from inputs to outputs) characteristics you require? Can it scale or does it provide sufficient "headroom" or is there a concern that while performance may be adequate today it might not be down the road?

2. Scalability
    How large do you expect your data model and data sets to grow? What data volumes and message rates need to be supported? Can the technology scale with the hardware? Is it 64 bit? Is it multi-threaded to take advantage of parallel processing on multiple cores and multiple CPUs? Can it be deployed across clusters of machines?

3. Versatility
    Are you only looking for technology that can support a single application, or do you want to select a technology that can be used as a platform for a number of different applications? Does the technology being considered have the breadth of functionality to allow it to be applied to a variety of different application needs?

4. Ease of Use: Authoring
    What authoring tools or languages are supported? How steep is the learning curve? Once past the learning curve, how efficiently can you implement new data models and change existing models? Are there choices in the language or tools to be used? Is it possible to build "wizard" type tools that allow a user to control the data model?

5. Ease of Use: Integration
    What application programming interfaces (APIs) are available? What languages are supported? Do the APIs provide sufficient functionality while remaining easy to use? What adapters are available?

6. Reliability
    If this will be deployed in mission-critical applications, what features are required for high availability and/or data security? Can the product be deployed in high-availability configurations using primary/secondary pairs? Can disk-based data persistence be used to ensure full state recovery after a failure? Do the interfaces support

transaction acknowledgements or is data only handled on a "best efforts" basis?

7. Security

   Are the security features adequate, allowing the system to do authentication, access control and encryption? Will the security features integrate with your overall security framework?

8. Support

   What support does the vendor provide? What are the hours of coverage? What is the experience level of the vendor's support staff? Is on-site support available?

9. Price

   This goes beyond simply a matter of how expensive/inexpensive, but includes aspects of how the pricing is structured. Is the product licensed for a one time license fee or only available through subscription? Is pricing per CPU, per user, other? What does the base price include? What are optional extras?

10. Features

    There are a range of features that may be important depending on the applications you plan to use the technology for. Just a few to consider include:

    a. Support for Updates and Deletes – *some event processors treat incoming messages as being independent of all previous messages. If they use data windows, the new message is always appended to the end of the window (or inserted if it's a sorted window). Some applications, however, may need the ability to treat incoming events as an update to an existing data element or as a signal to delete a data element. Examples of the types of applications that require this include: order book feeds or trade feeds that have cancellations and corrections.*

    b. Range of Built-in Operators, Data Types and Functions – *are they sufficient? extensible? Is there an interface for external or user-defined functions? Is there a way to go beyond standard operators for more complex logic?*

c.   Data analysis interfaces and tools – *what tools and interfaces are available for viewing and analyzing collected event data? Does the vendor provide tools? Can off-the-shelf tools be used?*

d.   Data Windows or Similar Temporal Operators - *does the technology allow you to specify time intervals over which operations will run? Can the time intervals be sufficiently long or short to meet your needs?*

Conclusion

Complex Event Processing is an invaluable new tool that can be applied to a range of applications across the trade lifecycle. Wherever there is a need to process, aggregate, analyze and respond to streaming event data in real-time, CEP should be considered. It provides for rapid implementation and deployment of new applications, the flexibility to quickly and easily adapt business logic to changing conditions, and the ability to deliver low latency results, even in the face of overwhelming data volumes and message rates. In short, we believe this new technology will soon be considered an "essential' platform for modern trading and trade processing applications.

References

[Baulier]   Gerald D. Baulier, Stephen M. Blott, Henry F. Korth, and Avi Silberschatz. *Sunrise: A Real-Time Event-Processing System*, Bell Labs Technical Journal, January-March 1998

[Luckham]   David C. Luckham and Brian Frasca, *Complex Event Processing Distributed Systems*, Stanford University Technical Report, March, 1998

Achieving Economies of Scale:
Building & Deploying Applications that are Reliable, Robust and Scaleable

By Philip Beevers, Technology Architect, Fidessa

Trading systems must be *reliable* (they must work in a repeatable manner), *robust* (they must be resilient to certain classes of failure) and *scalable* (their capacity must be able to grow significantly beyond current business levels). Building such systems can lead to cost and complexity, so how should these requirements best be achieved?

Reliability

The software industry is plagued by a reputation of unreliability, much of which is rightfully deserved. To produce reliable systems, we must understand why that is the case.

Computer systems are complicated. They require components, with multi-faceted interfaces, from different vendors, to interact coherently and predictably. Concurrency introduces further complexity, as well as non-deterministic behaviour which are difficult to test. Furthermore, formally proving correctness is not possible for anything other than the most trivial systems. In summary, building systems is difficult; testing them to an acceptable level is equally tough.

To produce reliable trading systems we must make them as simple as possible to build, and test them as thoroughly as we can. In this chapter we suggest techniques to turn this into reality.

Simplicity

The easiest way to build a reliable system is to build a simple system. Requirements which are simple to state are less likely to be misinterpreted; a simple design is easier to code; simple code is easier to test.

Simplicity starts with simple requirements. Requirements which are difficult to describe, or are ambiguous, rarely result in reliable software. Furthermore, although it goes against conventional wisdom, requirements need to be stated with simplicity of implementation in mind. A key part of the developer's role in interpreting requirements must be to challenge those which encourage or imply complexity. For example, users of trading systems are unlikely to enjoy using dialogs which are built from large numbers of controls.

In common with simple requirements, simple designs can usually be described easily. Documentation of simple designs should contain plenty of diagrams to clarify high-level concepts. Design patterns can help, as they form a common vocabulary for expressing ideas, but should not be adhered to religiously. Low-level design – interfaces between modules and classes – should also be simple but should be separated from high-level design. At a low level, it is more important to understand state transitions than the exact definition of methods on classes, which are likely to change in the coding phase anyway.

Simple code is hugely important. Simple code is easier to write, debug, test and review. Most importantly, simple code is easier to maintain. This is fundamental: successful projects will spend much more time maintaining old code (either fixing or enhancing) than was initially spent writing it.

Today's programming languages contain a number of sophisticated features, some of which simply are not useful or necessary for the majority of projects. In particular, C++ supports a wide range of esoterica, and continues to grow. Only true C++ enthusiasts have a good grasp of some of these features. Project leads have to take a pragmatic view on which features are beyond the knowledge of the average programmer, to ensure that all team members can understand code easily. Whilst sophisticated use of templates or exceptions might look clever, and be neat or elegant, they are unlikely to produce more comprehensible code. Simple logic expressed in simple programming constructs is always best. The important point here is to establish a corporate style; amongst your programming team, it should not be possible to determine who wrote which code simply by inspection.

Simple code requires good coding standards which are agreed and policed. Coding standards should cover naming and formatting, which are important in making code easy to read. Commenting guidance should also form part of coding standards; like design, the purpose of commenting is often misunderstood. Too many comments is often worse than too few; comments which state the obvious or simply rephrase code are not necessary. Equally, comments which bracket lines inserted on a particular change is just noise; such differences can be retrieved from the source code control system. Comments should describe interfaces and interactions which are not obvious, but good comments are no substitute for clarity.

Reducing Risk

Designs and code should be created with a view to reducing risk. Developers usually learn to appreciate that some implementations are simply more risky than others; indeed, some programming languages are more risky to use than others. For example, C and C++ require care when managing memory, to avoid referencing freed memory, freeing memory twice, or creating leaks. Managed languages like Java and C# do not have such risks.

Whichever programming language is chosen, some designs will always be more risky than others. For example, consider a market data subscriber application, which generates a list of stocks for which data should be retrieved by scanning a database table. The output of this scan is likely to be a set of objects, each modeling the state of a particular stock; these will probably be stored in a hash table, keyed by the stock's ticker symbol. The application will probably need to queue subscriptions; it will need to remove subscriptions from this queue if a stock is deleted before its price data is requested. If pointers to objects are used in this queue, the most obvious possible bug is that the object for a particular stock will be deleted, but the pointer will be left in the queue. However, this risk can be avoided completely by storing ticker symbols rather than pointers in the queue; if the stock is deleted, its object will simply not be found in the hash table when the symbol reaches the front of the queue. In a sense, this example borrows the concepts of managed languages for use in C++; it reduces risk when the outright performance of C++ is not necessary.

Reducing risk is a compromise; less risky designs often offer less performance, as indeed is true in this example. However, this performance might not be necessary, or the reduced risk implementation could be used in debug builds to verify the performance of the higher risk algorithm.

One way to manage risk is through code reviews. Code reviews are important in ensuring that coding standards are being adhered to, that designs are being implemented as agreed, and that low-level design details are sensible. Furthermore, they are an important feedback mechanism for all developers; as such, they must be done quickly once code is completed. A complete code review should include some form of testing by the reviewer, even if this is just viewing a demonstration of the new software by the developer. Such demonstrations are a useful tool in reinforcing the need for usability and sensible behavior when basic user mistakes are made; demonstrations in team meetings are particularly effective at providing feedback whilst simultaneously increasing self-esteem and team spirit.

One risk which is often overlooked is that of a program in an indeterminate state running amok. C and C++ programmers quickly learn that dangling pointers can lead to odd or seemingly random behavior; they are also lucky in that such programs usually crash quickly. However, in languages with strong exception handling features, like Java and C#, it is tempting for applications to catch every possible error condition and carry on regardless. An example illustrates why this is so dangerous.

Consider code written to validate user input in a particular dialog. The code might be structured to validate mandatory fields, then validate those which are optional. This validation might be surrounded by a try/catch construct, to make error handling easier; the results might then be sent to a server for processing. If an exception is thrown whilst validating the optional parameters, some of the user input might be missed off the message sent to the server. This could result in a fundamental semantic difference from what the user really wanted; in a trading system application, this could result in a financial loss.

To remove such possible risks, code should crash when it hits an unexpected runtime error, providing as much state as possible for diagnostic purposes. This offers an inconvenience to the end user, but this is almost always preferable to the unbounded risk of continuing processing when in an indeterminate state.

Testing

Software testing is a widely misunderstood discipline. Developers are typically unnecessarily disdainful of testers – they resent their code being broken during test cycles, but bitch about inadequate testing if problems are found in production. In fact, both are of course the fault of the developer.

Developers have to learn the fundamental lesson that *all code has bugs.* They then have to adopt techniques and train themselves to minimize the number of bugs they release into the field.

In *Writing Solid Code* [1], Steve Maguire argues that developers must coverage test their own code by stepping through it in a debugger, with the help of a listing and a pen. Most developers who join my team consider this some kind of heresy; how can this be an effective use of my time? It's boring; it's too hard to test all those error conditions. I have to remind those developers of the alternative – that the customer is the first to run that code. Few people would argue that this is desirable.

Stepping through code line-by-line in the debugger is the single most important thing the average developer could do to improve the quality of their code. When forced to inspect work this closely, and at a slow pace, bugs like the classic C single = become obvious. In addition, poor style and readability become clear, as does code which is hard to test.

As an example of how this feeds back into how you write code, experience shows that I often code while loops which do not terminate properly, typically because an iterator is not incremented within the loop body. I have seen this problem many times when single-stepping through my code. As a result, when writing such loops I take extra care, and make sure I know what will make the loop terminate. I make that mistake much less often, now.

I know a great consultant who makes a living out of optimizing applications. Given some technical talent and experience, this is often deceptively simple, because so few developers step through their code line-by-line. This means that very few coders truly understand the flow of their programs, and efficiency savings are therefore easily found. When shown the functions called by a simple operation, developers will often express surprise; "I never knew it went in **there**!" is the cry. Without the explicit check of control flow which stepping through the code gives you, mistakes in the flow are very likely.

Software developers learn about systems by maintaining them. However, maintenance can be risky without proper regression tests. In fact, the primary role of regression tests is to provide timely feedback on poor maintenance. Don't expect too much of regression tests: for example, they rarely find bugs in the changes of experienced developers; after all, they know the contents of the tests. Those tests are there to inform new developers of how the system is supposed to work, in a way more detailed than any specification ever could.

Test automation is something developers are very keen on, particular for release or regression tests. Whilst automated tests, when done well, have huge advantages in terms of reproducibility and ease of use, there is still a place for manual testing, even when scripted. A team leader reporting to me once described the design of a proposed automated release test suite, which he estimated would take 20 days to build. We subsequently agreed that the tests the suite would run only took a day to run manually; it would be 20 releases before the automated test suite actually saved us some effort, or more if the tests needed to change in that time. We continued to run the tests manually.

As well as being time consuming, test automation can also be invasive, as some test tools require significant edits to your source code. Such test tools should be avoided: clarity of your source code is sacrosanct.

Attitude

So, you have simplified your system, implemented it in a way which reduces risk, and tested it well, but you still suffer reliability problems. What is the magic missing ingredient?

Whilst all of the above technical disciplines contribute to software quality, by far the most important is the ability and particularly the attitude of your developers. If your developers are not keen to investigate and fix problems, and if they do not have a healthy paranoia when testing, they will continue to ship unreliable software.

Fostering the right attitude is thus a very important part of the development process. You can look for this attitude when recruiting; for example, does the candidate understand than complex constructs like threads are difficult and often lead to bugs? Are their solutions to problems simple? Do they describe their previous projects simply, or do they make them sound like rocket science?

However, you must also look to nurture this attitude within your team through the usual cycle of praising good behaviors and discouraging bad. Be aware that attitudes are contagious – a team full of developers convinced of the value of stepping through their code will soon pass this value on to new recruits.

Attitude is fundamental to reliability. Whilst it seems almost too obvious to state, your developers must *want* to produce reliable software.

Robustness

Robust applications are resilient to failures, with little or no impact on end-users. This section describes how robust systems are built, both in terms of the platforms and environments they run on and in, and how their software is engineered to achieve resilience.

Likely Hardware Failures and Avoidance

Fault-tolerant hardware used to be the ultimate in application robustness, with vendors like Stratus and Tandem providing fully dual-redundant machines with instant failover and phone-home capabilities. In recent times, such hardware has become rarer and rarer, as the resilience features of commodity hardware and operating systems have increased to levels which are sufficient for the vast majority of systems, particularly when allied with high-availability application architectures.

The following sections review hardware components in decreasing order of probability of failure, and recommends strategies for handling those failures gracefully.

Wide Area Communications Links

Any application which depends on wide area links should consider the impact of those links failing. Lines should be duplicated, with different providers, and tails rising at different ends of the building. Resilience should be built in at the network level (for example, routes should be migrated between lines using HSRP) to avoid the need for applications to recover state in the event of line failure (as the latter is likely to have more end-user impact).

PSUs and Fans

Commodity power supplies and fans have a life expectancy of a few years. Most server-class hardware can support one or more redundant hot-swappable power supplies relatively cheaply, and fitting these is an inexpensive way of avoiding an application problem because of the failure of a single fan.

Fans themselves are an important part of resilience. Technical specifications of all components will typically quote MTBF at a particular temperature; fan failures will increase temperatures and reduce time to failure. Again, hot-swappable fans are a standard feature on most server-class hardware.

It should also be considered that many application failures are caused by simple power failures. Dual PSUs should be connected to disparately-routed supplies if possible, and suitable UPS technology should be used to ensure resilience.

Disks

Like fans, disks have moving parts and thus are prone to mechanical failure. Disk failure has a huge impact on applications. Fatal disk failures often cause long outages, particularly when there is a need to rebuild an operating system disk. Non-fatal disk errors can cause data corruptions or application crashes which are difficult to trace.

The simplest approach to disk resilience is simply to mirror *all* disks. This is easy now that most machines support hardware mirroring of internal disks. External or SAN storage can also be mirrored, or can use an alternative resilience scheme like RAID-5. RAID-5 provides resilience to a single point of failure, but requires less spindles to do so: rather than mirroring every disk, resilience is provided through a parity scheme.

Once disks are mirrored, they can be replaced without application downtime. However, mirroring alone does not provide protection against read errors and other intermittent problems. One way to guard against such issues is to use the Solaris ZFS file system. ZFS protects against corruption at any point in the disk subsystem by using multiple checksums on each disk block; where mirrors are available, and one has a bad block, it will be repaired from the "good" mirror, invisibly to the application.

Local Area Network

Network resilience can be compromised by switches, network adaptors, routers or simply network cables failing. Resilience can be achieved by using resilient switches, plus IP multipathing to provide resilience to cable or adaptor failures.

Standby Datacentre

Fidessa's hosted service provides a very high level of resilience by running all applications in a primary/hot standby configuration. The primary and standby systems are located in separate datacenters, with a geographical separation of over 50 kilometers. Each datacenter is capable of sustaining the service in the event of the total loss of the other.

In addition to this explicit duplication of equipment, Fidessa's datacenters also provide dual-redundancy on critical components within a single site; for example, key connectivity services are doubled up, disks are mirrored, and dual power is used throughout.

Robust Application Architectures

This section discusses at a high level how applications can be architected for resilience.

Stateless Applications

The simplest applications in resilience terms are stateless applications; for example, a web farm or market data feed. Stateless applications can be _horizontally_ scaled; i.e. extra capacity or resilience can be added by simply adding further instances of the application running on separate hardware. Fidessa's Ticker Plant provides resilience to failure of any single market data feed by duplicating that data feed and the associated feed handler. In this case, the duplicate feeds are routed into datacenters separated by over 50 kilometers, providing an extremely high level of resilience to any single point of failure.

Statelessness is the panacea in that it involves little or no technology in either hardware or software to provide resilience. As such, it is simple, reliable and cheap. The downside is that few trading applications can be engineered to be truly stateless.

Stateful Clustering

The traditional solution for resilience of stateful applications is to use some kind of _clustering_. Clustering typically involves two or more closely-associated machines, connected by some common piece of hardware, which is typically a disk array. This disk array is usually known as the _quorum device_, in that whichever machine in the cluster controls the quorum device is the primary machine. Many clustering solutions are on the market, both from operating system vendors and third-parties.

Clustering software spots when the primary machine or application has failed. It then initiates a failover to another machine in the cluster, restarting the application as required. It has the advantage of simplicity at the application level: failover support is provided entirely by the clustering technology, assuming the application can start from its on-disk state. However, the disadvantage is the requirement for a shared disk array: this makes distributing the primary and standby application instances across disparate datacenters difficult and expensive.

Fidessa's Resilience Technology

Fidessa employs a proprietary resilience technology to address a number of issues with the standard, clustered solution. Fidessa's resilience technology is implemented entirely in application-level software and requires no specialized hardware support, or shared device between primary and standby systems. Persistent state is replicated in real-time from the primary to the standby system via TCP/IP; this means that primary and standby can easily be located in different datacenters with a significant geographical separation. Furthermore, this level of resilience can be achieved on inexpensive, entry-level hardware.

Fidessa also supports a third, disaster recovery system to which transactions can be fed on a best-effort basis. This could be in a third datacenter, providing an additional level of resilience.

Scalability

Data from Fidessa's Ticker Plant shows that the daily number of trades on every exchange has doubled in the last 12 to 24 months, and such increases seem likely to continue. Thus application scalability becomes ever more important. Scalability is much more than just efficiency; it implies the ability to overcome obvious bottlenecks by adding further hardware or duplicating key application components.

Types of Scalability

Horizontal

As mentioned above, *horizontal* scalability indicates the ability to increase an application's throughput by adding more machines. Horizontal scalability is simple, inexpensive and easy to understand. However, it typically only works for stateless applications.

Grid

Grid-based applications are similar to their horizontally scalable counterparts, in that their performance is increased by adding further machines. However, grid applications differ in that they take a single, large unit of work and divide it up into smaller, discrete units which can be progressed in parallel, on different machines. Typically scientific or numerical applications are best suited to the grid approach, where each discrete job is a large, numerically-intensive workload.

Vertical

Vertical scalability indicates the ability to increase throughput by adding further resources to the machine on which the application runs, typically by adding further processors. Vertically-scalable applications have typically run on large, expensive SMP hardware; however, with the advent of relatively inexpensive, powerful SMP computers using multi-core x86 processors, vertical scalability has come down in price. For example, in 2007 it will be possible to buy an SMP machine from a tier 1 vendor with 8 quad-core AMD Opteron CPUs. Similarly, CPU architectures like Sun's UltraSPARC T1 support massive vertical scalability.

Vertical scalability still requires workloads to be parallelizable and thus is not simple for all stateful applications. In particular, contention over shared state must be minimized to allow good vertical scalability.

Vertically scalable applications must choose whether to scale through multiple threads or multiple processes. These two contrasting methods offer similar levels of scalability, but have very different programming models. The biggest difference is how data is shared between the tasks.

When **multi-threading,** a process's address space is shared amongst all threads. This means that communication between threads is easy: all data structures are common. However, this also means that there is potential for data corruption when multiple threads update the same data structure concurrently. Such problems have to be solved by synchronization, which can lead to further problems such as deadlock.

Systems with **multiple processes** find it more difficult to share data, doing so by message passing through pipes or sockets, or IPC mechanisms such as shared memory, or via a database. However, this difficulty in sharing means that corruption of shared structures is much less likely, resulting in more reliable software.

Fidessa systems are inherently multi-process, with sharing of data being handled by Fidessa's proprietary in-memory database. This technology makes sharing of data between processes relatively simple, providing specialized features like real-time update notification to allow the database to be used like a lightweight message passing mechanism. In addition, the in-memory database provides a simple synchronization model, meaning that programmers rarely have to worry about the complexities of concurrency.

The Future

The ideal scalable application of the future should combine both vertical and horizontal scalability. Horizontal scalability takes advantage of the fact that uniprocessor machines will always have the best price/performance ratio. Vertical scalability is required to take advantage of the increasing core count on future processors, and the fact that horizontally scaling to a very large number of machines causes its own management problems.

Conclusion

Reliability, resilience and scalability are key operating parameters for today's trading systems. In this short overview we have seen how each area presents its own challenges, and how those can be met by systems now and in the future.

References

[1] *Writing Solid Code*, Steve Maguire, Microsoft Press.

Trading Floor Architecture:
Executive Overview

*By Mihaela Risca, Cisco Systems, Dave Malik Cisco Systems &
Andy Kessler Cisco Systems*

Increased competition, higher market data volume, and new regulatory demands are some of the driving forces behind industry changes. Firms are trying to maintain their competitive edge by constantly changing their trading strategies and increasing the speed of trading.

A viable architecture has to include the latest technologies from both network and application domains. It has to be modular to provide a manageable path to evolve each component with minimal disruption to the overall system. Therefore the architecture proposed by this paper is based on a services framework. We examine services such as ultra-low latency messaging, latency monitoring, multicast, computing, storage, data and application virtualization, trading resiliency, trading mobility, and thin client.

The solution to the complex requirements of the next-generation trading platform must be built with a holistic mindset, crossing the boundaries of traditional silos like business and technology or applications and networking.

This document's main goal is to provide guidelines for building an ultra-low latency trading platform while optimizing the raw throughput and message rate for both market data and FIX trading orders.

To achieve this, we are proposing the following latency reduction technologies:

- High speed inter-connect—InfiniBand or 10 Gbps connectivity for the trading cluster
- High-speed messaging bus
- Application acceleration via RDMA without application re-code [See Glossary at end of chapter for definition of acronyms]
- Real-time latency monitoring and re-direction of trading traffic to the path with minimum latency

Industry Trends and Challenges

Next-generation trading architectures have to respond to increased demands for speed, volume, and efficiency. For example, the volume of options market data is expected to double with the introduction of options penny trading. There are also regulatory demands for best execution, which require handling price updates at rates that approach 1M msg/sec.for exchanges. They also require visibility into the freshness of the data and proof that the client got the best possible execution.

In the short term, speed of trading and innovation are key differentiators. An increasing number of trades are handled by algorithmic trading applications, which need to be placed as close as possible to the trade execution venue. A challenge with these "black-box" trading engines is that they compound the volume increase by issuing orders, only to cancel them and re-submit them. The cause of this behavior is lack of visibility into which venue offers best execution.

The human trader is now a "financial engineer," a "quant" (quantitative analyst) with programming skills, who can adjust trading models on the fly. Firms develop new financial instruments like weather derivatives or cross-asset class trades and they need to deploy the new applications quickly and in a scalable fashion.

In the long term, competitive differentiation should come from analysis, not just knowledge. The star traders of tomorrow assume risk, achieve true client insight, and consistently beat the market (source IBM: http://www-935.ibm.com/services/us/imc/pdf/ge510-6270-trader.pdf).

Business resilience has been one main concern of trading firms since September 11, 2001. Solutions in this area range from redundant data centers situated in different geographies and connected to multiple trading venues to virtual trader solutions offering power traders most of the functionality of a trading floor in a remote location.

The financial services industry is one of the most demanding in terms of IT requirements. The industry is experiencing an architectural shift towards Services-Oriented Architecture (SOA), Web services, and virtualization of IT resources. SOA takes advantage of the increase in network speed to enable dynamic binding and virtualization of software components. This allows the creation of new applications without losing the investment in existing systems and infrastructure. The concept has the potential to revolutionize the way integration is accomplished, enabling significant reductions in the complexity and cost of such integration (http://www.gigaspaces.com/download/MerrilLynchGigaSpacesWP.pdf).

Another trend is the consolidation of servers into data center server farms, while trader desks have only KVM extensions and ultra-thin clients (e.g., SunRay and HP blade solutions). High-speed Metro Area Networks enable market data to be multicast between different locations, enabling the virtualization of the trading floor.

High-Level Architecture

Trading Architecture for a Buy Side/Sell Side Firm depicts the high-level architecture of a trading environment. The ticker plant and the algorithmic trading engines are located in the high performance trading cluster in the firm's data center or at the exchange. The human traders are located in the end-user applications area.

Functionally there are two application components in the enterprise trading environment, publishers and subscribers. The messaging bus provides the communication path between publishers and subscribers.

There are two types of traffic specific to a trading environment:

- Market Data—Carries pricing information for financial instruments, news, and other value-added information such as analytics. It is unidirectional and very latency sensitive, typically delivered over UDP multicast. It is measured in updates/sec. and in Mbps. Market data flows from one or multiple external feeds, coming from market data providers like stock exchanges, data aggregators, and ECNs. Each provider has their own market data format. The data is received by feed handlers, specialized applications which normalize and clean the data and then send it to data consumers, such as pricing engines, algorithmic trading applications, or human traders. Sell-side firms also send the market data to their clients, buy-side firms such as mutual funds, hedge funds, and other asset managers. Some buy-side firms may opt to receive direct feeds from exchanges, reducing latency.

Trading Architecture for a Buy Side/Sell Side Firm

There is no industry standard for market data formats. Each exchange has their proprietary format. Financial content providers such as Reuters and Bloomberg aggregate different sources of market data, normalize it, and add news or analytics. Examples of consolidated feeds are RDF (Reuters Data Feed), RWF (Reuters Wire Format), and Bloomberg Professional Services Data.

Trading Architecture

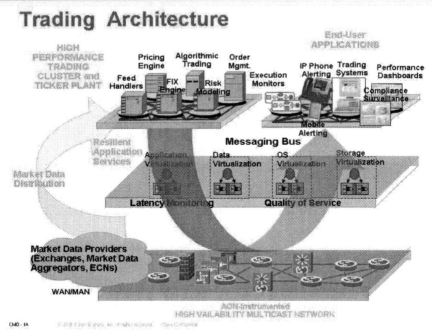

To deliver lower latency market data, both vendors have released real-time market data feeds which are less processed and have less analytics:

- RDF-D (Reuters Data Feed-Direct)
  (http://about.reuters.com/productinfo/datafeeddirect/)
- Bloomberg B-Pipe—With B-Pipe, Bloomberg de-couples their market data feed from their distribution platform because a Bloomberg terminal is not required for get B-Pipe. Wombat and Reuters Feed Handlers have announced support for B-Pipe.

A firm may decide to receive feeds directly from an exchange to reduce latency. The gains in transmission speed can be between 150 milliseconds to 500 milliseconds. These feeds are more complex and more expensive and the firm has to build and maintain their own ticker plant (http://www.financetech.com/featured/showArticle.jhtml?articleID=604043 06).

- Trading Orders—This type of traffic carries the actual trades. It is bi-directional and very latency sensitive. It is measured in messages/sec. and Mbps. The orders originate from a buy side or sell side firm and are sent to trading venues like an Exchange or ECN for execution. The most common format for order transport is FIX (Financial Information eXchange—http://www.fixprotocol.org/). The applications which handle FIX messages are called FIX engines and they interface with order management systems (OMS).

- An optimization to FIX is called FAST (Fix Adapted for Streaming), which uses a compression schema to reduce message length and, in effect, reduce latency. FAST is targeted more to the delivery of market data and has the potential to become a standard. FAST can also be used as a compression schema for proprietary market data formats.

To reduce latency, firms may opt to establish Direct Market Access (DMA). DMA is the automated process of routing a securities order directly to an execution venue, therefore avoiding the intervention by a third-party (http://www.towergroup.com/research/content/glossary.jsp?page=1&glossaryId=383). DMA needs a direct connection to the execution venue.

The messaging bus is middleware software from vendors such as Tibco, 29West, Reuters RMDS, or an open source platform such as AMQP. The messaging bus uses a reliable mechanism to deliver messages. The transport can be done over TCP/IP (TibcoEMS, 29West, RMDS, and AMQP) or UDP/multicast (TibcoRV, 29West, and RMDS). One important concept in message distribution is the "topic stream," which is a subset of market data defined by criteria such as ticker symbol, industry, or a certain basket of financial instruments. Subscribers join topic groups mapped to one or multiple sub-topics in order to receive only the relevant information. In the past, all traders received all market data. At the current volumes of traffic, this would be sub-optimal.

The network plays a critical role in the trading environment. Market data is carried to the trading floor where the human traders are located via a Campus or Metro Area high-speed network. High availability and low latency, as well as high throughput, are the most important metrics.

The high performance trading environment has most of its components in the Data Center server farm. To minimize latency, the algorithmic trading engines need to be located in the proximity of the feed handlers, FIX engines, and order management systems. An alternate deployment model has the algorithmic trading systems located at an exchange or a service provider with fast connectivity to multiple exchanges.

Deployment Models

There are two deployment models for a high performance trading platform. Firms may choose to have a mix of the two:

- Data Center of the trading firm (Traditional Deployment Model)— This is the traditional model, where a full-fledged trading platform is developed and maintained by the firm with communication links to all the trading venues. Latency varies with the speed of the links and the number of hops between the firm and the venues.
- Co-location at the trading venue (exchanges, financial service providers (FSP)) (Hosted Deployment Model)
- The trading firm deploys its automated trading platform as close as possible to the execution venues to minimize latency.

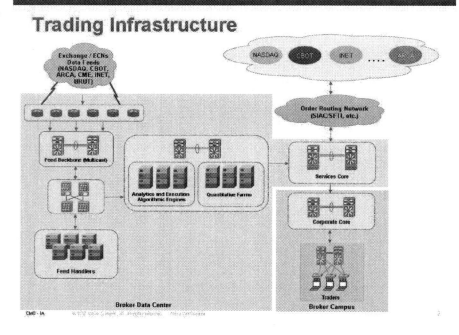

Figure 2   Traditional Deployment Model

Services-Oriented Trading Architecture

We are proposing a services-oriented framework for building the next-generation trading architecture. This approach provides a conceptual framework and an implementation path based on modularization and minimization of inter-dependencies.

This framework provides firms with a methodology to:

- Evaluate their current state in terms of services
- Prioritize services based on their value to the business

- Evolve the trading platform to the desired state using a modular approach

Figure 3 **Hosted Deployment Model**

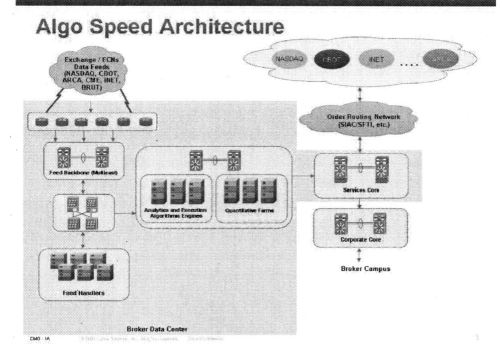

Ultra-Low Latency Messaging Service

This service is provided by the messaging bus, which is a software system that solves the problem of connecting many-to-many applications. The system consists of:

- A set of pre-defined message schemas
- A set of common command messages
- A shared application infrastructure for sending the messages to recipients. The shared infrastructure can be based on a message broker or on a publish/subscribe model.

Table 1   *The high performance trading architecture relies on the following services, as defined by the services architecture framework represented in* Error! Not a valid bookmark self-reference.*. Service Descriptions and Technologies*

Service Description	Technology
Ultra-low latency messaging	Middleware
Latency monitoring	Instrumentation—appliances, software agents, and router modules
Computing services	OS and I/O virtualization, Remote Direct Memory Access (RDMA), TCP Offload Engines (TOE)
Application virtualization	Middleware which parallelizes application processing
Data virtualization	Middleware which speeds-up data access for applications, e.g., in-memory caching
Multicast service	Hardware-assisted multicast replication through-out the network; multicast Layer 2 and Layer 3 optimizations
Storage services	Virtualization of storage hardware (VSANs), data replication, remote backup, and file virtualization
Trading resilience and mobility	Local and site load balancing and high availability campus networks
Wide Area application services	Acceleration of applications over a WAN connection for traders residing off-campus
Thin client service	De-coupling of the computing resources from the end-user facing terminals

Figure 4 Service Architecture Framework for High Performance Trading

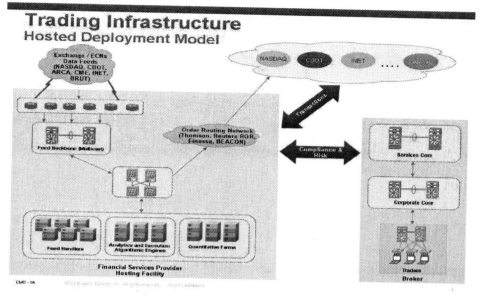

The key requirements for the next-generation messaging bus are (source 29West):

- Lowest possible latency (e.g., less than 100 microseconds)
- Stability under heavy load (e.g., more than 1.4 million msg/sec.)
- Control and flexibility (rate control and configurable transports)

There are efforts in the industry to standardize the messaging bus. Advanced Message Queueing Protocol (AMQP) is an example of an open standard championed by J.P. Morgan Chase and supported by a group of vendors such as Cisco, Envoy Technologies, Red Hat, TWIST Process Innovations, Iona, 29West, and iMatix. Two of the main goals are to provide a more simple path to inter-operability for applications written on different platforms and modularity so that the middleware can be easily evolved.

In very general terms, an AMQP server is analogous to an E-mail server with each exchange acting as a message transfer agent and each message queue as a mailbox. The bindings define the routing tables in each transfer agent. Publishers send messages to individual transfer agents, which then route the messages into mailboxes. Consumers take messages from mailboxes, which creates a powerful and flexible model that is simple (source: http://www.amqp.org/tikiwiki/tiki-index.php?page=OpenApproach#Why_AMQP_).

Latency Monitoring Service

The main requirements for this service are:

- Sub-millisecond granularity of measurements
- Near-real time visibility without adding latency to the trading traffic
- Ability to differentiate application processing latency from network transit latency
- Ability to handle high message rates
- Provide a programmatic interface for trading applications to receive latency data, thus enabling algorithmic trading engines to adapt to changing conditions
- Correlate network events with application events for troubleshooting purposes

Latency can be defined as the time interval between when a trade order is sent and when the same order is acknowledged and acted upon by the receiving party.

Addressing the latency issue is a complex problem, requiring a holistic approach that identifies all sources of latency and applies different technologies at different layers of the system.

Latency Management Architecture depicts the variety of components that can introduce latency at each layer of the OSI stack. It also maps each source of latency with a possible solution and a monitoring solution. This layered approach can give firms a more structured way of attacking the latency issue, whereby each component can be thought of as a service and treated consistently across the firm.

Maintaining an accurate measure of the dynamic state of this time interval across alternative routes and destinations can be of great assistance in tactical trading decisions. The ability to identify the exact location of delays, whether in the customer's edge network, the central processing hub, or the transaction application level, significantly determines the ability of service providers to meet their trading service-level agreements (SLAs). For buy-side and sell-side firms, as well as for market-data syndicators, the quick identification and removal of bottlenecks translates directly into enhanced trade opportunities and revenue.

Cisco Low-Latency monitoring tools

Traditional network monitoring tools operate with minutes or seconds granularity. Next generation trading platforms, especially those supporting algorithmic trading, require latencies less than 5 ms and extremely low levels of packet loss. On a Gigabit LAN, a 100ms microburst can cause 10,000 transactions to be lost or excessively delayed.

Cisco offers three approaches to address this challenge:

- Bandwidth Quality Manager (BQM), OEM'ed from Corvil
- Cisco AON based Financial Services Latency Monitoring Solution (FSMS)
- Cisco IP SLA

Figure 5   *Latency Management Architecture*

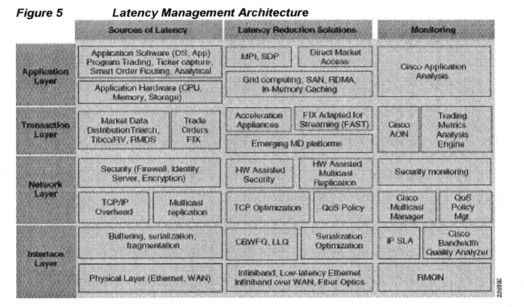

Bandwidth Quality Manager

Bandwidth Quality Manager (BQM) 4.0 is a next-generation network application performance management product that enables customers to monitor and provision their network for controlled levels of latency and loss performance. While BQM is not exclusively targeted at trading networks, its microsecond visibility combined with intelligent bandwidth provisioning features make it ideal for these demanding environments.

Cisco BQM 4.0 implements a broad set of patented and patent-pending traffic measurement and network analysis technologies that give the user unprecedented visibility and understanding of how to optimize the network for maximum application performance.

Cisco BQM is now supported on the product family of Cisco Application Deployment Engine (ADE). The Cisco ADE product family is the platform of choice for Cisco network management applications.

BQM Benefits

Cisco BQM micro-visibility is the ability to detect, measure, and analyze latency, jitter, and loss inducing traffic events down to microsecond levels of granularity with per packet resolution. This enables Cisco BQM to detect and determine the impact of traffic events on network latency, jitter, and loss. Critical for trading environments is that BQM can support latency, loss and jitter measurements one-way for both TCP and UDP (multicast) traffic. This means it reports seamlessly for both trading traffic and market data feeds.

BQM allows the user to specify a comprehensive set of thresholds (against microburst activity, latency, loss, jitter, utilization etc) on all interfaces. BQM then operates a background rolling packet capture. Whenever a threshold violation or other potential performance degradation event occurs, it triggers Cisco BQM to store the packet capture to disk for later analysis. This allows the user to examine in full detail both the application traffic that was affected by performance degradation ("the victims") and the traffic that caused the performance degradation ("the culprits"). This can significantly reduce the time spent diagnosing and resolving network performance issues.

BQM is also able to provide detailed bandwidth and quality of service (QoS) policy provisioning recommendations, which the user can directly apply to achieve desired network performance.

The BQM measurements illustrated

To understand the difference between some of the more conventional measurement techniques and the visibility provided by BQM, we can look at some comparison graphs. In the first set of graphs, we see the difference between the latency measured by BQM's Passive Network Quality Monitor (PNQM) and the latency measured by injecting ping packets every 1 second into the traffic stream.

In the first graph, we see the latency reported by 1-second ICMP ping packets for real network traffic. (It is divided by 2 to give an estimate for the one-way delay.) It shows the delay comfortably below about 5ms for almost all of the time.

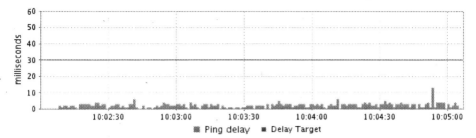

In the second graph, we see the latency reported by PNQM for the same traffic at the same time. Here we see that by measuring the one way latency of the actual application packets, we get a radically different picture. Here the latency is seen to be hovering around 20ms, with occasional bursts far higher than that. The explanation is that because ping is sending packets only every second, it is completely missing most of the application traffic latency. In fact, ping results typically only indicate round trip propagation delay rather than realistic application latency across the network.

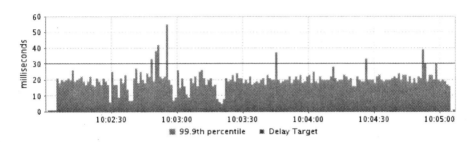

In the second example, we see the difference in reported link load or saturation levels between a 5-minute average view and a 5ms microburst view. (BQM can report on microbursts down to about 10-100 nanosecond accuracy.) The green line shows the average utilization at 5-minute averages to be low, maybe up to 5Mbits/s. The dark blue plot shows the 5ms microburst activity reaching between 75mbits/s and 100Mbits/s, the LAN speed effectively. BQM shows this level of granularity for all applications, and it also gives clear provisioning rules to enable the user to control or neutralize these microbursts.

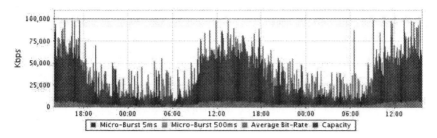

BQM Deployment in the Trading Network

This diagram shows a typical BQM deployment in a trading network.

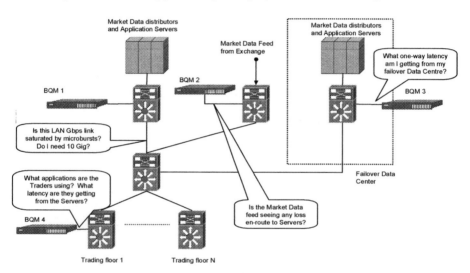

BQM can then be used to answer these types of questions:

- Are any of my Gigabit LAN core links saturated for more than X milliseconds? Is this causing loss? Which links would most benefit from an upgrade to Etherchannel or 10 Gigabit speeds?
- What application traffic is causing the saturation of my 1 Gigabit links?
- Is any of the Market Data experiencing end-to-end loss?
- How much additional latency does the failover Data Center experience? Is this link sized correctly to deal with microbursts?
- Are my Traders getting low latency updates from the Market Data distribution layer? Are they seeing any delays greater than X milliseconds?

Being able to answer these questions simply and effectively saves time and money in running the trading network.

BQM features at a glance

- PNQM (Passive Network Quality Monitoring)- Microsecond precision end-to-end measurement of packet latency, jitter and loss, as actually experienced by application packets
- Layer 7 Microvisibility - Microsecond application discovery, monitoring and analytics
- Event Analysis - Automatic detection, capture, analysis and alarm of congestion events with per packet (nanosecond) drilldown
- Expected Quality - Real-time estimation of queuing delay and loss conditions on downstream remote router interfaces.
- Corvil Bandwidth - Real-time estimation of bandwidth needed at router interfaces to achieve queuing delay and loss objectives.
- NSI - At a glance indexed view of overall performance health of interface or site against desired latency and loss objectives
- Live What-If: investigate in real time bandwidth upgrade, and/or migration to QoS

Cisco Financial Services Latency Monitoring Solution

Cisco and Trading Metrics have collaborated on a couple of latency monitoring solutions for FIX order flow and market data monitoring. Cisco AON technology is the foundation for a new class of network-embedded products and solutions that help merge intelligent networks with application infrastructure, based on either service-oriented or traditional architectures. Trading Metrics is a leading provider of analytics software for network infrastructure and application latency monitoring purposes (http://www.tradingmetrics.com/).

Cisco AON Financial Services Latency Monitoring Solution (FSMS) correlated two kinds of events at the point of observation:

- Network events correlated directly with coincident application message handling
- Trade order flow and matching market update events

Using time stamps inserted at the point of capture in the network, real-time analysis of these correlated data streams permits precise identification of bottlenecks across the infrastructure while a trade is being executed or market data is being distributed. By monitoring and measuring latency early in the cycle, financial companies can make better decisions about which network service—and which intermediary, market, or counterparty—to select for routing trade orders. Likewise, this knowledge allows more streamlined access to updated market data (stock quotes, economic news, etc.), which is an important basis for initiating, withdrawing from, or pursuing market opportunities.

The components of the solution are:

- AON hardware in three form factors:
- AON Network Module for Cisco 2600/2800/3700/3800 routers
- AON Blade for Cisco Catalyst 6500 series
- AON 8340 Appliance
- AON software
- Trading Metrics M&A 2.0 software, which provides the monitoring and alerting application, displays latency graphs on a dashboard, and issues alerts when slowdowns occur (http://www.tradingmetrics.com/TM_brochure.pdf).

Figure 6   AON-Based FIX Latency Monitoring

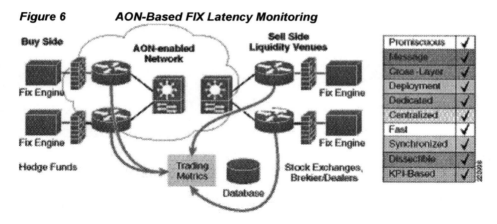

IP SLA

IP SLA is an embedded network management tool in Cisco IOS which allows routers and switches to generate synthetic traffic streams which can be measured for latency, jitter, packet loss, and other criteria (www.cisco.com/go/ipsla).

Two key concepts are the source of the generated traffic and the target. Both of these run an IP SLA "responder," which has the responsibility to timestamp the control traffic before it is sourced and returned by the target (for a round trip measurement). Various traffic types can be sourced within IP SLA and they are aimed at different metrics and target different services and applications. The UDP jitter operation is used to measure one-way and round-trip delay and report variations. As the traffic is time stamped on both sending and target devices using the responder capability, the round trip delay is characterized as the delta between the two timestamps.

A new feature was introduced in IOS 12.3(14)T, IP SLA Sub Millisecond Reporting, which allows for timestamps to be displayed with a resolution in microseconds, thus providing a level of granularity not previously available. This new feature has now made IP SLA relevant to campus networks where network latency is typically in the range of 300-800 microseconds and the ability to detect trends and spikes (brief trends) based on microsecond granularity counters is a requirement for customers engaged in time-sensitive electronic trading environments.

As a result, IP SLA is now being considered by significant numbers of financial organizations as they are all faced with requirements to:

- Report baseline latency to their users
- Trend baseline latency over time
- Respond quickly to traffic bursts that cause changes in the reported latency

Sub-millisecond reporting is necessary for these customers, since many campus and backbones are currently delivering under a second of latency across several switch hops. Electronic trading environments have generally worked to eliminate or minimize all areas of device and network latency to deliver rapid order fulfillment to the business. Reporting that network response times are "just under one millisecond" is no longer sufficient; the granularity of latency measurements reported across a network segment or backbone need to be closer to 300-800 micro-seconds with a degree of resolution of 100 μseconds.

IP SLA recently added support for IP multicast test streams, which can measure market data latency.

A typical network topology is shown in IP SLA Deployment with the IP SLA shadow routers, sources, and responders.

Computing Services

Computing services cover a wide range of technologies with the goal of eliminating memory and CPU bottlenecks created by the processing of network packets. Trading applications consume high volumes of market data and the servers have to dedicate resources to processing network traffic instead of application processing.

Figure 7   **IP SLA Deployment**

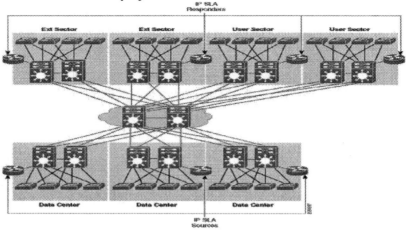

The problems:

- Transport processing—At high speeds, network packet processing can consume a significant amount of server CPU cycles and memory. An established rule of thumb states that 1Gbps of network bandwidth requires 1 GHz of processor capacity (source Intel white paper on I/O acceleration http://www.intel.com/technology/ioacceleration/306517.pdf).
- Intermediate buffer copying—In a conventional network stack implementation, data needs to be copied by the CPU between network buffers and application buffers. This overhead is worsened by the fact that memory speeds have not kept up with increases in CPU speeds. For example, processors like the Intel Xeon are approaching 4 GHz, while RAM chips hover around 400MHz (for DDR 3200 memory) (source Intel http://www.intel.com/technology/ioacceleration/306517.pdf).
- Context switching—Every time an individual packet needs to be processed, the CPU performs a context switch from application context to network traffic context. This overhead could be reduced if the switch would occur only when the whole application buffer is complete.

Figure 8   Sources of Overhead in Data Center Servers

Sources of Overhead in Server Networking	CPU Overhead
Transport Processing	40%
Intermediate Buffer Copying	20%
Application Context Switches	40%

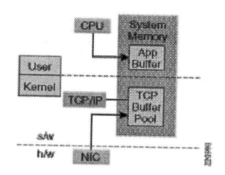

The solutions:

- TCP Offload Engine (TOE)—Offloads transport processor cycles to the NIC. Moves TCP/IP protocol stack buffer copies from system memory to NIC memory.
- Remote Direct Memory Access (RDMA)—Enables a network adapter to transfer data directly from application to application without involving the operating system. Eliminates intermediate and application buffer copies (memory bandwidth consumption).
- Kernel bypass —Direct user-level access to hardware. Dramatically reduces application context switches.

Figure 9   RDMA and Kernel Bypass

InfiniBand is a point-to-point (switched fabric) bidirectional serial communication link which implements RDMA, among other features. Cisco offers an InfiniBand switch, the Server Fabric Switch (SFS):

Figure 10 **Typical SFS Deployment**

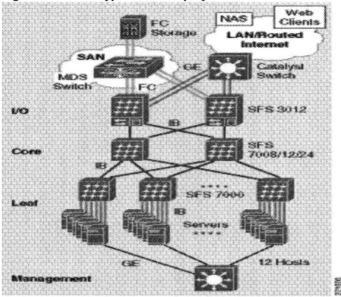

Trading applications benefit from the reduction in latency and latency variability, as proved by a test performed with the Cisco SFS and Wombat Feed Handlers by Stac Research:

Application Virtualization Service

De-coupling the application from the underlying OS and server hardware enables them to run as network services. One application can be run in parallel on multiple servers, or multiple applications can be run on the same server, as the best resource allocation dictates. This decoupling enables better load balancing and disaster recovery for business continuance strategies. The process of re-allocating computing resources to an application is dynamic. Using an application virtualization system like Data Synapse's GridServer, applications can migrate, using pre-configured policies, to under-utilized servers in a supply-matches-demand process

There are many business advantages for financial firms who adopt application virtualization:

- Faster time to market for new products and services
- Faster integration of firms following merger and acquisition activity
- Increased application availability
- Better workload distribution, which creates more "head room" for processing spikes in trading volume

- Operational efficiency and control
- Reduction in IT complexity

Currently, application virtualization is not used in the trading front-office. One use-case is risk modeling, like Monte Carlo simulations. As the technology evolves, it is conceivable that some of the trading platforms are going to adopt it.

Data Virtualization Service

To effectively share resources across distributed enterprise applications, firms must be able to leverage data across multiple sources in real-time while ensuring data integrity. With solutions from data virtualization software vendors such as Gemstone or Tangosol (now Oracle), financial firms can access heterogeneous sources of data as a single system image that enables connectivity between business processes and unrestrained application access to distributed caching. The net result is that all users have instant access to these data resources across a distributed network

This is called a data grid and is the first step in the process of creating what Gartner calls Extreme Transaction Processing (XTP)

Technologies such as data and applications virtualization enable financial firms to perform real-time complex analytics, event-driven applications, and dynamic resource allocation.

One example of data virtualization in action is a global order book application. An order book is the repository of active orders that is published by the exchange or other market makers. A global order book aggregates orders from around the world from markets that operate independently. The biggest challenge for the application is scalability over WAN connectivity because it has to maintain state. Today's data grids are localized in data centers connected by Metro Area Networks (MAN). This is mainly because the applications themselves have limits—they have been developed without the WAN in mind.

Figure 11   *GemStone GemFire Distributed Caching*

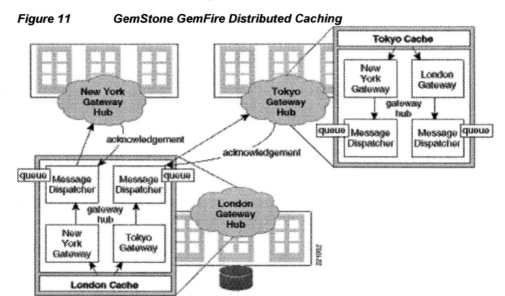

Before data virtualization, applications used database clustering for failover and scalability. This solution is limited by the performance of the underlying database. Failover is slower because the data is committed to disc. With data grids, the data which is part of the active state is cached in memory, which reduces drastically the failover time. Scaling the data grid means just adding more distributed resources, providing a more deterministic performance compared to a database cluster.

Multicast Service

Market data delivery is a perfect example of an application that needs to deliver the same data stream to hundreds and potentially thousands of end users. Market data services have been implemented with TCP or UDP broadcast as the network layer, but those implementations have limited scalability. Using TCP requires a separate socket and sliding window on the server for each recipient. UDP broadcast requires a separate copy of the stream for each destination subnet. Both of these methods exhaust the resources of the servers and the network. The server side must transmit and service each of the streams individually, which requires larger and larger server farms. On the network side, the required bandwidth for the application increases in a linear fashion. For example, to send a 1 Mbps stream to 1000recipients using TCP requires 1 Gbps of bandwidth.

IP multicast is the only way to scale market data delivery. To deliver a 1 Mbps stream to 1000 recipients, IP multicast would require 1 Mbps. The stream can be delivered by as few as two servers—one primary and one backup for redundancy.

There are two main phases of market data delivery to the end user. In the first phase, the data stream must be brought from the exchange into the brokerage's network. Typically the feeds are terminated in a data center on the customer premise. The feeds are then processed by a feed handler, which may normalize the data stream into a common format and then republish into the application messaging servers in the data center.

The second phase involves injecting the data stream into the application messaging bus which feeds the core infrastructure of the trading applications. The large brokerage houses have thousands of applications that use the market data streams for various purposes, such as live trades, long term trending, arbitrage, etc. Many of these applications listen to the feeds and then republish their own analytical and derivative information. For example, a brokerage may compare the prices of CSCO to the option prices of CSCO on another exchange and then publish ratings which a different application may monitor to determine how much they are out of synchronization.

Figure 12   *Market Data Distribution Players*

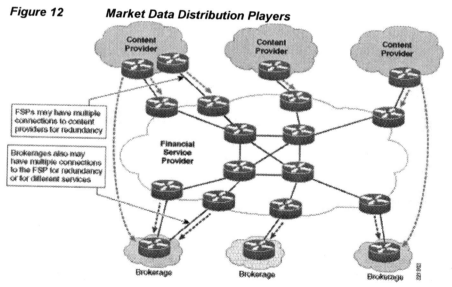

The delivery of these data streams is typically over a reliable multicast transport protocol, traditionally Tibco Rendezvous. Tibco RV operates in a publish and subscribe environment. Each financial instrument is given a subject name, such as CSCO.last. Each application server can request the individual instruments of interest by their subject name and receive just a subset of the information. This is called subject-based forwarding or filtering. Subject-based filtering is patented by Tibco.

A distinction should be made between the first and second phases of market data delivery. The delivery of market data from the exchange to the brokerage is mostly a one-to-many application. The only exception to the unidirectional nature of market data may be retransmission requests, which are usually sent using unicast. The trading applications, however, are definitely many-to-many applications and may interact with the exchanges to place orders.

Design Issues

Number of Groups/Channels to Use

Many application developers consider using thousand of multicast groups to give them the ability to divide up products or instruments into small buckets. Normally these applications send many small messages as part of their information bus. Usually several messages are sent in each packet that are received by many users. Sending fewer messages in each packet increases the overhead necessary for each message.

Figure 13   Market Data Architecture

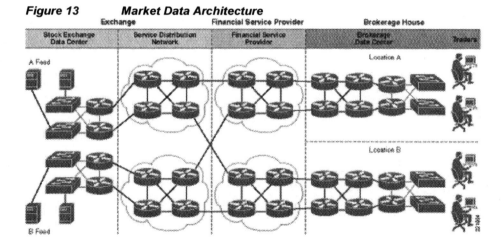

In the extreme case, sending only one message in each packet quickly reaches the point of diminishing returns—there is more overhead sent than actual data. Application developers must find a reasonable compromise between the number of groups and breaking up their products into logical buckets.

Consider, for example, the Nasdaq Quotation Dissemination Service (NQDS). The instruments are broken up alphabetically:

```
NQDS (A-E)   224.3.0.18
NQDS (F-N)   224.3.0.20
NQDS (O-Z)   224.3.0.22
```

Another example is the Nasdaq Totalview service, broken up this way:

```
Data Channel                  Primary Groups    Backup Groups
--------------------          --------------    -------------
NASDAQ TotalView (A)            224.0.17.32      224.0.17.35
NASDAQ TotalView (B-C)          224.0.17.48      224.0.17.49
NASDAQ TotalView (D-F)          224.0.17.50      224.0.17.51
NASDAQ TotalView (G-K)          224.0.17.52      224.0.17.53
NASDAQ TotalView (L-N)          224.0.17.54      224.0.17.55
NASDAQ TotalView (O-Q)          224.0.17.56      224.0.17.57
NASDAQ TotalView (R-S)          224.0.17.58      224.0.17.59
NASDAQ TotalView (T-Z)          224.0.17.60      224.0.17.61
```

This approach allows for straight forward network/application management, but does not necessarily allow for optimized bandwidth utilization for most users. A user of NQDS that is interested in technology stocks, and would like to subscribe to just CSCO and INTL, would have to pull down all the data for the first two groups of NQDS. Understanding the way users pull down the data and then organize it into appropriate logical groups optimizes the bandwidth for each user.

In many market data applications, optimizing the data organization would be of limited value. Typically customers bring in all data into a few machines and filter the instruments. Using more groups is just more overhead for the stack and does not help the customers conserve bandwidth. Another approach might be to keep the groups down to a minimum level and use UDP port numbers to further differentiate if necessary. The other extreme would be to use just one multicast group for the entire application and then have the end user filter the data. In some situations this may be sufficient.

Intermittent Sources
A common issue with market data applications are servers that send data to a multicast group and then go silent for more than 3.5 minutes. These intermittent sources may cause trashing of state on the network and can introduce packet loss during the window of time when soft state and then hardware shorts are being created.

PIM-Bidir or PIM-SSM
The first and best solution for intermittent sources is to use PIM-Bidir for many-to-many applications and PIM-SSM for one-to-many applications.
Both of these optimizations of the PIM protocol do not have any data-driven events in creating forwarding state. That means that as long as the receivers

are subscribed to the streams, the network has the forwarding state created in the hardware switching path.

Intermittent sources are not an issue with PIM-Bidir and PIM-SSM.

Null Packets

In PIM-SM environments a common method to make sure forwarding state is created is to send a burst of null packets to the multicast group before the actual data stream. The application must efficiently ignore these null data packets to ensure it does not affect performance. The sources must only send the burst of packets if they have been silent for more than 3 minutes. A good practice is to send the burst if the source is silent for more than a minute. Many financials send out an initial burst of traffic in the morning and then all well-behaved sources do not have problems.

Periodic Keepalives or Heartbeats

An alternative approach for PIM-SM environments is for sources to send periodic heartbeat messages to the multicast groups. This is a similar approach to the null packets, but the packets can be sent on a regular timer so that the forwarding state never expires.

S,G Expiry Timer

Finally, Cisco has made a modification to the operation of the S,G expiry timer in IOS. There is now a CLI knob to allow the state for a S,G to stay alive for hours without any traffic being sent. The (S,G) expiry timer is configurable. This approach should be considered a workaround until PIM-Bidir or PIM-SSM is deployed or the application is fixed.

RTCP Feedback

A common issue with real time voice and video applications that use RTP is the use of RTCP feedback traffic. Unnecessary use of the feedback option can create excessive multicast state in the network. If the RTCP traffic is not required by the application it should be avoided.

Fast Producers and Slow Consumers

Servers providing market data are attached at Gigabit speeds, while the receivers are attached at different speeds, usually 100Mbps. Receivers drop packets and ask for re-transmissions, which creates more traffic that slow consumers cannot handle, continuing the vicious circle.

The solution is to have the application limit the amount of data that one host can request.

Tibco Heartbeats

TibcoRV has had the ability to use IP multicast for the heartbeat between the TICs for many years. However, there are some brokerage houses that are still using very old versions of TibcoRV that use UDP broadcast support for the resiliency. This limitation is often cited as a reason to maintain a Layer 2 infrastructure between TICs located in different data centers. These older versions of TibcoRV should be phased out in favor of the IP multicast supported versions.

Multicast Forwarding Options

PIM Sparse Mode

The standard IP multicast forwarding protocol used today for market data delivery is PIM Sparse Mode. It is supported on all Cisco routers and switches and is well understood. PIM-SM can be used in all the network components from the exchange, FSP, and brokerage.

There are, however, some long-standing issues and unnecessary complexity associated with a PIM-SM deployment that could be avoided by using PIM-Bidir and PIM-SSM. These are covered in the next sections.

The main components of the PIM-SM implementation are:

- PIM Sparse Mode v2
- Shared Tree (spt-threshold infinity)
- A design option in the brokerage or in the exchange.
- Static RP
- Anycast RP
- Details of Anycast RP can be found in:
- Anycast RP

The classic high availability design for Tibco in the brokerage network is documented in:
Financial Services Design for High Availability

Bidirectional PIM

PIM-Bidir is an optimization of PIM Sparse Mode for many-to-many applications. It has several key advantages over a PIM-SM deployment:

- Better support for intermittent sources
- For more information, see Intermittent Sources.
- No data-triggered events

One of the weaknesses of PIM-SM is that the network continually needs to react to active data flows. This can cause non-deterministic behavior that may be hard to troubleshoot. PIM-Bidir has the following major protocol differences over PIM-SM:

- No source registration
- Source traffic is automatically sent to the RP and then down to the interested receivers. There is no unicast encapsulation, PIM joins from the RP to the first hop router and then registration stop messages.
- SPT switchover
- All PIM-Bidir traffic is forwarded on a *,G forwarding entry. The router does not have to monitor the traffic flow on a *,G and then send joins when the traffic passes a threshold.
- No need for an actual RP
- The RP does not have an actual protocol function in PIM-Bidir. The RP acts as a routing vector in which all the traffic converges. The RP can be configured as an address that is not assigned to any particular device. This is called a Phantom RP.
- No need for MSDP
- MSDP provides source information between RPs in a PIM-SM network. PIM-Bidir does not use the active source information for any forwarding decisions and therefore MSDP is not required.

Bidirectional PIM is ideally suited for the brokerage network in the data center of the exchange. In this environment there are many sources sending to a relatively few set of groups in a many-to-many traffic pattern.
The key components of the PIM-Bidir implementation are:

- Bidirectional PIM
- Static RP
- Phantom RP

Source Specific Multicast

PIM-SSM is an optimization of PIM Sparse Mode for one-to-many applications. In certain environments it can offer several distinct advantages over PIM-SM. Like PIM-Bidir, PIM-SSM does not rely on any data-triggered events. Furthermore, PIM-SSM does not require an RP at all—there is no such concept in PIM-SSM. The forwarding information in the network is completely controlled by the interest of the receivers.

Source Specific Multicast is ideally suited for market data delivery in the financial service provider. The FSP can receive the feeds from the exchanges and then route them to the end of their network.

Many FSPs are also implementing MPLS and Multicast VPNs in their core. PIM-SSM is the preferred method for transporting traffic in VRFs.

When PIM-SSM is deployed all the way to the end user, the receiver indicates his interest in a particular S,G with IGMPv3. Even though IGMPv3 was defined by RFC 2236 back in October, 2002, it still has not been implemented by all edge devices. This creates a challenge for deploying an end-to-end PIM-SSM service. A transitional solution has been developed by Cisco to enable an edge device that supports IGMPv2 to participate in an PIM-SSM service. This feature is called SSM Mapping and is documented in:

While SSM Mapping allows a end user running IGMPv2 to join an PIM-SSM service, there is no way for a router connected in a customer domain to request the service dynamically from a provider. A service like this would be called PIM Mapping and would allow a PIM *,G join to be translated into a PIM S,G join at the service edge. This is a feature that needs to be implemented to create an easy method to interface between providers and their customers.

Storage Services

The service provides storage capabilities into the market data and trading environments. Trading applications access backend storage to connect to different databases and other repositories consisting of portfolios, trade settlements, compliance data, management applications, Enterprise Service Bus (ESB), and other critical applications where reliability and security is critical to the success of the business. The main requirements for the service are:

- Storage virtualization
- Replication
- Backup services

Storage virtualization is an enabling technology that simplifies management of complex infrastructures, enables non-disruptive operations, and facilitates critical elements of a proactive information lifecycle management (ILM) strategy. EMC Invista running on the Cisco MDS 9000 enables heterogeneous storage pooling and dynamic storage provisioning, allowing allocation of any storage to any application. High availability is increased with seamless data migration. Appropriate class of storage is allocated to point-in-time copies (clones). Storage virtualization is also leveraged through the use of Virtual Storage Area Networks (VSANs), which enable the consolidation of multiple isolated SANs onto a single physical SAN infrastructure, while still partitioning them as completely separate logical entities. VSANs provide all the security and fabric services of traditional SANs, yet give organizations the flexibility to easily move resources from one VSAN to another. This results in increased disk and network utilization while driving down the cost of management. Integrated Inter VSAN Routing (IVR) enables sharing of common resources across VSANs.

Replication of data to a secondary and tertiary data center is crucial for business continuance. Replication offsite over Fiber Channel over IP (FCIP) coupled with write acceleration and tape acceleration provides improved performance over long distance. Continuous Data Replication (CDP) is another mechanism which is gaining popularity in the industry. It refers to backup of computer data by automatically saving a copy of every change made to that data, essentially capturing every version of the data that the user saves. It allows the user or administrator to restore data to any point in time. Solutions from EMC and Incipient utilize the SANTap protocol on the Storage Services Module (SSM) in the MDS platform to provide CDP functionality. The SSM uses the SANTap service to intercept and redirect a copy of a write between a given initiator and target. The appliance does not reside in the data path—it is completely passive. The CDP solutions typically leverage a history journal that tracks all changes and bookmarks that identify application-specific events. This ensures that data at any point in time is fully self-consistent and is recoverable instantly in the event of a site failure.

Backup procedure reliability and performance are extremely important when storing critical financial data to a SAN. The use of expensive media servers to move data from disk to tape devices can be cumbersome. Network-accelerated serverless backup (NASB) helps you back up increased amounts of data in shorter backup time frames by shifting the data movement from multiple backup servers to Cisco MDS 9000 Series multilayer switches. This technology decreases impact on application servers because the MDS offloads the application and backup servers. It also reduces the number of backup and media servers required, thus reducing CAPEX and OPEX. The flexibility of the backup environment increases because storage and tape drives can reside anywhere on the SAN.

Figure 14   High Performance Computing Storage

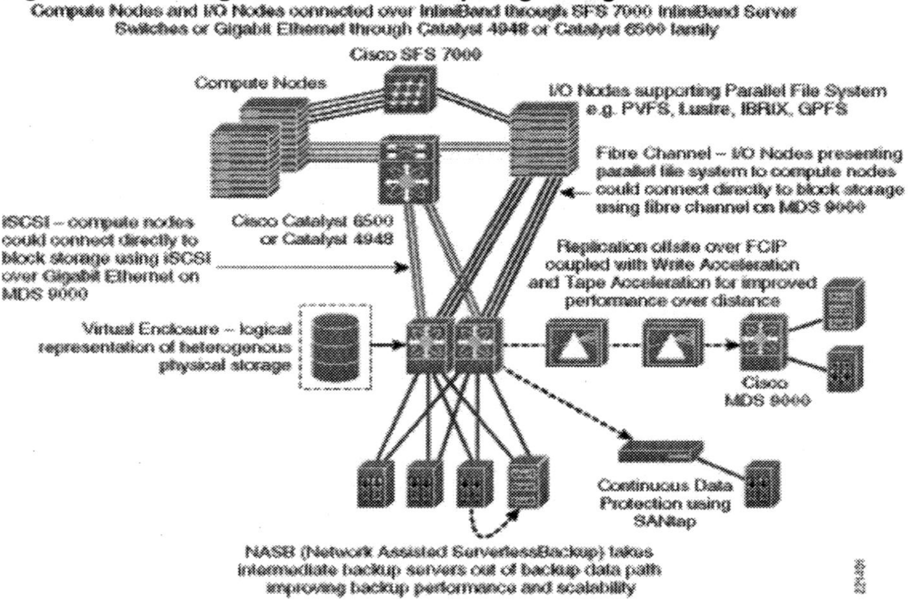

Compute Nodes and I/O Nodes connected over InfiniBand through SFS 7000 InfiniBand Server Switches or Gigabit Ethernet through Catalyst 4948 or Catalyst 6500 family

Cisco SFS 7000

Compute Nodes

I/O Nodes supporting Parallel File System e.g. PVFS, Lustre, IBRIX, GPFS

Fibre Channel – I/O Nodes presenting parallel file system to compute nodes could connect directly to block storage using fibre channel on MDS 9000

iSCSI – compute nodes could connect directly to block storage using iSCSI over Gigabit Ethernet on MDS 9000

Cisco Catalyst 6500 or Catalyst 4948

Replication offsite over FCIP coupled with Write Acceleration and Tape Acceleration for improved performance over distance

Virtual Enclosure – logical representation of heterogenous physical storage

Cisco MDS 9000

Continuous Data Protection using SANTap

NASB (Network Assisted ServerlessBackup) takes intermediate backup servers out of backup data path improving backup performance and scalability

Trading Resilience and Mobility

The main requirements for this service are to provide the virtual trader:

- Fully scalable and redundant campus trading environment
- Resilient server load balancing and high availability in analytic server farms
- Global site load balancing that provides the capability to continue participating in the market venues of closest proximity

A highly-available campus environment is capable of sustaining multiple failures (i.e., links, switches, modules, etc.), which provides non-disruptive access to trading systems for traders and market data feeds. Fine-tuned routing protocol timers, in conjunction with mechanisms such as NSF/SSO, provide sub-second recovery from any failure.

The high-speed interconnect between data centers can be DWDM/dark fiber, which provides business continuance in case of a site failure. Each site is 100km-200km apart, allowing synchronous data replication. Usually the distance for synchronous data replication is 100km, but with Read/Write Acceleration it can stretch to 200km. A tertiary data center can be greater than 200km away, which would replicate data in an asynchronous fashion.

A robust server load balancing solution is required for order routing, algorithmic trading, risk analysis, and other services to offer continuous access to clients regardless of a server failure. Multiple servers encompass a "farm" and these hosts can be added/removed without disruption since they reside behind a virtual IP (VIP) address which is announced in the network.

A global site load balancing solution provides remote traders the resiliency to access trading environments which are closer to their location. This minimizes latency for execution times since requests are always routed to the nearest venue.

Figure 15   Trading Resilience

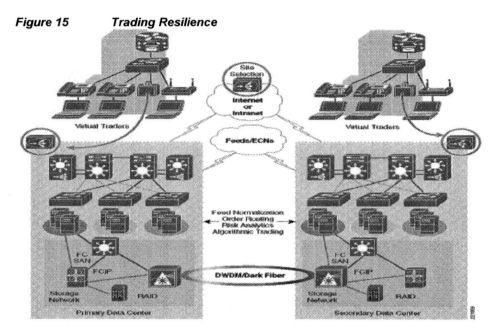

 A trading environment can be virtualized to provide segmentation and resiliency in complex architectures. Virtualization of Trading Environment illustrates a high-level topology depicting multiple market data feeds entering the environment, whereby each vendor is assigned its own Virtual Routing and Forwarding (VRF) instance. The market data is transferred to a high-speed InfiniBand low-latency compute fabric where feed handlers, order routing systems and algorithmic trading systems reside. All storage is accessed via a SAN and is also virtualized with VSANs, allowing further security and segmentation. The normalized data from the compute fabric is transferred to the campus trading environment where the trading desks reside.

Figure 16 **_Virtualization of Trading Environment_**

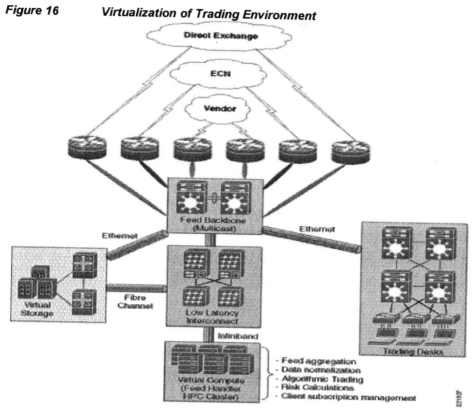

Wide Area Application Services

This service provides application acceleration and optimization capabilities for traders who are located outside of the core trading floor facility/data center and working from a remote office. To consolidate servers and increase security in remote offices, file servers, NAS filers, storage arrays, and tape drives are moved to a corporate data center to increase security and regulatory compliance and facilitate centralized storage and archival management. As the traditional trading floor is becoming more virtual, wide area application services technology is being utilized to provide a "LAN-like" experience to remote traders when they access resources at the corporate site. Traders often utilize Microsoft Office applications, especially Excel, in addition to Sharepoint and Exchange. Excel is used heavily for modeling and permutations where sometime only small portions of the file are changed. CIFS protocol is notoriously known to be "chatty," where several messages normally traverse the WAN for a simple file operation and it is addressed by Wide Area Application Service (WAAS) technology. Bloomberg and Reuters applications are also very popular financial tools,which access a centralized SAN or NAS filer to retrieve critical data, which is then fused together before represented to a trader's screen.

Figure 17   ***Wide Area Optimization***

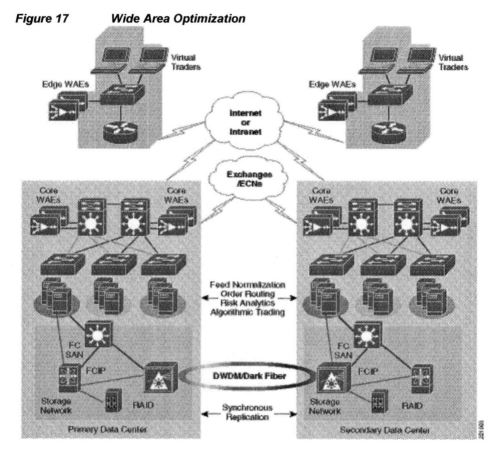

A pair of Wide Area Application Engines (WAEs) that reside in the remote office and the data center provide local object caching to increase application performance. The remote office WAEs can be a module in the ISR router or a stand-alone appliance. The data center WAE devices are load balanced behind an Application Control Engine module installed in a pair of Catalyst 6500 series switches at the aggregation layer. The WAE appliance farm is represented by a virtual IP address. The local router in each site utilizes Web Cache Communication Protocol version 2 (WCCP v2) to redirect traffic to the WAE that intercepts the traffic and determines if there is a cache hit or miss. The content is served locally from the engine if it resides in cache; otherwise the request is sent across the WAN the initial time to retrieve the object. This methodology optimizes the trader experience by removing application latency and shielding the individual from any congestion in the WAN.

WAAS uses the following technologies to provide application acceleration:

- Data Redundancy Elimination (DRE) is an advanced form of network compression which allows the WAE to maintain a history of previously-seen TCP message traffic for the purposes of reducing redundancy found in network traffic. This combined with the Lempel-Ziv (LZ) compression algorithm reduces the number of redundant packets that traverse the WAN, which improves application transaction performance and conserves bandwidth.
- Transport Flow Optimization (TFO) employs a robust TCP proxy to safely optimize TCP at the WAE device by applying TCP-compliant optimizations to shield the clients and servers from poor TCP behavior because of WAN conditions. By running a TCP proxy between the devices and leveraging an optimized TCP stack between the devices, many of the problems that occur in the WAN are completely blocked from propagating back to trader desktops. The traders experience LAN-like TCP response times and behavior because the WAE is terminating TCP locally. TFO improves reliability and throughput through increases in TCP window scaling and sizing enhancements in addition to superior congestion management.

Thin Client Service

This service provides a "thin" advanced trading desktop which delivers significant advantages to demanding trading floor environments requiring continuous growth in compute power. As financial institutions race to provide the best trade executions for their clients, traders are utilizing several simultaneous critical applications that facilitate complex transactions. It is not uncommon to find three or more workstations and monitors at a trader's desk which provide visibility into market liquidity, trading venues, news, analysis of complex portfolio simulations, and other financial tools. In addition, market dynamics continue to evolve with Direct Market Access (DMA), ECNs, alternative trading volumes, and regulatory changes, with Regulation National Market System (RegNMS) in the US and Markets in Financial Instruments Directive (MiFID) in Europe. At the same time, business seeks greater control, improved ROI, and additional flexibility, which creates greater demands on trading floor infrastructures.

Traders no longer require multiple workstations at their desk. Thin clients consist of keyboard, mouse, and multi-displays which provide a total trader desktop solution without compromising security. Hewlett Packard, Citrix, Desktone, Wyse, and other vendors provide thin client solutions to capitalize on the virtual desktop paradigm. Thin clients de-couple the user-facing hardware from the processing hardware, thus enabling IT to grow the processing power without changing anything on the end user side. The workstation computing power is stored in the data center on blade workstations, which provide greater scalability, increased data security, improved business continuance across multiple sites, and reduction in OPEX by removing the need to manage individual workstations on the trading floor. One blade workstation can be dedicated to a trader or shared among multiple traders depending on the requirements for computer power.

The "thin client" solution is optimized to work in a campus LAN environment, but can also extend the benefits to traders in remote locations. Latency is always a concern when there is a WAN interconnecting the blade workstation and thin client devices. The network connection needs to be sized accordingly so traffic is not dropped if saturation points exist in the WAN topology. WAN Quality of Service (QoS) should prioritize sensitive traffic. There are some guidelines which should be followed to allow for an optimized user experience. A typical highly-interactive desktop experience requires a client-to-blade round trip latency of <20ms for a 2Kb packet size. There may be a slight lag in display if network latency is between 20ms to 40ms. A typical trader desk with a four multi-display terminal requires 2-3Mbps bandwidth consumption with seamless communication with blade workstation(s) in the data center. Streaming video (800x600 at 24fps/full color) requires 9 Mbps bandwidth usage.

Management of a large thin client environment is simplified since a centralized IT staff manages all of the blade workstations dispersed across multiple data centers. A trader is redirected to the most available environment in the enterprise in the event of a particular site failure. High availability is a key concern in critical financial environments and the Blade Workstation design provides rapid provisioning of another blade workstation in the data center. This resiliency provides greater uptime, increases in productivity, and OpEx reduction.

Figure 18   *Thin Client Architecture*

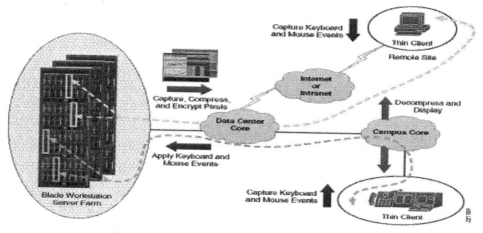

Glossary

Term	Description
AES	Advanced Encryption Standard
AMQP	Advanced Message Queueing Protocol
AON	Application Oriented Networking
ARCA	The Archipelago® Integrated Web book gives investors the unique opportunity to view the entire ArcaEx and ArcaEdge books in addition to books made available by other market participants.
BRUT	ECN Order Book feed available via NASDAQ.
CAPEX	Capital Expense
CBOT	Chicago Board of Trade
CBWFQ	Class-Based Weighted Fair Queueing
CDP	Continuous Data Replication

CME	Chicago Mercantile Exchange is engaged in trading of futures contracts and derivatives.
CPU	Central Processing Unit
DDR	Dual Data Rate
DDTS	Distributed Defect Tracking System
DMA	Direct Market Access
DRE	Data Redundancy Elimination
DWDM	Dense Wavelength Division Multiplexing
ECN	Electronic Communication Network
ESB	Enterprise Service Bus
ESE	Enterprise Solutions Engineering
FAST	FIX Adapted for Streaming
FCIP	Fibre Channel over IP
FIX	Financial Information Exchange
FSMS	Financial Services Latency Monitoring Solution
FSP	Financial Service Provider
ILM	Information Lifecycle Management
INET	Instinet Island Book
IOS	Internetworking Operating System
ISCSI	Internet SCSI
IT	Information Technology
IVR	Inter-VSAN Routing
KVM	Keyboard Video Mouse

LLQ	Low Latency Queueing
MAN	Metro Area Network
MDS	Multilayer Director Switch
MiFID	Markets in Financial Instruments Directive
MPI	Message Passing Interface is an industry standard specifying a library of functions to enable the passing of messages between nodes within a parallel computing environment.
NAS	Network Attached Storage
NASB	Network Accelerated Serverless Backup
NIC	Network Interface Card
NQDS	Nasdaq Quotation Dissemination Service
NSF	Non-Stop Forwarding
OMS	Order Management System
OPEX	Operational Expense
OS	Operating System
OSI	Open Systems Interconnection
PIM	Protocol Independent Multicast
PIM-Bidir	PIM-Bidirectional
PIM-SM	PIM-Sparse Mode
PIM-SSM	PIM-Source Specific Multicast
QoS	Quality of Service
RAM	Random Access Memory
RDF	Reuters Data Feed

RDF-D	Reuters Data Feed Direct
RDMA	Remote Direct Memory Access
RegNMS	Regulation National Market System
RGS	Remote Graphics Software
RMDS	Reuters Market Data System
RMON	Remote Monitoring
RTCP	RTP Control Protocol
RTP	Real Time Protocol
RWF	Reuters Wire Format
S,G	Source, Group
SAN	Storage Area Network
SCSI	Small Computer System Interface
SDP	Sockets Direct Protocol—Given that many modern applications are written using the sockets API, SDP can intercept the sockets at the kernel level and map these socket calls to an InfiniBand transport service that uses RDMA operations to offload data movement from the CPU to the HCA hardware.
SFS	Server Fabric Switch
SFTI	Secure Financial Transaction Infrastructure network developed to provide firms with excellent communication paths to NYSE Group, AMEX, Chicago Stock Exchange, NASDAQ, and other exchanges. It is often used for order routing.
SLA	Service Level Agreement
SOA	Services Oriented Architecture

SSL	Secure Sockets Layer
SSM	Storage Services Module
SSO	Stateful Switch-Over
TCP/IP	Transport Control Protocol/Internet Protocol
TFO	Transport Flow Optimization
TOE	TCP Offload Engine
UDP	User Datagram Protocol
VIP	Virtual IP
VRF	Virtual Routing and Forwarding
VSAN	Virtual Storage Area Network
WAAS	Wide Area Application Service
WAE	Wide area Application Engine
WAN	Wide Area Network
WCCP	Web Cache Communication Protocol
XTP	Extreme Transaction Processing

About the Authors

Mihaela Risca is an Industry Solutions Architect for the Financial Services vertical and can be reached at mrisca@cisco.com.

Dave Malik is a Technical Leader in the Advanced Services group and can be reached at dmalik@cisco.com.

Andy Kessler is a Technical Leader in the Systems and Architecture group and can be reached at kessler@cisco.com.

Case Study:

Lessons Learned from Implementing A State-of-the-Art Trading System – User Perspective

By James Doherty, Credit Suisse

When beginning to write this piece, we tried to separate the business from the technological aspects of algorithmic trading. But while the most elegant solutions to the problems faced in this burgeoning field are not necessarily technological ones, it would be inaccurate to say that the technology is not crucial to the overall process. Allow us to digress briefly from the business end, to address the role of the programmer in the success or failure of an algorithmic trading system.

There is often talk about the "art" of programming and something called the "elegance of design". Programmers are taught to aspire to these somewhat lofty ideals. Too little talk exists about what this art takes to achieve. Perhaps these textbook writers are loath to give aspiring programmers the cold, hard facts: that programming requires not only skill, but also vigilance and painstaking revision in order to produce something worthy of attention. Experience has taught us to expect to make mistakes but to do one's best to try to anticipate them, to head them off as early as possible, to track them and to test well and often. Like many programmers at the start of their career, we wrote effective yet amateurish programs. Back then, the mistakes—bugs in the jargon—usually caused only an embarrassment or a delay. Today, having moved from trade support systems to trade decision systems, these errors have a real and tangible track record, one that is dollar denominated and closely monitored by senior management. Such precise feedback and cost attribution is very much desired in many service industries, but it can seem like too much of a good thing to a programmer who must face a horde of very vocal, and understandably angry traders. Your system is going to crash, so the question, is what are you going to do about it now while you have the code in front of you?

For modern programmers, the entire process is supported by many tools. Helpful and productive as these tools are, they are not a substitute for discipline. Programmers, ***however, like to be first and this desire can cause us to make simple, avoidable mistakes.*** What a programmer really needs is a healthy dose of humility in order to create the type of "art" that lasts. In the not-so-distant past, programmers were not required to understand the purpose of the information systems they were building. Today the landscape is quite different. The data is now enriched with various analytics, delivered near real-time, and may feed automatic response mechanisms without human supervision, e.g. monitoring and restocking inventory. Complicated systems have many subtle design decisions embedded within them, decisions that are often not specified explicitly by requirements documentation. A programmer knowledgeable or experienced in the business for which he is coding will achieve a better result. Realistically, the jobs of those programmers who do not understand the business and don't add value directly to this complex process are in immediate jeopardy, as their work can be outsourced indirectly to a vendor or directly to a cheaper employee at home or abroad. In complicated systems, the programmer who takes the time to get to know the business will eventually become an expert, and the software creation effort will expose him to more of the details of the process than probably any other team member involved.

When it comes down to it, "art" is in the eye of the beholder. Programs are full of arcane-looking symbols and seemingly impenetrable lists of instructions. Not a very pretty picture. Code should be documented or commented, individual functions should be broadly understandable, and the code should follow some conventions of style. Even the lowliest initiate (read 'manager') should be able not only to read the code of any well-written system, but understand, at least on a basic level, how it works. Coding is a difficult thing to assess for quality, but reading code serves the dual purpose of surveying the quality and encouraging clear, better-written code. Such code reviews combined with testing are the only guides you really have to gauge quality before a system is developed enough to try out.

Measure twice, trade once.

Now that you understand the importance of the individual programmer, let's get to the big picture. The beauty and the bane of algorithmic trading is the ease with which trade performance can be tracked. Buy-side institutions are already measuring brokers using a battery of trade performance metrics: arrival price, VWAP, and so forth. In all likelihood, they are measuring their portfolio managers and in-house traders too. Therefore, it is critical to have your own in-house tools with a transparent methodology and quality reference data. Without your own accurate performance management and reporting infrastructure, you will be at a loss to compare your assumptions with those of any other and identify the source of differences.[cxlvi] Your approach to order modifications, e.g. limit changes, size changes or tactic changes, needs to be clear and rational. When measuring against VWAP performance, for instance, when a client's order size changes, we effectively begin a new trade for purposes of trade performance measurement because we believe it is unfair to expect the trading engine to be able to forecast these changes.

At the other end of the scale from the large institutional orders are the hundreds of micro trade decisions that go into trading one large order. Keeping track of the performance of these small slices is a stickier problem, since there are probably millions of these in a day. The bright side is that while the volume may be higher, the measurement is usually much simpler. In truth all scales of the trading system can be lumped into these three categories, from order routing to the macro trades mentioned above, but the clarity at the micro level will probably come from the following measurements.

What Price?
It's a straightforward measurement to compare against an independent benchmark. For small orders did you pay more than the offered price or as little as the inside bid? For large orders spread over a decent interval, did you pay more than the VWAP over that interval or did you buy near the local low or the local high?

How soon?
How long did you spend holding onto the order? Ten seconds? Ten minutes? For small orders ten seconds may be a reasonable amount of time trying to game the market, but for large orders they could take anywhere from fifteen to twenty minutes to finish. Was there an opportunity cost?

How much?
How much of the visible volume did you trade? Were you 50% of the available volume or 2%? On which trading venues did you source your liquidity? Granted, this is a little trickier. But participation rates can be insightful and are often the metric of choice for many styles of trading.

By keeping a careful eye on your performance measurements, how much, how soon and what price will not become too much, too soon and bad price.

Once you measure, you can determine which trade-offs you want to make. Metrics make your life easier in this regard; there's less guess work, more opportunities, and ultimately new and better ideas. Your system might eventually use real-time feedback of performance measurement to adapt trading style on-the-fly, probing markets for their responses and automatically responding with different behavior.

"Tell me what you eat, and I will tell you what you are."

Real-time data is the nourishment of any algorithmic trading system, and it needs careful preparation to get right. Because of its transience and volume, small errors in content and delivery problems are often ignored. With increasingly sophisticated modeling and more discriminating clients, these issues need constant attention. Real-time data surveillance is important. Actively monitoring the latency and discrepancies between different sources of the same data is just the first step in making your real-time data useful to an algorithm and reliable enough with which to trade. Frequent data format changes and micro outages lasting less than a second are constant issues. In many cases, we compare real-time data with official historical data the next day to benchmark our real-time quality. Vendors can add value in isolating format changes, but the added latency through their network make direct connections to the various exchanges a necessity in any leading system. With peak data rates in the U.S. doubling between February 2007 and July 2007 in the run up to RegNMS, this aspect of modern trading cannot get enough attention. We can't necessarily rely on hardware improvements to outrun this issue. The improved technology of trading has caused this growth, and we're therefore trapped in a spiral of increasing volumes driven by faster trading technology. Market data is sure to remain one the foremost fundamental technology issues for algorithmic trading desks in to the future.

No smart man is an island.

A U.S. algorithmic trading system worth its salt will connect to at least twenty different trading venues, probably with multiple circuits over different providers to each. It's a fact of life that these circuits are going to have problems, whether at your own end, that of the trading venue or the network carrier. With the different protocols over each connection, the volume of messages and the software at each end, you can expect connections to die completely or stall occasionally. If you have connections to twenty trading venues and five different paths along each (estimating 99.99% uptime on each path), you can still expect four minutes of outage on any given day.[cxlvii]

This variety of trading venues and the complexity of dealing with it all is an opportunity for the best of the algorithmic engines out there to shine. Exploiting direct connections and interconnections between the exchanges and ECNs is a responsibility that falls largely to systems called Smart Order Routers. These engines monitor market data and route your order or parts of it to the venue with the best price. (The topic of smart order routing is a whole chapter on its own so I won't labor the point here.)

Big iron?

Why a server? Why not a run-of-the-mill PC? To be honest, we are a bit zealous on this point. You probably have a PC at home. It doesn't take a specialist six months to install and configure a PC. They are cheap and don't require spare parts—they are the spare part. Specialized, rare or, heaven forbid, unique hardware requires trained support personnel. They are inevitably slower to repair and not necessarily any more reliable, e.g. highly available storage servers can be highly unavailable in a network outage. Specialized hardware is more trouble to manage and just as susceptible to many of the every day things that go wrong with common computer hardware.

Plenty of installations live or die by the success of the most visible part – the graphical user interface or GUI (pronounced 'gooey'). Since most people think of it as the tangible result of software development (naturally, since this is the part they get to interact with), they attract the most requests for changes. Even if not specifically about the GUI, the change will likely be put in terms, by the average user, of what it would look like within the context of the GUI. This is the problem with GUIs: they are the tip of the proverbial big system ice-berg. Not necessarily the most important part, they can be a huge source of what is known in the software business as 'feature creep', the inclination for users and developers alike to include as many functions as possible in one application. After only a few independently innocuous additions, the GUI can become enormously, and unnecessarily, complicated.

Compromising on new functionality may be sufficient. For example, if they want to be able to total up columns at the end of the day, offer them the ability to paste the data they need into a spread-sheet and they can do it there. Bargain the work down to the minimum necessary to get the job done. Refuse to combine operations that already exist in the application but must be applied serially into single button tasks. The per-user configurable GUI seems to be the objective of the many large rewrite efforts I've either witnessed or been a part of in the past. Resist this with all your might. If you are reading this article, I presume you work for a financial institution and you do not work for a software firm. Confusing the role of either institution never bodes well.

Programmers should be encouraged to use their own software as much as possible, including the GUI. Annoyances and bugs get corrected much more promptly, in my experience, if the programmer has to deal directly with the application's problems in day-to-day use

.

Getting any complicated system resilient is significant effort. Since problems are going to occur, and often, the most obvious solution to a software problem is going to be to restart. That's why I've strongly favored a rapid restart as a design goal of our algorithmic trading systems. This at least minimizes the outage period and allows for restart as an option in the face of system instability.

Fat fingers or how much control should a human being have?

This is a rhetorical question. Of course, the answer is complete control. In all those science-fiction movies where the machines rise up against humanity, the one effective and practical deterrent to their conquering us all is missing: a simple "off" switch. People need to be in control of any trading system. The members of your own trading desk are your most important users. When the application goes down, they're the ones who'll be able to cover your clients until you get the systems back up properly. For that reason, you need to ensure that they have the tools to do their job. On any reasonably sized algorithmic trading desk, there are going to be too many individual client orders for people to monitor entirely by eye. Whether built in to the trading systems directly, or as an independent side-by-side process with a proactive problem detection system (in addition to the tools to help correct the problems that do show up), you will need some proactive monitoring which will keep your clients from rising up against you.

Planning for system failure: Hope for best, plan for the worst

When the blow finally falls and you have a serious problem, the first stop on the diagnostic round is probably in log files. With any luck, they are all in a nice, clean, consistent format. Logs are meant to be read by people but often their size and the density of information within them create confusion. Better that they are in a consistent format with key reference data similarly formatted between them. This allows them to be brought together easily for a clear picture of the event and what led up to it. But logs should not be used only after the fact but as prophylactic tools. They should be reviewed for warnings frequently. Problems often reveal themselves overtly after lengthy periods of ignored or silent warnings. Look for issues before they become real problems and your boss comes looking for you.

Arthur C. Clarke, a renowned writer, said, "Any sufficiently advanced technology is indistinguishable from magic." I hope that someday our algorithmic tactics are this good. But in striving for this perfection, we must always remember that at the other end of the order is a real person. We may have got algorithmic trading to look like a little bit of alchemy so far, but it's not quite magic yet.

Lessons Learned From Building and Deploying a State of the Art Trading System

Steve Smith, CEO, 4th Story, LLC

My grandfather used to say, "good judgment comes from experience, and experience comes from bad judgment." This suggests how I and many others learned valuable lessons about building and deploying trading systems, and state of the art trading systems in particular.

If one looks up "State of the Art trading system" on Google the search returns more than 1000 references. That is a lot of references, but what is a state of the art trading system?

The dictionary says state of the art is: "the highest degree of development of a technique at a particular time".

Does that mean state of the art technology?

Great technology is important, but if someone came to you and said they had a trading system built on state of the art technology, would that be enough reason for you to run out and buy it? I have been in trading technology for 10 years, and I have to tell you that whenever I hear someone lead a pitch with the technology, I always think - "here is some technology looking for an application, resulting in this product." It should be the other way around - the application and need should drive the technology choice.

At 4th Story we chose to be on Microsoft's .Net platform. Years ago, in previous lives, we worked in Smalltalk, which was a state of the art object oriented development platform. We then worked with Java for a few years.

Again, state of the art, and probably still is. However, we chose .Net over other platforms like Java for two simple reasons that had less to do with technology and more to do with our needs:

7. It was a more productive development environment to work in, and,
8. it integrates very well with Microsoft Office tools like Excel. It is well-known that Excel is the most ubiquitous trading tool in the industry.

It was very important to us to allow clients to integrate with Excel in as many ways possible. We heard this early on from everyone we talked to. So because we are using .Net, users can push one button and a spreadsheet will pop up on their computer with the data from our applications. Now that is nice, but more importantly, users can write their strategy logic in an Excel macro and we can call Excel for the logic, or conversely, they can embed our software in Excel, so their front end becomes Excel and not our application. So suiting the technology to the need was one lesson learned.

Another one is that 'state of the art' is relative. As mentioned, the official definition of state of the art is "the highest degree of development of a technique at a particular time". I think this definition is incomplete. It should be: "the highest degree of development of a technique to suit *your particular needs* at a particular time."

With the double "particulars" - needs and time - what constitutes state of the art is bound to change, and that is what happens with trading systems. In a trading system, the features that you need are going to change almost a soon as you get your hands on that trading system. Not only that, the purpose of the system often changes.

For instance, a system may be put in to give a trader market access. Then another trader or two gets the system. Soon, the system ends up with a second objective, which is just as important as the first one - maybe allowing risk management across all the traders. The system could have been state of the art at market access, but that's not good enough anymore - it now has to do inter trader processing. And that is another lesson - not only will the features of your trading system change and expand, but so will its fundamental objectives.

The way everyone deals with this issue is to implement flexible, open systems. Almost any system you work with today, whether you are building or buying is going to be advertised as "open". But as George Orwell said, all animals are equal, but some are more equal than others." The lesson is that "open" is relative.

When you are talking about openness, you are really talking about integration and extensibility. All kinds of integration issues will come up, but the ones that are really annoying and dangerous are the little nit picky ones. These often show up way down the road, and sometimes it is too late to design for them. So dangerous shortcuts are taken, such as hardwiring a solution, which leads to reduced flexibility and openness later on. This makes it harder to stay sate of the art

An example is symbology. Take futures symbols. There is a rough standard here, but everyone has their own variation. So you might be using one symbol variant to get your market data, another one to talk to the broker or exchange, and maybe a third one internally, for you back office and risk management systems. A little thing like symbology can keep a system from going live.

The lesson here is to assume these issues will come up and have enough time and flexibility to deal with them. Flexibility is also a relative term. For instance, a system may be muti-currency capable. Sometimes, all that means is that the system can create orders for instruments denominated in different currencies. But a trading system may also need to let the user know what is going on, show a live running P&L, etc. Just because you can get a foreign instrument off to the market does not necessarily mean you can report on your portfolio real time in whatever currency you choose.

And no matter how state of the art your system is, at some point, something will go wrong. It could be user error, a piece of hardware or software could fail, it could be on your end or the other end, but something unexpected will happen. Lesson: you need to plan for this and build this planning into your trading system.

4th Story's software is a platform for automated algorithmic trading systems and runs our customers' very complex business logic. From the get go, we decided that we would not be a black box, but a transparent box just for this reason. So we built in all kinds of visibility features. This translated into much time saved in developing and implementing trading strategies by being able to look at the system and logs and see every decision the strategy made and what logical process it went through to make those decisions.

Finally, one needs to consider whether to build or buy. A commonly accepted wisdom is to build when it is strategic to your business or gives you competitive advantage. But in reality, organizations don't build everything that is strategic, though. For instance, a CRM system is strategic to many businesses, but there are not a lot of them that think it is a good idea to build one themselves.

Competitive advantage is another story. There is a case for building when you can gain a leg up on the competition. If you need an advanced strategy / trading system, it is usually because you want to do something unique – add your own special sauce. For instance, maybe you have some special strategies or algorithms you want to implement.

So if you have a great idea, should you build it out? Absolutely. But do you gain competitive advantage from writing the infrastructure around it? Only if that infrastructure lets you do something a commercial package does not.

The reality is that you will likely have to do some building if you have something special. The trick is building appropriately, and not re-inventing the wheel. Companies like 4th Story build so you can build less. If we do our job right, a lot less.

Here are some things one hears when discussing this issue.

- We are unique
  - Our stuff is like no-one else's
  - A commercial product will never be flexible enough for us

This cuts both ways – on the one hand all of us have had vendor relationships that promised more than they delivered.

On the other hand, from the vendor perspective, we often see clients over estimating or over complicating their problem. And the reality is, that in many cases, your needs are not too far off from next guy's – you just may have a different twist on the matter, or have implemented your special sauce better.

- If we work with a vendor, they might find out about our special sauce
- One advantage for customers to using open applications like from vendors to base their system on is that they were specifically designed to preserve the 'special-ness' of their special sauce.

But this also cuts both ways. Remember that the programmer or strategist on the team that built a spreadsheet or custom software can leave at any time. Unless people have been cross trained well, and/or the firm built its own internal standardized infrastructure, it is possible that no one there will have any idea how the spreadsheet or software works.

So when building, make sure to budget money and TIME for documentation

- We have more control & can do it right

Yes, maybe. But in our field of automated trading, we often find that the hedge funds and prop desks we talk to have hired quants and scientists (as they should). These folks may be able to get some code to work, but they are not experienced enterprise or commercial software developers. The other thing to remember is that commercial software probably has already accommodated use cases that you may have not anticipated yet, but may well need in the future and have not designed for.

Also, a good commercial application has to be supportable, as any support costs eat into the vendor's profit margin, while support for a bespoke application can also be thought of as job security for the developers.

- A commercial solution is more expensive

Could be, but push the numbers. Here is an example of an internally built system. The firm was semi happy with it, as it was completed on budget, but does not have all of the functionality they need.

> 6 person team for 1.5 years, now down to 4 persons
> Assume fully loaded cost of $120,000 per person

Year one		720
Year two	360 + 240 =	600
Years three – five		1,440
Total		2,760

The total cost is about 550k / year. On the plus side, costs won't be much above ~500k/year. On the minus side, costs won't be much below ~500k/year.

In addition, one needs to factor in these additional considerations:

- 18 months time to market
- $1M cost to develop
- 3 individuals who know how it works, and as maintenance is not a sexy role, they will probably move on soon

Where to draw the line between what to build vs. what to buy is one of the most difficult lessons. When making this decision, here are some issues to consider, remembering that state of the art means looking at your particular needs and abilities.

- What's the real cost, including opportunity cost in time to market?
- What is the expertise of your people resources?
- Where can you best add value?

- Where are you making trade offs?

The final lesson is that you have to be honest with yourself in considering these issues. It takes a pretty honest person to say that they cannot do something as well as someone else, and the right answer is to have someone/something else do it. That goes both for vendors as well as internal developers.

Outpacing Moore's Law – Reducing Latency and Jitter Using Advances in Operating Systems

By Ambreesh Khanna, Sun

1. Introduction

There is a parallel universe of IT consumers that is expanding rapidly. It contains unusually demanding customers such as Federal Express, which needs big computers to route trucks and aircraft efficiently; drug firms that need to model complex molecules; weather and climate forecasters; fast-growing 'Web 2.0' start-ups that handle huge amounts of data such as video and blogging sites[cxlviii]; and Capital Markets firms which have seen their "perfect storm" maturing, with demands for latency and throughput accelerating in the face of growing data volumes, whilst requiring their datacenters to be more green.

Greg Papadopoulos, Sun Microsystems CTO, calls this expanding constellation of clients a 'red-shift' market. As the universe expands, light from galaxies moving away from Earth appears to shift toward the longer (and hence redder) wavelengths of the spectrum[cxlix]. These clients are characterized by a common theme – their technology needs outpace Moore's Law, making "throwing hardware" at the problem a perfunctory exercise.

The growth in data volumes in Capital Markets can be attributed to a variety of factors – regulatory mandates such as RegNMS and MiFID, penny quoting of options, proliferation of trading venues, and electronic trading, which not only increases trading volumes but also sharply increases the ratio of quotes and cancellations to executions. The recent "sub-prime" crisis saw the volatility of the US markets, and subsequently of the global markets, reach a new high – resulting in abnormally high spikes in market data volumes. Systems designed to handle data volumes of last year could not keep up at most firms, as they were designed to handle a much smaller *throughput*[cl] of data.

External events create opportunities for profit, if one can take advantage of the arbitrage opportunities that arise. These opportunities dissipate within fractions of a second, and hence responding to these events within a very short period of time is critical. The meteoric rise of electronic trading is a testament to this fact, as computers can respond to events much quicker than humans can. *Latency* is defined as the time lag between an event occurring and the response to it (a more detailed definition is in Section 2 below). Systems that provide information about external events such as Market Data systems, and systems that respond such as CEP (complex event processing) systems and algorithmic trading systems must exhibit low latency.

Typically latency and throughput are negatively correlated. As one tries to increase the amount of data flow through a system, the time it takes to respond to each data packet increases. As an example, an 8-socket AMD based Sun Fire™ X4600 server with Solaris™ 10 can handle 282,000 OPRA messages/sec at 450µs (microsecond) latency, and can handle 359,000 OPRA messages/sec at 511µs latency[cli]. A standard technique for optimizing trading systems is to fix one of the two variables, and push the system and software to achieve the best result for the other. With the OPRA benchmark mentioned above, the goal was to achieve the highest possible throughput while keeping latency below the 1ms (millisecond) bound.

A critical trait of latency is its predictability, the guarantee that an application will respond within a bounded time interval to an external event. *Jitter* is defined as the variability from this interval. Jitter causes applications to behave in unpredictable ways, the anathema of a low latency trading environment. The proliferation of algorithmic trading is driving the focus on reducing or even eliminating jitter, thus allowing exploitation of arbitrage opportunities in a predictable fashion.

Cost is the final factor in deploying high throughput, low latency and low jitter systems. Acquisition costs are a small fraction of the total cost of implementing such systems – recurring costs such as power, cooling, datacenter space and networking infrastructure contribute a much larger percentage. Implementing niche and expensive technologies only provide transitory relief, as general purpose systems and advances in software technologies have a tendency of catching up quickly and providing similar reprieve at a much lower cost.

2. Latency Defined

Trading applications respond to external events, typically signalled via market data. Latency is defined as the time between the occurrence of the external event – such as the arrival of a market data packet – and the trading application's response to it.

A series of events occur when a Server receives the notification of an external event, broadly involving the hardware, Operating System (OS) and trading application.

- The network hardware adapter receives the network packet and uses a finite amount of time to pass this packet to the CPU via a hardware interrupt. The CPU subsequently passes this interrupt to the OS.
- The OS now needs to run its interrupt handler to process this packet, and likely bumps some running application off the CPU to accomplish this. The interrupt handler runs and queues the network packet for the trading application to consume and returns.

The trading application waiting for this packet is now put on a queue of applications which are "ready to run", since its dependence on the arrival of the network packet is satisfied. Depending on its priority, it could bump some other application currently running on the CPU. The trading application now begins processing this network packet, potentially causing yet another series of delays while its context is "faulted in" by the OS, and eventually responds.

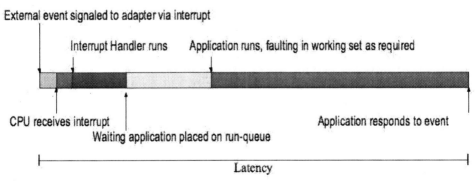

Figure A - Latency

As can be seen in Figure A, there are various contributors to latency. The hardware vendor is clearly responsible for the amount of time spent between the server receiving the interrupt and the OS being notified. The OS vendor is responsible for the time spent between the OS receiving this signal and the waiting application being put on the CPU to run. The remainder of the latency could be viewed as application specific – the time spent between the application being put on the CPU and it responding to the event. However the OS vendor is responsible for other runtime specifics, such as paging the application's working set in, allowing the application to lock its pages in memory to prevent paging, not bumping this latency sensitive application off the CPU for processing other higher priority tasks such as interrupts, allowing the application to use the CPU without lowering its priority etc. These factors contribute to the unpredictability of application latency, thus introducing jitter.

3. An Unusual Technology for Increasing Throughput, Reducing Latency and Reducing Cost – a Reuters RMDS Case Study

Reuters RMDS is one of the most prolific market data systems on the planet. Providing consolidated and direct market feeds, it is deployed at most major sell-side and buy-side firms. Due to its inherently single threaded nature, RMDS is an application that lends itself to horizontal scaling, with two-socket systems typically representing the optimum environment. This results in a large number of small systems being deployed, most of which are underutilized. With the number of CPU cores increasing, most of the CPU capacity of these systems remains unused while the systems continue to consume power, generate heat and use large amounts of datacenter space.

For most financial institutions, space and power constraints are an increasingly limiting factor in the deployment of new systems. Additionally there is an executive focus in many companies on their environmental impact . Alternative approaches are therefore needed to support continued volume growth and increases in performance, while addressing the need for more effective use of power and space by driving up utilization rates. It behooves systems vendors to suggest such approaches to effectively manage environmental effects of their systems, without negatively impacting the performance curve of these 'red-shift' applications.

The Solaris™10 Operating System from Sun Microsystems, released in March 2005, is supported on many platforms, including AMD and Intel based systems from Sun, IBM, HP and Dell. Many large banks have deployments of Solaris 10 Solaris 10 introduced a number of interesting features, such as Containers, DTrace, Service Management Facility, ZFS, networking enhancements such as FireEngine and Yosemite, and a number of security enhancements including Trusted Solaris. For some time, Solaris on SPARC, AMD and Intel based systems has been the preferred deployment platform for customers implementing RMDS and its predecessor products.

Solaris Containers are an interesting technology for consolidating multiple systems into one, without having a detrimental impact on performance. They are available on all platforms on which Solaris 10 is supported. Containers allow individual instances of Solaris 10 to be "installed" and "booted" within a single global instance of Solaris 10. Each of these non-global Containers appear as individual Solaris instances, each with their own identity, user namespace, inter-process communication namespace and network namespace (Figure B). They are security and fault contained; thus one non-global Container does not have the ability to view the data or resources of another Container. Faults inside one non-global Container cannot propagate into any other container.

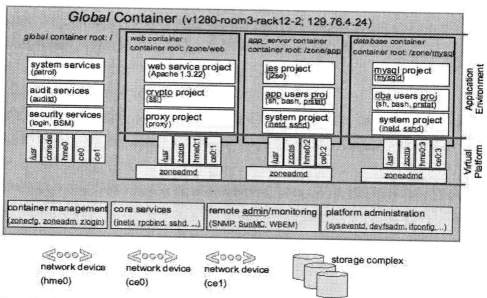

Figure B – Solaris Containers

The administration model of Containers is simple – the administrator for the global Container has the ability to affect the entire system, including all the non-global Containers. A kernel patch applied in the global Container instantly propagates to all installed non-global Containers, since the global and non-global Containers share the same copy of the kernel. Administrators of non-global Containers, however, have the ability to affect only the Container they are responsible for. They can apply application level patches, and can reboot their non-global Container. They however do not have the ability to make a change affecting the entire system such as changing the system time or rebooting the system.

Resources may be dedicated to Containers. These resources include CPU, memory and network bandwidth. Each Container has the ability to run with a different default scheduling class, thus affecting runtime behavior for only the applications running within that Container.

3.1 Increasing Throughput

A typical small RMDS installation is shown in Figure C, with eight dual-socket systems deployed. Each individual RMDS module is deployed on its own dedicated system, and certain modules are replicated for throughput and redundancy needs.

Since the RMDS modules are single-threaded, they typically end up consuming one of the four available cores (dual socket systems using dual-core CPUs). The transport software used for communication between the components such as TIBCO RV or Reuters RRCP consumes one more core. This leave two cores un-utlized.

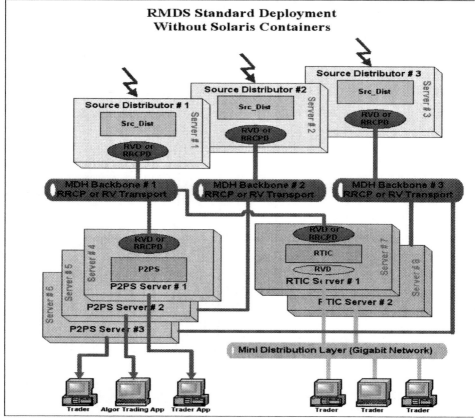

Figure C – Typical RMDS deployment

As an alternative deployment architecture one could use Solaris Containers and deploy each RMDS module in its own Container. Each Container behaves as a separate system, thus allowing RMDS to scale horizontally. As market data volumes increase and individual modules reach their processing limits, additional modules can be simply implemented in their own Container on the same system, as long as the system has available physical resources. This allows higher throughput to be driven through the same system.

Figure D shows the the eight RMDS modules from Figure C consolidated on a single Solaris 10 instance, using eight Containers. Each instance of the RMDS module still processes the incoming market data independently, exactly the same way it does on its own dedicated system. The total throughput of the consolidated system is the sum of the individual throughput rates of each relevant module. Using an eight socket server, this deployment would consume all available 16 cores, thus essentially doubling the throughput within a given footprint (look at the Performance per Rack Unit metric in Table 3 Section 3.3 – *Reducing Cost*).

3.2 Reducing Latency

Use of Solaris Containers also reduces the network latency between different RMDS modules when compared with the typical RMDS implementation using dedicated systems. When communicating between Containers, Solaris determines that the end-points are on the same physical system and uses the "short circuited" loopback interface. This approach significantly reduces the network latency introduced by the presence of physical network hops when modules are deployed on physically discrete systems.

The reduced latency benefits of Containers extend beyond communication between just RMDS modules. With the prolific use of electronic trading, the importance of minimizing latency across the entire trading ecosystem is increasingly important. In addition to implementing RMDS modules on a system with Containers, it is possible to create Containers which run other applications in the trading portfolio. As an example, a market data consuming trading application and the RMDS Point-To-Point Server (P2PS) module could be run on two Containers on the same system. The communication between P2PS and the trading application will now be at memory speeds, typically measured in nanoseconds, rather than over the physical network, typically measured in microseconds.

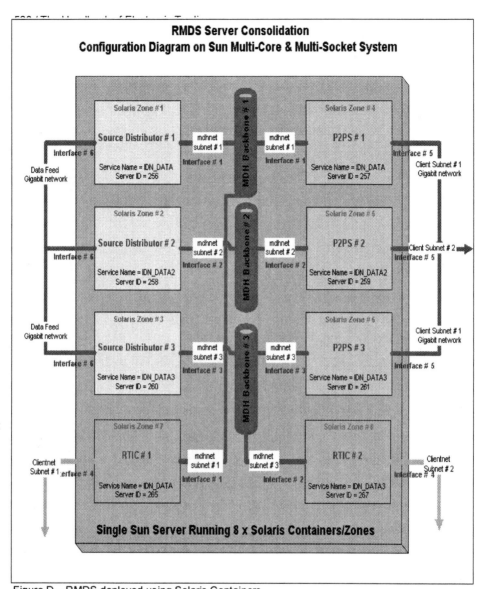

Figure D – RMDS deployed using Solaris Containers

3.3 Reducing Cost

Another significant advantage of deploying RMDS in Solaris Containers is the reduced power, cooling and space footprint. The example above proposes the use of a Sun Fire X4600, an 8-socket AMD system available today with dual-core CPUs. With this example deployment, the potential datacenter savings are tabulated below in Table 2. Table 1 shows the typical physical characteristics of the Sun Fire X4100, a 2-socket AMD system, and the Sun Fire X4600. Table 3 shows the performance characteristics for each deployment scenario on a per rack unit and per watt metric, assuming 1M messages/second being handled by each deployment. The Containers deployment would likely handle a higher throughput due to the latency considerations mentioned earlier.

Table 1 – Physical characteristics of the Sun Fire™ X4100 and X4600 servers

	CPU Sockets	Total Cores	Rack Units	Typical System Power Draw (Watts)	On-board Network Ports	Typical Cooling Power required (BTU/hr)
Sun Fire X4100	2	4	1	359	4	1396
Sun Fire X4600	8	16	4	1161	4	5296

Table 2 – Potential datacenter savings by deploying Containers

	Total Rack Units	Total System Power Draw	Total Network Drops required	Total Cooling Power required
Typical Deployment (using 8 X4100 servers)	8	2872	16	11168
Containers Deployment (using 8 Containers on 1 X4600)	4 (50% less)	1161 (60% less)	6 (62% less)	5296 (52% less)

Table 3 – Key performance metrics

	Aggregated Throughput	Performance/RU	Performance/Watt	Performance/Network Port
Typical Deployment	1000000	125000	348	62500
Containers Deployment	1000000	250000	841	166667

As is clearly evident from Table 3, the Containers deployment scenario offers 2X the performance per rack unit, and 2.5X the performance per Watt and per network port, thus significantly reducing the cost of deploying a market data application while improving throughput and latency.

Even though this case study uses Reuters RMDS as an example, any application that responds to external events signaled via the network and/or communicates with other applications using the network will benefit from this approach.

4. Other Techniques for Reducing Latency and Jitter

Application developers should look to Operating System vendors to provide features to help reduce latency and jitter. These include techniques to enable latency sensitive applications to get high priority over all other applications, for them to get preferential access to all resources on the system and to observe, analyze and debug latency and jitter problems in production. The following sections detail some of these available techniques in Solaris 10.

4.1 Scheduling Classes

Scheduling classes are a mechanism for an OS to make available a limited set of CPU resources to a larger set of applications. Different scheduling classes have different priority ranges; thus assigning an application to a class with a higher priority would allow it to get preferential treatment over applications assigned a lower priority within the same class, or a class with a lower priority range.

Solaris 10 defines six distinct scheduling classes, all with varying characteristics. Each Scheduling Class has a "local" or "user" range of priorities. Depending on the Class, the Scheduler can change the user priority of a running thread on the fly; moving a thread to a different class however requires manual intervention with appropriate privileges. The local priorities map onto a Global Priority range, and it is this range that determines the system-wide priority of the thread.

As can be seen from Figure E, Timesharing (TS), Interactive (IA), Fixed Priority (FX) and the Fair Share Scheduling (FSS) classes map onto the lowest global priority range. TS is the default scheduling class. The FX class introduces the concept of Fixed Priority scheduling. Processes in the FX class never have their priorities adjusted by the scheduler. Note that FX maps to the global priority range 0-60, whereas TS, IA and FSS map to 0-59. *This allows processes assigned to FX at priority 60 to run at higher priority than all user processes in the TS, IA and FSS classes.*

The Realtime (RT) class is fixed priority, and provides a priority range for user threads higher than all other user and OS threads on the system. The exception is the interrupt priority range, which maps to a global range higher than RT. The Solaris RT scheduling class is POSIX 1003.1b compliant, and allows users to specify First-In-First-Out or Round-Robin scheduling policy. The Solaris kernel is fully preemptable, which makes Solaris a true real time OS.

One source of jitter in an application is the preemption of its threads by higher priority threads. Another is the lowering of the priority of one or more of its threads by the Scheduler. Both can be mitigated by putting the relevant threads in a fixed high priority scheduling class – FX or RT. Using FX at priority 60 for these threads allow them to run at a priority level higher than any other user threads on the system, thus preventing them from being preempted by any other user threads. Unless there are RT threads running on the system, the only threads running at a higher priority are the threads in the SYS class and the interrupt threads, which is likely desirable for mature Operating Systems. Alternatively, running the relevant threads in RT make them higher priority than even the kernel threads, allowing rogue threads to hijack the system. The FX class at priority 60 is a safer alternative, and is available only on Solaris.

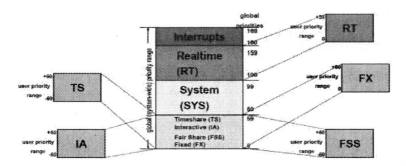

Figure E – Scheduling Classes

4.2 Processor Binding

Solaris allows applications to be bound to specific CPUs, ensuring that these applications only run on the CPUs they are bound to, thus giving these applications warm caches. However this mechanism does not prevent other unbound threads from running on these CPUs, thus somewhat reducing the warm cache effect. Solaris 2.6 introduced the concept of Processor Sets, which are groups of specific CPUs. Threads can be bound to a processor set, and only these bound threads run on the CPUs assigned to this processor set. This mechanism mitigates the processor binding problem mentioned above.

Creating one or more processor sets and binding applications to them eliminates jitter caused by cache misses.

4.3 Interrupt Shielding

Solaris 7 introduced the concept of preventing a CPU handling unbound interrupts – interrupt shielding. Shielding interrupts on a CPU ensures that any application running on this CPU would not be preempted by interrupt processing, since interrupt threads run at the highest priority on the system and will bump the latency sensitive application that might be running on this CPU. Both individual CPUs and Processor Sets can be interrupt shielded.

4.4 Memory Locking

All modern Operating Systems support the concept of virtual memory, which allows the OS to pretend to have more physical memory than is actually installed. It does this by using the disk as an extension of the physical memory, by paging on demand. Since paging involves the disk subsystem, one needs to be very aware of the detrimental effects of paging since disks are about 6 orders of magnitude slower than physical memory (nanosecond vs. millisecond access times). Solaris allows locking of an application's pages into memory. For any latency sensitive application, all memory should be pre-faulted (allocated and touched) and then locked down.

4.5 Observability

Solaris 10 introduced DTrace, a dynamic tracing mechanism. With DTrace, all of the above defined potential sources of jitter and latency can easily be identified and quantified. Since DTrace has no disabled probe-effect and very low enabled probe-effect, and can be used to dynamically instrument the system and any running application, it serves as the perfect tool to observe sources of unwanted latency and jitter affecting an application.

For instance, if one wanted to quantify the number and sources of preemption affecting an application, a few simple commands show which processes were preempted, by whom, and the number of times it occurred. Also, the current priorities of the preemptor and preempted are identified. This can be used as a clear picture to determine if, for instance, the FX scheduling class would be a candidate to address the issue. A few additional commands can show the amount of time the application spent waiting for a free CPU in the case of a preemption.

Another common source of latency and jitter is lock contention within an application. Heavily contended locks will cause competing threads to spin and then block (if the lock cannot be acquired) until the lock is released. This spin and block time can become quite substantial and cause serious jitter in an application as the number of threads competing for locks becomes larger, or if the critical sections are substantial. A single DTrace command can be used to identify heavily contended locks and to quantify the amount of time spent competing for these locks.

D-light is a Sun Studio DTrace GUI which makes DTrace data easier to observe and decipher. Another part of the Studio toolset, the Performance Analyzer is a premier performance analysis tool that allows clock based and hardware counter based statistical profiling of applications. A powerful GUI makes attribution of time to specific functions, source and assembler code straightforward. The Compiler Commentary Studio option explains what optimizations were done to compiled code. This significantly improves understanding of how the compiler optimizes code, and allows the user to make more optimal use of compiler options and determine what, if any, code should be reorganized.

4.6 Realtime Java

Java is used by financial firms worldwide for various applications, including trading applications. The inherent nature of Java makes it an ideal platform for application development, both due to the shortened application development lifecycle and application portability. However Java applications still suffer from the perception of being non-deterministic in nature, primarily due to the Garbage Collection process. As the name suggests, GC cleans up freed memory and places it in a free memory pool to be reused. However the GC routines run in an unpredictable fashion, depending primarily on the application's memory consumption and freeing patterns and the JVM tuning parameters.

The JVM thread runs at a high priority, which implies preemption and preference being given to the GC thread, thus introducing significant jitter.

Sun's implementation of the Real-Time Specification for Java (RTSJ), the Java RTS product, enables realtime processing by using techniques that protect low latency threads from the garbage collector. These threads will run at the highest priority and they will interrupt any and all other activity on the system to accomplish their tasks. This means that trading systems can confidently monitor the market and take action well within the window of opportunity. Sun's Java RTS system has a latency of 20 microseconds on it's reference platform, a relatively modest Sun Fire V240 running dual 1 GHz processors and Solaris 10.

Java RTS is fully compatible with standard J2SE applications, allowing customers to run their existing J2SE code on Java RTS without any failures. They can then add the necessary real-time components as needed.

5 Conclusion

Advances in Operating System technologies allow latency sensitive applications to keep pace with the ever increasing data rates in Capital Markets – even when these increases outpace Moore's law. These increasing data rates, coupled with space, power and cooling constraints being placed on datacenters, make it imperative that application developers pay closer attention to software techniques available today to improve throughput and lower latency of their applications, without relying solely on hardware upgrades. We have seen dramatic application performance improvements by simply applying software tuning techniques, in most cases without making code modifications. Tools such as Sun Studio Compilers and DTrace have been effective in identifying and eliminating bottlenecks in applications. Technologies such as Containers have been useful in consolidating and reducing network latencies in multi process applications.

Moore's Law makes available almost double the number of transistors to CPU designers every 18 to 24 months. All CPU manufacturers are now using these extra transistors to build multi-core CPUs, instead of dramatically increasing CPU frequency. As of today, Sun is shipping systems built using a 64-thread CPU. Intel is already shipping a 4-core CPU, and AMD will soon ship its 4-core CPU. It is nearly impossible to purchase a server which has fewer than 4 cores today, and soon the smallest enterprise class servers will have a minimum of 8 cores. Applications need to be built to take advantage of these large numbers of cores. Sun Studio 12 compilers have the ability to multi-thread C/C++ code, if recompiled with the appropriate options. Solaris is a highly scalable OS, , with proven ability to scale across hundreds of CPUs. Technologies such as Containers allow applications to be consolidated on multi-core systems if the applications are not capable of leveraging multi-core CPUs.

Many performance assumptions made about trading systems in 2006 are now invalid. No one anticipated the data rates that we are experiencing today. It behooves application developers and architects to re-examine their platform choices and to invest in technologies that will allow their applications to handle the throughput and latency requirements being demanded today and in the near future, while reducing datacenter footprint.

Buy vs. Build:
An Executive Approach to Business Strategy and Technology in the Capital Markets

by John Barun, Capital Markets Consulting

This chapter is devoted to the "buy vs. build" question for technical systems needed by capital markets companies. When does it make sense to buy an existing software product? When should you seriously consider building a custom system? Are there other choices? This discussion could quickly become complicated when you consider the many types of financial service firms that generally fall into the categories of buy-side, sell-side, exchanges, insurance and banks. It could be further complicated if you consider the various systems these firms have to choose, ranging from order management, execution management, direct market access, algorithmic trading, risk analysis, clearing, regulatory compliance & reporting, and many others. With so many combinations of firm and software types to choose from, we will not dive into the details of very specific firm needs and particular software comparisons. Instead we discuss the buy vs. build concepts at a high level so that they will be useful in various decision making situations.

Executives and owners of capital markets firms are witnessing a dramatic revolution as the industry migrates into the electronic realm. Generations to come will read about this time in the history books. Exchange floors are closing due to computerization, computer algorithms are replacing humans at an amazing rate, phones and fax machines might still be in use but they are obsolete, the list of changes goes on and on. It has become a global market and competitive pressures are forcing successful firms to work longer, harder and smarter to maintain their edge. Changes to the industry are accelerating with each passing year and capital markets firms are finding that successful business strategies have become heavily dependent on technology to achieve their goals. Exchanges, banks, mutual funds, clearing firms, hedge funds, proprietary trading companies, traditional asset managers and most other firms in the industry are finding they are unable to compete without innovative technology to create competitive advantages.

The question of buy vs. build is a multi-dimensional problem. We have separated the issue into several key aspects and will discuss each of them in turn. These dimensions include:

- Company and marketplace stages
- Strategic and tactical technology projects
- The risk of a hidden agenda
- We have decided to buy - what process should we follow?
- We have decided to build - what are the risks?
- The hybrid solution

Company and Marketplace Stages:

Companies can be classified into five categories. These categories relate to their competitive positions and actions in the overall marketplace, specifically:

1. Innovator
Innovators are doing things that most of their competitors have not even dreamed of yet. These are visionary firms that recognize new challenges and opportunities long before the rest of the marketplace.

2. Early Leader
Early leaders are doing things that many of their competitors have recognized as something needed in the marketplace, but the competition has not acted on it yet.

3. Mature Adopter
Mature adopters mostly stay with the pack of similar firms. They adopt new capabilities once the market has started to mature and they see the need to stay competitive. Much of their competition is adding similar capabilities.

4. Slow Adopter
Slow adopters are playing catch up since many of their competitors already have new capabilities and these firms have finally decided to bite the bullet and make the needed changes.

5. Late Adopter
Late adopters are firms that have lost customers or have not kept pace with the growth rate of their competitors due to the superior offerings of their competition. These firms have finally decided to make the changes the rest of the marketplace has already made.

While these categories are intended to provide a clear classification for a given firm, keep in mind that one firm could be an innovator in some areas of their business and simultaneously be a late adopter in other areas.

Some Rules of Thumb:

If a firm is an innovator or early adopter, there are no vendor solutions capable of meeting its needs. As a general rule, the only choice is to custom build a solution. In some cases, a hybrid approach might be possible.

If a firm is a mature adopter, there are now many vendors competing with "off-the-shelf" products to choose. In this stage, the vendor solutions might meet many of the firm's needs, but some capabilities might still be missing. Mature adopters can choose to buy a solution, custom build one, or a hybrid choice can be selected.

If a firm is a slow or late adopter, many vendors have sophisticated solutions that can meet most of the firm's needs. As a general rule, firms in these categories should buy a solution.

Strategic and Tactical Technology Projects:

In the financial markets industry, technology has become a mandatory enabler to achieve business goals. Success in today's capital markets environment comes down to strategic plans and leveraging technology to execute those plans. An important dimension of the buy vs. build choice requires an understanding of "strategic technology projects" and "tactical technology projects".

What is a "strategic technology project"? Strategic technology projects are those projects that will enable the execution of a company's business plans to create competitive advantages and ultimately yield greater profits. These are projects that are driven by the business need to compete and, if implemented correctly, will have significant and measurable benefits to the firm. They could be technology projects that execute tactical business functions in an innovative way, they could be projects to combine the technologies of two firms in a merger, they could be projects to improve efficiency and reduce costs, or they could be any number of projects to select and/or build technology that create competitive advantages for a business. Ultimately, capital markets firms will not thrive unless they can successfully execute their business strategy.

What is a "tactical technology project"? Tactical technology projects are those projects that are not tied directly to the execution of the company's strategic business plans and where the value to the business is relatively low. These projects might include cost reducing measures, improvement of efficiency, responses to external forces (such as regulatory changes), closing the gap with your competition (often by developing capabilities that resemble a competitor's current advantage) and many other projects that are really patches to outstanding issues. Generally speaking, the value of a tactical technology project is relatively low to the business. If the value to the business would be high, it would be considered a strategic technology project.

If you are about to launch a new project, you need to determine if you are dealing with a strategic technology project. What is the impact a successful project will have on the business? What are the consequences if there are project delays or failure? If the impact of success is small or the consequences of failure are minimal, don't sweat it. If the impact and consequences are significant and the strategic business plans depend on success, you have a strategic technology project on your hands.

Why was it important to define strategic technology and tactical technology projects in a build vs. buy discussion? Generally speaking, strategic technology projects have unique demands that require either a build or a hybrid approach. Tactical technology projects should lean in the direction of buying existing solutions.

The Risk of a Hidden Agenda:

When asked, a firm's management team member will almost never admit that there is a hidden agenda. The official answer will always be in the best interest of the company. Based on almost two decades of consulting experience, the reality of the situation is that some people in key roles will place a higher priority on their personal career goals than on corporate goals. The hidden agenda appears most frequently when the individual's personal goals are out of alignment with the corporate goals. In these instances, you might end up with decisions that are tainted by the hidden agenda.

Unfortunately, senior management at many firms do not delegate responsibilities to their technology groups, they abdicate their responsibilities. Delegation is the process of giving away responsibility for detailed tasks, but maintaining control of the overall goals, deadlines and constraints. Abdication of responsibilities means giving up control of the overall goals, deadlines and constraints. Many managers think they are delegating when in fact they are abdicating. Abdication often happens without the leader realizing it.

If you have ever seen a debate, certain facts get highlighted while others get ignored in the name of winning the argument. The same holds true in the case of a hidden agenda. Certain facts are highlighted and others get ignored in the name of achieving their agenda even if they could have a negative impact on the firm's future success. A few of the blatant examples include:

Empire Building

This is the case where your decision maker has a desire to grow the size of the staff reporting to him. A choice of building a custom system helps him achieve this goal if additional hires are required to complete the work. Even if there are available choices to buy a reasonable solution, this person will find ways to justify a build decision.

Resume Padding

This is the case where your decision maker has a desire to gain specific experience to make their resume look better. Depending on the experience this person is seeking, they could choose building or buying a system that meets their personal need. Again, this decision maker will find ways to justify their decision.

Helping Out a Friend

This is the case where your decision maker has a friend that they are looking to help. Their friend might work for a vendor and the decision will be skewed in their favor no matter how much better another solution might be. This decision maker will find creative ways to justify their decision.

Senior management needs to keep a constant lookout for the hidden agenda. Do not allow techno speak to prevent you from asking the right questions to ensure ultimate success. Your people should be able to explain and justify their technical decisions in business terms based on your highest priority business objectives. Don't allow the objectives or desired capabilities to be skewed in favor of a particular choice. Be cautious of the recommendations you receive in response to hidden agendas. There must be business justification for technology decisions! If they can't tie their technical decisions to the strategic goals of your business, you have trouble. If they give you techno babble and can't speak in business terms, don't walk away, run!

We Have Decided to Buy - What Process Should We Follow?

Assuming that you have multiple vendor choices, the buy process should be structured around making the best choice for your needs. For firms that have one decision maker, a common mistake often made is to simply get a demo of the vendor systems and allowing your gut reaction to make the decision for you. This runs the risk of making an emotional decision or basing the decision on a neat feature that might not even be a requirement (often neglecting the fact that a core requirement is not handled by the system).

For significant purchases, a multi-step process is often required to make a good choice. The following steps represent a typical buy process:

1. Requirements Definition
Before gathering information from vendors, you need to first define and document the capabilities that are required for the system to be useful. These should be prioritized into categories of "critical", "high priority" and "nice to have". All the stakeholders must participate in the definition of the requirements to ensure coverage and buy in.

2. Request For Information (RFI)
The RFI is often used to gather preliminary information from the various vendors. This allows you to gather information regarding the capabilities they bring to the table. A critical aspect to the RFI is the assessment of the vendor's health as a company. Before you enter into any important and long-term relationship with a vendor, it is critical in this stage to gather information about their health and staying power over the next several years.

3. Requirements Refinement
Now that you have gathered information about the vendor capabilities, you need to compare their capabilities to your documented requirements. This process usually helps identify additional critical capabilities that might have been missed in the requirements definition.

4. Request for Proposal (RFP)
The RFP is a formal request that is intended to gather very specific information about each vendor's capabilities in a way that will allow the different solutions to be compared to each other in a normalized way. An RFP is a structured process that sets expectations, deadlines and a process for all vendors to follow that will gather the critical information while efficiently using your resources.

By following a standard process for all of your significant buy decisions, the complexity in making a decision is greatly simplified. The process helps prioritize requirements and weeds out risky or bad choices. Most importantly, a formal decision making process that is properly managed can greatly reduce the risk of employee hidden agendas.

We Have Decided to Build – What Are The Risks?

Successful capital market firms understand risk and go to great lengths to protect themselves against exposure in their trading activities. Unfortunately, when it comes to their strategic technology projects, they very often underestimate or ignore the risks. Understanding the full financial impact of the inherent risks is essential to the success of these strategic projects. Many of the same risk management concepts that apply to money management also apply to technology project risk management. The parameters, controls and mitigation strategies are different, but the truth of the matter is most technology projects do not focus enough time and energy on eliminating or minimizing major risk factors.

There are many reasons that projects fail but they all fall under the general category of improper risk controls and management. Just as trading risks can be managed well, project risks can also be effectively managed. A few of these project risks include:

- Incorrect alignment with strategic business goals
- Conflicting goals between various project stakeholders or stakeholder politics
- Overly optimistic and unrealistic estimates
- Mismatched project team member skills
- Vague, changing or unidentified requirements
- Excessive commercial pressure causing irrational decisions
- Poor project management (including poor communication, lack of discipline in planning, tracking and reporting, lack of accountability practices, ignoring early warning signals or red flags, misrepresentation of progress, etc.)
- Poor project methodology (undisciplined design, development, testing and deployment practices)
- People issues (low morale, personality conflicts, unexpected health problems, disgruntled employees, etc.)
- Lack of change management
- Unidentified risks
- External dependencies
- "Techno sabotage" (both intentional and unintentional)
- Technology "religious wars"

Short of outright failure, cost overruns or delays cause serious consequences. It is quite typical for executives to be fully aware of the outright costs of these overruns, and not have an understanding of the lost opportunity costs. Costs include un-captured revenue, loss of first mover advantages or any number of other lost opportunities. These un-quantified opportunity costs could be significantly greater than any outright costs of the project. Unfortunately these hidden costs are often ignored in the early stages of planning a strategic technology project, and they are rarely woven into an integrated plan to merge strategic vision with technical implementation.

Given this laundry list of reasons that projects miss the intended mark, it might sound like all technology projects are doomed, however, they are not.

We have gathered some basic tips to help reduce the number of stressed out sleepless nights for management. Start by ensuring that your project team has identified all of the project's true stakeholders. Business stakeholders, operations staff, technology groups, and external customers all have interests and needs. Many projects are doomed to failure before they ever begin because the project did not take into consideration the various interests of all stakeholders. Do not underestimate the power of disgruntled or dissatisfied stakeholders! They can quietly bring the project down without you ever knowing what hit you. It is critical to understand, accommodate and align the interests of all true stakeholders very early in the project.

Ask your people if they have identified the major risks to the project's success. What are the people risks? What are the technical risks? What are the external dependencies? What are the unknowns? What contingencies have they built into the project? What are the key criteria they are tracking as early warning indicators of project troubles? What are the critical points of the project and how will they be involved to determine if these critical points are at risk? How are they monitoring and eliminating upcoming roadblocks?

Make sure that everyone (yes everyone) on the project understands the strategic business goals of the project and the definition of success in business terms. This knowledge will create a framework for technical decisions to be founded on the ultimate business goals.

Finally, ensure that your people follow a disciplined project management process and methodology that ensures consistent success.

The Hybrid Solution:

Many firms benefit from taking a hybrid approach to their technology projects. This approach involves buying a vendor solution to meet many of their needs and custom building the remaining features that are unique to their firm. This approach can get you up and running quickly with many of the needed capabilities while simultaneously reducing some of the risks associated with building the entire system from scratch. The decision to go with a hybrid approach requires all of the analysis of the buy decision and all of the risk management for the build aspects.

As a final comment, if you are uncertain about your capabilities or if your project is a strategic technology project, seek out experts to help ensure success.

The Converging Standards Myth of Electronic Trade Communication for Investment Managers

Bennett J. Kaplan, Principal, InvestTech Systems Consulting, Inc.

Introduction

The financial services industry spends billions of dollars on IT development to maintain its competitive edge. For some time now, buy-side investment managers at mutual funds, investment advisors, insurance companies, non-profit organizations and financial institutions have been focusing on automating business processes and building systems that reduce the time from negotiating a trade to settling it. This race to Straight Through Processing (STP), has been accelerated by numerous vendors and service providers all looking to put forth communication standards -- common industry file formats, protocols and other standards that promise a simpler move to STP[clii]. However, in their effort to create these standards and persuade investment managers to adopt them, industry groups, vendors and outsource providers have created overlapping capabilities, competing requirements and left the industry confused over what they do and what they plan to do in the future.

The majority of financial services firms have built a vast array of data feeds, transmissions, extracts and special loading processes in order to address a plethora of communication challenges surrounding electronic trading. The number of processing platforms and messaging standards is overwhelming for buy- and sell-side firms. Choosing a system can be a major issue. With the exception of more complex instruments, such as credit derivatives and leveraged loans, there are two or three sets of trade communication standards for each component of the trade cycle. While many of the systems are often relatively cheap or in some cases are free for the buy-side, the abundance of choices raises additional issues for some because of a reluctance to adopt a system or file format without an industry standard, increasing the amount of risk they assume.

Other firms have given up entirely and have engaged one of a growing number of third party providers to handle either all or a portion of their electronic trade communication needs. While we explore the middle and back office world of electronic trade communication at investment management firms, we'll also explore the latest offerings from leading providers that offer outsource solutions and measure their capabilities and level of success.

All Those "Standards" - A Brief Look Back:

Everyone acknowledges that communication standards are important; that's why we have so many of them - ISO15022, EDIFACT, FIX, ISO 15022, ISO 20022, FpML, MDDL, XBRL, TWIST, ACH and RTGS formats, OMGEO, ... - -- a patchwork of overlapping standards that are supposed to somehow work together. The naming conventions themselves seem geared towards creating confusion. Most of the standards that exist today arose in isolation – in different user communities with different objectives. FIX, for example, was a product of the securities industry, originally developed by Salomon Brothers and Fidelity Investments as a bilateral electronic protocol for pre-trade communication. Typically, users of a standard want to maintain a controlling interest in its content and technical direction because the standard determines to an extent what business they do and how that business is processed. Attempts to merge or rationalize standards often falter because the communities that created them are unwilling to cede control to another group, and, having already implemented them themselves, see little immediate benefit. Hence, the rise of multiple standards.

During the '80s and '90s, after the first electronic trade communication standards were first established, the original user communities expanded and the range of activities covered by each standard grew. As usage and coverage spread, standards began to overlap one another. Today the origination, confirmation, settlement and reconciliation of a transaction may involve the use of several standards, each with different rules, syntax, format, protocol, and communications requirements. The use of XML and the accessibility of cheap and secure connectivity have brought about more standards. Most recently, Service Oriented Architecture (SOA) has emerged and communication standards are once again morphing to adapt. SOA depends on services that produce and consume messages. SOA messages are also dictated by proprietary or public standards.

Supporting all these standards is a major headache for financial institutions. Institutions may not analyze what it costs to stay current; it is seen as an ongoing overhead, part of the cost of doing business and rarely looked at in isolation. But when the numbers are added up, many firms are surprised at the resources dedicated this effort.

Major Challenges of Electronic Trade Communication

So, what are the major challenges of electronic trade communication for investment managers? For starters, each investment manager deals with multiple external data sources and destinations – each requiring specific data layouts and content. Formats exist to communicate indications of interest (IOI), orders, notices of execution (NOE), allocations, settlement and delivery instructions, trade confirmations, trade affirmations and much more. Most every firm has some version of the "spaghetti diagram" that shows all of the connectivity points surrounding the trade process. For the purposes of this chapter, we're leaving all those market data feeds and feeds to/from analytical systems on the sidelines and will focus exclusively on the trade cycle (excluding reference data).

A significant portion of Investment Management Firms' IT budgets are spent on tracking and implementing standards: either interfacing between systems' proprietary data representations and standards, or mapping from one standard to another. The skills required to do this work are scarce and expensive, because with most of the current generation of standards, detailed business knowledge is required to identify correctly the meaning of data being mapped and detailed technical knowledge is required to implement mapping logic and manage the necessary technical infrastructure.

Connectivity points exist internally among investment accounting systems, trading systems, data warehouses or data hubs, but it is the external trade-related connectivity points that are impacted by the numerous standards and force investment management firms to select specific communication protocols. The typical electronic communication that is required of a buy-side investment management firm can be generically detailed as shown in figure 1 on the following page.

Firms have many choices on how to communicate different aspects of trade information throughout the trade process. Many of these connectivity mechanisms (e.g., SWIFT, ISO15022, ISITC, FTP, fax, etc.) are used for more than one part of the trade communication process and firms need to deal with multiple evolving standards (e.g.: SWIFT, XML) that may not address all security types or be accepted by certain institutions.

Figure 1

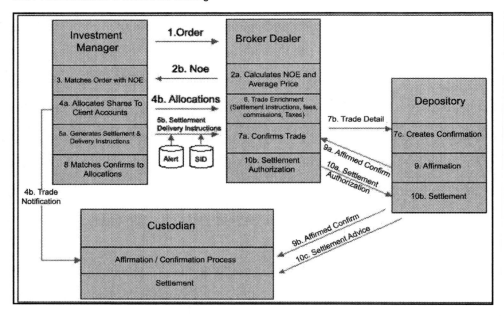

Despite the availability of trade support products in the commercial market today, numerous firms continue to submit, receive and process trade-related data, including allocations and confirms through manual procedures. This is particularly true for non-equity products such as fixed income instruments and derivatives, as well as firms that communicate with custodians that are not enabled to accept electronic files. In an effort to achieve straight through processing, the industry has promoted a central trade matching, electronic confirmation and settlement enrichment utility for processing of institutional trades. Adoption of the central utility has been strong for equities settled by The Depository Trust & Clearing Company ("DTCC"); however, it is not well-utilized for some other security types.

Security Type Impacts Trade Communication Methods

Industry wide higher rates of electronic allocation and affirmation are achieved for equity trades than for fixed income and international trades today. However firms are aiming to raise the rates across all instruments and are beginning to achieve this. Centralized matching is viewed as key to achieving true efficiencies (minimizing cost and errors and improving scalability) in the marketplace. Firms that are moving toward centralized matching feel that this is the answer to "getting away from the assembly line mentality" and developing a more real time, interactive environment.

Ideally the Order Management System should allow for fully integrated and configurable access to centralized matching utilities. While settlement is handled by trade support and settlements, it should ideally begin at the trade's inception in order to fully automate the process. Buy-side investment management best practices as it relates to the trade settlement process (including best practices from the Asset Manager's Forum STP Committee) includes the following:

- Trades matched using centralized matching at block level on Trade Date (90+% frequency)
- Trade allocations communicated on Trade Date - affirmation achieved (90+% frequency)
- Trades communicated electronically to custodian (90+% frequency)
- Trades affirmed with custodian on Trade Date (100% frequency)
- Block level matching, communication of allocations, confirmations and affirmations should all occur via automated systems to increase timeliness and accuracy.
- Block level match should occur within 30 minutes for electronic automatic matching and within one hour for manual matching post trade execution.
- Allocations should be communicated within one to three hours of the block level match based on the settlement timeframe as well as the allocation delivery method.
- Communications between participants are asynchronous (non-sequential)and electronic
- Industry standard electronic formats used for allocations
- Industry standard electronic formats used for confirmations/affirmations
- Internal systems and business processing supports sending trade notifications earlier to brokers (non-batch)
- Settlement systems(s) provide exception based correction GUI
- Manual processing exception based only
- Robust and seamless interfaces between firm's internal systems or vendor systems and Omgeo
- Procedures manual available to all relevant employees

The major trade communication methodologies used by investment managers are shown in Figure 2 on the next page.

Figure 2: Trade Communication Methodologies

Protocol / Communication Product	Used For...	Benefits
FIX (Financial Information eXchange) protocol.	A proprietary protocol to exchange information including allocations, confirmations, affirmations and settlements. This includes information such as getting quotes, market data, and trade orders. FIX covers the early stages of the securities trade life cycle from pre-trade to post-trade. Equities first, being extended to	Facilitates electronic communication through the use of a common language and messaging protocol. A vast number of orders and executions are presently being routed via FIX. Thus, FIX post trade messages become a logical and seamless extension from current FIX order routing flows.

	Fixed Income, Derivatives.	
FIXML	FIX Protocol in XML. FIXML takes a FIX tag value format and represents it in XML. These FIXML messages are then embedded within the traditional FIX headers and trailers.	By utilizing FIX, FIXML minimizes the impact on existing implementations of FIX, requiring just an XML parser for an existing FIX engine to communicate
FpML	FpML® (Financial products Markup Language) is the business information exchange standard for electronic dealing and processing of financial derivatives instruments. It establishes a new protocol for sharing information on, and dealing in swaps, derivatives and structured products. It is based on XML (Extensible Markup Language), the standard meta-language for describing data shared between applications	Provides the standard data content and structure to exchange derivatives transactions electronically. Product coverage includes: IRD: Interest Swaps, Swaptions, FRA's, Caps and Floors, Inflation Swaps and Bullet Payments. FX: Spots, Foreign Exchange Swaps, Forwards and FX Options. Credit: Credit Default Swaps, Credit Default Indexes, and Baskets. Equity: Equity Swaps, Equity Options, Variance Swaps and Total Return Swaps.
ISO 15022	Includes a range of messages covering the later stages starting from trade through to settlement and reconciliation. Second edition was developed to address the emergence of XML and to create a single XML industry standard. This is now a superset that covers the domains of ISO 15022, FIX and FpML.	Leverages the expertise of FPL in the pre-trade domain of orders and executions and leverages SWIFT in the post-trade domain of confirmations and affirmations. Created a standardized use of XML to ensure interoperability across the industry
ISO 20022	UNIFI does not describe the messages themselves; it is a 'recipe' to develop message standards. The main ingredients of this recipe are a development methodology, a registration process and a central repository.	UNIFI will first be used to cover areas not already covered – or poorly covered - by ISO 15022: investment funds, pre-trade/trade, proxy voting, etc... Cost savings benefit from using one message standard for all financial communications.
SWIFTNET	SWIFT is the messaging hub for many clearing and settlement systems in payments, securities, foreign exchange and derivatives.	Mostly used by investment managers and custodians to communicate trade confirmations / affirmations. Also used for bulk payments, cash reporting, collateral management, corporate actions and sending FIX over SWIFT
FTP	Protocol for exchanging files over any network that supports the TCP/IP protocol.	Virtually every computer supports the FTP protocol, but lacks any standardized file format.

Focusing on Emerging "Standards" – FIX:

One of the major protocols that has emerged and is widely utilized by investment managers is FIX. FIX Protocol, Ltd., (FPL) primary purpose is to facilitate electronic communication through the use of a common language and messaging protocol. FIX is a standardized message format designed for the automatic transfer of trading and dealing information. While FIX is a standard, it is by no means the standard. FIX will likely grow significantly in the next few years with new firms using the message protocol for communication and existing users expanding the use of the message protocol for other areas of the trade lifecycle, according to a 2007 report from the **TowerGroup**, a Needham, Mass., consulting firm. The increased use of FIX will result from small to medium sized firms starting to use the message protocol for the first time and existing FIX-enabled firms expanding the use of the message protocol to other asset classes (including fixed income and derivatives) and post-trade functions. The 4.4 version of the message protocol includes post-trade processing functionality.

To date, FPL's focus has been on automating the pre-trade through trade-execution aspects of the trade order life cycle. In these areas, users of FIX protocol have enjoyed great success in expediting equity orders and trade executions, while adoption is growing in fixed income and other product areas. As a result of electronic orders and trade executions using FIX, survey data has shown that FIX users have experienced a significant reduction in operational errors. These positive results can be improved further as FIX messaging is leveraged to perform post trade functions in an end-to-end electronic process flow.

The primary benefits of using FIX messages for allocations, confirmations, affirmations and settlements stem from the fact that a vast number of orders and executions are presently being routed via FIX. Thus, FIX post trade messages become a logical and seamless extension from current FIX order routing flows.

From a technology and straight-through processing perspective, the key advantages of using FIX post trade messages are:

- Post-trade messages can be distributed/received on the same single network utilized for pre-trade and trade execution messages;
- Multiple internal and vendor applications can be consolidated or more tightly integrated using FIX messages/network;
- FIX provides a single solution across many products;
- FIX provides a single solution for many end-points;
- Industry-wide best practices can be developed around a common and open standard rather than a proprietary model.

FIX projects are usually justified on:

- Reduced costs from fewer errors, and automation.
- Increased trading efficiency.
- Access to more liquidity pools.
- Greater ability to demonstrate best execution.

There are three main versions of FIX, and the table below shows the main differences between the most widely adopted versions. The most widespread version being used is 4.2. Most vendors are expecting to have version 4.4 capability in 2006 to 2007 and are just waiting for 'industry momentum' to get them kick-started on the upgrade.

Figure 3: FIX versions

	Version 4.0	Version 4.2	Version 4.4
Year of	1996	2000	2003

Release			
No. of Message Types	20	39	80
No. of Fields	140	442	956
Asset Classes Supported	• Equities	• Equities • Listed Derivatives • Forex	• Equities • Listed Derivatives • Forex • Fixed Income • OTC Derivatives
Functions Supported	• Basic Order Flow • IOIs • Quotes	• Market Data • Allocations • Program Trading	• Confirms/Affirms • Trade Reporting • Algorithmic Trading

The use of FIX for post trade processing enables firms to leverage existing in-house technology investments by utilizing current FIX engines, networks and processing capabilities. The opportunities have increased as FIX members have worked to extend FIX message types to support a wider range of functions in the trade life cycle, as well as broaden the types of instruments that can be accommodated using standard FIX messaging formats.

Slower Adoption of FIX by European Fund managers

Twelve years after it started, the acceptance of FIX by the fund management community within the US is strong and outside the US is growing, but still low. According to a recent Investit study, less than 60% of European fund management companies are said to be using FIX compared to around 70% in the US, and just under 50% of equity trade volume is executed using FIX. Figure 4 below shows this distribution.

Figure 4: Fund management companies' usage of FIX:

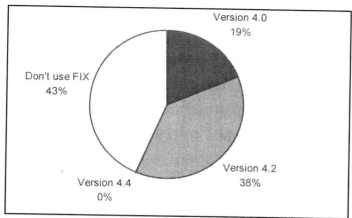

Source: Investit Intelligence, 2006

A recent **Celent** study titled, "European Post-Trade Processing: STP in the Back and Middle Office." confirmed these results. Out of 80 respondents from organizations whose primary markets include the U.K. and Germany, 17% said they would spend 50-75% of their IT budgets on back- and middle-office functionality. Just 8% said they would spend 76-100% of their budgets for these functions, while 50% said they would only spend up to 25% on these functions.

The key barriers to FIX adoption on the buy side is a lack of OMS support for FIX messaging, internal resistance to change and the fact that required functionality is perceived to always be in the next version. However, it is now widely accepted that FIX 4.4 has the capacity to manage most instruments being traded in the market and is scalable; the lack of community of FIX 4.4 users appears to be the greatest barrier with many in the market taking a "wait and see" approach. The key market drivers for FIX adoption are electronic trading, such as the increased use of algorithms and DMA, regulatory pressures, particularly MiFID and Reg NMS - and therefore best execution, cost pressures, and the fact that FIX can be implemented for fixed income, FX and derivatives.

The primary reasons given for the slow uptake are:

- Higher priority projects.
- Volumes not warranting the cost of implementation.
- The prior need for a system to integrate FIX into, usually an order management system.

FIX for Fixed Income

FIX has been far more widely adopted for equities than fixed income and usage is concentrated on the trade execution process. Use of the allocation messages is expected to be far more widespread going forward as they have only recently become available in version 4.4.

Figure 5: FIX use by instrument and function

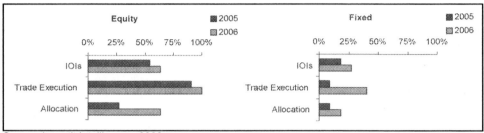

Source: Investit Intelligence, 2006

FIX use by fixed income fund managers is much lower than equities. It is expected that usage will increase, especially for trade execution, but not on the same scale as equities. There are several reasons for this:
There has been a much lower deployment of fixed income order management systems.

Where equities are traded on exchanges via brokers, fixed income instruments are traded directly between counterparties - there is no central exchange. TradeWeb and MarketAxess have created automatic markets - these products have been established for a while and linking to them does not necessarily require FIX.

FIX for fixed income has only just arrived. FIX version 4.4 was the first version to include all phases of fixed income trading from the simple dissemination of bid lists to the execution of complex swaps.

How have fund managers implemented FIX?

To fully implement FIX, an order management system that supports FIX messaging needs to be linked to a FIX engine which translates and routes messages. Examples of these engines are Javelin and Cameron. The main system vendors have integrated this into their application, so that companies do not have to acquire and maintain any additional servers or separate software. Affordability of FIX is improving dramatically because of cheaper technology, smaller scaled order management systems and web based solutions.

In addition to the FIX engine, a network needs to be selected to provide the broker connectivity linking the order management system to the broker's systems. Two examples are Radianz and TNS.

FIX can be implemented in two ways:

1. Through a direct connection to each broker dealer – 'point-to-point' (can be via an order management system network).
2. By using a hub-and-spoke solution where a vendor provides a hub that has already been connected to a large number of brokers, the fund manager only has to make the one connection to the hub.

Figure 6: FIX method of implementation

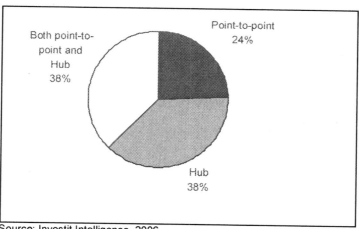

Source: Investit Intelligence, 2006

Point-to-point

Those that chose point-to-point often did so because they were early adopters of FIX, and at that time the hub vendors had not become established. While point-to-point gives more control of the connection to the broker, it is a more costly solution as a team is required to implement each connection and then subsequently test with each broker.

Hub

With a hub solution, only one connection is required. Testing connectivity to each broker should be quicker, as it has been done before, so this method should bring faster implementation, lower support and maintenance costs.
One of the downsides of the hub solution was it was not possible to know if the connection to the broker was available. This has now been resolved by the hub vendors, who provide a 'heartbeat' message showing that the broker is successfully connected. Hubs also used to suffer from performance problems and timeliness in getting additional brokers connected. Examples of hub solutions are AutEx, NYFIX and Ullink.

Both

Many companies implement both solutions, either:

- selecting point-to-point for the most frequently used brokers and hub-and-spoke for a large volume of alternative brokers; or
- selecting a hub-and-spoke solution for more standard connections and point-to-point for the more complex financial products and connections.

There are pros and cons with each model. Vendors will continue to add more features such as market data and other services within the network cloud such as transaction cost analysis and algorithms. The result will be an increasingly competitive battle between network providers to improve and differentiate their offering from that of the competition. The choice between hub and point-to-point is often guided by the order management system vendor, as shown in Figure 7 on the next page.

Figure 7 Driver for FIX implementation selection

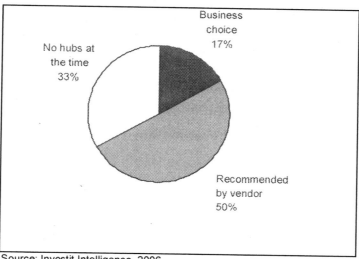

Source: Investit Intelligence, 2006

Future Mandate: Same Day Affirmation (SDA)

Mandated shorter settlement cycles is dormant (for now) in the US. Canadian Securities Association has pioneered the latest efforts to reduce costly errors for the greater good of the industry. It has mandated that institutional trade matching, or as it is sometimes called "Same Day Affirmation, (SDA)" be adopted by investment managers in the Canadian financial market by the summer of 2008, via straight-through processing (STP). The regulation, known as National Instrument 24-101, has turned attention to the back office in an effort to shore up one of the most risk-laden spaces in the trade lifecycle. National Instrument 24-101 mandates that Canadian investment managers must match their trades with counterparties on trade date (T). Centrally matching trades through automated solutions has been shown to dramatically increase firms' rates of SDA, the outcome when a buyer and seller capture and agree on trade details on trade date (T), independent of the settlement process. Higher rates of SDA mean operating costs and trade failures can be reduced dramatically, thus lowering systemic risk across the industry.

Another Attempt: Standards Convergence vs. Standards Interoperability:

Within the last several years the financial services industry talked about standards convergence. Initiatives were launched and working groups were formed to consolidate the existing communication formats. However, there was little success. Other attempts to merge standards have not succeeded. Standards convergence remains a myth, which means that firms must continue to track changes to existing standards, make the appropriate changes to their file formats and manage multiple trade communication standards.

One alternative to this dilemma is to create interoperability among the existing standards. The idea is that rather than all standards converging, each retains its own syntax and format, but measures are taken to ensure that conversion between them can be performed automatically. The most comprehensive attempt at Standards Interoperability is the ISO20022 Repository UNIversal Financial Industry message scheme (nicknamed "UNIFI). The objective of ISO20022 is one standard approach used by all – but it will not happen overnight. The standards and specifications of UNIFI have been around since December 2004 and the initial set of UNIFI messages developed by SWIFT was approved in November 2005. However, the adoption rates remain low.

The goal of UNIFI is to identify and standardize the 'data objects' (or 'words') that are shared between institutions and store them in the 'data dictionary' of the UNIFI Repository. For new standards at least ISO20022 offers some hope of automating the mapping between messages from different functional areas, reducing if not eliminating the need for laborious manual mapping. Using the agreed standard 'words' as Lego blocks, the developers can build syntax-independent message models, which can then be transformed into message formats according to the desired syntax. The current preferred UNIFI syntax is XML, but should a new and better syntax be chosen, the models would not need to be changed: only the rules to transform the message models in the desired message formats would change.

When work on the ISO20022 Repository began (it was originally part of the ISO15022 initiative) the aims were bolder. Rather than permitting interoperability between standards designed from scratch around its definitions, the belief was that if existing standards could be mapped in a one-off exercise to the repository, then all mapped standards could interoperate with one another.

Figure 8: The Future: Co-existence and Convergence:

FIX	Messages	ISO 15022
✓	Indication	
✓	Quotation	
✓	Order	✓
✓	Execution	✓
✓	(Pre-)Allocation	✓
✓	Confirmation	✓
	Settlement	✓
	Reconciliation	✓

Source: UNIFI (ISO 20022), 2007

The FIX protocol covers the early stages of the securities trade life cycle from pre-trade to post-trade, while ISO 15022 covers the later stages starting from trade through to settlement and reconciliation.
There are two interoperability problems:

- The information has to 'flow' throughout two different standards from the beginning to the end of the transaction life cycle,
- There is an overlap in the scope of the standards which may require the translation of a message in one syntax into the equivalent message in the other syntax.

Figure 9a: Current -- Co-existence: Convergence:

Figure 9b: Future --

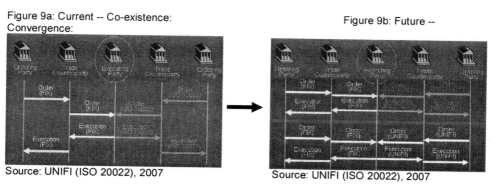

Source: UNIFI (ISO 20022), 2007

Source: UNIFI (ISO 20022), 2007

If the buyer and seller are not using the same standard (Figure 9a), the Executing Party in the middle would need to 'understand' the two standards, process them and eventually 'map' the information back into either standard.

The 'convergence table' (Figure 9b) can help the Executing Party to handle both syntaxes and eventually migrate to UNIFI.

The problem with such an ambitious undertaking as UNIFI is the amount of effort and time required to make it work and to keep it working. The benefit of UNIFI is that it does not impose a standard interface for communication, but introduces a central registration authority that is tasked with enabling communication interoperability between financial institutions, their market infrastructures and their end-user communities

Outsourced Options:

If a firm simply wants to avoid all of these "standards" headaches, they have an option to outsource their connectivity to one of dozens of firms that operate in this space, such as Brown Brothers Harriman (BBH) Infomediary, State Street, JP Morgan, Electra, Evare, ITG, SEI and many others.

The following highlights the core electronic trade communication services typically available from outsource providers:

Figure 8 Trade Cycle Outsource Provider Services:

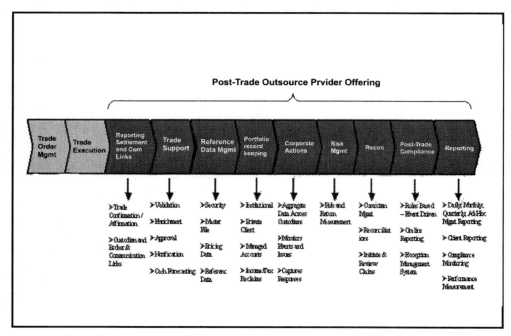

Source: State Street Investment Services

Figure 10: Top Functions Investment Managers Would Consider Outsourcing:

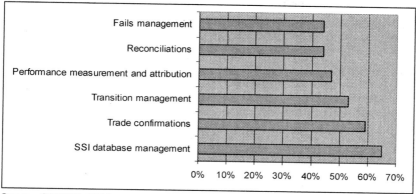

Source: OMGEO, 2006

Figure 11: Most Important Factors To Investment Management Firms In Choosing An Outsourcing Provider:

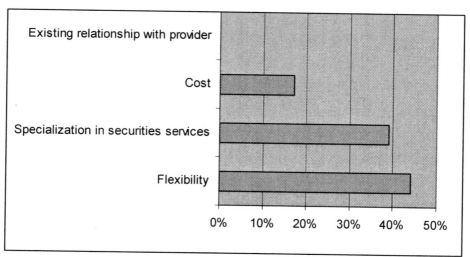

Source: OMGEO, 2006

Investment Managers are focusing more on their core competencies and therefore looking to lower their fixed costs by lowering the need to support multiple post-trade solutions required for STP. Outsourcing or "hubbing" these systems is a direction under consideration by many firms. The Primary Benefits of Outsourcing include STP Improvement, Process Automation, Flexibility, Scalability, Redundancy, Cost & Risk Reduction and Improved Focus on Core Business

Conclusion:

Today most buy-side investment management firms have a more controlled, structured process for communicating trade data electronically. The tolerance level for poor processes is much lower and the "STP rate" of firms has increased significantly. We have come a long way over the past few years towards increasing the number of standards and the capability to develop to standards for electronically communicating trade data for many of the basic security instruments. The growing number and variety of "standards" has now become a standardization problem itself. As the number of protocols increase, the complexity of the business they cover increases at the same time.

We have reached the stage where we are standardizing standards to reduce complexity and cost that are associated with building and supporting the systems that use messaging interfaces to communicate among themselves. It is no surprise that there is a growing interest among buy-side investment managers to outsource the trade communication process, rather than attempt to employ interface experts who can track the changing standards and spend time updating message formats for newly traded security types.

The holy grail of one electronic trade communication standard (standards convergence) is still in the distant future. Standards convergence only happens when market infrastructures merge and their individual users become part of the greater group. To alleviate the duplicate efforts of developing and maintaining multiple standards, the industry is moving towards standards interoperability. In most instances, standards interoperability seems to be a more fruitful way forward. However, interoperability between legacy standards is fraught with technical difficulties, such as manually mapping between standards using middleware and the demand for firms to have detailed business knowledge of the standards and specifications.

References:

- TowerGroup report "Decisions, decisions; FIX Network Models and the Outlook for FIX Connectivity."
- Federal Reserve Bank Of St. Louis *Review* – November/December 2006
- Investit Intelligence Paper: The Future Of Back Office Systems, Catherine Doherty, Investit, (www.investit.com), July 2006
- Canada's Regulatory environment – Changing the tide on a global scale? Lee Cutrone, OMGEO

- Outsourcing: Perspectives & Opportunities, OMGEO/Global Custodian
- Celent report "European Post-Trade Processing: STP in the Back and Middle Office.", David Easthope
- Financial Messaging and Integration, Steve Lindsay, Technical Architect, Misys
- Asset Managers Forum Panel Block Level Matching and Allocations Best Practices, AMF STP Committee, November, 2005
- Introduction to ISO 20022 – UNIversal Financial Industry message scheme (UNIFI), (www.iso20022.org) May, 2007
- www.fix-protocol.org

Measure It / Manage It:
Monitor and Control Trading Applications

By Don Mendelson, Capital Markets Consulting

System Management Challenges

Manage Your Business, Not Computers
In order to manage a trading system, you have to be able to measure its performance at a business level.

There are plenty of tools on the market for measuring and managing technical infrastructure, such as databases and networks. Those tools are necessary, and provide the means to deal with technical issues and crises. However, those tools don't tell you what you need to know about how your business is running. Even when appropriately dealing with a technical issue, they don't necessarily tell you its business impact.

A major success factor is aiming higher than just watching computing infrastructure. Don't think of system management tools as just failure catchers. Rather, you should monitor the business metrics that make a difference to your users and customers. Make it a part of a strategy for delivering quality service, and in the end, customer satisfaction.

Trading Application Trends and Risks

Trading systems are becoming more distributed at the same time they are becoming more time critical.
Application developers and IT operations personnel are challenged as never before by mega trends in trading system requirements. Some of the trends causing managers' headaches are:

- Multi asset classes, exchange destinations and lines of business force higher architectural complexity.

- Distributed, redundant data centers cut downtime risk, and co-location at market centers (physically placing computers at or near exchanges) cuts message latency but both require remote management of sites.
- Market data volumes grow exponentially, placing ever higher loads on systems.
- Algorithmic trading systems must respond to market conditions in milliseconds, or are even measured in nanoseconds scale.
- High volume and low latency performance characteristics demand more parallelism in systems designs, leading to more demanding requirements for coordination and synchronization.

All of these factors contribute to increased risk and cost of a problem. An outage can be very expensive if it prevents trading activities until resolved. Suboptimal design or a temporary performance slowdown can cause trading activities to miss market opportunities, directly limiting profitability.

Problem domains

Dealing with system unresponsiveness or outright failures is difficult because problems can originate from a number of domains.

- Application defects – the implementation didn't work as designed.
- Application deficiencies – the design missed a business requirement or got it wrong.
- User errors – the application works as designed, but a user made a bad decision. (However, allowing users to do the wrong thing may be a design deficiency.)
- Configuration or misconfiguration of servers, clients or network nodes
- Network faults, such as physical disconnection, routing errors or insufficient bandwidth.
- Platform resource constraints, such as memory or processor utilization.
- Third-party data resources, such as market data feeds.
- Partner or contra party failures (It's not always your own fault.)

Who's responsible?

To contain costs and business impact, you must identify problems immediately. You have to enlist the right experts in diagnosing and resolving it. This can be difficult since the responsibility for each problem domain may lie in different branches of your organization, with different cultures and reporting lines.

Problem diagnosis gets stickier when responsibility crosses organizational lines. For example, system performance involves a complicated interaction between platform resources and application logic. Application developers need to work closely with system operators since each of them knows only part of the picture. Taking outsourcing hosted facilities into account, the responsible party may not even be a member of your own firm.

Domain	Responsible parties	Typical issues
Application functionality	Software development staff	How can you give developers enough information about production problems without totally dropping security barriers?
Configuration	Software development staff and IT technical staff	Do operators have adequate instructions and training to reconfigure systems?
Network and platforms	IT technical staff or hosted facilities managers	Do operators recognize the business impact of a technical problem?
Business decisions	Users and software development staff	Is it a bug or a feature?
Application performance	Software development staff and IT technical staff	Is system load within the original requirements specification? Is there a known baseline for normal performance?
Data	Internal systems and vendors	What is the latency to deliver market data to its ultimate consumers? How can junk data be detected?

Ideally, each responsible party should detect and resolve problems in its own domain. However, in the real world, we know that is not always the case. In the worst case, a problem becomes highly visible to a customer before anyone inside the organization realizes it. Then a customer service contact must capture the problem and pass it off to the appropriate resource, while trying to assure the customer that something is being done. Obviously, having a problem evident to your customer before you know what is happening on your own system is a recipe for poor customer satisfaction, and ultimately lost business.

Islands of Data

Normally, all of the artifacts on a production system are owned by the IT operations staff. When a production problem occurs, access rights may be granted to applications developers to troubleshoot it.

Some of the artifacts viewed by support personnel are:

- System event logs
- System monitors
- Application event logs and audit trails
- Message logs and queues
- Data files
- Databases

These artifacts may be scattered across many machines in a data center and may be geographically distributed as well. Therefore, remote logins are necessary, even for authorized operations staff. Even if centrally located, access to systems must be restricted for security reasons.

As problem resolution is divided by responsibilities, understanding of system artifacts and reports is usually segregated along organizational lines. IT operations staff is trained in operating system and network monitoring facilities. Even though they have access rights to application artifacts, they may not be understandable to them, so they cannot resolve problems without outside help.

Getting the right information

- Managers need to know the business impact of a problem.
- Support staff needs to pull together the right experts with access to the right information to diagnose and resolve it.

Capital Markets Consulting, utilizes a concept that encapsulates problem resolution. We call it Problems/Causes/Solutions, or P/C/S for short. The words seem simple on their face, but their combination is the concept's strength. In a nutshell, it is worthless to report a problem without also reporting its possible causes and solutions.

The Problem
There are three branches to a well-formed problem report. The first is the business impact, such as "Failed to route order X from customer Y to exchange destination Z." That is the sort of information that is meaningful to customers and customer service contacts. You want to have that information

at hand, before receiving an angry customer call to the help desk. Having the business impact allows you to be prepared for dealing with the customer, because at least you know what they know. Without even knowing the technical cause of the problem, you can start thinking about ways to make the customer happy again.

The Cause

Of course, the technical troubleshooters also need to know the underlying cause of the problem. The second fork of the error report might be something like "Socket error 10054 on address x.x.x.x – connection reset by peer." This tells a technical person that the connection was closed by the party on the other end. There certainly can be more to the story, but at least it provides a starting point for troubleshooting. It could be a network issue that was coincidental to the order that failed. A network expert might look at collected statistics and routing information to determine that. Alternatively, it could be an application error either in your own system or at a counterparty's site. Within the context of the business problem, an application developer might look at the order fields to determine if they contained valid data. It might have been a message sent or received just before the order that was the actual cause of the problem. So the developer would want to look at message logs that correspond to the time of the disconnection to see it in context.

Often, problems are not caused by a single event, but by a whole chain of events. Programming techniques can be used to capture and log the whole chain rather than the most recent or visible link. In this scheme, the troubleshooter can start with the top level and drill down to finer levels of detail – what was the cause behind the scenes that led to the most immediate cause? Toyota manufacturing has long held the philosophy that when a problem occurs, you should ask "why" five times to get to its root cause[cliii].

The Solution

The third leg of the problem report supplies potential solutions to the problem. In the case of the session disconnection, it would be common to have standing instructions that tell an operator how to restart the aborted session. But what if the communications were incidental to the problem rather than its cause? Restarting the session would accomplish nothing if a bad order is resent, causing the connection to go down again. It is better if the potential solutions are tied to specific causes so the appropriate one is applied.

Of course, it is impossible to think of every possible failure point beforehand. However, it is still crucial to work with a client at the requirements gathering stage to think of as many possible failure scenarios as possible. It is surprising how this seemingly negative thought process leads to more precise requirements and better system designs. Potential disasters turn into avoidable or manageable situations. If not avoidable, the client at least determines in advance who should be alerted to a particular problem, rather than scrambling to figure it out while telephones are ringing off the hook.

Beyond fire fighting – business intelligence

IT operations staff should be monitoring network and hardware resources to avoid the most noticeable kinds of platform failures and traffic jams. But do you really know the performance of your applications as perceived by users and customers?

First, you have to develop metrics that directly reflect the users' needs. They are not necessarily correlated to statistics commonly reported by platform tools, such as CPU utilization or available network bandwidth.

To use a somewhat technical example, a key metric of black-box trading systems is low latency. Your system and your competitors are all reacting to the same market data at the same time. Assuming some of them follow similar trading strategies, the first to fire a message into the exchange hits the bid, while the others may miss the opportunity. That's not quite as serious as crashing an aircraft due to slow computing performance, but try and tell your CEO or investors that.

So to continue the black box example, how should latency be reported? The system itself could timestamp events; such as when a tick is received and the corresponding order or market maker quote is launched. Using that information, elapsed time can be calculated. (Time to propagate a signal to the marketplace could be a factor, but let's assume your black box system is co-located to eliminate that delay.) Another important fact to capture is whether the order succeeded, or was it too late for the market move? Now there are two facts to correlate: order entry latency and trade results. In most systems, the bits of data are stored in different places, perhaps different application logs, so the reporting system has to assemble the facts from different sources

You have to turn raw data into meaningful business information. In some cases, any event of a certain type calls for action immediately, irrespective of its context. In other cases, a large body of data must be summarized to make sense of it. Some kinds of data are only interesting with respect to a historical trend. Either the trend itself is of interest, or an outlier that runs counter to the trend indicates a problem.

At a less technological level, one can imagine all kinds of *financial* performance metrics to track. Metrics can be defined for pre-trade, trade, or post-trade processing .What is a trader's intraday P&L at the moment? What is the ratio of winning trades to losers? What are a customer's risk characteristics? Timely answers to these kinds of questions could be used to tweak a trading strategy or adjust trading limits.

The big picture is to turn around the old adage, "If you can't measure it, you can't manage it" to coin a new motto: *If you can think of a performance metric to describe your business, you can create a tool to manage it.*
The development tasks to achieve that goal include:

1. Define a performance metric that can be derived from system artifacts. If supporting facts are lacking, then some preparation work may be required to capture them.
2. Provide a system to capture the facts and correlate them for reporting. For example, let a customer service rep see all the transactions regarding a particular order of interest – the original order, its acknowledgement, a chain of cancel/replaces, and all the fills.
3. Calculate the performance metric using the gathered data. Summarize data as appropriate and look for trends.
4. Define alerts, which may be based on the summarized data but are triggered by specific events, possibly based on when a metric crosses a threshold.
5. Define who should be alerted about each event type and how they should be notified. An alert could take the form of a pop up window, an email, or a text message to a phone. It may be desirable to get an acknowledgement that the alert was received to hold a party accountable for handling it.
6. The obverse side of the alerting coin is to set policies for who should be prevented from receiving confidential information. Without explicit policies and awareness of organizational boundaries, it would be all too easy for an administrative assistant editing a notification list to inadvertently reveal company secrets Controlling applications

Trading applications are tweaked on the fly.

Trading applications today must stay up for a full day at a time at minimum. Traditionally, markets traded for several hours during daylight hours, and then closed overnight, giving the back office systems time to catch up. Even while that is still the case for some individual exchanges, trading strategies often require continuous trading as the focus shifts to markets around the globe. Many servers are required to run continuously or at least on a 24 X 5 basis.

The old practice of changing configuration and restarting an application no longer applies. Reconfiguration must be received by a running application on the fly. In particular, algorithmic trading systems must constantly be prepared to receive new parameters to control relative aggressiveness or risk aversion, and even to command it to switch to a different algorithm when the market changes direction.

For co-located black box systems, remote command and control is the only choice available.

Since critical systems are typically run as redundant pairs for safety or load balancing, a command that is sent to one running application must also be replicated to its redundant twin.

Choosing Tools

Off the shelf
Tools for IT operations staffers to manage infrastructure are readily available, but support for applications management is more sparse.

Data center tools
A broad spectrum of monitoring tools is available at a platform level for measuring hardware and network performance. Beyond the platform-specific tools, there are a number of tool suites geared to the management of large and distributed data centers. They are generally marketed to IT operations people rather than applications development managers or business leaders. Consequently, they tend to be quite technical in nature. Tools of this type are appropriate for large scale systems with sufficient depth in operational analysis to take advantage of their features.

Some of the leaders in the field:

- IBM Tivoli
- BMC Patrol
- CA Unicenter
- HP OpenView
- Microsoft Operations Manager (MOM)

These suites are sold as collections of modules. Although they share some common facilities and databases, each module manages a different aspect of the computing infrastructure, typically:

- Processes
- Servers
- Network
- Storage
- Security
- Web services

Management protocols

Management tools may either be wholly proprietary or may implement industry standards. Standards conformance offers the promise of interoperability between products from different vendors.

One industry standard protocol that has been around for years to manage network devices remotely is Simple Network Management Protocol (SNMP). It allows remote configuration of routers and the like and generates fault alerts. Although popular in the network world, it is not commonly used for business application monitoring, simply because it wasn't designed with applications in mind.

Another set of management protocols was standardized by the Distributed Management Task Force (DMTF). Among its many working groups dealing with infrastructure issues, one is dedicated to applications management. At least the need is recognized.

Microsoft developed Windows Management Instrumentation, based on DMTF standards. It can be used to control servers remotely and collect logged events from instrumented applications. This seems to be in Microsoft's long-range plans since they have provided an interface to it in the .NET framework. However, current emphasis still remains on hardware and device driver management rather than business level knowledge.

Starting with Java 1.5, Java Management Extensions (JMX) interfaces are provided as a standard part of every Java installation. Although pervasive in Java and therefore, cross-platform, it is not entirely based on a cross-language industry standards. (Some informal work has been done to link JMX to DMTF standards, but it is not fully interoperable with other systems.) JMX is only suitable for shops that develop most software in Java.

Monitoring applications

Despite their system administrator orientation, the big enterprise suites all claim to have some capability of monitoring business applications. Some have modules to capture application events by parsing logs, and they typically aggregate data in a database for later review and historical trends analysis.

An interesting approach is offered by Splunk Technology, which markets its product as the "search engine for IT data." Splunk is a commercial tool that charges users by the amount of raw data processed, but it also promotes an open source community for its users to share descriptions of events in operating systems and popular packages. It also provides APIs to capture events from custom applications in its database.

In short, the topics that matter to system administrators can be captured with off-the-shelf products of this sort. However, gathering true business intelligence on proprietary software would require significant customization of the monitoring tools.

Custom Monitors

One-off applications may require one-off business management tools.
One time-tested approach is to develop a custom system monitor along with the system to be monitored. Such a project has the best chance of meeting its goals since the combined system's requirements are worked out together. The monitor may also be able to share communications infrastructure and code with the monitored application.

Conversely, a custom monitor has the worst chance of integrating with other systems precisely because little is shared.

A challenge for managers is to get budget approval for monitor development along with the business system. You don't want to wait until the system is in production and you have to rush the development of the monitor to clean up all the problems that are occurring. Business leaders need to be sold on its benefits and quality of service attributes in general. Otherwise, given a choice between a monitor and another business feature, the monitor will usually lose.

A factor that could make the difference though is how much command and control is required on a project as compared to a view-only monitor.

Decision Points

Get started now.
There are several important decisions and assessments to be made. The first and most important is to decide what business factors need to be managed on the running system. What performance factors make a difference to the business? What controls are needed to affect operations?

Once you have decided what to measure and manage, you can evaluate the means. Can you use an off-the-shelf suite or should you develop a custom monitor? Can you use a proprietary management product or should it conform to industry standards? Is interoperability important?

Another decision point is to decide on an implementation strategy. Is it advantageous to instrument applications as they are developed, or is it acceptable to passively process its artifacts such as logs?

End Notes

i This is based upon Panasonic's Interactive TV Wall. See http://www.akihabaranews.com/en/review-63-Panasonic's+interactive+TV+wall,+the+demo.html for a demonstration and the image below gives a view:

ii See http://www.iwmi.cgiar.org/pubs/WWVisn/WWSDHtml.htm

iii PTV – Personal Transportation Vehicle. Each citizen is allowed to use biodegradable transportation services based upon non-water based emissions. These link to the government operated transport grid infrastructures. The early prototype was first demonstrated at Expo 1986 and is shown below courtesy of website http://www.geocities.com/exposcruff/green/france.html:

iv Housing had become unaffordable for many citizens due to demand far out-stripping supply during the 2000's. This was not only due to the population increases through economic migration, but also because more people were living on their own in single households due to the collapse of marriage as an institution. Marriage and 'having children' were viewed as a thing of the 20th Century and most people now lived alone. Therefore, the Government introduced the POD – Personal Ownership Development – Scheme in 2011. PODs are government-provided low-cost dwellings that comprise a kitchen, bathroom, lounge and bedroom. Each POD is built of combustible materials in a mix of aluminium and durable plastics. PODs could then be attached to each other to build larger developments and even high-rise block buildings where needed, almost like Lego sets. PODs are allocated to individuals as needed, with the basic form available for any adult over the age of 21. If adults wanted to cohabit, they are allocated two PODs. Should those adults replicate – who needed to go through the pain of childbirth so children are developed in beakers – then they could have an extra POD for every two replicates they raised.

v This is based upon Panasonic's Interactive TV Wall. The wall works on the basis of the user pointing and moving windows around on screen. Each window can be re-sized to suit what you are trying to view, and you simply move your hands in front of the wall to shape the window to the size you want.

vi Email gradually disappeared in usage in the early 2010's as the world moved toward video messaging. The result is that rather than 'calling' people you would 'view' them, as everyone is connected visually through video networking. Equally, you no longer post cards but view them, so you send viewcards. The term 'viewing' first appeared in Isaac Asimov's 1957 novel The Naked Sun, where people met through video networks rather than in person.

vii Some believe the end of the keyboard and typing is extreme, but if you think of the keyboard in context, it is not a natural interface at all. Just one we have learned to adapt to use. For example, we all type today because we have to. You cannot live in today's digital world without being able to press the QWERTY keyboard. As long ago as 1990 however, most financial institutions had typing pools and most managers had secretaries. The typists and secretaries were there to press the QWERTY keyboard, not the professionals. Even in 1995, most bank CEO's would be PC non-literate and would delegate such activities to their assistants. Ten years later, the world is a different place. Most bank CEO's could not survive without their Blackberry. Bank professionals at all levels rely on their laptops and PCs, and all of these are driven by keyboards. To Instant Message, Email or Text, you have to be keyboard-literate. This is just a temporary phase though as, since the inception of the computer era, the technology vision has been to create a virtual world that is as easy to live in as our physical world. In the 1930s, telephone firms were already experimenting with video telephony. Today, the world of video telephony has arrived. Equally, since the creation of typewriters, telex and fax, firms have tried to evolve to simple touch and point voice activated systems. Using simple point and touch systems today are mouse-based, but there are already experiments with haptic technologies, where the user wears gloves to interact with the system. A little like the way Tom Cruise moves information around in the film Minority Report using a pair of light emitting sensor gloves, these interfaces are in early experimentation today, but will gradually become more predominant. Combining such interface with voice commands and voice recognition will mean a movement away from typing. The result is that the keyboard will become more and more redundant as point and talk systems take over, driven by haptic technologies and reliable voice recognition.

viii After MiFID and RegNMS, Over-the-Counter (OTC) trading firms underwent extensive business process redesign to deliver best execution compliance. The result was a radical shake-up of most firms as buy-side to sell-side networking, linkage and operations all changed and TCA (Trade Cost Analysis) became the order of the day. In particular, sell-side charging was laid bare by these regulatory changes, and buy-side firms began to challenge charges for historically bundled services for connectivity, execution, research and commissions. The end result is that buy-side firms circumvented sell-side firms for many of these capabilities where they thought they could deliver more cost-efficiently or effectively. Soon, buy-side and sell-side and exchanges were all thrown into a competitive melting pot, with large brokers competing with traditional exchanges to gain institutional investors' liquidity. On the other hand, institutional investors were soon becoming technology powerhouses themselves and realised that they no longer needed to deal through accredited brokers on traditional exchanges – the old way of doing business – but just needed to have network connectivity to as many venues as possible. The outcome was that buy-side firms effectively became both trader and dealer houses, with the ability to order route directly to wherever they wanted to invest. This forced the large brokerage houses to reconsider their role and, as market-makers, they began to offer competitive fulfilment services to the traditional exchanges. In other words, there was no buy- and sell-side ... just investors and execution venues.

ix This is what best execution is all about, and was the result of RegNMS and MiFID with no-one considering their execution or execution venue requirements, but focusing on their investment and investment fulfilment requirements instead.

x Viewcalls are conference calls over the net and are based upon the currently dedicated services such as TelePresence by Cisco or Halo by HP. These products use ultra high definition 1080p video combined with end-to-end latency and wideband spatial audio. The result is an HDTV conferencing service that allows you to feel you are actually there in the room with the other callers. An example is provided below:

xi Alternative Trading System: A regulator approved non-exchange trading venue.

xii Investment Technology Group.

xiii Regulation NMS (or Reg NMS) is a regulation promulgated by the United States Securities and Exchange Commission (SEC). According to the SEC, Reg NMS is "a series of initiatives designed to modernize and strengthen the national market system for equity securities."

xiv Markets in Financial Instruments Directive.

xv "U.S. Equity Market Structure: Driving Change in Global Financial Markets," Larry Tabb, March 5, 2008.

xvi Dark Pool: A source of liquidity that is created by institutional trade orders not available to the public. It usually refers to block trades facilitated on an ATS and off the central exchange.

xvii Disclaimer: Timing figures quoted are based on information provided by those interviewed. They have not been measured or verified by Cisco and may differ from information published by a given exchange.

xviii NASDAQ's Electronic Crossing Network.

xix NYSE's Online Securities Exchange.

xx System clocks do not necessarily run consistently. One second may really be 100,000,000 beats. The first "second" generated by the clock, however, may be 99,999,999 beats, then the next may be 100,000,001 beats.

xxi Rosen and Wagner can attest to their lack of market power. Fidelity Investment and George Soros are put forth as icons without their consent. { Happy to leave my name in here if you left it in on purpose – your call, Wayne!}

xxii Paulden, Pierre; TRADING - Daggers, Dark Pools and Disintermediation, Institutional Investor, April 2007.

xxiii Friedman, Thomas F. The World Is flat, Farrar, Straus and Gireau, New York, 2005

xxiv Sorry, I just couldn't resist it.

xxv The Tragedy of the Commons, originally put forth by W. F. Lloyd, in 1833, concerns the situation where an asset is held communally, but the benefits accrue to the individuals who use it cost free. In the original formulation of the problem, the "Commons" was the communal grazing area in the center of a village, and the "tragedy" referred to the temptation for each villager to over-graze his own sheep to his individual benefit. The concept has seen wide applicability to modern problems such as air or water pollution, where polluters do not pay for the clean-up costs of the environmental damage they cause.

xxvi A similar argument has been made against index fund investing.

xxvii Sexton, Martin, The Handbook of World Stock, Derivative and Commodity Exchanges 2005 Edition

xxviii Picot, Arnold, Christine Bortenlanger and Heiner Roehrl, http://jcmc.indiana.edu/vol1/issue3/picot.html

xxix The Last Days of the Club, Chris Welles, E. P. Dutton & Co., New York, 1975, 460 pages
xxx Ditto
xxxi Ditto
xxxii "Big Board to Close 20% of Trading Floor", by Aaron Lucchetti, The Wall Street Journal, Nov. 1, 2006; "NYSE may close Extended Blue Room" by Melanie Wold, DowJones Financial News Online, June 21, 2007.
ii NY Post, Business section, 4/2/2006. There have been many articles like this one in the popular press discussing how "quants" have taken over trading on Wall Street.

xxxiv William G. Christie and Paul Schultz, "Why Do Nasdaq Market Makers Avoid Odd-Eighth Quotes?", Journal of Finance 49, 1994.

xxxv In July of 1996, the Dept. of Justice settled with 24 of the largest market-making firms for "anticompetitive conduct", after releasing findings showing substantial evidence of collusion and intimidation. See DOJ press release #343, July 17, 1996, available at www.usdoj.gov.

xxxvi Instinet would go on to try to correct its mistakes by buying Island in 2002. Almost all of the ECNs from that generation would go on to be gobbled up by Nasdaq and the NYSE in a massive consolidation game.

xxxvii See SEC press releases 2004-42 and 2004-99 for a summary of the civil violations, available at www.sec.gov

xxxviii For a detailed description of the charges, see the US Attorney's press release, "Two Former NYSE Specialists Plead Guilty to Federal Securities Fraud Charges", May 12, 2006, available at www.fbi.gov. As of July 2006, there were seven other specialists at various stages of criminal trials.

xxxix Source: Credit Suisse Quantitative Research

xl The big 5 Nasdaq market-makers in the late '90s bull market were Herzog, Troster, Sherwood, Knight, and Mayer-Schweitzer. By 2003, only Knight had survived as an independent entity.

xli See "UBS Cuts Floor Staff at NYSE", by Aaron Lucchetti, The Wall Street Journal Online, March 29, 2007. "Lehman is Latest to Get Off Floor", by Roddy Boyd, NY Post, June 1, 2007. "Bear Cleans Up the Floor", Forbes.com, May 14, 2007.

xlii See "Floor Exits: Specialists Walk as E-trading Takes Over", by Roddy Boyd, NY Post, May 14, 2007.

xliii The 10 exchanges as of mid-2007 were: NYSE, Nasdaq, Arca, Boston, Philadelphia, National, Chicago, American, International, CBOE.

xliv "Floor traders, feeling bitter and abandoned by the computerization of trading, have occasionally taken to booing Chief Executive John Thain when he brings honored guests to the balcony over the floor to ring the ceremonial bell.", Aaron Lucchetti, "Boos vs. Moos", The Wall Street Journal, April 6, 2007, page A1.

xlv In Aug. 2005 and March 2006, the SEC and the Dept. of Justice charged four former brokers from Merrill Lynch, Citigroup and Lehman Brothers with securities fraud for letting day traders eavesdrop on the firms' internal intercom, aka "squawk box". The first trial resulted in a hung jury. As of June 2007 they were awaiting a second trial. See SEC press release 2006-40, www.sec.gov.

xlvi for an interesting piece on signaling risk, see: Hora, Merrell, "The Practice of Optimal Execution", Institutional Investor Journal's Guide to Algorithmic Trading II, Spring 2006.

xlvii The Toronto Stock Exchange closed its trading floor in May 1997. The London Stock Exchange, which has been floor-less since Big Bang in 1996, introduced an electronic limit order book into its quote driven market in 1997. Nasdaq is currently planning to do the same. Floorless, electronic continuous trading now characterizes the equity markets of Toronto, Paris, Tokyo, Stockholm, Sidney, Switzerland, Madrid, Frankfurt and elsewhere. In the U.S., new alternative trading systems (commonly referred to as ATSs) and Electronic Communications Networks (ECNs) are also electronic, order driven systems.

xlviii It is important to assess liquidity impact costs in light of studies such as Amihud and Mendelson (1986), Brennan and Subrahmanyam (1996), and Amihud, Mendelson and Lauterbach (1997), among others, that have provided evidence of a liquidity premium in asset pricing.

xlixPast research has largely focused on comparing execution costs across various market structures such as auction versus dealer markets. See, for example, Huang and Stoll (1996), Bessembinder and Kaufman (1997) and Venkatraman (2001).

l Saul Hansell in the New York Times, March 16, 1998 wrote, "To compete with electronic markets, the New York Stock Exchange is giving traders on its floors all manner of hand-held computer and communication devices. 'The typical broker on the floor is starting to look like a space cadet,' said Greg Kipness..." (page D5).

li Explicit commission costs are typically higher for orders that are harder to handle. The fixed cost component is implicit in the fact that a customer must maintain a higher trading volume over time in order for the services of a floor broker to be readily available.

lii There may be other implicit costs of order handling such as the cost of delayed execution or non-execution that are beyond the scope of this study. In that sense our analysis may be viewed as comparing execution costs across two venues conditional on trade execution.

liii For further discussion of this approach, see Maddala (1996).

liv DOT (the NYSE's Designated Order Turnaround system) routes orders directly to specialists' posts on the NYSE trading floor and to the Amex's PER system which brings the orders for Amex stocks to the Amex specialists' posts.

lv The NBBO consists of the best prevailing bid, the size of the best bid and the exchange posting best bid, and similarly the best prevailing ask, the size of the best ask and the exchange posting the best ask.

lvi The Lee-Ready rule is that if the trade execution price is below the average of the prevailing NBBO bid and ask (the mid-quote), we classify it as buyer-initiated, and if the trade execution price is above the mid-quote we classify it as seller-initiated. If a trade occurs at the mid-quote, we use the tick test: if the execution price occurs on a plus tick or a zero-plus tick (i.e., it is higher than the last non-identical execution price), the trade is classified as buyer initiated, and if the execution price occurs on a minus tick or a zero-minus tick, the trade is classified as seller initiated.

lvii Our definition of temporary price impact incorporates one-half of the spread prevailing at the time of trade execution, a component that we refer to as the spread-related component of price impact. As a test of robustness, we also measured temporary price impact using the mid-quote for trade t to assess the component that is not spread related. The results were generally consistent with the findings reported here.

lviii A similar matched pair technique is also used by Venkatraman (2001) and Conrad et al. (2001).

lix Our results are robust to several alternative measures of order imbalance. For example, we also examine the ratio of the depth on own side of the book to the total depth at the both prevailing inside quotes. Our concern with the latter measure is that it could be corrupted by the possibility of the floor trader's own order being reflected in the quotes. Nevertheless, the two measures gave very similar results. We also found that changing the length of the window over which imbalance is measured to 5 minutes does not materially alter our results.

lx We thank the referee for this suggestion.

lxi See Maddala (1996) for examples of such applications in Finance.

lxii There are other possible proxies of a stock's liquidity such as price level, value of shares outstanding, etc. In our tests we found these variables to be highly correlated with a stock's trading volume.

lxiii The threshold value can be viewed as a constant. A more general interpretation is possible, however. It can be viewed as the cost of waiting to trade later and hence, as a function of the order characteristics and market conditions at the time of the decision. The model estimates are unaffected by the interpretation.

lxiv In other words,

$$\gamma' z_t = \gamma_0 + \gamma_1 q_{1t} + \gamma_2 q_{2t} + \gamma_3 q_{3t} + \gamma_4 Imb_t + \gamma_5 Preret_t + \gamma_6 D_{1t} + \gamma_7 D_{2t} + \gamma_8 Vol_t$$

lxv See Maddala (1983)

lxvi For details, please see pages 266-267, Maddala (1983).

lxvii SPDRs are now also traded on the NYSE.

lxviii Keim and Madhavan (1995) show that traders following momentum-based strategies trade more aggressively and incur higher trading costs relative to value traders.

lxix Following this finding, we estimated equation (2) using OLS, and the sign and significance of the explanatory variables was virtually identical to those in equation (11).

lxx In this context we define the average price as the trade-weighted transaction price in our sample.

lxxi For further discussion of this point, see Keim and Madhavan (1996).

lxxii In most cases the beneficial owners of institutional funds are endowments or those who are, or about to be, pensioners and their dependants.

lxxiii Kenneth R. French and Richard Roll, "Stock Return Variances: The Arrival of Information and the Reaction of Traders", Journal of Financial Economics, No. 17, pages 5-26.

lxxiv Richard Roll, "The International Crash of October 1987", Financial Analysts Journal, September/October, 1988, pages 19-35.

lxxv See the other chapters in this Handbook

lxxvi Notice that in a continuous market every trader is always a marginal trader, which is the driving consideration behind all the strategic behavior we observe among traders in continuous markets.

lxxvii Net Exchange, a California spinout from Caltech, has designed and implemented combinatorial call markets for pollution permits, trucking, fixed income instruments and information.

lxxviii The prices used to calculate these orders were $33.25 for AVID, $24.35 for CREE, $10.51 for TSM and $21.57 for INTC.

lxxix (i.e.) if the purchase for CREE can benefit from an aggressive seller in the market, the sell order for AVID can offer a reduced price and the overall order can still meet its budget constraint.

lxxx The traders knew their own portfolios but did not know the total number of shares available or the market portfolio, and so of course could not predict the CAPM equilibrium prices on their own.

lxxxi "Inducing Liquidity In Thin Financial Markets Through Combined-Value Trading Mechanisms," with Peter Bossaerts, and Leslie Fine. European Economics Review, 46(9): 1671-1695, October 2002. Prof. John Ledyard, a founder of the Mechanism Design field of Economics, has been a pioneer in the study and application of combinatoric markets.

lxxxii "Research" is no longer complementary, risk trades for commissions are an anachronism and coverage traders, who knew your portfolio and alerted you to news about securities of interest to you, have long gone.

lxxxiii It should be understood that knowledge of the orders submitted to a call market is exceedingly valuable. All participants have a vested interest is seeing this information remains confidential or is published immediately after the call. The market design solution to this problem will affect the behavior of traders.

lxxxiv And possibly a mid-day call. However, I do not believe the mid-day call adds any functionality for liquidity and restructuring traders, it will improve the lot for the wolves and hyenas.

lxxxv The authors gratefully acknowledge the generous and thorough assistance in providing statistics given by staff members at the exchanges: Joann Arena (NYMEX), John Harangody (CME), Pamela Plehn (CME) and Jireh Rey (CBOT).

lxxxvi An earlier version of this book chapter appeared in The Handbook of Fixed Income Technology, Joseph Rosen & Russell D. Glisker (editors), The Summit Group Press, 1999, pages 3-24.

lxxxvii Based on survey responses from 62 trading platform vendors. Some firms offer several types of platforms (e.g., Chicago Board of Trade).

lxxxviii The details in this case are based on the experiences of an actual company in the late 1990's. At the time, few electronic trading platforms for fixed income existed. The case shows, on the one hand, that some progress has been made. On the other hand, behavioral and technical issues (e.g., resistance to change) can still hamper progress. To protect the anonymity of the client for whom the work was done, the names of individual employees and the names of two companies featured in the case (Ridge and Summit) are fictitious.

lxxxix Personal communication, May 27, 1998

xc Wikipedia

xci Richard J. Teweles, Edward S. Bradley, and Ted M. Teweles (1992). The Stock Market (6th Edition), p. 97

xcii 1 With the addition of Bank of America, Bear Stearns, Credit Suisse, Deutsche Bank, JP Morgan and Knight to its original six broker dealer investors of Citi, Goldman, Lehman, Merrill, Morgan Stanley and UBS, the total number of investors in BIDS has gone to twelve. xcii

2 "It's logical to be an equity holder in a place where you're going to be a material customer," said Neil Fitzpatrick, head of retail execution at Citadel. "It increases your leverage over influencing the venue's policies and strategic direction." Fitzpatrick also said, it helps reduce the overall cost of execution, albeit indirectly." Given the choice between two ECNs with identical fees, it's logical to route toward one in which a firm has an ownership stake, since the additional volume over time would increase the ECN's valuation as an enterprise. Fitzpatrick said his firm has used DirectEdge for a while and, "when appropriate, we'll look for every opportunity to use it." Securities Industry News, July 23, 2007

xciii Advanced Trading, "The OMS: The system We Love to Hate" September 11, 2007.

xciv Bijan Monassebian is President of Ordex™ Systems, Inc. The company is in the process of building a new generation integrated order and execution management system. The author, Bijan Monassebian, is an industry veteran who has managed, built, and installed many trading and order management systems for financial services organizationsxciv. [this should be in bio as should the footnote]

The author has been involved in managing, building, and installing many order management and trading systems under many different operating system environments, including the following industry firsts:

First Automated Order/execution Matching and Routing System

First Block Trading and Allocation System

First Dynamic Smart Order Routing System

First Automated Third-Market Trading System

First Order Crossing "Box"

Prior to founding Ordex™ Systems, his responsibilities included:

President and CEO of TCAM Systems, Inc., a computer consulting and custom software development company that he co-founded

Chief Information Officer (CIO) at Smith Barney, a major Wall Street financial organization, responsible for managing all aspects of Information Technology Division

Senior Systems Engineer, Industry Specialist, Senior Marketing Representative and Project Manager at IBM Corporation

He can be reached at: Bijan@ordexsystems.com

xcv Advanced Trading, "Do You Need An Execution Management System Or Will The Order Management System Suffice?" September 16, 2007.

xcvi A facility is a structure in which a series of individual loan contracts can be funded. A facility defnes the characteristics to which each underlying contract must adhere, including rate structure, term and maximum borrowing.

xcvii Glenn Yago and Donald McCarthy, Milken Institute Research Report, October 2004

xcviii As with bonds, the number indicates the value expressed as a percentage of the loan's "face" or nominal amount

xcix Reuters LPC, March 30, 2007 press release

c *Business Week, September 17, 2007, p. 51*

ci *An "investor" can be a fund, not necessarily an individual or institutional account*

cii *There have been some attempts to create loans that do trade with interest, but market acceptance has not been widespread.*

ciii *There are several reasons for rejecting a specific lender, including confidentiality of information in the loan documents (i.e., the lender is affiliated with a competitor), a demonstrated unwillingness to work thru unanticipated loan performance issues, financial viability of the lender, and an "activist" agenda. Traders usually have a good sense of which lenders would not be approved by the agent and/or borrower.*

civ *ClearPar and Trade Settlement Inc.*

cv *These tools allow one party to a trade (usually the dealer) to post their understanding of the terms of a trade, which their counterparty can review and confirm on-line. This is obviously a manual process due to the complex nature of the trade. In fact, ClearPar offers a team of "loan closers" to help the counterparties close the trade.*

cvi *Loans, at least in the US, have a target of seven business days for a "standard" settlement after which "delayed compensation" calculations begin. For "distressed" loans, this window is 20 business days.*

cvii *There is one small exception to this generalization. There are parties who receive allocations in the primary market before the trade settles, and turn around and sell them before the primary offering has settled. In times of excess liquidity in the market, parties with these primary market allocations can profit from these transactions. Is this a short sale? Or is this really more like a TBA in the fixed income market?*

cviii *A credit default swap (CDS) is a bilateral contract under which two counterparties agree to isolate and separately trade the credit risk of at least one third-party Rreference Entity. Under a credit default swap agreement, a protection buyer pays a periodic fee to a protection seller in exchange for a contingent payment by the seller upon a credit event (such as a default or failure to pay) happening in the reference entity. When a credit event is triggered, the protection seller either takes delivery of the defaulted bond for the par value (physical settlement) or pays the protection buyer the difference between the par value and recovery value of the bond (cash settlement). In a LCDS, the underlying protection is sold on syndicated secured loans of the Reference Entity rather than the broader category of "Bond or Loan". A Total Return Swap is is a contract in which one party receives interest payments on a reference asset plus any capital gains and losses over the payment period, while the other receives a specified fixed or floating cash flow unrelated to the credit worthiness of the reference asset, especially where the payments are based on the same notional amount. The interest payments are floating payments and are usually based upon the LIBOR with a spread added according to the agreement between parties. The reference asset may be any asset, index, or basket of assets. [Definition courtesy of Wikipedia].*

cix *Both terms refer to the act of replacing one member of a contract with another. Novation is a cornerstone for many Central Counterparty clearinghouse operations. In derivatives instruments, "assign" refers to the transfer of a participation in an instrument to another party with the approval of the remaining counterparty to the transaction.*

cx *DTCC's Warehouse for OTC Derivatives is more of an information base rather than a legal record of ownership.*

cxi Bond statistics published by SIFMA; loan trading statistics by Reuters Loan Pricing Corporation courtesy of LSTA website   Loan trading volumes were running now at a rate approximately double that shown in the table at the time of this draft

cxii Wall Street Technology, "Prepare for Skyrocketing Data Volumes, Experts Warn," May 12, 2005

cxiii TABB Group "Institutional Equity Trading 2006"

cxiv I would like to thank my colleague Dr Harvey Westbrook for these insights. His research in this area is still ongoing, but I think the preliminary data is worth discussing. I anticipate that he will be publishing his results in detail in the next few months looking at the market as a whole. He has assured me that the data I have looked at is representative of the data of the market as a whole.

cxv Cf "Bayesian Adaptive Trading with a Daily Cycle", Robert Almgren and Julian Lorenz, Journal of Risk, July 26, 2006
cxvi Chung, A.; VanNess, R., "Order-Handling Rules, Tick Size and the Intraday Pattern of Bid-Ask Spreads for Nasdaq Stocks." Journal of Financial Markets, Vol. 4, (2001) p.143-161

cxvii Harris, Larry. Trading and Exchanges: Market Microstructure for Practitioners. New York: Oxford University Press, 2003.

cxviii Johnson, J.; Tabb, L. "Groping in the Dark: Navigating Crossing Networks and Other Dark Pools of Liquidity." TABB Group, Oct. 2006.

cxix Johnson, J.; Tabb, L. "Regulation NMS Order Protection Rule: Preparing for the Impact." TABB Group, Oct. 2006.

cxx Johnson, J.; Tabb, L. "Groping in the Dark: Navigating Crossing Networks and Other Dark Pools of Liquidity." TABB Group, Oct. 2006.

cxxi TABB Group estimates.

cxxii Harris, Larry. Trading and Exchanges: Market Microstructure for Practitioners. New York: Oxford University Press, 2003.

cxxiii Lundqist, S.; Clay, M. "Dark Liquidity Pools: Navigating the Dark Landscapes in Europe." European Pension & Investments News. London: Jun 4, 2007; p.1

cxxiv Allen, H.; Hawkins, J.; Sato S. "Electronic trading and its implications for financial systems." BIS Papers No. 7. Basel: Bank for International Settlements, 2007.

cxxv CFA Institute Trade Management Guidelines

cxxvi Davis, P.; Pagano, M.; Schwartz, R. "Life after the Big Board Goes Electronic." Financial Analysts Journal, Vol. 62, No. 5, 2006.

12 "Commission Guidance Regarding Client Commission Practices Under Section 28(e) of the Securities Exchange Act of 1934," Securities and Exchange Commission, [Release No. 34-54165; File No. S7-13-06] July 2006

13 Sussman, A. "Institutional Equity Trading in America 2006: The Return on Relationship." TABB Group, Oct. 2006

14 Johnson, J. "OMS, EMS or DMA? The Future of the Buy-Side Desktop." TABB Group, Dec. 2006

15 Craig, Susanne. "Prudential's Last Research Call: 'Bye.'" The Wall Street Journal. June 6, 2007, p. C1

cxxvii We thank Jeff Bacidore and Jatin Suryawanshi (Goldman, Sachs & Co.) for their comments.

cxxviii For a discussion of the choice of execution benchmark see Sofianos (2006).

cxxix See Bacidore and Sofianos (2002) and Sofianos (2005) for further discussion of ST alpha. ST alpha is also called trading alpha or momentum.

cxxx The example in Exhibit 1 uses the average characteristics of the high ST alpha orders in our sample (see Exhibit 4).

cxxxi For more details on VWAP algorithms see Bacidore & Su (2004), "VWAP Algorithms."

cxxxii For more details on shortfall algorithms see Bacidore & Su (2004), "Implementation Shortfall Algorithms."

cxxxiii The Goldman Sachs t-cost model gives a shortfall estimate. About a third of this shortfall estimate reflects the average ST alpha embedded in the t-cost model. Our impact estimate is 2/3rds of the model shortfall estimate.

cxxxiv The assumption of uniform execution underestimates the ST alpha loss of the VWAP strategy because the trading profile of HPQ (like most stocks) is U-shaped. Executing VWAP therefore between 12:00 and 16:00 will tilt executions towards the close increasing the loss of ST alpha.

cxxxv A more robust way of measuring ST alpha is to ignore the same day close and estimate ST alpha using prices further out (e.g. T+1 and T+2 closing prices as in Exhibit 1).

cxxxvi Or the execution ends at the close (16:00), whichever comes first. The estimates are from the Goldman Sachs t-cost model. For details on the model see Rodella (2005).

cxxxvii The 4Cast orders are smaller and have lower estimated impact than the VWAP orders, but the differences are small.

cxxxviii High ST-alpha orders are slightly larger and slightly lower-priced than the low ST-alpha orders. But the differences are small. For example, for VWAP, the average size of high ST-alpha orders is 3.3% ADV (23,470 shares) and average price $32, while for low ST-alpha average size is 2.9% ADV (19,859 shares) and average price $34. Consistent with Exhibit 3 the 4Cast orders are slightly smaller than the VWAP orders.

cxxxix The 5% non-fill rate represents orders that have been canceled or short-sales that did not execute.

cxl Using the average arrival of 12, the 4-hour alpha to close is 120 bps, or 30 bps per hour. The VWAP spreading the executions over roughly 3 hours compared to the VWAP spreading them over 1 hour gives up 30 bps of ST alpha relative to the more aggressive 4Cast algorithm.

cxli Using the average arrival of 12, the 4-hour alpha to close is 120 bps, or 30 bps per hour. The VWAP spreading the executions over roughly 3 hours compared to the VWAP spreading them over 1 hour gives up 30 bps of ST alpha relative to the more aggressive 4Cast algorithm.

cxlii Instead of being higher, the average ST-alpha of 4Cast orders is slightly lower than for VWAP orders.

cxliii The ratio normalizes for differences in volatility across orders that go to different algorithms. Again our hypothesis is that traders will tend to route orders in more volatile stocks to faster more aggressive algorithms. Looking at the normalized execution risk ratio, therefore, in comparing across algorithms corrects for this sample selection problem.

cxliv The Guide pre-trade tool available in REDIPlus® quantifies the trade-off between liquidity impact, execution risk and ST alpha loss (including a graphical representation). For details on The Guide see Bacidore & Su (2004) "Implementation Shortfall Algorithms."

cxlv Balanced buy-and-sell portfolio trades and "pairs trade" are examples of market neutral execution strategies.

cxlvi Another excellent reason to have your own trade performance tracking tool is for your own quality control. This was the first thing we devoted significant resources to other than the algorithms themselves at Credit Suisse.

cxlvii 20 venues times 5 circuits times 390 trading minutes a day times 0.01% outage rate ~ 4minutes of outage time per day

cxlviii http://www.cfo.com

cxlix http://www.cfo.com

cl Throughput is defined as the aggregate data volume that can be processed by a system with a given time unit, typically measured in units of bytes/seccond.

cli Detailed report is available at
http://www.stacresearch.com/index.php?option=com_content&task=view&id=43&Itemid=33

clii The current SIFMA definition for STP is as follows: "...the seamless integration of systems and processes to automate the trade process from end-to-end trade execution, confirmation and settlement – without the need for manual intervention or the re-keying of data." The process incorporates allocation communication, block trade matching, standing settlement instructions and post settlement event processing.

cliii For Toyota's quality philosophy, see ToyotaTraditions, especially this page: http://www.toyota.co.jp/en/vision/traditions/mar_apr_06.html

Joseph Rosen, President of RKA Inc., is a securities industry veteran with 25 years experience as an exchange executive, adviser, CIO & Quant, author, lecturer, as well as developer and marketer of electronic trading systems. He was most recently Managing Director, Trading Technology/Head of Technology Marketing at the New York Stock Exchange, where he developed and executed an Exchange-wide initiative to promote NYSE's trading/technology products, including a successful marketing campaign for the Hybrid Market initiative targeted at major sources of order flow and connectivity.

Previously, he was a partner for ten years at a financial technology consultancy, where he served as a strategic IT advisor, and built/deployed bespoke trading systems for a broad cross-section of international financial institutions, including global money managers, securities firms and market centers. Prior to this he was the founding Chief Information Officer & Director of Quantitative Research for Dubin & Swieca Capital Management and Highbridge Capital, and a senior IT manager at Nomura Securities. Before this he was a managing consultant and developer at TCAM Systems, where he developed one of the first electronic trading systems with automatic execution capabilities.

Joe has contributed in various capacities to nearly one hundred organizations across all segments of the global securities and investments industry, and has worked with scores of financial technology vendors across most functional areas. He has lectured globally, and been widely published, including five books, among them The Handbook of Investment Technology [McGraw-Hill]. His degrees include an MBA from Columbia University in Finance, International Business and Marketing, and a Masters as well as Doctoral Candidacy in Political Science from Stony Brook University, which included concentrations in Quantitative Methods, Middle East Politics and Civil-Military Relations.

Joe served as Adjunct Professor of Management at Polytechnic University, where he taught a course on Management of Technology & Innovation in Financial Services [MOTIFS] in their Executive Master's Degree Program. He served in a combat infantry brigade of the IDF between 1974 and 1976.